MAGILL INDEX
TO
CRITICAL SURVEYS

MAGILL INDEX
TO
CRITICAL SURVEYS

Cumulative Indexes

1981–1994

SALEM PRESS

Pasadena, California   Englewood Cliffs, New Jersey

Library of Congress Cataloging-in-Publication Data
Magill index to critical surveys, 1981-1994 : cumulative
indexes, 1981-1994
  p. cm.
ISBN 0-89356-698-5
  1. Literature—History and criticism—Dictionaries.
2. Literature—Bio-bibliography. 3. Authors—Biography. I. Magill, Frank Northen, 1907   .
PN524.M34 1994
016.809—dc20   93-18632
                                  CIP

PUBLISHER'S NOTE

This index to Magill's *Critical Survey* series combines and collates the indexes from the eleven multivolume reference sets in this comprehensive survey of both English-language and foreign-language writers. The series includes the Critical Surveys of Short Fiction (seven volumes), Long Fiction (thirteen volumes), Poetry (thirteen volumes), Drama (twelve volumes), their Supplements (one volume each for Long Fiction, Short Fiction, Poetry, and Drama), and Revised Editions of the Critical Surveys of English-language Long Fiction (eight volumes), Poetry (eight volumes), Drama (seven volumes), and the Critical Survey of Short Fiction (seven volumes). Magill's Critical Surveys of Mystery and Detective Fiction (four volumes) and Literary Theory (four volumes) are also included. Hence, the current index offers, in one location, a valuable guide to discussion of books, plays, stories, poems, and authors appearing in the eighty-seven volumes of the series, along with cross-references from foreign-language titles, alternative titles, and pseudonyms.

Entries are followed by a code indicating the Critical Survey in which the discussion appears, which in turn is followed by the page or pages locating the discussion:

DEng	Critical Survey of Drama: English Language Series (1985)
DFor	Critical Survey of Drama: Foreign Language Series (1986)
DSup	Critical Survey of Drama: Supplement (1987)
LFEng	Critical Survey of Long Fiction: English Language Series (1983)
LFFor	Critical Survey of Long Fiction: Foreign Language Series (1984)
LFSup	Critical Survey of Long Fiction: Supplement (1987)
LTh	Critical Survey of Literary Theory (1987)
M&D	Critical Survey of Mystery and Detective Fiction (1988)
PEng	Critical Survey of Poetry: English Language Series (1982)
PFor	Critical Survey of Poetry: Foreign Language Series (1984)
PSup	Critical Survey of Poetry: Supplement (1987)
RevDEng	Critical Survey of Drama: English Language Series, Revised Edition (1994)
RevLFEng	Critical Survey of Long Fiction: English Language Series, Revised Edition (1991)
RevPEng	Critical Survey of Poetry: English Language Series, Revised Edition (1992)
RevShF	Critical Survey of Short Fiction, Revised Edition (1993)
ShF	Critical Survey of Short Fiction (1981)
ShFSup	Critical Survey of Short Fiction: Supplement (1987)

Boldface entries signal the existence of a complete article on the topic in question.

Alphabetization is by word rather than letter, and transposed elements are disregarded; hence, "Jacob, Max," precedes "*Jacob and the Angel.*" Hyphenated compounds are treated as two separate words if the two elements could stand independently (as in "fifty-five") but are treated as one word if one of the elements could not stand alone (as in "non-being"). Numerals are alphabetized as though they were spelled out ("*1919*" under "nineteen-nineteen"), as are common abbreviations: "Mr." as "mister"; "Mrs." as "mistress"; "St." as "saint"; "Dr." as "doctor." The *Mc* particle in names such as McPherson is alphabetized as though it were spelled *Mac*.

There are two prominent exceptions to the alpha-by-word rule: First, surnames composed of more than one element are alphabetized as though one word; hence, "Le Carré, John" is preceded by "Leatherstocking Tales." Second, series of enumerated titles by the same author (such as the plays *Henry IV, Part I, Henry IV, Part II*, and *Henry V*, all by William Shakespeare) appear in numerical order rather than alphabetical order, for the sake of logical consistency.

Titles of books, plays, stories, essays, and poems are followed, in parentheses, by the author's surname; in an index of this size and scope, the editors found that further identification, by means of a first initial or a first name, was sometimes necessary to avoid confusion with another author.

Code System

ShF   *Critical Survey of Short Fiction.* 7 vols. Salem Press, Englewood Cliffs, N.J. 1981.

PEng   *Critical Survey of Poetry, English Language Series.* 8 vols. Salem Press, Englewood Cliffs, N.J. 1982.

LFEng   *Critical Survey of Long Fiction, English Language Series.* 8 vols. Salem Press, Englewood Cliffs, N.J. 1983.

PFor   *Critical Survey of Poetry, Foreign Language Series.* 5 vols. Salem Press, Englewood Cliffs, N.J. 1984.

LFFor   *Critical Survey of Long Fiction, Foreign Language Series.* 5 vols. Salem Press, Englewood Cliffs, N.J. 1984.

DEng   *Critical Survey of Drama, English Language Series.* 6 vols. Salem Press, Englewood Cliffs, N.J. 1985.

DFor   *Critical Survey of Drama, Foreign Language Series.* 6 vols. Salem Press, Englewood Cliffs, N.J. 1986.

LFSup   *Critical Survey of Long Fiction, Supplement.* 1 vol. Salem Press, Englewood Cliffs, N.J., and Pasadena, Calif. 1987.

ShFSup   *Critical Survey of Short Fiction, Supplement.* 1 vol. Salem Press, Englewood Cliffs, N.J., and Pasadena, Calif. 1987.

PSup   *Critical Survey of Poetry, Supplement.* 1 vol. Salem Press, Englewood Cliffs, N.J., and Pasadena, Calif. 1987.

DSup   *Critical Survey of Drama, Supplement.* 1 vol. Salem Press, Englewood Cliffs, N.J., and Pasadena, Calif. 1987.

LTh   *Critical Survey of Literary Theory.* 4 vols. Salem Press, Englewood Cliffs, N.J., and Pasadena, Calif. 1987.

M&D   *Critical Survey of Mystery and Detective Fiction.* 4 vols. Salem Press, Englewood Cliffs, N.J., and Pasadena, Calif. 1988.

RevLFEng   *Critical Survey of Long Fiction, English Language Series, Revised Edition.* 8 vols. Salem Press, Englewood Cliffs, N.J., and Pasadena, Calif. 1991.

RevPEng   *Critical Survey of Poetry, English Language Series, Revised Edition.* 8 vols. Salem Press, Englewood Cliffs, N.J., and Pasadena, Calif. 1992.

RevShF   *Critical Survey of Short Fiction, Revised Edition.* 7 vols. Salem Press, Englewood Cliffs, N.J., and Pasadena, Calif. 1993.

RevDEng   *Critical Survey of Drama, English Language Series, Revised Edition.* 7 vols. Salem Press, Englewood Cliffs, N.J., and Pasadena, Calif. 1994.

MAGILL INDEX
TO
CRITICAL SURVEYS

A

"*A*" (Zukofsky). PEng 3225-3226; RevPEng 3749-3750.

"A & P" (Updike). RevShF 2335-2336; ShF 98-99.

A ciascuno il suo. See *Man's Blessing, A.*

"A Cristo crucificado." *See* "To Christ Crucified."

"A halál lovai." *See* "Death's Horsemen."

"A Kolota partján." *See* "On the Banks of the Kalota."

"A la deriva." *See* "Drifting."

A la pintura (Alberti). PFor 23.

À la recherche du temps perdu. See *Remembrance of Things Past.*

"A la vida religiosa" (León). PFor 843.

"À la voix de Kathleen Ferrier" (Bonnefoy). PSup 46.

"A Leopoldo II." *See* "To Leopold II."

À l'ombre des jeunes filles en fleurs. See *Within a Budding Grove.*

"A Luigia Pallavicini caduta da cavallo." *See* "To Louise Pallavicini Fallen from a Horse."

"A mi hermano Miguel in memoriam." *See* "To My Brother Miguel in Memoriam."

"A mia figlia." *See* "To My Daughter."

"A mia moglie." *See* "To My Wife."

A minden titkok verseiből. See *Of All Mysteries.*

"A Nuestra Señora." *See* "To Our Lady."

"A parteneide" (Manzoni). PFor 958.

À rebours. See *Against the Grain.*

"A Roosevelt." *See* "To Roosevelt."

"A Santiago." *See* "To Santiago."

A secretio agravio, secreta venganza. See *Secret Vengeance for Secret Insult.*

"A Silvia." *See* "To Sylvia."

"A Sion-hegy alatt." *See* "Under Mount Sion."

"A stesso." *See* "To Himself."

"A szétszóródás elött." *See* "Before the Diaspora."

À toi, pour toujours, ta Marie-Lòu. See *Forever Yours, Marie-Lou.*

À vau-l'eau. See *Down Stream.*

"A veces una hoja des prendida . . ." (González Martínez). PFor 611.

"A Víctor Hugo" (Darío). PFor 421-422.

"À Villequier" (Hugo). PFor 736. See also *Contemplations, Les.*

"À Zurbarán" (Gautier). PFor 537-538.

Aarestrup, Emil. PFor 2166.

Abad, Per. *See* Per Abad.

Abaddón, el exterminador (Sabato). LFFor 1467-1468.

Abbas, K. A. ShF 649.

"Abbé Aubain, The" (Mérimée). RevShF 2692; ShF 198.

Abbé Mouret's Transgression (Zola). LFFor 1990.

Abbey, Kieran. *See* **Reilly, Helen.**

Abbot, Anthony. M&D 1-5.

"ABC to the Virgin, An" (Chaucer). RevShF 482; ShF 1101.

Abdelazer (Behn). RevDEng 211.

"Abduction, The" (Dove). RevPEng 957.

"Abduction, The" (Kunitz). PSup 249; RevPEng 1890.

Abe, Kōbō. DFor 2434; LFFor 1-9.

"Abe Lincoln" (Guest). PEng 1166; RevPEng 1326.

Abe Lincoln in Illinois (Sherwood). DEng 1807-1808; RevDEng 2241-2242.

Abel, Robert H. ShF 2487.

Abel et Bela (Pinget). DSup 306-307.

Abel Sánchez (Unamuno). LFEng 3302-3303; LFFor 1792-1793, 2391.

Abelard, Peter. LTh 1653.

Abell, Kjeld. DFor 1-10, 2480.

"Aben." *See* "Monkey, The" (Dinesen).

Abén Humeya (Martínez de la Rosa). DFor 1274-1275.

"Abend, Der." *See* "Evening."

"Abenjacán the Bojarí, muerto en su laberinto." *See* "Ibn Hakkan al-Bokhari, Dead in His Labyrinth."

"Abenland." *See* "Occident I, The."

Abenteuerliche Simplicissimus, Der. See *Adventurous Simplicissimus, The.*

Aber die Nachtigall jubelt (Kunze). PFor 805.

Abhijñānaśakuntalā. See *Śakuntalā.*

Abish, Walter. ShF 2488.

"Abominable" (Brown). ShF 564.

"Abominable History of the Man with the Copper Fingers, The" (Sayers). ShF 758.

Abominable Man, The (Sjöwall and Wahlöö). M&D 1499.

Abortion, The (Brautigan). LFEng 292-293; RevLFEng 375-376.

"Abou Ben Adhem" (Hunt). PEng 1464-1465; RevPEng 1675-1676.

1

About Face (Fo). DSup 114.

"About Marriage" (Levertov). RevPEng 1983.

About That (Mayakovsky). PFor 990-991.

About the House (Auden). PEng 78; RevPEng 89.

"About the Marionette Theater" (Kleist). LTh 815; RevShF 1372; ShF 1759-1760.

Above Suspicion (MacInnes). M&D 1169.

Abraham (Hroswitha). DFor 2153.

Abraham, Nelson Ahlgren. *See* **Algren, Nelson.**

Abraham Lincoln (Drinkwater). DEng 510-511; RevDEng 631-633.

Abraham Lincoln: The Prairie Years (Sandburg). PEng 2449; RevPEng 2852.

Abraham Lincoln: The War Years (Sandburg). PEng 2446, 2449; RevPEng 2849.

Abrams, M. H. LTh 1-6, 188, 306, 850, 1032, 1370.

"Abrasive" (Everson). PEng 987; RevPEng 1118.

"Abrazo de Vergara, El." *See* "Embrace at Vergara."

"Abricot, L'." *See* "Apricot, The."

"Abroad" (Gordimer). RevShF 1033-1034; ShFSup 108.

Absalom, Absalom! (Faulkner). LFEng 928-932, 3130, 3155-3156; RevLFEng 1102-1106, 3772, 3832, 3840-3841.

Absalom and Achitophel (Dryden). PEng 875-876, 3316, 3317; RevPEng 992-993.

"Abschied." *See* "Departure."

Abse, Dannie. PEng 1-5; RevPEng 1-6.

"Absences" (Tate, J.). PEng 2837.

Absences (Tate, J.). PEng 2837-2838; RevPEng 3308-3310.

"Absent-Minded Beggar, The" (Kipling). PEng 1609; RevPEng 1849.

"Absent-Minded Coterie, The" (Barr). M&D 92.

"Absent with Official Leave" (Jarrell). PEng 1482; RevPEng 1694.

Absentee, The (Edgeworth, M.). LFEng 861, 865-867; RevLFEng 1022, 1026-1028.

"Absentia animi" (Ekelöf). PFor 449-450.

"Absolution" (Sassoon). PEng 2471; RevPEng 2877.

Abstecher, Der. See *Detour, The.*

Absurd Person Singular (Ayckbourn). DEng 62; RevDEng 80, 83.

Absurda Comica (Gryphius). DFor 838.

Abu Telfan (Raabe). LFFor 1380, 1382.

Abuelo, El. See *Grandfather, The.*

Abyss, The (Yourcenar). LFFor 1970-1971.

AC/DC (Williams, H.). DEng 2494; RevDEng 3022-3023.

"Academic Squaw" (Rose). RevPEng 3936.

Acceptance World, The (Powell, A.). LFEng 2118; RevLFEng 2677.

Accidental Death of an Anarchist (Fo). DSup 112-113.

Accidental Man, An (Murdoch). LFEng 1937-1940; RevLFEng 2441, 2448-2452.

Accidental Tourist, The (Tyler). RevLFEng 3343-3344.

Accidental Woman, An (Neely). M&D 1270.

Accius, Lucius. DFor 2146.

"Accompanist, The" (Pritchett). RevShF 1936-1937.

Accomplices, The. See *Fellow-Culprits, The.*

"Account of Religion by Reason, An" (Suckling). PEng 2775; RevPEng 3240.

Account of the Growth of Popery and Arbitrary Government in England (Marvell). PEng 1910-1911; RevPEng 2214-2215.

"Accountability" (Dunbar, P.). PSup 113-114; RevPEng 1015-1016.

Achaeus of Ertria. DFor 2119.

Acharnés. See *Acharnians, The.*

Acharnians, The (Aristophanes). DFor 114-115, 2091, 2095, 2123-2124.

"Ache of Marriage, The" (Levertov). RevPEng 1983.

Achebe, Chinua. LFEng 1-14; LFFor 2039-2040, 2042-2044, 2048; LTh 1063; **RevLFEng 1-19; RevShF 1-6; ShF 819-823.**

Achievement of T. S. Eliot, The (Matthiessen). LTh 1012.

Achilles (Gay). DEng 735; RevDEng 914.

Achilles Tatius. LFFor 2004-2005.

"Achtzehnjährige, Der." *See* "Eighteen-Year-Old, The."

Ackerson, Duane. ShF 2489.

"Acon and Rhodope" (Landor). PEng 1644; RevPEng 1909.

Acquainted with Grief (Gadda). LFFor 606-608.

Acque e terre (Quasimodo). PFor 1306.

Acque Turbate (Betti). DFor 210-211.

Acres and Pains (Perelman). RevShF 1868; ShF 2081.

Acrobats, The (Richler). LFEng 2256; RevLFEng 2848.

Acropolis (Sherwood). RevDEng 2238-2239.

"Across Kansas" (Stafford). RevPEng 3170-3171.

"Act, The" (Oppenheimer). PEng 2146; RevPEng 2516.

Act of Fear (Collins, M.). M&D 383-384.

"Act of God, An" (Post). M&D 1346.

Act of Reading, The (Iser). LTh 732, 734.

"Act of Self-Defense, An" (Ford). ShF 1386.

"Adventure of the Egyptian Tomb, The" (Christie). ShF 1146-1147.

"Adventure of the Empty House, The" (Doyle). RevShF 770 771; ShF 1304

"Adventure of the Remarkable Worm, The" (Derleth). RevShF 709-710; ShF 1257-1258.

"Adventure of the Rudberg Numbers, The" (Derleth). RevShF 709; ShF 1256-1257.

"Adventure of the Speckled Band, The" (Doyle). RevShF 766; ShF 1299.

"Adventure of the Three R's, The" (Queen). RevShF 1978-1979.

Adventurer (Hawkesworth). RevShF 1137-1139; ShF 1605, 1606, 1607, 1608.

Adventurer, The (Johnson, S.). RevShF 1285; ShF 1708.

Adventures in the Letter I (Simpson). PEng 2605; RevPEng 3010-3011.

"Adventures of a Monkey, The" (Zoshchenko). RevShF 2558; ShFSup 379.

Adventures of Augie March, The (Bellow). LFEng 227, 3106; RevLFEng 278, 3775, 3808.

Adventures of Caleb Williams, The. See Caleb Williams.

Adventures of Ferdinand, Count Fathom, The. See Ferdinand, Count Fathom.

Adventures of Gil Blas of Santillane, The (Le Sage). LFEng 3103-3104; RevLFEng 3805-3806.

Adventures of Huckleberry Finn, The (Twain). LFEng 2667-2668, 3105; RevLFEng 3318-3319, 3323-3325, 3745, 3750, 3807; RevShF 2661; ShF 615.

Adventures of Master F. J., The (Gascoigne). PEng 1064-1065.

Adventures of Peregrine Pickle, The. See Peregrine Pickle.

Adventures of Pinocchio, The (Collodi). ShF 684-685.

Adventures of Roderick Random, The. See Roderick Random.

"Adventures of Shamrock Jolnes, The" (Henry). ShF 1630.

Adventures of Sir Launcelot Greaves, The. See Sir Launcelot Greaves.

Adventures of Tom Sawyer, The (Twain). LFEng 2664-2666; RevLFEng 3318-3319, 3321-3323.

Adventures of Wesley Jackson, The (Saroyan). LFEng 2337; RevLFEng 2946, 2952.

Adventurous Simplicissimus, The (Grimmelshausen). LFFor 754-761, 2152.

"Advice" (Smollett). PEng 2651, 2653-2654.

"Advice to King Lear" (Cassity). PSup 63; RevPEng 545.

"Advice to my best brother, Colonel Francis Lovelace" (Lovelace). PEng 1761; RevPEng 2054.

Ady, Endre. PFor 1-8, 1983-1984.

Æ. PEng 14-19; RevPEng 15-20.

"Aella: A Tragycal Enterlude" (Chatterton). PEng 472-473; RevPEng 568-569.

"Aeneas and Dido" (Brodsky). PFor 239.

Aeneid (Vergil). LTh 64-66, 515-517, 1650; PFor 399, 1606-1607, 1611-1617; RevShF 2351-2354, 2570; ShF 135, 2386-2389.

"Aeolian Harp, The" (Melville). PEng 1949, 1950; RevPEng 2256.

"Aerial Ways" (Pasternak). RevShF 1855.

Aerial Ways (Pasternak). ShF 2061.

"Aeroplanes at Brescia, The" (Davenport). RevShF 680; ShF 1247.

Aeschylus. DEng 2134-2135; DFor 20-30, 2090, 2099-2102, 2119-2120; RevDEng 2654-2655.

Aesclepius. LTh 21.

Aesop. RevShF 2567, 2576-2578; ShF 377-379.

Aesthetic as Science of Expression and General Linguistic (Croce). LTh 327, 330-331.

Aesthetic Experience and Literary Hermeneutics (Jauss). LTh 768.

"Aesthetic Relationship of Art to Reality" (Chernyshevsky). LTh 288, 1107.

"Aesthetica in Nuce" (Hamann). LTh 669.

Aethelston. PEng 3251.

Aethiopian History, An. See Ethiopian Story.

Aethiopica (Heliodorus). ShF 489.

Aetia (Callimachus). LTh 264; PFor 255-256.

Afer, Publius Terentius. *See* **Terence.**

"Affair of Honor, An" (Nabokov). RevShF 1703-1704; ShFSup 219-220.

Affaire Lerouge, L'. See Widow Lerouge, The.

"Affective Fallacy, The" (Wimsatt and Beardsley). LTh 1554.

Afranius. DFor 2145.

Africa (Petrarch). LTh 1093, 1662; PFor 1237-1238.

"Africa Africa Africa" (Baraka). PEng 88-89; RevPEng 99-100.

African Image, The (Mphahlele). LTh 1057.

African Millionaire, An (Allen). M&D 19.

"African Traveller, The" (Queen). RevShF 1979.

African Witch, The (Cary). LFEng 456; RevLFEng 574, 576.

After (Anderson, R.). RevDEng 52.

"After a Death" (Tomlinson). RevPEng 3380.

"After Apple-Picking" (Frost). PEng 1042-1045; RevPEng 1174-1177.

Aias. See *Ajax.*

Aichinger, Ilse. ShF 2491.

Aickman, Robert. ShF 2492.

Aigle à deux têtes, L'. See *Eagle Has Two Heads, The.*

Aiken, Conrad. LFEng 15-24; PEng 20-26; RevLFEng 28-38; RevPEng 21-27; RevShF 26-32; ShF 258-259, 836-841.

Ainsworth, William Harrison. LFEng 25-34; RevLFEng 39-48.

"Air and Fire" (Berry). PEng 153.

Air Raid (MacLeish). DEng 1219; RevDEng 1540.

"Airiños, airiños, aires." *See* "Breezes, Breezes, Little Breezes."

"Airship Boys in Africa, The" (Cassity). PSup 62-63; RevPEng 544-545.

Aissa Saved (Cary). LFEng 455; RevLFEng 574, 575.

Ajax (Sophocles), DFor 2103-2104.

Akalaitis, JoAnne. DSup 1-7. RevDEng 12-19.

Akhmatova, Anna. LTh 1607; PFor 9-16, 237, 2146.

Akhnaton, King of Egypt (Merezhkovsky), LFFor 1139.

Akiko, Yosano. See *Yosano Akiko.*

Akropolis (Wyspiański). DFor 2029-2031.

Aksakov, Sergey. LFFor 2315.

Aksyonov, Vassily. LFSup 16-21.

Akt des Lesens, Der. See *Act of Reading, The.*

Akt przerwany. See *Interrupted Act, The.*

"Akter." *See* "Actor, The."

Akutagawa, Ryūnosuke. RevShF 33-38; ShFSup 7-12.

Al gözüm seyreyle Salih. See *Seagull.*

Aladdin (Oehlenschläger). DFor 1439-1440.

Alaham (Greville). PEng 1157-1158; RevPEng 1316-1317.

Alain-Fournier. LFFor 24-39.

Alan of Lille. LTh 19-23; PFor 2114.

Alanus de Insulis. *See* Alan of Lille.

Alarcón, Pedro Antonio de. LFFor 2383; RevShF 39-44; ShF 842-848.

Alarcón y Mendoza, Juan Ruiz de. See **Ruiz de Alarcón, Juan.**

Alas, Leopoldo. *See* Clarín.

Alastor (Shelley). PEng 2551-2552; RevPEng 2964-2965.

Albany Cycle, The (Kennedy). LFSup 195-199; RevLFEng 1852-1856.

"Albatross, The" (Lem). RevShF 1461; ShFSup 153.

Albee, Edward. DEng 11-23, 2408-2409; DSup 407; RevDEng 20-34, 2929-3930.

Alberic. LTh 1651.

Albert von Stade. LTh 22.

Alberti, Leon Battista. LTh 1661.

Alberti, Rafael. DFor 2506; PFor 17-24.

Albertine disparue. See *Sweet Cheat Gone, The.*

Albertine in Five Times (Tremblay). DSup 356.

"Albertus: Soul and Sin" (Gautier). PFor 535.

Albigenses, The (Maturin). LFEng 1841; RevLFEng 2328.

Albine: Or, The Abbé's Temptation. See *Abbé Mouret's Transgression.*

"Albuquerque Graveyard, The" (Wright, Jay). RevPEng 3687.

Alcaeus. PFor 1759-1761.

Alcalde de Zalamea, El. See *Mayor of Zalamea, The.*

Alcayaga, Lucila Godoy. See **Mistral, Gabriela.**

Alceste (Quinault). DFor 1507-1508.

"Alceste in the Wilderness" (Hecht). RevPEng 1455.

Alcestis (Euripides). DFor 573-574, 2110-2111.

"Alchemist, The" (Bogan). PEng 236-237; RevPEng 283-284.

Alchemist, The (Jonson). DEng 1021-1023, 2285; RevDEng 1289-1291, 2804; ShF 1715-1716.

Alcibiades (Otway). DEng 1442-1443; RevDEng 1822-1823.

Alcman. PFor 1762.

Alcools (Apollinaire). PFor 53-54.

Alcuin. PFor 2113.

Alcyone (D'Annunzio). PFor 387-388. See also *Laudi, Le.*

Aldan, Daisy. ShF 2493.

Alden, Michele. *See* **Avallone, Michael.**

Aldington, Richard. LFEng 35-47. RevLFEng 49-62.

Aldiss, Brian. ShF 779-780, 2494.

Aldrich, Thomas Bailey. LFEng 48-58; M&D 11-15; PEng 27-36; RevLFEng 63-73; ShF 587.

Aleck Maury, Sportsman (Gordon). LFEng 1176; RevLFEng 1398.

Alecsandri, Vasile. DFor 2296-2297.

Alegría, Ciro. LFFor 40-48.

Alehouse Sonnets (Dubie). PSup 105; RevPEng 1001.

Aleichem, Sholom. RevShF 45-50; ShF 849-854.

Aleixandre, Vicente. PFor 25-32; PSup 403.

Aleksandriya. LFFor 2302.

Aleksandrov, Josip Murn. PFor 2269.

Alemán, Mateo. LFEng 3102; RevLFEng 3803, 3804.

Alencar, José de. LFFor 2281.

Alepoudhélis, Odysseus. *See* **Elýtis, Odysseus.**
Aleramo, Sibilla. LFFor 2238; PFor 2032.
Alexander, Sidney. ShF 2495.
Alexander, Campaspe and Diogenes. See *Campaspe.*
Alexander Romance (Pseudo-Callisthenes). LFFor 2014.
Alexanderplatz, Berlin (Döblin). LFFor 477-478, 2194.
Alexander's Feast (Dryden). PEng 878; RevPEng 995.
Alexandria Quartet, The (Durrell). LFEng 844-847; RevLFEng 1011-1014.
"Alexandrian Kings" (Cavafy). PFor 298-299, 1956.
Alfieri, Vittorio. DEng 2348; **DFor 39-49,** 2406-2407; PFor 2022-2024; RevDEng 2867.
Alfonso, King of Castile (Lewis). DEng 1129, 1135-1136; RevDEng 1421, 1427-1428.
Alfred Hitchcock Presents. RevDEng 3039.
Algabal (George). LTh 574; PFor 547-548.
Alger, Horatio. RevLFEng 3795.
Algren, Nelson. LFSup 22-30; RevLFEng 74-82; RevShF 51-54; ShF 269, **855-858.**
Alguma poesia (Drummond de Andrade). PSup 98.
Alguns Contos (Lispector). RevShF 1491; ShFSup 166.
Al-Hakim, Tawfiq. *See* **Hakim, Tawfiq al-.**
Ali Pacha (Payne). DEng 2397; RevDEng 2918.
Aliatar (Saavedra). DFor 1615.
Alibi for Murder. See *Dream Walker, The.*
"Alice Addertongue" (Franklin). RevShF 906-907; ShF 1410-1411.
Alice's Adventures in Wonderland (Carroll). PEng 440-443; RevPEng 509-513.
"Alicia Who Sees Mice" (Cisneros). RevShF 558.
"Alien Corn, The" (Maugham). RevShF 1628; ShF 1904.
Alighieri, Dante. *See* **Dante.**
Alison, Archibald. LTh 1745.
Alison's House (Glaspell). RevDEng 970-971.
Alive and Dead (Ferrars). M&D 601.
Aliya. See Second *Aliya* and Fifth *Aliya.*
Alkēstis. See *Alcestis.*
All About H. Hatterr (Desani). LFFor 2220.
"All Bread" (Atwood). PEng 69; RevPEng 76-77.
"All Choice Is Error" (Cunningham). PSup 77; RevPEng 806.
All Citizens Are Soldiers. See *Sheep-Well, The.*
"All Fires the Fire" (Cortázar). RevShF 634.
All Fools (Chapman). DEng 354-356; RevDEng 415-417.

All for Love (Dryden). DEng 521-522; RevDEng 643-644.
All God's Dangers (Rosengarten). ShF 627, 1430-1431.
All Green Shall Perish (Mallea). LFFor 1054-1056.
All Hallows Eve (Williams). RevLFEng 3860.
"All He Needs Is Feet" (Himes). RevShF 1202.
"All in a Maze" (Carr). RevShF 430-431.
"All-Knowing Rabbit" (Kennedy). PEng 1570-1571; RevPEng 1805-1806.
"All Legendary Obstacles" (Montague). PEng 2035.
All Men Are Brothers. See *Water Margin.*
All Men Are Enemies (Aldington). LFEng 42-43; RevLFEng 56-57.
All Men Are Mortal (de Beauvoir). LFFor 116-117.
All My Friends Are Going to Be Strangers (McMurtry). LFEng 1755-1756; RevLFEng 2223-2224.
"All My Pretty Ones" (Sexton). PEng 2523; RevPEng 2933.
All My Pretty Ones (Sexton). PEng 2523; RevPEng 2933-2934.
All My Sons (Miller). DEng 1338-1339, 2406; RevDEng 1677, 2927.
All Our Yesterdays. See *Dead Yesterdays.*
All Quiet on the Western Front (Remarque). LFFor 1398-1401, 2191.
"All-Seeing, The" (Nin). RevShF 1723; ShF 1950.
"All soul, no earthly flesh" (Nashe). PEng 2073; RevPEng 2422.
"All Souls' Day" (Pascoli). PFor 1141.
"All Strange Away" (Beckett). RevShF 192.
All That Fall (Beckett). DEng 153-154; DFor 161-162; RevDEng 190.
"All the Days of Our Lives" (Smith). RevShF 2155.
All the King's Men (Warren). LFEng 2775-2776; RevLFEng 3440-3441, 3772.
"All the Soul Indrawn . . ." (Mallarmé). PFor 926-927.
"'All You Zombies,'" (Heinlein). RevShF 1157; ShF 1619.
"Allal" (Bowles). ShF 992.
"All'amica risanata." *See* "To the Healed Friend."
"Allant châtier la rebellion des Rochelois" (Malherbe). PFor 921-922.
Allegiances (Stafford). RevPEng 3171.
Allegoria del Poema (Tasso). PFor 1501.
Allegories of Reading (de Man). LTh 349.
Allegory of Love, The (Lewis). LTh 896.

Allegria, L' (Ungaretti). PFor 1564-1566.
Allegria di naufragi. See *Allegria, L'.*
"Allegro, L'" (Milton). PEng 2007; RevPEng 2340.
Allegro Barbaro (Bartók). PEng 3505-3508, 3511, 3512.
"Alleluia Meadow, The" (Holz). PFor 694-695.
Allen, Grant. M&D 16-22.
Allen, Paula Gunn. RevPEng 3935.
Allen, Woody. RevShF 55-60.
Alley, Henry. ShF 2496.
Alley Jaggers (West, P.). LFSup 372; RevLFEng 3523.
Alleyn, Edward. DEng 2522-2523.
"Alligator Bride, The" (Hall). PEng 1202.
Alligator Bride, The (Hall). PEng 1197, 1201-1202; RevPEng 1372.
Allingham, Margery. M&D 23-28.
Allingham, William. PEng 37-46. RevPEng 28-37.
"All'Italia." See "To Italy."
All's Well That Ends Well (Shakespeare). DEng 1709-1710, 2280; RevDEng 2123-2124, 2799.
"Alma" (Prior). RevPEng 2671-2672.
Alma (Prior). PEng 2290-2291.
"Almanac, An" (Schuyler). PEng 2483; RevPEng 2889.
"Almanac of Pain, An" (Dazai). RevShF 692; ShFSup 93.
Almas perdidas (Hernández). DFor 2442.
Al-Mawākib. See *Procession, The.*
"Almohadón de plumas, El." See "Feather Pillow, The."
"Almond Blossom" (Lawrence, D. H.). PEng 1684; RevPEng 1954.
Almoran and Hamet (Hawkesworth). RevShF 1139-1140; ShF 1608-1609.
Almqvist, Carl Jonas Love. DFor 2469; LFFor 2337; PFor 2167.
Alnæs, Finn. LFFor 2363.
Alnilam (Dickey). RevLFEng 917-919.
Alonso, Dámaso. LTh 24-28.
Alouette, L'. See *Lark, The.*
Alpenkönig und der Menschenfeind. See Mountain King and Misanthrope.
"Alpha" (Brathwaite). PEng 272; RevPEng 334.
"Alpha" (Różewicz). PFor 1368-1369.
Alphabet of Elegies, An (Quarles). PEng 2299; RevPEng 2680.
Alphabetical Order (Frayn). DSup 127-128; RevDEng 831.
Alphonsus of Arragon (Greene, R.). DEng 2270; RevDEng 2789.

"Als der Krieg zu Ende war." See "As the War Ended."
Altamirano, Ignacio Manuel. LFFor 2284.
"Altar, The" (Herbert). PEng 1298, 1299; RevPEng 1478.
"Altar of the Dead, The" (James, H.). RevShF 1264.
"Altarwise by Owl-Light" (Thomas, D.). PEng 2884-2885; RevPEng 3352-3353.
"Alternative, The" (Baraka). ShF 923.
"Altes Blatt, Ein." See "Old Manuscript, An."
"Although by Night" (John of the Cross). PFor 766.
Althusser, Louis. LTh 416-417, 503-504, 845, 1767.
"Altura y pelos." See "Height and Hair."
Alurista. RevPEng 3922.
Álvarez Gardeazábal, Gustavo. LFFor 2300-2301.
Alvarez Journal, The (Burns). M&D 250.
Álvarez Quintero, Serafín, and Joaquín Álvarez Quintero. DFor 50-58, 2502-2503.
Alvaro, Corrado. DFor 2415; LFFor 2246.
"Always to Be Named" (Bobrowski). PFor 206.
Alyagrov. See **Jakobson, Roman.**
Alzire (Voltaire). DFor 1968-1969.
"Am I Insane?" (Maupassant). M&D 1209.
"Am Sonnabend Abend." See "On a Saturday Evening."
"Am/Trak" (Baraka). PEng 89-90; RevPEng 100-101.
Ama de la casa, El (Martínez Sierras). DFor 1284-1285.
Amade, László. PFor 1977.
Amadeus (Shaffer, P.). DEng 1685-1687; RevDEng 2093-2095, 2099-2101.
Amadis de Gaula (de Montalvo). ShF 144.
Amadis of Gaul (Vicente). DFor 1959.
Amado, Jorge. LFFor 49-56.
"Amado dueño mio" (Cruz). PFor 378.
"Amai." See "I Loved."
"Amante di Gramigna, L'." See "Gramigna's Mistress."
"Amante dulce del alma" (Cruz). PFor 380.
"Amaranta" (Alberti). PFor 20.
Amateur Cracksman, The (Hornung). M&D 906.
Amateurs (Barthelme). ShFSup 24.
"Amateur's Guide to the Night, An" (Robison). RevShF 2013-2014.
Amazing Stories. ShF 773-774.
Amazing Web, The (Keeler). M&D 956-957.
"Amazon, The" (Leskov). RevShF 1466-1467; ShFSup 159.
Amazoulous, Les (Kâ). DFor 2270.

Ambarvalia (Clough). PEng 519; RevPEng 617.

Ambassadors, The (James, H.). LFEng 1436, 1448-1449; RevLFEng 1715, 1727-1728.

"Amber Bead, The" (Herrick). PEng 1311; RevPEng 1491.

Ambiguous Adventure (Kane). LFFor 2035.

Ambitious Step-Mother, The (Rowe). DEng 1633-1634; RevDEng 2040-2041.

Ambito (Aleixandre). PFor 29.

Ambler, Eric. M&D 29-34.

Ambra (Poliziano). PFor 1256. See also *Sylvae*.

Ambrogini, Angelo. *See* **Poliziano.**

"Ambrose His Mark" (Barth). RevShF 154; ShF 928.

Ambrosio (Lewis, M.). ShF 730-731.

Ambrosio. See *Monk, The.*

Ambrosius Theodosius Macrobius. *See* **Macrobius.**

A.M.D.G. (Pérez de Ayala). LFFor 1256.

Âme enchantée, L'. See *Soul Enchanted, The.*

Âme romantique et la rêve, L' (Béguin). LTh 1151.

Amelia (Fielding, H.). LFEng 3073; RevLFEng 3782.

Amelia (Patmore). PEng 2194; RevPEng 2565.

Amen Corner, The (Baldwin). DEng 74-75; RevDEng 97-99.

America (Blake). PEng 213-214; RevPEng 257-258.

"America" (Ginsberg). RevPEng 1229.

"America" (Wheatley). PEng 3053; RevPEng 3540.

"America! America!" (Schwartz). RevShF 2084; ShF 2207-2208.

American, The (James, H.). DEng 994; RevDEng 1259.

"American Authors of Today" (Boynton). ShF 72.

American Buffalo (Mamet). DEng 1240-1243, 2413; RevDEng 1564-1565, 2934.

American Democrat, The (Cooper). LFEng 607; RevLFEng 732.

American Dream, The (Albee). DEng 2408; RevDEng 2929.

American Dream, An (Mailer). LFEng 1779-1781; RevLFEng 2252-2254.

"American Eagle, The" (Lawrence, D. H.). PEng 1683-1684; RevPEng 1953-1954.

"American Glamour" (Young). PEng 3216; RevPEng 3740.

"American History" (Harper). PSup 162; RevPEng 1402.

American Hunger (Wright, R.). ShF 579.

"American Letter" (MacLeish). PEng 1855; RevPEng 2155.

"American Literature" (Fuller). LTh 524-525.

"American Living Room, The" (Meredith). RevPEng 2275.

"American Portrait: Old Style" (Warren). PEng 3028.

American Renaissance (Matthiessen). LTh 1009-1012.

"American Rhapsody (2)" (Fearing). RevPEng 1140.

American Scene, The (James, H.). LFEng 1435; RevLFEng 1714.

American Scenes and Other Poems (Tomlinson). RevPEng 3378.

American Scholar, The (Emerson). LTh 455, 457-458; ShF 219.

"American Takes a Walk, An" (Whittemore). PEng 3079; RevPEng 3567.

American Tragedy, An (Dreiser). LFEng 836-838, 3051, 3180-3183; RevLFEng 1002-1004, 3759.

American Visitor, An (Cary). LFEng 456; RevLFEng 574, 576.

"American Way, The" (Corso). PEng 578; RevPEng 673.

Americana (DeLillo). LFSup 85-86; RevLFEng 863-864.

America's Coming-of-Age (Brooks, V.). LTh 226.

Amerika (Kafka). LFFor 898-900.

Amers. See *Seamarks.*

Âmes du Purgatoire, Les (Mérimée). LFFor 1148.

Âmes fortes, Les (Giono). LFFor 657.

Amichai, Yehuda. PSup 1-7.

Aminta (Tasso). DFor 1816-1819, 2399-2400; PFor 2015.

"Amirauté, L' " (Follain). PSup 128-129.

Amis, Ayfara. *See* **Behn, Aphra.**

Amis, Kingsley. LFEng 59-70; LFSup 401; RevLFEng 83-100, 3774, 3775, 3808.

Amis, Martin. RevLFEng 101-107.

"Amitié, L' " (Follain). PSup 128.

Ammianus Marcellinus. *See* Marcellinus, Ammianus.

Ammons, A. R. PSup 8-14; RevPEng 38-45.

"Among Ourselves" (Meredith). RevPEng 2275.

"Among School Children" (Yeats). PEng 3199-3203; RevPEng 3723-3727.

"Among Tenses" (Morgenstern). PFor 1058. See also *Gallows Songs, The.*

"Among the Dahlias" (Sansom). RevShF 2054.

"Among the Impressionists" (Wiggins). RevShF 2469-2470.

"Amor." *See* "Love."

"Amor dormido." *See* "Love Asleep."
Amor es más laberinto (Cruz). DFor 443-444.
Amore, Un. See *Love Affair, A.*
Amore della tre melarance, L'. See *Love of the Three Oranges, The.*
"Amore e morte." *See* "Love and Death."
Amores (Ovid). PFor 1122-1123, 1124.
"Amoret" (Congreve). PEng 555; RevPEng 647.
Amoretti (Spenser). PEng 2714-2715; RevPEng 3158-3159.
Amorous Prince, The (Behn). RevDEng 211.
Amos, Alan. *See* **Knight, Kathleen Moore.**
"Amos Barton" (Eliot, G.). RevShF 806; ShF 1334.
Amos 'n' Andy. RevDEng 3027.
"Amour." *See* "Love" (Colette).
Amour fou, L' (Breton). LTh 215.
"Amoureuse, L'." *See* "Woman in Love, A."
Amours de Voyage (Clough). PEng 520-521; RevPEng 618-619.
Amphitryon (Hacks). DFor 853.
Amphitryon (Kleist). DFor 1076-1078.
Amphitryon (Plautus). DFor 1484.
Amphitryon 38 (Behrman). DEng 187; RevDEng 224.
Amphitryon 38 (Giraudoux). DFor 725-726.
Amrita (Jhabvala). LFSup 171-172; RevLFEng 1753-1754.
Amtmandens døttre (Collett). LFFor 2338.
"Amuck in the Bush" (Callaghan). RevShF 385; ShFSup 69.
"Amusing Adventure, An" (Zoshchenko). RevShF 2559; ShFSup 380.
"Amy Foster" (Conrad). LFEng 3282-3284.
Amy Robsart (Hugo). DFor 969.
"An die Dichter." *See* "To the Poets."
"An die Freude." *See* "Ode to Joy."
"An ein fallendes Blatt." *See* "To a Falling Leaf."
An Giall (Behan). DEng 166.
"An Klopstock." *See* "To Klopstock."
"An Nelly Sachs." *See* "To Nelly Sachs."
"An Tieck." *See* "To Tieck."
Anabase. See *Anabasis.*
Anabasis (Perse). PFor 1195.
"Anaconda, A" (Quiroga). RevShF 1989.
Anacreon. PFor 33-39.
Anakomidhi (Pentzíkis). PFor 1190.
"Analyse structurale en linguistique et en anthropologie, L'." *See* "Structural Analysis in Linguistics and in Anthropology."
Anand, Mulk Raj. LFFor 2218-2220; ShF 645, 646.

"Anaphora" (Bishop). PEng 187; RevPEng 230.
"Anatomy Lesson, The" (Connell). ShF 1176-1177.
Anatomy Lesson, The (Roth). RevLFEng 2903
Anatomy of Criticism (Frye). LTh 508-509, 512, 1432, 1756-1757.
Anatomy of Nonsense, The (Winters). LTh 1568.
Anatomy of the World, An (Donne). PEng 834-835; RevPEng 940-941.
Anaya, Rudolfo A. ShF 2497.
Ancel, Paul. *See* **Celan, Paul.**
Anceschi, Luciano. LTh 29-35.
Ancestral Power (Awoonor). DEng 2421; RevDEng 2943-2944.
Ancestress, The (Grillparzer). DFor 821-822, 824.
Anciennes Odeurs, Les. See *Remember Me.*
Ancient Child, The (Momaday). RevPEng 2356.
Ancient Evenings (Mailer). RevLFEng 2260-2261.
"Ancient Hungarian Lament of Mary." PFor 1974.
"Ancient Lights" (Clarke). PSup 70-71; RevPEng 610-611.
"Ancient Torso of Apollo" (Rilke). PFor 1331. See also *New Poems.*
Ancius Manlius Severinus Boethius. *See* **Boethius.**
And Be a Villain (Stout). M&D 1543-1544.
And Come to Closure (Coulette). RevPEng 690-692.
"And Death Shall Have No Dominion" (Thomas, D.). PEng 2883-2884; RevPEng 3351-3352.
"And I Lounged and Lay on Their Beds" (Cavafy). PFor 300.
And Miss Reardon Drinks a Little (Zindel). DEng 2128-2131; RevDEng 2649-2651.
And on the Eighth Day (Queen). M&D 1380.
And Quiet Flows the Don. See *Silent Don, The.*
And So Ad Infinitum. See *Insect Play, The.*
"And So I Grew Up to Be Nineteen and to Murder" (Oates). RevPEng 2468.
"And the Rain Patters On" (Wang Anyi). RevShF 2395.
... And the Wife Ran Away (Weldon). RevLFEng 3475.
"And There Was the Evening and the Morning" (Böll). RevShF 237.
And They Put Handcuffs on the Flowers (Arrabal). DFor 128-129.
And Things That Go Bump in the Night (McNally). DEng 1228, 1229-1230; RevDEng 1550-1551.
"And You?" (Foscolo). PFor 493-494. *See also* "Sonetti."
Andersch, Alfred. ShF 2498.
Andersen, Benny. PFor 2197.

"Arabesque: The Mouse" (Coppard). RevShF 627-628; ShF 1199-1200.

Arabian Nights' Entertainments, The. ShF 138-139, 154, 407-414, 677.

"Araby" (Joyce). RevShF 1297; ShF 102-103, 114, 1720.

"Arachne" (Empson). PEng 970; RevPEng 1100.

Aragon, Louis. PFor 64-73, 1886-1887.

"Araignée mise au mur, L'." *See* "Spider Placed on the Wall, The."

Arany, János. PFor 74-84, 1982-1983.

Ararat (Glück). RevPEng 1249-1250.

Arbitration, The (Menander). DFor 2133.

Árbol de la ciencia, El. See *Tree of Knowledge, The.*

Árbol viejo, El (Hernández). DFor 2442.

Arbor of Amorous Devices, The (Breton, N.). PEng 279; RevPEng 341, 343.

Arbuthnott, John. *See* **Henry, O.**

Arcadia (Sidney). LFEng 3014-3015; RevLFEng 3722-3723; RevShF 2627, 2631; ShF 490-491, 495.

Arcadia (Stoppard). RevDEng 2318-2319.

Arcane 17 (Breton). LTh 214-215.

Arcangeli non giocano a flipper, Gli (Fo). DSup 110.

Arch Oboler's Plays. RevDEng 3031.

Arch of Triumph (Remarque). LFFor 1401-1402.

Archaeologist of Morning (Olson). PSup 310-311; RevPEng 2502.

Archaeology of Knowledge, The (Foucault). LTh 505.

"Archaischer Torso Apollos." *See* "Ancient Torso of Apollo."

Archéologie du savoir, L'. See *Archaeology of Knowledge, The.*

Archer in the Marrow (Viereck). RevPEng 3461.

"Archetype and Signature" (Fiedler). LTh 483-485.

Archilochus. DFor 2087; **PFor 85-92,** 712-713, 1758-1759.

Architect and the Emperor of Assyria, The (Arrabal). DFor 126-127.

Architecte et l'Empereur d'Assyria, L'. See *Architect and the Emperor of Assyria, The.*

"Arcturus" (Connell). RevShF 601-602; ShF 1178-1181.

Ardèle (Anouilh). DFor 80.

Arden, John. DEng 41-49, 2385, 2386; **RevDEng 54-63,** 2904.

Arden, William. *See* **Collins, Michael.**

Ardis Claverden (Stockton). M&D 1537.

"Are You a Doctor?" (Carver). ShFSup 77.

Aren't We All? (Lonsdale). DEng 1170-1171; RevDEng 1472-1473.

"Arethusa, the First Morning" (Viereck). RevPEng 3459.

Aretino, Pietro. DFor 93-102.

"Arfy i skripki" (Blok). PFor 197.

Argalus and Parthenia (Quarles). PEng 2298; RevPEng 2679.

Argonauten, Die. See *Golden Fleece, The.*

Argonautica (Apollonius Rhodius). PFor 57, 58-63.

Argonauts, The. DFor 825. See also *Golden Fleece, The.*

Argote, Luis de Góngora y. See **Góngora y Argote, Luis de.**

"Argument of His Book, The" (Herrick). PEng 1309-1311; RevPEng 1489-1491.

Ariadne auf Naxos (Ernst). DFor 559-560.

Arias, Ronald. ShF 2500.

Arias Gonzalo (Saavedra). DFor 1616.

Arias tristes (Jiménez). PFor 750.

Aridoshi (Zeami). DFor 2042.

Ariel (Rodo). LTFor 2286.

Arion of Lesbos. RevDEng 2653.

Arion. DFor 2088-2089.

Ariosto, Ludovico. DFor 103-110, 2396; LTh 131, 366, 584, 1040, 1662; **PFor 93-100,** 163, 2012-2014.

Aristocracy (Howard, B.). DEng 971-972; RevDEng 1208-1209.

Aristophanes. DEng 2137; **DFor 111-120,** 2091-2092, 2095, 2123-2130; RevDEng 2657.

Aristos, The (Fowles). LFEng 1008; RevLFEng 1199.

Aristotle. DEng 2138-2143; DFor 2094-2095; LTh 22, **36-44,** 77, 258, 272-274, 276-277, 280, 301-302, 305, 309-310, 323, 384, 405, 529, 584-587, 614, 779, 781-782, 840, 855, 862, 882, 906, 939, 952, 958, 1038-1041, 1111, 1143-1145, 1200, 1282-1283, 1285-1286, 1320, 1347, 1461, 1636-1637, 1648-1649, 1661, 1665, 1799, 1832; RevDEng 2658-2663; RevPEng 4006-4008.

"Aristotle and Phyllis" (Hollander). RevPEng 1547-1548.

"Aristotle and the Hired Thugs" (Gold). ShF 1503-1504.

Ariwara no Narihira. PFor 2059-2060.

"Arizona Midnight" (Warren). RevPEng 3524.

"Ark" (Johnson, R.). RevPEng 1717.

Ark (Johnson, R.). PSup 214-215.

Ark, The (Zhang Jie). RevShF 2543.

Arkansas Testament, The (Walcott). RevPEng 3501-3502.

Art of Prophesying, The (Perkins). **LTh** 1740-1741.

Art poétique, L' (Boileau). See *Art of Poetry, The.*

"Art poétique, L'" (Verlaine). **PFor** 1627.

Artaud, Antonin. DEng 2204-2205, 2239-2241; DFor 2238-2239, 2240-2241, 2256, 2352; **LTh 51-55;** RevDEng 2724-2725, 2759-2760.

Arte honeste amandi, De. See *Art of Courtly Love, The.*

Arte nuevo de hacer comedias en este tiempo, El. See *New Art of Writing Plays, The.*

Arte of English Poesie, The (Puttenham). **LTh** 1185-1187.

Arte of Rhetorique, The (Wilson). **LTh** 1666.

Arte poetica (Minturno). **LTh** 1039, 1669.

Artefactos (Parra). **PFor** 1134.

"Artémis" (Nerval). **PFor** 1088-1089.

Arthur Mervyn (Brown, C. B.). **LFEng** 316; RevLFEng 411.

"Arthur Mitchell" (Moore). **PEng** 2047; RevPEng 2377.

Arthur Rex (Berger). **LFEng** 257-258; RevLFEng 311-312.

"Artifex in Extremis" (Davie). **PSup** 91; RevPEng 857.

"Artificial Nigger, The" (O'Connor, Flannery). RevShF 1760-1761; ShF 1986-1987.

"Artist, The" (Wilde). **PEng** 3108; RevPEng 3599.

"Artist at Work, The" (Camus, A.). RevShF 402; ShF 1050-1051.

Artist Descending a Staircase (Stoppard). RevDEng 2314.

"Artist in the North, An" (Tranströmer). **PFor** 1528.

"Artist of the Beautiful, The" (Hawthorne). RevShF 1149.

Artist of the Floating World, An (Ishiguro). RevLFEng 1708-1709, 3793.

Artomonov Business, The (Gorky). **LFFor** 725-726.

Arts on the Level (Krieger). **LTh** 828.

Artsybashev, Mikhail. **LFFor** 2321.

"Aru kyuyu e okuru shuki." See "Memories Sent to an Old Friend."

As a Man Grows Older (Svevo). **LFFor** 1700, 1703-1704.

"As Children Together" (Forché). RevPEng 1159.

"As Fine as Melanctha" (Stein). RevShF 2200-2201; ShFSup 307-309.

As for Me and My House (Ross). **LFEng** 2284, 2286-2288, 2289-2291; RevLFEng 2882, 2883-2884, 2885-2887.

"As I Ebb'd with the Ocean of Life" (Whitman). **PEng** 3071; RevPEng 3558.

As I Lay Dying (Faulkner). **LFEng** 922-923; RevLFEng 1096-1097, 3832.

"As I Walked Out One Evening" (Auden). **PEng** 76; RevPEng 86.

As if by Magic (Wilson, Angus). **LFEng 2005;** RevLFEng 3595.

As the Crow Flies (Clarke, A.). DEng 376-377; RevDEng 464-465.

"As the Team's Head-Brass" (Thomas, E.). **PEng** 2892-2893; RevPEng 3360-3361.

"As the War Ended" (Böll). RevShF 237-238.

"As Toilsome I Wander'd Virginia's Woods" (Whitman). **PEng** 3072; RevPEng 3559.

"As weary pilgrim, now at rest" (Bradstreet). **PEng** 261; RevPEng 321.

"As Well as They Can Be" (Hope). **PSup** 190; RevPEng 1595.

As You Like It (Shakespeare). DEng 1708, 2278-2279; RevDEng 2122, 2797-2798.

Asachi, Gheorghe. **DFor** 2296.

"Ascendant Thought, The" (Leopardi). **PFor** 862-863. See also *Canti.*

Ascension. See *Christ II.*

Ascent of Mount Carmel, The (John of the Cross). **PFor** 763, 766-767.

Ascent to Omai (Harris, W.). **LFSup** 148-149; RevLFEng 1531.

Asch, Sholem. LFFor 72-80.

Ascham, Roger. **LTh** 1662-1663.

Aschenbrödel. See *Cinderella.*

Aschensommer (Ausländer). **PSup** 18.

Ascher, Sheila, and Dennis Straus. **ShF** 2501.

"Ash, The" (Heyen). **PEng** 1327; RevPEng 1507.

Ash Wednesday (Eliot). **PEng** 947; RevPEng 1076-1077.

Ashbery, John. PEng 57-62; PSup 403; **RevPEng 56-67.**

Ashdown, Clifford, *See* **Freeman, R. Austin.**

Ashe, Gordon. *See* **Creasey, John.**

Ashe, Mary Ann. *See* **Brand, Christianna.**

"Ashes" (Saba). **PSup** 347-348.

"Ashikari" (Tanizaki). RevShF 2247; ShFSup 316.

Así que pasen cinco años. See *When Five Years Pass.*

"Asian Shore, The" (Disch). RevShF 746; ShF 1289.

Asiatics, The (Prokosch). **LFEng** 2162, 2164; RevLFEng 2737.

Asimov, Isaac. RevShF 84-92; ShF 551, 775, **875-881;** ShFSup 387.

Ask Me Now (Young). **LFEng** 3010-3011; RevLFEng 3716-3717.

"At the Bottom of the River" (Kincaid). RevShF 1343.

"At the Circus" (Sinyavsky). RevShF 2139.

"At the Edge of the World" (Leskov). RevShF 1467-1468; ShFSup 160.

"At the End of September" (Petőfi). PFor 1224-1225.

At the End of the Open Road (Simpson). PEng 2603-2604; RevPEng 3009-3010.

"At the Executed Murderer's Grave" (Wright, James). PEng 3161-3163; RevPEng 3673-3675.

"At the Gynecologist's" (Pastan). RevPEng 2545.

"At the Indian Killer's Grave" (Lowell, R.). PEng 1788-1789; RevPEng 2082-2083.

"At the Market" (Arany). PFor 83.

"At the Prophet's" (Mann). ShF 1877.

"At the Rendezvous of Victory" (Gordimer). RevShF 1035; ShFSup 110.

"At the Seminary" (Oates). ShF 709-710.

"At the Theatre" (Cavafy). PFor 300.

"At the Tolstoy Museum" (Barthelme). RevShF 166-167.

At the Top of My Voice (Mayakovsky). PFor 991, 992.

At the Villa Rose (Mason). M&D 1197.

"At Twilight" (Monroe). PEng 2028.

At være eller ikke være. See *To Be, or Not to Be?*

Atala (Chateaubriand). LFFor 338-339.

Atalanta in Calydon (Swinburne). DEng 1897-1898; PEng 2813; RevDEng 2339-2340; RevPEng 3281.

Athawar House (Nagarajan). ShF 644.

Atheist, The (Otway). DEng 1449; RevDEng 1829.

Atheist's Tragedy, The (Tourneur). DEng 1941-1943, 2292; RevDEng 2400-2401, 2811.

"Athénaïse" (Chopin). RevShF 538-539; ShF 1134-1135.

Atlakviða. RevShF 2603. See *Lay of Atli*.

Atlantic Flyway (Galvin). PEng 1055-1057; RevPEng 1187-1189.

Atom Station, The (Laxness). LFFor 997.

"Atoms" (Wormser). RevPEng 3653-3654.

Atoms, Soul Music, and Other Poems (Wormser). RevPEng 3652-3654.

Atómstöðin. See *Atom Station, The*.

"Atrocity Exhibition, The" (Ballard). RevShF 144.

Atsumori (Zeami). DFor 2041-2042.

Atta Troll (Heine). LTh 663; PFor 648, 650.

"Attack on the Mill, The" (Zola). RevShF 2551; ShF 2486.

"Attempt About Us" (Lorenc). PFor 1823.

Atterbom, P. D. A. PFor 2165.

"Attis" (Bunting). PEng 370; RevPEng 444-445.

Atwood, Margaret. LFEng 94-102; LFSup 401; PEng 63-69; PSup 403; RevLFEng 132-143, 3871; RevPEng 68-79; RevShF 101-109; ShFSup 13-19.

"Au beau demi-jour." See "In the Lovely Half-light."

"Au hasard des oiseaux" (Prévert). PFor 1279.

"Au lecteur." See "To the Reader."

"Au regard des divinités." See "In the Eyes of the Gods."

"Au Tombeau de Charles Fourier" (Davenport). RevShF 683; ShF 1247-1248.

Aub, Max. DFor 2506; LFFor 2394.

"Aubade" (Empson). PEng 971; RevPEng 1101.

"Aubade" (Larkin). RevPEng 1945.

"Aubade" (Sitwell). PEng 2626-2627; RevPEng 3030-3031.

Aubrey-Fletcher, Henry Lancelot. See **Wade, Henry.**

Auchincloss, Louis. LFEng 103-114; LFSup 401; RevLFEng 144-156; RevShF 110-118.

Auden, W. H. DEng 50-58; PEng 70-80; RevDEng 64-73; RevPEng 80-91; ShF 543.

Audiberti, Jacques. DFor 2359.

Audience, The (García Lorca). DFor 660-662.

Audience (Havel). DFor 881.

Audun and the Bear. ShF 398.

Auerbach, Erich. LFEng 3214-3215, 3220; **LTh 56-61,** 712, 1394, 1512.

Auf dem Chimborazo (Dorst). DSup 96.

"Auf dem See." See "On the Lake."

Auf der Erde und in der Hölle (Bernhard). PFor 181-182.

"Auf der Galerie." See "Up in the Gallery."

Auf der Universität (Storm). LFFor 1681-1682.

"Auf dich im blauen Mantel." See "To You in a Blue Coat."

Auf eigene Hoffnung (Kunze). PFor 807-809.

"Auf Reisen." See "Travel."

Aufstand der Fischer von St. Barbara. See *Revolt of the Fishermen, The*.

Auftrag, Der (Dürrenmatt). See *Assignment, The*.

Auftrag, Der (Müller). DSup 262.

Augellino belverde, L' (Gozzi). DFor 797-798.

Augier, Émile. DFor 132-133, 2345-2346.

"Augsburg Chalk Circle, The" (Brecht). RevShF 323-325; ShF 1008-1009.

August (Hamsun). LFFor 768.

August, August, august (Kohout). DSup 223.

August Is a Wicked Month (O'Brien, E.). LFEng 2020; RevLFEng 2545.

"August 19, Pad 19" (Swenson). PEng 2797; RevPEng 3263.

August 1914 (Solzhenitsyn). LFEng 3154; RevLFEng 3839.

Augustine, Saint. LTh 62-67, 470, 565, 741, 1645-1646, 1653; PFor 2109; **ShF 889-894.**

Augustus. PFor 1607, 1610, 1615. *See also* Octavian.

Aukrust, Olav. PFor 2176.

Aulularia. See *Pot of Gold, The.*

Aulus Persius Flaccus. See **Persius.**

Aunt Dan and Lemon (Shawn). DSup 337-338; RevDEng 2170-2171.

Aunt Julia and the Scriptwriter (Vargas Llosa). LFFor 1851.

"Aunt Mara" (Dovlatov). RevShF 759, 760.

Aunt's Story, The (White, P.). LFEng 2866-2868; RevLFEng 3548-3549.

Aura (Fuentes). LFFor 595-596; RevShF 927-928; ShF 130.

Aurélia (Nerval). PFor 1085.

"Aurelia Frequenzia Reveals the Heart and Mind of the Man of Destiny" (Stern). RevShF 2215.

Aurelius Augustinus. *See* **Augustine, Saint.**

Aurelius Prudentius Clemens. *See* Prudentius.

Aureng-Zebe (Dryden). DEng 520-521; RevDEng 642-643.

Aureolus, Petrus. LTh 1653.

Aurobindo, Sri. PFor 1996-1997, 2000.

Aurora Dawn (Wouk). LFEng 2963-2965; RevLFEng 3666-3667.

Aurora Floyd (Braddon). M&D 182.

Aurora Leigh (Browning, E. B.). PEng 331-332; RevPEng 401-402.

"Auschwitz, Mon Amour." *See* "Welcoming Party, A."

"Auschwitz, Our Home" (Borowski). RevShF 256-257.

Ausflug der toten Mädchen, Der (Seghers). LFFor 1529.

Ausländer, Rose. PSup 15-21.

Ausonius, Decimus Magnus. PFor 2110.

Austen, Jane. LFEng 115-127, 3075, 3132, 3134; **RevLFEng 157-171, 3784; RevShF 119-123; ShF 895-898.**

"Austerity of Poetry" (Arnold). PEng 53; RevPEng 52.

Austin, Harry. *See* **McInerny, Ralph.**

Austin, J. L. LTh 1827-1828; L. RevPEng 3992.

"Australia" (Hope). PSup 188; RevPEng 1593, 3941.

"Author and Hero in Aesthetic Activity" (Bakhtin). LTh 86, 88.

"Author as Producer, The" (Benjamin). LTh 140.

"Author of the Acacia Seeds, The" (Le Guin). RevShF 1454.

Author's Farce, The (Fielding). DEng 607-608; RevDEng 750-751.

Auto da barca da glória. See *Ship of Heaven, The.*

Auto-da-Fé (Canetti). LFFor 268-271.

Auto da feira (Vicente). DFor 1958.

Auto da sibila Cassandra. See *Play of the Sibyl Cassandra, The.*

Auto de barca do inferno (Vicente). DFor 2173.

Auto de barca do purgatorio (Vicente). DFor 2177.

Auto de los Reyes Magos. DFor 2170.

"Autobiografia" (Saba). PSup 343, 345.

Autobiographies (Yeats). LTh 1589.

"Autobiography" (Barth). RevShF 154; ShF 929.

Autobiography (Hunt). PEng 1462.

"Autobiography: New York" (Reznikoff). RevPEng 2747.

"Autobiography" (Seifert). PSup 355.

"Autobiography of a Comedian" (Ciardi). PEng 503; RevPEng 592-593.

Autobiography of Leigh Hunt, The (Hunt). RevPEng 1673.

Autobiography of Miss Jane Pittman, The (Gaines). LFEng 1047-1048; RevLFEng 1243-1244; RevShF 931; ShF 1430-1431.

Autocracy of Mr. Parham, The (Wells). RevLFEng 3485.

"Automa, L'." *See* "Fetish, The."

"Automatons" (Hoffman). RevShF 1215-1216; ShF 1648.

Autonomia ed eteronomia dell'arte (Anceschi). LTh 31.

"Autor als Produzent, Der." *See* "Author as Producer, The."

Autre Monde, L' See *Other Worlds.*

Autre Tartuffe, L . See *Frailty and Hypocrisy.*

"Autumn Begins in Martin's Ferry, Ohio" (Wright, James). PEng 3165; RevPEng 3677.

"Autumn Day" (Gallant). RevShF 940; ShF 1439-1440.

Autumn Journal (MacNeice). PEng 1872-1875; RevPEng 2173-2176.

"Autumn Leaves" (Ignatow). RevPEng 1682.

"Autumn Maneuvers" (Bachmann). PFor 128. See also *Gestundete Zeit, Die.*

Autumn of the Patriarch, The (García Márquez). LFFor 619.

"Autumn Passed Through Paris" (Ady). PFor 6.

B

"B Negative" (Kennedy). PEng 1570; RevPEng 1805.

Baba Goya (Tesich). RevDEng 2376-2377.

"Babas del diable, Las." *See* "Blow-Up."

Babbitt (Lewis, S.). LFEng 1675-1677; RevLFEng 2071-2073.

Babbitt, Irving. LTh 68-74, 1011, 1256-1257, 1319, 1566, 1818.

"Babbo di Kafka, Il" (Landolfi). RevShF 1397.

Babe's Bed, The (Wescott). RevShF 2443-2444; ShF 2423.

Babel, Isaac. DFor 2462; ShF 899-904; RevShF 124-132, 2744-2745.

Babel-17 (Delany). LFEng 715, 717-718; RevLFEng 853-854.

Babelandia (Aguilera Malta). LFSup 13-14.

"Babette's Feast" (Dinesen). RevShF 741.

"Babettes Gæstebud." *See* "Babette's Feast."

Babička. See *Grandmother, The.*

Babits, Mihály. PFor 117-123, 1984.

"Babiy Yar" (Yevtushenko). PFor 1710.

Babouc (Voltaire). RevShF 2359-2360; ShFSup 329-330.

Babrius. RevShF 2578-2579; ShF 379, 380.

Babson, Marian. M&D 48-52.

"Baby H.P." (Arreola). RevShF 80.

"Baby Is Three" (Sturgeon). LFEng 2584; RevLFEng 3236.

"Baby Villon" (Levine). PEng 1715; RevPEng 1991.

Baby with the Bathwater (Durang). RevDEng 673.

"Babylon Revisited" (Fitzgerald). RevShF 862-863; ShF 1373-1374.

Babyloniaca (Iamblichus). LFFor 2001.

"Babysitter, The" (Coover). LFEng 3329; RevLFEng 3879; RevShF 2752; ShF 1191-1192.

Bacchae, The (Euripides). DFor 577, 2117-2119.

Bacchides. See *Two Bacchides, The.*

Bacchus (Cocteau). DFor 422.

"Bacchus" (Empson). PEng 970-971; RevPEng 1100-1101.

Bacchylides. PFor 1945.

Bachelard, Gaston. LTh 1149.

"Bachelor" (Meredith). PEng 1956-1957.

Bachelor of Arts, The (Narayan). LFEng 1968; RevLFEng 2483.

Bachman, Richard. See **King, Stephen.**

Bachmann, Ingeborg. LFFor 2199; **PFor 124-130,** 1934; ShF 2502.

"Back" (Corman). PEng 571; RevPEng 665.

Back Country, The (Snyder). PEng 2672-2674.

Back to Methuselah (Shaw). DEng 2382; RevDEng 2900.

Backtrack (Hansen). M&D 832-833.

Backward Place, A (Jhabvala). LFSup 174; RevLFEng 1756.

Bacon, Francis. **LTh 75-81,** 1675, 1677; PEng 596.

"Bad Blood" (Rimbaud). PFor 1339-1340. See also *Season in Hell, A.*

"Bad Characters" (Stafford). RevShF 2180; ShF 2262-2263.

"Bad Dreams" (Pinsky). PEng 2218.

Bad Habits (McNally). RevDEng 1552.

Bad Man, A (Elkin). LFEng 888-889; RevLFEng 1048.

Bad Man from Bodie. See *Welcome to Hard Times.*

Bad Seed (Anderson, M.). DEng 2202; RevDEng 2722.

Bad-tempered Man, The (Menander). DFor 1306-1308, 2133.

"Bad Time for Poetry" (Brecht). PFor 224-225.

Badenheim, 'ir nofesh. See *Badenheim 1939.*

Badenheim 1939 (Appelfeld). LFSup 33-35.

Badgers, The (Leonov). M&D 1059-1060.

Baggesen, Jens. PFor 2163.

Bagley, Desmond. M&D 53-58.

Bagrovy ostrov. See *Crimson Island, The.*

Bahía de silencio, La. See *Bay of Silence, The.*

Bahnwärter Thiel. See *Flagman Thiel.*

Bahr, Hermann. LFFor 2184.

Baikie Charivari, The (Bridie). DEng 278-279; RevDEng 333-334.

"Bailbondsman, The" (Elkin). LFEng 890; ShF 1341-1342; RevShF 813-814.

"Bailes y las comedias, Los" (Feijóo). LTh 476.

Bailey, H. C. M&D 59-66; ShF 755-756.

Baiser au lépreux, Le. See *Kiss for the Leper, A.*

Baitz, Jon Robin. RevDEng 85-92.

Bajazet (Racine). DFor 1518.

Bajazet, preface to (Racine). LTh 1199.

"Bajazzo, Der." *See* "Dilettante, The."

Bajka (Ćosić). LFFor 388-389.

Bajza, Jozef Ignác. LFFor 2068; PFor 1808.

Bakchai. See *Bacchae, The.*

Baker, Asa. See **Halliday, Brett.**

Baker, George Pierce. DEng 2399.

Baker, Houston A., Jr. LTh 546, 550.

Baker, Will. ShF 2503.

Bakhtin, Mikhail. LTh 82-89, 440, 832-833, 1437, 1799, 1821.

Bakke's Night of Fame (McGrath). RevDEng 1518-1519.

"Balaam and His Master" (Harris, J.). ShF 1590-1591; RevShF 1119.

"Balada de la placeta." *See* "Ballad of the Little Square."

"Balada del Andaluz perdido." *See* "Ballad of the Lost Andalusian."

Baladas de primavera (Jiménez). PFor 751.

Balaka. See *Flight of Swans, A.*

Balassi, Bálint. PFor 1976.

Balbín, Bohuslav. PFor 1798.

Balcony, The (Genet). DFor 683-685, 2260.

Balcony, The (Heiberg, G.). DFor 895.

Bald Soprano, The (Ionesco). DFor 995-997, 2248-2250, 2357.

Baldur hiin gode (Oehlenschläger). DFor 1441-1442.

Baldwin, James. DEng 70-78; LFEng 128-145, 3068; **RevDEng 93-102; RevLFEng 172-189,** 3776; **RevShF 133-139,** 2753; **ShF 556, 581, 905-910,** 1855.

Bale, John. DEng 79-91; RevDEng 103-116.

"Balek Scales, The" (Böll). ShF 974-975.

Balkonen. See *Balcony, The* (Heiberg, G).

Ball, Doris Collier. See **Bell, Josephine.**

Ball, John. M&D 67-73.

"Ball of Malt and Madame Butterfly, A" (Kiely). RevShF 1332-1334; ShF 1742-1744.

"Ballad" (Khodasevich). PSup 228.

Ballad and the Source, The (Lehmann). LFSup 231-234; RevLFEng 2020-2023.

"Ballad of a Streetwalker" (Manger). PFor 949-950.

"Ballad of a Sweet Dream of Peace" (Warren). PEng 3025.

"Ballad of Babie Bell, The" (Aldrich). PEng 30.

"Ballad of Billie Potts, The" (Warren). RevPEng 3521.

"Ballad of Birmingham" (Randall, D.). PEng 2316; RevPEng 2706.

"Ballad of Bouillabaise, The" (Thackeray). PEng 2874-2875.

"Ballad of Dead Ladies" (Villon). PFor 1658.

"Ballad of East and West, The" (Kipling). PEng 1608, 1609; RevPEng 1849.

"Ballad of Hanna'leh the Orphan, The" (Manger). PFor 950.

Ballad of Love, A (Prokosch). LFEng 2166; RevLFEng 2739.

Ballad of Reading Gaol, The (Wilde). PEng 3107-3108; RevPEng 3598-3599.

"Ballad of Sue Ellen Westerfield, The" (Hayden). PEng 1253; RevPEng 1437.

"Ballad of the Bridal Veil" (Manger). PFor 950.

"Ballad of the Children of the Czar, The" (Schwartz). PEng 2489; RevPEng 2896.

"Ballad of the Despairing Husband" (Creeley). RevPEng 778.

"Ballad of the Flexible Bullet, The" (King). RevShF 1349.

"Ballad of the Harp-Weaver, The" (Millay). PEng 2002; RevPEng 2326.

"Ballad of the Little Square" (García Lorca). PFor 516.

"Ballad of the Lost Andalusian" (Alberti). PFor 23.

"Ballad of the Oedipus Complex" (Durrell). PEng 923; RevPEng 1052.

Ballad of the Sad Café, The (McCullers). LFEng 1734-1736, 3309-3311; RevLFEng 2165-2167, 3877; RevShF 1544-1546; ShF 481, 1846-1847.

"Ballad of the White Horse, The" (Chesterton). PEng 493-494.

"Ballad of William Sycamore, The" (Benét). PEng 143; RevPEng 173.

"Ballad on the Gospel 'In the Beginning Was the Word'" (John of the Cross). PFor 766.

"Ballad on the Poet François Villon" (Biermann). PFor 190.

"Ballad on the Psalm 'By the Waters of Babylon'" (John of the Cross). PFor 766.

"Ballad upon a Wedding, A" (Suckling). PEng 2781-2782; RevPEng 3246-3247.

Ballade at the Reverence of Our Lady, Qwene of Mercy (Lydgate). RevPEng 2103; PEng 1808.

"Ballade auf den Dichter François Villon." *See* "Ballad on the Poet François Villon."

"Ballade des Äusseren Lebens" (Hofmannsthal). PFor 674.

"Ballade des dames du temps jadis." *See* "Ballad of Dead Ladies."

"Ballade von einem Traum" (Zweig). PFor 1726.

Ballades en jargon. See *Poems in Slang.*

Ballads (Stevenson). PEng 2757.

Ballads and Other Poems (Longfellow). PEng 1749; RevPEng 2034.

Ballads of a Bohemian (Service). PEng 2516; RevPEng 2925-2926.

Ballady i romanse (Mickiewicz). PFor 2124.

Balladyna (Słowacki). DFor 1715-1716, 2276.

Ballard, J. G. LFEng 146-154; LFSup 401; **RevLFEng 190-199; RevShF 140-146; ShF** 779-780, **911-916;** ShFSup 387.

Ballard, W. T. *See* **Carter, Nick.**

Balloon (Colum). DEng 386; RevDEng 485.

"Balloon, The" (Barthelme). RevShF 164-165; ShFSup 23.

"Baltazar's Marvellous Afternoon" (García Márquez). ShF 1455.

"Balthasar" (France). RevShF 899-900; ShF 1403-1404.

Balthazar (Balzac). See *Quest of the Absolute, The.*

Balthazar (Durrell). See *Alexandria Quartet, The.*

Baltics (Tranströmer). PFor 1528-1529.

"Balzac and Reality" (Butor). LTh 253.

Balzac, Honoré de. LFFor 89-102, 2126-2127, 2130, 2131; LTh 253, 554, 937, 1173, 1395, 1420, 1711; **M&D 74-81; RevShF 147-152,** 2667; ShF 172, 464, **917-921.**

Balzac, Jean-Louis Guez de. LTh 1687.

Bamboo Dancers, The (Gonzalez). LFEng 1143-1144; RevLFEng 1363-1364.

Bancroft, Marie Wilton. DEng 2350.

Bandello, Matteo. ShF 681.

Bandit, The (Hood). PEng 1382-1383; RevPEng 1580-1581.

Bang, Herman. LFFor 2339; LTh 1724.

"Bang-bang, You're Dead" (Spark). RevShF 2168; ShF 2255-2256.

"Bania." *See* "Bathhouse, The."

Bánk bán (Katona). DFor 2286.

Banker's Daughter, The (Howard, B.). DEng 969-970; RevDEng 1206-1207.

Bankrupt, The (Bjørnson). DFor 217-218.

"Banneker" (Dove). RevPEng 958.

Banquet, The (Dante). LTh 339, 342-345.

"Banshee, The" (Morgenstern). PFor 1057-1058. See also *Gallows Songs, The.*

Banville, John. LFSup 43-51; **RevLFEng 200-209.**

Banya. See *Bathhouse, The.*

Baotown (Wang Anyi). RevShF 2397.

Baptism, The (Baraka). DEng 96-97; RevDEng 121-123.

Bar-do thos-sgrol. See *Tibetan Book of the Dead, The.*

"Bar Giamaica, 1959-60" (Wright, C.). RevPEng 3662.

"Bar of Soap, A" (Lu Hsün). ShFSup 180-181.

Bar-20 (Mulford). RevLFEng 3852.

Barabbas (Lagerkvist). DFor 2442; LFFor 973-974; ShF 375-376.

Baraka, Amiri. DEng 92-103; PEng 81-91; **RevDEng 117-129,** 2950; **RevPEng 92-104,** 3903, 3908-3909; ShF 556, **922-926.**

Barba, Harry. ShF 2504.

"Barbados" (Marshall). RevShF 1613.

"Barbara of the House of Grebe" (Hardy). RevShF 1112-1113; ShF 1584-1585.

Barbare en Asie, Un. See *Barbarian in Asia, A.*

Barbarian in Asia, A (Michaux). PFor 999.

Barbarian Odes (Carducci). PFor 271.

Barbarian Within, The (Ong). LTh 1082.

Barbary Shore (Mailer). LFEng 1776-1778; RevLFEng 2250-2251.

Barber of Seville, The (Beaumarchais). DFor 148-150, 2340.

"Barberries" (Aldrich). PEng 31.

Barbour, John. PEng 3278.

Barca sin pescador, La (Casoná). DFor 357-359.

Barchester Towers (Trollope). LFEng 2653-2654; RevLFEng 3309-3310.

Barclay, Alexander. PEng 3286; RevPEng 3805.

"Bard, The" (Gray). PEng 1142; RevPEng 1300.

"Bardon Bus" (Munro). RevShF 1695-1696; ShFSup 212.

Bare and Ye Cubb, Ye (Darby). DEng 2394; RevDEng 2914.

Bare Hills, The (Winters). PSup 397; RevPEng 3626.

Barefoot in the Park (Simon). RevDEng 2263-2264.

Baretti, Giuseppe. LTh 90-94.

Barfield, Owen. LTh 95-101.

"Barishnya krestyanka." *See* "Squire's Daughter, The."

Bark (Popa). PFor 1269.

Barker, Harley Granville. *See* **Granville-Barker, Harley.**

Barker, James Nelson. DEng 104-114, 2397; **RevDEng 130-140,** 2918.

Barlow, Joel. LTh 1742.

"Barn Burning" (Faulkner). RevShF 854, 2731; ShF 802, 1365-1367.

Bàrnabo delle montagne. See *Bàrnabo of the Mountains.*

Bàrnabo of the Mountains (Buzzati). LFFor 225.

Barnaby Rudge (Dickens). M&D 503.

Barnard, Mary. PSup 22-32; **RevPEng 105-115.**

Barnard, Robert. M&D 82-87.

Barnes, Julian. RevLFEng 210-216.

Barnes, Peter. DSup 8-15; RevDEng 141-149.

Barnsley, Alan Gabriel. *See* Fielding, Gabriel.

Baroja, Pío. LFFor 103-111, 2389-2390.

Barolini, Helen. ShF 2505.

Barometer Rising (MacLennan). LFEng 1744-1745; RevLFEng 2213-2214.

Barometermacher auf der Zauberinsel, Der (Raimund). DFor 1529.

Baron, The (Moratín). DFor 1363.

Baron in the Trees, The (Calvino). LFFor 238-241. See also *Our Ancestors.*

Barone rampant, Il. See *Baron in the Trees, The.*

Barr, Robert. M&D 88-93.

Barr, Robert, and Stephen Crane. RevLFEng 779.

Barraca, La. See *Cabin, The.*

Barrage contre le Pacifique, Un. See *Sea Wall, The.*

Barranca abajo (Sánchez). DFor 2442.

Barrault, Jean-Louis. DFor 2352, 2354.

Barren Ground (Glasgow). LFEng 1122-1123; RevLFEng 1332-1333.

Barrett, Elizabeth. *See* Browning, Elizabeth Barrett.

Barretts of Wimpole Street, The (Besier). DEng 202-206; RevDEng 241-245.

Barrie, Sir James. DEng 115-127, 2382; RevDEng 150-163, 2900.

Barrons Wars, The (Drayton). PEng 851; RevPEng 966.

Barry, Philip. DEng 128-138; RevDEng 164-174.

Barsuki. See *Badgers, The.*

Barth, John. LFEng 155-169, 3327; RevLFEng 217-232, 3878-3879; RevShF 153-159, 2581, 2751; ShF 484, 927-933; ShFSup 35, 41.

Barthelme, Donald. LFEng 170-177; LFSup 401; RevLFEng 233-238; RevShF 160-170, 2671, 2752-2753; ShF 560; ShFSup 20-26.

Barthes, Roland. LTh 102-108, 269, 425, 503, 809, 832, 850, 1195-1196, 1236, 1274, 1280, 1372-1373, 1765, 1821, 1826, 1829.

Bartholomew Fair (Jonson). DEng 1023, 1024, 2285; RevDEng 1292, 2804; ShF 1716.

"Bartleby the Scrivener" (Melville). LFEng 3278-3280; RevLFEng 3875-3876; RevShF 1649-1652, 2700-2701; ShF 205, 207-208, 796-798, 1915-1918.

Bartlett, Paul Alexander. ShF 2506.

Bartolozzi, Lucia Elizabeth. *See* Vestris, Madame.

"Base and Superstructure in Marxist Cultural Theory" (Williams). LTh 1544.

"Base of the Wall, The" (Wang Anyi). RevShF 2396.

"Basement Room, The" (Greene, G.). RevShF 1071-1072, 2738; ShF 272-273, 786, 1543-1544.

Bashō, Matsuo. *See* Matsuo Bashō.

Basic Training of Pavlo Hummel, The (Rabe). DEng 1547-1548; RevDEng 1938-1939.

Basil (Collins, W.). M&D 388.

Basket Case, The (McInerny). M&D 1162.

Bass, Rochelle. *See* Owens, Rochelle.

Bassani, Giorgio. LFFor 2253.

Bassetto, Corno di. *See* Shaw, George Bernard.

Bašta, pepeo. See *Garden, Ashes.*

"Bat, The" (Sitwell). PEng 2629; RevPEng 3033.

Bataille, Henri. DFor 2349.

Bataille de Pharsale, La. See *Battle of Pharsalus, The.*

Batailles dans la montagne (Giono). LFFor 656.

"Bateau ivre, Le." *See* "Drunken Boat, The."

Bates, H. E. LFEng 178-186; E. RevLFEng 239-248; E. RevShF 171-177; ShF 270-271; ShFSup 27-34.

"Bath, The" (Carver). RevPEng 3108-3109; ShFSup 81.

Bathhouse, The (Mayakovsky). DFor 1296-1297.

"Bathhouse, The" (Zoshchenko). RevShF 2557; ShFSup 379.

Batiushkov, Konstantin. PFor 2136.

Batrachoi. See *Frogs, The.*

Battaile of Agincourt, The (Drayton). PEng 854; RevPEng 969-970.

"Batter my heart, three-personed God" (Donne). PEng 836; RevPEng 942.

Battered Wife and Other Poems, The (Davie). PSup 91; RevPEng 857.

Battle, The (Romains). LFFor 1444. See also *Men of Good Will.*

Battle of Agincourt, The. See *Battaile of Agincourt, The .*

Battle of Alcazar, The (Peele). DEng 1491-1492; RevDEng 1875-1876.

"Battle of Finney's Ford, The" (West). RevShF 2449-2450; ShFSup 362.

"Battle of Hastyngs" (Chatterton). PEng 471; RevPEng 567.

Battle of Maldon. RevShF 2603; ShF 431-432.

Battle of Pharsalus, The (Simon). LFFor 1609-1611.

Battle of the Books, The (Swift). LTh 1690.

"Battle of the Lake Regillus, The" (Macaulay). PEng 1827.

"Battle-Piece" (Belitt). RevPEng 157.

Battle Pieces and Aspects of the War (Melville). PEng 1945, 1950; RevPEng 2252-2257.

"Behold the Lilies of the Field" (Hecht). PEng 1279-1281.

Behrman, S. N. DEng 179-189; RevDEng 216-227.

Beiden Klingsberg, Die. See *Father and Son.*

"Beim Bau der Chinesischen Mauer." *See* "Great Wall of China, The."

Being and Nothingness (Sartre). LTh 1274.

Being There (Kosinski). LFEng 1563-1564; RevLFEng 1925-1926.

"Bekenntnis zur Trümmerliteratur." *See* "Defense of Rubble Literature."

Bela e a fera, A (Lispector). RevShF 1493; ShFSup 168.

Bela Lugosi's White Christmas (West, P.). LFSup 373; RevLFEng 3524.

Belaia staia (Akhmatova). PFor 12.

Belarmino and Apolonio (Pérez de Ayala). LFFor 1261-1263.

Belasco, David. DEng 190-199; RevDEng 228-238.

Belaya gvardiya. See *White Guard, The.*

Belfagor. See *Story of Belphagor the Arch Demon, The.*

Belfry of Bouges and Other Poems, The (Longfellow). PEng 1749; RevPEng 2034.

"Believe It" (Logan). PEng 1743; RevPEng 2027.

Belinda, Aunt. *See* **Braddon, M. E.**

Belinsky, Vissarion. LFFor 2314; LTh 115-123, 285, 288, 388, 394, 396-398, 946, 1104, 1108, 1122, 1179, 1446, 1502; PFor 2140-2141.

Belitt, Ben. RevPEng 154-160.

Bell, Josephine. M&D 99-106.

Bell for Adano, A (Hersey). LFEng 1352, 1355-1356; RevLFEng 1610, 1613-1614.

"Bella-Vista" (Colette). RevShF 581-582.

Bellamy, Edward. RevLFEng 3866.

Bellamy, Joe David. ShF 2509.

Bellarosa Connection, The (Bellow). RevLFEng 287-288.

Belle Saison, La (Martin du Gard). LFFor 1114-1115. See also *World of the Thibaults, The.*

"Belle Zoraïde, La" (Chopin). ShF 1133.

Belleau, Rémy. PFor 2115.

Bellefleur (Oates). LFEng 2015; RevLFEng 2538.

Belles Images, Les (de Beauvoir). LFFor 119.

Belles-sœurs, Les (Tremblay). DSup 349-350.

Bellman, Carl Michael. LFFor 2335; PFor 2161.

Belloc, Hilaire. PEng 132-139; RevPEng 161-169.

Bellow, Saul. LFEng 224-236, 3067; RevLFEng 275-290, 3775-3776, 3808; RevShF 202-208,

2757; ShF 549-550, **948-952**, 1855; ShFSup 387.

"Bells for John Whiteside's Daughter" (Ransom). PEng 2327-2329; RevPEng 2713-2715.

"Bells in Winter" (Milosz). PFor 1036.

"Bells of San Blas, The" (Longfellow). PEng 1748; RevPEng 2033.

Bellum civile. See *Pharsalia.*

Beloved (Morrison). RevLFEng 2433.

Beloved Hedgerose, The (Gryphius). DFor 839.

Bely, Andrey. LFFor 2320; **LTh 124-130**, 975.

"Belye nochi." *See* "White Nights."

Bembo, Pietro. LTh **131-136**, 1459, 1462-1463; PFor 160-169.

"Ben venga maggio." *See* "Oh, Welcome May."

Benavente y Martínez, Jacinto. DFor **174-182**, 2501-2502.

Bend in the River, A (Naipaul). LFEng 1962-1964; RevLFEng 2476-2477.

Bend Sinister (Nabokov). LFEng 1951-1952; RevLFEng 2464-2465.

Bendigo Shafter (L'Amour). LFSup 225; RevLFEng 1936.

Bending the Bow (Duncan). PEng 905; RevPEng 1041-1042.

"Beneath the Shelter" (Mahfouz). RevShF 1563-1564.

"Benediction" (Kunitz). PSup 243; RevPEng 1884.

Benediktsson, Einar. PFor 2175.

Benefactors (Frayn). DSup 130-131; RevDEng 833-834.

Benet, Juan. LFFor **133-143**.

Benét, Stephen Vincent. PEng **140-145**; RevPEng 170-176; RevShF 209-215; ShF 259, 543-544, **953-959**.

Benford, Gregory. RevLFEng 3871.

Beniak, Valentín. PFor 1811.

Beniowski (Słowacki). PFor 1445-1446, 2125.

"Benito Cereno" (Melville). LFEng 3311-3313; ShF 116.

Benjamin, Walter. LTh **137-143**; 416-417, 1366, 1808.

Benn, Gottfried. PFor **170-176**, 1929, 1933.

Bennett, Arnold. LFEng 237-248, 3052, 3082; M&D 107-111; RevLFEng 291-302, 3760.

Bennett, John. ShF 2510.

Benson Murder Case, The (Van Dine). M&D 1638.

"Benson Watts Is Dead and in Virginia" (Betts). RevShF 218-219; ShF 962-964.

"Bent Tree, The" (Manger). PFor 950.

Bentham, Jeremy. LTh 1030-1031, 1730.

Betsuyaku Minoru. DFor 2435.
"Bettelweib von Locarno, Das." *See*
"Beggarwoman of Locarno, The."
Bettelweib von Locarno, Das. See *Beggarwoman of Locarno, The.*
"Better Answer, A" (Prior). PEng 2289-2290; RevPEng 2670-2671.
Betterton, Thomas. DEng 2523.
Betti, Ugo. DFor 203-212, 2414.
Betts, Doris. RevShF 216-221; ShF 960-964.
Between Fantoine and Agapa (Pinget). LFFor 1287-1288, 1292-1293.
Between Life and Death (Sarraute). LFFor 1505-1506.
Between the Acts (Woolf). LFEng 1428, 2957-2959; RevLFEng 3658-3661.
"Between the Lines" (Smith). RevShF 2155.
Beulah Land (Davis). LFEng 677-678; RevLFEng 809-810.
Beulah Quintet, The (Settle). LFSup 345-349. See also *Killing Ground, The, Know Nothing, O Beulah Land, Prisons,* and *Scapegoat, The.*
Bevis of Hampton. ShF 141.
Beware the Curves (Gardner, E.). M&D 691.
Bewitched, The (Barnes). DSup 12-13; RevDEng 144-145.
"Bewitched Jacket, The" (Buzzati). RevShF 352; ShFSup 63-64.
Beyle, Marie-Henri. *See* **Stendhal.**
Beyond Culture (Trilling). LTh 1455.
Beyond Desire (Anderson). LFEng 79; RevLFEng 116.
Beyond Human Power. See *Beyond Our Power.*
Beyond Our Power (Bjørnson). DFor 216.
"Beyond the Alps" (Lowell, R.). PEng 1790; RevPEng 2084.
Beyond the Bedroom Wall (Woiwode). LFSup 395-396; RevLFEng 3622-3623; RevShF 2494.
"Beyond the Desert" (Rhodes). ShF 604.
"Beyond the Glass Mountain" (Stegner). RevShF 2191; ShF 2271-2272.
"Beyond the Pale" (Kipling). RevShF 1361-1362.
Beyond Therapy (Durang). DSup 104; RevDEng 673.
Bezdenezhe. See *Poor Gentleman, A.*
"Bezhin Meadow" (Turgenev). RevShF 2320, 2696-2697; ShF 201, 202-203, 2352-2354.
B. F.'s Daughter (Marquand). LFEng 1818; RevLFEng 2303.
Bhagavad Gītā. LFSup 172, 174.
Bhattacharya, Bhabani. ShF 651-652.
"Bi-focal" (Stafford). RevPEng 3167.
Białe małżeństwo. See *White Marriage.*

Bias of Communication, The (Innis). LTh 958.
"Bicycle Rider, The" (Davenport). RevShF 687.
Bidart, Frank. RevPEng 208-215.
Biedermann und die Brandstifter. See *Firebugs, The.*
"Biedny chrześcijanin patrzy na getto." *See* "Poor Christian Looks at the Ghetto, A."
Bierce, Ambrose. M&D 124-129; RevShF 222-227, 2677; ShF 182, 231-232, 536.
Biermann, Wolf. PFor 186-192, 1813, 1818, 1820.
Biernat of Lublin. PFor 2119.
Big as Life (Doctorow). LFEng 773-775; RevLFEng 935.
"Big Blonde" (Parker). RevShF 1849-1850; ShF 2054-2055.
Big Bow Mystery, The (Zangwill). M&D 1731-1733.
Big Clock, The (Fearing). M&D 596-597.
"Big Garage, The" (Boyle, T.). RevShF 293-294.
Big Heat, The (McGivern). M&D 1156-1157.
Big House, The (Robinson). DEng 1619-1621; RevDEng 2024-2026.
Big Knife, The (Odets). DEng 1402-1403; RevDEng 1778-1779.
"Big Mama's Funeral" (García Márquez). RevShF 952; ShF 1454.
"Big Meeting" (Hughes). RevShF 1228-1229; ShF 1660-1661.
Big Money, The (Dos Passos). LFEng 797-798; RevLFEng 961-962.
Big Night, The. See *Dreadful Summit.*
"Big Nose" (Slavitt). RevPEng 3053.
Big Rock Candy Mountain, The (Stegner). LFEng 2498, 2499-2500; RevLFEng 3130-3131.
Big Sin, The (Webb). M&D 1690-1691.
Big Sleep, The (Chandler). LFEng 492-494; M&D 304-305; RevLFEng 605, 606-607, 3846.
Big Toys (White). DSup 395-396; RevDEng 2515.
"Big Two-Hearted River" (Hemingway). LFEng 1339-1340; ShF 1624-1625; RevLFEng 1597-1598, 3763, 3769; RevShF 1172.
"Big-City Lights" (Zoshchenko). RevShF 2560; ShFSup 382.
Biggers, Earl Derr. M&D 130-135; RevLFEng 3845.
"Biggest Band, The" (Cassill). RevShF 445-446; ShF 1070-1071.
Biglow Papers, The (Lowell, J. R.). PEng 1780; RevPEng 2074.
Bijou (Madden). LFEng 1765-1766; RevLFEng 2237-2238.

Bijoux indiscrets, Les. See *Indiscreet Toys, The.*

Bila nemoc. See *Power and Glory.*

"Bildner, Der" (Zweig). PFor 1725-1726.

Bill, Max. PFor 592.

Bill of Rites, A Bill of Wrongs, A Bill of Goods, A (Morris). LFEng 1905; RevLFEng 2413.

Billard um halbzehn. See *Billiards at Half-Past Nine.*

Billiards at Half-Past Nine (Böll). LFFor 182-184.

"Billie" (Young). PEng 3218; RevPEng 3742.

Billy Bathgate (Doctorow). RevLFEng 939-942.

Billy Budd, Foretopman (Melville). LFEng 1859-1861, 3280-3282; PEng 1944; RevLFEng 2354-2356; RevPEng 2251.

Billy Liar (Hall and Waterhouse). DEng 869-871; RevDEng 1077-1079.

Billy Phelan's Greatest Game (Kennedy). LFSup 197-198; RevLFEng 1854. See also *Albany Cycle, The.*

Biloxi Blues (Simon). DEng 1831-1832; RevDEng 2267-2268.

Dilvav Yamin. See *In the Heart of the Seas.*

Dingham, Sallie. ShF 2516.

Bingo (Bond). RevDEng 292.

Biographia Literaria (Coleridge, S. T.). PEng 3478-3479; LTh 3, 303-304, 1696, 1701; RevPEng 4021.

Biography (Behrman). DEng 186, 187; RevDEng 223, 224.

Biography (Mi-la Ras-pa). PFor 2247-2248.

Biography of the Life of Manuel, The (Cabell). LFEng 406-407; RevLFEng 515-516.

Bios kai politela tou Alexe Zormpa. See *Zorba the Greek.*

Birchwood (Banville). LFSup 45-46; RevLFEng 202-203.

"Bird, The" (Paz). PFor 1172.

"Bird, The" (Simpson). RevPEng 3009.

Bird, Robert Montgomery. DEng 207-218; RevDEng 247-259.

Bird in Hand (Drinkwater). DEng 512; RevDEng 633.

Bird in the House, A (Laurence). RevShF 1409-1410.

"Bird Spider, The" (Arreola). RevShF 81.

"Birdbrain" (Ginsberg). RevPEng 1233.

Birds, The (Aristophanes). DFor 117-118, 2126-2127.

"Birds, The" (du Maurier). M&D 554-555.

"Birds, The" (Galvin). PEng 1057; RevPEng 1191.

Birds (Perse). PFor 1196-1197.

"Birds, The" (Sukenick). ShF 115.

"Birds and Roses Are Birds and Roses" (Heyen). RevPEng 1502.

Birds, Beasts and Flowers (Lawrence, D. H.). PEng 1081, 1603-1604, RevPEng 1951, 1953-1954.

"Birds in the Night" (Verlaine). PFor 1631.

Bird's Nest, The (Jackson). LFEng 1427-1428.

Birds of America (McCarthy, M.). LFEng 1724-1725; RevLFEng 2154-2155.

"Birds of Passage" (Longfellow). PEng 1750; RevPEng 2035.

Birney, Earle. PEng 174-180; PSup 403; RevPEng 216-223.

"Birth, The" (Berry). RevPEng 183.

"Birth" (Nin). RevShF 1724-1725; ShF 1951.

Birth and Afterbirth (Howe). RevDEng 1220.

Birth of a Grandfather, The (Sarton). LFEng 2348-2350; RevLFEng 2963-2965.

Birth of the Clinic, The (Foucault). LTh 504.

Birth of the Gods, The (Merezhkovsky). LFFor 1139.

Birth of the Poet (Foreman). DSup 123; RevDEng 824-825.

Birth of Tragedy, The (Nietzsche). DEng 2198; RevDEng 2717-2718.

Birth of Tragedy Out of the Spirit of Music, The (Nietzsche). LTh 1068-1069.

Birth Rate (Różewicz). DFor 1584-1585.

"Birthday, A" (Creeley). PEng 682-683.

Birthday King, The (Fielding, G.). LFSup 116-117; RevLFEng 1113, 1114-1115.

Birthday Party, The (Pinter). DEng 1512-1514; RevDEng 1899-1901.

"Birthmark, The" (Hawthorne). RevShF 1148-1149; ShF 475, 738, 1612.

"Birthmark, The" (Kavan). RevShF 1312.

"Birthplace Revisited" (Corso). PEng 576-577; RevPEng 671-672.

"Bisclayret" (Marie de France). RevShF 1607; ShF 1889-1890.

Bishop, Elizabeth. PEng 181-190; RevPEng 224-234.

"Bishop Blougram's Apology" (Browning, R.). PEng 341; RevPEng 412.

Bishop Murder Case, The (Van Dine). M&D 1639.

"Bishop Orders His Tomb at St. Praxed's Church, The" (Browning, R.). PEng 339-341; RevPEng 410-412.

Bishop's Bonfire, The (O'Casey). DEng 1391; RevDEng 1767.

"Bishop's Fool" (Lewis). RevShF 1484.

"Bitter Bread" (Ford). ShF 1384-1385.

Bloomers, The (Sternheim). DFor 1736-1737.

Bloomfield, Leonard. LTh 1441; PFor 1736.

Bloomingdale Papers, The (Carruth). RevPEng 526.

Blot in the 'Scutcheon, A (Browning). DEng 292-294; RevDEng 349-351.

"Blow, The" (Seifert). PSup 357.

"Blow-Up" (Cortázar). RevShF 634-635; ShF 786, 1203-1204.

"Blowing of the Seed, The" (Everson). PEng 989; RevPEng 1120-1121.

"Blue" (Heyen). RevPEng 1505.

Blue Boy (Giono). LFFor 655.

"Blue Cross, The" (Chesterton). RevShF 530-531.

Blue Hammer, The (Macdonald). LFSup 278-279; RevLFEng 2177-2178.

"Blue Hotel, The" (Crane, S.). LFEng 3305-3307; RevLFEng 3876-3877; RevShF 650-652, 2713-2714; ShF 598-599, 799-800, 1217, 1219-1220.

"Blue Island" (Powers). RevShF 1919; ShF 2120-2121.

Blue Juniata (Cowley, M.). PEng 603-605, 607; RevPEng 709-711.

Blue Juniata: Collected Poems (Cowley, M.). RevPEng 713-714.

"Blue Kimono, The" (Callaghan). RevShF 387; ShFSup 71.

Blue Knight, The (Wambaugh). RevLFEng 3428-3429.

"Blue Meridian" (Toomer). PEng 2918-2919; RevPEng 3390.

"Blue Moon" (Phillips). RevShF 1886.

Blue Movie (Southern). LFEng 2470-2472.

"Blue Rock" (Rich). RevPEng 2759-2760.

Blue Sash and Other Stories, The (Beck). ShF 935.

"Blue Swallows, The" (Nemerov). PEng 2087-2088.

Blue Swallows, The (Nemerov). RevPEng 2429.

"Blue Symphony" (Fletcher, J. G.). PEng 1027.

Blue Voyage (Aiken). LFEng 17-19; RevLFEng 13-32.

"Blue Wine" (Hollander). RevPEng 1552-1553.

Blue Wine and Other Poems (Hollander). RevPEng 1552-1553.

"Bluebeard's Egg" (Atwood). RevShF 105-106; ShFSup 17-18.

Bluebeard's Egg and Other Stories (Atwood). ShFSup 18.

"Bluebell Meadow" (Kiely). RevShF 1335-1336; ShF 1745-1747.

"Bluebirds, The" (Thoreau). PEng 2903; RevPEng 3371.

Blues for Mister Charlie (Baldwin). DEng 71, 75-78; RevDEng 93-94, 99-101.

Blues If You Want (Matthews). RevPEng 2246-2247.

Bluest Eye, The (Morrison). LFEng 1916-1917; RevLFEng 2425-2426.

Blumen-, Frucht- und Dornenstücke. See *Flower, Fruit, and Thorn Pieces.*

Blumenboot, Das (Sudermann). DFor 1765.

Blunck, Hans Friedrich. LFFor 2195.

"Bluspels and Flalansferes" (Lewis). LTh 895, 897.

Bly, Robert. PEng 220-228; PSup 403; RevPEng 266-275.

"Boarding House, The" (Joyce). ShF 1721.

Boas, Frederick S. PEng 1901, 1903.

"Boast no more, fond Love, thy Power" (D'Urfey). PEng 913.

Boat, The (Hartley). LFEng 1300-1301; RevLFEng 1554-1555.

"Bob, a Dog" (Smith). RevShF 2156-2157.

"Bob Summers' Body" (Stern). RevPEng 3199.

Bobette. See **Simenon, Georges.**

Bobrowski, Johannes. PFor 202-208, 1817, 1821.

Boccaccio, Giovanni. LFEng 3216-3218, 3219-3222; LTh 133-135, **168-173,** 283, 967, 1433, 1655-1656, 1661; PEng 3243; PFor 2009, 2114-2115; RevLFEng 3873; **RevShF 228-234; ShFSup 44-50.**

Bocksgesang. See *Goat Song.*

Bodas de sangre. See *Blood Wedding.*

Bodel, Jean. DFor 2163-2164, 2175.

Bödeln. See *Hangman, The.*

Bodelsen, Anders. LFFor 2367.

"Bodies" (Oates). ShF 1965-1966.

Bodily Harm (Atwood). LFEng 100-102; RevLFEng 138-140.

Bodmer, Johann Jakob. DFor 2363; **LTh 174-177.**

"Body, The" (King). RevShF 1349.

"Body, The" (Simic). PEng 2592.

Body in the Boudoir (Vulliamy). M&D 1660, 1662.

Body in the Library, The (Christie). LFEng 540; RevLFEng 657.

Body in the Silo, The (Knox). M&D 1000.

Body's Rapture, The (Romains). LFFor 1441.

Boesman and Lena (Fugard). DEng 700, 701-702; RevDEng 869, 870-871.

Boethius. LTh 20; PFor 2112.

"Bog Oak" (Heaney). RevPEng 1445.

Book of Settlements (Thorgilsson). RevShF 2585-2586; ShF 388.

Book of Songs (Confucius, editor). LTh 1773, 1785; PFor 1778-1779, 1781.

Book of Songs (Heine). PFor 644, 645, 647, 648-649.

Book of Stories. ShF 415.

Book of the Body, The (Bidart). RevPEng 210-211.

Book of the Courtier, The. See *Courtier, The*.

Book of the Duchess (Chaucer). PEng 481; RevPEng 577; RevShF 482-483; ShF 1102-1103.

Book of the Green Man, The (Johnson, R.). PSup 212-213; RevPEng 1714-1715.

Book of the Hopi (Waters). LFEng 2781; RevLFEng 3447.

Book of the Icelanders (Thorgilsson, Ari). RevShF 2585; ShF 387.

Book of the Pious. ShF 415-416, 417.

Book of Thel, The (Blake). PEng 209; RevPEng 253.

Booke of Ayres, A (Campion). PEng 427-428; RevPEng 491, 495-496.

Books Do Furnish a Room (Powell, A.). LFEng 2121; RevLFEng 2680.

Boom Boom Room. See *In the Boom Boom Room*.

Boomerang (Hannah). RevLFEng 1487.

Boors, The (Goldoni). DFor 760-761.

"Boot, The" (Giusti). PFor 574.

Booth, Edwin. DEng 2525, 2526.

Booth, Irwin. *See* **Hoch, Edward D.**

Booth, Philip. PSup 403; **RevPEng 300-309.**

Booth, Wayne C. LTh 184-189, 560, 1817, 1825.

"Bopeep: A Pastoral" (Howells). PEng 1422.

Bopp, Franz. PFor 1732.

Boquitas pintadas. See *Heartbreak Tango*.

Bor, Matej. PFor 2270.

Borchert, Wolfgang. DFor 2380; ShF 2522.

"Bordal." *See* "Wine Song."

Border Warfare (McGrath). RevDEng 1520-1521.

Bording, Anders. PFor 2158.

Borenstein, Audrey F. ShF 2523.

Borgen, Johan. LFFor 2352, 2353-2354.

Borges, Jorge Luis. LFEng 3225-3226; LFFor 2292, 2293; **LTh 190-197; M&D 161-167; RevShF 242-253,** 2747-2748; **ShF 997-982;** ShFSup 387.

"Borgo, Il" (Saba). PSup 347.

"Boring Story, A" (Chekhov). RevShF 514-515.

Boris Godunov (Pushkin). DFor 1496-1497, 2453; LTh 1178-1179; PFor 1292, 1293-1294.

Born Brothers (Woiwode). RevLFEng 3624-3625.

Born in the Gardens (Nichols). DSup 283-284; RevDEng 1732-1733.

"Born Yesterday" (Larkin). PEng 1672; RevPEng 1940.

Borough, The (Crabbe). PEng 641-643; RevPEng 730-731, 735-737.

Borowski, Tadeusz. RevShF 254-260.

"Borrowed Time" (Bachmann). PFor 128. See also *Gestundete Zeit, Die*.

Borrowed Time (Rasputin). RevShF 1994.

Boscán, Juan. PFor 2216-2217.

Bose, Buddhadeva. LFFor 2225, 2226.

Böse Geist Lumpazivagabundus, Der (Nestroy). DFor 1419-1422.

Böse Weib, Das (Sachs). DFor 1626.

Bösen Köche, Die. See *Wicked Cooks, The*.

Bosnian Chronicle (Andrić). LFFor 60-63.

Bosnian Story. See *Bosnian Chronicle*.

Bosoms and Neglect (Guare). DEng 862; RevDEng 1061.

Boston (Sinclair, U.). LFEng 2424-2425; RevLFEng 3054-3055.

Boston, Bruce. ShF 2524.

Bostonians, The (James, H.). LFEng 1446-1448; RevLFEng 1725-1727.

Boswell (Elkin). LFEng 888; RevLFEng 1047-1048.

Both Your Houses (Anderson, M.). DEng 28; RevDEng 39.

Bothie of Tober-na-Vuolich, The (Clough). PEng 518-519; RevPEng 616-617.

"Botschaft, Die." *See* "Breaking the News."

Bottega del caffe, La. See *Coffee-house, The*.

"Bottle" (Zoshchenko). RevShF 2557; ShFSup 379.

"Bottle of Milk for Mother, A" (Algren). RevShF 53; ShF 857.

Botto, Ján. PFor 1809.

Bottomley, Gordon. DEng 253-261; RevDEng 295-304.

Bouc émissaire, Le. See *Scapegoat, The*.

Boucher, Anthony. M&D 168-172.

Bouchon de cristal, Le. See *Crystal Stopper, The*.

Boucicault, Dion. DEng 262-270, 2360, 2398, 2526; **RevDEng 305-314,** 2878, 2919, 3050.

Bouge of Court, The (Skelton). PEng 2635, 2636-2637.

"Bought and Sold" (Moravia). RevShF 1673-1674; ShFSup 199.

Boughton, Rutland. DEng 2461.

"Boule de Suif" (Maupassant). RevShF 1635-1636.

"Brazil" (Marshall). RevShF 1614.

"Bread and Wine" (Hölderlin). PFor 687.

Bread and Wine (Silone). LFFor 1587-1588.

Bread of Time to Come, The (Malouf). RevLFEng 2291-2292.

Breadwinner, The (Maugham). DEng 1310; RevDEng 1639-1640.

"Break, The" (Sexton). PEng 2525; RevPEng 2935.

"Break-In, The" (Adams). RevShF 8.

Break of Noon (Claudel). DFor 408-409.

Breakers and Granite (Fletcher, J. G.). PEng 1027.

Breakfast at Tiffany's (Capote). LFEng 447-448; RevLFEng 559-560.

"Breakfast at Twilight" (Dick). ShF 1261-1262.

Breakheart Pass (MacLean). M&D 1175.

Breaking of the Vessels, The (Bloom). LTh 166.

"Breaking the Chain" (Harrison, T.). PSup 170; RevPEng 1424.

"Breaking the News" (Böll). RevShF 238.

Breast, The (Roth). LFEng 2305; RevLFEng 2900-2901.

"Breasts" (Simic). PEng 2592.

Breasts of Tiresias, The (Apollinaire). DEng 2203; RevDEng 2723.

"Breath of Lucifer, A" (Narayan). RevShF 1718; ShFSup 228.

Breathing It In (Machado). RevDEng 1532.

Breathing Lessons (Tyler). RevLFEng 3344-3345.

Breathing the Water (Levertov). RevPEng 1984.

Brébeuf and His Brethren (Pratt). PEng 2284-2285; RevPEng 2657.

Brecht, Bertolt. LTh 140-141, 144, 147-148, **204-211,** 937-938, 1815; DEng 2205-2206, 2239; **DFor 230-245,** 611-612, 615, 2240, 2378-2379; DSup 17, 25, 116, 118-119, 321; **PFor 218-227,** 1813, 1817, 1819, 1822, 1931-1932; RevDEng 2725-2726, 2759; **RevShF 320-327; ShF 1004-1010.**

"Breefe balet touching the traytorous takynge of Scarborow Castell, A" (Heywood, J.). PEng 1335-1336; RevPEng 1516-1517.

Breen, Jon L. M&D 198-202.

"Breeze Anstey" (Bates). RevShF 174; ShF 270; ShFSup 31.

Breeze from the Gulf, A (Crowley). DSup 71-72; RevDEng 535-536.

"Breezes, Breezes, Little Breezes" (Castro). PFor 278. See also *Cantares gallegos.*

Breitinger, Johann Jakob. DFor 2363; LTh 174-175.

Brekke, Paal. LFFor 2363; PFor 2190.

Brekkukotsannáll. See *Fish Can Sing, The.*

Bremer, Fredrika. LFFor 2337.

Bremond, Claude. LTh 1762.

Brendan (Buechner). RevLFEng 452.

Brennan, Joseph Payne. ShF 2528.

Brentano, Clemens. PFor 1917-1918.

Brenton, Howard. DEng 2491, 2492-2493; **DSup 28-37; RevDEng 315-325,** 3019-3022.

"Breslauer Ausarbeitung" (Dilthey). LTh 378.

"Brethren" (Bunin). RevShF 345.

Breton, André. DEng 2203; **LTh 212-216,** 1492, 1710, 1830; **PFor 228-234,** 1547, 1885; RevDEng 2723.

Breton, Nicholas. PEng 274-282; RevPEng 338-347.

Bretón de los Herreros, Manuel. DFor 2498.

Breton's Bowre of Delights (Breton, N.). PEng 278.

Brett, Simon. M&D 203-209.

"Bréviaire des nobles, Le." *See* "Breviary for Nobles, The."

"Breviary for Nobles, The" (Chartier). PFor 348.

Brewsie and Willie (Stein). LFEng 2516-2517; RevLFEng 3148-3149.

Brewster, Harry. ShF 566.

Breytenbach, Breyten. PSup 50-58.

Březina, Otokar. PFor 1803.

"Brick Moon, The" (Hale). ShF 770.

"Brickdust Row" (Henry). ShF 230.

Bridal Canopy, The (Agnon). LFFor 14-17.

Bridal Dinner, The (Gurney). DSup 164-165; RevDEng 1066-1067.

"Bridal Measure, A" (Dunbar, P.). PSup 111; RevPEng 1013.

"Bridal Photo, 1906" (Ciardi). PEng 503; RevPEng 592.

Bridal Wreath, The (Undset). LFFor 1803.

"Bride, The" (Chekhov). RevShF 517-518.

"Bride Comes to Yellow Sky, The" (Crane, S.). RevShF 650; ShF 599-600, 1220-1221.

"Bride Waits, The" (Venkataramani). ShF 644.

"Bride Without a Dowry, A" (Amichai). PSup 4.

Bridegroom's Body, The (Boyle, K.). LFEng 277-278; RevLFEng 342-343.

Bridel, Bedřich. PFor 1798.

"Brides, The" (Hope). PSup 189; RevPEng 1594.

Brides of Reason (Davie). PSup 85; RevPEng 850.

"Bride's Prelude, The" (Rossetti, D. G.). PEng 2428-2429; RevPEng 2821-2822.

Bride's Tragedy, The (Beddoes). PEng 111; RevPEng 131.

Brideshead Revisited (Waugh). LFEng 2798-2799; RevLFEng 3465-3466.

Bridge, The (Crane, H.). PEng 651-652, 3365-3366, 3391; RevPEng 745, 746-753, 3883-3884

"Bridge Builders, The" (Kipling). ShF 1751.

"Bridge of Dreams, The" (Tanizaki). RevShF 2248; ShFSup 317-318.

Bridge of Lost Desire, The (Delany). RevLFEng 854.

Bridge of San Luis Rey, The (Wilder). LFEng 2883; RevLFEng 3572, 3573.

"Bridge of Sighs, The" (Hood). PEng 1388-1389; RevPEng 1586-1587.

Bridge of Years, The (Sarton). LFEng 2347-2348; RevLFEng 2962-2963.

Bridge on the Drina, The (Andrić). LFFor 63-64.

Bridgeman, Richard. *See* Davies, L. P.

Bridges, Robert. PEng 283-291; RevPEng 348-357.

Bridges at Toko-Ri, The (Michener). LFSup 300-301; RevLFEng 2372-2373

Bridie, James. DEng 271-280, 2383; RevDEng 326-336, 2901.

"Bridle, The" (Carver). RevShF 440-441.

Brief an den Vater. See *Letter to His Father.*

"Brief eines Dichters an einen Andern." *See* "Letter from One Poet to Another."

"Brief Fall, A" (Woiwode). RevShF 2496.

Brief Life, A (Onetti). LFFor 1211-1212.

Brief-Wechsel von der Natur des poetischen Geschmackes (Bodmer). LTh 176.

"Briefcase History" (Middleton, C.). PEng 1990; RevPEng 2312.

Briefe, die neueste Litteratur betreffend (Lessing). LTh 668, 880.

Briefe über die ästhetische Erziehung des Menschen in einer Reihe von Briefen. See *On the Aesthetic Education of Man.*

Briefe zu Beförderung der Humanität. See *Letters for the Advancement of Humanity.*

Briefing for a Descent into Hell (Lessing). LFEng 1640; RevLFEng 2037.

Brieux, Eugène. DFor 246-255, 2348.

Brigadier, The (Fonvizin). DFor 633-635.

"Brigadier and the Golf Widow, The" (Cheever). RevShF 505-506.

Briggflatts (Bunting). PEng 367, 371; RevPEng 445.

Briggs, Charles F. ShF 588.

"Bright and Morning Star" (Wright, R.). ShF 579.

Bright Center of Heaven (Maxwell). RevLFEng 2342-2343.

Bright Day (Priestley). LFEng 2143-2144; RevLFEng 2715-2716.

"Bright Field, The" (Walcott). PEng 3006.

Bright Orange for the Shroud (MacDonald, J.). M&D 1132

Brighton Beach Memoirs (Simon). DEng 1831; RevDEng 2267-2268.

Brighton Rock (Greene, G.). LFEng 1217-1219; M&D 791; RevLFEng 1443-1445.

"Brim Beauvais" (Stein). RevShF 2201-2202; ShFSup 309.

"Brindisi di Girella, Il." *See* "Girella's Toast."

Bringing It All Back Home (McNally). RevDEng 1551.

"Bringing Up" (Harrison, T.). PSup 168-169; RevPEng 1422.

Brissac, Malcolm de. *See* Dickinson, Peter.

Bristo (Ferreira). DFor 591.

"Bristowe Tragedie: Or, The Deth of Syr Charles Bawdin" (Chatterton). PEng 471.

Britannia's Pastorals (Browne). PEng 320.

Britannicus (Racine). DFor 1516-1518.

Britannicus, prefaces to (Racine). LTh 1197, 1199.

"British Guiana" (Marshall). RevShF 1613-1614.

British Museum Is Falling Down, The (Lodge). RevLFEng 2091.

Britten, Benjamin. DEng 2462-2463; RevDEng 2987.

Britting, Georg. PFor 1931.

Britton's Bowre of Delights (Breton). RevPEng 342.

"Britva." *See* "Razor, The."

Broad and Alien Is the World (Alegría). LFFor 46-47.

"Broadsheet Ballad, A" (Coppard). RevShF 626; ShF 1197.

Broadway Bound (Simon). RevDEng 2267-2269.

Broadway, Broadway (McNally). See *It's Only a Play.*

Broch, Hermann. LFFor 190-201, 2194.

Brock, Rose. *See* Hansen, Joseph.

Brockport, New York (Heyen). RevPEng 1508.

"Brodeuse d'abeilles, La" (Follain). PSup 130.

Brodkey, Harold. RevShF 328-334.

Brodsky, Joseph. PFor 235-243.

"Broken Connections" (Oates). PEng 2119.

"Broken Dark, The" (Hayden). PEng 1248-1249; RevPEng 1432-1433.

Broken Eggs (Machado). RevDEng 1530-1531.

Broken Face Murders, The (Teilhets). M&D 1577.

"Broken Ground, The" (Berry). PEng 150.

Broken Ground, The (Berry). PEng 149-150; RevPEng 179-181.

Broken Gun, The (L'Amour). LFSup 224; RevLFEng 1935.

Broken Heart, The (Ford). DEng 655-658, 2289; RevDEng 800-803, 2808.

"Broken Homes" (Trevor). RevShF 2308-2309; ShFSup 324.

Broken Pieces. See *Cinq* and *Like Death Warmed Over.*

Broken Water (Hanley). LFEng 1245; RevLFEng 1473.

"Broken World, A" (O'Faoláin). ShF 2000-2001.

Brokenbrow. See *Hinkemann.*

Broker of Bogotá, The (Bird). DEng 217-218; RevDEng 257-258.

Brome, Richard. DEng 281-288, 2298-2299; RevDEng 337-345, 2817-2818.

"Bromeliads" (Williams, J.). RevShF 2475.

Brontë, Charlotte. LFEng 296-305; RevLFEng 380-389.

Brontë, Emily. LFEng 306-311, 3145-3146; PEng 292-300; RevLFEng 390-396; RevPEng 358-366.

Bronze Horseman, The (Pushkin). PFor 1300-1301.

Brook Kerith, The (Moore, G.). LFEng 1902; RevLFEng 2409.

Brook, Peter. DEng 2489-2490, 2531-2532.

Brooke, C. F. Tucker. PEng 1903.

Brooke, Fulke Greville, First Lord. See **Greville, Fulke.**

Brooke, Rupert. PEng 301-308; RevPEng 367-374.

Brookhouse, Christopher. ShF 2529.

"Brooklyn" (Marshall). RevShF 1613.

Brooklyn Murders, The (Coles). M&D 371.

Brookner, Anita. LFSup 60-69; RevLFEng 397-406.

Brooks, Ben. ShF 2530.

Brooks, Cleanth. LTh 158, 217-222, 306, 1011, 1148, 1424-1425, 1521-1523, 1554-1556, 1753-1754, 1818; RevPEng 3975-3976, 3977-3978.

Brooks, Gwendolyn. PEng 309-317; RevPEng 375-385, 3905, 3911.

Brooks, Van Wyck. LTh 223-230, 316-319, 1011, 1550.

"Broom, The" (Leopardi). PFor 864-865. See also *Canti.*

"Brooms" (Simic). RevPEng 3000-3001.

Brorson, Hans Adolph. PFor 2159-2160.

Brot und Wein. See *Bread and Wine.*

"Brother Jacob" (Eliot, G.). RevShF 808; ShF 1336.

"Brother John" (Harper). PSup 162; RevPEng 1401-1402.

Brother to Dragons (Warren). PEng 3025-3027; RevPEng 3522-3523.

"Brotherhood of Men" (Eberhart). RevPEng 1060-1061.

Brotherly Love (Fielding, G.). LFSup 116; RevLFEng 1114.

Brotherly Love (Hoffman). PEng 1360-1361; RevPEng 1535-1536.

Brothers, The (Terence). DFor 1826, 2143.

Brothers and Sisters (Compton-Burnett). LFEng 566-567; RevLFEng 694-695.

Brothers in Arms (Denison). DEng 500-501; RevDEng 621-622.

Brothers in Confidence (Madden). LFEng 1761, 1764-1765; RevLFEng 2233, 2236-2237.

Brothers Karamazov, The (Dostoevski). LFFor 515-517; M&D 524.

Brouette du vinaigrier, La (Mercier). DFor 1316-1317, 2342.

Brown, Charles Brockden. LFEng 312-324; LTh 524; RevLFEng 407-419; ShF 528, 529.

Brown, Douglas. See **Gibson, Walter B.**

Brown, Fredric. M&D 210-214; ShF 2531.

Brown, Morna Doris. See **Ferrars, E. X.**

Brown, Rosellen. ShF 2532.

Brown, Sterling. RevPEng 386-392, 3910-3911.

Brown, William Hill. LFEng 3039.

Brown, William Wells. RevDEng 2947.

Brown Dog (Harrison). RevShF 1125-1126.

Browne, Barum. See **Beeding, Francis.**

Browne, William. PEng 318-322.

Browning, Elizabeth Barrett. PEng 323-333; RevPEng 393-404.

Browning, Robert. DEng 289-297; LTh 524; PEng 325, 334-347; RevDEng 346-355; RevPEng 405-419.

Browning Version, The (Rattigan). DEng 1561; RevDEng 1953. See also *Playbill.*

Brownsville Raid, The (Fuller). RevDEng 881.

Bruce, The (Barbour). PEng 3255, 3278.

Bruce, Leo. M&D 215-222.

Bruckner, Ferdinand. DFor 256-265.

Bruder Eichmann (Kipphardt). DFor 1055-1057.

Brulls, Christian. See **Simenon, Georges.**

Brumby Innes (Prichard). DEng 2433; RevDEng 2956.

Brunetière, Ferdinand. LTh 231-236, 859, 1421.

"Brunettina mia, La." See "My Brunette."

Bruno, Giordano. DFor 2397.

"Brush Fire" (Cain). RevShF 365-366; ShF 1025-1027.

"Brushwood Boy, The" (Kipling). RevShF 1363; ShF 1751.

Brut (Layamon). PEng 1689-1694; RevPEng 1061 1065; RevShF 2612.

"Bruto Minore." *See* "Younger Brutus, The."

Brutus (Cicero). LTh 294-295, 1638.

Brutus (Payne). DEng 1486-1487; RevDEng 1869-1870.

Brutus, Dennis. RevPEng 3943.

Bruyn, Günter de. LFFor 2203.

Bryant, William Cullen. LTh 1744, 1746; **PEng 348-353; RevPEng 420-426.**

Bryosov, Valery. LFFor 2320; LTh 975; PFor 2143.

Buccaneers, The (Wharton, Edith). LFEng 2858; RevLFEng 3540.

Buch der Bilder, Das (Rilke). PFor 1328.

Buch der Lieder. See *Book of Songs.*

"Buch vom mönchischen Leben, Das." *See* "Of the Monastic Life."

"Buch von der Armut und vom Tod, Das." *See* "Of Poverty and Death."

Buch von der deutschen Poeterey, Das (Opitz). PFor 1908.

"Buch von der Pilgerschaft, Das." *See* "Of Pilgrimage."

Buchan, John. LFEng 325-337; M&D 223-230; **RevLFEng 420-433.**

Büchner, Georg. DFor 266-275, 2371.

Büchse der Pandora, Die. See *Pandora's Box.*

Buck (Ribman). DSup 315.

Buck, Pearl S. LFEng 338-346; **RevLFEng 434-442; RevShF 335-341; ShF 1011-1016.**

"Buck in the Hills, The" (Clark). RevShF 563-564; ShF 1151-1152.

"Buckdancer's Choice" (Dickey, J.). PEng 798.

Buckdancer's Choice (Dickey, J.). PEng 797, 798.

"Bucket Rider, The" (Kafka). RevShF 1305-1306.

Buckingham, George Villiers, second Duke of. *See* **Villiers, George.**

Buckley, William F., Jr. M&D 231-237.

Buckower Elegies (Brecht). PFor 226.

Buckstone, John Baldwin. DEng 2358; RevDEng 2876.

Bucolics. See *Eclogues.*

Bucolicum carmen. See *Eclogues.*

"Bud Parrot" (Robison). RevShF 2012.

Buda halála. See *Death of King Buda, The.*

Buddenbrooks (Mann). LFFor 1077-1079, 2186.

Budding Prospects (Boyle, T.). RevLFEng 350.

Budō denraiki (Saikaku). RevShF 2030; ShFSup 270.

Buechner, Frederick. LFEng 347-356; **RevLFEng 443-453.**

Buenaventura, Enrique. DFor 2445.

"Buenaventura, La." *See* "Prophecy, The."

Buenos Aires Affair, The (Puig). LFFor 1353-1357; M&D 1371-1374.

Buero Vallejo, Antonio. DFor 276-286. DFor 2507.

Bufera e altro, La. See *Storm and Other Poems, The.*

"Buffalo, 12.7.41" (Howe). PSup 196; RevPEng 1632.

Buffeting, The (Wakefield Master). DEng 1995; RevDEng 2458.

"Bufords, The" (Spencer). RevShF 2175.

Bug-Jargal. See *Noble Rival, The.*

Bugayev, Boris. *See* Bely, Andrey.

Bugles in the Afternoon (Haycox). LFEng 3195; RevLFEng 3852.

"Builders, The" (Orr). PEng 2153; RevPEng 2523.

"Building, The" (Larkin). PEng 1670-1671, 1675-1676; RevPEng 1938-1939, 1943-1944.

Buke giri monogatari. See *Tales of Samurai Honor.*

Bukowski, Charles. PEng 354-365; PSup 403; **RevPEng 427-439.**

Bukowski Sampler, A (Bukowski). PEng 360-361; RevPEng 433-434.

"Buladelah-Taree Holiday Song Cycle, The" (Murray). PSup 290; RevPEng 2411-2412.

Bulgakov, Mikhail. DFor 287-296, 2462; **LFFor 202-210,** 2327.

Bulgarin, Fadey. LFFor 2310.

Bull, Olaf. PFor 2176.

Bull from the Sea, The (Renault). LFEng 2220-2221; RevLFEng 2811.

Bullet Park (Cheever). LFEng 508-510; RevLFEng 621-623.

Bullins, Ed. DEng 298-308, 2411, 2424, 2428, 2429; **RevDEng 356-368, 2932, 2946-2947.**

Bulwer-Lytton, Edward. DEng 309-317; **RevDEng 369-377.**

"Bums in the Attic" (Cisneros). RevShF 558.

Bungei Kyōkai. DFor 2432.

"Bungeijō no shizen shugi" (Hōgetsu). LTh 681.

Bunin, Ivan. LFFor 2321; **RevShF 342-347.**

Bunte Steine (Stifter). LFFor 1669, 1671.

Bunting, Basil. PEng 366-372; PSup 404; **RevPEng 440-446.**

Bunyan, John. LFEng 357-363, 3018; **RevLFEng 454-461,** 3726.

"Buoy, The" (Zoshchenko), 2560; ShFSup 382.

Burbage, James. DEng 2267.

Burbage, Richard. DEng 2522-2523.
"Burden of Itys, The" (Wilde). PEng 3105-3106; RevPEng 3596-3597.
"Bureau d'Echange de Maux, The" (Dunsany). ShF 743-744.
Bürger, Gottfried. LTh 1304-1305.
Bürger Schippel. See *Paul Schippel Esq.*
Bürger von Calais, Die. See *Citizens of Calais, The.*
Burger's Daughter (Gordimer). LFEng 1168-1170; RevLFEng 1389-1391.
Burgess, Anthony. LFEng 364-372; LFSup **401-402; RevLFEng 462-471.**
Burgess, Trevor. See **Trevor, Elleston.**
Burglar in the Closet, The (Block). M&D 151.
"Burglar of Babylon, The" (Bishop). PEng 187-188; RevPEng 230-231.
Burgomaster of Stilemonde, The (Maeterlinck). DFor 1241-1242.
Burgraves, The (Hugo). DFor 970-971.
"Burial" (Woiwode). RevShF 2495-2496.
"Burial of Orgaz, The" (Rítsos). PFor 1349.
Buried Child (Shepard). DEng 1762, 1765-1766; RevDEng 2197-2198.
Buried City (Moss). PEng 2066; RevPEng 2398.
Buried for Pleasure (Crispin). M&D 414.
Buried Land, A (Jones, M.). LFEng 1490-1491; RevLFEng 1813-1814.
"Buried Life, The" (Arnold). PEng 52-53; RevPEng 51-52.
Buried Treasure, A (Roberts). LFEng 2279-2280; RevLFEng 2874-2875.
Burke, Edmund. LTh 237-241, 722-723, 1218, 1601, 1700.
Burke, Kenneth. LTh 188, 242-248, 306, 315, 349, 980, 1222.
Burlador de Sevilla, El. See *Trickster of Seville, The.*
Burley, W. J. M&D 238-241.
Burlyuk, David. PFor 987.
Burmese Days (Orwell). LFEng 2057-2058; RevLFEng 2593-2594.
Burn, The (Aksyonov). LFSup 19-20.
Burn, David. DEng 2431; RevDEng 2954.
Burn This (Wilson, L.). RevDEng 2614.
Burnett, W. R. M&D 242-248.
Burney, Fanny. LFEng 373-382; RevLFEng 472-481, 3738.
Burning (Johnson, D.). RevLFEng 1773.
"Burning" (Snyder). PEng 2672; RevPEng 3105.
"Burning Babe, The" (Southwell). PEng 2690-2691; RevPEng 3133-3134.
Burning Beach, A (Machado). RevDEng 1531.

"Burning Bush" (Untermeyer). PEng 2949; RevPEng 3417.
Burning Court, The (Carr). ShF 728.
Burning Fountain, The (Wheelwright). LTh 1756.
Burning Heart: Women Poets of Japan, The (Rexroth, trans.). PFor 1716.
Burning House, The (Beattie). RevShF 181-183; ShFSup 39.
Burning in Water, Drowning in Flame (Bukowski). PEng 362; RevPEng 435.
"Burning Light, The" (Varnalis). PFor 1959.
Burning Mountain, The (Fletcher, J. G.). PEng 1028.
"Burning of Paper Instead of Children, The" (Rich). RevPEng 2756.
"Burning Poem, The" (MacBeth). PEng 1835; RevPEng 2114.
"Burning the Letters" (Jarrell). PEng 1482; RevPEng 1694.
"Burning the Tomato Worms" (Forché). RevPEng 1156-1157.
Burning World, The. See *Drought, The.*
Burns, Rex. M&D 249-254.
Burns, Robert. PEng 373-383, 3322, 3334-3335, 3341-3342; **RevPEng 447-457,** 3853-3854, 3859-3860.
Burr (Vidal). LFEng 2719-2721, 3154; RevLFEng 3374.
Burroughs, Edgar Rice. LFEng 3209; RevLFEng 3868.
Burroughs, William S. LFEng 383-391; LFSup **402; RevLFEng 482-492.**
"Burrow, The" (Kafka). ShF 1733-1734.
Burton, Miles. *See* **Rhode, John.**
"Bus Along St. Clair: December, A" (Atwood). PEng 67.
Bus Stop (Inge). DEng 985-986; RevDEng 1238-1239.
"Busca en todas las cosas" (González Martínez). PFor 611.
Busch, Frederick. ShF 2534.
Bush, Thomas. RevDEng 2961.
"Bush Trembles, Because, The" (Petőfi). PFor 1223-1224.
Bushman Who Came Back, The. See *Bony Buys a Woman.*
Bushrangers, The (Burn). DEng 2431; RevDEng 2954.
Bushwhacked Piano, The (McGuane). LFSup 292; RevLFEng 2199.
Busie Body, The (Centlivre). DEng 347-349; RevDEng 408-410.
Busman's Honeymoon (Sayers). LFEng 2362-2363; RevLFEng 2978.

C

Cab at the Door, A (Pritchett). LFEng 2152; RevLFEng 2724.

Cabal and Love (Schiller). DFor 1658.

Cabala, The (Wilder). LFEng 2882-2883; RevLFEng 3572-3573.

"Caballero, El." See "Gentleman, The."

Caballero de Olmedo, El. See *Knight from Olmedo, The.*

Caballo del rey don Sancho, El (Zorrilla y Moral). DFor 2064.

Cabbages and Kings (Henry). M&D 854-855.

Cabell, James Branch. LFEng 401-410; RevLFEng 510-520.

Cabellos de Absolón, Los (Calderón). DFor 307-308.

Cabin, The (Blasco Ibáñez). LFFor 171-173.

Cable, George Washington. LFEng 411-419; RevLFEng 521-530; RevShF 356-363; ShF 225-226, 534, 586, 616, **1017-1023.**

Cables to Rage (Lorde). RevPEng 2042.

Cables to the Ace (Merton). PEng 1976-1977; RevPEng 2294-2295.

Cabot Wright Begins (Purdy). LFEng 2172; RevLFEng 2746.

Cabrera Infante, Guillermo. LFFor 2298.

Cabrujas, José Ignacio. DFor 2445.

Caccia al lupo, La. See *Wolf Hunt, The.*

Caccia alla volpe, La (Verga). DFor 1947.

Cadenus and Vanessa (Swift). PEng 2806-2807; RevPEng 3273-3274.

Cadillac Jack (McMurtry). LFEng 1756-1757; RevLFEng 2224.

Cadle, Dean. ShF 2535.

Cady, Jack. ShF 2536.

Caecilius of Calacte. LTh 904-905.

Caecilius Statius. DFor 2144-2145.

Caedmon. PEng 416-420; RevPEng 483-488.

Caeiro, Alberto. *See* **Pessoa, Fernando.**

Caelica (Greville). PEng 1156-1157, 3291; RevPEng 1316.

Caesar, Gaius Julius. PFor 2093-2094.

"Caesar and His Legionnaire" (Brecht). RevShF 322-323; ShF 1006-1007.

Caesar's Apostasy. See *Emperor and Galilean.*

Caesar's Column (Donnelly). LFEng 3207; RevLFEng 3866.

Cæsars frafald. See *Emperor and Galilean.*

Cage aux Folles, La (Fierstein). DEng 2409; RevDEng 2930.

"Cage of Sand, The" (Ballard). RevShF 142-143.

Cahier d'un retour au pays natal. See *Return to My Native Land.*

Cahier gris, Le (Martin du Gard). LFFor 1114. See also *World of the Thibaults, The.*

Caída de los Limones, La. See *Fall of the House of Limón, The.*

Cain (Byron). DEng 330; RevDEng 389-390.

Cain, James M. M&D 255-261; RevShF 364-367; ShF 1024-1027.

Caine, Hall. DEng 2372; RevDEng 2890.

Caine Mutiny, The (Wouk). LFEng 2965-2967; RevLFEng 3667-3669.

Caius Gracchus (Knowles). DEng 1060-1061; RevDEng 1338-1339.

"Cake, The" (Baudelaire). PFor 139.

Cakes and Ale (Maugham). LFEng 1848-1849, 1850; RevLFEng 2336-2337.

Cakes for Your Birthday (Vulliamy). M&D 1660.

"Cakewalk" (Smith), 2156.

"Calamus" (Whitman). PEng 3069; RevPEng 3556-3557.

Calderón de la Barca, Pedro. DEng 2162; DFor 297-309, 2494-2495; LTh 637; PFor 244-250; RevDEng 2682.

Caldwell, Erskine. LFEng 420-428; LFSup 402; RevLFEng 531-539; RevShF 368-374, ShF 261-262, **1028-1033;** ShFSup 387.

Cale (Wilkinson). LFEng 2892-2893.

Caleb Williams (Godwin). M&D 751-755.

"Caliban" (Brathwaite). PEng 266; PFor 210, 215; RevPEng 328.

Caliban's Filibuster (West, P.). LFSup 373-374; RevLFEng 3524-3525.

California Suite (Simon). DEng 1829-1830; RevDEng 2265-2267.

Caligula (Camus). DFor 315-317, 2356-2357.

Calisher, Hortense. RevShF 375-381; ShF 548, 1034-1040; ShFSup 387.

Calisto and Meliboea. DEng 2259.

Call for the Dead (le Carré). LFEng 1611-1612; RevLFEng 1985-1986.

Call Girls, The (Koestler). LFEng 1554-1555; RevLFEng 1915-1916.

"Call of Cthulhu, The" (Lovecraft). RevShF 1509-1511; ShF 1823-1825.

Casa verde, La. See *Green House, The.*

Casamiento, El. See *Marriage, The.*

Casanova's Chinese Restaurant (Powell, A.). LFEng 2119; RevLFEng 2678.

Case, The (Sukhovo-Kobylin). DFor 1774-1776. See also *Trilogy of Alexander Sukhovo-Kobylin, The.*

Case for Three Detectives (Bruce). M&D 218.

Case Is Altered, The (Jonson). DEng 2285; RevDEng 2804.

Case of Kitty Ogilvie, The (Stubbs). M&D 1549.

"Case of Laker, Absconded, The" (Morrison). M&D 1243-1244.

"Case of Mr. Foggatt, The" (Morrison). M&D 1242-1243.

"Case of Oscar Brodski, The" (Freeman). M&D 669.

Case of Rebellious Susan, The (Jones, H. A.). DEng 1004; RevDEng 1270.

Case of the Baker Street Irregulars, The (Boucher). M&D 170.

Case of the Missing Brontë, The (Barnard). M&D 85.

"Case of the Missing Hand, The" (Morrison). M&D 1244.

Case of the Russian Diplomat, The (Cunningham). M&D 442.

Case of the Seven of Calvary, The (Boucher). M&D 170.

Case of the Solid Key, The (Boucher). M&D 170-171.

Case of the Velvet Claws, The (Gardner, E.). M&D 691.

Casey, John. See **O'Casey, Sean.**

Casibus Illustrium Virorum, De (Boccaccio). PEng 1809-1810.

Casina (Plautus). DFor 1485.

Cask, The (Crofts). M&D 419.

"Cask of Amontillado, The" (Poe). RevShF 2687; ShF 192-193.

Casona, Alejandro. DFor 352-360, 2506.

Caspary, Vera. M&D 289-294.

Cassandra Singing (Madden). LFEng 1763-1764; RevLFEng 2235-2236.

Cassaria, La. See *Coffer, The.*

Cassill, R. V. LFEng 464-471; LFSup 402; **RevShF 444-449; ShF 1069-1074;** ShFSup 388.

"Cassinus and Peter" (Swift). PEng 2808; RevPEng 3275.

Cassiodorus. PFor 2113.

Cassirer, Ernst. LTh 790, 1756; RevShF 2679-2680; ShF 184-185.

Cassity, Turner. PSup 59-65; RevPEng 541-548.

"Castaway, The" (Cowper). PEng 615-616; RevPEng 721-723.

Castaway (Cozzens). LFEng 632-633; RevLFEng 765-766.

Castaway and Other Poems, The (Walcott). RevPEng 3498.

Caste (Robertson). DEng 1609-1610; RevDEng 2013-2014.

Castellano, Il (Trissino). LTh 1462.

Castello dei destini incrociati, Il. See *Castle of Crossed Destinies, The.*

Castelvetro, Lodovico. DEng 2156, 2158; DFor 2199-2200; **LTh 272-278,** 310, 1664-1665; RevDEng 2676, 2678.

Castiglione, Baldassare. LTh 131-132, 1462.

Castigo sin venganza, El. See *Justice Without Revenge.*

Castigos y ejemplos de Catón. PFor 2210.

Casting of Bells, The (Seifert). PSup 356.

Castle, The (Kafka). LFFor 902-904.

Castle Corner (Cary). LFEng 456; RevLFEng 576.

Castle Gay (Buchan). LFEng 334; RevLFEng 429.

Castle Keep (Eastlake). LFEng 853-855.

Castle of Crossed Destinies, The (Calvino). LFFor 246-247.

Castle of Hearts, The (Flaubert). LFFor 547.

Castle of Otranto, The (Walpole). LFEng 3121, 3124-3125, 3257-3259; RevLFEng 3736. RevLFEng 3782, 3783, 3823, 3826-3827. RevLFEng 3874; ShF 179, 474, 730.

Castle of Perseverance, The. DEng 2253; RevDEng 2773.

Castle of the Carpathians, The (Verne). LFFor 1876.

Castle Rackrent (Edgeworth, M.). LFEng 863-865; RevLFEng 1022-1023, 1024-1026.

Castle Spectre, The (Lewis). DEng 1132-1135; RevDEng 1424-1427.

Castle to Castle (Céline). LFFor 306, 311-313.

Castles of Athlin and Dunbayne, The (Radcliffe). LFEng 2199-2200; M&D 1390; RevLFEng 2778-2779.

Castro, A. See *Ignez de Castro.*

Castro, Rosalía de. PFor 273-281.

Castro y Bellvís, Guillén de. DFor 2488.

Casualties of Peace (O'Brien, E.). LFEng 2020-2021; RevLFEng 2545-2546.

Cat, The (Colette). LFFor 370.

"Cat, The" (Matthews). RevPEng 2244.

Cat and Mouse (Grass). LFFor 736.

MAGILL INDEX TO CRITICAL SURVEYS

Cat and Shakespeare, The (Rao). LFEng 2212-2213; RevLFEng 2792-2793.

Cat Man (Hoagland). LFSup 153; RevLFEng 1630.

Cat of Many Tails (Queen). M&D 1379-1380.

Cat on a Hot Tin Roof (Williams, T.). DEng 2076-2080; RevDEng 2577-2581.

"Cat-Goddesses" (Graves). PEng 1132; RevPEng 1289.

Cataline (Ibsen). DFor 2471.

"Catastrophe" (Buzzati). RevShF 351-352; ShFSup 63.

"Catastrophe de l'Igitur, La" (Claudel). PFor 359.

"Catch, The" (Ōe). RevShF 1776-1777; ShFSup 232-234.

Catch-22 (Heller). LFEng 1329-1330, 1331-1334; RevLFEng 1588-1590, 3808.

Catcher in the Rye, The (Salinger). LFEng 2321, 2325-2329; RevLFEng 2932, 2934-2939, 3808.

"Categories" (Kennedy). PEng 1575; RevPEng 1810.

Catharina von Georgien (Gryphius). DFor 836.

Cathay (Pound). PEng 2268; RevPEng 2643.

"Cathedral" (Carver). ShFSup 80-81.

Cathedral, The (Lowell, J. R.). PEng 1780-1781; RevPEng 2074.

Cathedral Folk, The (Leskov). RevShF 1467; ShFSup 159.

Cather, Willa. LFEng 472-484, 3054; RevLFEng 585-597, 3762; RevShF 450-456; ShF 10, 587, 605, **1075-1081,** 1569.

Catherine Carmier (Gaines). LFEng 1044-1045; RevLFEng 1240-1242.

Catherine Howard (Dumas *père*). DFor 491.

Catherine the Great. LFFor 2308-2309; LTh 1694.

Cathleen ni Houlihan (Yeats and Gregory). DEng 2118-2119; RevDEng 2638-2639.

Catholic, The (Plante). LFSup 311; RevLFEng 2647.

Catholics (Moore, B.). LFEng 1891; RevLFEng 2397.

Cathy Come Home (Sanford). DEng 2506.

Cathy of Heilbronn (Kleist). DFor 1078-1080.

Catiline His Conspiracy (Jonson). DEng 2286; RevDEng 2805.

Cato. PFor 2088.

Cato (Addison). DEng 4, 7-9, 2342; RevDEng 4, 7-9, 2861.

Cat's Cradle (Flower). M&D 632.

Cat's Cradle (Vonnegut). LFEng 2727-2728; RevLFEng 3382-3384.

Cat's Eye (Atwood). RevLFEng 141.

"Cat's Meow, The" (Morris). RevShF 1680-1681; ShFSup 204-205.

Catsplay (Örkény). DSup 298-299; Cattafi, Bartolo. PFor 2051.

Catullus. DFor 2147; PFor 282-291, 2094-2095.

Caucasian Chalk Circle, The (Brecht). DFor 241-244.

Caudwell, Christopher. LFEng 3161; LTh 1540.

"Caupolicán" (Darío). PFor 422-423. See also *Azul.*

Cavafy, Constantine P. PFor 292-301, 1954-1957.

"Cavalcanti" (Pound). LTh 1156.

Cavalcanti, Guido. LTh 341-342; PFor 302-307.

Cavaliere inesistente, Il. See *Nonexistent-Knight, The.*

"Cavalla storna, La." *See* "Dapple-grey Mare, The."

"Cavalleria rusticana." *See* "Rustic Chivalry."

"Cave, The" (Zamyatin). LFFor 1978-1979; RevShF 2536; ShFSup 371-372.

Cave Birds (Hughes, T.). RevPEng 1654.

Cave Dwellers, The (Saroyan). DEng 1658; RevDEng 2066, 2068-2069.

Cave of Salamanca, The (Cervantes). DFor 366.

Caveat for Common Cursetors, Vulgarly Called Vagabonds, A (Harman). ShF 453-454.

Cavendish, Margaret. *See* **Newcastle, Margaret Cavendish, Duchess of.**

"Cavern, The" (Tomlinson). RevPEng 3378.

Caversham Entertainment, The (Campion). PEng 427; RevPEng 495.

Caves du Vatican, Les. See *Lafcadio's Adventures.*

Caviare at the Funeral (Simpson). PEng 2608-2609; RevPEng 3011.

Caxton, William. LTh 1185; PEng 3269; ShF 143, 382.

"Ce que dit la bouche d'ombre." *See* "What the Mouth of the Shadow Says."

"Cebu" (Creeley). PEng 688-689.

Čech, Svatopluk. PFor 1802.

"Ceci n'est pas un conte." *See* "This Is No Yarn" *and* "This Is Not a Story."

Cecilia (Burney). LFEng 379-380; RevLFEng 478-479.

Cefalu. See *Dark Labyrinth, The.*

"Ceil" (Brodkey). RevShF 332-333.

Cela, Camilo José. LFFor 289-301, 2393.

Celan, Paul. PFor 308-315, 1372, 1934-1935.

"Celebrated Jumping Frog of Calaveras County, The" (Twain). RevShF 2327-2328, 2704; ShF 211-212, 2361-2362.

"Celebration, The" (Dickey, J.). PEng 798.
Celebration (Settle). LFSup 349-350; RevLFEng 3004-3005, 3010-3011.
"Celebrations" (Clarke). PSup 70; RevPEng 610.
Celestial Navigation (Tyler). LFEng 2679-2680; RevLFEng 3338-3339.
"Celestial Omnibus, The" (Forster). RevShF 888; ShF 521, 1391.
Celestina, La (Rojas). See *Comedia de Calisto y Melibea, La.*
"Celibacy" (Clarke). PSup 69; RevPEng 609.
Céline, Louis-Ferdinand. LFFor 302-314.
Celle qui n'était plus. See *Woman Who Was No More, The.*
Celles qu'on prend dans ses bras (Montherlant). DFor 1354.
Celos infundados, Los (Martínez de la Rosa). DFor 1272-1273.
Celtic Twilight, The (Yeats). LTh 1587; RevShF 2525; ShF 656-657.
Cement (Müller). DSup 260.
"Cemetery, The" (Gill). ShF 1487.
"Cena miserable, La." *See* "Wretched Supper, The."
Cena Trimalchionis (Petronius). RevShF 1879, 1882-1883; ShF 2092, 2095-2096.
Cenci, The (Shelley). DEng 1746, 1747, 1752-1753; RevDEng 2177, 2184-2187.
Cendrars, Blaise. LFFor 315-323; PFor 1880.
"Ceneri." *See* "Ashes."
"Ceneri di Gramsci, Le." *See* "Gramsci's Ashes."
"Census Taker, The" (Oates). RevShF 1738.
Cent Ballades (Christine de Pisan). PFor 352-353.
Centaur, The (Updike). LFEng 2687, 2699-2703; RevLFEng 3351-3352.
"Center" (Miles). PSup 279; RevPEng 2319.
Center of Attention, The (Hoffman). PEng 1358; RevPEng 1533-1534.
"Centerfold Reflected in a Jet Window" (McPherson). RevPEng 2186.
Centlivre, Mrs. Susannah. DEng 343-350, 2177; **RevDEng 404-411,** 2697, 2830.
Centuries of Meditations (Traherne). PEng 2925-2926; RevPEng 3396, 3397-3399.
Century. ShF 585, 586, 588.
Century of Hero-Worship, A (Bentley). LTh 146.
Cerco de Numancia, El. See *Siege of Numantia, The.*
Ceremonies in Dark Old Men (Elder). RevDEng 676, 677-680.
Ceremony (Parker). M&D 1301.
"Ceremony" (Stafford). PEng 2723-2724.

Ceremony of Innocence, The (Ribman). DSup 314; RevDEng 1978.
Cerenio, Virginia. RevPEng 3918.
Cernuda, Luis. PFor 316-324.
"Cero." *See* "Zero."
Certain Bokes of Virgiles Aenis (Surrey). PEng 2790-2791; RevPEng 3256-3257.
Certain Notes of Instruction Concerning the Making of Verse or Rime in English (Gascoigne). PEng 3285.
Certain Sleep (Reilly). M&D 1404.
Certain Smile, A (Sagan). LFFor 1473-1474.
Certain Sourire, Un. See *Certain Smile, A.*
Certain Tragicall Discourses (Fenton). ShF 487-489.
Certayne Eglogus (Barclay). PEng 3286; RevPEng 3805.
Certayne Notes of Instruction Concerning the Making of Verse (Gascoigne). RevPEng 1196, 1197.
"Certayne Notes of Instruction Concerning the Making of Verse or Rhyme in English" (Gascoigne). LTh 543.
Cervantes, Miguel de. DFor 361-368, 2486-2487; LFEng 3222-3223, 3225-3227, 3231; **LFFor 324-332,** 2024-2026, 2373; PEng 3313; RevLFEng 3873; **RevShF 457-466; ShF 1082-1092.**
Ces plaisirs. See *Pure and the Impure, The.*
Césaire, Aimé. DSup 38-44; LTh 1056, 1058; **PFor 325-330;** PSup 404.
Cesta kolem světa za 80 dni (Kohout). DSup 223.
Cetro de José, El (Cruz). DFor 444.
Cette Voix. See *That Voice.*
Cézanne, Paul. LTh 1493.
Chabon, Michael. RevShF 467-473.
Chabot, Admiral of France (Chapman and Shirley). DEng 2287, 2288; RevDEng 2806, 2807.
"Chac Mool" (Fuentes). RevShF 926.
Chaereas and Callirhoe (Chariton). RevShF 2573.
Chaffin, Lillie D. ShF 2542.
Chaikin, Joseph. DEng 2483.
"Chain of Love, A" (Price). RevShF 1923-1924; ShF 2123.
"Chain Saw at Dawn in Vermont in Time of Drouth" (Warren). PEng 3027.
"Chained Stream, The" (Hölderlin). PFor 686. See also *Nachtgesänge.*
"Chainsaw" (Everson). PEng 993; RevPEng 1124.
Chairs, The (Ionesco). DFor 998-999, 2251, 2357.
Chaises, Les. See *Chairs, The.*

Charakteristiken und Kritiken (Schlegel, F.). LTh 1311.

Charcot, Jean-Martin. PFor 229-230.

Chareas and Callirhoe (Chariton). LFFor 2002-2003.

"Charges Against Cock Robin, The" (Snodgrass). RevPEng 3095.

Charing Cross Mystery, The (Fletcher). M&D 625.

Charioteer, The (Renault). LFEng 2218-2219; RevLFEng 2809-2810.

Chariton. LFFor 2002-2003.

Charlatanisme, Le (Scribe). DFor 1681-1682.

"Charles" (Jackson). ShF 1670.

Charles, Franklin. *See* **Adams, Cleve F.**

"Charles Baudelaire's 'Les Chats'" (Jakobson). LTh 749.

Charles Demailly (Goncourts). LFFor 712.

Charles d'Orléans. PEng 3272; PFor 337-343, 1845, 1846; RevPEng 3791.

Charles Men, The (Heidenstam). LFFor 821-822.

Charles of Orleans. *See* **Charles d'Orléans.**

"Charles Simic" (Simic). PEng 2594-2595.

Charles XII (Planché). DEng 1525-1526; RevDEng 1913-1914.

Charley Is My Darling (Cary). LFEng 457-458.

Charlie (Mrożek). DFor 1381.

Charlie Is My Darling (Cary). RevLFEng 577-578.

Charlotte Corday (Ponsard). DFor 1490, 1492.

Charlotte Löwensköld (Lagerlöf). LFFor 986-989. See also *Ring of the Löwenskölds, The.*

"Charlotte Russe" (Hale, N.). RevShF 1098; ShF 1570.

Charlotte Temple (Rowson). LFEng 2314-2316; RevLFEng 2909-2912.

Charmed Circle, A (Kavan). LFEng 1510; RevLFEng 1835.

Charmed Life, A (McCarthy, M.). LFEng 1722-1723; RevLFEng 2153.

Charnel Rose, The (Aiken). PEng 23; RevPEng 24.

"Charogne, Une." *See* "Carcass, A."

Charon's Cosmology (Simic). RevPEng 3001.

Charterhouse of Parma, The (Stendhal). LFFor 1660-1663.

Charteris, Leslie. M&D 312-318; ShF 764-765.

Chartēs, Ho (Sinópoulos). PFor 1972.

Chartier, Alain. PFor 344-349, 1844.

Chartreuse de Parme, La. See *Charterhouse of Parma, The.*

Chase, James Hadley. M&D 319-324.

Chase, Richard. LTh 1756.

Chase of the Golden Plate, The (Futrelle). M&D 676.

"Chaser, The" (Collier). RevShF 590; ShF 121, 1169.

"Chassidische Schriften." *See* "Hasidic Scriptures."

Chast' rechi. See *Part of Speech, A.*

Chaste Maid in Cheapside, A (Middleton). DEng 1329-1330; RevDEng 1666-1667.

Chastelard (Swinburne). DEng 1898-1899; RevDEng 2340-2341.

Château, The (Maxwell). RevLFEng 2345.

Château des Carpathes, Le. See *Castle of the Carpathians, The.*

Château des cœurs, Le. See *Castle of Hearts, The.*

Chateaubriand, François René de. LFEng 3142; **LFFor 333-342;** LTh 1181, 1243, 1698.

Châtiments, Les (Hugo). PFor 735.

Chatte, La. See *Cat, The.*

Chatterton (Vigny). DFor 2344.

Chatterton, Thomas. PEng 464-474; RevPEng 560-570.

Chattopadhyaya, Harindranath. PFor 2000.

Chaucer, Geoffrey. DEng 2149; LTh 22-23, 279-284, 967; **PEng 475-489,** 1288, 1802-1803, 1804, 3260-3267, 3490; PFor 1467; RevPEng 2669; **RevPEng 571-586,** 3779-3786; **RevShF 481-497;** ShF 138-140, 142-143, 381, 447, **1100-1117.**

Chaulieu, Guillaume Amfryl. PFor 1859.

Chaussée, Pierre-Claude Nivelle de La. *See* **La Chaussée, Pierre-Claude Nivelle de.**

Chaves (Mallea). LFFor 1057-1058.

Chayefsky, Paddy. RevDEng 3037.

Chayka. See *Seagull, The.*

"Che Guevara" (Lowell, R.). PEng 1795; RevPEng 2089.

Cheat, The (Čapek). LFFor 278-279.

"Cheat's Remorse, The" (Callaghan). RevShF 388-389; ShFSup 72-73.

"Cheating the Gallows" (Zangwill). M&D 1733.

Checkmate (Le Fanu). M&D 1049.

Chee-Chee (Rodgers and Hart, L.). DEng 902-903; RevDEng 1125.

Cheer, The (Meredith). PEng 1956; RevPEng 2273-2274.

Cheery Soul, A (White). DSup 394-395; RevDEng 2515.

Cheever, John. LFEng 500-512; RevLFEng 613-628; RevShF 498-508, 2754; ShF 553-554, **1118-1123.**

Chef-d'œuvre inconnu, Le. See *Unknown Masterpiece, The.*

Chekhov, Anton. DFor 369-383, 782, 2457; LFEng 3172, 3300; RevShF 509-519, 2718-2721; ShF 462, 1124-1130.

"Chelkash" (Gorky). RevShF 1047.

Chelsea Murders, The (Davidson). M&D 457-458.

Chemins de la liberté, Les. See *Roads to Freedom.*

Chemmeen (Pillai). LFFor 2226.

Ch'ên Tu-hsiu. LTh 704, 1781.

Chêng Hsüan. LTh 1774.

Chêng Kuang-chu. DFor 2316.

Chénier, André-Marie. PFor 1859, 1861, 1864.

Chéreau, Patrice. DFor 2355.

Chéri (Colette). LFFor 371-372.

Chérie (Goncourt, E.). LFFor 717.

Chernyshevsky, Nikolay. LFFor 2318; LTh 121, 285-291, 386-388, 390, 396, 398, 946, 1104-1108, 1123, 1125, 1447, 1502.

Cherokee Night, The (Riggs). DEng 1592, 1596-1597; RevDEng 1996, 2000-2001.

Cheronis-Selz, Thalia. ShF 2543.

Cherry, Kelly. ShF 2544.

Cherry Orchard, The (Chekhov). DFor 380-383.

"Cherrylog Road" (Dickey, J.). PEng 797.

"Cherty dlia kharakteristiki russkogo prostonarod'ia." *See* "Features for Characterizing the Russian Common People."

Chesapeake (Michener). LFSup 302-303; RevLFEng 2374-2375.

Chesnutt, Charles Waddell. LFEng 513-522; RevLFEng 629-638; RevShF 520-527; ShFSup 83-90.

Chessmaster and His Moves, The (Rao). RevLFEng 2794-2795.

Chester Cycle. DEng 2248-2249; RevDEng 2768-2769.

Chesterfield, Lord (Phillip Dormer Stanhope). LTh 1218.

Chesterton, G. K. M&D 325-332; PEng 490-497; RevShF 528-535; ShF 754.

"Chestnut casts his flambeaux, The" (Housman). PEng 1415; RevPEng 1625.

Chestnut Rain, The (Heyen). RevPEng 1507-1508.

Chetki (Akhmatova). PFor 11-12.

Chetyrnadtsatoye dekabrya. See *December the Fourteenth.*

Cheuse, Alan. ShF 2545.

Chevengur (Platonov). LFFor 2323.

Cheviot, the Stag, and the Black, Black Oil, The (McGrath). RevDEng 1520.

"Chèvre, La." *See* "Goat, The."

"Chèvre de M. Seguin, La." *See* "M. Seguin's Goat."

"Chèvrefeuille." *See* "Honeysuckle, The."

Cheyney, Peter. M&D 333-339.

Cheyney, Reginald Southhouse. *See* Cheyney, Peter.

Chez Nous (Nichols). DSup 282; RevDEng 1731.

Chi, Juan. *See* Juan Chi.

Ch'i Ju-shan. DFor 2334.

Chia. See *Family, The.*

Chiabrera, Gabriello. PFor 2018.

Ch'iang K'uei. LTh 1777.

Chiang-chai shin-hua (Wang Fu-chih). LTh 1779-1780.

Chiao-jan. LTh 1776.

Chiarelli, Luigi. DFor 384-391.

Chiaroscuro (Deledda). LFFor 436-437.

Chiave a stella, La. See *Monkey's Wrench, The.*

Chicago (Shepard). RevDEng 2193.

Chicago Poems (Sandburg). PEng 2449, 2451; RevPEng 2854.

"Chicago Train, The" (Glück). PSup 134; RevPEng 1245.

"Chickamauga" (Bierce). RevShF 225; ShF 793, 968-969.

Chicken Soup with Barley (Wesker). DEng 2016-2017; RevDEng 2506-2508.

Chickencoop Chinaman, The (Chin). DSup 46-48; RevDEng 425-428.

Chief Joseph of the Nez Percé (Warren). RevPEng 3524-3525.

Chief Thing, The. See *Main Thing, The.*

Ch'ien, T'ao. *See* T'ao Ch'ien.

Chien couchant, Le (Sagan). LFFor 1477-1478.

"Chiens ont soif, Les" (Prévert). PFor 1280.

Chijin no ai (Tanizaki). LFFor 1712-1713.

Chikamatsu Monzaemon. DFor 392-400, 2426-2431; LTh 1790.

"Child, The" (Bates). ShF 270.

"Child and the Shadow, The" (Le Guin). RevShF 1451, 1453.

"Child by Fever" (Foote). LFEng 979; RevLFEng 1161-1162.

"Child in the Hills" (Still). PEng 2764; RevPEng 3227.

"Child in the House, The" (Pater). LFEng 2065; RevLFEng 2602.

"Child My Choice, A" (Southwell). PEng 2688; RevPEng 3131-3132.

"Child Next Door, The" (Warren). RevPEng 3522.

"Child of Europe, A" (Miłosz). PFor 1033.

Child of God (McCarthy, C.). LFSup 268; RevLFEng 2144-2145.

"Child of God, The" (O'Flaherty). RevShF 1794; ShF 2008-2009.

Child of Pleasure, The (D'Annunzio). LFFor 409-411.

Child Story (Handke). LFFor 790.

"Child Who Favored Daughter, The" (Walker). RevShF 2380; ShFSup 337.

Childe Byron (Linney). DSup 238; RevDEng 1448.

Childe Harold's Pilgrimage (Byron). LTh 1709; PEng 407-411; RevPEng 473-477.

"Childe Roland to the Dark Tower Came" (Browning, R.). PEng 343-344; RevPEng 414-415.

Childermass, The (Lewis, W.). LFEng 1685-1686; RevLFEng 2082-2083.

Childers, Erskine. M&D 340-344.

"Childhood: At Grandmother's" (Babel). RevShF 126.

"Childhood" (Justice). PEng 1533; RevPEng 1758.

"Childhood of a Boss" (Sartre). LFFor 1514; RevShF 2067-2069.

"Childhood of Luvers, The" (Pasternak). PFor 1159; RevShF 1854-1855; ShF 2060-2061. See also *My Sister, Life.*

"Childish Recollections" (Byron). PEng 405; RevPEng 471.

Children (Gurney). DSup 166-167; RevDEng 1068-1069.

"Children" (McPherson). RevPEng 2185.

"Children, The" (Oates). ShF 707.

Children at the Gate, The (Wallant). LFEng 2763-2764; RevLFEng 3421-3422.

Children of a Lesser God (Medoff). DSup 244; RevDEng 1648.

"Children of Adam" (Whitman). PEng 3068, 3069; RevPEng 3555-3556.

Children of Heracles, The (Euripides) 2113-2114.

Children of Light (Stone). RevLFEng 3202.

Children of the Albatross (Nin). LFEng 1994; RevLFEng 2516, 2518.

Children of the Ash-Covered Loam (Gonzalez). LFEng 1139; RevLFEng 1359.

Children of the Black Sabbath (Hébert). LFFor 812-813, 814.

Children of the Game (Cocteau). LFFor 361-362.

"Children of the Great" (Lewis). RevShF 1486.

Children of Violence (Lessing). RevLFEng 2035.

Children's Hour, The (Hellmann). DEng 916-920; RevDEng 1140-1144.

Child's Garden of Verses, A (Stevenson). PEng 2755, 2756; RevPEng 3217-3218.

Child's Play (Malouf). RevLFEng 2291.

Child's Play (Slavitt). RevPEng 3051.

Childwold (Oates). RevLFEng 2537-2538.

"Childybawn" (O'Faolain). RevShF 1785-1786.

Chill, The (Macdonald). LFSup 275-276; RevLFEng 2174-2175.

Chilly Scenes of Winter (Beattie). LFEng 190-192; RevLFEng 250-251.

Chimera (Barth). LFEng 3327-3328.

Chimères, Les (Nerval). PFor 1087-1089.

"Chimes for Yahya" (Merrill). PEng 1964-1966.

Chimmoku. See *Silence.*

Chin, Frank. DSup 45-51; RevDEng 424-432.

Chin P'ing Mei (Wang Shih-chen). LFFor 2091, 2097-2099.

Chin Shêng-t'an. LTh 1779.

China Governess, The (Allingham). M&D 26-27.

China Trace (Wright, C.). PEng 3152-3153; RevPEng 3659-3661.

"Chinaman, The" (Wideman). RevShF 2463.

Chinese des Schmerzes, Der (Handke). LFFor 790.

Chinese Lake Murders, The (van Gulik). M&D 1643.

Chinese Nail Murders, The (van Gulik). M&D 1646.

"Chinese Nightingale, The" (Lindsay). PEng 1725-1726; RevPEng 2009-2010.

Chinese Wall, The (Frisch). DFor 643-645, 2261-2262.

Chinese Written Character as a Medium for Poetry, The (Pound). LTh 1159.

Ch'ing shan lei (Ma). DFor 2316.

Ch'ing-chao, Li. See **Li Ch'ing-chao.**

"Ch'ing-p'ing yüeh." *See* "Tune: Pure, Serene Music."

"Chiocciola, La." *See* "Snail, The."

"Chip of Glass Ruby, A" (Gordimer). RevShF 1033; ShFSup 107.

"Chiron" (Hölderlin). PFor 686. See also *Nachtgesänge.*

Chłopi. See *Peasants, The.*

"Chœur des cèdres du Liban" (Lamartine). PFor 835-836.

Choephoroi. See *Libation Bearers.*

Choice of a Tutor, The (Fonvizin). DFor 638.

Choirboys, The (Wambaugh). RevLFEng 3429-3430.

Choise of Valentines, The (Nashe). PEng 2074; RevPEng 2421, 2423.

"Chomei at Toyama" (Bunting). PEng 370; RevPEng 444.

Chomsky, Noam. LTh 1437, 1801, 1803, 1813, 1830; PFor 1736; RevPEng 3986-3987.

Chopin, Frédéric. LFFor 1489-1490.

Chopin, Kate. LFEng 523-532; RevLFEng 639-649; RevShF 536-541; ShF 1131-1136.

"Chor der Steine." *See* "Chorus of the Stones."

"Chorus Girl, The" (Chekhov). RevShF 312.

Chorus of Disapproval, A (Ayckbourn). RevDEng 82.

"Chorus of the Stones" (Sachs). PFor 1373-1374.

"Choruses Descriptive of Dido's State of Mind" (Ungaretti). PFor 1571. See also *Terra promessa, La.*

Chosen, The (Potok). LFSup 314-315; RevLFEng 2660-2661.

Chosen Light, A (Montague). RevPEng 2361-2362.

Chosen Poems (Monroe). PEng 2029.

"Ch'ou Ch'ang shaofu." *See* "In Response to Vice-Magistrate Chang."

Chou Shou-jen. *See* Lu Hsün.

Chou-kung shê-chêng (Chêng). DFor 2316.

Chouans, The (Balzac). M&D 75.

Chrétien de Troyes. LFFor 2110; PFor 632, 1838; ShF 444, 1137-1142; RevShF 542-547, 2615; ShF 444, 1137-1142.

Christ and Antichrist (Merezhkovsky). LFFor 1138-1139.

Christ Legends (Lagerlöf). LFFor 979.

Christ Recrucified (Kazantzakis). LFFor 920.

Christ Stopped At Eboli (Levi). LFFor 2248.

Christ II (Cynewulf). PEng 720-721; RevPEng 816, 822-823.

Christabel (Coleridge, S. T.). PEng 540-541; RevPEng 631-632.

Christian Ethicks (Traherne). PEng 2926-2927; RevPEng 3399-3400.

Christian Hero, The (Steele, R.). RevShF 2186; ShF 2268.

Christianity at Glacier (Laxness). LFFor 1001-1002.

Christie, Agatha. LFEng 533-543, 3187-3188; M&D 345-353; RevLFEng 650-660, 3844-3845; RevShF 548-555; ShF 756, 1143-1149.

Christie in Love (Brenton). DSup 32-33; RevDEng 319-320.

Christine (Dumas, *père*). DFor 487.

Christine (King). LFSup 207-208; RevLFEng 1889-1890.

Christine de Pisan. PFor 350-354, 1844.

"Christmas" (Herbert). PEng 1301; RevPEng 1480.

Christmas Carol, A (Dickens). RevShF 724-725; ShF 1272-1273.

"Christmas Eve in Whitneyville" (Hall). PEng 1199.

"Christmas Eve Service at Midnight at St. Michael's" (Bly). RevPEng 272.

Christmas Garland, Woven by Max Beerbohm, A (Beerbohm). RevShF 199-200; ShF 946-947.

"Christmas Gift" (Himes). ShF 1642.

Christmas Murder, The. See *English Murder, An.*

"Christmas 1944" (Levertov). RevPEng 1982.

"Christmas Story, A" (Bates). RevShF 175-176; ShFSup 32.

"Christmas Tree and a Wedding, A" (Dostoevski). RevShF 752.

"Christmas Trees" (Hill). RevPEng 1527.

Christopher Columbus (Jensen). LFFor 883. See also *Long Journey, The.*

Christos xanastauronetai, Ho. See *Christ Recrucified.*

Christ's Company and Other Poems (Dixon). PEng 817-818.

Chronica maiora (Isidore of Seville). LTh 742.

Chronicle of a Death Foretold (García Márquez). LFFor 619-620; RevShF 953.

"Chronicle of Division, The" (Everson). PEng 988-989; RevPEng 1119-1120.

Chronicle of the Drum, The (Thackeray). PEng 2872-2873.

Chronicle of the Reign of Charles IX, A (Mérimée). LFFor 1147-1148.

Chronicle of the Times of Charles the Ninth, A. See *Chronicle of the Reign of Charles IX, A.*

Chronicles, The (Froissart). LFFor 2111.

Chronicles of Hell (Ghelderode). DFor 698.

Chronicles of Japan. LTh 1784.

Chronicles of St. Bernard (Ruskin). ShF 2165-2166.

Chronik der Sperlingsgasse, Die (Raabe). LFFor 1379-1380.

Chronique du règne de Charles IX. See *Chronicle of the Reign of Charles IX, A.*

Chroniques. See *Chronicles, The.*

"Chronopolis" (Ballard). ShF 912-913.

"Chrysalis" (Montale). PFor 1049. See also *Bones of the Cuttlefish.*

Chrysanthemum Chain, The (Melville). M&D 1217.

"Chrysanthemums, The" (Steinbeck). RevShF 2208-2209.

"Chthonian Revelation: A Myth" (Warren). PEng 3025.

Chto delat'? See *What Is to Be Done?*

"Chto takoe oblomovshchina?" *See* "What Is Oblomovism?"

Chto takoe sotsialisticheskii realizm. See *On Socialist Realism.*

Chto takoye iskusstvo? See *What Is Art?*

Ch'ü Yüan. PFor 1781-1782.

Chu Yüan-chang. *See* Hung Wu.

Ch'uan ch'i. DFor 1039, 1042, 1046-1047, 2306, 2311, 2320, 2322-2325.

Ch'üan Yüan tsa-chü (Yang). DFor 2318.

"Chu-fu." *See* "New Year's Sacrifice, The."

Chulkov, Mikhail. LFFor 2305.

Chung Jung. LTh 1775.

"Church, The" (Herbert). PEng 1297-1299, 1300, 1302-1303; RevPEng 1476-1483.

Church, Francis Pharcellus. ShF 587.

Church, William Conant. ShF 587.

"Church Going" (Larkin). PEng 1672-1673; RevPEng 1940-1941.

"Church Militant, The" (Herbert). PEng 1297; RevPEng 1476.

"Church-monuments" (Herbert). PEng 1300; RevPEng 1477, 1478-1479.

"Church-porch, The" (Herbert). PEng 1297; RevPEng 1476.

Churchill, Caryl. RevDEng 433-439.

Churchill, Charles. PEng 3333; RevPEng 3852.

Churchill Plays, The (Brenton). DSup 36; RevDEng 323-324.

Chute, B. J. ShF 2546.

Chute, La. See *Fall, The.*

Chyornye maski. See *Black Maskers, The.*

Ciabattari, Jane. ShF 2547.

Ciardi, John. PEng 498-505; PSup 404; RevPEng 587-595.

Ciascuno a suo modo. See *Each in His Own Way.*

Cibber, Colley. DEng 362-369, 2177; RevDEng 440-448, 2697.

"Cicely's Dream" (Chesnutt). RevShF 526; ShFSup 89-90.

Cicero. LTh 133-134, **292-297,** 411-412, 470-471, 741, 963-967, 1039, 1045, 1092-1093, 1190, 1192, 1638-1639, 1650-1651, 1653, 1665; PFor 2093-2094.

"Ciceronian, The (Erasmus). LTh 411, 470.

Ciceronis Amor. See *Tullies Love.*

Cicognani, Bruno. LFFor 2240.

Cid, El. ShF 138.

Cid, The (Corneille). DEng 2171; DFor 428-430, 1246; LTh 308-310; RevDEng 2691.

Cidade e as serras, A. See *City and the Mountains, The.*

Cider House Rules, The (Irving, J.). RevLFEng 1702-1703.

Cien años de soledad. See *One Hundred Years of Solitude.*

Cíger-Hronský, Jozef. LFFor 2069.

Cimbrernes tog (Jensen). LFFor 883. See also *Long Journey, The.*

Cimbrians, The. See *Long Journey, The.*

Cimetière des voitures, La. See *Car Cemetery, The.*

"Cimetière marin, Le." *See* "Graveyard by the Sea, The."

Cinco horas con Mario (Delibes). LFFor 450-451.

"Cinderella" (Grimm). RevShF 1088; ShF 1561.

"Cinderella" (Jarrell). PEng 1483; RevPEng 1695.

"Cinderella" (McPherson). RevPEng 2185.

Cinderella (Walser, R.). RevShF 2389-2390; ShFSup 347.

"Cinderella Waltz, The" (Beattie). RevShF 182; ShFSup 39.

Cinna (Corneille). DFor 432-433.

Cinnamon Shops (Schulz). RevShF 2074-2077; ShFSup 274-279.

Cino, Joseph. DEng 2480.

Cinq (Tremblay). DSup 353-354.

Cinq Cents Millions de la Bégum, Le. See *Begum's Fortune, The.*

Cinq Grandes Odes. See *Five Great Odes.*

"Cinque maggio, Il." *See* "Napoleonic Ode, The."

Cinthio, Giambattista Giraldi. *See* **Giraldi Cinthio, Giambattista.**

Cioso (Ferreira). DFor 591.

Cipreses creen en Dios, Los. See *Cypresses Believe in God, The.*

Circle, The (Maugham). DEng 1311-1312; RevDEng 1640-1641.

"Circle Game, The" (Atwood). PEng 64-65.

Circle Game, The (Atwood). RevPEng 70-72.

Circle Home, The (Hoagland). LFSup 153-154; RevLFEng 1630-1631.

"Circular Ruins, The" (Borges). RevShF 249.

Circular Staircase, The (Rinehart). M&D 1430-1431.

Circular Study (Green). M&D 785.

"Circus, The" (Koch). PEng 1628; RevPEng 1867.

"Circus, The" (Porter). RevShF 1912; ShF 261.

Circus, Anthony. *See* **Hoch, Edward D.**

"Circus in the Attic, The" (Warren). RevShF 2413; ShF 2406-2407.

"Circus Performers, The" (Tzara). PFor 1551.

Cisneros, Sandra. RevShF 556-561.

Citadel, The (Cronin). LFEng 653, 656-658, 661; RevLFEng 786, 789-791, 794.

Citadelle. See *Wisdom of the Sands, The.*

Cithara sanctorum (Tranovský, comp.). PFor 1807.

"Cities" (Hacker). PEng 1190-1191.

"Cities and Thrones and Powers" (Kipling). PEng 1608; RevPEng 1847-1848.

Cities of the Interior (Nin). LFEng 1992-1993; RevLFEng 2516-2518.

Cities of the Plain (Proust). LFFor 1334-1337. See also *Remembrance of Things Past.*

Cities of the Red Night (Burroughs). RevLFEng 489-490.

"Cities, Plains and People" (Durrell). PEng 920-921; RevPEng 1050-1051.

Citizen Kane (Welles). DEng 2517.

Citizen of the World, The (Goldsmith). RevShF 1024-1028; ShF 1512-1516.

Citizen Tom Paine (Fast). RevLFEng 3838

Citizens of Calais, The (Kaiser). DFor 1019.

Città invisibili, Le. See *Invisible Cities.*

Città morta, La. See Dead City, The.

"Città vecchia." *See* "Old Town."

"City, The" (Æ). PEng 18; RevPEng 18.

City, The (Claudel). DFor 406-407.

City, The (Fitch). DEng 622-624; RevDEng 766-768.

"City, The" (Updike). RevShF 2342.

City and the House, The (Ginzburg). LFSup 131.

City and the Mountains, The (Eça de Queiróz). LFFor 546.

City and the Pillar, The (Vidal). LFEng 2718-2719; RevLFEng 3372.

City Boy, The (Wouk). LFEng 2965; RevLFEng 3667.

"City in the Sea" (Poe). PEng 2246; RevPEng 2619.

City Looking Glass, The (Bird). DEng 214; RevDEng 254.

City Madam, The (Massinger). DEng 2291; RevDEng 2810.

City of God, The (Augustine). LTh 1646; ShF 892-894.

City of Illusions (Le Guin). LFEng 1633-1634; RevLFEng 2009-2010.

City of Pleasure, The (Bennett). M&D 109.

"City of Satisfactions, The" (Hoffman). PEng 1359; RevPEng 1534.

"City of the Dead, a City of the Living, A" (Gordimer). RevShF 1035-1036; ShFSup 110.

"City of the Living, The" (Stegner). RevShF 2191; ShF 2272.

City of Trembling Leaves, The (Clark). LFEng 550; RevLFEng 664, 667.

City Politiques (Crowne). DEng 439-441; RevDEng 546-548.

City Primeval (Leonard). M&D 1056.

City Romance (Furetière). LFFor 2028.

City Solitary, A (Freeling). M&D 663-664.

Ciudad y los perros, La. See *Time of the Hero, The.*

Civil Poems (Miles). PSup 270; RevPEng 2310.

Civil War, The (Foote). LFEng 969; RevLFEng 1152; ShF 288.

Civil War (Montherlant). DFor 1356-1357.

CIVIL warS, The (Wilson, Robert). DSup 402; RevDEng 2621.

"Civilities" (Booth). RevPEng 307.

"Civilization" (Snyder). PEng 2674.

Cixous, Helen. RevPEng 3968.

Clacson, trombette è pernacchi. See *About Face.*

Claiborne, Sybil. ShF 2548.

"Clair de lune." *See* "Moonlight."

Clam Shell, The (Settle). LFSup 347; RevLFEng 3004, 3008.

"Clamming" (Whittemore). PEng 3080; RevPEng 3568.

Clamor (Guillén). PFor 625.

Clanvowe, Sir John. RevPEng 3791.

"Clara" (O'Brien, Edna). ShF 1974-1975.

"Clara Milich" (Turgenev). RevShF 2324.

Clare, John. PEng 506-515; RevPEng 596-605.

Clarel (Melville). PEng 1949; RevPEng 2256.

Clarín. LFFor 343-355, 2385.

Clarissa (Richardson, S.). LFEng 2246-2247, 2250-2251; LTh 887; RevLFEng 2841-2842, 3816; ShF 471.

Clark, Alfred Alexander Gordon. *See* **Hare, Cyril.**

Clark, Curt. *See* **Westlake, Donald E.**

Clark, Howard. *See* **Henry, O.**

Clark, Jean C. ShF 2549.

Clark, John Pepper. DSup 52-59. *See also* **Clark-Bekederemo, John Pepper.**

Clark, LaVerne Harrell. ShF 2550.

Clark, Walter Van Tilburg. LFEng 544-552; RevLFEng 661-671; RevShF 562-568; ShF 547, 1150-1155.

Clark-Bekederemo, John Pepper. RevDEng 449-457. *See also* **Clark, John Pepper.**

Clarke, Anna. M&D 354-359.

Clarke, Arthur C. RevShF 569-575; ShF 1156-1162; ShFSup 388.

Clarke, Austin. DEng 370-379; PSup 66-72; RevDEng 458-467; RevPEng 606-613.

Clarke, Martha. DSup 60-67; RevDEng 468-478.

Claro enigma (Drummond de Andrade). PSup 100.

Clash by Night (Odets). DEng 1402; RevDEng 1778.

"Classic" (Herbert). PFor 656.

"Classic Ballroom Dances" (Simic). RevPEng 3001.
Classic Vision, The (Krieger). LTh 826.
"Classical Walpurgis Night" (Verlaine). PFor 1629.
Claudel, Paul. DFor **401-413,** 2352; LFFor 1124; **PFor 355-365,** 1881, 1882-1883.
Claude's Confession (Zola). LFFor 1988-1989.
Claudianus, Claudius. PFor 2110.
Claudine à l'école. See *Claudine at School.*
Claudine à Paris. See *Claudine in Paris.*
Claudine and Annie (Colette). LFFor 371.
Claudine at School (Colette). LFFor 370-371.
Claudine en ménage. See *Claudine Married.*
Claudine in Paris (Colette). LFFor 371.
Claudine Married (Colette). LFFor 371.
Claudine s'en va. See *Claudine and Annie.*
Claudius Namatianus. *See* Namatianus, Claudius.
Claudius the God (Graves, R.). LFEng 1200-1201; RevLFEng 1424-1425.
Claussen, Sophus. PFor 2172-2173.
Clavigo (Goethe). DFor 736.
"Clavo, El." *See* "Nail, The."
"Clay" (Joyce). ShF 115.
Clay's Ark (Butler, O.). RevLFEng 497.
Clayhanger (Bennett). LFEng 244-245; RevLFEng 298-299.
Clayton, Richard Henry Michael. *See* **Haggard, William.**
Clea. See *Alexandria Quartet, The.*
"Clean, Well-Lighted Place, A" (Hemingway). ShF 1625-1626; ShFSup 40.
"Cleaning Out the Garage" (Booth). RevPEng 302.
Cleanness (Pearl-Poet). PEng 2197, 2200, 2202-2204, 3254; RevPEng 2568, 2573-2575; ShF 2068, 2069, 2070-2072.
Clear Light of Day (Desai). LFEng 731-732; RevLFEng 873, 877-878.
Clearing (Berry). PEng 154; RevPEng 183.
Clearing in the Woods, A (Laurents). DEng 1104-1105; RevDEng 1383-1385.
"Clearing the Title" (Merrill). PEng 1968; RevPEng 2285.
Cleary, Jon. M&D 360-364.
Cleek, the Man of the Forty Faces. See *Man of the Forty Faces, The.*
Cleek, the Master Detective. See *Man of the Forty Faces, The.*
Clem Anderson (Cassill). LFEng 469.
Clemens, Samuel Langhorne. *See* **Twain, Mark.**
Cleng Peerson (Hauge). LFFor 799.
Cleopatra (Daniel). PEng 728; RevPEng 831.

Cléopâtre captive (Jodelle). DEng 2160; RevDEng 2680.
"Clepsydra" (Ashbery). PEng 61.
Clerambault (Rolland). LFFor 1429-1430.
Clerihew, E. See **Bentley, E. C.**
"Clerk's Quest, The" (Moore, George). RevShF 2727.
"Clerk's Tale, The" (Chaucer). RevShF 494; ShF 1113, 1114-1115.
Cleve, Anders. LFFor 2370.
Cleveland, Grover. LFEng 1025-1026; RevLFEng 1218-1219.
"Cleveland Wrecking Yard, The" (Brautigan). RevShF 315; ShFSup 54-55.
"Clickety-Clack" (Blackburn). PEng 199; RevPEng 243.
"Cliff, The" (Lermontov). PFor 874.
Cliges (Chrétien de Troyes). RevShF 545-546; ShF 1141.
"Climbing Mount E-mei" (Li Po). PFor 888-889.
"Climbing the Peak of Mount T'ai-po" (Li Po). PFor 889.
"Clinic" (Pastan). RevPEng 2546.
Clitophon and Leucippe (Tatius). ShF 489.
Clizia (Machiavelli). DFor 1224-1225.
"CLM" (Masefield). PEng 1924; RevPEng 2229.
"Clock, The" (Beer). PEng 117-118; RevPEng 137-138.
"Clock, The" (Dučić). PFor 429.
Clock Winder, The (Tyler). LFEng 2679; RevLFEng 3337-3338.
Clock Without Hands (Kersh). M&D 980.
Clock Without Hands (McCullers). LFEng 1737; RevLFEng 2168.
Clockwork Orange, A (Burgess). LFEng 370-371; RevLFEng 468-469.
Clope (Pinget). DSup 305.
Clorinda. See *His Excellency.*
Close of Play (Gray). DEng 812; RevDEng 1004.
Close Quarters (Golding). RevLFEng 1356.
Close to the Sun Again (Callaghan). LFEng 432, 437-439; RevLFEng 543, 548-550.
Closed Garden, The (Green). LFFor 744-745.
Closed Harbour, The (Hanley). LFEng 1250-1251; RevLFEng 1478.
Clothes Make the Man (Keller). LFFor 932-934. See also *People of Seldwyld, The.*
"Cloud, The" (Fowles). LFEng 1020; RevLFEng 1211; RevShF 894-895; ShF 1398.
"Cloud, Castle, Lake" (Nabokov). RevShF 1704; ShFSup 220-221.
Cloud in Pants, A (Mayakovsky). PFor 989.
Cloud Nine (Cain). M&D 260.

Colette. LFFor 365-374, 2142; RevShF
576-585; ShF 1163-1167.
Colin Clout (Skelton). PEng 2638-2639, 3286.
Coliphizacio. See *Buffeting, The.*
Collaborators (Mortimer). DEng 1358-1359;
RevDEng 1697-1698.
Collages (Nin). LFEng 1996-1997; RevLFEng
2520-2521.
"Collapsars" (McPherson). PEng 1882.
"Collar, The" (Herbert). PEng 1300, 1301;
RevPEng 1479, 1480.
Collected Longer Poems, The (Rexroth). PEng
2352; RevPEng 2739-2740.
Collected Poems (Barnard). PSup 24; RevPEng
107.
Collected Poems (Betjeman). PEng 167;
RevPEng 202-204.
Collected Poems (Davie). RevPEng 850, 853.
Collected Poems (Eberhart). RevPEng 1059.
Collected Poems (Winters). PSup 399-400;
RevPEng 3628-3629.
Collected Poems, 1950-1970 (Davie). PSup 88.
Collected Poems, 1930-1983 (Miles). PSup 279;
RevPEng 2319.
*Collected Poems and Epigrams of J. V.
Cunningham, The* (Cunningham). PSup 74-75;
RevPEng 803-807.
Collected Shorter Poems, The (Rexroth). PEng
2351; RevPEng 2738-2739.
Collected Stories, The (Stafford). RevShF 2178;
ShF 2260.
Collected Stories (Taylor). ShF 550.
Collector, The (Fowles). LFEng 1014-1016;
RevLFEng 1205-1207.
Colleen Bawn, The (Boucicault). DEng 269;
RevDEng 312.
Colliander, Tito. LFFor 2369.
Collier, Jeremy. DEng 2177.
Collier, John. RevShF 586-593; ShF 258,
1168-1170.
Collier, Old Cap. *See* Hanshew, Thomas W.
Colline. See *Hill of Destiny.*
Collins, Hunt. *See* McBain, Ed.
Collins, Michael. M&D 379-386. *See also*
Carter, Nick.
Collins, Wilkie. LFEng 553-562; M&D
387-393; RevLFEng 680-690, 3788, 3843.
Collins, William. LFEng 553-555; PEng
546-552, 3331-3332; RevLFEng 680-681;
RevPEng 638-644.
Collinson, Peter. *See* Hammett, Dashiell.
"Colloque sentimentale." *See* "Sentimental
Colloquium."

"Colloquy of The Dogs" (Cervantes). RevShF
460-463; ShF 1086-1089.
Collyn Clout (Skelton). RevPEng 3043-3044.
Colmena, La. See *Hive, The.*
Cologne Epode (Archilochus). PFor 91-92.
Colomba (Mérimée). LFFor 1149-1150; RevShF
1657; ShF 1922.
Colombe's Birthday (Browning). DEng 295-296;
RevDEng 352-353.
"Colomber, The" (Buzzati). RevShF 352; ShFSup
63.
"Colombre, Il." *See* "Colomber, The."
"Colonel, The" (Forché). RevPEng 1158.
Colonel Jack (Defoe). LFEng 690; RevLFEng
824.
Colonel Julian and Other Stories (Bates). RevShF
175-176; ShFSup 31.
Colonel Mint (West, P.). LFSup 374-375;
RevLFEng 3525-3526.
Colonel's Daughter, The (Aldington). LFEng
41-42; RevLFEng 55-56.
Colonel's Dream, The (Chesnutt). LFEng
521-522; RevLFEng 637.
"Color of Darkness" (Purdy). RevShF 1956; ShF
2136-2137.
Color Purple, The (Walker). LFEng 2750,
2754-2756; RevLFEng 3407-3408, 3412-3414.
Colossus of Maroussi, The (Miller). LFEng 1873;
RevLFEng 2381.
Colour of Murder, The (Symons). M&D 1563.
Colours in the Dark (Reaney). DEng 1576;
RevDEng 1969.
Colton, James. *See* Hansen, Joseph.
Colum, Padraic. DEng 380-394; RevDEng
479-493.
Columbian Ode, The (Monroe). PEng 2027.
Come and Kill Me. See *Brat Farrar.*
Come Back, Little Sheba (Inge). DEng 982-984;
RevDEng 1235-1237.
"Come Back to the Raft Ag'in, Huck Honey!"
(Fiedler). LTh 485.
Come le foglie. See *Like Falling Leaves.*
Come Morning (Gores). M&D 762.
"Come On, Ye Sons of Art" (Paley). RevShF
1838; ShF 2043.
Comedia de Calisto y Melibea, La (Rojas). DEng
2161; LFFor 2376-2377; RevDEng 2681.
Comedia Himenea. See *Hymen.*
Comedia nueva, La (Moratín). DFor 1362-1363.
Comedia soldadesca (Torres Naharro). DFor
1872-1873.
Comédie de la mort, La. See *Drama of Death,
The.*

Comptesse Coquette (Bracco). DFor 226.

Compton-Burnett, Ivy. LFEng 563-572; RevLFEng 691-701; ShF 521.

"Computer's Karl Marx" (Middleton, C.). PEng 1988; RevPEng 2310.

Comrade Kirillov (Rao). LFEng 2213-2214; RevLFEng 2793-2794.

Comte, Auguste. LTh 1417, 1712, 1718, 1732.

Comte de Monte-Cristo, Le. See *Count of Monte-Cristo, The.*

Comus (Milton). PEng 2007; RevPEng 2340.

Con il piedo straniero sopra il cuore (Quasimodo). PFor 1307.

"Concentration Camps, The" (Sarton). RevPEng 2867.

"Concentration City" (Ballard). RevShF 142.

Concept of Irony, The (Kierkegaard). ShFSup 24.

"Concept of Romanticism in Literary History, The" (Wellek). LTh 1538.

"Conception" (Miles). PSup 278; RevPEng 2318.

"Conception and Technique" (Beck). ShF 71.

"Concepts of 'Tension,' 'Intensity,' and 'Suspense' in Short-Story Theory" (Dollerup). ShF 74.

"Concerning Short Stories" (Strong). ShF 90.

Concerning the Angels (Alberti). PFor 20.

"Concord Hymn" (Emerson). PEng 960; RevPEng 1090.

Concrete (Bernhard). LFFor 161-162.

Concrete Island (Ballard). LFEng 151; RevLFEng 195.

"Condemned, The" (Allen). RevShF 58-59.

"Condemned Librarian, The" (West). RevShF 2451; ShFSup 364.

Condemned of Altona, The (Sartre). DFor 1644-1645, 1650-1651.

Condendado por desconfiado, El (Tirso). DFor 1847-1848.

"Condition Botanique, La" (Hecht). PEng 1278-1279; RevPEng 1454-1455.

Condition humaine, La. See *Man's Fate.*

"Condition of Art, The" (Conrad). ShF 814.

"Condominium, The" (Elkin). LFEng 890-891.

"Condor and the Guests, The" (Connell). ShF 1177.

Condor Passes, The (Grau). LFEng 1187-1188; RevLFEng 1410-1411.

Coney Island of the Mind, A (Ferlinghetti). RevPEng 1149.

Confess, Fletch (Mcdonald). M&D 1128.

Confessio Amantis (Gower). PEng 1114, 1115, 1121-1123, 3259-3260; RevPEng 1268-1271, 3778-3779.

"Confession, A" (MacBeth). PEng 1835; RevPEng 2114.

Confession (Simms). LFEng 2414; RevLFEng 3044.

Confession de Claude, La. See *Claude's Confession.*

Confession of a Child of the Century, The (Musset). LTh 1709.

"Confessional" (Bidart). RevPEng 212.

Confessions (Augustine). LTh 62-66, 1645-1646; ShF 890-892.

Confessions of a English Opium Eater (De Quincey). LTh 1709.

Confessions of a Fool, The (Strindberg). LFFor 1691-1693.

Confessions of a Mask (Mishima). LFFor 1156-1157.

"Confessions of Fitz Boodle" (Thackeray). RevShF 2260-2261; ShF 2315-2316.

Confessions of J.-J. Rousseau (Rousseau). LTh 1709.

Confessions of Nat Turner, The (Styron). LFEng 2589-2590, 2599-2601, 3154-3155; RevLFEng 3244-3245, 3251-3253, 3839-3840.

Confessions of Zeno (Svevo). LFFor 1700-1702, 1705-1707.

Confianza (Salinas). PFor 1389.

Confidential Clerk, The (Eliot). DEng 554-555; RevDEng 695-696.

Conformist, The (Moravia). LFFor 1170-1171.

Confucius. LTh 1773; PFor 1779-1780.

Congiura dei Pazzi. La. See *Conspiracy of the Pazzi, The.*

"Congo" (Senghor). PFor 1427. See also *Hosties noires.*

Congreve, William. DEng 395-412, 2310; PEng 553-558; RevDEng 494-512, 2829; RevPEng 645-651; RevShF 594-597; ShF 503, 504, 1171-1174.

Conjectures on Original Composition (Young). LTh 1596-1599, 1601.

Conjuración de Venecia año de 1310, La. (Martínez de la Rosa). DFor 1269, 1275-1276.

Conjure Woman, The (Chesnutt). LFEng 513; RevLFEng 629; RevShF 522-524; ShF 575-576; ShFSup 85.

"Conjurer's Revenge, The" (Chesnutt). RevShF 523-524; ShFSup 86-87.

Connaissance de l'est. See *East I Know, The.*

Connecticut General from Big Sur, A (Brautigan). LFEng 291-292; RevLFEng 374-375.

Connecticut Yankee in King Arthur's Court, A (Twain). LFEng 2668-2669; RevLFEng 3325-3326, 3860.

Contrast, The (Tyler). DEng 1950-1954, 2396-2397; RevDEng 2408-2413, 2917-2918.

Contre Sainte-Beuve, suivi de nouveaux mélanges. See *By Way of Sainte-Beuve.*

Controversia. RevDEng 1654-1655.

Conul Leonida fata cu reactiunea. See *Mr. Leonida and the Reactionaries.*

"Convergence of the Twain, The" (Hardy). PEng 1221; RevPEng 1394.

Conversación en la catedral. See *Conversation in the Cathedral.*

"Conversation, A" (Aiken). RevShF 30; ShF 840-841.

Conversation (Aiken). LFEng 18, 22-23; RevLFEng 31, 35-36.

"Conversation in Crisis" (Lorde). RevPEng 2043.

Conversation in Sicily. See *In Sicily.*

Conversation in the Cathedral (Vargas Llosa). LFFor 1849-1850.

"Conversation in the Drawing Room, The" (Kees). PEng 1563-1564; RevPEng 1791-1792.

"Conversation of Eiros and Charmion, The" (Poe). ShF 770.

Conversation on the Highway, A (Turgenev). DFor 1906.

Conversations (Jonson). LTh 780, 782.

Conversations of German Emigrés (Goethe). LFEng 3238; ShF 460-528.

Conversazione in Sicilia. See *In Sicily.*

"Conversion of an English Courtizan, The" (Greene, R.). RevShF 1080; ShF 1553-1554.

"Convict and His Radio, The" (Bly). PEng 227.

Convivial Poems (Pascoli). PFor 1142-1143.

Convivio, Il. See *Banquet, The.*

"Convoy" (Booth). PEng 245.

Conway, Troy. *See* **Avallone, Michael.**

Cooke, H. O. *See* **Hanshew, Thomas W.**

Cooke, Margaret. *See* **Creasey, John.**

Cooke, M. E. *See* **Creasey, John.**

Cool Million, A (West, N.). LFEng 2844-2845; RevLFEng 3516-3517.

"Cool Web, The" (Graves). PEng 1128-1129; RevPEng 1285-1286.

"Cooled Heels Lament Against Frivolity, the Mask of Despair," (Dugan). PEng 884; RevPEng 1008.

Cooper, Anthony Ashley. *See* **Shaftesbury, Third Earl of.**

Cooper, Henry St. John. *See* **Creasey, John.**

Cooper, James Fenimore. LFEng 602-616, 3040, 3091, 3192; LTh 525; **RevLFEng 732-747,** 3700, 3748, 3753-3754, 3800.

"Cooper's Hill" (Cleveland). RevPEng 3830.

Coover, Robert. LFEng 617-625, 3227, 3328-3329; LFSup 402; **RevLFEng 748-758,** 3878-3879; RevShF 616-622; ShF 1189-1193.

"Cop and the Anthem, The" (Henry). ShF 230.

Cop Killer (Sjöwall and Wahlöö). M&D 1498.

Cop-Out (Guare). RevDEng 1056-1057.

Copains, Les. See *Boys in the Back Room, The.*

Cope, Wendy. RevPEng 3902.

Copeau, Jacques. DEng 2237; DFor 2351.

Copeland, Ann. ShF 2556.

Cophetua (Drinkwater). DEng 508-509; RevDEng 629-630.

"Copley-Plaza, The" (Hale, N.). RevShF 1098; ShF 1570.

Coppard, A. E. RevShF 623-630; ShF 257-258, **1194-1201.**

"Copper Ferule, The" (Otero). PFor 1114.

Coppia aperta, quasi spalancata. See *Open Couple—Very Open, An.*

"Copulating Gods, The" (Kizer). RevPEng 1855.

Coquelin, Benoît-Constant. DEng 2525-2526.

Coral, The (Kaiser). DFor 1021-1023, 2378. See also *Gas* and *Gas II.*

Corbeaux, Les. See *Vultures, The.*

"Cord of Birch" (Wormser). RevPEng 3650.

"Cords" (O'Brien, E.). RevShF 1746.

Corey, Paul. ShF 2557.

"Cori descrittivi di stati d'animo di Didone." *See* "Choruses Descriptive of Dido's State of Mind."

"Corinna's Going A-Maying" (Herrick, R.). PEng 1315-1317; RevPEng 1495-1496.

Coriolanus (Shakespeare). DEng 1722-1723, 2283; RevDEng 2136-2137, 2802.

Corman, Cid. PEng 567-573; PSup 404; **RevPEng 661-668.**

"Corn" (Lanier). PEng 1661-1662; RevPEng 1928-1929.

Corn Is Green, The (Williams, E.). DEng 2063-2065; RevDEng 2563-2565.

"Corn Planting, The" (Anderson). RevShF 74; ShF 873.

Corneille, Pierre. DEng 2171-2173; DFor 424-437, 1246; LTh **308-313,** 403-404, 669, 708, 775, 838, 840, 880, 882, 1196-1197, 1393; RevDEng 2691-2693.

Cornelia (Garnier). DFor 669-670.

Cornelia (Kyd). DEng 1094-1095; RevDEng 1373-1374.

Cornelius Nepos. *See* Nepos, Cornelius.

Corner of Paradise, A (Holton). M&D 900.

Cornhuskers (Sandburg). PEng 2451; RevPEng 2854.

Corning, Kyle. *See* **Gardner, Erle Stanley.**
"Cornwall" (Davie). PSup 89; RevPEng 855.
Cornwell, David John Moore. *See* **Le Carré, John.**
"Corona" (Celan). PFor 312. See also *Mohn und Gedächtnis.*
"Corona, La" (Donne). PEng 836; RevPEng 942.
Corona de fuego (Usigli). DFor 2442-2443.
Corona de luz (Usigli). DFor 2442-2443.
Corona de sombra. See *Crown of Shadows.*
Corona trágica, La (Vega). PFor 1603.
Coronation (Donoso). LFFor 492-495.
"Coronation, The" (Giusti). PFor 574-575.
Coronel no tiene quien le escriba, El. See *No One Writes to the Colonel.*
"Coronet for his Mistress Philosophy, A" (Chapman). PEng 459; RevPEng 554-555.
"Corpo, O" (Lispector). ShFSup 168.
"Corporal" (Brautigan). RevShF 315-316; ShFSup 55-56.
"Corpse on the Wheat-Field" (Ady). PFor 6.
Correction (Bernhard). LFFor 160-161.
Correspondance, 1830-1880 (Flaubert). LFFor 547-548.
"Corridor, The" (Gunn). PEng 1170.
"Corridor, A" (Robbe-Grillet). ShF 2156.
Corridors of Power (Snow). LFEng 2463; RevLFEng 3089.
Corrington, John Williams. ShF 2559.
Corruption in the Palace of Justice (Betti). DFor 209-210.
Corso, Gregory. PEng 574-579; RevPEng 669-676.
"Corsons Inlet" (Ammons). PSup 10; RevPEng 40.
Cortázar, Julio. LFFor 375-384, 2292, 2298; LFSup 402; **RevShF 631-637; ShF 1202-1205;** ShFSup 388.
Corte de los milagros, La. See *Ruedo ibérico, El.*
Cortegiano, Il. See *Courtier, The.*
Cortigiana, La. See *Courtesan, The.*
Corvo, Il (Gozzi). DFor 795-796.
Corwin, Norman. RevDEng 3030-3031.
Coryell, John Russell. *See* **Carter, Nick.**
Cosa e altri racconti, La. See *Erotic Tales.*
Cosa é una cosa, Una. See *Command and I Will Obey You.*
Coscienza di Zeno, La. See *Confessions of Zeno.*
Così è (se vi pare). See *Right You Are (If You Think So.)*
Ćosić, Dobrica. LFFor 385-392.
Cosmic Rape, The (Sturgeon). LFEng 2585-2586; RevLFEng 3237-3238.

Cosmicomiche, Le. See *Cosmicomics.*
Cosmicomics (Calvino). LFFor 244-245.
Cosmopolitan. ShF 589, 771, 773.
Cosmos (Gombrowicz). LFFor 699.
Cosroès (Rotrou). DFor 1575.
"Cost, The" (Hecht). PEng 1281-1282.
"Côte Basque: 1965, La" (Capote). LFEng 450; RevLFEng 561-562.
Côté de Guermantes, Le. See *Guermantes Way, The.*
"Cotter's Saturday Night, The" (Burns). PEng 377; RevPEng 451.
Cotton, Charles. PEng 580-587; RevPEng 677-685.
Coulette, Henri. RevPEng 686-692.
Coulter, John. DEng 2441; RevDEng 2964.
Coulton, James. *See* **Hansen, Joseph.**
"Councillor Krespel" (Hoffman). RevShF 1215; ShF 1647-1648.
Counselman, Mary Elizabeth. ShF 2560.
Counselor Ayres' Memorial (Machado de Assis). LFFor 1046-1047.
"Counsels" (Miłosz). PFor 1035.
Count Belisarius (Graves, R.). LFEng 1198-1199; RevLFEng 1422-1423.
Count Julian (Landor). PEng 1642; RevPEng 1907.
"Count Magnus" (James, M. R.). RevShF 1271; ShF 743.
Count of Monte-Cristo, The (Dumas, père). LFFor 526-528; M&D 544-547.
"Count the Almonds" (Celan). PFor 312. See also *Mohn und Gedächtnis.*
"Count's Wife, The" (Buzzati). RevShF 353; ShFSup 64.
"Counter-Attack" (Sassoon). PEng 2471; RevPEng 2877.
Counter Spy Murders, The. See *Dark Duet.*
"Counterfactual Proposal, A" (Stern). RevShF 2214.
Counterfeiters, The (Gide). LFFor 641-642, 646-649, 2139.
Counterlife, The (Roth). RevLFEng 2900, 2904.
Countess Julie. See *Miss Julie.*
Countess of Pembroke's Passion, The (Breton, N.). PEng 280; RevPEng 344.
"Counting Small-Boned Bodies" (Bly). RevPEng 269.
Country, The (Plante). LFSup 309-310; RevLFEng 2645-2646. See also *Francoeur Novels, The.*
Country and the City, The (Williams, R.). PEng 3412-3413.

Country Between Us, The (Forché). RevPEng 1158-1159.

"Country Burying" (Warren). RevPEng 3522.

Country Comets (Day Lewis). PEng 757-758; RevPEng 875.

Country Doctor, A (Jewett). LFEng 1456-1459; RevLFEng 1743-1746.

"Country Doctor, A" (Kafka). RevShF 1306-1308; ShF 1734.

"Country Doctor, The" (Turgenev). RevShF 2320, 2695-2696; ShF 201-202.

Country Girl, The (Odets). DEng 1403-1404; RevDEng 1779-1780.

Country Girls, The (O'Brien, E.). LFEng 2018-2019; RevLFEng 2544.

"Country Husband, The" (Cheever). RevShF 504-505; ShF 1121-1122.

"Country Love Story, A" (Stafford). RevShF 2180; ShF 2262.

Country of a Thousand Years of Peace, The (Merrill). RevPEng 2278.

Country of Marriage, The (Berry). PEng 153-154; RevPEng 182-183.

Country of the Pointed Firs, The (Jewett). LFEng 1459-1461; ShF 1694; RevLFEng 1746-1748; RevShF 1277.

"Country Passion, A" (Callaghan). RevShF 385; ShFSup 68-69.

"Country Sunday, A" (Darley). PEng 733; RevPEng 837.

"Country Town" (Wright, Judith). RevPEng 3941.

"Country Walk, A" (Kinsella). PSup 234; RevPEng 1836.

Country Wife, The (Wycherley). DEng 2109-2111; RevDEng 2628-2630.

"County Ball, The" (Praed). PEng 2278.

County Kill (Gault). M&D 714-715.

Coup, The (Updike). RevLFEng 3357-3358.

Coup d'aile, Le (Curel). DFor 452-453.

Coup de dés jamais n'abolira le hasard, Un. See *Dice Thrown Never Will Annul Chance.*

Coup de Grâce (Yourcenar). LFFor 1962-1965.

Coup de lune, Le. See *Tropic Moon.*

"Couple, The" (Olds). RevPEng 2492-2493.

Couples (Updike). LFEng 2689, 2690, 2691; RevLFEng 3355-3356.

Courage (Grimmelshausen). LFFor 762.

Courrier sud. See *Southern Mail.*

Cours de linguistique générale. See *Course in General Linguistics.*

Cours de littérature dramatique. See *Vorlesungen über dramatische Kunst und Literatur.*

Cours de philosophie positive (Comte). LTh 1712.

Course in General Linguistics (Saussure). LTh 1761-1762.

"Course of a Particular, The" (Stevens). PEng 2749-2750; RevPEng 3210-3211.

Course of Lectures on Dramatic Art and Literature, A (Schlegel, A. W.). LTh 710, 1360-1361, 1707.

"Course of True Love Never Did Run Smooth, The" (Aldrich). PEng 34.

"Court Day" (Still). PEng 2763; RevPEng 3226.

Courteline, Georges. DFor 2350.

Courtesan, The (Aretino). DFor 97-98.

Courtier, The (Castiglione). LTh 131-132, 1462; PFor 162-163; ShF 681-682.

Courtois d'Arras. DFor 2175.

Courts of the Morning, The (Buchan). LFEng 332; RevLFEng 427.

"Courtship" (Dove). RevPEng 959.

Courtship of Miles Standish, The (Longfellow). PEng 1752; RevPEng 2037.

"Courtship of the Family, The" (Stevenson). LTh 887.

"Courtship of the Yonghy-Bonghy-Bò, The" (Lear). PEng 1700; RevPEng 1972.

"Courtyard in Winter" (Montague). RevPEng 2364.

Cousin Bazilio (Eça de Queiróz). LFFor 543-544.

Cousin Bette (Balzac). LFFor 100-101.

Cousin Phillis (Gaskell). LFEng 1101; RevLFEng 1304.

"Cousin Theresa" (Saki). RevShF 2034-2035; ShF 2171-2172.

"Cousins" (Bellow). RevShF 207.

Covenant with Death, A (Becker). LFEng 199-200.

"Cover for Trout Fishing in America, The" (Brautigan). RevShF 314; ShFSup 53-54.

Cover Her Face (James). M&D 933.

Covetous Knight, The (Pushkin). DFor 1497-1498. See also *Little Tragedies.*

"Cow in the House, A" (Kiely). RevShF 1332; ShF 1742.

"Cow of the Barricades, The" (Rao). ShF 648-649.

Coward, Noël. DEng **423-431**, 2380-2381, 2382-2383; **RevDEng 523-531**, 2898-2899, 2900-2901; **ShF 1206-1209.**

Cowboys #2 (Shepard). RevDEng 2193-2194.

Cowled Lover, The (Bird). DEng 214; RevDEng 254.

Cowley, Abraham. LTh 1349; **PEng 588-597; RevPEng 693-703.**

Cowley, Hannah. DEng 2335; RevDEng 2854.

Crimes of the Heart (Henley). DSup 195-196;
RevDEng 1153-1154.

Criminals, The (Bruckner). DFor 262-263.

Crimson Alibi, The (Cohen). M&D 366-367.

Crimson Island, The (Bulgakov). DFor 293-294.

"Crisalide." *See* "Chrysalis."

Crisi dell'eroe nel romazo vittoriano, La. See
Hero in Eclipse in Victorian Fiction, The.

"Crisis, The" (Zoshchenko). RevShF 2559;
ShFSup 381.

Crisis Achaiōn (Dionysius). LTh 1643.

"Crisis in Comparative Literature, The" (Wellek).
LTh 1535, 1537.

"Crisis in London" (Gallico). ShF 1443-1444.

"Crisis of Culture, The" (Bely). LTh 128.

Crispin, Edmund. M&D 412-417.

Crispin, Rival of His Master (Lesage). DFor
1186-1187.

Cristo de Velázquez, El (Unamuno). PFor 1558.

Cristo si è fermato a Eboli. See *Christ Stopped at
Eboli.*

Critic, The (Sheridan). DEng 1780-1781;
RevDEng 2213-2214.

"Critic and Society: Barthes, Leftocracy, and
Other Mythologies, The" (Soyinka). LTh 1372.

*Critical and Historical Principles of Literary
History* (Crane, R. S.). ShF 173-174.

"Critical Approach to the Short Story, A"
(Stroud). ShF 91.

Critical Understanding (Booth). LTh 188.

"Criticism: A Many-Windowed House"
(Cowley). LTh 316.

"Criticism and Crises" (de Man). LTh 350.

Criticism and Ideology (Eagleton). LTh 415.

"Criticism and Symbolism" (Bely). LTh 126.

Criticism and Truth (Barthes). LTh 103, 106.

Criticism in the Wilderness (Hartman). LTh 645.

Critics and Criticism (Crane). LTh 322, 1755.

Critique de la critique. See *Literature and Its
Theorists.*

Critique et vérité. See *Criticism and Truth.*

Critique of Judgment, The (Kant). LTh 791, 1296.

Critique of the School for Wives, The (Molière).
DFor 1334-1335.

*Critische Abhandlung von dem Wunderbaren in
der Poesie und dessen Verbindung mit dem
Wahrscheinlichen* (Bodmer). LTh 176.

Critische Briefe (Bodmer). LTh 176.

Crnjanski, Miloš. PFor 2256.

"Croatoan" (Ellison). RevShF 826-827.

Croce, Benedetto. LTh 31, **326-333**; 362-363,
627, 630, 982, 1100, 1129, 1168-1169, 1512.

Crocodile on the Sandbank (Peters, Elizabeth).
M&D 1314.

"Croeso i Gymru" (Wiggins). RevShF 2470.

Croft-Cooke, Rupert. *See* **Bruce, Leo.**

Crofts, Freeman Wills. M&D 418-424.

Crome Yellow (Huxley). LFEng 1400-1401;
RevLFEng 1676-1677.

Cromedeyre-le-vieil (Romains). DFor 1551-1552.

Cromwell (Hugo). DFor 967-968.

Cronica Tripertita (Gower). PEng 1114;
RevPEng 1267-1268.

Crónica de una muerte anunciada. See *Chronicle
of a Death Foretold.*

Crónica del alba (Sender). LFFor 1551-1552.

**Cronin, A. J. LFEng 648-662; RevLFEng
781-795.**

Cronyn, George W. RevPEng 3932.

Crooked Lines of God, The (Everson). PEng 990;
RevPEng 1121.

Cross, The (Undset). LFFor 1804.

Cross, Amanda. M&D 425-430.

Cross Purpose. See *Misunderstanding, The.*

"Cross Ties" (Kennedy). PEng 1572; RevPEng
1807.

"Crossed Apple, The" (Bogan). PEng 233;
RevPEng 280.

"Crossing Brooklyn Ferry" (Jewett). ShF 1698.

"Crossing Brooklyn Ferry" (Whitman). PEng
3070; RevPEng 3557.

"Crossing into Poland" (Babel). RevShF 128; ShF
900-901.

Crossing to Safety (Stegner). RevLFEng
3134-3135.

Crotchet Castle (Peacock). LFEng 2084-2085;
LTh 1710; RevLFEng 2622-2623.

Crow (Hughes, T.). PEng 1445, 3368-3369;
RevPEng 1651-1652, 3886.

"Crow, The" (Meckel). RevShF 1643; ShFSup
188-189.

"Crow Comes Last, The" (Calvino). RevShF 394.

"Crow Jane" (Baraka). PEng 86; RevPEng 97.

Crowds and Power (Canetti). LFFor 266.

Crowe, C. B. *See* **Gibson, Walter B.**

Crowe, John. *See* **Collins, Michael.**

Crowley, Mart. DSup 68-73; RevDEng 532-538.

"Crown, The" (Lawrence). RevShF 1424.

"Crown Is Older Than King Philip, The"
(Walther). PFor 1678.

Crown of Shadows (Usigli). DFor 2442-2443;
DSup 363-364.

**Crowne, John. DEng 432-441; RevDEng
539-549.**

Croxton *Play of the Sacrament.* DEng 2248, 2252; RevDEng 2768, 2772.
"Cruche, La." *See* "Pitcher, The."
Crucible, The (Miller). DEng 1342-1343, 2407; RevDEng 1680-1681, 2928.
Crucifix in a Deathhand (Bukowski). PEng 359; RevPEng 432.
"Cruel and Barbarous Treatment" (McCarthy). RevShF 1534-1535; ShF 1835-1836.
Cruikshank, George. LFEng 31; RevLFEng 45.
Cruise of a Deathtime, The (Babson). M&D 50.
Cruise of the Breadwinner, The (Bates). LFEng 185; RevLFEng 246.
"Cruise of the 'Idlewild,' The" (Dreiser). RevShF 776; ShF 1308.
"Cruising 99" (Hongo). RevPEng 1572.
Crumbling Idols (Garland). ShF 234.
Crumley, James. M&D 431-436.
"Crusoe in England" (Bishop). PEng 189; RevPEng 232.
Cruz, Sor Juana Inés de la. DFor 438-446; PFor 375-381, 2220.
Cry Killer! See *Dagger of the Mind.*
Cry of Absence, A (Jones, M.). LFEng 1492-1493; RevLFEng 1815-1816.
Cry, The Peacock (Desai). LFEng 725, 728; RevLFEng 872, 873-874.
Crying Game, The (Braine). LFEng 283; RevLFEng 366-367.
Crying of Lot 49, The (Pynchon). LFEng 2191-2192; RevLFEng 2765, 2768-2770, 3771, 3777.
Crystal, David. PEng 3456-3457; RevPEng 3991.
Crystal Age, A (Hudson). LFEng 1384-1385, 1387; RevLFEng 1660-1661.
Crystal and Fox (Friel). DEng 674-675; RevDEng 841-842.
"Crystal Palace, The" (Thackeray). PEng 2875-2876.
Crystal Stopper, The (Leblanc). M&D 1038.
Crystal World, The (Ballard). LFEng 149-150; RevLFEng 194.
"Családi kör." *See* "Family Circle."
"Csárda romjai, A." *See* "Ruins of the *Csárda.*"
"Csatában." *See* "In Battle."
Csíky, Gergely. DFor 2287.
Csokonai Vitéz, Mihály. PFor 1978.
Csongor és Tünde (Vörösmarty). PFor 1667.
Csurka, István. DFor 2289.
Ctisis (Apollonius Rhodius). PFor 57.
"Cuartilla." *See* "Sheet of Paper."
Cuatro jinetes del Apocalipsis, Los. See *Four Horsemen of the Apocalypse, The.*

"Cuba" (Muldoon). RevPEng 2405.
Cuban Thing, The (Gelber). DEng 744; RevDEng 924.
Čubranović, Andrija. PFor 2260.
Cueca larga, La (Parra). PFor 1133.
Cuentos andinos (López Albújar). ShF 699.
Cuentos de amor. See *Tales of Love.*
Cuernos de don Friolera, Los (Valle-Inclán). DFor 1925-1926.
Cuestión palpitante, La (Pardo Bazán). LFFor 1217-1218.
Cueva, Juan de la. DFor 2486.
Cueva de Salamanca, La. See *Cave of Salamanca, The.*
Cujo (King). LFSup 206; RevLFEng 1889.
Cullen, Countée. PEng 692-700; RevPEng 783-791.
Culler, Jonathan. LTh 425, 1801-1802, 1829.
Cultivation of Ideas, The (Gourmont). LTh 623.
"Cultural Center." *See* "Musée Imaginaire."
"Culture and Anarchy" (Rich). RevPEng 2759.
Culture and Anarchy (Arnold). PEng 3482; RevPEng 50.
Culture des idées, La. See *Cultivation of Ideas, The.*
"Cultured Nation" (Kunze). PFor 806.
Culver, Kathryn. *See* **Halliday, Brett.**
Culver, Timothy J. *See* **Westlake, Donald E.**
Cumandá (Mera). LFFor 2283.
Cumberland, Richard. DEng 442-452; RevDEng 550-561.
Cummings, E. E. PEng 701-710; RevPEng 792-801.
Cumpleaños (Fuentes). RevShF 928.
Cunningham, E. V. M&D 437-444.
Cunningham, J. V. PSup 73-82.; RevPEng 802-812.
Cuomo, George. ShF 2561.
Cuore. See *Heart.*
Cup, The (Tennyson). DEng 1919-1920; RevDEng 2362-2363.
"Cupid and my Campaspe played" (Lyly). PEng 1818.
"Cupid and Psyche" (Apuleius). LFFor 2016.
Cupid's Revenge (Beaumont and Fletcher). DEng 631; RevDEng 776.
Cupido Conquered (Googe). PEng 3289; RevPEng 3808.
Curandero de su honra, El. See *Tiger Juan.*
Cure (Foreman). RevDEng 825.
Cure for Love (Ovid). PFor 1123-1125.
Curé de Tours, Le. See *Vicar of Tours, The.*
Curée, La. See *Kill, The.*

Curel, François de. DFor 447-454, 2347-2348.

Curious Savage, The (Patrick, J.). DEng 1466-1467; RevDEng 1848-1849.

Curnow, Allen. RevPEng 3942.

"Currency" (Dazai). RevShF 694.

Curry, Peggy Simson. ShF 2562.

Curse of Kehama, The (Southey). PEng 2682; RevPEng 3125.

Curse of the Pharaohs, The (Peters, Elizabeth). M&D 1314-1315.

Curse of the Starving Class, The (Shepard). DEng 1762-1764; RevDEng 2193, 2196-2197.

Cursor Mundi. PEng 3490.

"Curtain Blown by the Breeze, The" (Spark). RevShF 2167-2168.

Curtin, Philip. *See* **Lowndes, Marie Belloc.**

Curtis, George William. ShF 588.

Curtis, Louisa Knapp. ShF 589.

Curtis, Natalie. RevPEng 3931-3932.

Curtius, Ernst Robert. LTh 334-338.

Curve, The (Dorst). DSup 93.

Curzon, Daniel. ShF 2563.

Cusack, Dymphna. RevDEng 2956.

"Custom House, The" (Hawthorne). LFEng 1320-1321; RevLFEng 1575-1576; ShF 813.

Custom of the Country, The (Wharton, Edith). LFEng 2857-2858; RevLFEng 3539-3540.

"Cutting Edge" (Purdy). RevShF 1957.

Cutting of an Agate, The (Yeats). LTh 1588.

"Cutting the Firebreak" (Everson). PEng 993; RevPEng 1124.

Cuttlefish, The (Kantor). DSup 210.

Cyankali, Paragraph 218 (Wolf). DFor 2020.

Cyberiad, The (Lem). LFFor 1014; RevShF 1462.

"Cybernetics and Ghosts" (Calvino). LTh 270.

"Cycle des saisons, Le." *See* "Cycle of the Seasons, The."

Cycle for Mother Cabrini (Logan). PEng 1740; RevPEng 2024.

"Cycle of Dust" (Tate, J.). PEng 2838.

"Cycle of the Seasons, The" (Ponge). PFor 1262.

"Cyclists' Raid" (Rooney). ShF 549.

Cyclone, The. See *Strong Wind.*

Cyclone and Other Stories (Narayan). RevShF 1718; ShFSup 227.

Cyclops (Euripides). DFor 2120.

Cygnaeus, Fredrik. DFor 1060-1061.

"Cygne, Le." *See* "Swan, The."

Cymbeline (Shakespeare). DEng 1711-1712; RevDEng 2125-2126; ShF 2217.

Cynewulf. PEng 711-721.; RevPEng 813-824.

Cynthia's Revels (Jonson). DEng 2285; RevDEng 2804.

Cypresse Grove, A (Drummond of Hawthornden). PEng 866; RevPEng 982.

Cypresses Believe in God, The (Gironella). LFFor 661-663.

Cyrano de Bergerac (Rostand). DFor 1564-1566, 2350; LFFor 393-403.

Cyropaedia (Xenophon of Athens). LFFor 2000.

Czaczkes, Shmuel Yosef. *See* **Agnon, Shmuel Yosef.**

Czarowna noc. See *Enchanted Night.*

D

Da (Leonard). DSup 230-233; RevDEng 1411-1413.

Da Ungaretti a D'Annunzio (Anceschi). LTh 34.

Dachniki. See *Summer Folk.*

"Da-Da-Dee" (Himes). ShF 1643.

"Daddy" (Plath). PEng 2229, 3374; RevPEng 2596, 2601, 3892.

Daddy Goriot. See Father Goriot.

"Daddy Long-Legs and the Fly, The" (Lear). PEng 1699; RevPEng 1971.

Dadié, Bernard. DFor 2269, 2270.

"Dados eternos, Los." See "Eternal Dice, The."

"Daffodil Sky, The" (Bates). RevShF 176.

Daffodil Sky, The (Bates). ShFSup 32.

"Daffy Duck in Hollywood" (Ashbery). RevPEng 64-65.

Dage på en sky. See *Days on a Cloud.*

Dagerman, Stig. LFFor 2359.

Dagger of the Goth (Zorrilla y Moral). DFor 2064.

Dagger of the Mind (Fearing). M&D 595-596.

Dahl, Roald. RevShF 655-662; ShF 1222-1228; ShFSup 388.

Dahl, Tor Edvin. LFFor 2364.

Dahlstierna, Gunno. PFor 2158.

Dahn, Felix. LFFor 2174.

Dahomean, The (Yerby). LFEng 2990-2992; RevLFEng 3696-3698.

"Dahomey" (Lorde). RevPEng 2044.

Dain Curse, The (Hammett). LFEng 1237; RevLFEng 1465.

Dainty Shapes and Hairy Apes (Kantor). DSup 210.

Daisy Miller (James, H.). LFEng 1442-1443; RevLFEng 1721-1722; RevShF 1260-1261, 2707-2708; ShF 215-216.

Daisy's Necklace and What Came of It (Aldrich). LFEng 50; RevLFEng 65.

Daiyon kampyōki. See *Inter Ice Age 4.*

Dakghar. See *Post Office, The.*

Dal tuo al mio (Verga). DFor 1947-1948.

"Dalaim." *See* "My Songs."

D'ale carnavalului. See *Carnival Scenes.*

Daleko je sunce. See *Far Away Is the Sun.*

"Daleko u nama." *See* "Far Within Us."

D'Alembert, Jean. LTh 78.

Dalin, Olof von. DFor 2467.

Dalkey Archive, The (O'Brien, F.). LFEng 2031; RevLFEng 2557-2558.

Dallas. RevDEng 3041.

Dalton, James. RevLFEng 3858.

Dalton, Priscilla. *See* **Avallone, Michael.**

Dalva (Harrison). RevLFEng 1546.

Daly, Carroll John. M&D 445-449.

Daly, Elizabeth. M&D 450-454.

Daly, Maureen Patricia. ShF 551-552.

Dama boba, La. See *Lady Nit-Wit, The.*

Dama del alba, La. See *Lady of Dawn, The.*

Dama duende, La. See *Phantom Lady, The.*

Damaged Goods (Brieux). DFor 253-254.

Damask Drum, The (Mishima). DFor 1323.

Damask Drum, The (Zeami). DFor 2040-2041.

Damballah (Wideman). RevShF 2463-2465. See also *Homewood Trilogy, The.*

Dame aux camélias, La. See *Camille.*

Dame Sirith. DEng 2256; RevDEng 2776.

"Damnation of Byron, The" (Hope). PSup 191; RevPEng 1596.

Damnation of Theron Ware, The (Frederic). LFEng 1029-1033; RevLFEng 1222-1226.

"Damned Thing, The" (Bierce). RevShF 226; ShF 969-970.

Damnée Manon, Sacée Sandra (Tremblay). DSup 355.

"Damoetas" (Hollander). RevPEng 1549.

Damon and Pithias (Edward). DEng 2260-2261; RevDEng 2780-2781.

Dämonen, Die. See *Demons, The.*

Damy i huzary. See *Ladies and Hussars.*

Dana, Freeman. *See* **Taylor, Phoebe Atwood.**

Dana, R. H., Sr. LTh 1744.

Dana, Richard Henry, Jr. ShF 530.

Dance, Charles. *See* **Planché, James Robinson.**

Dance and the Railroad, The (Hwang). RevDEng 1227-1228.

"Dance for Militant Dilettantes, A" (Young). PEng 3212; RevPEng 3736.

Dance of the Forests, A (Soyinka). DEng 1848-1851; RevDEng 2288-2290.

"Dance of the Happy Shades" (Munro). RevShF 1693; ShFSup 209.

Dance of the Machines, The (O'Brien, Edward). ShF 84.

Dance of the Seasons, The (Monroe). PEng 2028.

"Dance of the Sevin Deidly Synnis, The"
(Dunbar, W.). PEng 895; RevPEng 1031.

Dance to the Music of Time, A (Powell, A.).
LFEng 2110-2112, 2114-2116, 2117-2122;
RevLFEng 2673-2675, 3773.

"Dancer" (Sachs). PFor 1375.

Dancer, Russell. *See* **Pronzini, Bill.**

"Dancer's Life, A" (Justice). PEng 1532;
RevPEng 1757.

"Dancing" (Young). PEng 3214-3215; RevPEng
3738-3739.

Dancing Bear (Crumley). M&D 433-435.

"Dancing Day to Day" (Young). PEng 3212;
RevPEng 3736.

Dancing Floor, The (Buchan). LFEng 334-335;
RevLFEng 429-430.

"Dancing Girls" (Atwood). RevShF 103-105;
ShFSup 15-16.

Dancing Girls and Other Stories (Atwood).
RevShF 102-105; ShFSup 16.

Dancing on the Grave of a Son of a Bitch
(Wakoski). PEng 2998; RevPEng 3489-3490.

"Dancing Pierrot" (Young). PEng 3213; RevPEng
3737.

Dancourt, Florent Carton. DFor 2338.

Dandelion Wine (Bradbury). RevLFEng 360-361.

Dane, Mark. *See* **Avallone, Michael.**

*Dangerous Acquaintances. See Dangerous
Liaisons.*

Dangerous Connections. See Dangerous Liaisons.

Dangerous Liaisons (Laclos). LFEng 3117-3120;
LFFor 2121-2122; RevLFEng 3819-3822.

Dangerous to Know (Babson). M&D 50.

"Dangers of Waking" (Middleton, C.). PEng
1987-1988; RevPEng 2309-2310.

Dangling in the Tournefortia (Bukowski). PEng
364; RevPEng 437.

Dangling Man (Bellow). LFEng 226; RevLFEng
277.

Daniel, Samuel. LTh 1663-1664; **PEng 722-730;
RevPEng 825-834.**

Daniel Deronda (Eliot). LFEng 881-883;
RevLFEng 1043-1045.

Daniel Martin (Fowles). LFEng 1020-1021;
RevLFEng 1211-1212.

Daníelsson, Guðmundur. LFFor 2370.

Dannay, Frederic. *See* **Queen, Ellery.**

D'Annunzio, Gabriele. DFor 455-462,
2411-2412; **LFFor 404-415**, 2237-2238; LTh
995-996; **PFor 382-389**, 2030-2032; ShF 687.

D'Annunzio intime (Marinetti). LTh 995.

"Dans le vide." *See* "In Space."

*Dans un mois, dans un an. See Those Without
Shadows.*

Danse de Sophocle, La (Cocteau). PFor 370.

Dansk students eventyr, En (Møller). LFFor 2336.

Dante Alighieri. LTh 58-59, 66, 91-92, 169-172,
193, 275, **339-347**, 448-450, 967, 1018, 1511,
1655, 1660-1661; PEng 3243; **PFor 390-417**,
2006-2008, 2116; **RevShF 663-670; ShF
1229-1235.**

"Dante and the Lobster" (Beckett). ShF 674-675.

Dante's Divine Comedy (Ciardi, trans.). PEng
498; RevPEng 587.

D'Ântibes, Germain. *See* **Simenon, Georges.**

Danton's Death (Büchner). DFor 269-271, 2371.

Daphnis and Chloë (Longus). LFFor 2008-2009,
2017; RevShF 2574; ShF 489.

"Dapple-grey Mare, The" (Pascoli). PFor 1142.

Dar. See Gift, The.

D'Arblay, Madame. *See* **Burney, Fanny.**

Darby, William. RevDEng 2915.

D'Arcy, Margareta. DEng 42, 44; RevDEng 55,
57, 61.

Dare e avere. See To Give and to Have.

"Dare I Weep, Dare I Mourn?" (le Carré). LFEng
1606.

"Dare's Gift" (Glasgow). RevShF 1003; ShF
1492-1493.

"Daring Young Man on the Flying Trapeze, The"
(Saroyan). RevShF 2059-2060; ShF
2189-2190.

Darío, Rubén. PFor 418-425, 748, 749,
2225-2226.

Dark at the Top of the Stairs, The (Inge). DEng
986-987; RevDEng 1239-1240.

"Dark August" (Walcott). PEng 3006.

Dark Carnival (Bradbury). RevLFEng 357-358.

Dark Child, The (Laye). LFFor 2035, 2041.

Dark Dancer, The (Prokosch). LFEng 2167;
RevLFEng 2740-2741.

Dark Duet (Cheyney). M&D 337-338.

"Dark Eyes of Daughters, The" (Smith, D.). PEng
2644-2645; RevPEng 3067.

Dark Flower, The (Galsworthy). LFEng 1062;
RevLFEng 1261.

Dark Frontier, The (Ambler). M&D 30.

Dark Half, The (King). RevLFEng 1894-1895.

Dark Hero (Cheyney). M&D 337.

Dark Hollow (Green). M&D 786-787.

Dark Houses, The (Hall). PEng 1196-1197,
1199-1200; RevPEng 1372.

Dark Is Light Enough, The (Fry). DEng 688;
RevDEng 855-856.

Dark Journey, The (Green). LFFor 745-746.

Davita's Harp (Potok). LFSup 319-320; RevLFEng 2661, 2665-2666.

Davor. See *Max.*

Dawkins, Cecil. ShF 2564.

Dawn (Butler, O.). RevLFEng 497, 498-499.

"Dawn" (Purdy). RevShF 1957.

"Dawn in Erewhon, The" (Davenport). RevShF 681-683.

"Dawn of Remembered Spring" (Stuart). RevShF 2231-2232; ShF 2292-2293.

Dawn's Left Hand (Richardson, D.). LFEng 2241-2242; RevLFEng 2832-2833.

"Day, The" (Kraus). PFor 797.

"Day at Harmenz" (Borowski). RevShF 257.

"Day Before, The" (Endō). RevShF 836.

Day by Day (Lowell, R.). PEng 1798-1800; RevPEng 2092.

"Day Cools . . ., The" (Södergran). PSup 363-365.

Day for Anne Frank, A (Williams, C. K.). PSup 389; RevPEng 3603.

Day for Surprises, A (Guare). RevDEng 1057-1058.

"Day He Himself Shall Wipe My Tears Away, The" (Ōe). RevShF 1778-1780; ShFSup 234-236.

"Day I Was Older, The" (Hall). RevPEng 1376.

"Day in Late October, A" (Van Duyn). PEng 2964; RevPEng 3443.

Day in the Death of Joe Egg, A (Nichols). DSup 278-289; RevDEng 1727-1729.

"Day in the Open, A" (Bowles, J.). RevShF 271.

"Day Lady Died, The" (O'Hara). PEng 2127-2128; RevPEng 2478-2479.

"Day of Judgment, The" (Watts). PEng 3047; RevPEng 3533.

Day of the Leopards (Wimsatt). LTh 1555-1558.

Day of the Locust, The (West, N.). LFEng 2841, 2845-2847; RevLFEng 3517-3519.

Day Sailing (Slavitt). RevPEng 3050-3051.

"Day They Eulogized Mahalia, The" (Lorde). RevPEng 2043.

"Day with the Foreign Legion, A" (Whittemore). PEng 3078; RevPEng 3566-3567.

Daybook, A (Creeley). PEng 688; RevPEng 780.

"Daybreak" (Dickey). RevPEng 911.

Daybreakers, The (L'Amour). LFSup 222-223; RevLFEng 1933-1934.

Day Lewis, Cecil. PEng 755-762; RevPEng 873-881. *See also* **Blake, Nicholas.**

"Days" (Emerson). PEng 956-957; RevPEng 1086-1087.

"Days, The" (Hall). RevPEng 1372.

Day's End and Other Stories (Bates). RevShF 173-174; ShFSup 30.

"Days of Foreboding" (Kunitz). PSup 249-250; RevPEng 1890-1891.

Days of Hope. See *Man's Hope.*

"Days of 1971" (Merrill). RevPEng 2280.

"Days of 1935" (Merrill). RevPEng 2280.

"Days of Perky Pat, The" (Dick). ShF 1262-1263.

Days of the Turbins (Bulgakov). DFor 291-293.

Days on a Cloud (Abell). DFor 8.

Days Run Away Like Wild Horses over the Hills, The (Bukowski). PEng 361; RevPEng 434.

"Day's Work, A" (Porter). RevShF 1912.

"Dayspring Mishandled" (Kipling). RevShF 1367.

Dazai, Osamu. LFFor 428-435, 2278; RevShF 690-695; ShFSup 91-96.

D'Azeglio, Massimo. LFFor 2231.

De Alfonce Tennis (Donleavy). RevLFEng 950-951.

De amore (André le Chapelain). PFor 1836.

De arte poetica explicationes (Robortello). LTh 1664.

De Baudelaire au surréalisme. See *From Baudelaire to Surrealism.*

De civitate dei. See *City of God, The.*

De Constantia Jurisprudentis Liber Alter (Vico). LTh 1510.

De Copia. See *De Duplici Copia Verborum ac Rerum.*

De differentiis verborum (Isidore of Seville). LTh 741.

De Duplici Copia Verborum ac Rerum (Erasmus). LTh 411, 469, 471.

De imitations (Bembo). LTh 133

De inventione (Cicero). LTh 1651.

De la grammatologie. See *Of Grammatology.*

De la littérature considérée dans ses rapports avec les institutions sociales. See *Influence of Literature upon Society, The.*

De l'Allemagne. See *Germany.*

De l'idéal dans l'art. See *Ideal in Art, The.*

De l'influence des passions sur le bonheur des individus et des nations. See *Treatise on the Influence of the Passions upon the Happiness of Individuals and Nations, A.*

"De los álamos y los sauces" (Alberti). PFor 22.

De monarchia. See *On World Government.*

"De Mortuis" (Collier). RevShF 589; ShF 1170.

De mundi universitate (Bernard Silvestris). LTh 20.

De nos oiseaux (Tzara). PFor 1550.

De Nuptiis Mercurii et Philologiae. See *On the Marriage of Mercury and Philology.*

Del Valle-Inclán, Ramón Maria. *See* **Valle-Inclán, Ramón María del.**

De Man, Paul. LTh 165, 348-352, 645-647, 828, 1033, 1035, 1152-1153, 1436, 1766, 1833

De Marchi, Emilio. LFFor 2236.

Demesne of the Swans, The (Tsvetayeva). PFor 1535, 1536-1537.

Demetrios (Ernst). DFor 556-558.

Demian (Hesse). LFFor 828-829.

De Mille, Richard. ShF 2569.

Deming, Richard. *See* Queen, Ellery.

Demitrius (Metastasio). DSup 251-252.

Democracy (Didion). RevLFEng 931-932.

Democracy (Linney). RevDEng 1447-1448.

Democracy and Esther (Linney). DSup 238; RevDEng 1447-1448.

Democracy and Poetry (Warren). LTh 1525.

Démocrite (Regnard). DFor 1541-1542.

Demoiselle à marier, La (Scribe). DFor 1678-1679.

Demolirte Literatur, Die (Kraus). PFor 793.

Demon, The (Lermontov). PFor 871-873.

"Demon Lover, The" (Bowen). RevShF 264-266; ShF 987-989.

Demons, The (Doderer). LFFor 484-488; M&D 518-520.

Demosthenes. LTh 1643.

Denied a Country (Bang). LFFor 2339.

Denier du rêve. See *Coin in Nine Hands, A.*

Denison, Merrill. DEng 493-505, 2439; RevDEng 614-626, 2962.

Dennis, John. LTh 908, 1688; RevDEng 2960-2961.

"Dennis O'Shaughnessy Going to Maynooth" (Carleton). ShF 1060-1061.

"Dennitsa." *See* "Morning Star."

Dent, Lester. M&D 483-488.

Dentinger, Stephen. *See* **Hoch, Edward D.**

'dentity Crisis (Durang) DSup 102; RevDEEng 671-672.

D'entre les morts. See *Living and the Dead, The.*

Denuestos del agua y del vino. See *Razón de amor.*

Deobe (Ćosić). LFFor 387-388.

"Deodand, The" (Hecht). PEng 1281; RevPEng 1461.

"Departmental" (Frost). ShF 106.

"Departure" (Benn). PFor 174-176.

"Departures" (Belitt). RevPEng 156.

Departures (Justice). PEng 1532; RevPEng 1756-1758.

Dépeupleur, Le. See *Lost Ones, The.*

De Pre, Jean-Anne. See **Avallone, Michael.**

"Depressed by a Book of Bad Poetry, I Walk Toward an Unused Pasture and Invite the Insects to Join Me" (Wright, James) PEng 3159; RevPEng 3671.

"Depression" (Annensky). PFor 42.

Deptford trilogy. See *Fifth Business, Manticore, The,* and *World of Wonders.*

Depth of Field (Heyen). RevPEng 1502-1503.

Deputy, The (Hochhuth). DFor 917-921, 2380.

De Quincey, Thomas. LTh 1705, 1709.

Derleth, August. M&D 489-496; RevShF 707-712; ShF 746, 1255-1259, 1827.

Dernier de l'empire, Le. See *Last of the Empire, The.*

Dernière Aimée, La (Njoya). DFor 2271.

"Dernière Classe, La." *See* "Last Class, The."

Derniers vers (Laforgue). PFor 827-828.

De Robertis, Giuseppe. PFor 2038.

De Roberto, Federico. LFFor 2223.

deRoo, Robert. RevPEng 3943.

Derozio, Henry Louis Vivian. PFor 1994.

Derrida, Jacques. LTh 348, 353-361, 417, 503, 506, 527, 529, 645-647, 824-825, 828, 850, 890, 1033, 1035, 1070, 1152, 1436, 1628-1629, 1764-1766, 1802, 1820-1821, 1832.

Dersonne, Jacques. *See* **Simenon, Georges.**

Déry, Tibor. LFFor 2073.

Derzhavin, Gavrila. LTh 1694; PFor 2135.

Des bleus à l'âme. See *Scars on the Soul.*

Des Choses cachées depuis la fondation du monde. See *Things Hidden Since the Foundation of the World.*

Des fleurs de bonne volonté (Laforgue). PFor 826-827.

Desa aquests llibres al calaix de baix (Foix). PFor 489.

Desai, Anita. LFEng 725-732; LFFor 2223; LFSup 402; RevLFEng 871-880.

De Sanctis, Francesco. LTh 362-368, 630-631.

Desatino, El (Gambaro). DSup 151.

"Descendant of El Cid, A" (Pardo Bazán). RevShF 1842; ShF 2048.

Descending Figure (Glück). PSup 136-137; RevPEng 1247-1248.

"Descent in a Parachute" (Belitt). RevPEng 156-157.

"Descent into the Maelström, A" (Poe). RevShF 1898-1900.

"Descent Through the Carpet, A" (Atwood). PEng 65.

Deschamps brothers. LTh 1707.

"Describing Poetic Structures" (Riffaterre). LTh 889.

"Description of a City Shower, A" (Swift). PEng 2086; RevPEng 3273.

"Description of a Salamander, The" (Swift). PEng 2805-2806; RevPEng 3272-3273.

"Description of the Morning, A" (Swift). PEng 2806; RevPEng 3273.

Desdén con el desdén, El. See *Love's Victory.*

"Desdichado, El" (Nerval). PFor 1087.

Desengaño en un sueño, El (Saavedra). DFor 1618-1619.

"Desert Breakdown, 1968" (Wolff). RevShF 2509.

Désert de l'amour, Le. See *Desert of Love, The.*

Desert of Love, The (Mauriac). LFFor 1127.

"Deserted Church, The" (Coleridge, H.). PEng 530.

Deserted Village, The (Goldsmith). PEng 1109-1110, 3332; RevPEng 1256-1257, 3851.

Déserteur, Le. See *Point of Honor, The.*

Deserto dei Tartari, Il. See *Tartar Steppe, The.*

Desheredada, La. See *Disinherited Lady, The.*

"Design" (Frost). PEng 1045-1046; RevPEng 1177-1178.

"Design for Departure" (Algren). RevShF 52; ShF 856.

Design for Living (Coward). DEng 429-430; RevDEng 529-530.

"Design of a House, The" (Berry). RevPEng 181.

"Desire and Pursuit of the Part, The" (Coulette). RevPEng 691.

"Desire and the Black Masseur" (Williams, T.). RevShF 2482-2483; ShF 2437, 2438.

Desire in Language (Kristeva). LTh 833.

Desire to Kill (Clarke). M&D 355-356.

Desire Under the Elms (O'Neill). DEng 1410-1414, 2401; RevDEng 1787-1790, 2922.

"Désirée's Baby" (Chopin). RevShF 538; ShF 1133-1134.

Desmond, Gail Whang. RevPEng 3916.

Desnos, Robert. PFor 1886.

"Desnudo." See "Nude."

Desolación (Mistral). PFor 1040-1042.

"Desperate Character, A" (Turgenev). ShF 2357-2358.

"Despicable Bastard" (Endō). RevShF 837.

"Despondency" (Arnold). PEng 51; RevPEng 50.

Desportes, Philippe. LTh 970-973.

Despot Vodă (Alecsandri). DFor 2297.

"Desquite." See "Revenge, The."

"Destination" (Wang Anyi). RevShF 2396.

Destinées, Les (Vigny). PFor 1640-1643.

Destinies of Darcy Dancer, Gentleman, The (Donleavy). LFEng 786-787; RevLFEng 950.

Destouches, Louis-Ferdinand. See **Céline, Louis-Ferdinand.**

"Destroying Literary Studies" (Wellek). LTh 1538-1539.

Destrucción o el amor, La. See *Destruction or Love.*

Destruction of Jerusalem by Titus Vespasian, The (Crowne). DEng 434-437; RevDEng 541-544.

Destruction or Love (Aleixandre). PFor 30.

"Destructors, The" (Greene, G.). RevShF 1072-1073, 2738; ShF 1545-1546.

Destry Rides Again (Faust). RevLFEng 3851-3852.

"Detective Stories Gone Wrong—The Adventures of Sherlaw Kombs." See "Great Pegram Mystery, The."

Detective Story (Kingsley). DEng 1042-1044; RevDEng 1318-1320.

"Detective Story Decalogue, A" (Knox). M&D 999.

"Detective's Wife, The" (Hoch). RevShF 1210.

"Detente, sombra de mi bien esquivo" (Cruz). PFor 378.

Detour, The (Davis). DEng 477-478; RevDEng 588-589.

Detour, The (Walser, M.). DSup 384-385.

"Detour in the Dark" (Beck). ShF 936.

"Detroit Skyline, 1949" (Mason). RevShF 1619.

Detstvo. See *My Childhood.*

"Detstvo: U babushki." See "Childhood: At Grandmother's."

"*Detstvo i otrochestvo:* 'Voennye rasskazy' grafa L. N. Tolstogo." See "L. N. Tolstoy's *Childhood* and *Boyhood* and *Military Tales.*"

"Detstvo Liuvers." See "Childhood of Liuvers, The."

Deutsche Dichtung (George). LTh 575.

Deutsche Mythologie. See *German Mythology.*

Deutsche poetische Literatur seit Klopstock und Lessing, Die (Gelzer). LTh 436.

Deutsche Roman des achtzehnten Jahrhunderts in seinem Verhältnis zum Christentum, Der (Eichendorff). LTh 437.

Deutschland. See *Germany.*

Deutschland: Ein Wintermärchen (Biermann). PFor 191.

Deutschland: Ein Wintermärchen (Heine). See *Germany: A Winter's Tale.*

Deux Amis, Les. See *Two Friends, The.*

Deux amis de Bourbonne, Les. See *Two Friends from Bourbonne, The.*

"Deux Barques" (Bonnefoy). PSup 47.

"Disdaine returned" (Carew). PEng 434; RevPEng 502.
"Disent les imbéciles." *See* "Fools Say."
"Disillusionment of Ten O'Clock" (Stevens). PEng 2746; RevPEng 3207.
Disinherited Lady, The (Pérez Galdós). LFFor 1276-1280.
D'Isly, Georges. *See* **Simenon, Georges.**
"Disorder and Early Sorrow" (Mann). RevShF 2739-2740.
"Displaced Orpheus, A" (Untermeyer). PEng 2952-2953; RevPEng 3420-3421.
"Displaced Person, The" (O'Connor, Flannery). LFEng 3270-3272; ShF 798.
Displaced Person, The (O'Connor, Flannery). RevShF 1761-1762.
Dispossessed, The (Le Guin). LFEng 1636; RevLFEng 2011-2012.
Disputation Between a Hee-Conny-catcher and a Shee-Conny-catcher, A (Greene, R.). RevShF 1079-1080; ShF 1553.
Disraeli, Benjamin. LFEng 3078-3079.
"Dissentient Voice" (Davie). PSup 88; RevPEng 853.
Dissertations Moral and Critical (Beattie, J.). ShF 470.
"Distance" (Creeley). PEng 684.
"Distance" (Paley). RevShF 1837; ShF 2042-2043.
Distance from Loved Ones (Tate, J.). RevPEng 3312-3313.
"Distant Episode, A" (Bowles, P.). RevShF 277-278; ShF 992.
Distant Horns of Summer, The (Bates). LFEng 184-185; RevLFEng 245-246.
Distant Music, The (Davis). LFEng 679-680; RevLFEng 807, 811-812.
"Distant Orgasm, The" (Tate, J.). PEng 2837-2838.
Distant Relations (Fuentes). LFFor 596.
"Distant Steps, The" (Vallejo). PFor 1588, 1589.
Distant Trumpet, A (Horgan). LFSup 160-161; RevLFEng 1639-1640.
Distortions (Beattie). RevShF 179-180; ShFSup 36.
"Distracted Preacher, The" (Hardy). RevShF 1111-1112; ShF 1582-1583.
Distrait, Le (Regnard). DFor 1540-1541.
Distressed Family, The (Mercier). DFor 1315-1316.
"District Doctor, The" (Turgenev). ShF 2354-2355.
"District in the Rear, A" (Pasternak). RevShF 1856; ShF 2062.

"Dithyramb to Women" (Illyés). PFor 744.
"Ditirambus a nőkhöz." *See* "Dithyramb to Women."
Ditte Menneskenbaren (Nexø).
"Dittié de Jeanne d'Arc, Le" (Christine de Pisan). PFor 353-354.
Divan (Hafiz). PSup 149, 152-157.
Divan-e Shams-e Tabriz (Rumi). PSup 340-341.
"Diver, The" (Hayden). PEng 1252-1253; RevPEng 1436-1437.
"Diver, The" (Pritchett). RevShF 1936.
"Diver, The" (Schiller). PFor 1409.
"Diverting History of John Gilpin, The" (Cowper). PEng 616-617, 3330; RevPEng 723-724.
"Divided Heart, The" (Etherege). PEng 978-979; RevPEng 1109.
Divided Heaven (Wolf). LFFor 1934-1935.
Dividend on Death (Halliday). M&D 811-813.
"Dividends" (O'Faolain). RevShF 1787.
Divina commedia, La. See *Divine Comedy, The.*
Divinas palabras. See *Divine Words.*
Divine Comedies (Merrill). RevPEng 2280.
Divine Comedy, The (Dante). LTh 66, 340-342, 345-346; PEng 498, 3243; PFor 397-416, 1467, 2006-2007; RevShF 664-669; ShF 1230-1235.
Divine Fancies (Quarles). PEng 2298; RevPEng 2679.
"Divine Mistress, A" (Carew). PEng 2779; RevPEng 3244.
Divine Narcissus, The (Cruz). DFor 444; PFor 376, 381.
Divine Tragedy, The (Longfellow). PEng 1752-1753; RevPEng 2037-2038.
Divine Words (Valle-Inclán). DFor 1922-1924, 2503.
Diviners, The (Laurence). LFEng 1570-1571, 1574-1576; RevLFEng 1943-1944, 1947-1949.
"Diving into the Wreck" (Rich). PEng 2368-2369.
Diving into the Wreck (Rich). RevPEng 2756-2757.
"Divining Rod" (Eichendorff). PFor 439.
"Divinity School Address" (Emerson). RevPEng 1084.
Divinity School Address (Emerson). LTh 455; PEng 954.
Divino Narciso, El. See *Divine Narcissus, The.*
"Division of Parts, The" (Sexton). PEng 2522; RevPEng 2932.
Division Street (Tesich). RevDEng 2377-2378.
"Divorce" (Lu Hsün). RevShF 1524; ShFSup 181-183.

"Divorce of Lovers, A" (Sarton). PEng 2461; RevPEng 2865.

Dīwān över fursten av Emgión (Ekelöf). PFor 452-453.

Dixon, Richard Watson. PEng 814-820.

Djinn (Robbe-Grillet). LFFor 1421.

"Djinns, The" (Hugo). PFor 733. See also *Orientales, Les.*

Djulabije (Vraz). PFor 2262.

Djurdjević, Ignjat. PFor 2261.

"Dnevnik lishnega cheloveka." *See* "Diary of a Superfluous Man, The."

Dnevnik pisatelya. See *Diary of a Writer, The.*

Dni Turbinykh. See *Days of the Turbins.*

Do Androids Dream of Electric Sheep? (Dick). LFSup 97; RevLFEng 893, 897.

"Do ksiedza Ch." (Miłosz). PFor 1032.

Do, Lord, Remember Me (Garrett). LFEng 1093-1094; RevLFEng 1295-1296.

"Do Robinsona Jeffersa." *See* "To Robinson Jeffers."

Dobell Folio (Traherne). PEng 2927-2928; RevPEng 3400-3401.

Döblin, Alfred. LFFor 468-480, 2194, 2201.

Dobrolyubov, Nikolay. LTh 286-287, 289, **386-391,** 395, 1104, 1106, 1108-1109, 1447, 1502.

"Dobrorozhelatel" (Zoshchenko). RevShF 2559.

Dobrovský, Josef. PFor 1799.

"Dobrozhelatel" (Zoshchenko). ShFSup 380.

Docherty, James L. *See* **Chase, James Hadley.**

Dock Brief, The (Mortimer). DEng 1354-1355; RevDEng 1694.

Docker noir, Le (Sembène). LFFor 1536-1538.

"Dockery and Son" (Larkin). PEng 1674; RevPEng 1942.

Doctor Cobb's Game (Cassill). LFEng 470.

Doctor Copernicus (Banville). LFSup 46-47; RevLFEng 203-204.

Doctor Faustus (Mann). LFFor 1083-1084;

Doctor Faustus (Marlowe). DEng 1260-1263, 2273; RevDEng 1585-1588, 2791.

"Dr. Havel Twenty Years Later" (Kundera). RevShF 1388-1389.

Dr. Jekyll and Mr. Hyde (Stevenson). ShF 478, 479, 480.

Dr. Knock (Romains). DFor 1552-1553.

Doctor Zhivago (Pasternak). LFFor 1234-1238, 2327; PFor 1160-1161.

Doctorow, E. L. LFEng 768-780; LFSup 403; RevLFEng 934-943.

"Doctor's Son, The" (O'Hara). RevShF 1803-1804; ShF 2018-2019.

Documents Relating to the Sentimental Agents in the Volyen Empire (Lessing). RevLFEng 2039.

Dodekalogos tou gynthou, Ho. See Twelve Words of the Gypsy, The.

Dödens arlekin (Bergman). DFor 186.

Doderer, Heimito von. LFFor 481-488; M&D 515-521.

Dødes rige, Die (Pontoppidan). LFFor 2340.

Dodgson, Charles Lutwidge. *See* **Carroll, Lewis.**

Dodsworth (Lewis, S.). LFEng 1680; RevLFEng 2076.

"Dodu" (Narayan). RevShF 1717; ShFSup 227.

Dodu and Other Stories (Narayan). RevShF 1717-1718; ShFSup 227.

"Dodwells Road" (Wilbur). PEng 3095; RevPEng 3585.

"Dog" (Ferlinghetti). PEng 1008-1009; RevPEng 1149-1151.

"Dog, The" (Stern). RevPEng 3198-3199.

Dog Beneath the Skin, The (Auden and Isherwood). DEng 53-56; RevDEng 67-70.

"Dog Fox Field" (Murray). RevPEng 2414-2415.

Dog in the Manger, The. See *Gardener's Dog, The.*

"Dog Named Ego, the Snowflakes as Kisses, A" (Schwartz). PEng 2492; RevPEng 2899.

"Dog Sleeping on My Feet, A" (Dickey, J.). PEng 796.

Dog Soldiers (Stone). RevLFEng 3200-3201, 3202.

Dog Years (Grass). LFFor 736.

"Doge and Dogaressa" (Hoffman). RevShF 1216; ShF 1648.

"Dogood Papers, The" (Franklin). RevShF 905-907, 2644; ShF 1409.

"Dogwood Tree, A" (Updike). RevShF 2754.

"Doklad o zhurnalakh *Zvezda* i *Leningrad.*" *See* "On the Journals *Zvezda* and *Leningrad.*"

Doktor Faustus. See *Doctor Faustus.*

"Doktor Murkes gesammeltes Schweiger." *See* "Murke's Collected Silences."

Doktor Zhivago. See *Doctor Zhivago.*

Doll, The. See *Summer of the Seventeenth Doll, The.*

Doll Trilogy, The (Lawler). DEng 1116; RevDEng 1396. See also *Kid Stakes; Other Times;* and *Summer of the Seventeenth Doll.*

Doll's House, A (Ibsen). DFor 981-982.

"Doll's House, The" (Mansfield). RevShF 1601-1602.

Dolore, Il (Ungaretti). PFor 1569-1570.

"Dolores" (Swinburne). PEng 2818-2819; RevPEng 3286-3287.

Dorfman, Ariel. ShF 693.
"Doris" (Congreve). PEng 555; RevPEng 647.
Dorn, Edward. PEng 839-846, RevPEng 945-953.
Dorothée (Camus, J. P.). ShF 498.
"Dorothy Q." (Holmes). PEng 1372-1373; RevPEng 1561-1562.
Dorsage, Jean. See Simenon, Georges.
Dorsan, Luc. See Simenon, Georges.
"Dorset" (Davie). PSup 90; RevPEng 855.
Dorst, Tankred. DSup 90-97.
Dorval (Diderot). DSup 84-85.
Dos caras del patroncito, Las (Valdez). DSup 370; RevDEng 2428-2429.
"Dos Elenas, Las." See "Two Elenas, The."
Doskonała próżnia. See Perfect Vacuum, A.
Dos Passos, John. LFEng 789-799; LTh 1273; RevLFEng 953-963, 3763, 3766.
Dostoevski, Fyodor. LFEng 3147-3148; LFFor 503-517, 2314-2315, 2316-2317; LTh 120, 288, 290, 389, 392-400, 947, 985, 1478; M&D 522-528; RevShF 749-755; ShF 204, 1291-1296.
Dostoevskii i Gogol (k teorii parodii) (Tynyanov). LTh 1477.
Dosunmu, Sanya; God's Deputy. RevDEng 2943.
Dosutoefuskii no seikatsu (Kobayashi). LTh 821.
"Double, The" (Annensky). PFor 43.
"Double, The" (de la Mare). PEng 776; RevPEng 896.
Double, The (Dostoevski). LFEng 3296-3298; ShF 477.
"Double Axe, The" (Jeffers). PEng 1493-1494; RevPEng 1703, 1706-1707.
Double-Barrel (Freeling). M&D 663.
Double Barrelled Detective Story, A (Twain). M&D 1611-1612.
"Double Charley" (Stern). RevShF 2214.
Double Dealer, The (Congreve). DEng 404-406; RevDEng 503-505.
Double Double (Yglesias). LFEng 3000-3001; RevLFEng 3705-3707.
"Double Happiness Bun, The" (Gilchrist). RevShF 987.
Double Honeymoon (Connell). LFEng 581-582; RevLFEng 710-711; RevShF 600; ShF 1181.
Double Image, The (MacInnes). M&D 1169.
"Double Image, The" (Sexton). PEng 2522; RevPEng 2932.
Double Inconstance, La. See Double Infidelity.
Double Indemnity (Cain). M&D 258.
Double Infidelity (Marivaux). DFor 1264-1265.

Double Invention of Komo, The (Wright, Jay). RevPEng 3690-3691.
Double Méprise, La. See Slight Misunderstanding, A.
Double PP, The (Dekker). PEng 771; RevPEng 890.
Double Solitaire (Anderson, R.). RevDEng 52.
Double Vision. RevLFEng 1137-1138.
"Doubles" (Moravia). RevShF 1673; ShFSup 198.
Douglas, Gavin. PEng 3280; RevPEng 3799.
Douglas, John. See Collins, Michael.
"Doux pays" (González Martínez). PFor 611-612.
Dove, Rita. RevPEng 954-961.
"Dove in the Head, A" (Popa). PFor 1273.
"Dove of the East, A" (Helprin). RevShF 1162-1163; ShFSup 116-117.
Dove of the East and Other Stories, A (Helprin). RevShF 1160-1163; ShFSup 114-116.
"Dover Beach" (Arnold). PEng 54-55, 3229-3230; RevPEng 53-54.
"Dover Bitch, The" (Hecht). RevPEng 1459-1460.
Dover One (Porter). M&D 1340.
Dover Three (Porter). M&D 1340.
Dovlatov, Sergei. RevShF 756-763.
Dowd, T. B. See Henry, O.
Down and Out. See Lower Depths, The.
"Down at the Dinghy" (Salinger). ShF 2180.
"Down in My Heart" (Stafford). RevPEng 3167.
Down Stream (Huysmans). LFFor 862-863.
Down the Long Hills (L'Amour). LFSup 225; RevLFEng 1935-1936.
"Down Then By Derry" (Kiely). RevShF 1336-1337; ShF 1747.
Down There. See Là-Bas.
"Downlook, The" (Lowell, R.). PEng 1800; RevPEng 2094.
Downstream (Kinsella). PSup 233-234; RevPEng 1835-1836.
"Downward Path to Wisdom, The" (Porter). RevShF 1912.
Dowson, Ernest. ShF 517.
Doyle, Arthur Conan. LFEng 800-813, 3079-3080; M&D 529-537; RevLFEng 964-978, 3861, 3788-3789, 3843; RevShF 764-773; ShF 728, 751-752.
D'Oyly Carte, Richard. See Carte, Richard D'Oyly.
Dozens (Slavitt). RevPEng 3052-3053.
Dożywocie. See Life Annuity, The.
Drabble, Margaret. LFEng 814-827; RevLFEng 979-993.
Drachmann, Holger. LFFor 2338, 2339; PFor 2169.

"Dublin Mystery, The" (Orczy). M&D 1283.

Dubliners (Joyce). LFEng 1496; RevLFEng 1820; RevShF 1292-1298; ShF 242, 661-663, 1719, 1722-1723.

Dubois, Rochelle H. ShF 2574.

Du Bouchet, André. PFor 1893.

Dubrolyubov, Nikolay. LFFor 2318.

"Dubrovačke poeme" (Dučić). PFor 429.

Dubrovsky (Pushkin). LFFor 1363-1364, 1366-1368.

Dubus, Andre. RevShF 781-786.

"Duchess and the Jeweller, The" (Woolf). ShF 2458-2459.

Duchess de la Vallière, The (Bulwer-Lytton). DEng 313; RevDEng 373.

Duchess of Malfi, The (Webster). DEng 2009-2010; RevDEng 2488-2493.

Duchesse de Langeais, La (Tremblay). DSup 354.

Dučić, Jovan. PFor 426-434, 2255.

Duck Variations (Mamet). RevDEng 1564.

Dudevant, Amandine-Aurore-Lucile Dupin, Baronne. *See* **Sand, George.**

Dudintzev, Vladimir. LFFor 2328.

Dudley-Smith, Trevor. *See* **Trevor, Elleston.**

Due zitelle, Le. See *Two Old Maids, The.*

"Duel, The" (Chekhov). LFEng 3300-3301; RevShF 515-516.

"Duel, The" (Conrad). RevShF 611-612.

Duenna, The (Sheridan). DEng 1776-1778; RevDEng 2209-2211.

Dueño de las estrellas, El (Ruiz de Alarcón). DFor 1609-1610.

Duffy, Marguerite. *See* **Terry, Megan.**

"Dug Out, The" (Sassoon). PEng 2472-2473; RevPEng 2878-2879.

Dugan, Alan. PEng 881-885; PSup 404; RevPEng 1005-1010.

Duineser Elegien. See *Duino Elegies.*

Duino Elegies (Rilke). PFor 1329, 1331-1332.

Duke, Will. *See* **Gault, William Campbell.**

Duke Humphrey's Dinner (O'Brien, F.). RevShF 1754; ShF 1980.

Duke of Gandia, The (Swinburne). DEng 1899; RevDEng 2341.

Dukkehjem, Et. See *Doll's House, A.*

"Dulce et Decorum Est" (Owen). PEng 2160-2161; RevPEng 2530-2531.

"Dulcima" (Bates). LFEng 185; RevLFEng 246.

Dulcy (Kaufman and Connelly). DEng 417-418; RevDEng 517-518.

Dullin, Charles. DFor 2351.

"Duma." *See* "Meditation."

Dumas, Alexandre, *fils.* **DFor 494-506, 2346.**

Dumas, Alexandre, *père.* **DFor 480-493,** 2343-2345; LFEng 3152-3153; **LFFor 518-530; M&D 543-550;** RevLFEng 3837-3838.

Du Maurier, Daphne. M&D 551-556.

Dumb Gods Speak, The (Oppenheim). M&D 1274.

Dumb Waiter, The (Pinter). DEng 1514-1517; RevDEng 1901-1903.

"Dun, The" (Edgeworth). RevShF 802-803; ShF 1328-1329.

D'un château l'autre. See *Castle to Castle.*

"D'una letteratura europea." *See* "Of an European Literature."

Dunbar, Paul Laurence. PEng 3399-3400; PSup 109-118; RevPEng 1011-1021, 3907-3908.

Dunbar, William. PEng 886-896, 3279-3280; RevPEng 1022-1033, 3797, 3798-3799.

Duncan, Isadora. PFor 476.

Duncan, Robert. PEng 897-907; PSup 404; RevPEng 1034-1044.

Duncan, Robert L. *See* **Roberts, James Hall.**

Duncan, W. R. *See* **Roberts, James Hall.**

"Duncan spoke of a process" (Baraka). PEng 84-86; RevPEng 95-97.

Dunciad, The (Pope). PEng 2262; RevPEng 2636.

Dunelawn (McNally). See *Bad Habits.*

Dunlap, William. DEng 526-534, 2397; RevDEng 649-657, 2918.

Dunne, Finley Peter. ShF 537.

Dunne, John Gregory. LFEng 758-759; RevLFEng 923-924.

"Duns Scotus's Oxford" (Hopkins). PEng 1401; RevPEng 1610.

Dunsany, Lord. DEng 535-542; ShF 665, 743, 744, 1313-1318; RevDEng 658-666; RevShF 787-793.

"Dunwich Horror, The" (Lovecraft). RevShF 1511-1512; ShF 1825-1827.

"Dunya Allah." *See* "God's World."

Dunyazadiad (Barth). RevLFEng 3878.

Du Perry, Jean. *See* **Simenon, Georges.**

Dupin, Amandine-Aurore-Lucile, Baronne Dudevant. *See* **Sand, George.**

Dupin, Jacques. PFor 1893.

Duplex, The (Bullins). DEng 308; RevDEng 366. *See also* Twentieth-Century Cycle.

Duplicate Death (Heyer). M&D 863.

Duque de Aquitania, El (Saavedra). DFor 1615-1616.

Durang, Christopher. DSup 98-105; RevDEng 667-675.

Duras, Marguerite. DFor 507-514; LFFor 531-539, 2146; LFSup 403.

D'Urfey, Thomas. PEng 908-915, Durrant, Theo. *See* **Teilhet, Darwin L.**

Durrell, Lawrence. LFEng 840-848; LFSup 403; PEng 916-924; PSup 404; **RevLFEng 1007-1017; RevPEng 1045-1054.**

Dürrenmatt, Friedrich. DFor 515-525, 2262-2263, 2380-2382; **M&D 557-561.**

Durych, Jaroslav. LFFor 2067.

Duse, Eleonora. DFor 457-458.

"Dushechka." *See* "Darling, The."

"Dusk" (Æ). PEng 18; RevPEng 18-19.

Dusklands (Coetzee). LFSup 78-79; RevLFEng 673-674.

Dusty Answer (Lehmann). LFSup 228-229; RevLFEng 2017-2018.

"Dusty Braces" (Snyder). PEng 2675.

Dutch Courtesan, The (Marston). DEng 1270-1271; RevDEng 1595-1596.

Dutch Lover, The (Behn). DEng 175; RevDEng 211.

Dutch Uncle (Gray). DEng 806-807; RevDEng 999.

Dutchman (Baraka). DEng 97-99; RevDEng 123-125, 2950.

Dutiful Daughter, A (Keneally). LFSup 190-191; RevLFEng 1846-1847.

Dutt, Govin Chunder. PFor 1995.

Dutt, Michael Madhusan. PFor 1994-1995.

Dutt, Toro. PFor 1995-1996.

"Duty Was His Lodestar" (Smith, S.). RevPEng 3079-3080.

Dux Moraud. DEng 2252; RevDEng 2772.

Dva brata. See *Two Brothers.*

"Dva chasa v rezervuare." *See* "Two Hours in a Reservoir."

"Dva gusara." *See* "Two Hussars."

"Dvadtsat'shest' i odna." *See* "Twenty-six Men and a Girl."

Dvärgen. See *Dwarf, The.*

Dvenadtsat. See *Twelve, The.*

"Dvoinik." *See* "Double, The."

"Dvořákovo requiem." *See* "Requiem for Dvořák, A."

Dvoryanskoye gnezdo. See *House of Gentlefolk, A.*

Dwarf, The (Lagerkvist). LFFor 972-973; ShF 481.

"Dwarf House" (Beattie). RevShF 179-180; ShFSup 36-37.

"Dwelling Place in Heaven" (León). PFor 843.

Dwight, Timothy. LTh 1739.

Dworzan, Hélène. ShF 2575.

Dwyer, Deanna. *See* **Koontz, Dean R.**

Dwyer, K. R. *See* **Koontz, Dean R.**

Dyadya Vanya. See *Uncle Vanya.*

Dybek, Stuart. ShF 2576.

Dying: An Introduction (Sissman). PEng 2615-2616; RevPEng 3018-3020.

"Dying" (Stern). RevShF 2215.

"Dying Goddess, The" (Kizer). RevPEng 1855.

Dying Inside (Silverberg). LFEng 3212.

"Dying Man's Confession, A" (Twain). M&D 1611.

"Dykes, The" (Kipling). PEng 1608; RevPEng 1848.

Dym. See *Smoke.*

Dynamics of Literary Response, The (Holland). LTh 684-686, 1764.

"Dynamite" (Smiley). RevShF 2146-2147.

Dynamite Voices (Madhubuti). PEng 1888; RevPEng 2192.

Dynasts, The (Hardy). DEng 888-891; PEng 1222-1223; RevDEng 1098-1101; RevPEng 1395-1396.

Dyskolos. See *Bad-tempered Man, The.*

"Dyvers thy death do dyversely bemoan" (Surrey). PEng 2788; RevPEng 3254.

Dziady. See *Forefathers' Eve.*

"Dziecie Europy." *See* "Child of Europe, A."

"Dzień na Hermenzach." *See* "Day at Harmenz."

"Dzwony w zimie." *See* "Bells in Winter."

E

E. Kology (Koch). PEng 1623; RevPEng 1862.

È stato così. See *Dry Heart, The.*

"E tu?" *See* "And You?"

"Each and All" (Emerson). PEng 958; RevPEng 1088.

Each in His Own Way (Pirandello). DFor 1470-1471.

Each Man's Son (MacLennan). LFEng 1745-1746; RevLFEng 2214-2215.

Eagle Has Two Heads, The (Cocteau). DFor 420-422.

"Eagle in New Mexico" (Lawrence, D. H.). PEng 1683; RevPEng 1953.

Eagle on the Coin, The (Cassill). LFEng 468.

Eagle or Sun? (Paz). PFor 1172-1173.

"Eagles" (Hoffman). RevPEng 1533.

Eagles' Nest (Kavan). LFEng 1511-1512; RevLFEng 1836-1837.

Eagleton, Terry. LTh 137, **414-419**, 758-759, 762, 912, 1541.

Early Americana (Richter). ShF 600, 602.

Early Autumn (Parker). M&D 1301.

Early Graves (Hansen). M&D 832.

Early Lessons (Edgeworth). RevShF 797; ShF 1322-1323.

"Early Morning" (Bachmann). PFor 127-128.

Early Morning (Bond). DEng 247; RevDEng 288.

"Early Noon" (Bachmann). PFor 127. See also *Gestundete Zeit, Die.*

"Early Poems" (Justice). PEng 1531; RevPEng 1756.

Early Sunday Morning (Hopper). PEng 3510, 3511, 3512.

Earmarked for Hell. See *Pro Patria.*

Earth Poetry (Everson). PEng 987; RevPEng 1118.

Earth Spirit (Wedekind). DFor 1976-1977.

"Earth Walk" (Meredith). RevPEng 2271-2272.

Earth Walk (Meredith). RevPEng 2271-2272.

Earth Worms (Innaurato). DSup 201-202; RevDEng 1247.

Earthbreakers, The (Haycox). LFEng 3196; RevLFEng 3853.

Earthly Paradise, The (Morris). PEng 2055, 2056, 2057-2058; RevPEng 2386-2389.

Earthly Possessions (Tyler). LFEng 2682; RevLFEng 3340-3341.

Earthly Powers (Burgess). LFEng 369-370; RevLFEng 467.

"Earthquake in Chile, The" (Kleist). RevShF 1371-1372.

Earthquake in Chile, The (Kleist). LFEng 3248-3249; ShF 1759.

Earthsea series, The (Le Guin). RevLFEng 2013-2014.

East, Charles. ShF 2577.

East I Know, The (Claudel). PFor 359-360.

East Is East (Boyle, T.). RevLFEng 352-353.

"East of the Sun and West of the Moon" (Merwin). PEng 1981; RevPEng 2299.

East River (Asch). LFFor 79.

"Eastbourne" (Montale). PFor 1051. See also *Occasioni, Le.*

"Easter Morning" (Ammons). PSup 13; RevPEng 43.

"Easter Procession, The" (Solzhenitsyn). RevShF 2163; ShF 2250.

"Easter-wings" (Herbert). PEng 1298, 1299; RevPEng 1478.

Eastlake, William. LFEng 849-856; ShF 2578.

Eastman, Charles A. (Ohiyesa). ShF 567.

Eastward Ho! (Chapman, Jonson, and Marston). DEng 2286-2287; RevDEng 2806-2806.

"Eating the Pig" (Hall). PEng 1206; RevPEng 1374.

Eaton, Charles Edward. ShF 2580.

Eaux et forêts, Les. See *Rivers and Forests, The.*

Eberhart, Mignon G. M&D 562-567.

Eberhart, Richard. PEng 925-935; PSup 404-405; **RevPEng 1055-1064.**

Ebert, Adolf. LTh 335.

Ebner-Eschenbach, Marie von. LFFor 2188.

Ebony Box, The (Fletcher). M&D 623-624.

"Ebony Tower, The" (Fowles). LFEng 1018-1020; RevLFEng 1209-1210; RevShF 892-893; ShF 1395, 1396.

Ebony Tower, The (Fowles). LFEng 1008, 1018-1020; RevLFEng 1209-1211; RevShF 891-895; ShF 1394.

Eça de Queiróz, José Maria de. LFFor 540-546.

"Ecce Puer" (Joyce). PEng 1526; RevPEng 1750.

Ecclesiastes 1-5 (Surrey, paraphrase). PEng 2791; RevPEng 3257.

"Egri hangok." *See* "Sounds of Eger."

"Egy estém otthon." *See* "One Evening at Home."

Egy mondat a zsarnokságról. See *One Sentence on Tyranny.*

Eh? (Livings). DEng 1153-1154; RevDEng 1453-1454.

Ehe des Herrn Mississippi, Die. See *Marriage of Mr. Mississippi, The.*

Ehre, Die. See Honor.

Ehrenburg, Ilya. LFFor 2325, 2327.

Ehrengard (Dinesen). ShF 1284.

Eich, Günther. PFor 1930-1931.

Eiche and Angora. See *Rabbit Race, The.*

Eichendorff, Joseph von. LTh 433-439; PFor 435-444, 1918.

Eigenart des Ästhetischen, Die (Lukács). LTh 939.

Eight Men (Wright, R.). LFEng 2974; RevLFEng 3679.

Eight Million Ways to Die (Block). M&D 152-153.

"Eight O'clock One Morning" (Grau). ShF 1533.

Eight Strokes of the Clock (Leblanc). M&D 1037-1038.

"Eight Views of Tokyo" (Dazai). RevShF 693; ShFSup 94.

1876 (Vidal). RevLFEng 3375-3376.

"Eighteen-Year-Old, The" (Morgenstern). PFor 1060.

"Eighth Air Force" (Jarrell). PEng 1481-1482; RevPEng 1693-1694.

Eighth Circle, The (Ellin). M&D 576.

Eighth Day, The (Wilder). LFEng 2886-2887; RevLFEng 3576-3577.

"Eighth Eclogue" (Radnóti). PFor 1314-1315.

Eighth Satire (Oldham, trans.). PEng 2134; RevPEng 2486-2487.

87 pesama (Pavlović). PFor 1164-1165.

"Eighty-Yard Run, The" (Shaw). RevShF 2101; ShF 2223.

Eikhenbaum, Boris. LTh 440-444, 913, 1505, 1758-1760, 1822.

1 Konstellation: 15 (Gomringer). PFor 595.

Ein Mord den jeder begeht. See *Every Man a Murderer.*

"Ein Wort." *See* "One Word."

Einar Elkær (Jensen). LFFor 882.

Einarsson, Indrioi. DFor 2474-2475.

Einleitung in die Geisteswissenschaften (Dilthey). LTh 378.

Einstein (MacLeish). RevPEng 2153-2154.

Einstein Intersection, The (Delany). LFEng 718; RevLFEng 854.

Einstein on the Beach (Wilson R.). DSup 402; RevDEng 2620-2621.

"Einzige, Der." *See* "Only One, The."

Eirēnē. See *Peace.*

"Eisenhower's Visit to Franco, 1959" (Wright, James). PEng 3165-3166; RevPEng 3677-3678.

Eiszeit (Dorst). DSup 95.

"Éjfeli párbaj." *See* "Midnight Duel."

Èjxenbaum, B. M. LFEng 3214, 3277-3278, 3331; RevShF 2670; ShF 174.

Ekbom, Torsten. LFFor 2360.

Ekelöf, Gunnar. PFor 445-454, 2180.

Ekelund, Vilhelm. PFor 2175.

Ekkehard I. PFor 2114.

Ekklesiazousai. See *Ecclesiazusae.*

Ekwensi, Cyprian. LFFor 2046-2048.

Elaine's Book (Wright, Jay). RevPEng 3691.

Elämä ja aurinko (Sillanpää). LFFor 1578-1579.

Elder, Gary. ShF 2582.

Elder, Lonne, III. RevDEng 676-683.

Elder Edda. PFor 1747, 1762-1764, 2153.

Elder Statesman, The (Eliot). DEng 555-557; RevDEng 696-698.

"Eleanoure and Juga" (Chatterton). PEng 469; RevPEng 567.

Elective Affinities (Goethe). LFFor 676-678.

Electra (Euripides). DFor 2115.

Electra (Sophocles). DFor 2108.

"Electric Ant, The" (Dick). ShF 1263-1264.

Eleftheroi poliorkimenoi (Solomòs). PFor 1456-1457, 1949-1950.

Eleghia ke satires (Karyotákis). PFor 1960.

"Elegía a doña Juana la Loca" (García Lorca). PFor 515-516.

"Elegía interrumpida." *See* "Interrupted Elegy."

Elegie (Walther). PFor 1680.

"Élégie de l'eau." *See* "Elegy of Water."

"Élégie de minuit." *See* "Elegy of Midnight."

"Elegie upon the Death of the Deane of Pauls, Dr. John Donne, An" (Carew). LTh 1675; PEng 435; RevPEng 503.

Elegies (Propertius). PFor 1286-1290.

"Elegies" (Senghor). PFor 1427. See also *Nocturnes.*

"Elegies for the Hot Season" (McPherson). PEng 1879-1880; RevPEng 2182-2183.

"Elegy" (Berry). PEng 149; RevPEng 184.

"Elegy" (Bidart). RevPEng 211.

"Elegy" (Hacker). RevPEng 1361.

"Elegy for Neal Cassady" (Ginsberg). PEng 1094.

"Elegy for Wesley Wells" (Hall). RevPEng 1371-1372.

"Elegy Just in Case" (Ciardi). PEng 502; RevPEng 591.

"Elegy of Fortinbras" (Herbert). PFor 656.

"Elegy of Midnight" (Senghor). PFor 1428. See also *Nocturnes.*

"Elegy of Water" (Senghor). PFor 1428. See also *Nocturnes.*

"Elegy on the Death of a Mad Dog, An" (Goldsmith). PEng 1107, 1108; RevPEng 1255.

"Elegy on the Glory of Her Sex: Mrs. Mary Blaize, An" (Goldsmith). PEng 1107-1108; RevPEng 1255.

Elegy to the Memory of an Unfortunate Lady (Pope). PEng 3322; RevPEng 3841.

Elegy Written in a Country Churchyard (Gray). PEng 1140-1142, 3321-3322; RevPEng 1298-1300, 3840-3841, 3847.

Elemental Odes, The (Neruda). PFor 1076-1077, 1078-1079.

"Elementary Cosmogony" (Simic). PEng 2592.

"Elementary School Classroom in a Slum, An" (Spender). PEng 2700; RevPEng 3144.

Elene (Cynewulf). PEng 718-720; RevPEng 820-822; RevShF 2604-2605; ShF 433-434.

Elettra (D'Annunzio). PFor 387. See also *Laudi, Le.*

"Elevated" (Nims). RevPEng 2456.

"Eleven" (Cisneros). RevShF 559.

"Elf King" (Goethe). PFor 583, 587.

"11th: and last booke of the Ocean to Scinthia, The" (Raleigh). RevPEng 2695-2696.

"Eli, the Fanatic" (Roth). RevShF 2019-2020; ShF 2159-2160.

Elias Portolu (Deledda). LFFor 442-443.

"Eliduc" (Fowles). RevShF 893; ShF 1395-1396.

"Eliduc" (Marie de France). RevShF 1608; ShF 1890-1891.

"Elinda's Glove" (Lovelace). PEng 1760; RevPEng 2053.

Elingsson, Thorsteinn. PFor 2169.

Eliot, George. LFEng 870-883, 2903, 2905, 3033, 3035; **RevLFEng 1032-1045**, 3741, 3743; **RevShF 805-809; ShF 1333-1337.**

Eliot, T. S. DEng 543-558, 2377-2379; LTh 158, 160, 264, **445-452,** 795, 896, 979-980, 1012, 1090, 1206, 1261, 1413-1414, 1426, 1492, 1523, 1549, 1554, 1556, 1566-1568, 1752-1753, 1804-1805, 1818; PEng 158, 170, **936-949,** 3356, 3358-3359, 3389, 3485-3488; **RevDEng 684-699,** 2895-2897; **RevPEng 1065-1079,** 3874, 3974-3975, 4028-4031; RevShF 2673; ShF 177-178, 292.

Elisa (Goncourt, E.). LFFor 716-717.

Elixiere des Teufels, Die. See *Devil's Elixirs, The.*

"Elixir du Révérend Père Gaucher, L'." *See* "Reverend Father Gaucher's Elixir, The."

"Elizabeth" (Jackson). RevShF 1252; ShF 1669.

Elizabeth of England (Bruckner). DFor 263-264.

Elizabeth the Queen (Anderson, M.). DEng 27-28; RevDEng 38-39.

Elizabethan World Picture (Davies). RevPEng 3809.

"Elka i svad'ba." *See* "Christmas Tree and a Wedding, A."

Elkin, Stanley. LFEng 884-893; LFSup 403; **RevLFEng 1046-1052; RevShF 810-815;** ShF 1338-1343; ShFSup 388.

"Ellen West" (Bidart). RevPEng 211-212.

Ellin, Stanley. M&D 574-578.

Elliott, George P. RevShF 816-823; ShF 1344-1350.

Elliott, William D. ShF 2538.

Ellis, Henry Havelock. LTh 1737.

"Ellis Island" (Helprin). RevShF 1165-1166; ShFSup 119-120.

Ellis Island and Other Stories (Helprin). RevShF 1163-1166; ShFSup 117-118.

Ellison, Harlan. RevShF 824-830; ShF 780, 781

Ellison, Ralph. LFEng 894-905; LFSup 403; **RevLFEng 1053-1064,** 3776, 3808; ShF 555-556.

Elmer Gantry (Lewis, S.). LFEng 1678-1680; RevLFEng 2074-2076.

"Éloge de Richardson" (Diderot). LFFor 2120.

Éloges (Perse). PFor 1195.

Eloisa. See *New Héloïse, The.*

"Elpenor" (Sinópoulos). PFor 1971. See also *Metaichmio I.*

"Elsa's Eyes" (Aragon). PFor 70-71.

"Else Lasker-Schüler" (Bobrowski). PFor 205.

"Elsie in New York" (Henry). ShF 1630.

Elster, Kristian. LFFor 2340.

Éluard, Paul. PFor 455-460, 1886.

Elverhøj (Heiberg, J.). DFor 907.

"Elvis Presley" (Gunn). PEng 1172.

Ely, David. ShF 2584.

Elytis, Odysseus. PFor 461-466, 1965-1968; PSup 405.

E. M. Forster (Trilling). LTh 500.

Emaux et camées. See *Enamels and Cameos.*

"Ember az embertelenségben." *See* "Man in Inhumanity."

Ember tragédiája, Az. See *Tragedy of Man, The.*

Embers (Beckett). DEng 154; RevDEng 190.

Embezzled Heaven (Werfel). LFFor 1911-1912.

Embezzler, The (Auchincloss). LFEng 111-112; RevLFEng 152-153.

"End of August, The" (Pavese). RevShF 1863-1864.

"End of Autumn, The" (Ponge). PFor 1265.

End of Beauty, The (Graham). RevPEng 1276, 1278.

"End of Chronos, The" (Ungaretti). PFor 1568. See also *Sentimento del tempo.*

End of Summer (Behrman). DEng 185-186; RevDEng 222-223.

"End of Summer School, The" (Nemerov). PEng 2079.

End of the Affair, The (Greene, G.). DEng 827-828; RevDEng 1021-1022.

End of the Battle, The (Waugh). LFEng 2803; RevLFEng 3470.

End of the Day (Baitz). RevDEng 87, 90-91.

End of the Game. See *Judge and His Hangman, The.*

End of the Road, The (Barth). LFEng 161-162; RevLFEng 223-224.

"End of the Road, The" (Belloc). PEng 138; RevPEng 167.

"End of the Tether, The" (Conrad). ShF 1186.

"End of the World, The" (MacLeish). PEng 3501-3502, 3504, 3508-3509, 3511-3512.

End Zone (DeLillo). LFSup 86; RevLFEng 864.

Endangered Species (Clarke, M.). RevDEng 477.

Endgame (Beckett). DEng 152-153, 2385; DFor 160-162, 2246-2247, 2359; RevDEng 17, 187-188, 2902-2903.

Endimion and Phoebe (Drayton). PEng 849; RevPEng 964.

Endō, Shusaku. LFSup 100-107; RevShF 831-839.

Endymion (Heidenstam). LFFor 820.

Endymion (Lyly). DEng 1184-1185, 2269; PEng 1819; RevDEng 1486-1487, 2788; RevShF 1530; ShF 1832.

Enemies (Singer, Isaac). LFEng 2437-2439; LFFor 1623-1625; RevLFEng 3064-3065.

Enemigos de alma, Los (Mallea). LFFor 1056-1057.

Enemy, The (Bagley). M&D 55-57.

"Enemy, The" (Buck). RevShF 336-337; ShF 1012-1014.

"Enemy Joy, The" (Belitt). RevPEng 157.

Enemy of the People, An (Ibsen). DFor 2472.

Enemy of the People, An (Miller). DEng 1341-1342, 2406; RevDEng 1680, 2927.

"Enfance d'un chef, L'." *See* "Childhood of a Boss."

"Enfant au tambour, L'" (Follain). PSup 128.

Enfant noir, L'. See *Dark Child, The.*

Enfant prodigue, L' (Becque). DFor 170.

"Enfantement" (Follain). PSup 130.

Enfants du sabbat, Les. See *Children of the Black Sabbath.*

Enfants terribles, Les. See *Children of the Game.*

"Enfermé, seul" (Éluard). PFor 459.

"Enfin" (Reverdy). PSup 325.

Engañados, Los (Rueda). DFor 1598-1600.

Engels, Friedrich. LTh 1712.

"Engführung." *See* "Stretto."

"England" (Davie). PSup 88; RevPEng 853-854.

England's Heroical Epistles (Drayton). PEng 850; RevPEng 965-966.

English Bards, and Scotch Reviewers (Byron). LTh 256, 258, 261; PEng 406; RevPEng 472.

English Literature in the Sixteenth Century, Excluding Drama (Lewis). LTh 896-897.

English Murder, An (Hare). M&D 844-845.

English Poetry (Bateson). PEng 3408-3410.

English Teacher, The (Narayan). LFEng 1968-1969; RevLFEng 2483-2484.

English Traveler, The (Heywood, T.). DEng 2291; RevDEng 2810.

"Englishman in Texas, An" (Middleton, C.). PEng 1988; RevPEng 2310.

"Engraving" (Rítsos). PFor 1348-1349.

"Enigma, The" (Fowles). LFEng 1019; RevLFEng 1210-1211; RevShF 894; ShF 1397-1398.

Enigma of Arrival, The (Naipaul). RevLFEng 2477-2478.

Enneads (Plotinus). LTh 1129-1130, 1645.

Ennius, Quintus. DFor 546-551, 2139; LTh 1511; PFor 905, 2089-2090.

Ennodius. PFor 2111.

"Enoch Soames" (Beerbohm). RevShF 197-198; ShF 943-944.

Enomoto Kikaku. *See* Takarai Kikaku.

"Enormous Radio, The" (Cheever). RevShF 501, 2734; ShF 1122.

Enough Is Enough (Henshaw). DEng 931-933; RevDEng 1164-1166.

Enough Stupidity in Every Wiseman. See *Scoundrel, The.*

"Enough" (Creeley). PEng 684-685.

Enquist, Per Olov. LFFor 2361.

Enrico IV. See *Henry IV.*

"Enslaved Besieged, The" (Varnalis). PFor 1959.

Enter Solly Gold (Kops). DEng 1082; RevDEng 1361.

"Entered as Second-class Matter" (Perelman). RevShF 1869; ShF 2082.

Entered from the Sun (Garrett). RevLFEng 1298.

Epistola del Trissino de le lettre nuovamente aggiunte ne la lingua italiana (Trissino). LTh 1401.

Epistolae metricae. See *Metrical Letters.*

"Epistolary Essay from M. G. to O. B. upon their Mutual Poems" (Rochester). PEng 2403-2404; RevPEng 2795-2796.

"Epitaph, An" (Shalamov). RevShF 2096; ShFSup 292.

"Epitaph for the Tomb of El Greco" (Góngora). PFor 602.

Epitaph of a Small Winner. See *Posthumous Memoirs of Brás Cubas.*

"Epitaph on a Jacobite" (Macaulay). PEng 1828.

"Epitaph on Hogarth" (Johnson, S.). PEng 1506; RevPEng 1727.

"Épitaphe, Villon, L'." See "Villon's Epitaph."

Epitaphios (Rítsos). PFor 1348, 1968-1969.

Epithalamion (Spenser). PEng 2715-2716; RevPEng 3159-3160.

"Epithalamion Made at Lincoln's Inn" (Donne). PEng 833-834; RevPEng 939-940.

"Epithalamium" (Harrison, J.). PEng 1235; RevPEng 1416.

Épître à Huet (La Fontaine). LTh 856.

Épître IX (Boileau). LTh 179.

"Épître première" (Nerval). PFor 1088.

Epitrepontes. See *Arbitration, The.*

Épîtres (Corneille). LTh 311.

Epodes (Horace). PFor 713-714.

Epsom-Wells (Shadwell). DEng 1670-1672; RevDEng 2083-2085.

"Epstein" (Roth). RevShF 2020-2021; ShF 2160-2161.

Equal Danger (Sciascia). LFFor 1521-1522.

"Equanimity" (Murray). PSup 292-293; RevPEng 2413-2414.

Equations of Love, The. See *Tuesday and Wednesday* and *Lilly's Story.*

"Equilibrists, The" (Ransom). PEng 2331-2332; RevPEng 2717-2718.

"Equinox" (Lorde). RevPEng 2043.

"Equitan" (Marie de France). RevShF 1607; ShF 1889.

Equus (Shaffer, P.). DEng 1683-1685; RevDEng 2093-2095, 2098-2099.

"Eraser" (Simic). PEng 2579.

Erasers, The (Robbe-Grillet). LFFor 1413-1414; M&D 1435-1436.

Erasmus, Desiderius. LFFor 2021-2022; LTh 411, **467-472,** 932, 1662; ShF 450-451.

Erasmus Montanus (Holberg). DFor 949-950, 2466.

Erba, Luciano. PFor 2050.

Erben, Karel Jaromír. PFor 1800.

Erbförster, Der. See *Hereditary Forester, The.*

"Erdbeben in Chili, Das." See "Earthquake in Chile, The."

Erdbeben in Chili, Das. See *Earthquake in Chile, The.*

Erdgeist, Der. See *Earth Spirit.*

Erdman, Nikolai. DFor 2460.

Erdrich, Louise. RevLFEng **1065-1072;** RevPEng 3935.

"Ere Sleep Comes Down to Soothe the Weary Eyes" (Dunbar, P.). PSup 113; RevPEng 1015.

Erec (Hartmann von Aue). PFor 632-633.

Erec et Enide (Chrétien de Troyes). PFor 1838; RevShF 543.

Erechtheus (Swinburne). PEng 2813; RevPEng 3281.

Erewhon (Butler, S.). LFEng 393, 394-396; RevLFEng 503-505.

Erewhon Revisited (Butler, S.). LFEng 396-397; RevLFEng 505-506.

Erica (Vittorini). LFFor 1888-1889.

Erica e i suoi fratelli. See *Erica.*

Ericson, Walter. See **Cunningham, E. V.**

"Erinnerung an die Maria A." See "Remembering Maria A."

"Erlebnis." See "Experience, An."

"Erlkönig." See "Elf King."

Ermine, The (Anouilh). DFor 71.

Ermittlung, Die. See *Investigation, The.*

Ermordete Majestät (Gryphius). DFor 837.

Erneuerung, Die. (Kaiser). DFor 1023-1024.

Ernst, Paul. DFor **552-562,** 2377.

Eröffnung des indischen Zeitalters (Hacks). DFor 852.

Eros (Verga). LFFor 1860-1861.

Eros at Breakfast (Davies). DEng 469, 2441; RevDEng 579, 2964.

"Eros to Howard Nemerov" (Van Duyn). PEng 2964; RevPEng 3443.

"Eros Turannos" (Robinson). PEng 2389-2391; RevPEng 2780-2782.

Erosion (Graham). RevPEng 1276-1278.

"Erosion" (Pratt). PEng 2282-2283; RevPEng 2655-2656.

"Erostratus" (Sartre). RevShF 2067.

Erotic Tales (Moravia). RevShF 1670; ShFSup 199.

Erotica pathemata (Parthenius). LFFor 2000.

Erotika (Cankar). PFor 2269.

"Erotikos Logos" (Seferis). PFor 1415.

Erpingham Camp, The (Orton). DEng 1424-1425; RevDEng 1802-1803.

"*Errata*" (Simic). PEng 2597.

"Errigal Road, The" (Montague). PEng 2038-2039.

Ertel, Aleksandr. LFFor 2319.

Ervine, John Greer. *See* **Ervine, St. John.**

Ervine, St. John. DEng 559-565; RevDEng 700-706.

Erwin (Solger). LTh 1360.

"Erziehung der Hirse, Die." *See* "Education of Millet, The."

"Es färbte sich die Wiese grün." *See* "Meadow Turned Green, The."

Es lebe das Leben! See *Joy of Living, The.*

"Escalator, The" (Robbe-Grillet). ShF 2156.

"Escapade, An" (Callaghan). RevShF 385; ShFSup 69.

Escape (Galsworthy). DEng 716; RevDEng 893.

"Escaped Cock, The" (Lawrence). RevShF 1427.

"Escapes" (Williams, J.). RevShF 2474-2475.

Escapes (Williams, J.). RevShF 2474-2476.

"Escargots." *See* "Snails."

Esclusa, L'. See *Outcast, The.*

Escurial (Ghelderode). DFor 694-695.

Esenin, Sergei. PFor 473-481, 2148-2149.

Esfera, La. See *Sphere, The.*

Esmond in India (Jhabvala). LFFor 2222-2223; LFSup 172-173; RevLFEng 1754-1755.

Espadas como labios (Aleixandre). PFor 29.

España (Gautier). PFor 536-538.

España, aparta de mí este cáliz. See *Spain, Take This Cup from Me.*

"Español habla de su tierra, Un." *See* "Spaniard Speaks of His Homeland, A."

"Esperanto" (Shalamov). RevShF 2094; ShFSup 290.

Espoir, L'. See *Man's Hope.*

Espriu, Salvador. PFor 1775.

Espurgatoire Seint Patriz (Marie de France). RevShF 1609.

Essai sur les fables de La Fontaine. See *La Fontaine et ses fables.*

Essai sur les fictions. See *Essay on Fiction.*

Essais (Montaigne). ShF 155.

Essais de critique et d'histoire (Taine). LTh 1417-1418, 1420.

Essais de psychologie contemporaine (Bourget). LTh 200, 1391.

Essais sur la littérature contemporaine (Brunetière). LTh 233.

"Essay at War, An" (Duncan). PEng 902; RevPEng 1038.

Essay Concerning Human Understanding, An (Locke). LTh 1700.

Essay on Criticism, An (Pope). LTh 909, 1142-1143, 1145, 1689; PEng 2253-2255, 3323, 3472; RevPEng 2627-2629, 3842.

"Essay on Criticism, An" (Van Duyn). PEng 2963; RevPEng 3442-3443.

Essay on Fiction (Staël). LTh 1380, 1382.

Essay on Literature (Lu Chi). LTh 920, 922-923, 1774.

Essay on Man, An (Pope). LTh 1349; PEng 2258-2261, 3325; RevPEng 2632-2635, 3844.

"Essay on Psychiatrists" (Pinsky). RevPEng 2587-2588.

"Essay upon Epitaphs" (Wordsworth). LTh 1581.

Essayes in Divinity (Donne). PEng 822; RevPEng 928.

Essays, The (Montaigne). LTh 1042, 1044, 1046-1047.

Essays and Studies (Swinburne). LTh 1401.

Essays in Criticism (Arnold). LTh 47-48, 1733; PEng 3484-3485; RevPEng 4027.

Essays on European Literature (Curtius). LTh 336.

Essays on Shakespeare (Empson). LTh 464.

Essays on the Gogol Period of Russian Literature (Chernyshevsky). LTh 121, 287.

Essays Speculative and Suggestive (Symonds). LTh 1408.

"Essex" (Davie). PSup 89; RevPEng 855.

"Essex and Bacon" (Landor). PEng 1643; RevPEng 1908.

Esson, Louis. DEng 2432; RevDEng 2955.

Est-il bon? Est-il méchant? (Diderot). DSup 86-88.

"Est' tselomudrennye chary." *See* "There Are Chaste Charms."

Esta noche juntos, amándonos tanto. See *Together Tonight, Loving Each Other So Much.*

"Esta tarde, mi bien" (Cruz). PFor 378.

Estación total, La (Jiménez). PFor 753-754.

Estate, The (Singer). RevLFEng 3061-3063.

"Estatuto del vino." *See* "Ordinance of Wine."

Este domingo. See *This Sunday.*

Estetica come scienza dell'espressione e linguistica generale. See *Aesthetic as Science of Expression and General Linguistic.*

Esteticheskie otnosheniya iskusstva k deistvitel'nosti. See "Aesthetic Relationship of Art to Reality."

Esther. ShF 356-358.

"Esther" (Toomer). RevShF 2298-2299; ShF 2341.

Esther Waters (Moore, G.). LFEng 1900-1901; RevLFEng 2402, 2407-2408.

Esthétique de la langue française. See *What Is Pure French?*

Estío (Jiménez). PFor 752.

Esto no es un libro (Otero). PFor 1116.

"Estrellas y grillos." *See* "Stars and Cricket."

"Estuary, The" (Beer). PEng 120-121; RevPEng 140-141.

Et ils passerent des menottes aux fleurs. See *And They Put Handcuffs on the Flowers.*

Et les chiens se taisaient (Césaire). DSup 41-42.

"Et Maintenant" (Reverdy). PSup 326.

Été 1914, L' (Martin du Gard). LFFor 1116-1118. See also *World of the Thibaults, The.*

"Eterna" (Lavin). RevShF 1417; ShF 1785.

"Eternal" (Ungaretti). PFor 1565-1566. See also Allegria, L'.

"Eternal Dice, The" (Vallejo). PFor 1589.

Eternal Feminine. PFor 194, 196-197, 199-200.

"Eternal Moment, The" (Forster). RevShF 886-887; ShF 1389-1390.

Eternal Road, The (Werfel). DFor 1999.

"Eterno." *See* "Eternal."

"Ethan Brand" (Hawthorne). RevShF 1150; ShF 477, 738-739, 1611-1612.

Ethan Frome (Davis). DEng 479-480; RevDEng 590-591.

Ethan Frome (Wharton, Edith). LFEng 2855; RevLFEng 3537.

Ethelstan (Darley). PEng 734; RevPEng 838.

Etherege, Sir George. DEng 566-578; PEng 974-980; RevDEng 707-720; RevPEng 1105-1111.

Ethics of Reading, The (Miller). LTh 1037.

Ethiopian History, An (Heliodorus of Emesa). RevShF 2574.

Ethiopian Story (Heliodorus of Emesa). LFFor 2005-2008, 2017.

Ethiopica. See *Ethiopian Story.*

Étranger, L'. See *Stranger, The.*

Être et le néant, L'. See *Being and Nothingness.*

Ett drömspel. See *Dream Play, A.*

Études critiques sur l'histoire de la littérature française (Brunetière). LTh 233-235.

Études et portraits (Bourget). LTh 201.

Etymologies (Isidore of Seville). LTh 740-741; ShF 425.

Euba, Temi. RevDEng 2944.

"Euclid Alone Has Looked on Beauty Bare" (Millay). PEng 2000-2001; RevPEng 2324-2325.

"Eufori." *See* "Euphoria."

Eugen, Berthold. *See* **Brecht, Bertolt.**

Eugène (Jodelle). DEng 2160; RevDEng 2681.

Eugene Onegin (Pushkin). LFFor 1363-1366, 2312; PFor 873, 1293, 1298-1299.

Eugénie. See *School of Rakes, The.*

Eugénie Grandet (Balzac). LFFor 98.

Eumenides (Aeschylus). DFor 2102. See also *Oresteia.*

Eumenides (Ennius). DFor 549.

Eunuch, The (Terence). DFor 1826-1827, 2143.

"Euphoria" (Ekelöf). PFor 449. See also *Färjesång.*

Euphues and His England (Lyly). RevShF 1528-1529, 2627; ShF 1830-1831.

Euphues, the Anatomy of Wit (Lyly). LFEng 3014; RevLFEng 3722; RevShF 1528-1529, 2627-2628; ShF 491-492, 1830, 1831.

Eupolis. DFor 2121-2122.

"Eupompus Gave Splendour to Art by Numbers" (Huxley). ShF 245.

Euripides. DEng 2135, 2137, 2138; DFor 563-578, 2110-2119, 2120; LTh 1198; RevDEng 2655, 2657, 2658.

"Europe" (Ashbery). RevPEng 58.

Europe (Blake). PEng 214-215; RevPEng 258.

European Literature and the Latin Middle Ages (Curtius). LTh 335-337.

Europeans, The (James, H.). RevLFEng 3750.

Eurydice (Fielding). DEng 604; RevDEng 747.

"Eurydice" (Patmore). PEng 2193-2194; RevPEng 2564-2565.

Eusebius Hieronymum. *See* Jerome, Saint.

Eustace and Hilda (Hartley). LFEng 1300; RevLFEng 1554.

Eustace Chisholm and the Works (Purdy). LFEng 2172-2173; RevLFEng 2746-2747.

Eustace Diamonds, The (Trollope). LFEng 2657-2659; RevLFEng 3313-3315.

Eustis, Helen. M&D 579-584.

Euthymiae Raptus (Chapman). PEng 461-462; RevPEng 556-557.

"Eva." *See* "Eve" (Arreola).

Eva (Verga). LFFor 1860.

Eva Trout (Bowen). LFEng 268; RevLFEng 324.

Evander, Per Gunnar. LFFor 2362.

Evangeline (Longfellow). PEng 1751-1752; RevPEng 2036-2037.

"Evangeline's Mother" (Kinsella). RevShF 1354.

Evans, Mary Ann. *See* **Eliot, George.**

Evans, Morgan. *See* **Davies, L. P.**

"Eve" (Arreola). RevShF 80-81.

Ève (Péguy). PFor 1183.

"Eve" (Soto). RevPEng 3116.

"Exhortation" (Bogan). PEng 237-238; RevPEng 284.

Ἐᾱͺ ᾱͺ ᾱͺ τίρεῖς γία τοη ουρανό. See *Six and One Remorses for the Sky.*

Exile, An (Jones, M.). LFEng 1491-1492; RevLFEng 1814-1815.

Exile and the Kingdom (Camus, A.). RevShF 399; ShF 1047.

Exile of the Sons of Uisliu. RevShF 2606; ShF 434-435.

"Exiles" (Cavafy). PFor 298.

Exiles and Marriages (Hall). PEng 1198-1199; RevPEng 1371.

Exile's Return (Cowley). LTh 314, 317-319.

Exister (Follain). PSup 126, 128.

Exit Lines (Hill). M&D 875.

Exit the King (Ionesco). DFor 1002-1003, 2255-2256, 2357.

Exodus. ShF 342-344.

Expedition of Humphrey Clinker, The. See *Humphrey Clinker.*

"Expelled, The" (Beckett). ShF 939.

Expensive People (Oates). LFEng 2011-2012; RevLFEng 2535-2536.

"Experience, An" (Hofmannsthal). PFor 675.

Experiment in Criticism, An (Lewis). LTh 895.

"Experiment in Misery, An" (Crane). RevShF 646-647.

"Experiment with a Rat, The" (Rakosi). RevPEng 2685-2686.

Experimental Novel, The (Zola). LTh 1618, 1711.

"Expiation, L'" (Hugo). PFor 735. See also *Châtiments, Les.*

Explanation of America, An (Pinsky). PEng 2211-2212; RevPEng 2588-2589.

Explications/Interpretations (Wright, Jay). RevPEng 3687-3689.

Explorations (Yeats). LTh 1588.

"Exploring the Province of the Short Story" (Elliott, G. P.). ShF 75-76.

"Explosion of Seven Babies, An" (Crane, S.). ShF 1217.

Expositio Virgilianae continentiae secundum philosophos moralis. See *Content of Virgil.*

Exposition of the Content of Virgil According to Moral Philosophy, The. See *Content of Virgil.*

"Expostulation" (Byrom). PEng 396.

"Expounder of the Way" (Yosano Akiko). PFor 1717.

"Express, The" (Spender). PEng 2701-2702; RevPEng 3145.

"Expulsion, The" (Stern) PEng 337; RevPEng 3197.

Exterminator! (Burroughs). LFEng 390; RevLFEng 489.

Extracts from Adam's Diary (Twain). ShF 374.

Extravagant Shepherd, The (Sorel). LFFor 2027.

"Eye, The" (Powers). RevShF 1919; ShF 2120.

"Eye Altering, The" (Le Guin). RevShF 1453.

"Eye and Tooth" (Lowell, R.). PEng 1792.

"Eye-Beaters, The" (Dickey, J.). PEng 800.

Eye-Beaters, Blood, Victory, Madness, Buckhead and Mercy, The (Dickey, J.). PEng 799.

Eye in the Darkness, The (Chance). M&D 298-299.

Eye in the Sky (Dick). LFSup 94-95; RevLFEng 894-895.

"Eye of Apollo, The" (Chesterton). RevShF 531-532.

Eye of the Needle (Follett). M&D 636-638.

Eye of the Scarecrow, The (Harris, W.). LFSup 148-149; RevLFEng 1530-1531.

Eye of the Storm, The (White, P.). LFEng 2860, 2874-2876; RevLFEng 3554-3555.

Eyeless in Gaza (Huxley). LFEng 1406-1407; RevLFEng 1682-1683.

"Eyes, The" (Wharton). RevShF 2457; ShF 2429-2430.

Eyes and Objects (Johnson, R.). PSup 214; RevPEng 1716.

"Eyes in the Grass" (Still). PEng 2762; RevPEng 3225.

"Eye's Journey, The" (Nin). RevShF 1723; ShF 1950.

Eyes of Darkness (Highwater). RevLFEng 1625.

Eyes of the Dragon, The (King). LFSup 211; RevLFEng 1893.

Eyes of the Interred, The (Asturias). LFFor 87.

"Eyes of the World, The" (Beer). PEng 118; RevPEng 138.

"Eyes to See" (Cozzens). RevShF 641-642; ShF 1213-1214.

Eyrbggja Saga. RevShF 2590; ShF 392.

Ezechial. DFor 2134.

Ezekiel. ShF 349-351.

Ezekiel, Nissim. PFor 2001; RevPEng 3946.

Ezra (Kops). DEng 1083-1084; RevDEng 1362-1363.

F

Fabbri, Diego. DFor 2414.

Fabeln (Lessing, Gotthold). RevShF 2580-2581; ShF 382.

"Faber Book of Modern Short Stories, The" (Bowen). ShF 71-72.

Fabiola (Machado). RevDEng 1527-1529.

"Fable, The" (Winters). PSup 398; RevPEng 3627.

Fable for Critics, A (Lowell, J.). RevPEng 2073-2074.

"Fable from the Cayoosh Country" (Barnard). PSup 29-30; RevPEng 112-113.

"Fable of Pyramus and Thisbe, The" (Góngora). PFor 601.

Fable of the Bees, The (Mandeville). PEng 3406-3407.

"Fable of the Goat" (Agnon). RevShF 21-22; ShF 831-833.

Fables, The, preface to (Dryden). LTh 406-407.

Fables (Gay). PEng 1075; RevPEng 1210.

Fables (Henryson). PEng 1288-1290, 3279; RevPEng 1466-1468, 3798.

Fables (La Fontaine). PFor 810, 812-813, 816-818.

Fables (Marie de France). PFor 971; ShF 1891.

Fables and Fantasies for Adults (Das). ShF 643.

Fables of La Fontaine, The (Moore, trans.). PEng 2046-2047; RevPEng 2376.

"Fábula de Píramo y Tisbe." *See* "Fable of Pyramus and Thisbe, The."

Fábula de Polifemo y Galatea. See *Polyphemus and Galathea.*

Fabulous Beasts, The (Oates). PEng 2119.

Fabulous Miss Marie, The (Bullins). DEng 308; RevDEng 366. See also Twentieth-Century Cycle.

Façade (Sitwell). PEng 2627-2629; RevPEng 3031-3033.

Faccio, Rina. *See* Aleramo, Sibilla.

Face of Another, The (Abe). LFFor 7.

Face of Fear, The (Koontz). M&D 1007.

"Face of Helen, The" (Christie). ShF 1144-1145.

"Face of Helene Bournouw, The" (Ellison). RevShF 827-828.

"Face of Stone, A" (Williams, W. C.). RevShF 2488-2489; ShF 2443-2444.

"Face on the Barroom Floor, The" (Algren). RevShF 52; ShF 856.

"Faces" (Koch). PEng 1627; RevPEng 1866.

Facing the Tree (Ignatow). PEng 1475; RevPEng 1687-1688.

"Facino Cane" (Balzac). RevShF 150; ShF 920-921.

Fackel, Die. PFor 791-792, 792-793.

"Facts Concerning the Recent Carnival of Crime in Connecticut, The" (Twain). RevShF 2328; ShF 2362-2363.

"Facts in the Case of M. Valdemar, The" (Poe). ShF 739-740.

Fadeout (Hansen). M&D 830-831.

Fadeyev, Aleksandr. LFFor 2324.

Fadren. See Father, The.

Faerie Queene, The (Spenser). PEng 387-388, 2706, 2707-2708, 2710-2714; RevPEng 3151-3152, 3154-3158; ShF 146.

Fahrenheit 451 (Bradbury). RevLFEng 360.

"Fahrgast, Der." *See* "On the Tram."

Fair, A. A. *See* **Gardner, Erle Stanley.**

Fair Blows the Wind (L'Amour). LFSup 223-224; RevLFEng 1934.

"Fair Chloris in a pigsty lay" (Rochester). PEng 2400; RevPEng 2792.

Fair Eckbert (Tieck, Ludwig). RevShF 2646.

Fair Game (Johnson, D.). RevLFEng 1771.

Fair Grit, The (Darin). DEng 2438; RevDEng 2961.

Fair Haven, The (Butler, S.). LFEng 393, 397; RevLFEng 506.

Fair Jilt, The (Behn). LFEng 222; RevLFEng 272; ShF 502.

Fair Maid of the West, The (Heywood, T.). DEng 952-953; RevDEng 1186-1187.

Fair Penitent, The (Rowe). DEng 1635-1636; RevDEng 2042-2043.

Fairbairn, Roger. *See* **Carr, John Dickson.**

"Faire roome, the presence of sweet beauty's pride" (Nashe). PEng 2072; RevPEng 2421.

"Fairies, The" (Allingham). PEng 42; RevPEng 33.

Fairly Dangerous Thing, A (Hill). M&D 875-876.

Fairly Good Time, A (Gallant). LFEng 1054-1055; RevLFEng 1252-1253.

Fairly Honourable Defeat, A (Murdoch). LFEng 1933-1937; RevLFEng 2444-2448.

"Fairmount Cemetery" (Untermeyer). PEng 2949; RevPEng 3417.

Family and a Fortune, A (Compton-Burnett). LFEng 569-570; RevLFEng 697-698.

Family and Friends (Brookner). LFSup 67-68; RevLFEng 404-405.

Family Arsenal, The (Theroux). LFEng 2630, 2632-2633; RevLFEng 3285-3286.

Family at Gilje, The (Lie). LFFor 2342.

"Family Circle" (Arany). PFor 79.

Family Dancing (Leavitt). RevShF 1438-1440.

Family Devotions (Hwang). RevDEng 1228.

Family Goldschmitt, The (Coulette). RevPEng 689.

Family Happiness (Tolstoy). RevShF 2283.

Family Idiot, The (Sartre). LTh 1274.

Family in Renaissance Florence, The (Alberti). LTh 1661.

Family Madness, A (Keneally). LFSup 191; RevLFEng 1847.

Family Moskat, The (Singer). RevLFEng 3061-3063.

Family of Pascual Duarte, The (Cela). LFFor 292-295.

"Family Portrait, Three Generations" (Rakosi). RevPEng 2686-2687.

Family Reunion, The (Eliot). DEng 550-552; RevDEng 691-693.

Family Sayings (Ginzburg). LFSup 129-130.

Family Talk (Terry). RevDEng 2371.

Family Ties (Lispector). RevShF 1491-1492; ShFSup 166-167.

"Family Tree" (Pastan). RevPEng 2542.

Family Vault, The (MacLeod). M&D 1180-1181.

"Famous Poll at Jody's Bar, The" (Gilchrist). RevShF 986-987.

Famous Tragedy of the Queen of Cornwall, The (Hardy). DEng 891-893; RevDEng 1101-1103.

Famous Victories of Henry V, The. DEng 2265; RevDEng 2784-2785.

Fan Kuai p'ai chün nan (Chao Tsung). DFor 2305.

Fanatic Heart, A (O'Brien, E.). RevShF 1748-1749.

Fancies and Goodnights (Collier). RevShF 590-592.

"Fanciullino, Il" (Pascoli). PFor 1136-1137.

"Fancy Woman, The" (Taylor). ShF 2310.

"Fanny" (Kizer). RevPEng 1857-1858.

Fanny's Consent. See *When a Girl Says Yes.*

Fanon, Frantz. LTh 1062.

Fanshawe (Hawthorne). LFEng 1319-1320; RevLFEng 1574-1576.

Fanshawe, Sir Richard. PEng 995-1003; RevPEng 1127-1136.

Fanshen (Hare). DSup 184; RevDEng 1108.

Fantasia of the Unconscious (Lawrence, D. H.). LFEng 1583-1584; RevLFEng 1957.

Fantasio (Musset). DFor 1402-1403.

Fantastic, The (Todorov). LTh 1432, 1435; ShF 92.

Fantasticks, The. See *Romantics, The.*

"Fantasy, to Laura" (Schiller). PFor 1406.

Fantazy (Słowacki). DFor 1719-1721, 2276.

Fantesca, La (Della Porta). DFor 477-478.

Far Away Is the Sun (Ćosić). LFFor 386-387.

"Far Cry from Africa, A" (Walcott). RevPEng 3496-3497.

Far Cry from Kensington, A (Spark). RevLFEng 3116.

"Far East" (Snyder). PEng 2673.

Far from Cibola (Horgan). LFSup 159-160; RevLFEng 1638-1639.

Far from the Madding Crowd (Hardy). LFEng 1264-1266; RevLFEng 1500-1502.

Far Journey of Ouidin, The (Harris, W.). LFSup 147; RevLFEng 1529. See also *Guiana Quartet, The.*

Far-off Hills, The (Robinson). DEng 1617-1618; RevDEng 2022-2023.

Far Princess, The (Rostand). DFor 1561-1562.

"Far Rockaway" (Schwartz). PEng 2490; RevPEng 2897.

Far Tortuga (Matthiessen). LFEng 1822-1823, 1826, 1827, 1830-1832; RevLFEng 2308-2309, 2312, 2313, 2316-2318.

"Far West, The" (Snyder). PEng 2672.

"Far Whistle, The" (Beck). ShF 936.

"Far Within Us" (Popa). PFor 1271.

Farce de Maître Pierre Panthelin. DFor 2177.

"Fare to the Moon" (Price). RevShF 1926-1927.

Farewell and Return, The (Crabbe). PEng 646; RevPEng 740.

"Farewell, Go with God!" (Unamuno). PFor 1558.

Farewell, My Lovely (Chandler). LFEng 490; M&D 306-307, 309; RevLFEng 603.

Farewell Party, The (Kundera). LFFor 954.

Farewell to Arms, A (Hemingway). LFEng 1338, 1343-1346; RevLFEng 1601-1603, 3763, 3769.

"Farewell to Cuba" (Cozzens). RevShF 640-641; ShF 1212-1213.

Farewell to Matyora (Rasputin). RevShF 1995.

"Farewell to Tobacco, A" (Lamb). PEng 1636; RevPEng 1900.

"Farewell Without a Guitar" (Stevens). PEng 2750-2751; RevPEng 3211-3212.

Farigoule, Louis-Henri-Jean. *See* **Romains, Jules.**

"Faris" (Mickiewicz). PFor 1020-1021.

Färjesång (Ekelöf). PFor 449, 453.

Farmacia di turnor (De Filippo). DFor 467-468.

Farmer (Harrison). LTEng 1200, 1201; RevLFEng 1537-1539.

Farmer Forsworn, The (Anzengruber). DFor 89-90.

Farmer in His World, The. See *King and the Farmer, The*.

"Farmer's Daughter, The" (D'Urfey). PEng 913.

"Farmers' Daughters, The" (Williams, W. C.). RevShF 2489; ShF 2444-2445.

Farming (Berry). PEng 152-153; RevPEng 182-183.

Farmyard (Kroetz). DFor 1123-1124.

Farquhar, George. RevDEng 721-728, 2697; DEng 579-585, 2177.

Farr, John. *See* **Webb, Jack.**

Farrell, James T. LFEng 906-913, 3062; RevLFEng 1073-1081, 3770; RevShF 841-847; ShF 265-266, 545, 1351-1357.

Farrell, J. G. LFSup 108-113; RevLFEng 1082-1087.

Farsa de Santa Susaña (Sánchez de Badajoz). DFor 2172.

Farther Off from Heaven. See *Dark at the Top of the Stairs, The*.

"Farys." *See* "Faris."

Fashionable Lover, The (Cumberland). DEng 448-450; RevDEng 556-558.

Fashionable Prejudice (La Chaussée). DFor 1141-1142.

Fassbinder, Rainer Werner. DFor 2383.

Fast, Howard. RevLFEng 3838. *See also* **Cunningham, E. V.**

"Fast Lanes" (Phillips). RevShF 1886.

"Fast Train" (Kraus). PFor 797-798.

Fastes d'enfe. See *Chronicles of Hell*.

"Fastest Runner on Sixty-First Street, The" (Farrell). RevShF 844-845; ShF 1355-1356.

"Fat" (Carver). RevShF 436.

Fat Woman's Joke, The. See *. . . And the Wife Ran Away*.

Fata Morgana (Breton). PFor 234.

Fatal Curiosity (Lillo). DEng 1142-1143, 1147-1150, 2178; RevDEng 1434-1435, 1439-1442, 2698.

Fatal Interview (Millay). PEng 2001; RevPEng 2325-2326.

Fatal Inversion, A (Rendell). M&D 1408-1409.

Fatal Revenge (Maturin). LFEng 1838-1839; RevLFEng 2325-2326.

Fatal Skin, The. See *Wild Ass's Skin, The*.

"Fate" (Olds). RevPEng 2492.

Fate at the Wedding. See *Blood Wedding*.

Fate of a Cockroach (Hakim). DSup 177.

Fate of the Jury, The (Masters). PEng 1933; RevPEng 2239.

Fates of the Apostles, The (Cynewulf). PEng 715-717; RevPEng 817-819.

Father, The (Dunlap). DEng 529-530, 2397; RevDEng 652-653, 2918.

"Father, A" (Mukherjee). RevShF 1687-1688.

Father, The (Strindberg). DFor 1750.

Father and Son (Kotzebue). DFor 1088.

"Father and Son" (Kunitz). PSup 243-244; RevPEng 1883-1885.

Father Goriot (Balzac). LFEng 3164; LFFor 98-100; M&D 77.

Father Guzman (Stern). PSup 374-376; RevPEng 3194-3196.

Father Hubburd's Tale (Middleton, T.). PEng 1995-1996.

Father of an Only Child, The (Dunlap). DEng 530-531; RevDEng 653-654.

"Father of My Country, The" (Wakoski). RevPEng 3486.

Father of the Family, The (Diderot). DSup 85-87.

Father of the Plague-Stricken, The (Slowacki). PFor 1443-1444.

Fathers and Sons (Turgenev). LFFor 1775-1777, 2316.

"Father's Story, A" (Dubus). RevShF 784-785.

Father's Words, A (Stern). LFSup 366-367; RevLFEng 3169-3170.

Fauchono. See *Bristo*.

Faulkner, William. LFEng 914-937, 3058, 3063-3064, 3130-3131, 3155-3156; LTh 316, 1273; **M&D 585-591; RevLFEng 1088-1111,** 3766, 3771-3772, 3832-3833, 3840, 3875; **RevShF 848-857;** ShF 250-251, 544-545.

Fausses Confidences, Les. See *False Confessions, The*.

Faust (Goethe). DFor 741-743, 2366-2367.

Faust (Reynolds). ShF 732.

Faust, Frederick Schiller. RevLFEng 3851-3852. *See also* **Brand, Max.**

Faust, Irvin. ShF 2586.

Faustin, La (Goncourt, E.). LFFor 717.

"Faustina" (Bishop). PEng 187; RevPEng 230.

"Faustus" (Hope). PSup 191; RevPEng 1596.

Faustus and the Censor (Empson). LTh 465.

Faute de l'abbé Mouret. See *Abbé Mouret's Transgression*.

Faux-monnayeurs, Les. See *Counterfeiters, The*.

Favores del mundo, Los (Ruiz de Alarcón). DFor 1608-1609.

Fawn, The (Marston). DEng 1271-1273; RevDEng 1596-1598.

Fazendeiro do ar (Drummond de Andrade). PSup 100.

Fear of Heaven, The (Mortimer). DEng 1359; RevDEng 1699.

Fearful Joy, A (Cary). LFEng 458; RevLFEng 578.

Fearing, Kenneth. M&D 592-598; RevPEng 1137-1144.

"Fears in Solitude" (Coleridge, S. T.). PEng 541; RevPEng 632.

Feast in Time of the Plague, The (Pushkin). DFor 1500. See also *Little Tragedies.*

Feast of Lupercal, The (Moore, B.). LFEng 1887-1888; RevLFEng 2392-2394.

"Feast of Stephen, The" (Hecht). PEng 1282.

Feather Cloak Murders, The (Teilhet). M&D 1576-1577.

"Feather Pillow, The" (Quiroga). RevShF 1986-1987.

"Features for Characterizing the Russian Common People" (Dobrolyubov). LTh 389.

"February 1st, 1842" (Coleridge, H.). PEng 529-530.

Fecamps, Elise. *See* **Creasey, John.**

Federman, Raymond. ShF 2587.

Fedin, Konstantin. LFFor 2323.

Fédor, La (Daudet). ShF 1241.

Fedra. See *Phaedra.*

"Feed My Lambs" (O'Faoláin). ShF 2002.

"Feel of Rock, The" (Whittemore). RevPEng 3569.

Féerie pour une autre fois (Céline). LFFor 310-311.

Fegefeuer in Ingolstadt (Fleisser). DFor 610, 615-620.

"Fei-tsao." *See* "Bar of Soap, A."

Feijóo y Montenegro, Benito Jerónimo. LTh 473-477.

Felderman, Eric. ShF 2589.

"Feleségem és kardom." *See* "My Wife and My Sword."

Felhok. See *Clouds.*

Felicidade clandestina (Lispector). RevShF 1492; ShFSup 167-168.

"Félig csókolt csók." *See* "Half-Kissed Kiss."

"Felix Krull" (Mann). ShF 1877.

"Felix Randal" (Hopkins). PEng 1401; RevPEng 1610.

"Feliz anniversário." *See* "Happy Birthday."

Fellow-Culprits, The (Goethe). DFor 735.

Fellow Passengers (Auchincloss). RevShF 117.

Fellowship of the Ring, The. See *Lord of the Rings, The.*

Female Consistory of Brockville, The (Caroli Candidus). DEng 2438; RevDEng 2961.

"Female, Extinct" (Beer). PEng 121-122; RevPEng 141-142.

Female Imagination, The (Spacks). LTh 1769.

Female Imagination and the Modernist Aesthetic, The (Gilbert and Gubar). LTh 581.

Femme fardée, La. See *Painted Lady, The.*

"Femme noire." *See* "Black Woman."

Fen (Churchill). RevDEng 437.

Fences (Wilson, A.). RevDEng 2601-2602.

"Fenchurch Street Mystery, The" (Orczy). M&D 1281-1282.

Fénelon, François de Salignac de La Mothe-. LTh 478-482.

Fenoglio, Beppe. LFFor 2252.

Ferber, Edna. RevDEng 729-738; DEng 586-595.

Ferdinand, Count Fathom (Smollett). LFEng 2449; RevLFEng 3074.

Ferdowsi. *See* **Firdusi.**

Ferdydurke (Gombrowicz). LFFor 698-699.

Ferguson, Helen. *See* **Kavan, Anna.**

Fergusson, Francis. LTh 242, 1756.

Ferlin, Nils. PFor 2178-2179.

Ferlinghetti, Lawrence. PEng 1004-1010, 3381; PSup 405; RevPEng 1145-1152, 3899.

Fermenty (Reymont). LFFor 1407-1408.

Fermo e Lucia. See *Betrothed, The.*

Fernández, Lucas. DFor 2172.

Fernández de Moratín, Leandro. *See* Moratín, Leandro Fernández de.

Feron, Jacques. ShF 640.

Ferrars, Elizabeth. *See* Ferrars, E. X.

Ferrars, E. X. M&D 599-604.

Ferreira, António. DFor 588-595.

Ferrements. See *Shackles.*

"Festival, The" (Duncan). PEng 901; RevPEng 1038.

Fêtes galantes. See *Gallant Parties.*

"Fetish, The" (Moravia). RevShF 1672-1673; ShFSup 197-198.

"Fetish for Love, A" (Laurence). ShF 1778.

Fetterley, Judith. LTh 1807; RevPEng 3970.

Feud, The (Berger). RevLFEng 315.

Feuilles d'automne, Les (Hugo). PFor 733-734.

Fever, The (Shawn). RevDEng 2171-2172.

"Fever" (Wideman). RevShF 2465-2466.

"Few Crusted Characters, A" (Hardy). RevShF 1112; ShF 1583-1584.

Feydeau, Georges. DFor 596-607, 2349.

Fin de Chéri, La. See *Last of Chéri, The.*

"Fin de l'automne, La." *See* "End of Autumn, The."

Fin de partie. See *Endgame.*

Fin de Satan, La (Hugo). PFor 737-738.

Fin del mundo, El (Valdez). DSup 371; RevDEng 2429-2430.

"Fin du Globe" (MacBeth). PEng 1832; RevPEng 2111.

Fin du Potomak, Le (Cocteau). LFFor 362-363.

Final Beast, The (Buechner). LFEng 352; RevLFEng 448-449.

"Final Problem, The" (Doyle). RevShF 769-770; ShF 1302-1303.

"Final Unpleasantness, A" (Zoshchenko). RevShF 2559; ShFSup 381.

Financial Expert, The (Narayan). LFEng 1970-1971; RevLFEng 2485-2486.

Financier, The (Dreiser). LFEng 835-836; RevLFEng 1001-1002.

Fincke, Gary. ShF 2590.

"Find the Woman" (Macdonald). ShF 764.

"Finding a Girl in America" (Dubus). RevShF 784.

Finding Them Lost and Other Poems (Moss). PEng 2066; RevPEng 2398.

Findings (Berry). PEng 151-152; RevPEng 181.

"Findling, Der." *See* "Foundling, The."

Fine! (Mayakovsky). PFor 991-992.

"Fine Accommodations" (Hughes). RevShF 1228; ShF 1659-1660.

"Fine d'agosto." *See* "End of August, The."

"Fine di Crono." *See* "End of Chronos, The."

"Finest Story in the World, The" (Kipling). ShF 1751.

Finger of Destiny and Other Stories (Ayyar). ShF 643.

"Fingers in the Door" (Tuohy). RevShF 2313; ShF 2347-2348.

Finished Man, The (Garrett). LFEng 1091-1092; RevLFEng 1295.

Finishing School, The (Godwin). LFSup 140; RevLFEng 1344-1345.

"Finjamos que soy feliz" (Cruz). PFor 379-380.

Finnegans Wake (Joyce). LFEng 1505-1507, 3057-3058; LTh 424; RevLFEng 1829-1831, 3765-3766.

Firdausi. *See* **Firdusi.**

Firdusi. PSup 119-124.

"Fire and Cloud" (Wright, R.). RevShF 2519-2520; ShF 2463-2465.

"Fire and Ice" (Frost). PEng 1048; RevPEng 1180.

Fire and Ice (Jensen). See *Long Journey, The.*

Fire and the Sun, The (Murdoch). LFEng 1943; RevLFEng 2441, 2452.

"Fire Balloons, The" (Bradbury). RevShF 305.

Fire Down Below (Golding). RevLFEng 1356-1357.

Fire-Dwellers, The (Laurence). LFEng 1574; RevLFEng 1947.

Fire from Heaven (Renault). LFEng 2222; RevLFEng 2813.

"Fire in the Wood, The" (Welch). RevShF 2427.

"Fire Is Dying Down, The" (Brodsky). PFor 238.

Fire Lake (Valin). M&D 1623.

Fire on the Mountain (Desai). LFEng 726-727, 730-731; RevLFEng 872, 873, 876-878.

Fire-Raiser, The. See *Blaze of Roses, A.*

Fire Screen, The (Merrill). RevPEng 2279.

Fire Storm (Roberts). M&D 1443-1445.

"Firebombing, The" (Dickey, J.). PEng 798.

Firebugs, The (Frisch). DFor 645-648, 2262.

Fires (Carver). RevPEng 533-535.

Fires of St. John (Sudermann). DFor 1768-1769.

"First Anniversary" (Donne). PEng 3492.

[First] Book of Urizen, The (Blake). PEng 215; RevPEng 259.

First Circle, The (Solzhenitsyn). LFFor 1645-1646.

First Cities, The (Lorde). RevPEng 2042.

"First Confession" (Kennedy). PEng 1571; RevPEng 1806.

"First Confession" (O'Connor, Frank). RevShF 1771; ShF 1992.

"First Dark" (Spencer). RevShF 2173.

"First-Day Thoughts" (Whittier). PEng 3088; RevPEng 3577.

First Days Entertainment at Rutland House, The (Davenant). DEng 457; RevDEng 566.

First Deadly Sin, The (Sanders). RevLFEng 3847.

"First Death" (Justice). PEng 1533-1534; RevPEng 1758.

"First Eclogue" (Garcilaso). PFor 525-528.

First Fast Draw, The (L'Amour). LFSup 222; RevLFEng 1933.

"First Fish, The" (Beck). ShF 936.

First Fowre Bookes of the Civile Warres, The (Daniel). PEng 723, 729, 3295; RevPEng 826-827, 831-832, 3814.

"First Hour of the Night, The" (Bidart). RevPEng 213-214.

First Hymn to Lenin and Other Poems (MacDiarmid). PSup 263; RevPEng 2123.

"First Lesson" (Booth). RevPEng 302.

"First Love" (Babel). RevShF 126.

"First Love" (Beckett). RevShF 190-191.

Flaubert's Parrot (Barnes). RevLFEng 212-213.

Flavius Magnus Aurelius Cassiodorus Senator. *See* Cassiodorus.

"Flea, The." *See* "Lefty."

"Flea, The" (Donne). PEng 830; RevPEng 936.

"Flea, The" (Leskov). *See* "Lefty."

Flea in Her Ear, A (Feydeau). DFor 600-603.

"Flee on Your Donkey" (Sexton). PEng 2524; RevPEng 2934.

"Fleeing" (Sachs). PFor 1374-1375.

Flegeljahre. See *Walt and Vult.*

Fleisser, Marieluise. DFor 608-626.

Fleming, Ian. M&D 611-616; RevLFEng 3774.

Fleming, Joan. M&D 617-620.

"Flemish Garden, A" (Fuentes). RevShF 926.

Flesh and Blood (Williams, C. K.). PSup 391-392; RevPEng 3606-3607.

"Flesh and the Spirit, The" (Bradstreet). PEng 260-261; RevPEng 321-322.

Fletch and the Widow Bradley (Mcdonald). M&D 1125.

Fletch, Too (Mcdonald). M&D 1127.

Fletcher, Alice. RevPEng 3930.

Fletcher, Giles. PEng 3309.

Fletcher, John. DEng 626-639; PEng 1011-1020; RevDEng 771-784.

Fletcher, John, and Francis Beaumont. DEng 2290, 2299-2301; RevDEng 2809, 2818.

Fletcher, John Gould. PEng 1021-1029.

Fletcher, J. S. M&D 621-628.

Fleurs du Mal, Les. See *Flowers of Evil.*

Flies, The (Sartre). DFor 1641-1642, 1645-1646, 2356.

Flight (Bulgakov). DFor 294-295.

"Flight, The" (Levertov). RevPEng 1985.

"Flight" (Steinbeck). RevShF 2209.

"Flight" (Updike). RevShF 2335.

Flight from Nevèrÿon (Delany). RevLFEng 854.

Flight of Swans, A (Tagore). PFor 1483-1484, 1485.

Flight to Arras (Saint-Exupéry). LFFor 1485.

Flight to Canada (Reed). LFSup 340; RevLFEng 2804.

"Flights of Fancy" (Trevor). RevShF 2308; ShFSup 323-324.

"Flip of a Coin, The" (Maugham). M&D 1202-1203.

Floating Admiral, The (Whitechurch, with others). M&D 1715.

Floating Island series (Machado). See *Modern Ladies of Guanabacoa, The; Fabiola; In the Eye of the Hurricane; Broken Eggs.*

Floating Opera, The (Barth). LFEng 159-161; RevLFEng 221-223.

Fløgstad, Kjartan. LFFor 2364.

Flood (Grass). DSup 156-157.

"Flood, The" (Richter). ShF 601-602.

"Flood, The" (Tomlinson). RevPEng 3381.

"Flood, The" (Zamyatin). RevShF 2537; ShFSup 372-373.

Floodtide of Fate (Duun). LFFor 2351.

"Flophouse" (Fearing). RevPEng 1141.

Flor de mayo. See *Mayflower, The.*

Floricanto en Aztlán (Alurista). RevPEng 3922.

Florus. PFor 2104.

Floss der Medusa, Das. See *Raft of the Medusa, The.*

Flounder, The (Grass). LFFor 737.

Flow My Tears, the Policeman Said (Dick). LFSup 98; RevLFEng 898.

Flower, Pat. M&D 629-633.

"Flower-fed Buffaloes, The" (Lindsay). PEng 1727; RevPEng 2011.

Flower, Fist and Bestial Wail (Bukowski). PEng 357; RevPEng 430.

Flower, Fruit, and Thorn Pieces (Jean Paul). LFFor 875-876.

"Flower Given to My Daughter, A" (Joyce). PEng 1525, 1526; RevPEng 1750.

"Flower Herding on Mount Monadnock" (Kinnell). PEng 1596.

"Flower of Buffoonery, The" (Dazai). LFFor 433-434.

"Flower Piece, A" (Bates). RevShF 174; ShFSup 30.

"Flowering Judas" (Porter). RevShF 1909; ShF 2112-2113.

Flowering Peach, The (Odets). DEng 1404; RevDEng 1780.

Flowers Are Not for You to Pick, The (Guthrie). RevDEng 3033.

Flowers of Evil (Baudelaire). PFor 133-139.

Flowres of Sion (Drummond of Hawthornden). PEng 866; RevPEng 982.

Flush Times of Alabama and Mississippi, The (Baldwinblack, J. G.). ShF 613.

"Flux" (Eberhart). RevPEng 1062.

"Fly, The" (Mansfield). RevShF 1599, 2725-2726.

Flying Goat, The (Bates). RevShF 175; ShFSup 31.

"Flying Home" (Ellison, R.). ShF 580.

Flying Islands of the Night, The (Riley). PEng 2372; RevPEng 2762.

Flynn's In (Mcdonald). M&D 1128.

F. M. (Linney). DSup 238. See also *Laughing Stock.*
Fo, Dario. DFor 2415; **Dsup 106-115.**
F.O.B. (Hwang). RevDEng 1227.
"Foetal Song" (Oates). RevPEng 2466.
Fog (Patrick, R.). DEng 1478; RevDEng 1860-1861.
"Fog Horn, The" (Bradbury). ShF 565.
Fog of Doubt (Brand). M&D 194.
Fogazzaro, Antonio. LFFor 2234-2235.
Foggage (McGinley). RevLFEng 2191, 2192.
Foix, J. V. PFor 482-490, 1775.
Folded Leaf, The (Maxwell). RevLFEng 2344.
Folie du sage, La (Tristan). DFor 1895.
Folie et déraison. See *Madness and Civilization.*
Folies amoureuses, Les (Regnard). DFor 1542-1543.
"Folk Singer of the Thirties, A" (Dickey, J.). PEng 797.
Folke, Will. *See* **Bloch, Robert.**
Folktale, The (Thompson). ShF 153-154.
Folkungaträdet. See *Tree of the Folkungs, The.*
Follain, Jean. PSup 125-132.
Follas novas (Castro). PFor 279-280.
"Folle, La." *See* "Madwoman, The."
Folle de Chaillot, La. See *Madwoman of Chaillot, The.*
Folle Journée. See *Marriage of Figaro, The.*
Follett, Ken. M&D 634-639.
Follies of a Day. See *Marriage of Figaro, The.*
Follow Me Down (Foote). LFEng 974-975; RevLFEng 1157-1158.
"Follow That Stagecoach" (Wakoski). RevPEng 3485.
"Follower" (Heaney). RevPEng 1442.
Folly or Saintliness (Echegaray). DFor 529-531, 2500.
Foma Gordeyev (Gorky). LFFor 724-725.
"Fonction et champ de la parole et du langage en psychoanalyse." *See* "Language of the Self, The."
Fong and the Indians (Theroux). LFEng 2630-2631; RevLFEng 3283-3284.
"Fontaine de Vaucluse, La" (Hacker). RevPEng 1363.
Fontamara (Silone). LFFor 1586-1587.
Fontane, Theodor. LFFor 559-569, 2176-2178; LTh 1718, 1720.
Fontenelle, Bernard de. LTh 841, 1683.
Fonvizin, Denis Ivanovich. DFor 627-639, 2452; LFFor 2308.
F.O.O. *See* Rhode, John.

"Food for Fire, Food for Thought" (Duncan). PEng 903; RevPEng 1039.
Food for the Millions (Hakim). DSup 178.
"Food of Love" (Kizer). RevPEng 1859.
Food of the Gods, and How It Came to Earth, The (Wells). RevLFEng 3482.
Fool, The (Bond). DEng 251; RevDEng 292.
Fool for Love (Shepard). DEng 1766, 1767; RevDEng 2198-2199.
Fool in Christ, Emanuel Quint, The (Hauptmann). LFFor 2183.
Fool Killer, The (Eustis). M&D 583-584.
"Foolish Pride" (Castro). PFor 278. See also *Follas novas.*
Fools of Time (Frye). LTh 512.
"Fools Say" (Sarraute). LFFor 1506-1507.
Foote, Samuel. DEng 640-649, 2337; **RevDEng 785-794,** 2856.
Foote, Shelby. LFEng 968-981; **RevLFEng 1151-1164;** ShF 288.
Footnote to Youth: Tales of the Philippines and Others (Villa). PEng 2976-2977; PFor 1644 RevPEng 3463-3464.
Footsteps of Doves, The (Anderson, R.). DEng 38; RevDEng 50. See also *You Know I Can't Hear You When the Water's Running.*
"For a Breath I Tarry" (Zelazny). ShF 373.
"For a Freshman Reader" (Justice). PEng 1530; RevPEng 1755.
"For a Lamb" (Eberhart). RevPEng 1058-1059.
"For a Marriage" (Bogan). PEng 232; RevPEng 279.
For a New Novel (Robbe-Grillet). LTh 1233-1234.
"For a Young Artist" (Hayden). PEng 1247; RevPEng 1431-1432.
"For Anna Mae Pictou Aquash . . ." (Harjo). RevPEng 3936.
"For Anne at Passover" (Kumin). RevPEng 1873.
"For Black People" (Madhubuti). PEng 1896; RevPEng 2200.
for colored girls who have considered suicide/ when the rainbow is enuf (Shange). DSup 328-329; RevDEng 2141-2142.
"For Esmé—with Love and Squalor" (Salinger). RevShF 2040-2041; ShF 290-291, 2178-2179.
"For Esther" (Plumly). PEng 2237; RevPEng 2609.
"For Fran" (Levine). PEng 1714; RevPEng 1990.
"For George Lamming" (Birney). PEng 179-180; RevPEng 221.
"For Homer" (Corso). PEng 579; RevPEng 675.
"For Jan, in Bar Maria" (Kizer). PEng 1618.

Fourteen Sonnets (Bowles). PEng 251; RevPEng 311-312.

Fourth Commandment, The (Anzengruber). DFor 91-92, 2373.

Fourth Deadly Sin, The (Sanders). M&D 1464.

Fourth Postman, The (Rice). M&D 1423-1424.

Fourth Protocol, The (Forsyth). M&D 648.

Fous des Bassan, Les. See *In the Shadow of the Wind.*

Fowler, Roger. PEng 3458-3459; RevPEng 3993-3994.

Fowles, John. LFEng 1008-1022; LFSup 403; RevLFEng 1199-1215; Rev ShF 890-896; ShF 1393-1399.

Fowre Hymnes (Spenser). PEng 2707; RevPEng 3151.

"Fox, The" (Lawrence, D. H.). LFEng 3315-3317.

Fox, The (Lawrence, D. H.). RevShF 2737.

Fox, Robert. ShF 2593.

Fox Fables (Berechiah ben Natronai ha-Nakdan, Rabbi). RevShF 2579; ShF 380-381.

"Fox Hunt" (Still). PEng 2763; RevPEng 3226.

Foxe, John. ShF 498.

Foxes of Harrow, The (Yerby). LFEng 2987-2988; RevLFEng 3693-3694.

Foxprints (McGinley). M&D 1150-1152; RevLFEng 2191, 2192.

Fox's Paw, The (Pérez de Ayala). LFFor 1256-1257.

Foxx, Jack. *See* **Pronzini, Bill.**

Foxybaby (Jolley). LFSup 180-181; RevLFEng 1793-1794.

Fra det moderne Amerikas aandsliv. See *Spiritual Life of Modern America, The.*

Fracastoro, Girolamo. PFor 499-510.

"Fragment of the Lives of Three Friends, A" (Hoffman). RevShF 1215; ShF 1648.

"Fragment on Death" (Swinburne). PEng 2822; RevPEng 3290.

Fragments (Anacreon). PFor 35-38.

Fragments (Archilochus). PFor 88-91.

Fragments (Armah). LFEng 86-88; RevLFEng 124-126.

Fragments (Sappho). PFor 1396-1400.

"Fragments of a Liquidation" (Howe). PSup 195-196; RevPEng 1631.

Frailty and Hypocrisy (Beaumarchais). DFor 153.

Frana allo scalo nord. See *Landslide.*

France, Anatole. LFFor 570-580; RevShF 897-903; ShF 1400-1407.

Francesca da Rimini (Boker). DEng 222-224, 2398; RevDEng 263-265, 2919.

Francesca da Rimini (D'Annunzio). DFor 2412.

Francesco's Fortunes (Greene). PEng 1149-1150, 1151; RevPEng 1307-1308.

Franchiser, The (Elkin). LFEng 891-892; RevLFEng 1049.

Francis, Dick. M&D 651-655.

Francis, H. E. ShF 2594.

Franco, Marjorie. ShF 2596.

Francoeur Novels, The (Plante). LFSup 307-310; RevLFEng 2643-2646.

Frank (Edgeworth). ShF 1323.

"Frank Courtship, The" (Crabbe). PEng 644; RevPEng 738.

Frank, I-IV (Edgeworth). RevShF 797-798.

Frank, Joseph. RevPEng 3995.

Frank, Leonhard. ShF 2597.

Frankenstein (Shelley, M.). LFEng 2386, 2388-2389, 3129, 3139-3140, 3141; RevLFEng 3016-3017, 3831; ShF 179, 475, 735.

"Frankie and Johnnie" (Brown). RevPEng 390.

Frankie and Johnnie (Kirkland). DEng 1048-1049; RevDEng 1325-1326.

Frankie and Johnny in the Clair de Lune (McNally). RevDEng 1555-1556.

Franklin, Benjamin. LTh 1741; RevShF 904-909, 2644; ShF 1408-1414.

"Franklin's Tale, The" (Chaucer). PEng 3265-3266; RevPEng 584, 3784-3785; RevShF 495-496; ShF 1113, 1115-1116.

"Franny" (Salinger). RevShF 2043-2045.

Franzén, Frans Mikael. PFor 2162.

Fraser, Lady Antonia. M&D 656-660.

Fraternity (Galsworthy). LFEng 1061-1062; RevLFEng 1260-1261.

Frau Jenny Treibel. See *Jenny Treibel.*

Frau Jutta (Schernberg). DFor 2169-2170.

Frayn, Michael. DSup 125-132; RevDEng 828-836.

Frazer, Fred. *See* **Avallone, Michael.**

Frazer, Robert Caine. *See* **Creasey, John.**

Freaky Deaky (Leonard). RevLFEng 2029.

Freddy's Book (Gardner, J.). LFEng 1079-1080; RevLFEng 1279-1280.

Frederic, Harold. LFEng 1023-1033; RevLFEng 1216-1227.

"Frederic and Elfrida" (Austen). RevShF 120.

Frederic and Elfrida (Austen). ShF 896-897.

"Fredericksbury" (Aldrich). PEng 34.

Fredro, Aleksander. DFor 2277; DSup 133-141.

Free Fall (Golding). LFEng 1133-1134; RevLFEng 1353.

Free Fall in Crimson (MacDonald, J.). M&D 1132.

"Free Fiction" (Canby). ShF 72.
"Free Joe and the Rest of the World" (Harris, J.). RevShF 1118-1119; ShF 1589-1590.
Free-Lance Pallbearers, The (Reed). LFSup 337; RevLFEng 2801-2802.
Free Union (Breton). PFor 233-234.
"Free Will" (Pavese). RevShF 1863.
"Freedom and Discipline" (Carruth). RevPEng 527.
Freedom for Clemens (Dorst). DSup 93.
"Freedom Kick, The" (Foote). LFEng 979; RevLFEng 1162.
Freedom of the City, The (Friel). DEng 675-676; RevDEng 842-843.
Freedom or Death (Kazantzakis). LFFor 920.
"Freedom's a Hard-Bought Thing" (Benét). RevShF 212-213; ShF 956-957.
Freeing of the Dust, The (Levertov). PEng 1709.
Freeling, Nicholas. M&D 661-666.
Freeman, Mary E. Wilkins. RevShF 910-917, 2711; ShF 228-229, **1415-1422.**
Freeman, R. Austin. M&D 667-673; ShF 753.
Freeman, Susannah. *See* **Centlivre, Mrs, Susannah.**
Freeway, The (Nichols). DSup 282; RevDEng 1731.
"Freezing" (Meredith). PEng 1957.
Freiheit für Clemens. See *Freedom for Clemens.*
Fremsynte, Den. See *Visionary, The.*
"French Lessons" (Rasputin). RevShF 1994.
French Lieutenant's Woman, The (Fowles). LFEng 1016-1018; RevLFEng 1207-1209.
French Revolution, The (Blake). PEng 213; RevPEng 257.
French Vulgate Cycle. LFEng 1802; RevLFEng 2279.
French Without Tears (Rattigan). DEng 1559-1561; RevDEng 1951-1953.
Freneau, Philip. PEng 1030-1038; RevPEng 1161-1170.
Frenssen, Gustav. LFFor 2182.
Frères Zemganno, Les. See *Zemganno Brothers, The.*
Frescoes for Mr. Rockefeller's City (MacLeish). PEng 1857; RevPEng 2156-2157.
"Fresh Snow, A" (Humphrey). RevShF 1235.
Freud, Sigmund. LTh 214, 359, 685, 760, 833-834, 844-851, 890-891, 988, 1273, 1318, 1712, 1737, 1763-1764, 1767, 1822-1823; PEng 3419-3420; PFor 229-230.
Freund, Edith. ShF 2598.
Freyre, Isabel. PFor 523-524.
Freytag, Gustav. LFFor 2174.

Friar Bacon and Friar Bungay (Greene, R.). DEng 840-841, 2270-2271; PEng 1150; RevDEng 1035-1036, 2789-2790; RevPEng 1308.
"Friar Jerome's Beautiful Book" (Aldrich). PEng 31.
Fribytaren på Östersjön (Rydberg). LFFor 2337.
Friday (Tournier). LFFor 1740-1743.
Friday the Rabbi Slept Late (Kemelman). M&D 968.
Fridegård, Jan. LFFor 2349.
Friedman, Bruce Jay. RevShF 918-923; ShF 1423-1428.
Friedman, Thomas. ShF 2599.
Friel, Brian. DEng 671-679, 2449; **RevDEng 837-846,** 2973.
"Friend of the Family, A" (Simpson). RevPEng 3010.
Friendly Persuasion, The (West). RevShF 2449-2450; ShFSup 362.
Friends (Abe). DFor 2434.
"Friends" (Williams, C. K.). PSup 390; RevPEng 3605.
"Friend's Song" (Otero). PFor 1111.
"Friendship" (Thoreau). PEng 2902; RevPEng 3370.
Friendship in Fashion (Otway). DEng 1447-1448; RevDEng 1827-1828.
"Frightened Man, The" (Bogan). PEng 234; RevPEng 281.
Fringe of Leaves, A (White, P.). LFEng 2876-2877; RevLFEng 3555-3556.
Frisch, Max. DFor 640-650, 2261-2262, 2380-2382; **LFFor 581-590,** 2199, 2201, 2209-2210; LFSup 403.
Fritenkjar, Ein (Garborg). LFFor 2341.
Frithofs saga. LFFor 2333.
Fritz Kochers Aufsätze (Walser, R.). RevShF 2389; ShFSup 346.
Fröding, Gustaf. PFor 2171-2172.
Frogs, The (Aristophanes). DFor 119-120, 2129.
Fröhliche Weinberg, Der (Zuckmayer). DFor 2071-2073.
Fröken Julie. See *Miss Julie.*
"Frol Skobeev, The Rogue." LFFor 2303.
"From a Notebook" (Levertov). PEng 1709.
From a View to a Death (Powell, A.). LFEng 2117; RevLFEng 2676.
"From all these events, from the slum, from the war, from the boom" (Spender). PEng 2702; RevPEng 3146.
"From an Airplane" (Akhmatova). PFor 13.

G

Gaboriau, Émile. M&D 680-686.

Gabriel (Pushkin). PFor 1296.

Gabriela, Clove and Cinnamon (Amado). LFFor 53-54.

Gabriela, cravo e canela. See *Gabriela, Clove and Cinnamon.*

Gadamer, Hans-Georg. LTh 527-532, 766, 1770.

Gadda, Carlo Emilio. LFFor 602-611, 2253.

Gaddis, William. LFEng 1034-1041; LFSup 403; RevLFEng 1228-1237.

Gaines, Ernest J. LFEng 1042-1049; LFSup 403; ShF 582, 1429-1436; RevLFEng 1238-1247; RevShF 931-937, 2753.

Gaius Cornelius Gallus. *See* Gallus.

Gaius Julius Caesar. *See* Caesar, Gaius Julius.

Gaius Plinius Caecilius Secundus. *See* Pliny the Younger.

Gaius Sallustius Crispus. *See* Sallust.

Gaius Valerius Catullus. *See* **Catullus.**

Gaius Vetteius Aquilinus Juvencus. *See* Juvencus.

Gaj, Ljudevit. PFor 2262.

Gala (West, P.). LFSup 375; RevLFEng 3526.

Galanskov, Yuri. PFor 2151.

Galanteries du duc d'Ossonne, Les (Mairet). DFor 1248-1249.

Galathea (Lyly). DEng 1182-1184; RevDEng 1182-1184, 1484, 1485-1486.

Galaxy. ShF 585, 587-588, 767, 776.

Galdós, Benito Pérez. LFEng 3171.

"Galeso et Maximo, De" (Bembo). PFor 168.

Galgenlieder. See *Gallows Songs, The.*

Galich, Manuel. DFor 2445.

Galileo. See *Life of Galileo.*

Gallant, Mavis. LFEng 1050-1056; RevLFEng 1248-1255; RevShF 938-942; ShF 551, 640, 1437-1440; ShFSup 388;

Gallant Parties (Verlaine). PFor 1629-1631.

Gallery, The (Burns). ShF 274.

Gallicanus (Hroswitha). DFor 2153.

Gallico, Paul. ShF 1441-1445.

Gallina, Giacinto. DFor 2410.

"Gallina degollada, La." *See* "Decapitated Chicken, The."

Gallows of Chance, The (Oppenheim). M&D 1275.

Gallows Songs, The (Morgenstern). PFor 1057.

Gallus. PFor 2097.

"Galope muerto." *See* "Dead Gallop."

Galsworthy, John. DEng 709-717; LFEng 1057-1066, 3052, 3082; RevDEng 886-895; RevLFEng 1256-1266, 3760, 3791; RevShF 943-948; ShF 1446-1451.

Galton Case, The (Macdonald). LFSup 274-275; RevLFEng 2173-2174.

Gálvez, Manuel. LFFor 2287.

Galvin, Brendan. PEng 1050-1057; PSup 405; RevPEng 1183-1192.

Gambaro, Griselda. DFor 2444; DSup 142-152.

Gambler, The (Betti). DFor 210.

Gamboa, Federico. DFor 2442; LFFor 2285.

Game, The (Euba). DEng 2422; RevDEng 2944.

"Game After Supper" (Atwood). RevPEng 75.

Game at Chess, A (Middleton). DEng 1326; RevDEng 1663.

Game of Love and Chance, The (Marivaux). DFor 1265-1266, 2339.

"Games" (Popa). PFor 1270.

"Games Without End" (Calvino). RevShF 395.

Gamester, The (Centlivre). DEng 346-347; RevDEng 407-408.

Gamlet (Sumarokov). DFor 1785-1786.

Gammer Gurton's Needle (Stevenson?). DEng 2257, 2264; RevDEng 2777, 2783.

Ganar amigos (Ruiz de Alarcón). DFor 1606-1607.

"Gander-pulling, The" (Longstreet). RevShF 1503-1504; ShF 1816-1817.

Gandhi (Trivadi). DFor 2391.

Gandhi, Mahatma. ShF 643.

"Gangrene" (Levine). PEng 1714; RevPEng 1990.

"Gangu." *See* "Toys."

"Ganymed" (Goethe). PFor 585-586.

"Ganymed" (Hölderlin). PFor 686. See also *Nachtgesänge.*

Gao Ming. See **Kao Ming.**

Gao Tsê-ch'êng. See **Kao Ming.**

Gaol Gate, The (Gregory). DEng 853-854; RevDEng 1049-1050.

Går an, Det. See *Sara Videbeck.*

"Garbage" (Slavitt). RevPEng 3053.

Garber, Eugene K. ShF 2602.

Garborg, Arne. DFor 2470-2471; LFFor 2341; PFor 2170.

García Guitiérrez, Antonio. DFor 2498.

Gathering Storm, The (Empson). PEng 965, 971; RevPEng 1101.

"Gathering the Bones Together" (Orr). PEng 2151-2152; RevPEng 2519, 2521-2522.

Gathering the Tribes (Forché). RevPEng 1155-1158.

Gatomachia (Vega). PFor 1603-1604.

Gatti, Armand. DFor 2360.

Gatto, Alfonso. PFor 2045, 2048.

Gattopardo, Il. See *Leopard, The*.

Gaudette (Hughes, T.). PEng 1445; RevPEng 1652-1654.

Gaudy Night (Sayers). LFEng 2361-2362; M&D 1477-1478; RevLFEng 2977-2978.

Gault, William Campbell. M&D 711-716.

Gaunt, Graham. *See* **Gash, Jonathan.**

Gauntlet, A (Bjørnson). DFor 218.

"Gautami" (Bunin). RevShF 344.

Gauthier-Villars, Henri. LFFor 367-368.

Gautier, Théophile. LTh 113, **551-557,** 1732; PFor **529-541,** 1872-1873; RevShF 2667; ShF 172.

"Gavin O'Leary" (Collier). RevShF 590-591.

Gavriiliada. See *Gabriel*.

Gawain-Poet. *See* **Pearl-Poet, The.**

Gay, John. DEng **729-736,** 2179; PEng **1069-1078;** RevDEng **908-916,** 2699; **RevPEng 1204-1214;** ShF 143, 455.

"Gazebo" (Carver). ShFSup 78.

"Gazing at Yellow Crane Mountain" (Li Po). PFor 891.

Gde tonko, tam i rvyotsya. See *Where It Is Thin, There It Breaks*.

Gdzie wschodzi słońce i kędy zapada (Miłosz). PFor 1035-1036.

Ge-sar epic, The. PFor 2245-2246.

"Gebet, Das." See "Prayer, The."

"Gebet des Zoraster." *See* "Prayer of Zarathustra."

"Gebildete Nation." *See* "Cultured Nation."

Gebir (Landor). PEng 1643; RevPEng 1908.

Geburt der Tragödie aus dem Geiste der Musik, Die. See *Birth of Tragedy Out of the Spirit of Music, The*.

"Gedali" (Babel). RevShF 128-129.

Gedanken über die Nachahmung der griechischen Werke in der Malerei und Bildhauerkunst. See *Reflections on the Paintings and Sculpture of the Greeks*.

"Gedicht, Das." *See* "Poem, The."

Gedichten, gezangen en gebeden (Gezelle). PFor 555-557.

"Geese, The" (Graham). RevPEng 1274.

"Gefesselte Strom, Der." *See* "Chained Stream, The."

Geijer, Erik Gustaf. PFor 2165-2166.

Geijerstam, Gustaf af. LFFor 2340.

Geistliche Lieder (Luther). See *Spiritual Songs*.

Geistliche Lieder (Novalis). See *Devotional Songs*.

Gelber, Jack. DEng **737-746,** 2481; **RevDEng 917-926,** 3008.

"Gelding of the Devil, The" (D'Urfey). PEng 912.

Geller, Ruth. ShF 2604.

Gellius, Aulus. LTh 1681.

Gelzer, Johann Heinrich. LTh 436.

"Gemeine, Das" (Dazai). RevShF 694; ShFSup 95-96.

Gemini (Giovanni). PEng 1097, 1099, 1100, 1101-1102; RevPEng 1240-1241.

Gemini (Innaurato). DSup 202-203; RevDEng 1247-1248.

Gemini (Tournier). LFFor 1745-1746.

Gemini Contenders, The (Ludlum). M&D 1109-1110.

Genealogia deorum gentilium (Boccaccio). LTh 172, 1655, 1668-1669.

General Confession (Davies). DEng 469, 470; RevDEng 579-580, 470.

"General Prologue" to *The Canterbury Tales* (Chaucer). PEng 486, 3262-3263; RevPEng 582, 3781-3782.

"General William Booth Enters into Heaven" (Lindsay). PEng 1721, 1723-1724; RevPEng 2007-2008.

"General's Day, The" (Trevor). RevShF 2305; ShFSup 320-321.

General's Ring, The. See *Ring of the Löwenskölds, The*.

Generation Without Farewell (Boyle, K.). LFEng 279-280; RevLFEng 344.

"Generations" (Gurney). PEng 1180; RevPEng 1341.

Generous Man, A (Price). LFEng 2131-2132; RevLFEng 2700, 2703-2704.

Genesis. ShF 330-335, 337-342.

"Genesis" (Elýtis). PFor 465, 1967. See also *Axion Esti, The*.

"Genesis" (Hill, G.). PEng 1349-1352; RevPEng 1520.

Genet, Jean. DFor **674-690,** 2258-2260, 2358; LFFor **621-634;** LFSup 404; LTh 1274.

Genette, Gérard. LTh 195, **558-564,** 1437.

Genezis z Ducha (Słowacki). PFor 1446.

Gengandere. See *Ghosts*.

"Genial Host, The" (McCarthy). ShF 124-125.

Génie du Christianisme, Le. See *Genius of Christianity, The.*

"Genio e tendenze di Tommasco Carlyle." *See* "On the Genius and Tendency of the Writing of Thomas Carlyle."

Genitrix (Mauriac). LFFor 1126-1127.

Genius, The (Brenton). DSup 34-35; RevDEng 322.

Genius and the Goddess, The (Huxley). LFEng 1409-1410; RevLFEng 1685-1686.

Genius of Christianity, The (Chateaubriand). LFFor 333-334, 2124.

Genius of the Crowd, The (Bukowski). PEng 359; RevPEng 432.

Genji monogatari. See *Tale of Genji, The.*

"Genoveva" (Trench). PEng 2934-2935.

Gente conocida (Benavente). DFor 177.

Gentile, Giovanni. LTh 328.

"Gentilesse" (Chaucer). RevShF 482; ShF 1101-1102.

Gentle Grafter, The (Henry). M&D 855-856; ShF 1632-1633.

Gentle Weight Lifter, The (Ignatow). PEng 1471; RevPEng 1683.

"Gentleman, The" (Guillén). PFor 626-627.

Gentleman Dancing-Master, The (Wycherley). DEng 2107-2109; RevDEng 2626-2628.

"Gentleman from Cracow, The" (Singer). RevShF 2741-2742.

"Gentleman from San Francisco, The" (Bunin). RevShF 345-346.

"Gentleman of Shalott, The" (Bishop). PEng 185; RevPEng 228.

Gentleman Usher, The (Chapman). DEng 356-357; RevDEng 417-418.

"Gentlemen and Players" (Hornung). M&D 907.

Gentlemen, I Address You Privately (Boyle, K.). LFEng 276-277; RevLFEng 341-342.

Gentlemen in England (Wilson, A. N.). LFSup 390-391; N.). RevLFEng 3584-3585.

Gentlemen in Their Season (Fielding, G.). LFSup 117-118; RevLFEng 1113, 1114, 1115-1116.

Geoffrey of Vinsauf. LTh 22, **565-570,** 1652.

"Geographer" (Hacker). PEng 1189-1190; RevPEng 1362.

Geography of a Horse Dreamer (Shepard). RevDEng 2195-2196.

Geography of Lograire, The (Merton). PEng 1977; RevPEng 2295.

Geography of Poets, A (Field, ed.). ShF 316.

"Geography of the Near Past" (Young). PEng 3216-3217; RevPEng 3740-3741.

Geography of the Near Past (Young). PEng 3215; RevPEng 3739-3742.

"Geometry" (Dove). RevPEng 956.

"George" (Randall, D.). PEng 2314-2315; RevPEng 2704-2705.

George, Albert. RevShF 2690.

George, Stefan. LTh **571-577,** 639-641; **PFor** **542-550,** 670-671, 1924.

George Mills (Elkin). RevLFEng 1049-1050.

George Silverman's Explanation (Dickens). RevShF 723-724; ShF 1270-1271.

George Washington Poems, The (Wakoski). PEng 2997; RevPEng 3485-3486.

Georges, Georges-Martin. *See* **Simenon, Georges.**

George's Mother (Crane). LFEng 641; RevLFEng 774.

Georgia Scenes (Longstreet). RevShF 1502-1505, 2660; ShF 613, 1814.

"Georgia Theatrics" (Longstreet). RevShF 1502-1503; ShF 1815-1816.

Georgics (Vergil). LTh 1043; PFor 1606, 1609-1611; RevShF 2350, 2351; ShF 2385.

Gerald's Party (Coover). RevLFEng 756-757.

Gerammelten Gedichte (Zweig). PFor 1725-1726.

Gerber, Merrill Joan. ShF 2605.

German Mythology (Grimm, J.). ShF 1556.

"German Refugee, The" (Malamud). RevShF 1573.

Germania Tod in Berlin (Müller). DSup 260-261.

"Germanic Materials and Motifs in the Short Story" (Pochman). ShF 87.

Germanicus. DFor 2147.

Germany (Staël). LTh 1380, 1382-1383, 1696, 1704.

Germany: A Winter's Tale (Heine). LTh 663-664; PFor 648, 650.

Germinal (Zola). LFFor 1994. See also *Rougon-Macquart, Les.*

Germinie Lacerteux (Goncourts). LFFor 714-715.

Gernsback, Hugo. LFEng 3209.

Geronimo Rex (Hannah). RevLFEng 1482-1483.

"Gerontion" (Eliot). PEng 943; RevPEng 1072.

Gerould, Katherine Fullerton. RevShF 2672-2673; ShF 177.

Geroy nashego vremeni. See *Hero of Our Time, A.*

Gerpla. See *Happy Warriors, The.*

Gershwin, George, and Ira Gershwin. RevDEng 1167, 1170-1171, 2996.

Gerusalemme conquistata. See *Jerusalem Conquered.*

Gerusalemme liberata. See *Jerusalem Delivered.*

Gervinus, Georg Gottfried. LTh 436.

Gesammelte Werke in sieben Bänden (Ausländer). PSup 18.

"Gesang für meine Genossen." *See* "Song for My Comrades."

Geschichte der alten und neuen Literatur. See Lectures on the History of Literature Ancient and Modern.

Geschichte der Kunst des Alterthums. See History of Ancient Art.

Geschichte der Poesie der Griechen und Römer (Schlegel, F.). LTh 1310.

Geschichte der poetischen Literatur Deutschlands (Eichendorff). LTh 436-438.

Geschichte der poetischen National-Literatur der Deutschen (Gervinus). LTh 436.

Geschichte des Fräuleins von Sternheim. See History of Lady Sophia Sternheim.

Geschichte und Klassenbewusstsein. See History and Class Consciousness.

Geschichten aus dem Wiener Wald. See Tales from the Vienna Woods.

Geschichten Jakobs, Die. See Tales of Jacob, The.

Gesellschaft im Herbst (Dorst). DSup 93-94.

Gespräch im Hause Stein über den abwesenden Herrn von Goethe, Ein (Hacks). DFor 854.

Gespräch über die Poesie. See "Dialogue on Poetry."

"Gest Historiale of the Destruction of Troy, The." ShF 447.

Gesta Danorum (Saxo Grammaticus). LFFor 2333.

Gesta Regum Anglorum. See Acts of the Kings.

Gestalt am Ende des Grundstücks, Die. See Figure on the Boundary Line, The.

Gesticulador, El (Usigli). DFor 2443; DSup 362-363.

Gestiefelte Kater, Der. See Puss-in-Boots.

Gestohlene Bachern, Der (Sachs). DFor 1625-1626.

Gestundete Zeit, Die (Bachmann). PFor 126-127.

"Get on with the Sleeping" (Zoshchenko). RevShF 2556; ShFSup 377-378.

Get Ready for Battle (Jhabvala). LFSup 174; RevLFEng 1756.

Get Shorty (Leonard). RevLFEng 2029-2030.

Geteilte Himmel, Der. See Divided Heaven.

Getting a Way with Murder (McInerny). M&D 1162-1163.

Getting Away with Murder? See Murder Post-Dated.

"Getting into Death" (Disch). RevShF 745; ShF 1288.

Getting into Death (Disch). RevShF 745-747; ShF 1289-1290.

Getting Out (Norman). DSup 290; RevDEng 1740-1741.

Gewicht der Welt, Das. See Weight of the World, The.

"Gezeiten." *See* "Tides."

Gezelle, Guido. PFor 551-561.

Ghare baire. See Home and the World.

"Ghaselen II." *See* "Ghazel II."

"Ghazals" (Rich). RevPEng 2755-2756.

"Ghazel II" (Hofmannsthal). PFor 673-674.

Ghelderode, Michel de. DFor 691-699.

Ghetto (Heijermans). DFor 813.

Ghose, Aurobindo. *See* Aurobindo, Sri.

Ghose, Kasiprasad. PFor 1994.

Ghose, Manmohan. PFor 1999.

Ghost Horse Cycle, The (Highwater). RevLFEng 1625-1626.

Ghost in the Machine, The (Koestler). LFEng 1550; RevLFEng 1916.

Ghost It Was, The (Hull). M&D 917.

Ghost of Lucrece, The (Middleton, T.). PEng 1995.

Ghost Sonata, The (Strindberg). DFor 1754-1755.

Ghost Stories and Tales of Mystery (Le Fanu). RevShF 1443; ShF 1796.

Ghost Way, The (Hillerman). M&D 881-882.

Ghost Writer, The (Roth). LFEng 2308-2309; RevLFEng 2901-2902, 3877-3878.

"Ghostly Father, I Confess" (McCarthy). RevShF 1536-1537; ShF 1837-1838.

Ghostly Lover, The (Hardwick). LFEng 1256-1257; RevLFEng 1492.

"Ghosts, The" (Dunsany). RevShF 2722-2723.

Ghosts (Ibsen). DFor 982-983, 2472.

Ghosts of the Heart (Logan). PEng 1740; RevPEng 2025.

"Giacca stregata, La." *See* "Bewitched Jacket, The."

"Giacchetta di cuoio, La." *See* "Leather Jacket, The."

Giacosa, Giuseppe. DFor 700-710, 2410.

Giall, An (Behan). RevDEng 201.

Giambi ed epodi (Carducci). PFor 270-271.

"Giardino incantato, Il" (Calvino). ShF 1043-1044.

Gibbs, Henry. *See* **Harvester, Simon.**

Giboyer's Son (Augier). DFor 138-140.

Gibran, Kahlil. PEng 1079-1087; PFor 562-570. RevPEng 1215-1223.

Gibson, Morgan. ShF 2606.

Gibson, Walter B. M&D 717-724.

Gibson, William. DEng 747-755; DSup 407; RevDEng 927-936.

Gide, André. LFFor 635-650, 2138-2140; LTh 1171.

Gierow, Karl Ragner. DFor 2479.

Gift, The (Nabokov). LFEng 1950-1951; RevLFEng 2463-2464.

Gift of Asher Lev, The (Potok). RevLFEng 2666-2667.

"Gift of Gravity, The" (Berry). RevPEng 184.

"Gift of the Magi, The" (Henry). LFEng 3218; RevShF 1179-1180; ShF 230, 1630, 1631, 1632.

Gift Shop, The (Armstrong). M&D 39.

"Gifts of Rain" (Heaney). RevPEng 1445.

Giganti della montagna, I. See *Mountain Giants, The.*

Gigi (Colette). LFFor 372-373; RevShF 581; ShF 1164-1165.

Gil Blas (Lesage). LFFor 1030-1035, 2029-2030, 2118.

Gilbert, Anthony. M&D 725-730.

Gilbert, Michael. M&D 731-738.

Gilbert, Nicolas-Joseph-Laurent. PFor 1862-1863.

Gilbert, Sandra. ShF 2607.

Gilbert, Sandra M., and Susan Gubar. LTh 578-582, 1769.

Gilbert, W. S. RevDEng 937-950, 2993.

Gilbert, W. S. DEng 756-768, and Sir Arthur Sullivan. DEng 2460-2461, 2467.

Gilchrist, Ellen. RevShF 984-990; ShF 2608.

Gilded Age, The (Twain). RevLFEng 3795.

"Gilded Six-Bits, The" (Hurston). RevShF 1243.

Gilder, Richard Watson. ShF 586, 588.

Giles Goat-Boy (Barth). LFEng 165-167; RevLFEng 227-229.

Gilgun, John. ShF 2609.

Gill, B. M. M&D 739-744.

Gill, Brendan. ShF 1484-1487.

Gill, Claes. PFor 2189.

Gill, Patrick. *See* Creasey, John.

Gilles et Jeanne (Tournier). LFFor 1747.

Gillette, William; *Secret Service.* RevDEng 2919-2920.

Gilliatt, Penelope. RevShF 991-998.

Gilman, Dorothy. M&D 745-749.

Gilman, George. LFEng 3198; RevLFEng 3855.

Gilroy, Frank D. DEng 769-782. RevDEng 951-965.

"Gimiendo." *See* "Groaning."

"Gimpel the Fool" (Singer). RevShF 2132, 2741; ShF 2242-2243.

"Ginestra, La." *See* "Broom, The."

Ginger Man, The (Donleavy). LFEng 783-784; RevLFEng 946-947.

Ginger, You're Barmy (Lodge). RevLFEng 2090-2091.

"Gingillino." *See* "Trifler, The."

Ginsberg, Allen. PEng 1088-1096; PSup 405; RevPEng 1224-1235, 3897-3898.

Ginzburg, Natalia. DFor 2415-2416; LFFor 2255-2256; LFSup 127-132.

Giocatore, Il. See *Gambler, The.*

"Giochi senza fine." *See* "Games Without End."

Gioconda (D'Annunzio). DFor 460.

Giono, Jean. LFFor 651-659.

Giorno, Il (Parini). LTh 1691; PFor 2021-2022.

Giorno della civetta, Il. See *Mafia Vendetta.*

Giovanni, Nikki. PEng 1097-1104; PSup 405; RevPEng 1236-1243, 3908.

Giovanni da Procida (Niccolini). DFor 1431-1432.

Giovanni Episcopo. See *Episcopo and Company.*

Giraffe (Plumly). PEng 2233, 2234, 2235-2237; RevPEng 2605, 2607-2608.

Giraldi, Cinthio, Giambattista. DEng 2157; DFor 711-719, 2395; LTh 583-588, 1667; RevDEng 2677.

Giraldus Cambrensis. LTh 22.

Girard, James P. ShF 2610.

Girard, René. LTh 589-594.

Giraudoux, Jean. DFor 721-730, 2353.

"Girella's Toast" (Giusti). PFor 575.

"Girl" (Kincaid). RevShF 1341.

"Girl at the Center of Her Life, A" (Oates). RevPEng 2465.

Girl from Samos, The (Menander). DFor 1304-1306, 2133.

"Girl in a Library, A" (Jarrell). PEng 1483; RevPEng 1695.

"Girl in the Storm, The" (Cain). ShF 1025.

"Girl Named Peter, A" (Bates). RevShF 175; ShFSup 31.

Girl of the Golden West, The (Belasco). DEng 197-199; RevDEng 235-237.

"Girl on the Bus, The" (Sansom). RevShF 2053.

Girl Who Was Shorn, The (Menander). DFor 2133.

"Girls at War" (Achebe). RevShF 4-5; ShF 822-823.

Girls in Their Married Bliss (O'Brien, E.). LFEng 2019-2020; RevLFEng 2544-2545.

"Girls in Their Summer Dresses, The" (Shaw). RevShF 2102-2103; ShF 2224-2225.

"Girl's Song" (Bogan). PEng 233; RevPEng 280.

Gironella, José María. LFFor 660-666.

Gísla Saga Súrssonar. See *Saga of Gisli, The.*

Gisli's Saga. See *Saga of Gisli, The.*

Gissing, George. LFEng 1108-1116; RevLFEng 1318-1326; ShF 516.

Gitanjali (Tagore). PFor 1482-1483, 1485.

"Giulia Lazzari" (Maugham). M&D 1203-1204.

Giusti, Giuseppe. PFor 571-577.

"Give All to Love" (Emerson). PEng 958-959; RevPEng 1088-1089.

"Give It Up!" (Kafka). RevShF 1304-1305.

"Give Me Your Eyes" (Ady). PFor 5.

"Given Grace, A" (Tomlinson). RevPEng 3378.

"Giving Birth" (Atwood). RevShF 105; ShFSup 16-17.

"Giving Blood" (Updike). ShF 2371-2373.

"Giving Myself Up" (Strand). RevPEng 3234.

Gjedsted, Rolf. PFor 2198.

Gjuzel, Bogomil. PFor 2273.

"Glad Day (After a Color Print by Blake)" (Untermeyer). PEng 2951; RevPEng 3419.

Gladiator, The (Bird). DEng 215-216; RevDEng 255-256.

Gladiators, The (Koestler). LFEng 1550-1551; RevLFEng 1911-1912.

"Gladius Dei" (Mann). ShF 1877.

Glance Away, A (Wideman). LFSup 380-381; RevLFEng 3562-3563.

Glas (Derrida). LTh 645.

Glaser, Isabel Joshlin. ShF 2611.

Glasgow, Ellen. LFEng 1117-1125, 3054; RevLFEng 1327-1336, 3762; RevShF 999-1005; ShF 1488-1494.

Glaspell, Susan. RevDEng 966-972; ShF 541.

Glasperlenspiel, Das. See *Glass Bead Game, The.*

Glass Bead Game, The (Hesse). LFFor 833-834.

Glass Key, The (Hammett). LFEng 1239-1240; M&D 827; RevLFEng 1467-1468.

Glass Menagerie, The (Williams, T.). DEng 36-37, 2068-2071, 2405; RevDEng 49, 2569-2572, 2926; RevShF 2481; ShF 2436.

Glass of Blessings, A (Pym). LFEng 2181-2182, 2183-2184, 2185; RevLFEng 2757, 2759.

Glass of Water, The (Scribe). DFor 1679-1680, 2345.

Glass People (Godwin). LFSup 135-136; RevLFEng 1339, 1340-1341.

"Glass Pigeon, The" (Johnson, J.). ShF 1703-1705.

"Glass Scholar, The" (Cervantes). RevShF 463-464; ShF 1089-1090.

Glass-Sided Ants' Nest, The (Dickinson). M&D 510-511.

Glasse of Governement, The (Gascoigne). DEng 726-727; LTh 542; RevDEng 904-905.

Glaube Liebe Hoffnung (Horvath). DFor 960-961.

Glengarry Glen Ross (Mamet). DEng 1243-1244, 2394, 2413; RevDEng 1565-1566, 2915, 2934-2935.

Glidden, Frederick Dilley. *See* Short, Luke.

Glimm, Adele. ShF 2612.

"Glimpse into Another Country" (Morris). RevShF 1681; ShFSup 205-206.

"Glimpses" (Stafford). RevPEng 3172.

Glitter Dome, The (Wambaugh). M&D 1680-1681.

Glittering Gate, The (Dunsany). DEng 539-540; RevDEng 662-663.

Gloria Mundi (Frederic). LFEng 1027; RevLFEng 1220.

Gloria Star. See *Cinq.*

"Gloria" (Elýtis). PFor 465, 1967. See also *Axion Esti, The.*

"Glorias de España, Las" (Feijóo). LTh 476.

"Glory at Twilight" (Bhattacharya). ShF 651.

Glory of Columbia—Her Yeomanry!, The (Dunlap). DEng 533; RevDEng 656.

Glory of Hera, The (Gordon). LFEng 1180; RevLFEng 1402.

Glory of the Hummingbird, The (De Vries). LFEng 741; RevLFEng 889.

Glory's Course (Purdy). RevLFEng 2750.

"Glove, The" (Schiller). PFor 1409.

"Gloworm, The" (Stanley). PEng 2729.

Glück, Louise. PSup 133-139; RevPEng 1244-1251.

Glynn, Thomas. ShF 2613.

Gnaeus Naevius. *See* Naevius, Gnaeus.

Gnomes and Occasions (Nemerov). RevPEng 2430-2431.

Gnomology. See *Theognidea.*

Gnomon (Kenner). LTh 801.

"Go-Away Bird, The" (Spark). RevShF 2169.

Go-Away Bird, The (Spark). ShF 2256-2257.

"Go Back to Your Precious Wife and Son" (Vonnegut). RevShF 2368-2370; ShF 2396-2397.

Go-Between, The (Hartley). LFEng 1301-1302; RevLFEng 1555-1556.

Go Down, Moses (Faulkner). LFEng 932-935; RevLFEng 1106-1109, 3766, 3771.

Go in Beauty (Eastlake). LFEng 850-851.

Go, Lovely Rose (Potts). M&D 1349-1350.

"Go, lovely rose" (Waller). PEng 3015; RevPEng 3512.

Go Tell It on the Mountain (Baldwin). LFEng 134-137; RevLFEng 178-181, 3776.

Goalie's Anxiety at the Penalty Kick, The (Handke). LFFor 784-785.

"Goat, The" (Ponge). PFor 1265.
"Goat, The" (Saba). PSup 346.
Goat Song (Werfel). DFor 1997-1998.
"Goblin Market" (Rossetti, C.). PEng 2418, 2419; RevPEng 2811-2812.
Goblin Market and Other Poems (Rossetti, C.). PEng 2416; RevPEng 2811.
Goblins and Pagodas (Fletcher, J. G.). PEng 1027.
"God" (Lawrence, D. H.). PEng 1685; RevPEng 1955.
"God Abandons Antony, The" (Cavafy). PFor 299.
God and His Gifts, A (Compton-Burnett). RevLFEng 699.
"God and the Bayadere, The" (Goethe). PFor 587-588.
God Bless You, Mr. Rosewater (Vonnegut). LFEng 2728-2729; ShF 2392-2393; RevShF 2365-2366.
"God Blesses Everything, Child" (Castro). PFor 278. See also *Cantares gallegos.*
God Knows (Heller). RevLFEng 1592-1593.
God of Quiet, The (Drinkwater). DEng 509; RevDEng 630.
"God Sees the Truth, but Waits" (Tolstoy). ShF 2333-2334.
God Without Thunder (Ransom). PEng 2324; RevPEng 2710.
Godey's Lady's Book. ShF 585.
"Godfather Death" (Grimm). RevShF 1085-1086; ShF 1557-1558.
Godfrey, Thomas. RevDEng 2916.
"Godhead as Lynx, The" (Sarton). PEng 2461-2462; RevPEng 2866.
"Godliness" (Anderson). RevShF 71-72; ShF 871.
Godric (Buechner). LFEng 354-355; RevLFEng 451-455.
Gods Are Athirst, The (France). LFFor 577-578.
Gods Are Not to Blame, The (Rotimi). DEng 1625, 1627-1629; RevDEng 2031, 2033-2035.
God's Bits of Wood (Sembène). LFFor 1540-1542, 2052, 2056.
Gods, Demons and Others (Narayan). ShF 643.
God's Deputy (Dosunmu). DEng 2421; RevDEng 2943.
"Gods Determinations" (Taylor). PEng 2852; RevPEng 3323-3326.
God's Gentry (MacDonagh). DEng 1211; RevDEng 1514.
God's Grace (Malamud). LFEng 1799-1800; RevLFEng 2275.
"God's Grandeur" (Hopkins). PEng 1400; RevPEng 1609.

God's Little Acre (Caldwell). LFEng 425-427; RevLFEng 536-537.
"Gods of Greece, The" (Schiller). PFor 1408.
Gods of the Mountain, The (Dunsany). DEng 540; RevDEng 663.
God's Promises (Bale). DEng 84-86; RevDEng 108-110.
"God's Spies" (Howe). PSup 196; RevPEng 1631.
"God's Visit" (Cernuda). PFor 322. See also *Nubes, Las.*
"God's World" (Mahfouz). RevShF 1562.
"God's Wrath" (Malamud). RevShF 1575.
"God's Youth" (Untermeyer). PEng 2948-2949; RevPEng 3416-3417.
Godwin, Gail. LFSup 133-141. RevLFEng 1337-1347.
Godwin, William. M&D 750-757.
Godzinna myśli (Slowacki). PFor 1442.
Goethe, Johann Wolfgang von. DEng 2185, 2229; DFor 731-744, 1838-1839, 2366-2367; LFEng 3234-3235, 3238-3239, 3240-3241; **LFFor 667-682,** 2159, 2162, 2163; LTh 60, 118, 337, 437, **595-602,** 641-642, 663-664, 667-668, 790, 984-986, 1018, 1298, 1302, 1304-1306, 1382, 1698, 1710; **PFor 578-589,** 1403, 1913-1914; RevDEng 2705-2706, 2749; RevLFEng 3736, 3817-3819, 3873-3874; **RevShF 1006-1012; ShFSup 97-103.**
"Gog" (Praed). PEng 2277-2278.
Goggan, John Patrick. *See* **Patrick, John.**
Gogol, Nikolai. DFor 745-753, 1771, 2453-2454; LFEng 3267, 3277-3278; **LFFor 683-692,** 2312; LTh 119-120, 287, 442, 1108, 1180, 1448, 1478, 1614; **RevShF 1013-1022,** 2665-2666.ShF 187-188, 460, **1495-1500.**
"Gogol's Wife" (Landolfi). RevShF 1397-1398; ShFSup 132-133.
Gogol's Wife and Other Stories (Landolfi). RevShF 1394; ShFSup 129.
Going Abroad (Macaulay). LFSup 262; RevLFEng 2139.
"Going Back to the River" (Hacker). RevPEng 1366.
"Going, Going" (Larkin). PEng 1675; RevPEng 1943.
Going to Meet the Man (Baldwin, James). ShF 556, 907; RevShF 134-137.
"Going to Meet the Man" (Baldwin, James). RevShF 135-136; ShF 907-908.
Going to Pot (Feydeau). DFor 606.
"Going Up in the World" (Kavan). RevShF 1312.
Gökçeli, Yaşar Kemal. *See* **Kemal, Yashar.**
"Gold" (Hall). PEng 1203.

Gold, Herbert. ShF 1501-1505; ShFSup 389.

"Gold Bug, The" (Poe). M&D 1333.

Gold by Gemini (Gash). M&D 708.

Gold Cell, The (Olds). RevPEng 2493-2494.

"Gold Coast" (McPherson). RevShF 1555-1556; ShF 1855-1856.

Gold Coast Customs (Sitwell). PEng 2630; RevPEng 3034.

Goldberg, Lester. ShF 2614.

Golden Apples, The (Welty). ShF 2418.

Golden Apples of the Sun, The (Bradbury). RevLFEng 359; RevShF 305-306.

Golden Ass, The. See *Metamorphoses.*

Golden Bowl, The (James, H.). LFEng 3047-3048; RevLFEng 3755-3756.

Golden Boy (Odets). DEng 1400-1401; RevDEng 1776-1777.

"Golden Chain, The" (Peretz). ShF 2085.

Golden Crucible, The (Stubbs). M&D 1550-1551.

Golden Fleece, The (Graves, R.). See *Hercules, My Shipmate.*

Golden Fleece, The (Grillparzer). DFor 822-826.

Golden Flower Pot, The (Hoffman). RevShF 1214-1215; ShF 1646.

Golden Fruits, The (Sarraute). LFFor 1503-1504.

"Golden Honeymoon" (Lardner). RevShF 1403; ShF 1772-1773.

"Golden Hour, The" (Claudel). PFor 360. See also *East I Know, The.*

Golden Keel, The (Bagley). M&D 54.

Golden Legend, The (Longfellow). PEng 1753-1754; RevPEng 2038-2039.

Golden Lotus, The. See *Chin P'ing Mei.*

Golden Notebook, The (Lessing). LFEng 1640, 1643-1645; RevLFEng 2036.

Golden Serpent, The (Alegría). LFFor 41-43.

Golden Spur, The (Powell, D.). RevLFEng 2687-2688.

"Golden State" (Bidart). RevPEng 209-210.

Golden State (Bidart). RevPEng 209.

"Golden Verses" (Nerval). PFor 1089.

Goldene Vliess, Das. See *Golden Fleece, The.*

"Goldfish" (Chandler). RevShF 479; ShF 1097.

Golding, William. LFEng 1126-1138; LFSup 404; RevLFEng 1348-1358, 3768; ShF 1506-1510; ShFSup 389.

Goldmann, Lucien. LTh 1421.

Goldoni, Carlo. DEng 2333; DFor 754-763, 790, 2403-2405; RevDEng 2852.

Goldsmith, Jeanette Erlbaum. ShF 2615.

Goldsmith, Oliver. DEng 783-794, 2334; LFEng 3073; PEng 1105-1111, 3332; RevDEng 973-985, 2853; RevLFEng 3736, 3782;

RevPEng 1252-1259; RevShF 1023-1029, 2643; ShF 1511-1517.

Goldsmith, Peter. See **Priestley, J. B.**

Goldstone, Lawrence A. See **Treat, Lawrence.**

"Goldyn Targe, The" (Dunbar, W.). PEng 890, 891-892; RevPEng 1026-1028.

"Golem Death!" (Sachs). PFor 1374.

"Golem Tod!" See "Golem Death!"

Golk (Stern). LFSup 361-362; RevLFEng 3164-3165.

Golob, Zvonimir. PFor 2266.

"Gololeditsa." See "Icicle, The."

Golos iz khora. See *Voice from the Chorus, A.*

"Golubaia zhizu." See "Sky-Blue Life."

Goluben' (Esenin). PFor 478-479.

Goly god. See *Naked Year, The.*

Goly koral. See *Naked King, The.*

Gombrowicz, Witold. DFor 764-776; LFFor 693-700, 2064; LTh 603-608.

Gommes, Les. See *Erasers, The.*

Gomringer, Eugen. PFor 590-597, 1935.

Goncharov, Ivan. LFFor 701-708, 2315-2316; LTh 389.

Goncourt, Edmond de. LFFor 709-718; LTh 1711.

Goncourt, Edmond de and Jules de. LFFor 709-718.

Goncourt, Jules de. LTh 1711.

Gondibert (Davenant). PEng 736, 740-741; RevPEng 840, 844-846.

"Gondolatok a könyvtárban." See "Thoughts in the Library."

Gondoliers, The (Gilbert and Sullivan). DEng 767; RevDEng 948.

Gondreville Mystery, The. See *Historical Mystery, An.*

Gone, No Forwarding (Gores). M&D 760-761.

Gone Out (Różewicz). DFor 1586-1587.

Gone with the Wind (Mitchell). LFEng 3151-3152; RevLFEng 3836-3837.

Góngora y Argote, Luis de. LTh 26-27; PFor 598-604, 1384, 2218-2219.

"Gonzaga Manuscripts, The" (Bellow). RevShF 204-205; ShF 950-951.

Gonzalez, N. V. M. LFEng 1139-1144; ShF 2616; RevLFEng 1359-1365.

González, Rodolfo. RevPEng 3921.

González Martínez, Enrique. PFor 605-613, 2226.

Good and Faithful Servant, The (Orton). DEng 1421-1422; RevDEng 1799-1800.

Good Apprentice, The (Murdoch). RevLFEng 2455-2456.

Good as Gold (Heller). LFEng 1335-1336; RevLFEng 1592.
Good Companions, The (Priestley). LFEng 2142; RevLFEng 2714-2715.
"Good Corn, The" (Bates). RevShF 176; ShFSup 32.
"Good Country People" (O'Connor, Flannery). RevShF 1761; ShF 720-721, 1985.
Good Day to Die, A (Harrison). LFEng 1289-1290; RevLFEng 1537.
"Good Deed, The" (Buck). RevShF 338-340; ShF 1014-1016.
Good Earth, The (Buck). LFEng 339, 342-343; RevLFEng 435, 437-439.
Good Fight, The (Kinsella). PSup 236-237; RevPEng 1838-1839.
Good Friday (Masefield). DEng 1287-1288; RevDEng 1614-1615.
"Good Friday, 1954" (Booth). RevPEng 301-302.
"Good Friday, 1613" (Donne). PEng 837; RevPEng 943.
Good Hope, The (Heijermans). DFor 914.
"Good ladies, ye that have your pleasure in exyle" (Surrey). PEng 2788; RevPEng 3254.
"Good Man Is Hard to Find, A" (O'Connor, Flannery). RevShF 1759-1760, 2733; ShF 624, 1983-1985.
Good Man Is Hard to Find, A (O'Connor, Flannery). RevShF 1759-1762.
Good Man Is Hard to Find and Other Stories, A (O'Connor, Flannery). ShF 1569.
Good Morning, America (Sandburg). PEng 2452; RevPEng 2855.
Good Morning, Midnight (Rhys). LFEng 2228; RevLFEng 2819.
"Good Morrow, Swine" (Stern). RevShF 2213.
Good-Natured Man, The (Goldsmith). DEng 787-789; RevDEng 977-979.
Good News of Death and Other Poems (Simpson). RevPEng 3007-3008.
"Good-Night to the Season" (Praed). PEng 2278.
Good Samaritan, The. ShF 363.
"Good Samaritan, The" (Newman). PEng 2102.
Good Soldier, The (Ford, F.). LFEng 985-988; RevLFEng 1168-1171.
Good Soldier Schweik, The (Hašek). DSup 222; LFFor 795-796.
Good Spirit of Laurel Ridge, The (Stuart). LFEng 2576; RevLFEng 3227-3228.
Good Terrorist, The (Lessing). RevLFEng 2040.
"Good Time, The" (Friedman, B.). RevShF 920; ShF 1426.
Good Trembling (Wormser). RevPEng 3651-3652.
Good Will (Smiley). RevShF 2149-2150.

"Good Woman, A" (Purdy). ShF 2138-2139.
"Good Women, The" (Sillitoe). RevShF 2116; ShF 2227, 2229-2230.
"Good" (Matthews). RevPEng 2245-2246.
"Goodbye" (Creeley). PEng 679.
"Goodbye and Good Luck" (Paley). RevShF 1836-1837; ShF 2041-2042.
Goodbye, Chicago (Burnett). M&D 245-246.
Goodbye, Columbus (Roth). LFEng 3323-3325.
Goodbye, Fidel (Sackler). DEng 1652-1653; RevDEng 2061-2062.
Goodbye, Howard (Linney). DSup 238. See also *Laughing Stock.*
"Goodbye, My Brother" (Cheever). RevShF 502; ShF 1120-1121.
Good-Bye Wisconsin (Wescott). RevShF 2442; ShF 2422, 2423, 2424.
Good-Bye World (Kops). DEng 1080; RevDEng 1359-1360.
Goodman, Paul. LFEng 1145-1156; RevLFEng 1366-1377.
Googe, Barnabe. PEng 3289; RevPEng 3808.
"Goophered Grapevine, The" (Chesnutt). RevShF 522; ShFSup 85-86.
"Goose Fish, The" (Nemerov). PEng 2080.
Goosefoot (McGinley). M&D 1149-1151; RevLFEng 2191, 2192.
Gora (Tagore). LFFor 2217.
Gorbanevskaya, Natalya. PFor 2151.
Gorboduc (Norton and Sackville). DEng 1371, 1375-1380, 2163-2164, 2260, 2264-2265; PEng 2435; RevDEng 1747, 1751-1756, 2683-2684, 2780, 2783-2784.
"Gorbunov and Gorchakov" (Brodsky). PFor 241.
Gordimer, Nadine. LFEng 1157-1172; RevLFEng 1378-1394; RevShF 1030-1037; ShFSup 104-112.
Gordon, Caroline. LFEng 1173-1181; ShF 236, 543, 1518-1524; RevLFEng 1395-1404; RevShF 1038-1044.
Gordon, George. *See* **Byron, George Gordon, Lord.**
Gordone, Charles. RevDEng 2950.
Gore ot uma. See *Mischief of Being Clever, The.*
Gorenko, Anna Andreyevna. *See* **Akhmatova, Anna.**
Gores, Joe. M&D 758-763.
Gorgias (Plato). LTh 1113-1114.
Gorkaya Sudbina. See *Bitter Fate, A.*
Gorky (Tesich). RevDEng 2377.
Gorky, Maxim. DFor 777-787; LFFor 719-729, 2320, 2321; LTh 947; RevShF 1045-1056.
Gorky Park (Smith). M&D 1504-1506.

"Gorod" (Blok). PFor 197.

Görres, Johann Joseph. LTh 1699, 1704-1705.

Gospodica. See *Woman from Sarajevo, The.*

"Gospodin -bov i vopros ob iskusstve." *See* "Mr.
-bov and the Question of Art."

Gosse, Edmund. LTh 1735.

Gossip from the Forest (Keneally). LFSup
185-186; RevLFEng 1841-1842.

Gosson, Stephen. LTh 609-614, 1345, 1671.

Gösta Berling's Saga (Lagerlöf). LFFor 982-984,
2344.

Gothic Tradition in Fiction, The (MacAndrew).
ShF 724.

Gotovac, Vlado. PFor 2266.

"Gott und die Bajadere, Die." *See* "God and the
Bayadere, The."

"Götter Griechenlands, Die." *See* "Gods of
Greece, The."

Gottfried von Strassburg. PFor 1900, 1901.

Gotthelf, Jeremias. ShF 463.

Gottschalk of Orbais. PFor 2113.

Gottsched, Johann Christoph. DEng 2184,
2343; DFor 2362; LFFor 2154; LTh 175, 599,
615-619, 668, 880-881, 883, 1697; PFor 1911;
RevDEng 2704, 2862.

Götz von Berlichingen with the Iron Hand
(Goethe). DFor 738.

Goulart, Ron. M&D 764-768.

Gourmont, Remy de. LTh 620-626.

Goux, Jean-Joseph. LTh 1832.

Gover, Robert. ShF 2617.

Government Inspector, The. See *Inspector
General, The.*

Government of the World in the Moon, The. See
Other Worlds.

Governo della famiglia. See *Family in
Renaissance Florence, The.*

Govinda Samantha (Day). LFFor 2216-2217.

Govoni, Corrado. PFor 2037, 2048.

**Gower, John. PEng 1112-1123; RevPEng
1260-1272.**

Goy, The (Harris, M.). LFEng 1280-1281;
RevLFEng 1517-1518.

**Goyen, William. RevShF 1051-1056; ShF
1525-1529; ShFSup 389.**

Goytisolo, Juan. LFFor 2393.

Gozzano, Guido. PFor 2037.

Gozzi, Carlo. DFor 788-798; ShF 683.

Gozzi, Gaspare. RevShF 2648.

Grabbe, Christian Dietrich. DFor 799-808.

"Grace" (Joyce). RevShF 1295.

Grace Abounding to the Chief of Sinners
(Bunyan). LFEng 359-361; RevLFEng
456-458.

Grace Notes (Dove). RevPEng 959-960.

Grace of Mary Traverse, The (Wertenbaker).
RevDEng 2497-2498.

Gradnik, Alojz. PFor 2270.

Grady, Tex. *See* **Webb, Jack.**

Graeme, Bruce. M&D 769-773.

Graeme, David. *See* **Graeme, Bruce.**

Graff, Gerald. LTh 810-811.

Graham, Jorie. RevPEng 1273-1280.

Graham, Winston. M&D 774-779.

Grain of Wheat, A (Ngugi wa Thiong'o). LFEng
1980-1983; LFFor 2052; RevLFEng
2504-2506.

"Gramigna's Mistress" (Verga). RevShF 2347;
ShF 2381.

Grammaire du Décaméron (Todorov). LTh
1432-1433.

"Grammar of Love" (Bunin). RevShF 344.

Grammar of Motives, A (Burke, K.). LTh 244-245.

Grammar of Stories, A (Prince). ShF 87.

Grammatica Slavica (Bernolák). PFor 1807.

"Grammatika liubvi." *See* "Grammar of Love."

Gramsci, Antonio. LTh 363, 627-632, 1543.

"Gramsci's Ashes" (Pasolini). PFor 1144,
1148-1150.

"Gran aventura, La." *See* "Sublime Adventure,
The."

Gran carpa de los rasquachis, La (Valdez). DSup
371.

Gran Galeoto, El. See *Great Galeoto, The.*

Gran teatro del mundo, El. See *Great Theater of
the World, The.*

Granby (Lister). LFEng 3134-3137.

Grand Écart, The (Cocteau). LFFor 360.

"Grand Galop" (Ashbery). PEng 60.

Grand Meaulnes, Le. See *Wanderer, The.*

Grand Piano, The (Goodman). RevLFEng
1369-1371. See also *Empire City, The.*

Grand Testament, Le. See *Great Testament, The.*

Grand Troupeau, Le. See *To the Slaughterhouse.*

"Grande Bretèche, The" (Balzac). RevShF
149-150; ShF 920.

Grande ritratto, Il. See *Larger than Life.*

Grandfather, The (Pérez Galdós). DFor
1458-1461, 2501.

"Grandfather and Grandson" (Singer). RevShF
2133-2134.

Grandissimes, The (Cable). LFEng 416-417;
RevLFEng 526-527.

Grandmother, The (Němcová). LFFor 2065.

Grandmothers, The (Wescott). LFEng 2832, 2834-2836; RevLFEng 3505-3507.

Grandower, Elissa. *See* Waugh, Hillary.

Grangecolman (Martyn). DEng 1280-1281; RevDEng 1606-1607.

Grant, Ambrose. *See* **Chase, James Hadley.**

Grant, John. *See* **Gash, Jonathan.**

Grant, Maxwell. *See* **Collins, Michael,** and **Gibson, Walter B.**

Granville-Barker, Harley. DEng 795-803; RevDEng 986-995.

Grapes of Wrath, The (Steinbeck). LFEng 2525-2526, 3062; RevLFEng 3158-3159, 3770; ShF 2275.

Grasemann, Ruth. *See* **Rendell, Ruth.**

Grass, Günter. DSup 153-161; LFFor 730-739, 2199, 2201.

Grass Harp, The (Capote). LFEng 446-447; RevLFEng 558-559.

Grass Is Singing, The (Lessing). LFEng 1641-1643; RevLFEng 2034-2035.

Grass-Widow's Tale, The (Peters, Ellis). M&D 1320-1321.

"Grasshopper" (Cummings). PEng 3230.

"Grasshopper, The" (Lovelace). PEng 1758-1759; RevPEng 2051-2052.

Grateful to Life and Death. See *English Teacher, The.*

"Gratiana, dancing and singing" (Lovelace). PEng 1759, 1760; RevPEng 2053.

"Gratulatory to Mr. Ben Johnson for His adopting of Him to be His Son" (Randolph). PEng 2322.

Grau, Shirley Ann. LFEng 1182-1190; RevLFEng 1405-1414; RevShF 1057-1061; ShF 552, 1530-1534; ShFSup 389.

Grau Delgado, Jacinto. DFor 2504.

"Grauballe Man, The" (Heaney). RevPEng 1447-1448.

"Grave, A" (Moore). PEng 2044; RevPEng 2373.

"Grave, The" (Porter). RevShF 1912.

Grave of the Right Hand, The (Wright, C.). RevPEng 3657.

Graves, Caroline Elizabeth. LFEng 556-557; RevLFEng 683-684.

Graves, Robert. LFEng 1191-1204; LFSup 404; PEng 167, 1124-1134; PSup 405; RevLFEng 1415-1429, 3838-3839; RevPEng 1281-1292; ShF 2618.

"Graveyard by the Sea, The" (Valéry). LTh 1491-1493; PFor 1578-1582.

Graveyard for Lunatics, A (Bradbury). RevLFEng 361-362.

Gravina, G. W. PFor 2019.

"Gravities" (Heaney). PEng 1268.

Gravity's Rainbow (Pynchon). LFEng 2192-2194; RevLFEng 2765, 2770-2771, 3771, 3777.

Gray, Simon. DEng 804-813; DSup 407; RevDEng 996-1006.

Gray, Thomas. PEng 1135-1143, 3329, 3331, 3332; RevPEng 1293-1301.

"Grayling" (Simms). RevShF 2122-2123; ShF 2236-2237.

Grayson, Richard. ShF 2619.

Grazie, Le (Foscolo). PFor 496-497.

Grażyna (Mickiewicz). PFor 1019.

"Great American Novel, The" (De Forest). LFEng 700-701; RevLFEng 834-835.

Great American Novel, The (Roth). LFEng 2305-2306; RevLFEng 2900.

"Great Bear, The" (Hollander). RevPEng 1547.

"Great Blue Heron, The" (Kizer). PEng 1620; RevPEng 1858.

"Great Breath, The" (Æ). PEng 12; RevPEng 19.

Great Circle (Aiken). LFEng 17-18, 19-20; RevLFEng 30-31, 32-33.

Great Cloak, The (Montague). RevPEng 2365.

"Great Cossack Epic, The" (Thackeray). PEng 2873-2874.

Great Days (Barthelme). ShFSup 24.

Great Exhibition, The (Hare). DSup 184.

Great Expectations (Dickens, C.). LFEng 3163-3165.

"Great Falls" (Ford). RevShF 880.

Great Galeoto, The (Echegaray). DFor 531-532, 2500.

Great Gatsby, The (Fitzgerald, F. S.). LFEng 956, 961-964, 3060-3061, 3087; RevLFEng 1138, 1143-1146, 3768, 3796, 3799; RevShF 861-862; ShF 1317, 1372.

Great Goodness of Life (Baraka). DEng 101; RevDEng 126-127.

Great Hunger, The (Kavanagh). PEng 1539-1540; RevPEng 1765-1766.

Great Instauration, The (Bacon). LTh 77.

Great Jones Street (DeLillo). LFSup 86-87; RevLFEng 864-865.

Great Meadow, The (Roberts). LFEng 2278-2279; RevLFEng 2873-2874.

"Great Pax Whitie, The" (Giovanni). PEng 1103; RevPEng 1242.

Great Peace, The (Braun). DSup 25-26.

"Great Pegram Mystery, The" (Barr). M&D 89.

Great Testament, The (Villon). PFor 1654, 1655, 1657-1659.

Great Theater of the World, The (Calderón). DFor 303-304.

Great Tirade at the Town-Hall (Dorst). DSup 93-94.

Great Victorian Collection, The (Moore, B.). LFEng 1891-1892; RevLFEng 2397-2398.

"Great Wall of China, The" (Kafka). ShF 1733-1734.

Great Wash, The (Kersh). M&D 981.

Great White Hope, The (Sackler). DEng 1651-1652; RevDEng 2060-2062.

Great World, The (Malouf). RevLFEng 2293.

"Great World and Timothy Colt, The" (Auchincloss). RevShF 114-115.

Greban, Arnoul. DFor 2166.

Greed (Wakoski). RevPEng 3491-3492.

"Greedy Milkwoman, The" (Zoshchenko). RevShF 2559; ShFSup 380.

Greek feet, **4063.**

Greek Passion, The. See *Christ Recrucified.*

Green, Anna Katharine. M&D 780-788.

Green, Charles M. *See* **Gardner, Erle Stanley.**

Green, Geoffrey. ShF 2620.

Green, Henry. LFEng 1205-1212; RevLFEng 1430-1438.

Green, Julien. LFFor 740-750.

Green, Paul. DEng 814-823; RevDEng 1007-1017.

Green Card (Akalaitis). DSup 5; RevDEng 16-17.

Green Centuries (Gordon). LFEng 1178; RevLFEng 1400.

"Green Eye, The" (Merrill). PEng 1961.

Green Flash, The (Graham). M&D 778.

Green for Danger (Brand). M&D 194.

Green Grow the Lilacs (Riggs). DEng 1591, 1594-1595; RevDEng 1995, 1998-1999.

Green Henry (Keller). LFFor 928-930.

"Green Hills of Earth, The" (Heinlein). RevShF 1155-1156; ShF 1617-1618.

Green House, The (Vargas Llosa). LFFor 1848-1849.

"Green Lampshade" (Simic). PEng 2596.

Green Man, The (Amis, K.). LFEng 64, 68-69; RevLFEng 94-95.

Green Mansions (Hudson). LFEng 1385-1386; RevLFEng 1661-1663.

"Green Park" (Wiggins). RevShF 2469.

Green Pastures, The (Connelly). DEng 413-414, 420-422; RevDEng 513-514, 520-522, 2948.

Green Pope, The (Asturias). LFFor 87.

"Green Shelf, The" (Hall). PEng 1204; RevPEng 1373.

"Green Tea" (Le Fanu). RevShF 1446-1448; ShF 728, 1798, 1800-1802.

Green Water, Green Sky (Gallant). LFEng 1053-1054; RevLFEng 1251-1252.

Green Years, The (Cronin). LFEng 653, 659-660, 661; RevLFEng 786, 792-794.

Greenberg, Alvin. ShF 2621.

Greenberg, Barbara L. ShF 2622.

Greenberg, Joanne. RevShF 1062-1067; ShF 1535-1539.

Greene, Graham. DEng 824-835; LFEng 1213-1222; LFSup 403; M&D 789-794; RevDEng 1018-1030; RevLFEng 1439-1449, 3768, 3771; RevShF 1068-1075, 1191, 2737-2738; ShF 523, 1540-1547.

Greene, Robert. DEng 836-846, 1364, 2270-2271; LFEng 3014, 3016; **PEng 1144-1152; RevDEng 1031-1042,** 1705, 2789-2790; RevLFEng 3722; **RevPEng 1302-1311; RevShF 1076-1082,** 2629; ShF 454, 455, 491, 495, **1548-1554.**

Greene's Groatsworth of Wit (Greene, R.). DEng 839; RevDEng 1034.

"Greenleaf" (O'Connor, Flannery). RevShF 1763; ShF 107.

Greenmantle (Buchan). LFEng 332-333; RevLFEng 427-428.

Gregorčič, Simon. PFor 2268-2269.

Gregorius (Hartmann von Aue). PFor 633-635.

Gregory, Lady Augusta. DEng 847-856, 2445; **RevDEng 1043-1052,** 2969; ShF 658.

Greimas, A. J. LTh 1762.

Grendel (Gardner, J.). LFEng 1073-1074; RevLFEng 1273-1274.

Grendon, Stephen. *See* **Derleth, August.**

Gressmann, Uwe. PFor 1817, 1822.

"Gretel in Darkness" (Glück). PSup 135; RevPEng 1246-1247.

Grettir's Saga. See *Grettis Saga.*

Grettis Saga. RevShF 2584, 2590-2591; ShF 393.

Greve, Felix Paul. *See* Grove, Frederick Philip.

Grevenius, Herbert. DFor 2479.

Greville, Fulke. PEng 1153-1159; RevPEng 1312-1319.

Grey, Mostyn. *See* **Christie, Agatha.**

Grey, Romer Zane. *See* **Pronzini, Bill.**

Grey, Zane. LFEng 3193-3194; RevLFEng 3850-3851.

"Grey Light, The" (Sinópoulos). PFor 1972.

"Greyhound People" (Adams). RevShF 9; ShFSup 3.

Griboyedov, Alexander. DFor 807-817.

Gridr's Fostering, Illugi. RevShF 2595-2596; ShF 399.

"Grief of Men, The" (Bly). RevPEng 274.

Grieg, Nordahl. DFor 2480; PFor 2183.

Grieve, Christopher Murray. *See* **MacDiarmid, Hugh.**

"Grifel' naia oda." *See* "Slate Ode."

Griffi, Giuseppe Patroni. DFor 2415.

Griffin's Way (Yerby). LFEng 2988-2989; RevLFEng 3694-3695.

Griffith, George. RevLFEng 3866-3867.

Griffith, Patricia Browning. ShF 2623.

Grigorovich, Dmitrí. LFFor 2314.

Grigoryev, Apollon. LTh 395.

Grile, Dod. *See* **Bierce, Ambrose.**

Grillparzer, Franz. DFor 818-828, 2371-2372; **LTh 633-638.**

Grimes, Martha. M&D 795-800.

Grimke, Angelina. RevDEng 2947.

Grimm, Jakob. LTh 1502, 1704.

Grimm, The Brothers. RevShF 1083-1090; ShF 1555-1562.

Grimmelshausen, H. J. C. von. LFFor 751-764, 2152; RevLFEng 3805.

Grimm's Fairy Tales (Grimm). RevShF 1084-1089, 2651; ShF 1556, 1558, 1559-1562.

Grimus (Rushdie). RevLFEng 2919.

Grindel, Eugène. *See* **Éluard, Paul.**

Gringa, La (Sánchez). DFor 2442.

Gripenberg, Bertil. PFor 2174.

"Groaning" (Alberti). PFor 20.

Gról Agamemnona. See *Agamemnon's Grave.*

Gröber, Gustav. LTh 335.

"Grobovshchik" *See* "Undertaker, The."

"Grocer's Daughter" (Wiggins). RevShF 2470-2471.

Grooks (Hein). PFor 640.

Grosse Fahrt, Die (Blunck). LFFor 2195.

"Grosse Fifi, La" (Rhys). RevShF 1999-2000; ShFSup 259-260.

Grosse Schmährede an der Stadtmauer. See *Great Tirade at the Town-Hall.*

Grosser Frieden. See *Great Peace, The.*

Grossmüttiger Rechts-Gelehrter (Gryphius). DFor 837-838.

Grotesque in Art and Literature, The (Kayser). ShF 712.

Grotowski, Jerzy. DEng 2241; DFor 2241-2242.

Ground Work (Duncan). RevPEng 1042-1043.

"Groundhog, The" (Eberhart). PEng 929-930; RevPEng 1057-1058.

"Groundhog Revisiting, The" (Eberhart). PEng 933; RevPEng 1061-1062.

Group, The (McCarthy, M.). RevLFEng 2153-2154; LFEng 1723-1724.

"Group Life: Letchworth" (Betjeman). PEng 171-172; RevPEng 205.

Group of Noble Dames, A (Hardy). RevShF 1112; ShF 1584.

Group Portrait with Lady (Böll). LFFor 186-188.

Grove, Frederick Philip. LFEng 1223-1231; RevLFEng 1450-1459; ShF 637.

Groves of Academe, The (McCarthy, M.). LFEng 1722; RevLFEng 2152-2153.

"Growing Season, The" (Caldwell). RevShF 371-372; ShF 1031.

"Growing Stone, The" (Camus, A.). RevShF 401-402; ShF 1049-1050.

Growth of Love, The (Bridges). PEng 287; RevPEng 352.

Growth of the Soil (Hamsun). LFFor 774-775, 2346.

Groza. See *Storm, The.*

Gruber, Ludwig. See **Anzengruber, Ludwig.**

Gruk. See *Grooks.*

Grumbler. *See* **Twain, Mark.**

Grün, Max von der. LFFor 2199.

Grundtvig, N. F. S. PFor 2165.

Grüne Heinrich, Der. See *Green Henry.*

Grupa Laokoona (Różewica). DFor 1582-1583.

Gruppenbild mit Dame. See *Group Portrait with Lady.*

"Gruselett." *See* "Scariboo."

Gryll Grange (Peacock). LFEng 2085-2086; RevLFEng 2623-2624.

Gryphius, Andreas. DFor 829-840; PFor 1909.

Guard of Honor (Cozzens). LFEng 634-635; RevLFEng 767-768.

"Guardagujas, El." *See* "Switchman, The."

"Guardapelo, El." *See* "Locket, The."

Guardian, The (Steele, R.). RevShF 2186; ShF 2267-2268.

Guardsman, The (Molnár). DFor 1346.

Guare, John. DEng 857-864; RevDEng 1053-1063.

Guareschi, Giovanni. LFFor 2253.

Guarini, Giambattista. DEng 2157; DFor 841-848, 2400; PFor 2016.

"Guatemalan Idyll, A" (Bowles, J.). RevShF 270-271.

Guattari, Félix. LTh 850.

Gubar, Susan. *See* **Gilbert, Sandra M.**

Gucio zaczarowany (Miłosz). PFor 1034.

Guðjónsson, Halldór Kiljan. *See* **Laxness, Halldór.**

Guðmundsson, Kristmann. LFFor 2357, 2358.

Gudrun (Jensen). LFFor 882.

Guerillas (Hochhuth). DFor 922.

Guerillas (Naipaul). LFEng 1962; RevLFEng 2475-2476.

Guermantes Way, The (Proust). LFFor 1330-1334. See also *Remembrance of Things Past.*

Guerra del fin del mundo, La. See *War of the End of the World, The.*

Guerras de nuestros antepasados, Las (Delibes). LFFor 452-453.

"Guerre" (Reverdy). PSup 322-323.

Guerre civile, La. See *Civil War.*

Guerre de Troie n'aura pas lieu, La. See *Tiger at the Gates.*

"Guest, The" (Camus, A.). RevShF 400-401, 2743-2744; ShF 1048-1049.

Guest, The (Grillparzer). DFor 825. See also *Golden Fleece, The.*

Guest, Edgar A. PEng 1160-1167. RevPEng 1320-1327.

Guest for the Night, A (Agnon). LFFor 17-19.

Guest of Honor, A (Gordimer). LFEng 1164-1166; RevLFEng 1386-1387.

"Guests" (Taylor). ShF 2305-2307.

"Guests of the Nation" (O'Connor, Frank). RevShF 1768-1769, 2739; ShF 1989-1991.

Guevara (Braun). DSup 25.

Guevara, Luis Veléz de. DEng 2162; RevDEng 2682.

Guffey, George. LFEng 220; RevLFEng 270.

Guiana Quartet, The (Harris, W.). LFSup 144-148; RevLFEng 1526-1530.

Guide, The (Narayan). LFEng 1969-1970; RevLFEng 2484-2485.

Guide to the Ruins (Nemerov). RevPEng 2428.

Guide to the Underworld (Ekelöf). PFor 453.

Guillaume d'Angleterre (Chrétien de Troyes). RevShF 545; ShF 1140.

Guillaume de Lorris and Jean de Meung. PFor 614-621, 1839.

Guillén, Jorge. PFor 622-628.

Guilleragues, Gabriel. LFEng 3109-3110; RevLFEng 3811.

Guilt Its Own Punishment. See *Fatal Curiosity.*

"Guilty Party, The" (Henry). ShF 1630.

"Guilty Woman, A" (Wescott). RevShF 2443.

Guimarães Rosa, João. LFFor 2300; RevShF 1091-1095. ShF 1563-1567.

Guizot, François. DEng 2188; RevDEng 2708.

Gulf and Other Poems, The (Walcott). RevPEng 3498.

"Gulfport" (Smith). RevShF 2155-2156.

Gulistan. See *Rose Garden, The.*

Gullason, Thomas A. ShF 690; RevShF 2678-2679.

Gullberg, Hjalmar. PFor 2178.

Gulliver's Travels (Swift). LFEng 2609-2611; RevLFEng 3262-3264.

Gumilyov, Nikolay. PFor 2146.

Gun for Sale, A (Greene). M&D 791-792.

Gundelfinger, Friedrich. See **Gundolf, Friedrich.**

Gundling's Life Frederick of Prussia Lessing's Sleep Dream Scream (Müller). DSup 261.

Gundolf, Friedrich. LTh 639-643.

Gundulić, Ivan. DFor 2292; PFor 2260-2261.

"Gunga Din" (Kipling). PEng 1608-1609; RevPEng 1848-1849.

Gunn, Thom. PEng 1168-1177; PSup 405; **RevPEng 1328-1338.**

Gunnarsson, Gunnar. DFor 2480; LFFor 2357-2358.

Gunnarsson, Pétur. PFor 2200-2201.

"Guns at Cyrano's" (Chandler). RevShF 476-477; ShF 1096.

Guns of Navarone, The (MacLean). M&D 1173-1174.

Gunslinger (Dorn). PEng 844-845; RevPEng 950-951.

Gunsmoke. RevDEng 3038, 3040.

Gurney, Albert. DSup 162-168.

Gurney, A. R. RevDEng 1064-1072.

Gurney, Ivor. PEng 1178-1185; RevPEng 1339-1347.

Gus and Al (Innaurato). RevDEng 1250-1251.

Gusai. LTh 1787.

Gustafsson, Lars. LFFor 2361-2362; PFor 2194.

Gusto neoclassico. See *On Neoclassicism.*

Gut, Gom. See **Simenon, Georges.**

"Gutenberg as Card Shark" (Cassity). RevPEng 543.

Guthmundsson, Tómas. PFor 2185-2186.

Guthrie, Tyrone. RevDEng 3033.

Gutiérrez, Jorge Díaz. DFor 2443.

Gutzkow, Karl. DFor 2371; LFFor 2167, 2169.

Guy Domville (James, H.). DEng 995; RevDEng 1250-1261.

Guy of Warwick. ShF 141.

Guy Rivers (Simms). LFEng 2412; RevLFEng 3042.

Guzmán de Alfarache (Alemán). LFEng 3102; RevLFEng 3804; ShF 451, 1083.

G'wissenswurm, Der (Anzengruber). DFor 90.

"Gyakusetsu to iu mono ni tsuite" (Kobayashi). LTh 821.

Gyges and His Ring (Hebbel). DFor 889.

Gyllenborg, Carl. DFor 2467.

Gyllenborg, Gustaf Fredrik. PFor 2160.
Gyllensten, Lars. LFFor 2359-2360.
"Gyofukuki." *See* "Transformation."
Gyöngyösi, Istvá. PFor 1977.
"Gypsies" (Clare). PEng 509-510; RevPEng
   599-600.

Gypsy (Laurents and Sondheim). DEng 2474;
   RevDEng 3000.
Gypsy Ballads (García Lorca). PFor 317.
"Gypsy Delegate, The" (Hoch). RevShF 1210.
Gypsy in Amber (Smith). M&D 1506.
"Gyrtt in my giltlesse gowne" (Surrey). PEng
   2787; RevPEng 3253.

H

H As in Hangman (Treat). M&D 1598.
H As in Hunted (Treat). M&D 1600.
"H. Scriptures, The" (II) (Herbert). PEng 1297; RevPEng 1476.
Ha estallado la paz. See *Peace After War.*
"Ha férfi vagy, légy férfi." *See* "If You Are a Man, Then Be One."
Haablǿse Slægter (Bang). LFFor 2339.
Håakansson, Björn. PFor 2192.
Haavikko, Paavo. LFFor 2368; PFor 2191; **PSup 140-148.**
Haavio, Martti. See Mustapää, P.
"Habit of Angels, The" (Belitt). RevPEng 156.
"Habit of Loving, The" (Lessing). RevShF 1474.
Hachnasat Kala. See *Bridal Canopy, The.*
Hacker, Marilyn. LFEng 714-715; **PEng 1186-1193; PSup 405;** RevLFEng 850-851; **RevPEng 1358-1367.**
Hacks, Peter. DFor 849-855.
Haddon, Christopher. *See* **Beeding, Francis.**
Hadrian's Memoirs. See *Memoirs of Hadrian.*
"Haecceity" (Cunningham). PSup 77; RevPEng 806.
Hafiz. PSup 149-157.
Hafstein, Hannes. PFor 2170.
"Häftlinge, Die." See *Irren-die Häftlinge, Die.*
"Hag of Beare, The" (Montague). PEng 2036; RevPEng 2362-2363.
Hagedorn, Jessica. RevPEng 3918.
Hager, Stan. ShF 2624.
Haggard, H. Rider. LFEng 3202; Rider. RevLFEng 3860.
Haggard, William. M&D 801-807.
Hagiwara Sakutarō. PFor 2075, 2076.
"Haguruma." *See* "Cogwheels."
"Haha maru mono." *See* "Mothers."
Hail and Farewell (Moore, G.). LFEng 1895-1896; RevLFEng 2402-2403.
Haindl, Marieluise. *See* **Fleisser, Marieluise.**
"Hair, Lips, Eyes" (Vörösmarty). PFor 1666-1667.
"Haircut" (Lardner). RevShF 1402-1403; ShF 108, 1772.
"Hairless Mexican, The" (Maugham). M&D 1203.
"Haj, száj, szem." *See* "Hair, Lips, Eyes."
Hakim, Tawfiq al-. DSup 169-180.
Hakon Jarl (Oehlenschläger). DFor 1440-1441.
Hákonarmál. See *Lay of Hákon, The.*

Hakootoko. See *Box Man, The.*
Hale, Nancy. RevShF 1096-1102; ShF 1568-1574.
Ha-Levy, Judah. See **Judah ha-Levi.**
"Half an Hour" (Cavafy). PFor 300.
"Half-Kissed Kiss" (Ady). PFor 5. See also *New Verses.*
Haliburton, Thomas Chandler. ShF 635.
Halidon Hill (Minot). PEng 3255.
Hall, Adam. *See* **Trevor, Elleston.**
Hall, Donald. PEng 1194-1206; PSup 405; **RevPEng 1368-1378.**
Hall, James Byron. ShF 2625.
Hall, John. LTh 908.
Hall, Willis. DEng 865-873; **RevDEng 1073-1082.**
Hall of Mirrors, A (Stone). RevLFEng 3200.
Hallam, Arthur Henry. PEng 1207-1211, 2861, 2864-2865; **RevPEng 1379-1384.**
Halle, Morris. PEng 3456; RevPEng 3991.
"Hallelujah" (Sachs). PFor 1374.
"Hallelujawiese, Die." *See* "Alleluia Meadow, The."
Hallgrímsson, Jónas. PFor 2167-2168.
Halliday, Brett. M&D 808-814.
Halliday, M. A. K. PEng 3454-3455; RevPEng 3989.
Halliday, Michael. *See* **Creasey, John.**
Hallinan, Nancy. ShF 2627.
Hall-Stevenson, John. LFEng 2531; RevLFEng 3174.
"Halt in the Wilderness, A" (Brodsky). PFor 242.
Halvfärdiga himlen, Den (Tranströmer). PFor 1529.
Ham Funeral, The (White). DSup 394; RevDEng 2514.
"Hamann" (Bobrowski). PFor 205.
Hamann, Johann Georg. LTh 437, 669.
"Hamatraya" (Emerson). PEng 957; RevPEng 1087.
Hamblen, Abigail Ann. ShF 2628.
Hamburg Dramaturgy (Lessing). LTh 881-882.
Hamburgische Dramaturgie. See *Hamburg Dramaturgy.*
Hamdismál. RevShF 2601; ShF 429.
Hamilton, Donald. M&D 815-821.
Hamlet (Döblin). LFFor 479-480.

Hamlet (Shakespeare). DEng 1716, 2281-2282; RevDEng 2130, 2800; ShF 2214-2216.

"Hamlet and His Problems" (Eliot). LTh 448, 450.

Hamlet of A. MacLeish, The (MacLeish). PEng 1853; RevPEng 2153.

"Hamlet of Shchigrov, The" (Turgenev). RevShF 2320.

Hamlet of Stepney Green, The (Kops). DEng 1079-1080; RevDEng 1358-1359.

"Hamlet of the Shchigrov District, The" (Turgenev). ShF 2355-2356.

Hamlet, Revenge! (Innes). M&D 924.

Hamletmachine (Müller). DSup 261-262.

"Hammer of God, The" (Chesterton). RevShF 532-533.

Hammer of the Village, The (Petőfi). PFor 1219.

Hammerstein, Oscar, II. RevDEng 1995, 1599, 2995-2997.

Hammett (Gores). M&D 761.

Hammett, Daghull. *See* **Hammett, Dashiell.**

Hammett, Dashiell. LFEng 1232-1242; M&D **822-828; RevLFEng 1460-1470,** 3771, 3845-3846; **RevShF 1103-1107;** ShF 543, 761, **1575-1578.**

Hammett, Mary Janc. *See* **Hammett, Dashiell.**

Hāmojō no umi. See *Sea of Fertility, The.*

Hamri, Thorsteinn fra. PFor 2200.

Hams al-junun (Mahfouz). RevShF 1561-1562.

Hamsun, Knut. DFor 2476; **LFFor 765-777,** 2345-2346.

Han d'Islande. See *Hans of Iceland.*

Han kung ch'iu. See *Sorrows of Han, The.*

Han sidder ved smeltediglen. See *He Sits at the Melting Pot.*

Han som fick leva om sitt liv. See *Man Who Lived His Life Over, The.*

Han Yü. PFor 1787.

"Hana." *See* "Nose, The."

"Hand, The" (Maupassant). M&D 1208.

Hand and Glove (Machado de Assis). LFFor 1042.

Hand and Ring (Green). M&D 784.

"Hand at Callow Hill Farm, The" (Tomlinson). PEng 2909.

"Hand-Rolled Cigarettes" (Yevtushenko). PSup 247.

Handel, George Frederick. DEng 2457, 2458.

Handful of Blackberries, A (Silone). LFFor 1588-1589.

Handful of Dust, A (Waugh). LFEng 2796-2798; RevLFEng 3463-3465.

Handful of Rice, A (Markandaya). LFFor 2222.

"Handing Down, The" (Berry). PEng 152; RevPEng 181.

Handke, Peter. DFor **856-864,** 2243, 2383; **LFFor 778-791,** 2207; LFSup 404.

Handmaid's Tale, The (Atwood). RevLFEng 140-141.

"Hands" (Anderson). RevShF 70; ShF 870.

Hands of Its Enemy, The (Medoff). DSup 244; RevDEng 1648-1649.

"Handschuh, Der." *See* "Glove, The."

Handske, En. See *Gauntlet, A.*

"Handsome Is as Handsome Does" (Pritchett). RevShF 1932.

"Handsomest Drowned Man, The" (García Márquez). RevShF 953; ShF 1455-1456.

Handy, Lowney. LFEng 1477-1478; RevLFEng 1799-1800.

Hanged Man's House (Ferrars). M&D 601.

Hanging Captain, The (Wade). M&D 1667.

Hangman, The (Lagerkvist). DFor 1156, 2477-2478.

"Hangover Mass" (Kennedy). RevPEng 1811.

Hanjo (Mishima). DFor 1324-1325.

Hanka, Václav. PFor 1798.

"Hank's Woman" (Wister). ShF 596.

Hanley, James. LFEng 1243-1252; **RevLFEng 1471-1480.**

Hannah, Barry. RevLFEng **1481-1488;** RevShF 2759.

Hannibal (Grabbe). DFor 806-807.

Hannon, Ezra. *See* **McBain, Ed.**

Hans Alienus (Heidenstam). LFFor 820-821.

"Hans Carvel" (Prior). PEng 2290; RevPEng 2671.

Hans Faust. See *Hinze und Kunze.*

Hans of Iceland (Hugo). LFFor 851-853.

Hansberry, Lorraine. DEng **874-884,** 2427-2428; **RevDEng 1083-1094,** 2949-2950.

Hansen, Joseph. M&D **829-834;** ShF 2629.

Hansen, Martin Alfred. LFFor 2356.

Hansen, Thorkild. LFFor 2366-2367.

Hanshew, Thomas W. M&D 835-840. *See also* **Carter, Nick.**

Hansson, Ola. PFor 2170.

"Hap" (Hardy). PEng 1219; RevPEng 1392.

Hapgood (Stoppard). RevDEng 2318.

"Happie obtaining the Great Galleazzo, The" (Deloney). PEng 785.

"Happiest Man on Earth, The" (Maltz). ShF 1872-1873.

"Happily Neighing, the Herds Graze" (Mandelstam). PFor 936.

"Happiness" (Glück). PSup 137; RevPEng 1248.

Hart, Julius. LFFor 2179 Lth 1719.

Hart, Lorenz. DEng 895-905; RevDEng 1118-1128,

Hart, Lorenz, and Richard Rodgers. DEng 896, 898-899, 900, 901.

Hart, Moss, and George S. Kaufman. DEng 906-907; RevDEng 1129-1130

Hart, Moss. DEng 906-913; RevDEng 1129-1137.

Harte, Bret. LTh 1749; PEng 1237-1245; RevShF 1129-1135; ShF 210, 222-223, 533, 594, 1592-1597.

Harter, Penny. ShF 2632.

Hartley, L. P. LFEng 1296-1302; RevLFEng 1550-1557.

Hartman, Geoffrey H. LTh 165, 306, 351, **644-648,** 909, 1033, 1492, 1766, 1833.

Hartmann von Aue. PFor 629-636, 1900.

Hartzenbusch y Martínez, Juan Eugenio de. DFor 2498.

Haru no yuki. See *Spring Snow.*

"Haru to shura." *See* "Spring and Asura."

Harvest (Giono). LFFor 654.

"Harvest" (Soto). RevPEng 3113.

Harvest on the Don. See *Virgin Soil Upturned.*

"Harvest Song" (Toomer). PEng 2917-2918; RevPEng 3389-3390.

Harvester, Simon. M&D 847-851.

Harvesters, The (Pavese). LFFor 1246-1247.

Harvey, Anne Gray. *See* **Sexton, Anne.**

"Harzreise, Die." *See* "Journey to the Harz, The."

Hasdeu, Bogdan Petriceicu. DFor 2297.

Hašek, Jaroslav. LFFor 792-796, 2066.

"Hasidic Scriptures" (Sachs). PFor 1374.

Haslam, Gerald. ShF 2633.

Haste to the Wedding. See *Italian Straw Hat, The.*

Hastings, Roderic. See **Graeme, Bruce.**

Hasty Heart, The (Patrick, J.). DEng 1467-1468; RevDEng 1849-1850.

Hate of Treason (Breton, N.). PEng 282; RevPEng 346.

Hateful Contraries (Wimsatt). LTh 1556.

"Hateful Word, The" (Welch). RevShF 2427-2428.

Hatter's Castle (Cronin). LFEng 648, 650-651, 652-653, 654-655, 661; RevLFEng 781, 783-784, 785-786, 787-788, 794.

Hattyú, A. See *Swan, The.*

Hauch, Johannes Carsten. DFor 2469.

Hauge, Alfred. LFFor 797-804.

Hauge, Olav H. PFor 2194.

Haugen, Paal-Helge. LFFor 2364.

"Haunted" (de la Mare). PEng 778; RevPEng 898.

"Haunted and the Haunters, The" (Bulwer-Lytton). RevShF 2693-2694; ShF 199-200.

"Haunted House, The" (Hood). PEng 1388; RevPEng 1586.

Haunted House, The (Plautus). DFor 1486-1487, 2141.

"Haunted House, A" (Woolf). RevShF 2515; ShF 2455.

Haunted House and Other Short Stories, A (Woolf). ShF 2455.

Haunted Man, The (Dickens). RevShF 724; ShF 1272.

"Haunted Palace, The" (Poe). PEng 2247; RevPEng 2620.

"Haunted Valley, The" (Bierce). M&D 125.

Haunting of Hill House, The (Jackson). LFEng 1430-1431.

Hauptmann, Gerhart. DFor 865-875, 2375-2376; LFFor 2180-2181, 2183; LTh 986-987, 1721-1722, 1726.

Hauptmann von Köpenick, Der. See *Captain of Köpenick, The.*

Hauschner, Auguste. LFFor 2189.

Hauser, Marianne. ShF 2634.

Hausierer, Der (Handke). LFFor 784.

Haute Surveillance. See *Deathwatch.*

Hávamál. See *Sayings of the High One, The.*

Have Come, Am Here (Villa). PEng 2979-2981; PFor 1647; RevPEng 3466-3468.

Have with You to Saffron Walden (Nash). ShF 494-495.

Havel, Václav. DFor 876-882, 2283.

Havelok the Dane. RevShF 2618; ShF 448.

Havlíček Borovský, Karel. PFor 1800-1801.

Haw Lantern, The (Heaney). RevPEng 1451.

Hawes, Stephen. RevPEng 3791-3792, 3804.

"Hawk in the Rain, The" (Hughes, T.). RevPEng 1649-1650.

Hawk in the Rain, The (Hughes, T.). RevPEng 1648-1649.

"Hawk Roosting" (Hughes, T.). PEng 1443-1445.

Hawkes, John. LFEng 1303-1313; LFSup 404; RevLFEng 1558-1568; ShF 1598-1604; ShFSup 389.

Hawkesworth, John. RevShF 1136-1141; ShF 1605-1609.

Hawkline Monster, The (Brautigan). LFEng 293-294; RevLFEng 376-377.

Hawthorne, Nathaniel. LFEng 1314-1328, 1855, 3041; LTh 524, 1012, 1567; **RevLFEng 1569-1584,** 3749, 3798, 3831; **RevShF 1142-1152,** 2619, 2656-2657, 2680-2681; ShF 112, 114, 160-161, 163, 181, 182-183,

185-187, 188-191, 449, 530-531, 769, 812-814, **1610-1614.**

Hawthorne and the Modern Short Story (Rohrberger). ShF 88, 182-183.

"Hay Fever" (Hope). PSup 191; RevPEng 1596.

Haycox, Ernest. LFEng 3195-3196; RevLFEng 3852-3853.

Hayden, Robert. PEng 1246-1254; RevPEng 1430-1439, 3909.

"Haystack in the Floods, The" (Morris). PEng 2054; RevPEng 2385.

Hayward, Richard. *See* **Kendrick, Baynard H.**

Hazard of New Fortunes, A (Howells). LFEng 1376-1378; RevLFEng 1652-1654.

Hazard, the Painter (Meredith). RevPEng 2272-2273.

Hazards of Holiness, The (Everson). PEng 990-991; RevPEng 1122.

Hazlitt, William. LTh 649-654, 798, 1701, 1705-1706, 1710.

H. D. LFEng 37-38; PEng 1255-1263; RevLFEng 51-52; RevPEng 1348-1357.

"H. D. Book, The" (Duncan). PEng 897, 901; RevPEng 1034, 1037.

"He?" (Maupassant). M&D 1209; ShF 1910-1911.

"He" (Porter). RevShF 1909; ShF 2113-2114.

"He Came into Her Line of Vision Walking Backward" (Backus). ShF 69-70.

"He Don't Plant Cotton" (Powers). RevShF 1919; ShF 2120.

He Sent Forth a Raven (Roberts). LFEng 2282-2283; RevLFEng 2877-2878.

He Sits at the Melting Pot (Munk). DFor 1392-1393.

"He Swung and He Missed" (Algren). RevShF 52; ShF 856.

He Wants Shih! (Owens). DEng 1460; RevDEng 1841.

He Who Gets Slapped (Andreyev). DFor 65-66.

Head of a Traveller (Blake). M&D 140-141.

"Head of the Bed, The" (Hollander). RevPEng 1551.

Head of the Bed, The (Hollander). PEng 1364, 1365.

Headbirths (Grass). LFFor 738.

Headlights (Terry). RevDEng 2371.

Headlong Hall (Peacock). LFEng 2079-2080; RevLFEng 2617-2618.

"Headwaiter" (Himes). RevShF 1201.

"Headwaters" (Momaday). PEng 2020-2021; RevPEng 2354-2355.

Healers, The (Armah). LFEng 91-92; RevLFEng 129-130.

Healing Art, The (Wilson, A. N.). LFSup 388; RevLFEng 3582-3583.

Healing Song for the Inner Ear (Harper). PSup 164; RevPEng 1404.

"Health Card" (Yerby). ShF 2477-2478.

"Healthiest Girl in Town, The" (Stafford). RevShF 2180; ShF 2262.

Heaney, Seamus. PEng 1264-1273, 3369-3370; PSup 405; **RevPEng 1440-1452,** 3887.

"Hearing" (Koch). PEng 1627; RevPEng 1866.

Hearing Secret Harmonies (Powell, A.). LFEng 2121-2122; RevLFEng 2681.

Heart (De Amicis). ShF 684.

"Heart" (Robison). RevShF 2013.

Heart for the Gods of Mexico, A (Aiken). LFEng 18, 21-22; RevLFEng 31, 34-35.

Heart Is a Lonely Hunter, The (McCullers). DEng 1190; LFEng 1732-1733; RevDEng 1492; RevLFEng 2163-2164.

Heart of a Dog, The (Bulgakov). LFFor 209.

"Heart of Darkness" (Booth). RevPEng 302.

Heart of Darkness (Conrad). LFEng 229-230, 585, 589-593, 3048, 3284-3286; RevDEng 3029; RevLFEng 714, 718-722, 3756, 3875-3876; RevShF 609-610, 2673; ShF 1184-1186.

Heart of Maryland, The (Belasco). DEng 195-196; RevDEng 233-234.

Heart of Midlothian, The (Scott). LFEng 2377-2382; RevLFEng 2995-3000.

"Heart of Stone, A" (Zoshchenko). RevShF 2557-2558; ShFSup 379.

"Heart of the Artichoke, The" (Gold). ShF 1502-1503.

Heart of the Matter, The (Greene, G.). LFEng 1219-1220; M&D 792; RevLFEng 1445-1446.

"Heart of Thomas Hardy, The" (Betjeman). PEng 169-170; RevPEng 203.

Heartbreak Tango (Puig). LFFor 1351-1353.

Heartland (Harris, W.). LFSup 148-149; RevLFEng 1530.

"Hearts' and Flowers'" (MacLeish). PEng 1854; RevPEng 2154.

"Hearts Come Home" (Buck). RevShF 337-338; ShF 1014.

Heart's Garden, The Garden's Heart, The (Rexroth). PEng 2353; RevPEng 2740.

"Heart's Needle" (Snodgrass). PEng 2659-2660, 3372-3373; RevPEng 3088-3089, 3890-3891.

Heart's Needle (Snodgrass). PEng 2658; RevPEng 3087.

Heat and Dust (Jhabvala). LFSup 175; RevLFEng 1757.

"Heat Lightning" (Smith). RevShF 2156.

Hello (Creeley). PEng 688.

Hello America (Ballard). LFEng 152-153; RevLFEng 196.

Hello, Darkness (Sissman). PEng 2618-2622; RevPEng 3022.

Hello, La Jolla (Dorn). PEng 843-844; RevPEng 949-950.

Hello Out There (Saroyan). DEng 1658; RevDEng 2068.

Helmets (Dickey). RevPEng 906-908.

"Helmsman, The" (Cunningham). PSup 77-78; RevPEng 806-807.

"Heloise." *See* "Heroine, The" (Dinesen).

Héloïse (Hébert). LFFor 814.

Héloise and Abélard (Moore, G.). LFEng 1902; RevLFEng 2409.

"Helping Hand, A" (Sansom). ShF 2184.

Helprin, Mark. RevShF 1159-1167, 2758; ShFSup 113-121.

Helység-kalapácsa, A. See *Hammer of the Village, The.*

Hemingway, Ernest. LFEng 490, **1337-1349,** 3061-3062; LFSup 404; **RevLFEng 1595-1607,** 3763, 3769-3770, 3797, 3799, 3875; **RevShF 1168-1177;** ShF 249-250, 544, 815, **1621-1628.**

Hemligheter på vägen (Tranströmer). PFor 1529.

Hemlock and After (Wilson, Angus). LFEng 2900-2901; RevLFEng 3590-3591.

Hemmer, Jarl. LFFor 2346-2347.

Hemsöborna. See *Natives of Hemsö, The.*

"Hen-Pecked" (Zoshchenko). RevShF 2557; ShFSup 378.

"Henceforth, from the Mind" (Bogan). PEng 238-239; RevPEng 285-286.

Henceforward (Ayckbourn). RevDEng 82, 83.

Henderson, Philip. PEng 1904.

Henderson the Rain King (Bellow). LFEng 229-231; RevLFEng 280-282, 3775.

Henley, Beth. DEng 2411-2412; **DSup 192-197; RevDEng 1150-1157, 2932-2933.**

Hennissart, Martha. *See* **Lathen, Emma.**

Henri Christoph (Walcott, D. A.). DEng 2453; RevDEng 2978.

Henrietta, The (Howard, B.). DEng 970-971; RevDEng 1207-1208.

Henry, O. LTh 443; **M&D 852-858; RevShF 1178-1182;** ShF 223, 229-230, 537-539, **1629-1633.**

Henry, Olivier. *See* **Henry, O.**

"Henry and Emma" (Prior). RevPEng 2671.

Henry and Emma (Prior). PEng 2290.

Henry James: A Life (Edel). LTh 428.

Henry of Ofterdingen (Novalis). LFFor 2166; LTh 1701.

Henry Stillings Jugend (Jung). LFFor 2156.

Henry III and His Court (Dumas, *père*). DFor 486-487, 2343.

Henry IV (Pirandello). DFor 1469-1470; LTh 1101.

Henry IV, Part I (Shakespeare). DEng 1701, 2277; RevDEng 2115-2116, 2796.

Henry IV, Part II (Shakespeare). DEng 1701-1702, 2277; RevDEng 2115-2116, 2796.

Henry V (Shakespeare). DEng 1702-1703; RevDEng 2116-2117, 2796.

Henry V (Shakespeare, adapted by Olivier). DEng 2519-2520.

Henry VI, Part I (Shakespeare). DEng 1697-1698; RevDEng 2111-2112.

Henry VI, Part II (Shakespeare). DEng 1698; RevDEng 2112.

Henry VI, Part III (Shakespeare). DEng 1698-1699; RevDEng 2112-2113.

Henry VIII (Shakespeare and Fletcher). DEng 636, 1703, 2284; RevDEng 781, 2117, 2803.

Henryson, Robert. PEng **1287-1293,** 3278-3279; **RevPEng 1465-1472,** 3797-3798.

Henshaw, James Ene. DEng 925-933. **RevDEng 1158-1166.**

Hepta epi Thebas. See *Seven Against Thebes.*

Heptameron, The (Marguerite de Navarre). LFFor 2111; ShF 144.

Heptateuchon (Thierry of Chartres). LTh 20.

"Hêr Bâbest." *See* "Sir Pope."

"Hêr Keiser." *See* "Sir Emperor."

"Her Person" (Guillén). PFor 627.

"Her Pure Fingernails on High Offering Their Onyx" (Mallarmé). PFor 928.

"Her Table Spread" (Bowen). RevShF 263-264; ShF 985-987.

Her Victory (Sillitoe). LFEng 2402.

"Her Whole Existence: A Story of True Love" (Himes). RevShF 1201.

"Hera, Hung from the Sky" (Kizer). PEng 1619; RevPEng 1855.

Heracles (Euripides). DFor 2114-2115.

Hērakleidai. See *Children of Heracles, The.*

Hērakles (Euripedes). See *Heracles.*

Herakles (MacLeish). DEng 1224; RevDEng 1545.

Heraldos negros, Los (Vallejo). PFor 1587-1589.

Herberge, Die (Hochwälder). DFor 930.

Herbert, George. PEng **1294-1305; RevPEng 1473-1485.**

Herbert, Victor. DEng 2467; RevDEng 2993.

"Herbert White" (Bidart). RevPEng 209.

Herbert, Zbigniew. PFor 653-661; PSup 406.

"Herbstmanöver." *See* "Autumn Manouvero."

Herceg, hátha megjön a tél is! (Babits). PFor 119-120.

"Hercules and Antaeus" (Heaney). PEng 1271.

Hercules furens. See *Mad Hercules.*

Hercules, My Shipmate (Graves, R.). LFEng 1201; RevLFEng 1425.

Hercules on Oeta (Seneca). DFor 2149.

Herder, Johann Gottfried. LFFor 2158; LTh 437, 596-597, **666-671,** 1560, 1697, 1699; PFor 1912-1913.

"Here" (Salinas). PFor 1386-1387.

"Here Comes the Maples" (Updike). ShF 2373.

"Here with the Long Grass Rippling" (Cowley, M.). PEng 607-608; RevPEng 713-714.

Hérédia, José-Maria de. PFor 1874.

Hereditary Forester, The (Ludwig). DFor 1214-1215.

Heritage (Cullen). PEng 696-697.

"Heritage" (Still). PEng 2764; RevPEng 3227.

Heritage of the Desert, The (Grey). RevLFEng 3850.

Herlihy, James Leo. ShF 559.

Herman, William. *See* **Bierce, Ambrose.**

"Herman Melville" (Auden). PEng 76-77; RevPEng 86-87.

Hermannschlacht, Die (Grabbe). DFor 807.

Hermes, pies i gwiazda (Herbert). PFor 657.

Hermine, L'. See *Ermine, The.*

Hermippus. DFor 2122.

"Hermit, The" (Updike). RevShF 2337; ShF 2368.

Hermlin, Stephan. PFor 1817, 1818, 1822, 1823, 1824, 1826.

Hermosura de Angélica, La (Vega). PFor 1601-1602.

Hernández, Antonio Acevedo. DFor 2442.

Hernani (Hugo). DEng 2188, 2189; DFor 968; LFFor 847; LTh 1710; RevDEng 2708-2709.

Hero and Leander (Chapman). PEng 460-461; RevPEng 555-556.

Hero and Leander (Marlowe). PEng 1902-1905; ShF 1893; RevPEng 2207-2210.

Hero in Eclipse in Victorian Fiction, The (Praz). LTh 1167.

Hero of Our Time, A (Lermontov). LFEng 3142-3144; LFFor 1021-1024, 2314; PFor 866.

Herod and Mariamne (Hebbel). DFor 888-889.

Herod the Great (Wakefield Master). DEng 1994; RevDEng 2463-2464.

Herod the King (Munk). DFor 1390.

Herodas. DFor 2135.

"Hérodias" (Flaubert). RevShF 874-875; ShF 1381.

Herodias (Mallarmé). PFor 928 930.

Heroes and Heroines (Whittemore). PEng 3077-3078; RevPEng 3566.

Heroes and Villains (Carter). LFSup 74; RevLFEng 568.

Heroic and Elegiac Song for the Lost Second Lieutenant of the Albanian Campaign (Elýtis). PFor 1966.

"Heroic Poem in Praise of Wine" (Belloc). PEng 134-136; RevPEng 162, 163-165.

Heroica de Buenos Aires (Dragún). DFor 2444.

"Heroine, The" (Dinesen). RevShF 740-741.

"Heroine, The" (Highsmith). RevShF 1192.

Herr Sleeman kommer. See *Mr. Sleeman Is Coming.*

"Herrick" (Aldrich). PEng 32-33.

Herrick, Robert. PEng 1306-1318; RevPEng 1486-1499.

Herrington, John. LTh 1184.

Herself Surprised (Cary). LFEng 458-459; RevLFEng 578-579.

Hersey, John. LFEng 1350-1358; LFSup 404-405; RevLFEng 1608-1616.

Hertha (Bremer). LFFor 2337.

"Hertha" (Swinburne). PEng 2819-2820; RevPEng 3287-3288.

Hertz, Henrick. DFor 2469.

Hervey, Evelyn. *See* **Keating, H. R. F.**

Hervieu, Paul. DFor 2348.

"Herzeliebez Frowelîn." *See* "Little Maid So Dear."

Herzen, Aleksandr. LFFor 2318.

Herzog (Bellow). LFEng 231-232; RevLFEng 282-283.

Herzog Theodor von Gothland (Grabbe). DFor 800-801.

Hesiod. PFor 662-669, 1757; ShF 135.

"Hesitations Outside the Room" (Atwood). PEng 67.

Hesperus (Jean Paul). LFFor 873-874.

Hesse, Hermann. LFFor **825-835,** 2185, 2191-2193; **RevShF 1183-1189; ShF 1634-1639.**

"Hessian Prisoner, The" (Bates). RevShF 174; ShFSup 30.

"Hester" (Lamb). PEng 1636; RevPEng 1900.

Het Pantser (Heijermans). DFor 914-915.

Hetty Dorval (Wilson, E.). LFEng 2911; RevLFEng 3602.

"Heure jaune, L'." *See* "Golden Hour, The."

Hext, Harrington. *See* **Phillpotts, Eden.**

Hey Jack! (Hannah). RevLFEng 1487.
"Hey Sailor, What Ship?" (Olsen). RevShF 1813-1814; ShF 2021-2022.
Heyduk, Adolf. PFor 1802.
Heyen, William. PEng 1319-1328; PSup 406; RevPEng 1500-1509.
Heyer, Georgette. M&D 859-864.
Heym, Georg. PFor 1927-1928.
Heym, Stefan. LFFor 2204.
Heynen, Jim. ShF 2637.
Heyse, Paul. LFEng 3236-3237; LFFor 2172-2173.
Heyward, DuBose. DEng 934-939; RevDEng 1167-1172.
Heywood, John. DEng 940-947, 2154, 2256-2257; **PEng 1329-1336; RevDEng 1173-1181,** 2674, 2776-2777; **RevPEng 1510-1518.**
Heywood, Thomas. DEng 948-956, 2291; **PEng 1337-1343; RevDEng 1182-1191,** 2810.
"Hi!" (de la Mare). PEng 776; RevPEng 896.
"Hi, Kuh" (Zukofsky). PEng 3223; RevPEng 3747.
Hidden God, The (Brooks, C.). LTh 221.
"Hidden Things" (Cavafy). PFor 299.
"Hiding of Black Chief, The" (Henry). ShF 1630.
"Hiding Our Love" (Kizer). PEng 1618-1619.
Hiding Place (Wideman). LFSup 383-384. See also *Homewood Trilogy, The.*
Hier régnant désert (Bonnefoy). PSup 46.
Hierarchy of the Blessed Angels, The (Heywood, T.). PEng 1341-1342.
Hieroglyphikes of the Life of Man (Quarles). PEng 2297; RevPEng 2678.
Hieronymous Fracastorius. *See* **Fracastoro, Girolamo.**
Higgins, Dick. ShF 2638.
"Higgler, The" (Coppard). RevShF 626-627; ShF 1198-1199.
"High and Low Brows" (Lewis). LTh 895.
High Bid, The (James, H.). DEng 996-997; RevDEng 1261.
High Citadel (Bagley). M&D 54, 57.
High Commissioner, The (Clery). M&D 362-363.
High Crime and Misdemeanor (Greenberg). RevShF 1065; ShF 1539.
"High Dive" (Empson). PEng 969; RevPEng 1099.
High Malady (Pasternak). PFor 1159.
"High Modes" (Harper). PSup 163; RevPEng 1403.
High Rise (Ballard). LFEng 151; RevLFEng 195.
High Road, The (O'Brien, E.). RevLFEng 2548.

High Sierra (Burnett). M&D 246.
High Stakes. See Dead at the Take-Off.
"'High-Toned Gentleman,' The" (De Forest). LFEng 700-701; RevLFEng 834-835.
"High-Toned Old Christian Woman, A" (Stevens). PEng 3392.
High Tor (Anderson, M.). DEng 28-29; RevDEng 39-40.
High Window, The (Chandler). LFEng 491, 493; RevLFEng 604, 606.
Highland, Dora. *See* **Avallone, Michael.**
"Highland Widow, The" (Scott). RevShF 2088-2089; ShFSup 283-284.
Highsmith, Patricia. M&D 865-871. RevShF 1190-1198.
Highwater, Jamake. LFEng 1359-1367; RevLFEng 1617-1627; ShF 2639.
Highway to the Spital-House, The (Copland). ShF 453.
Hijikata Yoshi. DFor 2433.
Hijo de Don Juan, El. See Son of Don Juan, The.
Hiketides. See Suppliants, The.
Hikmet, Nazim. PSup 173-183.
Hilarius. DFor 2162.
Hilarius of Poitiers. *See* Hilary.
Hilary. PFor 2111.
Hilda Lessways (Bennett). LFEng 245; RevLFEng 299.
Hilda Wade (Allen and Doyle). M&D 18-19.
Hildebrandslied. PFor 1897; RevShF 2601-2602; ShF 429-430.
Hildesheimer, Wolfgang. LFFor 2199.
"Hill, A" (Hecht). PEng 1283-1284; RevPEng 1459.
Hill, Archibald A. PEng 3447-3448; RevPEng 3982-3983.
Hill, Geoffrey. PEng 1344-1354, 3369; **PSup 406; RevPEng 1519-1529,** 3887.
Hill, Grimes. *See* **Nebel, Frederick.**
Hill, John. *See* **Koontz, Dean R.**
Hill, Reginald. M&D 872-877.
Hill of Destiny (Giono). LFFor 654.
Hill Street Blues. RevDEng 3041-3042.
Hiller, Catherine. ShF 2640.
Hillerman, Tony. M&D 878-883.
"Hills Like White Elephants" (Hemingway). RevShF 1170-1171, 2731; ShF 5-6, 7-8, 16, 110-111.
Him (Cummings). PEng 701; RevPEng 792.
"Him with His Foot in His Mouth" (Bellow). RevShF 206.
Himari qala li (Hakim). DSup 176.
Himbeerpflucker, Der. See Raspberry Picker, The.

History of Henry Esmond, Esquire, The (Thackeray). LFEng 2621-2623; RevLFEng 3274-3276.

History of Italian Literature (De Sanctis). LTh 362-363, 366.

History of Lady Sophia Sternheim, The (La Roche). LFFor 2155-2156.

History of Mr. Polly, The (Wells). LFEng 2811-2812; RevLFEng 3483-3484.

"History of My Heart" (Pinsky). RevPEng 2589.

History of Pendennis, The (Thackeray). LFEng 2620-2621; RevLFEng 3273-3274.

History of Rasselas, The (Johnson, S.). PEng 3473; ShF 1709-1711.

History of the Adventures of Joseph Andrews, and of His Friend Mr. Abraham Adams. See *Joseph Andrews.*

History of the American Film, A (Durang). DSup 101-102; RevDEng 671.

History of the Franks (Gregory of Tours). RevShF 2598-2599; ShF 427.

History of the French Novel, A (Saintsbury). LTh 1265-1266.

History of the Kings of Britain (Geoffrey of Monmouth). PEng 1688-1689; RevShF 2612; ShF 441.

History of the Life of the Late Mr. Jonathan Wild the Great, The. See *Jonathan Wild.*

History of the Lombards (Paul the Deacon). RevShF 2600; ShF 428.

History of the Nun, The (Behn). LFEng 221; RevLFEng 271; ShF 502.

History of the Royal Society (Sprat). PEng 3493.

History of the Valorous and Wittie Knight-Errant, Don Quixote of the Mancha. See *Don Quixote de la Mancha.*

History of the World (Raleigh). PEng 2301; RevPEng 2690, 2697.

History of the World in 10-1/2 Chapters, A (Barnes). RevLFEng 215.

History of Tom Jones, a Foundling, The. See *Tom Jones.*

"History of Yesterday, A" (Tolstoy). LFFor 1721.

"Hiszek hitetlenül Istenben." *See* "I Believe, Unbelieving, in God."

Hitchcock, George. ShF 2641.

"Hitchhiking Game, The" (Kundera). RevShF 1387-1388.

"Hitler Spring, The" (Montale). PFor 1051-1052. See also *Storm and Other Poems, The.*

Hitomaro, Kakinomoto no. *See* Kakinomoto no Hitomaro.

"Hitotsu hako ni." *See* "Laying."

Hive, The (Cela). LFFor 295-298.

"Hiver qui vient, L'" (Laforgue). PFor 827-828.

"Hiway Poesy LA-Albuquerque-Texas-Wichita" (Ginsberg). PEng 1094.

Hjelmslev, Louis. LTh 422.

Hjemløs. See *Homeless.*

Hjulet (Jensen). LFFor 881. See also *Long Journey, The.*

H. M. Pulham, Esquire (Marquand). LFEng 1817-1818; RevLFEng 2302-2303.

H.M.S. Parliament (Fuller, W. H.). DEng 2438; RevDEng 2961.

H.M.S. Pinafore (Gilbert and Sullivan). DEng 763; RevDEng 944.

Ho Ching-chih. DFor 2333.

Ho Ching-ming. LTh 1777.

Hoagland, Edward. LFSup 151-156; RevLFEng 1628-1635.

Hobart, George V. RevDEng 729, 732.

Hobbes, Thomas. LTh 1677.

Hobbit, The (Tolkien). LFEng 2642-2644; RevLFEng 3298-3299, 3862.

Hobson, Geary. ShF 2642.

Hoch, Edward D. M&D 891-897; RevShF 1205-1211; ShF 2643. *See also* Queen, Ellery.

Hochhuth, Rolf. DFor 916-923, 2380.

Hochstein, Rolaine. ShF 2644.

Hochwälder, Fritz. DFor 924-936; DSup 407.

Hochwasser. See *Flood.*

Hockaby, Stephen. *See* Mitchell, Gladys.

Hoddis, Jakob von. PFor 1927.

Hodgson, William Hope. ShF 772.

Hododarje (Pavlović). PFor 1166.

Hoel, Sigurd. LFFor 2352.

Hoffman, Daniel. PEng 1355-1361; RevPEng 1530-1537.

Hoffmann, E. T. A. LFEng 3246, 3247; LFFor 836-844, 2166; RevLFEng 3874; RevShF 1212-1218; ShF 714, 1644-1650.

Hofmannsthal, Hugo von. DFor 935-943, 2377; LTh 672-678; PFor 670-678, 1924-1925.

Hofmannswaldau, Christian Hofmann von. PFor 1909-1910.

Hofmeister, Der. See *Tutor, The.*

"Hog Heaven" (Williams, C. K.). PSup 390; RevPEng 3605.

Hogan, Linda. RevPEng 1538-1544, 3936.

Hogarth, Charles. *See* Creasey, John.

Hōgetsu, Shimamura. LTh 679-683.

Hogg, James. LFEng 3146-3147; RevLFEng 3858.

Hojarasca, La. See *Leaf Storm.*

Højholt, Per. PFor 2197-2198.

"Hokuro no Tegami." *See* "Mole, The."

Holan, Vladimír. PFor 1805.

Holberg, Ludvig. DFor 944-952, 2466.

Holcroft, Thomas. DEng 2001, RevDEng 2840, 2850.

Hölderlin (Weiss). DFor 1990-1991.

Hölderlin, Friedrich. LTh 1698; PFor 679-688, 1914-1915.

"Holdfast, The" (Herbert). PEng 1301; RevPEng 1480.

Holding Talks (Rotimi). RevDEng 2032.

"Holding the Mirror Up to Nature" (Nemerov). PEng 2085.

"Hole in the Floor, A" (Wilbur). PEng 3096; RevPEng 3586.

Holiday (Barry). DEng 134; RevDEng 170.

"Holiday" (Kincaid). RevShF 1342.

"Holiday" (Porter). RevShF 1913; ShF 2115-2116.

Holiday, Grant. *See* **Gardner, Erle Stanley.**

Holland, Norman N. LTh 684-689, 768, 1764; PEng 3422; RevPEng 3957.

Hollander, John. LTh 165; PEng 1362-1367; PSup 406; **RevPEng 1545-1556.**

Hölle Weg Erde (Kaiser). DFor 1019-1020.

Holliday, James. *See* **Gray, Simon.**

"Hollow Men, The" (Eliot). PEng 946-949; RevPEng 1076.

Hollow Sea (Hanley). LFEng 1249-1250; RevLFEng 1471.

Hollý, Ján. PFor 1808.

Holmåas, Stig. PFor 2196.

Holmes, H. H. *See* **Boucher, Anthony.**

Holmes, Oliver Wendell. PEng 1368-1376; RevPEng 1557-1566.

Holmsen, Bjarne P. See *Before Dawn.*

Holocaust (Reznikoff). PEng 2356-2362; RevPEng 2748-2749.

Holton, Leonard. M&D 898-904.

Holy City, The (Lagerlöf). LFFor 985. See also *Jerusalem.*

Holy Ghosts (Linney). DSup 237; RevDEng 1446-1447.

Holy Grail, The. RevLFEng 2284.

Holy Place (Fuentes). LFFor 596-597; RevShF 928.

Holy Terror, The. See *Empire City, The.*

Holy Terror, The (Goodman). RevLFEng 1373-1374.

Holz, Arno. LFFor 2180-2187; LTh 573, **690-694,** 1719-1720; **PFor 689-697.**

"Homage to Clotho: A Hospital Suite" (Sissman). PEng 2619-2620; RevPEng 3023-3024.

"Homage to Ezra Pound" (Wright, C.). RevPEng 3657.

Homage to Mistress Bradstreet (Berryman). PEng 162-164; RevPEng 194-196.

"Homage to Paul Cézanne" (Wright, C.). PEng 3153; RevPEng 3661.

Homage to Sextus Propertius (Pound). PEng 2268-2269, 3364-3365; RevPEng 2643-2644, 3882-3883.

"Homage to William Cowper" (Davie). PSup 85; RevPEng 850.

"Hombre muerto, El." *See* "Dead Man, The."

Hombres de maíz. See *Men of Maize.*

"Hombres necios" (Cruz). PFor 379.

"Home" (Beer). PEng 122; RevPEng 142.

"Home" (Guest). PEng 1165-1166; RevPEng 1325.

"Home" (Phillips). RevShF 1886.

Home (Storey). DEng 1887-1889.; RevDEng 2328-2330.

Home and Beauty (Maugham). DEng 1310; RevDEng 1639.

Home and the World (Tagore). LFFor 2218.

Home as Found (Cooper). LFEng 606-607; RevLFEng 736-737.

Home at Seven (Sherriff). DEng 1791; RevDEng 2225.

Home Course in Religion (Soto). RevPEng 3117.

Home Fires (Guare). RevDEng 1057.

"Home Front, The" (Helprin). RevShF 1161-1162; ShFSup 115-116;

"Home Is Where" (Adams). RevShF 8; ShFSup 2.

Home of the Brave (Laurents). DEng 1101-1102; RevDEng 1380-1382.

"Home on the Range" (Dorn). PEng 842; RevPEng 948.

Home Place, The (Morris). LFEng 1904; RevLFEng 2412.

"Home Sickness" (Moore). ShF 660-661.

Home Truths (Gallant). LFEng 1053; RevLFEng 1251.

"Home/World" (Niedecker). PSup 299; RevPEng 2448.

Homecoming (Ngugi). LTh 1062-1063.

"Homecoming, The" (Yerby). ShF 2478-2479.

Homecoming Singer, The (Wright, Jay). RevPEng 3685-3686.

"Homeland" (Hölderlin). PFor 681-682.

Homeless (Goldschmidt). LFFor 2337.

Homenaje (Guillén). PFor 625-626.

Homer. DFor 2087-2088; LFFor 1999; LTh 1143-1144, 1511; PFor 62, 85-86, **698-708,** 1750-1754; **RevShF 1219-1224,** 2568-2569; ShF 135, **1651-1655.**

Horozsco, Sebastián de. DFor 2172.

Horribilicribrifax (Gryphius). DFor 838-839.

Horror Stories. ShF 741.

Horse and His Boy, The (Lewis, C. S.). LFEng 1657; RevLFEng 2049.

"Horse and Two Goats, A" (Narayan). RevShF 1718.

Horse and Two Goats and Other Stories, A (Narayan). RevShF 1718-1719; ShFSup 228.

"Horse Chestnut Tree, The" (Eberhart). PEng 933.

"Horse Dealer's Daughter, The" (Lawrence, D. H.). RevShF 2737; ShF 1791-1792.

Horse Eats Hat. See *Italian Straw Hat, The.*

"Horse That Could Whistle 'Dixie,' The" (Weidman). RevShF 2419-2420; ShF 2411-2412.

"Horseback in the Rain" (Still). PEng 2764; RevPEng 3227.

Horseman on the Roof, The (Giono). LFFor 658.

Horseman, Pass By (McMurtry). LFEng 1751-1752; RevLFEng 2220.

"Horses in Central Park" (Swenson). PEng 2795; RevPEng 3261.

Horse's Mouth, The (Cary). LFEng 458, 460; RevLFEng 578, 580.

"Horses of Achilles, The" (Sikelianos). PFor 1957-1958.

"Horseshoe Finder, The" (Mandelstam). PFor 939-940.

Horsky hotel (Havel). DFor 881.

"Horus" (Nerval). PFor 1087.

Horvath, Odon von. DFor 953-962.

Horvatić, Dubravko. PFor 2266.

Horwitz, Julius. ShF 2645.

Hosanna (Quarles). PEng 2298; RevPEng 2679.

Hosanna (Tremblay). DSup 354-355.

Hose, Die. See *Bloomers, The.*

Hospital, The (Fearing). M&D 594.

"Hospital Window, The" (Dickey, J.). PEng 796.

Hostage, The (Behan). DEng 165-167; RevDEng 200-202.

"Hostages" (Wideman). RevShF 2465.

Hosties noires (Senghor). PFor 1426.

Hostrup, Jens Christian. DFor 2469.

Hot l Baltimore, The (Wilson, L.). DEng 2100-2101; RevDEng 2611-2612.

Hotel, The (Bowen). LFEng 264; RevLFEng 320.

Hotel du Lac (Brookner). LFSup 66-67; RevLFEng 402-404.

Hotel New Hampshire, The (Irving, J.). LFEng 1413, 1423-1425; RevLFEng 1700-1702.

Hotel Play, The (Shawn). DSup 336-337; RevDEng 2169-2170.

Hotel Universe (Barry). DEng 136-137; RevDEng 172-173.

Hottentot Ossuary (Tate, J.). PEng 2838-2839.

Hound of the Baskervilles, The (Doyle). LFEng 807; M&D 532-535; RevLFEng 974.

"Hound of Ulster, The" (Smith, S.). RevPEng 3078-3077.

"Hounds of Tinaldos, The" (Long). ShF 565.

Hounds on the Mountain (Still). PEng 2762-2765; RevPEng 3225.

"Hour, The" (Blackburn). PEng 195; RevPEng 239.

"Hour of Feeling, The" (Simpson). PEng 2608.

Hour of the Star, The (Lispector). LFSup 247.

Hours of Idleness (Byron). LTh 258; PEng 405; RevPEng 471-472.

Hous of Fame, The. See *House of Fame, The.*

"House, The" (Berry). PEng 151-152.

"House, The" (Creeley). PEng 690.

House Behind the Cedars, The (Chesnutt). LFEng 518-520; RevLFEng 634-636.

House by the Churchyard, The (Le Fanu). LFEng 1624-1625; M&D 1050; RevLFEng 1999-2000.

House by the Medlar Tree, The (Verga). DFor 2411; LFFor 1861-1864, 2232-2233; LTh 1497-1498.

House for Mr. Biswas, A (Naipaul). LFEng 1960; RevLFEng 2473-2474.

House in Clewe Street, The (Lavin). ShF 1780.

House in Paris, The (Bowen). LFEng 265-266; RevLFEng 321-322.

House in the Country, A (Donoso). LFFor 500-501.

"House in the Trees, The" (Booth). PEng 246; RevPEng 306.

"House in Turk Street, The" (Hammett). RevShF 1105-1106; ShF 1577-1578.

House Made of Dawn (Momaday). RevPEng 3929.

House of Bernarda Alba, The (García Lorca). DFor 665, 2506.

House of Blue Leaves, The (Guare). DEng 861; RevDEng 1058-1059.

House of Cards (Ellin). M&D 577-578.

House of Children, A (Cary). LFEng 458; RevLFEng 577-578.

House of Dust, The (Aiken). PEng 24; RevPEng 25.

"House of Ecstacy, The" (Farley). ShF 129-130.

House of Fame, The (Chaucer). LTh 282; PEng 481-482; RevPEng 577-578; RevShF 483-484; ShF 1103.

House of Five Talents, The (Auchincloss). LFEng 106-107; RevLFEng 147-148.

House of Fourchambault, The (Augier). DFor 140-142.

House of Gentlefolk, A (Turgenev). LFFor 1774.

House of Incest (Nin). LFEng 1990-1991; RevLFEng 2514-2515.

House of Life, The (Rossetti, D. G.). PEng 2431-2432, 2433; RevPEng 2824-2826.

House of Mirth, The (Wharton, Edith). LFEng 2852-2854; RevLFEng 3534, 3535-3536.

"House of Night, The" (Freneau). PEng 1035; RevPEng 1166.

House of Sleep, The (Kavan). RevShF 1313-1314.

House of Sleeping Beauties, The (Hwang). RevDEng 1229.

House of the Arrow, The (Mason). M&D 1197-1198.

House of the Dead, The (Dostoevski). LFFor 2317.

House of the Four Winds, The (Buchan). LFEng 334; RevLFEng 429.

House of the Prophet, The (Auchincloss). LFEng 112-113; RevLFEng 153-154.

House of the Seven Gables, The (Hawthorne). LFEng 1322-1324; RevLFEng 1577-1579, 3831.

House of the Sleeping Beauties, The (Kawabata). LFFor 911-912; RevShF 1321.

House of the Solitary Maggot, The (Purdy). LFEng 2174-2175; RevLFEng 2747, 2748-2749.

House on Coliseum Street, The (Grau). LFEng 1185; RevLFEng 1408.

House on Mango Street, The (Cisneros). RevShF 557-559.

House on Marshland, The (Glück). PSup 135-136; RevPEng 1246-1247.

House on the Hill, The (Pavese). LFFor 1248-1250.

"House on the Hill, The" (Robinson). PEng 2388-2389; RevPEng 2779-2780.

House with Two Doors Is Difficult to Guard, A (Calderón). DFor 301-302.

"Houseboat" (Nin). RevShF 1723; ShF 1949.

"Housebreaker of Shady Hill, The" (Cheever). RevShF 503-504.

Household, Geoffrey. M&D 911-915.

Household Plagued by Love, A (Cruz). DFor 443.

Householder, The (Jhabvala). LFSup 173-174; RevLFEng 1757.

Houseman, John. RevDEng 3027, 3030.

"Houses" (Leavitt). RevShF 1438.

Housman, A. E. PEng 1405-1416; RevPEng 1615-1627.

"How Annandale Went Out" (Robinson). PEng 2391, 2392-2393; RevPEng 2779, 2783-2784.

"How Come?" (Ignatow). PEng 1472; RevPEng 1684.

"How Cruel Is the Story of Eve" (Smith, S.). RevPEng 3074.

"How Dunbar Was Desired to Be a Friar" (Dunbar, W.). PEng 888; RevPEng 1024.

How Far Can You Go? (Lodge). RevLFEng 2092.

"How I Contemplated the World from the Detroit House of Correction and Began My Life Over Again" (Oates). RevShF 1739-1740; ShF 1962-1963.

"How I Finally Lost My Heart" (Lessing, D.). RevShF 1474-1476; ShF 1806-1807.

How It Is (Beckett). LFEng 213; LFFor 129; RevLFEng 262-264.

"How It Was Done in Odessa" (Babel). RevShF 127.

How Like a God (Stout). ShF 128.

How Like an Angel (Millar). M&D 1221-1222.

How Mister Mockingpott Was Cured of His Suffering (Weiss). DFor 1990.

"How Mr. Rabbit Saved His Meat" (Harris, J.). RevShF 1116; ShF 1587-1588.

"How Much Land Does a Man Need?" (Tolstoy). ShF 2334-2335.

"How Pearl Button Was Kidnapped" (Mansfield). ShF 1881.

"How Sharp Snaffles Got His Capital and His Wife" (Simms). RevShF 2120-2122; ShF 2233-2236.

How the Ancients Represented Death (Lessing). LTh 882.

"How the Devil Came Down Division Street" (Algren). RevShF 52-53; ShF 857.

How the Other Half Loves (Ayckbourn). RevDEng 78, 79.

How the Plains Indians Got Horses (Plumly). PEng 2235; RevPEng 2607.

"How the Rain Is Falling Lightly" (Castro). PFor 279. See also *Cantares gallegos.*

How to Do Things with Words (Austin). LTh 1827.

"How to Eat an Orange" (MacBeth). PEng 1834; RevPEng 2113.

"How to Get on in Society" (Betjeman). PEng 171; RevPEng 204-205.

"How to Get Through Reality" (Blackburn). PEng 196; RevPEng 240.

"How to Get Up Off It" (Blackburn). PEng 198; RevPEng 242.

"How to Read" (Pound). LTh 1156, 1158.

"How to See Deer" (Booth). RevPEng 305.

"How We Heard the Name" (Dugan). PEng 882-883; RevPEng 1006-1007.

Howard, Bronson. DEng 965-972; RevDEng 1202-1210.

Howard, Hartley. See **Carmichael, Harry.**

Howard, Henry. See **Surrey, Henry Howard, Earl of.**

Howard, Robert E. RevLFEng 3862.

Howard, Sidney. DEng 973-978; RevDEng 1211-1217.

Howard Nemerov Reader, A (Nemerov). RevPEng 2432.

Howard's End (Forster). LFEng 1001-1003; RevLFEng 1191-1193.

Howe, Irving. LFEng 3252-3253.

Howe, Susan. PSup 193-199; RevPEng 1628-1635.

Howe, Tina. RevDEng 1218-1224.

Howells, William Dean. LFEng 1368-1379, 3042-3043, 3049, 3173; LTh 1750; PEng 1417-1427; RevLFEng 1644-1655, 3751, 3757, 3795; ShF 221, 233-234, 575, 586, 587, 589;

"Howl" (Ginsberg). RevPEng 1226-1229, 3897, 3898.

Howl (Ginsberg). PEng 1091-1092, 3380, 3393.

Howling at the Moon (Sakutarō). PFor 2075, 2076-2077.

Hrabal, Bohumil. LFFor 2067.

Hrafnkel's Saga. RevShF 2592-2593; ShF 395-396.

Hreidar the Fool. RevShF 2594; ShF 396-397.

Hristić, Jovan. PFor 2257.

Hroswitha of Gandersheim. DEng 2244; DFor 2153-2154; PFor 2114; RevDEng 2764.

"Hsiao-ch'ung-shan." See "Tune: Manifold Little Hills."

"Hsi furen." See "Lady Hsi."

Hsi-Chou-shêng. See **P'u Sung-ling.**

Hsieh Ling-yün. PFor 720-726.

Hsi-hsiang chi. See *Romance of the Western Chamber, The.*

Hsi-hsiang chi chu kung-tiao (Tung). DFor 2309.

Hsing-shih yin-yüan chuan (P'u Sung-ling). RevShF 1940; ShFSup 238.

Hsi-yu chi. See *Journey to the West, The.*

Hsü Wei. DFor 2323.

Hu Shih. LTh 701-706, 1781.

Hu Ying-lin. LTh 1779.

"Hua ma." See "Picture Horse, The."

"Hua p'i." See "Painted Skin, The."

Huang Fang-yü. DFor 2324.

Huch, Friedrich. LFFor 2185.

Huch, Ricarda. LTFor 2104.

Huchel, Peter. PFor 1815, 1817, 1821, 1930.

Huddle, David. ShF 2646.

Hudibras (Butler). PEng 384-385, 386-390; RevPEng 460-464.

Hudson, W. H. LFEng 1380-1397; RevLFEng 1656-1664.

"Hue and Cry" (McPherson). RevShF 1556; ShF 1856-1857.

Hue and Cry (McPherson). RevShF 1555-1558; ShF 1855.

Huellas (Reyes). PFor 1321.

Huge Season, The (Morris). LFEng 1911-1912; RevLFEng 2419-2420.

Hugh Selwyn Mauberley (Pound). PEng 2269, 3365, 3390; RevPEng 2644, 3882-3883.

Hughes, Colin. See **Creasey, John.**

Hughes, Langston. PEng 1428-1436, 3393, 3400, 3401, 3402; RevDEng 2948-2949; RevPEng 1636-1645, 3908, 3909, 3910; RevShF 1225-1231; ShF 266-267, 555, 578, 1656-1661.

Hughes, Matilda. See **MacLeod, Charlotte.**

Hughes, Ted. PEng 1437-1446; PSup 406; RevPEng 1646-1657, 3886.

Hughes, Thomas. RevDEng 2784.

Hugo (Bennett). M&D 108.

Hugo, Richard. PEng 1447-1459; PSup 406; RevPEng 1658-1670.

Hugo, Victor. DEng 2188, 2189; DFor 963-972, 2344; LFFor 845-857; LTh 707-713, 1383, 1395, 1696-1697, 1705-1707, 1709-1710, 1733; PFor 727-739, 1870-1871; RevDEng 2708-2709; ShF 464.

Huguenots, Les (Scribe). DFor 1682-1684.

Huidobro, Vicente. LFFor 2291.

Huis-clos. See *No Exit.*

Huis van die dowe, Die (Breytenbach). PSup 53-54.

Huit Coups de l'horloge, Les. See *Eight Strokes of the Clock.*

"Huître, L'." See "Oyster, The."

Huldén, Lars. PFor 2200.

Hull, Richard. M&D 916-921.

"Hulla a búza-földön." See "Corpse on the Wheat-Field."

Hulme, T. E. LTh 306, 714-720, 1554, 1810.

Human Age, The (Lewis, W.). LFEng 1688-1689; RevLFEng 2085-2086.

Human, All Too Human (Nietzsche). LTh 1069.

Human Comedy, The (Balzac). LFFor 90-91, 92-94, 2126-2127; RevShF 150; ShF 921.

Human Comedy, The (Saroyan). LFEng 2336-2337; RevLFEng 2946, 2951-2952.

"Human Condition" (Gunn). PEng 1173.

"Human Element, The" (Maugham). RevShF 1628; ShF 1905.

Human Factor, The (Greene, G.). LFEng 1220-1221; RevLFEng 1446-1447.

Human Landscapes (Hikmet). PSup 180-181.

Human Poems (Vallejo). PFor 1561, 1592-1593.

Human Season, The (Wallant). LFEng 2761-2762; RevLFEng 3419-3420.

"Human Universe" (Olson). PSup 307; RevPEng 2499-2500, 2501.

Human Universe and Other Essays (Olson). LTh 1074.

Human Vibration (Richter). LFEng 2266-2267; RevLFEng 2860-2861.

"Humanism and the Religious Attitude" (Hulme). LTh 716, 718.

"Humanitad" (Wilde). PEng 3106-3107; RevPEng 3597-3598.

"Humanitarians, The" (Giusti). PFor 575.

"Humble Bee, The" (Emerson). PEng 959-960; RevPEng 1089-1090.

Humble Romance and Other Stories (Freeman, M.). RevShF 911-912; ShF 228.

Humboldt's Gift (Bellow). LFEng 234-235; RevLFEng 285-286.

Hume, David. LTh 240, **721-725.**

"Hummingbirds" (Dubie). PSup 107; RevPEng 1003.

Humor (Pirandello). LTh 148, 1097-1101.

Humourous Day's Mirth, An (Chapman). DEng 354; RevDEng 415.

Humphrey, William. RevShF **1232-1237.**

Humphreys, David. LTh 1742.

Humphry Clinker (Smollett). LFEng 2450-251; RevLFEng 3075-3076.

Hunchback of Notre Dame, The (Hugo). LFFor 853-854, 2125.

Hund des Generals, Der (Kipphardt). DFor 1055.

Hundejahre. See *Dog Years.*

Hundevakt (Hauge). LFFor 799-800. See also *Cleng Peerson.*

Hundred Sundrie Flowers Bound Up in One Small Poesie (Gascoigne). ShF 489-490.

Hundred-Thousand Songs (Mi-la Ras-pa). PFor 2247-2248.

Hundreth Sundrie Flowres, A (Gascoigne). LTh 541.

Hung Shêng. DFor 2326.

Hung Wu. DFor 2319-2320.

Hunger (Hamsun). LFFor 769-771, 2345-2346.

Hunger and Thirst (Ionesco). DFor 2357.

Hunger Artist, The (Clarke, M.). DSup 66-67; RevDEng 475.

"Hunger Artist, A" (Kafka). ShF 1733.

Hunger-Pastor, The (Raabe). LFFor 1380, 1381-1382.

"Hungerfield" (Jeffers). RevPEng 1707.

Hung-lou meng. See *Dream of the Red Chamber.*

"Hungry Man's Wheel, The" (Vallejo). PFor 1593. See also *Human Poems.*

Hunt, Kyle. See **Creasey, John.**

Hunt, Leigh. PEng 1460-1465; RevPEng **1671-1677.**

Hunt, William Holman. LTh 1245.

Hunter, Evan. See **McBain, Ed.**

"Hunter Trials" (Betjeman). PEng 171; RevPEng 205.

Hunters, The (Salter). RevLFEng 2940-2941.

"Hunters in the Snow" (Wolff). RevShF 2508.

"Hunting" (Snyder). PEng 2672; RevPEng 3105.

"Hunting of the Hare, A" (Newcastle). PEng 2095; RevPEng 2439.

Hunting of the Snark, The (Carroll). PEng 447-452; RevPEng 516-521.

"Hunting Season" (Greenberg). RevShF 1065; ShF 1538-1539.

Huntingtower (Buchan). LFEng 333-334; RevLFEng 428-429.

Hurlyburly (Rabe). DEng 1553-1554; RevDEng 1945.

"Hurrahing in Harvest" (Hopkins). PEng 1399-1400; RevPEng 1608-1609.

"Hurricane, The" (Freneau). PEng 1035; RevPEng 1166.

Hurricane Lamp (Cassity). PSup 64-65; RevPEng 545, 546.

"Hurricane Watch" (Pastan). RevPEng 2542.

Hurry Home (Wideman). LFSup 381-382; RevLFEng 3563-3564.

Hurry on Down (Wain). LFEng 2738, 2739-2740; RevLFEng 3395-3397, 3808.

"Hurry Up Please It's Time" (Sexton). PEng 2526; RevPEng 2936.

Hurskas kurjuus. See *Meek Heritage.*

Hurston, Zora Neale. LFEng 1389-1397;; RevLFEng **1665-1673; RevShF 1238-1244;** ShF 577-578.

Husband and Wife (Fredro). DFor 2277; DSup 138.

Husfrue. See *Mistress of Husaby, The* and *Kristin Lavransdatter.*

I

"I skuchno i grustno . . ." *See* "It's Boring and Sad . . ."

"I Stand Here Ironing" (Olsen). RevShF 1813; ShF 113, 2021.

"I started Early—Took my Dog" (Dickinson). PEng 809; RevPEng 921.

"I, the Mournful God." See *Laughable Loves.*

"I Try to Waken and Greet the World Once Again" (Wright, James). RevPEng 3676-3677.

"I Used to Have a Nail" (Castro). PFor 277.

"I Used to Live Here Once" (Rhys). RevShF 2002; ShFSup 262-263.

"I Wake and Feel the Fell of Dark, Not Day" (Hopkins). PEng 1402; RevPEng 1611.

"I Walk Out Alone onto the Road" (Lermontov). PFor 875.

"I Was in Love" (Oates). ShF 1964.

"I Was Reading a Scientific Article" (Atwood). PEng 66.

"I Was Riding at Full Gallop Around the City Walls, Pursued by a Throng of Superstitious Coalmongers" (Foix). PFor 489-490.

"I Was Sitting upon a Rock" (Walther). PFor 1678-1679.

I Wear the Morning Star (Highwater). RevLFEng 1625-1626.

"I went into the Maverick Bar" (Snyder). PEng 2675.

"I Went A-Roaming, Maidens, One Bright Day" (Poliziano). PFor 1254.

I Will Marry When I Want (Ngugi wa Thiong'o and Ngugi wa Mirii). DEng 2419; DSup 267-268, 272-274 RevDEng 1720-1722, 2941.

I Would, and Would Not (Breton, N.). PEng 281; RevPEng 345.

"Ia ne slyxal rasskazov Ossiana." *See* "I Have Not Heard the Tales of Ossian."

"Ia slova pozabyl, chto ia khotel skazat." *See* "I Have Forgotten the Word I Wanted to Say."

Iaia Garcia (Machado de Assis). LFFor 1042.

Iambi (Callimachus). PFor 256-257.

Iamblichus. LFFor 2001.

Iamvi kai anapaisti (Palamàs). PFor 1953.

"Iazvital'nyi." *See* "Stinger, The."

Ibn Ezra, Moses. PFor 777.

Ibn Gabirol, Solomon. PFor 777.

"Ibn Hakkan al-Bokhari, Dead in His Labyrinth" (Borges). M&D 163.

Ibn Nagrillah, Samuel. PFor 776-777.

Ibsen, Henrik. DEng 2191-2192; DFor 973-988, 2237, 2471-2472; LTh 1327-1329, 1724; RevDEng 2711-2712.

Icarus's Mother (Shepard). RevDEng 2194.

Ice (Kavan). LFEng 1512-1513; RevLFEng 1837-1838.

Ice Age, The (Drabble). LFEng 825-826, RevLFEng 990-991.

"Ice Eagle, The" (Wakoski). RevPEng 3487.

"Ice-Floes, The" (Pratt). PEng 2284; RevPEng 2657.

"Ice House, The" (Gordon). RevShF 1042-1043; ShF 1522-1524.

"Ice Storm" (Ashbery). RevPEng 65-66.

Icebound (Davis). DEng 478-479; RevDEng 589-590.

Iceman Cometh, The (O'Neill). DEng 1414-1417; RevDEng 1790-1793.

"Iceplants" (Hacker). RevPEng 1360.

"Ich bin ein Pferd." *See* "I Am a Horse."

"Ich saz ûf eine Steine." *See* "I Was Sitting upon a Rock."

"Ichabod" (Whittier). PEng 3087; RevPEng 3576.

Ichikawa Sadanji II. DFor 2432-2433.

"Ichinaka wa." *See* "In the City."

Ici ou ailleurs. See *Clope.*

"Icicle, The" (Sinyavsky). RevShF 2140-2141.

"Icicles" (Gass). ShF 1480.

Iconographs (Swenson). PEng 2795-2796; RevPEng 3261-3263.

"¡Id con Dios!" *See* "Farewell, Go with God!"

"I'd Know You Anywhere" (Hoch). RevShF 1207.

Ida, A Novel (Stein). LFEng 2516; RevLFEng 3148.

Ida Brandt (Bang). LFFor 2339.

"Idea, The" (Carver). ShFSup 77.

Idea (Drayton). PEng 853; RevPEng 968-969.

"Idea of Order at Key West, The" (Stevens). PEng 3392.

Idea of the Humanities and Other Essays Critical and Historical, The (Crane). LTh 322.

Idea, the Shepheard's Garland (Drayton). PEng 849; RevPEng 964.

"Ideal Craftsman, An" (de la Mare). RevShF 699-700; ShF 1253-1254.

"Ideal Father, The" (Olds). RevPEng 2492.

Ideal Husband, An (Wilde). DEng 2037, 2038; RevDEng 2537.

Ideal in Art, The (Taine). LTh 1420.

Idealist, En. See *Herod the King.*

Ideas Mirrour (Drayton). PEng 849; RevPEng 964.

Ideas of Good and Evil (Yeats). LTh 1587.

Ideen über eine beschreibende und zergliedende Psychologie (Dilthey). LTh 378.

Idées de Madame Aubray, Les. See *Madame Aubray's Ideas.*

Identité (Pinget). DSup 305-306.

"Identities" (Muldoon). RevPEng 2405.

"Ides of March, The" (Hornung). M&D 908.

Ides of March, The (Wilder). LFEng 2885-2886; RevLFEng 3575-3576.

Idiot, The (Dostoevski). LFFor 511-513.

Idiot de la famille, L'. See *Family Idiot, The.*

Idiot Lady, The. See *Lady Nit-Wit, The.*

Idiot's Delight (Sherwood). DEng 1806-1807; RevDEng 2240-2241.

"Idiots First" (Malamud). RevShF 1572.

Idiots Karamazov, The (Durang and Innaurato). DSup 101, 203; RevDEng 1248.

"Idle Days on the Yann" (Dunsany). RevShF 791; ShF 1317.

Idler, The (Johnson, S.). LTh 774, 1685; RevShF 1285; ShF 771, 1708-1709.

Idō. See *Move, The.*

"Idolaters, The" (D'Annunzio). ShF 687.

"Idyll" (Roethke). PEng 2409-2410; RevPEng 2802-2803.

"Idyll" (Tomlinson). RevPEng 3378.

Idylls (Theocritus). PFor 1508-1509.

Idylls of the King (Tennyson). PEng 2868; RevPEng 3342.

If (Rotimi). RevDEng 2031-2032

"if I have made, my lady, intricate" (Cummings). PEng706; RevPEng 797.

"If from my lips some angry accents fell" (Lamb). RevPEng 1898-1899; PEng 1634-1635.

If I Could Sleep Deeply Enough (Miller). RevPEng 2333.

If I Had Wheels or Love (Miller). RevPEng 2335.

"If I must die" (Nashe). PEng 2072; RevPEng 2421.

If Morning Ever Comes (Tyler). LFEng 2676; RevLFEng 3334.

"If Not Higher" (Peretz). RevShF 1875-1876; ShF 2089.

If Not Now, When? (Levi). LFSup 237-239.

If on a Winter's Night a Traveler (Calvino). LFFor 247-249.

"If poisonous minerals" (Donne). PEng 836; RevPEng 942.

"If There Were Not Death, but Oblivion" (Annensky). PFor 43.

"If They Knew Yvonne" (Dubus). RevShF 782-783.

"If We Must Die" (McKay). PEng 1845, 3392-3393, 3400; RevPEng 2144, 3908.

"If You Are a Man, Then Be One" (Petőfi). PFor 1226.

"If You Don't Want to Live I Can't Help You" (Calisher). RevShF 378-379; ShF 1037-1038.

"If You Forget the Germans" (Stern). RevPEng 3191.

"If you would seek a friend among men" (Crane, S.). PEng 663; RevPEng 760.

Ifigenia cruel (Reyes). PFor 1322.

"I. G." LTh 1668.

Igitur (Mallarmé). PFor 926-930.

Ignatow, David. PEng 1466-1477; PSup 406; **RevPEng 1678-1689.**

Ignez de Castro (Ferreira). DFor 592-594.

Ignjatović, Jakov. LFFor 2075.

"Igre." *See* "Games."

Ihara Saikaku. See **Saikaku, Ihara.**

Ihmiselon ihanuus ja kurjuus (Sillanpää). LFFor 1580.

Ihmiset suviyössä. See *People in the Summer Night.*

"Ihr Worte" (Bachmann). PFor 129.

"Iisusov grekh." *See* "Sin of Jesus, The."

Ikiddeh, Imme; *Blind Cyclos.* RevDEng 2944.

Ikones (Pentzíkis). PFor 1187-1189.

"Ilama de amor viva." *See* "Living Flame of Love, The."

Île des esclaves, L' (Marivaux). DFor 1262-1263.

Île des pingouins, L'. See *Penguin Island.*

Île mystérieuse, L'. See *Mysterious Island, The.*

Iles, Francis. See **Berkeley, Anthony.**

Ilf, Ilya. LFFor 2325.

Iliad (Homer). PFor 698-702, 704-708, 1747, 1750-1751, 1756-1757; RevShF 1220-1221, 2566-2567, 2569; ShF 1652-1653.

Ilić, Jovan. PFor 2254.

Ilić, Vojislav. PFor 2255.

Ílios o protos, mazi me tis parallayiés páno se mián ahtídha (Elýtis). PFor 464, 1966.

I'll Be Home for Christmas (Anderson, R.). DEng 39-40, RevDEng 51-52. See also *You Know I Can't Hear You When the Water's Running.*

Ill Seen Ill Said (Beckett). LFEng 215; LFFor 131; RevLFEng 263.

"Illinois Village, The" (Lindsay). PEng 1725; RevPEng 2009.

Illness as Metaphor (Sontag). LTh 1366-1367.

Illuminations (Rimbaud). PFor 1341, 1342-1343.

"Illusion, The" (Everson). PEng 987; RevPEng 1118.

Illusion and Reality (Caudwell). PEng 3411-3412.

Illusion comique, L' (Corneille). DFor 427-428.

Illustrated Man, The (Bradbury). RevLFEng 359; RevShF 304-305.

Illustrations, The (Dubie). PSup 106; RevPEng 1002.

Illustrious House of Ramires, The (Eça de Queiróz). LFFor 545-546.

Illyés, Gyula. DFor 2288; **PFor 740-746,** 1987.

Ilusiones del doctor Faustino, Las (Valera). LFFor 1821-1822.

Ilustre casa de Ramires, A. See Illustrious House of Ramires, The.

I'm Expecting to Live Quite Soon (West, P.). LFSup 372-373; RevLFEng 3523-3524.

I'm Herbert (Anderson, R.). DEng 38-39; RevDEng 50-51. See also *You Know I Can't Hear You When the Water's Running.*

Im Land der Umbramauten (Meckel). RevShF 1642-1643; ShFSup 188.

I'm Not Stiller (Frisch). LFFor 583-585.

I'm Talking About Jerusalem (Wesker). DEng 2018; RevDEng 2508.

"Im Unterreich." *See* "In the Subterranean Kingdom."

Im Westen nichts Neues. See All Quiet on the Western Front.

"Im Winter." *See* "In Winter."

Image and the Law, The (Nemerov). RevPEng 2428.

Image Maker, The (Merrill). RevPEng 2285-2286.

"Image-Vendor, The" (Okri). RevShF 1809.

"Images, The" (Rich). PEng 2371.

Images of Truth (Westcott). ShF 2423.

Imaginary Friends (Lurie). LFSup 254-255; RevLFEng 2128-2133.

"Imaginary Iceberg, The" (Bishop). PEng 184, 188; RevPEng 227, 231.

Imaginary Life, An (Malouf). RevLFEng 2290-2291.

Imaginary Magnitude (Lem). RevShF 1458; ShFSup 150.

"Imagination Dead Imagine" (Beckett). RevShF 192.

Imago (Butler, O.). RevLFEng 498-499.

Imán. See Pro Patria.

Imitation de Notre-Dame la lune, L' (Laforgue). PFor 825-826.

Immanuel Kant (Bernhard). DFor 200-201.

"Immanuel Kant and the Hopi" (Stern). PSup 369; RevPEng 3189.

Immensee (Storm). LFFor 1680-1681.

"Immer zu benennen." *See* "Always to Be Named."

Immermann, Karl Leberecht. LTh 1710.

Immobile Wind, The (Winters). PSup 396; RevPEng 3625.

"Immoral Proposition, The" (Creeley). RevPEng 776-777.

Immoralist, The (Gide). LFFor 640, 642-643, 2139-2140.

"Immortal Strangeness" (Everson). PEng 991; RevPEng 1123.

"Immram" (Muldoon). RevPEng 2405-2406.

Imnos is tin eleftheria. See Hymn to Liberty, The.

"Imperfect Conflagration, An" (Bierce). M&D 127.

"Imperfect Paradise, The" (Pastan). RevPEng 2544.

Imperfect Paradise, The (Pastan). RevPEng 2543, 2544-2545.

"Imperial Adam" (Hope). PSup 189; RevPEng 1594.

"Imperial Delhi" (Naidu). RevPEng 3945.

"Imperial Message, An" (Kafka). ShF 1733.

"Imperialism" (Graham). RevPEng 1278.

Imperium Pelagi (Young). LTh 1597.

Implied Reader, The (Iser). LTh 732-733.

Implizite Leser, Der. See Implied Reader, The.

Importance of Being Earnest, The (Wilde). DEng 2036, 2038-2040, 2366; RevDEng 2535, 2537-2539, 2884.

Imposteur, L'. See Tartuffe.

"Impostor" (Dick). ShF 1263.

"Impressions of Africa" (Koch). RevPEng 1868.

Impromptu of Outrement, The (Tremblay). DSup 355-356.

Improvisatore, The (Andersen). LFFor 2336.

Improvisatore, The (Beddoes). PEng 110-111; RevPEng 130-131.

"In a Dark Time" (Roethke). PEng 2413-2414; RevPEng 2806.

In a Free State (Naipaul). LFEng 1961-1962; RevLFEng 2475.

In a Garden (Barry). RevDEng 172.

"In a Garden" (McPherson). PEng 1883.

"In a Glass Darkly" (Christie). RevShF 551.

In a Glass Darkly (Le Fanu). RevShF 1445; ShF 1798.

In a Green Night (Walcott). RevPEng 3496-3498.

"In a Grove" (Akutagawa). RevShF 36; ShFSup 10.

"In a Hard Intellectual Light" (Eberhart). PEng 929.

"In a Hole" (Elliott). RevShF 821.

In a Shallow Grave (Purdy). LFEng 2175; RevLFEng 2749.

"In a Thicket" (Wescott). RevShF 2442.

"In a Townsip of Asia Minor" (Cavafy). PFor 298.
In a Yellow Wood (Vidal). LFEng 2717-2718.
In Abraham's Bosom (Green). DEng 819-820; RevDEng 1012-1013.
"In Alexandria, 31 B.C." (Cavafy). PFor 298-299.
"In Another Country" (Hemingway). RevShF 1171-1172.
In Any Case (Stern). LFSup 362-363; RevLFEng 3165-3166.
"In Battle" (Petőfi). PFor 1228.
"In Beirut" (Durrell). PEng 920-921; RevPEng 1049.
"In Bertram's Garden" (Justice). PEng 1530; RevPEng 1755.
In Broken Country (Wagoner). PEng 2988, 2989; RevPEng 3476-3477, 3479.
"In California" (Simpson). PEng 2604-2605; RevPEng 3009.
In Celebration (Storey). DEng 1883-1885; RevDEng 2324-2326.
In Chancery (Galsworthy). LFEng 1064; RevLFEng 1263-1264.
In Cold Blood (Capote). LFEng 448-449; RevLFEng 560-561.
"In Dark Times" (Brecht). PFor 224.
In Defence of Shelley and Other Essays (Read). LTh 1212.
In Defense of Materialism (Plekhanov). LTh 1121.
"In Defense of the Short Story" (Hartley). ShF 79.
"In der blauen Ferne." *See* "In the Blue Distance."
"In der Flucht." *See* "Fleeing."
In der Sache J. Robert Oppenheimer. See In the Matter of J. Robert Oppenheimer.
"In der Strafkolonie." *See* "In the Penal Colony."
"In deserto" (Gautier). PFor 536-537. See also *España.*
"In Distrust of Merits" (Moore). PEng 2046; RevPEng 2376.
"In Dreams Begin Responsibilities" (Schwartz, D.). RevShF 2081-2084; ShF 549.
In Dreams Begin Responsibilities (Schwartz, D.). ShF 549, 2204.
In Dubious Battle (Steinbeck). LFEng 2522-2523; RevLFEng 3155-3156, 3770.
In Evil Hour (García Márquez). LFFor 616-617.
"In Excelsis" (Lowell, A.). PEng 1771; RevPEng 2064.
"In Faith of Rising" (Kennedy). PEng 1571; RevPEng 1806.
"In finsteren Zeiten." *See* "In Dark Times."
"In Gallarus Oratory" (Heaney). PEng 1269.
In Goethes Hand (Walser, M.). DSup 388-390.

"In Greenwich There Are Many Gravelled Walks" (Calisher). RevShF 376-378; ShF 1035-1037.
"In Her Own Image" (Boland). PSup 36-38; RevPEng 292-293.
In Her Own Image (Boland). PSup 34, 36-40; RevPEng 289, 290-295.
In His Own Country (Callaghan). RevShF 386; ShFSup 70.
"In His Own Image" (Boland). PSup 37; RevPEng 292-293.
"In Honour of Du Bartas" (Bradstreet). PEng 259-260; RevPEng 320-321.
"In Honour of St. Alphonsus Rodriguez: Laybrother of the Society of Jesus" (Hopkins). PEng 1401; RevPEng 1610.
In hora mortis (Bernhard). PFor 182-183.
"In Jewel" (Robison). RevShF 2014.
In Love and Trouble (Walker). RevShF 2378-2381; ShFSup 335-336.
"In memoriam" (Senghor). PFor 1428. See also *Chants d'ombre.*
In Memoriam (Tennyson). PEng 2868-2870; RevPEng 3342-3344.
In Memoriam James Joyce (MacDiarmid). PSup 266; RevPEng 2126.
"In Memory of Barry Cornwall" (Swinburne). PEng 2821; RevPEng 3289.
"In memory of my dear grand-child Elizabeth Bradstreet" (Bradstreet). PEng 262-263; RevPEng 323, 324.
"In Memory of W. H. Auden" (Stern). PSup 376; RevPEng 3196.
"In morte di Carlo Imbonati" (Manzoni). PFor 958.
In My Father's House (Gaines). LFEng 1048-1049; RevLFEng 1244-1245.
"In My Own Album" (Lamb). PEng 1637; RevPEng 1901.
In New England Winter (Bullins). DEng 308; RevDEng 366. *See also* Twentieth-Century Cycle.
"In Old Russia" (Zamyatin). RevShF 2536; ShFSup 371.
In Ole Virginia (Page). ShF 616.
In Other Worlds (Spivak). RevPEng 3969.
"In Petersburg We Shall Meet Again" (Mandelstam). PFor 938-939. See also *Tristia.*
"In Praise of Cities" (Gunn). RevPEng 1331.
In Praise of Krishna (Levertov). RevPEng 1984.
In Praise of Love (Rattigan). DEng 1563-1564; RevDEng 1955-1956.
"In railway halls, on pavement near the traffic" (Spender). PEng 2700; RevPEng 3144.

"In Response to Vice-Magistrate Chang" (Wang Wei). PFor 1689-1690.

"In Sant' Ambrogio's" (Giusti). PFor 376-377.

"In Santa Maria del Popolo" (Gunn). PEng 1174-1175; RevPEng 1332.

"In Savage Wastes" (Everson). PEng 991; RevPEng 1122.

In Search of Love and Beauty (Jhabvala). LFSup 175-176; RevLFEng 1754.

In Search of Theatre (Bentley). LTh 149.

In Sicily (Vittorini). LFFor 1885-1886, 2244.

"In Snow, a Possible Life" (Smith, D.). PEng 2644; RevPEng 3067.

In somnium Scipionis. See *Commentary on the "Dream of Scipio."*

"In Space" (Arp). PFor 106.

"In Summer" (Dunbar, P.). PSup 116-117; RevPEng 1018-1019.

In Switzerland (Slowacki). PFor 1443.

"In the Alley" (Elkin). RevShF 812-813; ShF 1341.

"In the Autumn of the Year" (Oates). RevShF 1740-1741.

"In the Basement" (Babel). RevShF 126-127.

In the Beginning (Potok). LFSup 317-318; RevLFEng 2663-2664.

"In the Beginning Was the Word" (Fiedler). LTh 483-484.

In the Best Families (Stout). M&D 1544-1545.

"In the Blue Distance" (Sachs). PFor 1376.

In the Boom Boom Room (Rabe). DEng 1550-1551; RevDEng 1942-1943.

In the Burning Darkness (Buero Vallejo). DFor 276-279.

"In the Cathedral" (Castro). PFor 281. See also *Follas novas.*

"In the Central Blue" (Cassill). RevShF 446-447; ShF 1070, 1071-1072.

"In the City" (Matsuo Bashō). PFor 983. See also *Monkey's Raincoat.*

"In the City of Red Dust" (Okri). RevShF 1810.

"In the Clay" (Moore). ShF 660.

"In the Corridors of the Metro" (Robbe-Grillet). ShF 2156.

In the Days of the Comet (Wells). RevLFEng 3483.

"In the Dream's Recess" (Everson). PEng 990; RevPEng 1121.

In the Eye of the Hurricane (Machado). RevDEng 1529-1530.

"In the Eyes of the Gods" (Breton). PFor 232-233.

"In the Fleeting Hand of Time" (Corso). PEng 576; RevPEng 671.

"In the Forest" (de la Mare). RevShF 698-699; ShF 1252-1253.

In the Frame of Don Cristobal (García Lorca). DFor 658.

"In the Garden" (Paley). RevShF 1838-1839; ShF 2043-2044.

"In the Garden of the North American Martyrs" (Wolff). RevShF 2508.

"In the Grave No Flower" (Millay). PEng 2002; RevPEng 2326.

In the Heart of the Country (Coetzee). LFSup 79; RevLFEng 674-675.

"In the Heart of the Heart of the Country" (Gass). LFSup 121; ShF 1482-1483; RevLFEng 1312; RevShF 979, 982.

In the Heart of the Heart of the Country and Other Stories (Gass). LFSup 121; RevLFEng 1312.

In the Heart of the Seas (Agnon). LFFor 19-22.

In the Heat of the Night (Ball). M&D 68-70.

In the Hollow of His Hand (Purdy). RevLFEng 2750-2751.

"In the Holy Nativity of Our Lord" (Crashaw). PEng 669-670; RevPEng 766-767.

In the Labyrinth (Robbe-Grillet). LFFor 1416-1417.

In the Last Analysis (Cross). M&D 428.

"In the Lovely Half-light" (Breton). PFor 233.

In the Matter of J. Robert Oppenheimer (Kipphardt). DFor 1053-1055, 2382.

In the Mecca (Brooks). PEng 3393.

"In the Miro District" (Taylor). ShF 624-635, 2309-2310.

"In the Mountain Tent" (Dickey). PEng 3566.

"In the Mountains: Question and Answer" (Li Po). PFor 890.

"In the Naked Bed, in Plato's Cave" (Schwartz). PEng 2489-2490; RevPEng 2896-2897.

In the Native State (Stoppard). RevDEng 2318.

"In the Night" (Kincaid). RevShF 1341-1342.

"In the Night" (Schorer). ShF 2198-2199.

"In the Orchard" (Woolf). RevShF 2513.

In the Outer Dark (Plumly). PEng 2234-2235; RevPEng 2606-2607.

"In the Penal Colony" (Kafka). ShF 1734.

"In the Region of Ice" (Oates). RevShF 1738-1739; ShF 1965.

In the Room We Share (Simpson). RevPEng 3013.

In the Shadow of the Glen (Synge). DEng 1906-1907; RevDEng 2349-2350.

In the Shadow of the Wind (Hébert). LFFor 811, 813-814.

"In the Shadow of War" (Okri). RevShF 1809.

"In the Steppe" (Gorky). RevShF 1048.

"In the Stopping Train" (Davie). PSup 90-91; RevPEng 856.

"In the Subterranean Kingdom" (George). PFor 547. See also *Algabal.*

In the Tennessee Mountains (Murfree). ShF 226.

"In the Terror of the Night" (Pessoa). PFor 1208.

"In the Thicket" (Wescott). ShF 2423.

In the Time of Greenbloom (Fielding, G.). LFSup 115-116; RevLFEng 1113, 1114.

"In the Train" (O'Connor, Frank). RevShF 1769-1770; ShF 672, 1991.

In the Valley (Frederic). LFEng 1025, 1027; RevLFEng 1218, 1220.

"In the Village" (Bishop). PEng 181.

"In the Waiting Room" (Bishop). PEng 188; RevPEng 231.

In the Western Night (Bidart). RevPEng 213.

In the Wilderness (Undset). LFFor 1805. See also *Master of Hestviken, The.*

In the Wine Time (Bullins). DEng 307-308; RevDEng 366. *See also* Twentieth-Century Cycle.

In the World (Gorky). LFFor 727.

In Their Wisdom (Snow). LFEng 2464; RevLFEng 3090.

"In Time and Place" (Hollander). RevPEng 1553-1554.

"In Time of Grief" (Reese). PEng 2344; RevPEng 2731.

"In Vain" (Reese). PEng 2345; RevPEng 2732.

In Watermelon Sugar (Brautigan). LFEng 292; RevLFEng 375.

"In Winter" (Trakl). PFor 1519-1520.

"In Your Bad Dream" (Hugo, R.). PEng 1456; RevPEng 1667.

Inadmissible Evidence (Osborne). DEng 1434-1435; RevDEng 1813-1814.

"Incautious Burglar, The" (Carr). RevShF 431.

Ince Memed. See Memed, My Hawk.

Inchbald, Elizabeth. DEng 2331; RevDEng 2850.

"Incident at Krechetovka Station" (Solzhenitsyn). RevShF 2160-2161; ShF 2248-2249.

Incident at Vichy (Miller). DEng 1347-1348; RevDEng 1686-1687.

"Incidents at the Shrine" (Okri). RevShF 1807-1809.

"Incidents in the Life of My Uncle Arly" (Lear). PEng 1701; RevPEng 1973.

Incognita (Congreve). RevShF 595-596, 2638; ShF 151, 502-503, 506-507, 1172-1173.

Inconnus dans la maison, Les. See Strangers in the House.

"Incoronazione, L.'" *See* "Coronation, The."

Increased Difficulty of Concentration, The (Havel). DFor 880.

"Incredible Voyage" (Endō). RevShF 837-838.

Incrimination (Hakim). DSup 177.

Independent People (Laxness). LFFor 998-1001.

India Song (Duras). DFor 511-513; LFFor 538-539.

Indian (Ryga). DEng 1642-1643; RevDEng 2050-2052.

"Indian Burying Ground, The" (Freneau). PEng 1036; RevPEng 1167.

"Indian Camp" (Hemingway). ShF 1623-1624.

Indian Princess, The (Barker). DEng 110-112, 2397; RevDEng 136-138, 2918.

"Indian Summer of a Forsyte, The" (Galsworthy). RevShF 946; ShF 1449-1450.

"Indian Uprising, The" (Barthelme). RevShF 163-164; ShFSup 23.

Indian Wants the Bronx, The (Horovitz). DEng 960-961; RevDEng 1196-1197.

"Indian Well, The" (Clark). RevShF 565-566; ShF 1153-1154.

Indiana (Sand). LFFor 1491.

Indians (Kopit). DEng 1071-1073; RevDEng 1350-1352.

Indians in the Woods, The (Lewis). PSup 254-255; RevPEng 1999-2000.

Indifferenti, Gli. See Time of Indifference, The.

Indigent, L'. See Distressed Family, The.

Indiscreet Toys, The (Diderot). LFFor 462-463.

"Induction" (Sackville). PEng 2439, 2440-2441, 2442; RevPEng 2842-2844.

Indulgent Husband, The. See *Claudine Married.*

"Inexorable Progress" (Hood). RevShF 2759.

"Infant Prodigy, The" (Mann). RevShF 1586; ShF 1877.

"Infant Sorrow" (Blake). PEng 3439-3440; RevPEng 3997.

"Infantile Influence" (Hugo). PFor 734. See also *Feuilles d'automne, Les.*

Infedele. See Comptesse Coquette.

"Inference of Mexico, An" (Hayden). PEng 1251-1252.

"Inferiae" (Swinburne). PEng 2821; RevPEng 3289.

Infernal Desire Machines of Doctor Hoffman, The (Carter). LFSup 74; RevLFEng 568.

Inferno (Dante). PFor 398-405. See also *Divine Comedy, The.*

Inferno (Strindberg). LFFor 1694-1695.

"Infinitati Sacrum" (Donne). PEng 835; RevPEng 941.

"Intentional Fallacy, The" (Wimsatt and Beardsley). LTh 1554.

Inter Ice Age 4 (Abe). LFFor 5-6.

Intercom Conspiracy, The (Ambler). M&D 32-33.

Intereses creados, Los. See *Bonds of Interest, The.*

Interface (Gores). M&D 762.

Interfaces of the Word (Ong). LTh 1083.

"Interference of Mexico, An" (Hayden). RevPEng 1435-1436.

Interior (Maeterlinck). DFor 1239.

Interludium de Clerico et Puella. DEng 2256; RevDEng 2776.

Interlunar (Atwood). RevPEng 77-78.

Intermezzo (D'Annunzio). PFor 386.

Intermezzo (Giraudoux). See *Enchanted, The.*

"Intermission" (Coover). RevShF 620-621.

"Interpretations of Dreams, The" (Koch). PEng 1627; RevPEng 1866.

Interpreters, The (Soyinka). LFFor 2037, 2054-2055; LFSup 353-356; RevLFEng 3094-3097.

Interrupted Act, The (Różewicz). DFor 1584.

"Interrupted Cadence, An" (Hoffman). RevShF 1216; ShF 1648.

"Interrupted Elegy" (Paz). PFor 1172.

"Interruption, The" (Jacobs). M&D 929-930.

Intimate Relations (Cocteau). DFor 419-420.

"Into the Cone of Cold" (Elliott, G.). RevShF 819-820; ShF 1347-1348.

"Into the Dusk-Charged Air" (Ashbery). PEng 60.

Into the Stone and Other Poems (Dickey, J.). PEng 795; RevPEng 905-906.

Into the Valley (Hersey). LFEng 1352; RevLFEng 1610.

Into Thin Air (Beck). ShF 934.

Intrigue and Love. See *Cabal and Love.*

"Introduction, An" (Das). RevPEng 3946.

Introduction à la littérature fantastique. See *Fantastic, The.*

Introduction à l'architexte (Genette). LTh 563.

Introduction à l'étude de la médecine expérimentale. See *Introduction to the Study of Experimental Medicine.*

Introduction to Poetics, An (Todorov). LTh 1435, 1437.

Introduction to the Study of Experimental Medicine (Bernard). LTh 1713.

Intruder, The (D'Annunzio). LFFor 411.

"Intruder, The" (Gordimer). RevShF 1033; ShFSup 107-108.

"Intruder, The" (Kizer). PEng 1620.

'ntruder The (Maeterlinck). DFor 1238-1239.

"Intruder in the Discotheque, The" (Joshi). ShF 653.

Intruder in the Dust (Faulkner). M&D 589.

Intruse, L'. See *Intruder, The.*

Invasion, L' (Adamov). DFor 14-15, 2257.

"Inverno di malato" (Moravia). RevShF 1668; ShFSup 195.

Investigation, The (Weiss). DFor 1988-1989.

"Investigations of a Dog" (Kafka). ShF 1733.

Invincible, The (Lem). LFFor 1013.

Invisible Bond, The (Nuwa). DEng 2417; RevDEng 2939.

Invisible Cities (Calvino). LFFor 245-246.

"Invisible Father, The" (Coulette). RevPEng 690.

Invisible Lodge, The (Jean Paul). LFFor 872-873.

"Invisible Lover, The" (Queen). RevShF 1980-1981.

Invisible Man (Ellison). LFEng 896-904, 3106; RevLFEng 1055-1063, 3776, 3808.

Invisible Man, The (Wells). RevLFEng 3482.

Invisible Threads (Yevtushenko). PFor 1712.

"Invitation" (Fearing). RevPEng 1141.

Invitation to a March (Laurents). DEng 1105-1107; RevDEng 1385-1386.

Invitation to the Waltz (Lehmann). LFSup 229-231; RevLFEng 2018-2020.

"Invite to Eternity, An" (Clare). PEng 514; RevPEng 604.

Invitée, L'. See *She Came to Stay.*

"Invocation" (McKay). PEng 1843; RevPEng 2142.

"Invocation to Kali, An" (Sarton). PEng 2463-2464; RevPEng 2867-2868.

I.O. *See* **Rhode, John.**

Iolanthe (Gilbert and Sullivan). DEng 765; RevDEng 946.

Ion (Euripides). DFor 576-577, 2116.

Ion (Plato). LTh 1115-1116.

Ion of Chios. DFor 2119.

Ionesco, Eugène. DEng 2204; DFor 989-1005, 2241, 2248-2256, 2357-2358; RevDEng 2724.

Iphigenia (Ennius). DFor 549-550.

Iphigenia in Aulis (Euripides). DFor 2117.

Iphigenia in Aulis (Racine). DFor 1519.

Iphigenia in Tauris (Euripides). DFor 2116.

Iphigenia in Tauris (Goethe). DFor 739, 2366.

Ipocrito, Lo (Aretino). DFor 99.

Ippolito, Donna. ShF 2648.

"Ir Sult sprechen." *See* "Speak a Welcome."

"Irás sobre la vida de las cosas . . ." (González Martínez). PFor 610-611.

"Ireland with Emily" (Betjeman). PEng 171; RevPEng 204.

Istituzioni della poesia, Le (Anceschi). LTh 32.
Istoria della volgar poesia (Crescimbeni). LTh 1691.
Istoricheskaya poetika (Veselovsky). LTh 1506.
"Istoriia bolezni." *See* "History of an Illness."
"Istoriia moei golubiatni." *See* "Story of My Dovecote, The."
"István Öcsémhez." *See* "To My Younger Brother, István."
Isvaran, Manjeri. ShF 644.
It (King). LFSup 210; RevLFEng 1892-1893.
It Catches My Heart in Its Hand (Bukowski). PEng 359; RevPEng 432.
"It Don't Mean a Thing If It Ain't Got That Swing" (Matthews). RevPEng 2247.
"It Had to Be Murder" (Woolrich). M&D 1726.
"It Is Not Beauty I Demand" (Darley). PEng 733-734; RevPEng 837-838.
It Is So (If You Think So). See *Right You Are (If You Think So).*
"It may be good, like it who list" (Wyatt). PEng 3176-3177; RevPEng 3699, 3700-3701.
"It May Never Happen" (Pritchett). ShF 2130-2131.
"It sifts from Leaden Sieves" (Dickinson). PEng 806; RevPEng 918.
It Walks by Night (Carr). M&D 268-269.
"It was not Death, for I stood up" (Dickinson). PEng 806-807; RevPEng 918-919.
Italian, The (Radcliffe). LFEng 2202-2203; M&D 1393; RevLFEng 2781-2782.
"Italian Morning" (Bogan). PEng 236; RevPEng 283.
Italian Straw Hat, The (Labiche). DFor 1131-1133.
Italian Visit, An (Day Lewis). PEng 760-761; RevPEng 878-879.

Italienische Nacht (Horvath). DFor 955-958.
Itching Parrot, The (Lizardi). LFFor 2281-2282, 2286, 2296.
"Item from Norwich" (Slavitt). RevPEng 3049.
It's a Family Affair (Ostrovsky). DFor 1448.
"It's a Woman's World" (Boland). PSup 36-37; RevPEng 290-291.
"It's Boring and Sad . . ." (Lermontov). PFor 874-875.
"It's easy to invent a Life" (Dickinson). PEng 808; RevPEng 920.
Its Image on the Mirror (Gallant). LFEng 1054; RevLFEng 1252.
"Its Many Fragments" (Pinsky). RevPEng 2588.
"It's Nation Time" (Baraka). PEng 88-89; RevPEng 99-100.
It's Only a Play (McNally). RevDEng 1554, 1555.
"Iudol." *See* "Vale of Tears."
Ivaanov, Vyacheslav. PFor 2145.
"Ivan Fyodorovich Shponka and His Aunt" (Gogol). RevShF 1017.
Ivan Vejeeghen (Bulgarin). LFFor 2310.
Ivan Vyzhigin. See *Ivan Vejeeghen.*
Ivanovskiye sitsi (Yevtushenko). PFor 1711-1712.
Ivar's Story. RevShF 2594; ShF 397.
"I've Brought to Art" (Cavafy). PFor 299.
Ivona (Gombrowicz). DFor 770-771.
"Ivy Day in the Committee Room" (Joyce). RevShF 1296, 1297-1298.
"Ivy Gripped the Steps" (Bowen). ShF 255.
Iwein (Hartmann von Aue). PFor 633.
Iwona, ksiezniezka Burgunda. See *Ivona.*
"Iz Andreya Shenie." *See* "From André Chénier."
"Izu Dancer, The" (Kawabata). RevShF 1319-1320.
"Izu no Odoriko." *See* "Izu Dancer, The."

J

"Jabberwocky" (Carroll). PEng 445-448; RevPEng 514-516.

"Jack and the Other Jack" (Hall). PEng 1200.

Jack Gelber's New Play: Rehearsal (Gelber). DEng 745; RevDEng 925.

Jack Juggler (Udall?). DEng 2264; RevDEng 2783.

Jack of Newbury (Deloney). LFEng 3016; RevLFEng 3723, 3724.

"Jack Straw's Castle" (Gunn). RevPEng 1335.

Jack Straw's Castle and Other Poems (Gunn). PEng 1169-1170, 1171; RevPEng 1335.

Jackson, Shirley. LFEng 1426-1433; 1668-1674; RevShF 1251-1257; ShF 552.

Jacob, Max. PFor 1887-1888.

"Jacob and the Angel" (Everson). PEng 991; RevPEng 1122.

"Jacob o la idea de la poesía" (Reyes). PFor 1322.

Jacobowsky, Ludwig. LFFor 2182.

Jacobowsky and the Colonel (Behrman). DEng 186-187; RevDEng 223-224.

Jacobs, W. W. M&D 928-931.

Jacob's Room (Woolf). LFEng 2947-2949; RevLFEng 3648-3649.

Jacobsen, Jens Peter. LFFor 2338-2339; PFor 2169.

Jacobsen, Josephine. ShF 2650.

Jacobsen, Rolf. PFor 2189.

Jacobwsky and the Colonel (Werfel). DFor 1999-2000.

Jacques le fataliste et son maître. See *Jacques the Fatalist and His Master.*

Jacques the Fatalist and His Master (Diderot). LFFor 465-466.

"Jade Buddhas, Red Bridges, Fruits of Love" (Gilchrist). RevShF 987.

Jagdgesellschaft, Die (Bernhard). DFor 198-200.

Jagua Nana (Ekwensi). LFFor 2047-2048.

Jahier, Piero. PFor 2038, 2045.

Jahr der Seele, Das. See *Year of the Soul, The.*

Jahrestage. See *Anniversaries.*

Jailbird (Vonnegut). LFEng 2730-2731.

"Jailer, The" (Plath). PEng 2224; RevPEng 2596.

Jakobson, Roman. LFEng 3214-3215, 3331; LTh 744-749, 828, 849, 889-890, 913, 1477, 1758, 1761-1762, 1800, 1815, 1822; PEng 3448-3450; RevPEng 3983-3985, 3997.

Jakšić, Djura. PFor 2254.

Jalousie, La. See *Jealousy.*

Jama (Kovačić). PFor 2265.

Jamaica Inn (du Maurier). M&D 553.

James, C. L. R. RevDEng 2977.

James, Henry. DEng 989-998; LFEng 994, 1434-1451, 2848-2849, 2851-2852, 3035, 3042, 3043, 3047-3049, 3055, 3082-3083, 3251-3252, 3262-3265, 3298; LTh 556, 750-757, 926-927, 1012, 1454, 1549, 1568, 1750-1751; RevDEng 1254-1264; RevLFEng 1713-1730, 3743, 3750, 3751, 3755-3757, 3763, 3791-3792, 3800, 3874-3875; RevShF 1258-1267, 2705, 2712; ShF 182, 213-214, 232, 518-519, 740-741, 1675-1687, 2427-2428.

James, M. R. RevShF 1268-1274; ShF 743, 1688-1693.

James, P. D. LFSup 164-169; M&D 932-938; RevLFEng 1731-1738.

James, William. LFEng 3223-3224; LTh 146; PEng 900; RevLFEng 3763.

James I. PEng 3272, 3278; RevPEng 3791.

James IV (Greene, R.). DEng 842-844; PEng 1150-1151; RevDEng 1037-1039; RevPEng 1308-1309.

Jameson, Fredric. LTh 414, 758-763, 1770, 1814.

Jammersminde. See *Memoirs of Leonora Christina.*

Jammes, Francis. PFor 1880.

Jandl, Ernst. PFor 1936.

"Jane at Pigall's" (Hall). PEng 1204.

"Jane" (Maugham). RevShF 1628; ShF 1904.

Jane Clegg (Ervine). DEng 561, 562, 563; RevDEng 702, 703, 704.

Jane Eyre (Brontë, C.). LFEng 301-302, 2228-2229, 2230, 2231-2232, 3162, 3163; RevLFEng 385-386.

Jane Shore. See *Tragedy of Jane Shore, The.*

Janet, Pierre. PFor 229-230.

"Janet Waking" (Ransom). PEng 2329-2330; RevPEng 2715.

"Janet's Repentance" (Eliot, G.). RevShF 807; ShF 1335-1336.

Janevski, Slavko. PFor 2272-2273.

Janos the Hero (Petőfi). PFor 1219-1220.

János Vitéz. See *Janos the Hero.*

"January 1919" (Middleton, C.). PEng 1988; RevPEng 2310.

"Janus" (Beattie). RevShF 184; ShFSup 41-42.
"Jap, The" (Beck). ShF 935.
Japanese Family Storehouse, The (Saikaku).
 RevShF 2030; ShFSup 270-271.
"Japanese Way, The" (Pastan). PEng 2175.
Jardiel Poncela, Enrique. DFor 2506.
"Jardín de senderos que se bifurcan, El." *See*
 "Garden of the Forking Paths, The."
Jardines lejanos (Jiménez). PFor 750-751.
Jarnés, Benjamín. LFFor 2392.
Jarrell, Randall. PEng 1478-1486; RevPEng
 1690-1699.
Jarry, Alfred. DFor 1006-1015, 2349-2350; LTh
 622, 996; RevDEng 2723.
Jarvis, E. K. *See* **Bloch, Robert.**
"Jasmine" (Mukherjee). RevShF 1688-1689.
Jason, Stuart. *See* **Avallone, Michael.**
Jason, Veronica. *See* **Johnston, Velda.**
Jatadharan (Venkataramani). ShF 644.
Játék a kastélyban. See *Play's the Thing, The.*
Jauss, David. ShF 2651.
Jauss, Hans Robert. LTh 685, 731, 733,
 764-768, 1763, 1770, 1801.
"Javni" (Rao). ShF 648.
"Jaws of the Dog, The" (Greenberg). RevShF
 1066; ShF 1539.
Jay, Martin. LTh 138.
J.B. (MacLeish). DEng 1220-1224; RevDEng
 1540-1545.
"Je ne parle pas français" (Mansfield). RevShF
 1597.
"Je Suis le Plus Malade des Surrealistes" (Nin).
 RevShF 1723; ShF 1950.
"Je suis un cheval." See "I Am a Horse."
Je vous écris d'un pays lointain. See *I Am Writing
 to You from a Far-Off Country.*
Jealous God, The (Braine). LFEng 283, 286,
 287-288; RevLFEng 369, 370-371.
"Jealous Hidalgo, The" (Cervantes). LFEng 3227,
 3228-3230.
Jealous Old Husband, The (Cervantes). DFor 366.
Jealousy (Robbe-Grillet). LFFor 1415-1416, 2146.
Jean Barois (Martin du Gard). LFFor 1111-1112.
"Jean Beicke" (Williams, W. C.). RevShF
 2487-2489; C.). ShF 2443.
Jean de Meung and **Guillaume de Lorris.** PFor
 614-621; PFor 1839.
Jean le bleu. See *Blue Boy.*
Jean Paul. LFFor 868-878, 2162.
"Jean-ah Poquelin" (Cable). RevShF 360-361;
 ShF 1021-1023.
Jean-Christophe (Rolland). LFFor 1427-1429,
 2141-2142.

Jeannot and Colin (Voltaire). RevShF 2360;
 ShFSup 330.
"Jean-Pierre" (Spencer). RevShF 2175.
"Jean's TV" (Carver). RevPEng 536.
Jeeves and Wooster novels (Wodehouse). LFEng
 2922-2925; RevLFEng 3613-3615.
Jeffers, Robinson. PEng 1487-1497; RevPEng
 1700-1711.
Jefferson, Ian. *See* **Davies, L. P.**
Jefferson and/or Mussolini (Pound). LTh 1156.
Jeffrey, Lord. LTh 1708.
Jeffrey, William. *See* **Pronzini, Bill.**
"Jeffrey, Believe Me" (Smiley). RevShF 2146.
Jeffries, Graham Montague. *See* **Graeme, Bruce.**
"Jeffty Is Five" (Ellison). RevShF 828-829.
"Jen jednou." *See* "Once Only."
Jenko, Simon. PFor 2268.
Jenneval (Mercier). DEng 2183; RevDEng 2703.
Jennie Gerhardt (Dreiser). LFEng 833-835;
 RevLFEng 999-1001.
"Jenny" (Rossetti, D. G.). PEng 2430; RevPEng
 2823.
Jenny (Undset). LFFor 1799.
Jenny Treibel (Fontane). LFFor 563-564,
 2177-2178.
Jensen, Johannes V. LFFor 879-884,
 2347-2348; PFor 2176-2177.
Jeppe of the Hill (Holberg). DFor 948-949, 2466.
"Jerboa, The" (Moore). PEng 2044-2045;
 RevPEng 2374-2375.
"Jeremiah Desborough: Or, The Kentuckian"
 (Richardson, J.). ShF 635.
Jeremy's Version (Purdy). LFEng 2173;
 RevLFEng 2747.
Jerome, Saint. LTh 1193; PFor 2110.
Jersild, Per Christian. LFFor 2361.
Jerusalem (Blake). PEng 218-219; RevPEng 260,
 262-263.
Jerusalem (Lagerlöf). LFFor 984, 2344.
Jerusalem Conquered (Tasso). PFor 1501; PFor
 1494-1495, 1496, 1498-1501, 2015.
Jerusalem the Golden (Drabble). LFEng 817-820;
 RevLFEng 982-985.
"Jerusalem's Lot" (King). RevShF 1347.
Jerusalén conquistada (Vega). PFor 1602.
Jest of God, A (Laurence). LFEng 1573-1574;
 RevLFEng 1946-1947.
Jest, Satire, Irony, and Deeper Significance
 (Grabbe). DFor 801-803.
"Jesu" (Herbert). PEng 1301; RevPEng 1480.
Jeu d'Adam, Le. DFor 2162-2163.
Jeu de la feuillée (La Halle). DFor 2175.

Jeu de l'amour et du hasard, Le. See *Game of Love and Chance, The.*
Jeu de Robin et Marion, Le (La Halle). DFor 2175-2176.
Jeu de Saint-Nicolas, Le (Bodel). DFor 2163-2164, 2175.
Jew of Denmark, The (Goldschmidt). LFFor 2336.
Jew of Malta, The (Marlowe). DEng 1253-1256, 2272-227; RevDEng 1578-1581, 2791-2792; ShF 1896.
"Jew of Persia, A" (Helprin). RevShF 1162; ShFSup 116.
"Jewbird, The" (Malamud). RevShF 1573-1574.
Jewett, Sarah Orne. LFEng 1452-1463; RevLFEng 1739-1751; RevShF 1275-1282, 2711; ShF 227-228, 547, 1694-1699.
Jews, The (Lessing). DFor 1200-1201.
Jew's Beech Tree, The (Droste-Hülshoff). M&D 539-541.
Jews in Babylonia (Reznikoff). PEng 2361; RevPEng 2748.
Jhabvala, Ruth Prawer. LFFor 2222; **LFSup 170-176; RevLFEng 1752-1759;** ShF 650.
Jidaimono. DFor 2427, 2430.
Jig of Forslin, The (Aiken). PEng 23-24; RevPEng 24-25.
Jig-Saw. See *Marylebone Miser, The.*
"Jigokuhen." *See* "Hell Screen."
"Jilting of Granny Weatherall, The" (Porter). RevShF 1909; ShF 801, 2114.
Jiménez, Juan Ramón. PFor 747-755, 2227.
Jimmy Shine (Schisgal). DEng 1664; RevDEng 2076.
Jin xin gu zhi lian (Wang Anyi). RevShF 2398.
Jingling in the Wind (Roberts). LFEng 2282; RevLFEng 2877.
"Jinny the Just" (Prior). PEng 2291; RevPEng 2672.
Jirásek, Alois. LFFor 2066.
Jiyugeki Kyōkai. DFor 2432-2433.
"Joal" (Senghor). PFor 1424. See also *Chants d'ombre.*
Job. ShF 346-348, 373.
Job (Roth). LFFor 1450-1452.
Job, the Victim of His People (Girard). LTh 592.
Jocasta (Gascoigne and Kinwelmershe). DEng 725-726, 2265; RevDEng 903, 2784.
Jocelyn (Lamartine). PFor 835.
Jochumsson, Matthiás. DFor 2474.
"Jockey, The" (McCullers). RevShF 1540; ShF 1841.
Jøde, En. See *Jew of Denmark, The.*
Jodelle, Étienne. RevDEng 2680.

Joe, Rita. RevPEng 3943-3944.
"Joe Eliot" (Farrell). RevShF 843-844; ShF 1333-1335.
Joe Turner's Come and Gone (Wilson, A.). RevDEng 2602-2603.
Joel Brand (Kipphardt). DFor 1055.
Johan Johan (Heywood, J.). DEng 945-946, 2256; RevDEng 1178-1179, 2776.
Johannessen, Georg. PFor 2194-2195.
Johannisfeuer. See *Fires of St. John.*
Johannsson, Ulrika Wilhelmina. *See* **Canth, Minna.**
John (Barry). DEng 136; RevDEng 172.
John Brown (Warren). LFEng 2770, 2773; RevLFEng 3438.
John Brown's Body (Benét). PEng 143-144; RevPEng 173-174.
"John Coltrane Dance, The" (Young). PEng 3212-3213; RevPEng 3736-3737.
"John Deth: A Metaphysical Legend" (Aiken). PEng 25; RevPEng 26.
"John Dryden" (Eliot). LTh 896.
John Ferguson (Ervine). DEng 561, 562, 563; RevDEng 702, 703, 704.
"John Gardner" (Gardner). RevShF 960.
"John Keats, Surgeon" (Belitt). RevPEng 156.
John Macnab (Buchan). LFEng 334-335; RevLFEng 429-430.
John of Bordeaux (Greene, R.). DEng 844-845; RevDEng 1039-1040.
John of Salisbury. LTh 966, 1650.
John of the Cross, Saint. PFor 756-768.
"John Redding Goes to Sea" (Hurston). RevShF 1241-1242.
"John Sherman" (Yeats). RevShF 2526-2527; ShF 2471.
Johnno (Malouf). RevLFEng 2289-2290.
Johnny Johnson (Green). DEng 820-821; RevDEng 1013-1014.
Johnny Mangano and His Astonishing Dogs. See *Cinq.*
"Johnny Pye and the Fool-Killer" (Benét). RevShF 213-214; ShF 957-959.
"Johnny Thomas" (Brown). RevPEng 390.
Johnson, Bengt Emil. PFor 2193.
Johnson, Charles. RevLFEng 1760-1769.
Johnson, Colin. *See* Mudrooroo Narogin.
Johnson, Diane. RevLFEng 1770-1777.
Johnson, Eyvind. LFFor 2349-2350.
Johnson, Joe. ShF 2652.
Johnson, Josephine. ShF 1700-1705.
Johnson, Ronald. PSup 210-216; RevPEng 1712-1718.

Johnson, Samuel. LFEng **1464-1474**, 3026, 3027; LTh 91-92, 260, 403, **769-778**, 1140, 1216, 1259, 1528-1529, 1533, 1684-1686, 1690; PEng 588, **1498-1507**, 3332; **RevLFEng 1778-1789**, 3734, 3735; **RevPEng 1719-1730**, 3838, 3851, 4015-4018; **RevShF 1283-1289**; ShF **1706-1712.**

Johnson, Uwe. LFFor **885-893.**

Johnson Over Jordan (Priestley). DEng 1540-1541; RevDEng 1929-1930.

Johnston, Velda. M&D **939-942.**

Jókai, Mór. LFFor 2071-2072.

Joke, The (Kundera). LFFor 952-953.

Joker of Seville, The (Walcott, D. A.). DEng 2002; RevDEng 2471-2472.

Joking Apart (Ayckbourn). DEng 67-68.

Jokond ile Si-Ya-U (Hikmet). PSup 177.

Jolley, Elizabeth. LFSup **177-183**; RevLFEng **1790-1796.**

"Jolly Corner, The" (James, H.). LFEng 3298-3299; RevShF 1265-1266; ShF 477, 741, 800, 1685-1686.

Jonah. ShF 358-360.

Jonah's Gourd Vine (Hurston). LFEng 1393, 1394-1395; RevLFEng 1669, 1670-1671.

"Jonas" (Camus). LFFor 264.

Jónás könyve (Babits). PFor 122.

Jónasson, Jóhannes B. PFor 2186.

Jonathan Wild (Fielding, H.). LFEng 949-950; RevLFEng 1130-1131.

Jones, Annabel. *See* **Brand, Christianna.**

Jones, Everett Le Roi. *See* **Baraka, Amiri.**

Jones, Henry Arthur. DEng **999-1006**; **RevDEng 1265-1273.**

Jones, Inigo. DEng 2223.

Jones, James. LFEng **1475-1484**; RevLFEng **1797-1807.**

Jones, LeRoi. *See* **Baraka, Amiri.**

Jones, Madison. LFEng **1485-1495**; RevLFEng **1808-1819.**

Jones, Preston. DEng **1107-1013**; RevDEng **1274-1281.**

Jones, William. PFor 1732, 1989-1990.

"Jongleur de Notre-Dame, Le." *See* "Juggler of Our Lady, The."

Jonson, Ben. DEng 283, **1014-1025**, 2167, 2285-2287, 2297, 2298; DFor 2227; LTh 450, **779-784**, 1184, 1665, 1676; PEng 93, **1508-1519**, 3305-3308, 3317-3318; RevDEng 339, **1282-1293**, 2687, 2804-2806, 2816, 2817; **RevPEng 1731-1743**, 3819-3820, 3824-3827; ShF **1713-1717.**

Jordan County (Foote). LFEng 978-979; RevLFEng 1160-1162.

"Jordan's End" (Glasgow). RevShF 1003-1004; ShF 1493-1494.

Jordi de Sant Jordi. PFor 1771.

Jørgensen, Johannes. LFFor 2347; PFor 2172.

Jörn Uhl (Frenssen). LFFor 2182.

Jōruri. DFor 392-394.

"Joscelyn" (Simms). LFEng 2410-2411; RevLFEng 3040-3041.

Josef Švejk (Kohout). DSup 222-223.

"Joseph" (Forché). RevPEng 1159.

Joseph, Edward Lanza. DEng 2451; RevDEng 2976.

Joseph and His Brothers (Mann). LFFor 1082.

Joseph Andrews (Fielding, H.). LFEng 947-949; RevLFEng 1128-1130, 3815.

Joseph, der Ernährer. See *Joseph the Provider.*

Joseph in Ägypten. See *Joseph in Egypt.*

Joseph in Egypt (Mann). LFFor 1082. See also *Joseph and His Brothers.*

Joseph the Provider (Mann). LFFor 1082-1083. See also *Joseph and His Brothers.*

Joseph und seine Brüder. See *Joseph and His Brothers.*

"Josephine the Singer, or the Mouse Folk" (Kafka). ShF 1733.

Josephson, Ragnar. DFor 2479.

Josh. *See* **Twain, Mark.**

Joshi, Arun. ShF 653.

"Joshua" (Grau). RevShF 1058-1059; ShF 1531-1532.

Joshua Then and Now (Richer). LFEng 2260-2262; RevLFEng 2849, 2852-2854.

Joudrey, Patricia. RevDEng 2963.

Joueur, Le (Regnard). DFor 1539-1540.

"Joujou du pauvre, Le." *See* "Poor Child's Plaything, The."

Journal (Goncourts). LFFor 709.

Journal d'un curé de campagne. See *Diary of a Country Priest.*

"Journal for My Daughter" (Kunitz). PSup 246-247; RevPEng 1887-1888.

Journal in time (Queneau). LFSup 327-329.

Journal of the Plague Year, A (Defoe). LFEng 686-688; RevLFEng 819-821.

"Journal of the Year of the Ox, A" (Wright, C.). RevPEng 3663-3664.

Journalists, The (Wesker). RevDEng 2509-2510.

Journals of Susanna Moodie, The (Atwood). RevPEng 73-74.

"Journey, The" (Boland). RevPEng 297-298.

"Journey" (Oates). ShF 131.

"Journey, The" (Winters). PSup 398-399; RevPEng 3627-3628.

Julian (Vidal). LFEng 2719; RevLFEng 3373-3374.
Julian and Maddalo (Shelley). PEng 2548-2550; RevPEng 2961-2964.
"Julian M. to A. G. Rochelle." *See* "Prisoner, The."
Julian the Apostate. See Death of the Gods, The.
Juliana (Cynewulf). PEng 717-718; RevPEng 819-820.
"Julia's Petticoat" (Herrick). PEng 1312-1314; RevPEng 1492-1494.
Julie: Or, The New Eloise. See New Héloïse, The.
Julie: Ou, La Nouvelle Héloïse. See New Héloïse, The.
Ju-lin wai-shih. See Scholars, The.
"Julinatt, En." *See* "July Night, A."
Julius Caesar (Shakespeare). DEng 1715-1716; RevDEng 2129-2130, 2800.
"July 14" (Ponge). PFor 1265-1266.
"July Night, A" (Ekelöf). PFor 450. See also *Non serviam.*
July's People (Gordimer). LFEng 1170-1171; RevLFEng 1391-1392.
"Jumblies, The" (Lear). PEng 1699; RevPEng 1971.
"Jumbo" (Smith, S.). RevPEng 3076-3077.
Jūmon saihi shō (Yoshimoto). LTh 1595.
Jumpers (Stoppard). DEng 1870, 1874-1875; RevDEng 2312-2314.
"Jumping the Grave-Sized Hole" (Galvin). PEng 1055; RevPEng 1189.
"June 1940" (Spender). PEng 2698-2699; RevPEng 3142-3143.
Jung, Carl. LTh 1798; PEng 3414-3417.
Junge Joseph, Der. See Young Joseph, The.
Jungfrau von Orleans, Die. See Maid of Orleans, The.
Jungle, The (Sinclair, U.). LFEng 2421-2422, 3088; RevLFEng 3050-3052, 3761, 3797.
Jungle Book, The (Kipling). RevShF 1363.
"Jüngling und die Spinne, Der" (Hofmannsthal). PFor 677.
Jungmann, Josef. PFor 1799.

"Junior" (Lewis). RevShF 1485.
"Junior Life Saving" (Kumin). RevPEng 1871-1872.
"Junius Maltby" (Steinbeck). RevShF 2208.
"Junk Shop, The" (Coulette). RevPEng 687.
Junkie (Burroughs). LFEng 387; RevLFEng 486.
Juno and the Paycock (O'Casey). DEng 1389; RevDEng 1765.
Juntacadáveres (Onetti). LFFor 1213.
Jurčič, Josip. LFFor 2077-2078.
Jurgen (Cabell). LFEng 404, 408-410; RevLFEng 513, 517-519.
"Jūrokusai no Nikki." *See* "Diary of a Sixteen-Year-Old."
"Just a Whack at Empson" (Sissman). PEng 2614-2615; RevPEng 3018-2019.
Just Above My Head (Baldwin). LFEng 139-144; RevLFEng 183-188.
Just and the Unjust, The (Cozzens). LFEng 629, 634; RevLFEng 762, 767.
Just Assassins, The (Camus). DFor 319-320.
"Just Like a Tree" (Gaines). RevShF 935-936; ShF 1435-1436.
Just So Stories (Kipling). RevShF 1363-1364.
Justes, Les. See Just Assassins, The.
Justice, Donald. PEng 1528-1534; RevPEng 1753-1760.
Justice Enough (Carmichael). M&D 264.
"Justice Is Reason Enough" (Wakoski). RevPEng 3485.
Justice Without Revenge (Vega). DFor 1938-1939.
Justine. See Alexandria Quartet, The.
Juvenal. PFor 2104; ShF 1724-1728.
Juvencus. PFor 2111.
Juvenilia (Carducci). PFor 270.
"Juvenilia" (Day Lewis). PEng 758; RevPEng 876.
Juventud, divino tesoro (Martínez Sierras). DFor 1284.
Juvik, Thomas. ShF 2653.
Juvikfolke. See People of Juvik, The.
Jux will er sich machen, Einen. See Matchmaker, The.

K

K voprosu o razvitii monisticheskogo vzgliada na istoriiu. See In Defense of Materialism.

K zvezdam. See To the Stars.

Kâ, Abdou Anta. DFor 2268-2269, 2270.

Kaalø, Steen. PFor 2198.

Kabale und Liebe. See Cabal and Love.

Kabaphēs, Kōnstantionos Petrou. See Cavafy, Constantine P.

"Kabnis" (Toomer). RevShF 2300-2302; ShF 2343-2344.

"Kaddish" (Ginsberg). PEng 1092-1093; RevPEng 1229-1231.

Kafka, Franz. LFFor 199, 894-905, 2189-2190; LTh 938, 1316; ShF 1729-1735; RevLFEng 3877; RevShF 1300-1309.

"Kafkas" (Wiggins). RevShF 2469.

"Kagebōshi." See "Shadow Figure, The."

Kagi. See Key, The.

Kaicho-on (Ueda Bin). PFor 2074.

Kailas, Uuno. PFor 2182.

Kains, Josephine. See Goulart, Ron.

Kaiser, Georg. DFor 1016-1027, 2239-2240, 2377-2378.

Kaiser Friedrich Barbarossa (Grabbe). DFor 804.

Kaiser Heinrich VI (Grabbe). DFor 804.

"Kaiserliche Botschaft, Eine." See "Imperial Message, A."

"Kak sdelana 'Shinel' Gogolia" (Eikhenbaum). LTh 442.

Kakinomoto no Hitomaro. PFor 2055-2057.

Kaksikymmentä ja yksi (Haavikko). PSup 146.

Kälberbrüten, Das (Sachs). DFor 1624-1625.

Kalechofsky, Roberta. ShF 2654.

Kalendergeschichten. See Tales from the Calendar.

Kalevala (Lönnrot). DFor 1063; PFor 2157; ShF 137.

Kaliber, Der (Müllner). M&D 1259-1262.

Kālidāsa. DFor 1028-1037, 2387-2388.

Kalinčiak, Ján. LFFor 2068.

Kalkwerk, Das. See Lime Works, The.

Kallimachos. See Callimachus.

Kallman, Chester. DEng 53; RevDEng 67, 70-71.

Kallocain (Boye). LFFor 2351.

Kálvos, Andreas. PFor 1950-1952.

"Kamakapala" (Rao). ShF 643.

Kamban, Guðmundur. DFor 2480; LFFor 2347.

Kamen no kokuhaku. See Confessions of a Mask.

"Kamennoe serdtse." See "Heart of Stone, A."

Kamera Obskura. See Laughter in the Dark.

"Kamienny świat." See "World of Stone."

Kamin. See Stone.

Kamin, Franz. ShF 2655.

Kaminsky, Stuart M. M&D 943-947.

Kammersänger, Der. See Tenor, The.

Kamo no Mabuchi. LTh 785-789, 1050-1052.

Kamouraska (Hébert). LFFor 812.

"Kampf mit dem Drachen, Der." See "Battle with the Dragon, The."

Kampmann, Christian. LFFor 2367.

Kamyenny gost. See Stone Guest, The.

Kan'ami Kiyotsugu. DFor 2422-2423.

"Kanbatsu to zazen." See "Drought and Zazen."

Kane, Cheikh Hamidou. LFFor 2035.

Kane, Wilson. See Bloch, Robert.

Kangaeru hinto (Kobayashi). LTh 821.

Kanjō-no maki. LFFor 2266. See also Tale of Genji, The.

Kant, Immanuel. LFFor 2160; LTh 378, 455, 531, 790-794, 1019, 1296-1297, 1315, 1321-1322, 1697, 1756, 1810.

Kantan (Mishima). DFor 1324.

Kanteletar (Lönnrot). PFor 2157.

Kantemir, Antioch. PFor 2134.

Kanthapura (Rao). LFEng 2208-2210; LFFor 2220; RevLFEng 2788-2790; ShF 648.

Kantor, Tadeusz. DSup 206-211.

Kao Ming. DFor 1038-1049, 2319-2321.

Kao Tsê-ch'êng. See Kao Ming.

Kapetan Michales, Ho. See Freedom or Death.

Kapitanskaya dochka. See Captain's Daughter, The.

Kaplan, Bernard. ShF 2656.

Kappa (Akutagawa). RevShF 36; ShFSup 11.

"Karamazov" (Belitt). RevPEng 156.

Karamzin, Nikolay. LFFor 2307-2308; LTh 1694.

"Karintha" (Toomer). PEng 2915-2917; RevPEng 3387-3389.

Karkurit (Kivi). DFor 1067.

Karl Marx Play, The (Owens). DEng 1459-1460; RevDEng 1840-1841.

Karl Stuart (Fleisser). DFor 624.

Karlfeldt, Erik Axel. PFor 2171-2172.

"Karma" (Singh). ShF 650.

Killing Time (Berger). LFEng 254-255; RevLFEng 308-309.

Killshot (Leonard). RevLFEng 2026, 2029.

Kilpi, Eeva. LFFor 2369.

Kilpi, Volter. LFFor 2357.

"Kilroy" (Viereck). RevPEng 3459.

Kim. *See* **Simenon, Georges.**

Kim (Kipling). LFEng 1543-1545; RevLFEng 1904-1906, 3789.

Kim Tong Il, 3916.

"Kimi shinitamō koto nakare." *See* "Never Let Them Kill You, Brother!"

Kimitake Hiraoka. *See* **Mishima, Yukio.**

Kincaid, Jamaica. RevShF 1339-1344.

Kinck, Hans Ernst. DFor 2476; LFFor 2345.

Kind of Testament, A (Gombrowicz). LTh 606.

"Kind pity chokes my spleen" (Donne). PEng 828; RevPEng 934.

"Kind Sir: These Woods" (Sexton). PEng 2523; RevPEng 2933.

Kinder- und Hausmärchen. See Grimms' Fairy Tales.

Kindergeschichte. See Child Story.

Kinderspiel, Ein (Walser, M.). DSup 388.

Kindheitsmuster. See Patterns of Childhood, A.

Kindly Ones, The (Powell, A.). LFEng 2119-2120; RevLFEng 2678-2679.

"Kindness" (McPherson). RevPEng 2188.

Kindred (Butler, O.). RevLFEng 495.

Kinds of Affection (Miles). PSup 278; RevPEng 2318.

Kineji, Maborushi. *See* **Gibson, Walter B.**

"King, The" (Babel). RevShF 127; ShF 900.

King, The (Barthelme). RevLFEng 236-237.

King, The (Lagerkvist). DFor 1155.

King, Henry. PEng 1577-1588; RevPEng 1813-1824.

King, Stephen. LFSup 201-211; M&D 985-989; RevLFEng 1883-1897, 3863; RevShF 1345-1351; ShF 2662; ShFSup 122-126.

King and His Campaigners, A. See Charles Men, The.

King and No King, A (Beaumont and Fletcher). DEng 632; RevDEng 777.

King and the Farmer, The (Vega). DFor 1935.

King Coal (Sinclair, U.). LFEng 2423-2424; RevLFEng 3053-3054.

King Coffin (Aiken). LFEng 17-18, 20-21; RevLFEng 30-31, 33-34.

"King Constantine Gave So Much" (Walther). PFor 1679-1680.

King Horn. ShF 141.

King Hunger (Andreyev). DFor 64.

King Jesus (Graves, R.). LFEng 1201-1202; RevLFEng 1425-1426.

King Johan (Bale). DEng 80-81, 88-90, 2260; RevDEng 104-105, 112-114, 2780.

King John (Shakespeare). DEng 1700, 2276; RevDEng 2114, 2795.

King Lear (Shakespeare). DEng 1719-1720, 2281, 2282; RevDEng 2133-2134, 2801-2802.

"King Lear of the Steppes" (Turgenev). RevShF 2322.

King Lear's Wife (Bottomley). DEng 258-261; RevDEng 300-303.

King Leir and His Three Daughters. DEng 2266; RevDEng 2785.

King Log (Hill, G.). PEng 1352, 1353; RevPEng 1521.

King Must Die, The (Renault). LFEng 2220-2221; RevLFEng 2811-2812.

King Oedipus (Hakim). DSup 176.

"King of Asine, The" (Seferis). PFor 1416.

King of Spain, The (Wilson, R.). RevDEng 2619.

"King of the Bingo Game" (Ellison, R.). ShF 580-581.

"King of the Comics" (Moose). RevShF 2759.

King of the Dark Chamber, The (Tagore). DFor 1796-1797.

King of the Fields, The (Singer). RevLFEng 3065-3066.

King of the Golden River, The (Ruskin). ShF 2164, 2167-2168.

"King of the River" (Kunitz). PSup 245; RevPEng 1886.

"King of the Trenches, The" (Lewis). RevShF 1486.

King Otakar's Rise and Fall (Grillparzer). DFor 826-827.

King, Queen, Knave (Nabokov). LFEng 1949; RevLFEng 2462.

King Stag, The (Gozzi). DFor 796.

King, the Greatest Alcalde, The (Vega). DFor 1935.

"King Travicello" (Giusti). PFor 575.

"Kingdom, The" (MacNeice). PEng 1868-1869; RevPEng 2169.

Kingdom Come, The (George). LTh 576.

"Kingdom of Darkness, The" (Dobrolyubov). LTh 388.

Kingdom of God in Bohemia, The (Werfel). DFor 1999.

Kingdom of This World, The (Carpentier). LFFor 281-282.

Kingdoms of Elfin (Warner). ShFSup 358.

Kingery, Margaret. ShF 2663.

"Kingfisher Flat" (Everson). PEng 992-993; RevPEng 1124.

"Kingfishers, The" (Olson). PSup 309-310; RevPEng 2501.

Kingo, Thomas. PFor 2158-2159.

"King's Indian, The" (Gardner). RevShF 960-961; ShF 1461-1462.

Kingsley, Charles. LFEng 3078.

Kingsley, Charlotte May. See **Hanshew, Thomas W.**

Kingsley, Sidney. DEng 1035-1044; RevDEng 1311-1321.

"Kingsmeat" (Card). RevShF 411-413.

"Kinjū." See "Of Birds and Beasts."

Kinkakuji. See *Temple of the Golden Pavilion, The.*

Kinnell, Galway. PEng 1589-1601; PSup 406; RevPEng 1825-1831.

"Kinneret" (Hollander). RevPEng 1554.

Kinoshita Junji. DFor 2434.

Kinsella, Thomas. PSup 230-238; RevPEng 1832-1841.

Kinsella, W. P. RevShF 1352-1358; ShF 2664.

"Kinsman of His Blood, A" (Wolfe). RevShF 2501-2502; ShF 2451.

Kinwelmershe, Francis. RevDEng 903, 904, 2784.

Kipling, Rudyard. LFEng 1537-1546; PEng 1602-1611; RevLFEng 1898-1907, 3789; RevPEng 1842-1851; RevShF 1359-1368; ShF 518, 1748-1755, 1901.

"Kipling's World" (Lewis). LTh 896.

Kipper, Die (Braun). DSup 20-22.

Kipphardt, Heinar. DFor 1050-1057, 2382.

Kipps (Wells). RevLFEng 3483.

Kireyevsky, Ivan Vasilyevich. LTh 1179.

Kirk, Hans. LFFor 2355.

Kirk, John Foster. ShF 588.

Kirkland, Jack. DEng 1045-1054. RevDEng 1322-1332.

Kirshner, Sidney. See **Kingsley, Sidney.**

Kirstinä, Väinö. PFor 2199.

Kiš, Danilo. LFSup 212-217.

Kisfaludy, Károly. DFor 2286.

Kisfaludy, Sándor. PFor 1979-1980.

"Kiss, The" (Chekhov). ShF 110.

Kiss, The (Nims). PEng 2113-2114; RevPEng 2458-2460.

Kiss, József. PFor 1983.

Kiss for the Leper, A (Mauriac). LFFor 1124-1126.

"Kiss me, sweet: the wary lover" (Jonson). PEng 1510; RevPEng 1733.

Kiss of Kin, The (Settle). LFSup 345; RevLFEng 3004, 3006, 3010.

"Kiss of the Cross, The" (Everson). PEng 991; RevPEng 1122-1123.

Kiss of the Spider Woman (Puig). LFFor 1357.

Kit Brandon (Anderson). LFEng 79; RevLFEng 116.

"Kite and Paint" (Robison). RevShF 2011-2012.

"Kith of the Elf-folk, The" (Dunsany). RevShF 790-791; ShF 1316-1317.

Kittredge, G. L. LFEng 1803-1804; RevLFEng 2280-2281.

Kivi, Aleksis. DFor 1058-1070, 2474.

Kizer, Carolyn. PEng 1612-1622; PSup 406; RevPEng 1852-1861.

Kjær, Nils. DFor 2477.

Kjærlighedens tragedie. See *Tragedy of Love, The.*

Klage, Die (Hartmann von Aue). PFor 631.

Kleider machen Leute. See *Clothes Make the Man.*

Kleist, Heinrich, von. DFor 1071-1078, 2369; LFEng 3247-3248, 3249; LTh 437-438, 812-817, 986, 1704; RevShF 1369-1376; ShF 1756-1763.

Kline, Nancy. ShF 2665.

Klop. See *Bedbug, The.*

Klopstock, Friedrich Gottlieb. DEng 2349; LTh 175, 670, 1699; PFor 1911-1912; RevDEng 2868.

Knack to Know a Knave, A (Greene, R.). DEng 844; RevDEng 1039.

Knapp, Samuel. LTh 1746, 1770.

"Knee-Deep in June" (Riley). PEng 2379; RevPEng 2769.

Knee Plays (Wilson). DSup 402.

"Kneel to the Rising Sun" (Caldwell). RevShF 370-371; ShF 1030-1031.

"Kneeling Down to Look into a Culvert" (Bly). RevPEng 274.

"Knife, The" (Gill). ShF 1485-1486.

Knife of the Times and Other Stories, The (Williams, W. C.). RevShF 2487; ShF 2442.

"Knife That Killed Po Hancy, The" (Stockton). M&D 1537-1538.

Knight, Kathleen Moore. M&D 990-995.

Knight from Olmedo, The (Vega). DFor 1937-1938.

Knight of the Burning Pestle, The (Beaumont). DEng 143-145; RevDEng 179-181.

Knights, The (Aristophanes). DFor 117, 2124.

"Knights and Dragons" (Spencer). RevShF 2174-2175.

Knights of the Cross, The (Sienkiewicz). LFFor 1570-1572.

"Knights of the Open Palm" (Daly, C.). M&D 449; ShF 760.

"Knight's Tale, The" (Chaucer). PEng 3263-3264; RevPEng 583, 3782-3783; RevShF 489-490; ShF 1109-1110, 1111.

Kniha smichu a zapomnění. See *Book of Laughter and Forgetting, The.*

Knister, Raymond. ShF 638.

Knjiga boccadoro (Begović). PFor 2263.

Knock. See *Dr. Knock.*

"Knot, The" (Kunitz). PSup 247-248; RevPEng 1888-1889.

Know Nothing (Settle). LFSup 346-347; RevLFEng 3006-3007. See also *Beulah Quintet, The.*

Knowledge of the Evening (Nims). PEng 2112; RevPEng 2458.

Knowles, James Sheridan. DEng 1055-1063. RevDEng 1333-1341.

Knowles, John. RevShF 1377-1382; ShF 1764-1769.

Knox, Ronald A. M&D 996-1004.

Knuckle (Hare). DSup 185-186; RevDEng 1109-1110.

Knudsen, Erik. PFor 2189.

Knudsen, Jakob. LFFor 2347.

Knyaginya Ligovskaya. See *Princess Ligovskaya.*

Kobayashi Hideo. LTh 818-822, 1053.

Kobayashi Issa. PFor 2073.

Kobayashi Yatarō. See **Issa.**

"Kobutori." See "Taking the Wen Away."

Kocbek, Edvard. PFor 2270.

Koch, Claude. ShF 2666.

Koch, Kenneth. PEng 1623-1629; PSup 407; RevPEng 1862-1869.

Kochanowski, Jan. PFor 2119-2120.

Koestler, Arthur. LFEng 1547-1555; **RevLFEng 1908-1917.**

"Kogda b ne smert', a zabyt'e." See "If There Were Not Death, but Oblivion."

"Kogda Psikheia-zhizn' spuskaetsia k teniam." See "When Psyche-Life Descends to the Shades."

Kogdá razguliayetsa. See *When the Skies Clear.*

"Kogda zhe pridet nostoiashchii den'?" See "When Will the Real Day Come?"

"Kohei." See "Currency."

Kohout, Pavel. DSup 218-225.

Kohu, Rosemary. RevPEng 3943.

Kojiki. See *Records of Ancient Matters.*

Kojinteki na taiken. See *Personal Matter, A.*

Kokinshū (Tsurayuki). LTh 1470.

Kokusenya kassen. See *Battles of Coxinga, The.*

"Kolacje." See "Supper, The."

Kolbenheyer, Erwin Guido. PFor 1932.

Kölcsey, Ferenc. PFor 1980.

Kollár, Ján. PFor 1799, 1808.

Kolodny, Annette. RevPEng 3970.

Kolonne Hund (Wolf). DFor 2019-2020.

"Kolybel'naia Treskovogo Mysa." See "Lullaby of Cape Cod."

Komachi, Ono no. See Ono no Komachi.

Komedia rybałtowska. DFor 2274.

Komediantka. See *Comedienne, The.*

Komenský, Jan Ámos. See Comenius.

Komet, Der (Jean Paul). LFFor 877.

Kommandørans døttre. See *Commodore's Daughters, The.*

Komornicka, Maria. PFor 2128.

Kompleks polski. See *Polish Complex, The.*

Konecky, Edith. ShF 2667.

Koneski, Blaže. PFor 2272-2273.

Kongens fald. See *Fall of the King, The.*

König Ottokars Glück und Ende. See *King Otakar's Rise and Fall.*

Konigsburg, Allen Stewart. See Allen, Woody.

Konrad Wallenrod (Mickiewicz). PFor 1020.

Konstantinov-Džinov, Jordan Hadži. DFor 2294.

"Konstnär i norr, En." See "Artist in the North, An."

Kontraption (Owens). DEng 1460-1461; RevDEng 1841-1842.

Konungen. See *King, The.*

Konwicki, Tadeusz. LFFor 944-949.

"Kool-Aid Wino, The" (Brautigan). RevShF 314; ShFSup 54.

Koontz, Dean R. M&D 1005-1009.

Köp den blindes säng (Ekelöf). PFor 449.

Kopfgeburten. See *Headbirths.*

Kopit, Arthur. DEng 1064-1076; DSup 407; RevDEng 1342-1355.

Kops, Bernard. DEng 1077-1085; RevDEng 1356-1364.

Kora. See *Bark.*

Koralle, Die. See *Coral, The.*

Korbal pravednykho. See *Ship of the Righteous, The.*

Kordian (Słowacki). DFor 1714-1715.

"Korean Declaration of Independence" (Desmond). RevPEng 3916.

Koreni (Ćosić). LFFor 387.

"Korf's Clock" (Morgenstern). PFor 1058-1059. See also *Gallows Songs, The.*

"Korfsche Uhr, Die." *See* "Korf's Clock."

Korn, Henry. ShF 2668.

"Korol." *See* "King, The."

Korol', dama, valet. See *King, Queen, Knave.*

Korolenko, Vladimir. LFFor 2319.

Korpela, Jorma. LFFor 2368.

Korrektur. See *Correction.*

Korset. See *Cross, The,* and *Kristin Lavransdatter.*

Korzeniowski, Jósef Teodor Konrad Nałęcz. *See* Conrad, Joseph.

"Koshka i liudi." *See* "Stove, The."

Kōshoku gonin onna. See *Five Women Who Loved Love.*

Kōshoku ichidai otoko. See *Life of an Amorous Man, The.*

Kosinski, Jerzy. LFEng 1556-1566; RevLFEng 1918-1928.

Kosmos. See *Cosmos.*

Kosoelv, Srečko. PFor 2270.

"Kost kosti." *See* "One Bone to Another."

Kosta, Victor. *See* **Simenon, Georges.**

Kostić, Laza. PFor 2254.

Kostrowitzky, Wilhelm Apollinaris de. *See* **Apollinaire, Guillaume.**

Kosztolányi, Dezső. PFor 1984.

Kötlum, Jóhannes úr. PFor 2186.

Kotzebue, August von. DEng 2178, 2332; DFor 1083-1093, 2370; LTh 1306; RevDEng 2698, 2851.

Kouevuur (Breytenbach). PSup 54-55.

Kovačić, Ivan Goran. PFor 2265.

Kovan onnen lapsia (Canth). DFor 326-327.

Kozačinski, Emanuil. DFor 2291.

Kōzui wa waga tamashii ni oyobi (Ōe). LFFor 1200-1202.

"Krähe, Die." *See* "Crow, The."

"Kral Majales" (Ginsberg). RevPEng 1231.

Kralická Bible. PFor 1797.

Králik, Štefan. DFor 2285.

Králv, Janko. PFor 1809.

"Kranich and Bach" (Hollander). RevPEng 1551.

"Kraniche des Ibykus, Die." *See* "Cranes of Ibycus, The."

Kranjčević, Silvije Strahimir. PFor 2263.

Krankheit der Jugend (Bruckner). DFor 260-261.

Kransen. See *Bridal Wreath, The* and *Kristin Lavransdatter.*

Krapp's Last Tape (Beckett). DEng 154-155; DFor 162-163, 2247; RevDEng 188.

Krasicki, Ignacy. LFFor 2061; PFor 2122-2123.

Krasiński, Zygmunt. DFor 1094-1106, 1705, 1709-1710, 2276; PFor 2126.

"Krasnoe koleso" (Solzhenitsyn). LFFor 1646.

Kraszewski, Józef Ignacy. LFFor 2062.

Kraus, Karl. DFor 1107-1118; PFor 791-800.

Krechinsky's Wedding (Sukhovo-Kobylin). DFor 1773-1774. See also *Triology of Alexander Sukhovo-Kobylin, The.*

Křest svatého Vladimíra (Havlíček). PFor 1801.

Kretzer, Max. LFFor 2181.

Kreutzer Sonata, The (Tolstoy). RevShF 2285-2286.

Kreuzelschreiber, Die. (Anzengruber). DFor 90-91.

Krieger, Murray. LTh 823-830.

Kristensen, Tom. LFFor 2354; PFor 2184.

Kristeva, Julia. LTh 423, 831-835, 850, 1812, 1832.

Kristin Lavransdatter (Undset). LFFor 1803-1804, 2352.

Kristnihald undir Jökli. See *Christianity at Glacier.*

Kristuslegender. See *Christ Legends.*

Kritik der Urteilskraft. See *Critique of Judgment, The.*

Kritische Waffengänge (Harts). LTh 1719.

Kritische Wälder (Herder). LTh 669.

"Krizis." *See* "Crisis, The."

Krleža, Miroslav. DFor 2293; LFFor 2077; PFor 2264.

Krntikos, To (Solomòs). PFor 1456.

Kroetz, Franz Xaver. DFor 1119-1128, 2382-2383; DSup 407.

Krog, Helge. DFor 2480.

Król-Duch (Słowacki). PFor 1446-1447.

Krol Popiel i inne wiersze (Miłosz). PFor 1034.

Krolow, Karl. PFor 1934.

"Krône ist elter danne der künec Philippes sî, Diu." *See* "Crown Is Older Than King Philip, The."

Krst pri Savici (Prešeren). PFor 2268.

Krysl, Marilyn. ShF 2670

Krzyżacy. See *Knights of the Cross, The.*

"Który skrzywdziłeś." *See* "You Who Have Wronged."

Kuan Han-ch'ing. DFor 2314-2315.

"K'uang-jên jih-chi." *See* "Diary of a Madman, The."

"Kübelreiter, Der." *See* "Bucket Rider, The."

"Kubla Khan" (Coleridge, S. T.). PEng 539-540; RevPEng 630-631.

"Kubla Khan" (Wheatley). PEng 3060; RevPEng 3547.

Kubly, Herbert. ShF 2671.

Kuća nasred druma (Popa). PFor 1272.

Kuchibue o fuku toki. See *When I Whistle.*
"Kudzu" (Dickey, J.). PEng 797.
"Kugelmass Episode, The" (Allen). RevShF 57-58.
Kuhn, Thomas. LTh 765, 1819.
Kuhner, Herbert. ShF 2672.
Kukučín, Martin. LFFor 2068-2069.
Kulcskeresok (Örkény). DSup 300.
Kulisakh dushi. See *Theatre of the Soul, The.*
Kullervo (Kivi). DFor 1063-1064.
Kumbell, Kumbel. See **Hein, Piet.**
Kumin, Maxine. RevPEng 1870-1879.
"Kumo no ito." *See* "Spider's Thread, The."
Kun en spillemand. See *Only a Fiddler.*
"Künc Constantin der gap sô vil." *See* "King Constantine Gave So Much."
Kundan the Patriot (Venkataramani). ShF 643.
Kundera, Milan. LFFor 950-957, 2067; **RevShF 1383-1391.**
Kunert, Günter. PFor 1813, 1817, 1820, 1823, 1824.
"K'ung I-chi" (Lu Hsün). RevShF 1520-1521; ShFSup 175-176.
K'ung Shang-jên. DFor 2327.
Kungaskald (Dahlstierna). PFor 2158.
Kunitz, Stanley. PSup 239-251; RevPEng 1880-1893.
"Kuno no nenkan." *See* "Almanac of Pain, An."
Kunst, Die (Holz). LTh 692-693, 1719-1720.

"Kunstwerk im Zeitalter seiner Reproduzierbarkeit, Das." *See* "Work of Art in the Age of Mechanical Reproduction, The."
Kuntsnmakher fun Lubin, Der. See *Magician of Lublin, The.*
Kunze, Reiner. PFor 801-809.
"Kuo Hsiangchi ssu." *See* "Visiting the Temple of Gathered Fragrance."
Kuo Mo-jo. LTh 1782.
Kuprin, Aleksandr. LFFor 2320-2321.
Kurka wodna. See *Water Hen, The.*
"Kuroi kyū-jū. *See* "Old Friends."
Kuruo paideía. See *Cyropaedia.*
Kurve, Die. See *Curve, The.*
Kurze Brief zum langen Abschied, Der. See *Short Letter, Long Farewell.*
Kusika's Short Stories (Madhaviah). ShF 643.
"Kusok mysa." *See* "Piece of Meat, A."
"Kusuteki kokai." *See* "Incredible Voyage."
Kutonet veha-pasim. See *Tzili.*
Kuzari (Judah). PFor 779, 780.
Kvaran, Einar Hjörleifsson. LFFor 2343.
"Kvartiranty." *See* "Tenants."
Kyd, Thomas (1558-1594). DEng 1086-1097, 2270; **RevDEng 1365-1376, 2789.**
Kyd, Thomas (1901-1976); M&D 1010-1016
Kyng Alisaunder. RevShF 2617; ShF 446.
"Kyōfu." *See* "Terror."
Kyūshū mondō (Yoshimoto). LTh 1594.

L

L. Tolstoy i Dostoyevsky. See *Tolstoy as Man and Artist, with an Essay on Dostoievski.*

Là-Bas (Huysmans). LFFor 865-866, 2136-2137.

"La Belle Zoraïde" (Chopin). RevShF 537-538.

La Bruyère, Jean de. LTh **836-842,** 1259.

La Chaussée, Pierre-Claude Nivelle de. DEng 2181; DFor **1139-1145,** 2340.

La Chaussée, Pierre-Claude Nivelle de. RevDEng 2701.

La Cour, Paul. PFor 2184.

La Fayette, Madame de. LFFor **958-965,** 2028-2029, 2117.

La Fontaine, Jean de. LTh 481, **853-858,** 1419; PFor **810-818,** 1856-1857; RevShF 2580; ShF 382.

La Fontaine et ses fables (Taine). LTh 1419.

La Halle, Adam de. DFor 2175-2176.

La Harpe, Jean-François de. LTh **859-864,** 1180.

L.A. Law. RevDEng 3042.

La Mesnardière, Jules de. LTh 310.

Laberius, Decimus. DFor 2147.

Labiche, Eugène. DFor **1129-1138,** 2349.

Labirynt (Ważyk). PFor 1695.

"Labor Day Dinner" (Munro). RevShF 1696-1698; ShFSup 213-214.

Labrunie, Gérard. See **Nerval, Gérard de.**

Labyrinten (Baggesen). LFFor 2335.

"Labyrinth, The" (King). PEng 1586-1587; RevPEng 1822-1823.

"Labyrinth, The" (Nin). RevShF 1723; ShF 1950.

Labyrinthine Ways, The. See *Power and the Glory, The.*

"Lac, Le." See "Lake, The."

Lacan, Jacques. LTh 503, 833-834, **843-852,** 1767-1768, 1826; PEng 3424-3425; RevPEng 3959-3960.

Lacayos ladrones, Los. See *Registro de representantes.*

"Lachrimae" (Hill). RevPEng 1526-1527.

Laclos, Pierre Choderlos de. LFEng 3117-3120; LFFor 2121; RevLFEng 3819-3822.

Laços de familia. See *Family Ties.*

Lacy, Ed. M&D **1017-1020.**

Ladders to Fire (Nin). LFEng 1993-1994; RevLFEng 2516, 2518.

Ladies and Hussars (Fredro). DSup 138-139.

Ladies' Home Journal. ShF 589.

Lady, The (Richter). LFEng 2270; RevLFEng 2864.

"Lady and the Lion, The" (Grimm). RevShF 1085; ShF 1557.

Lady Aoi, The (Mishima). DFor 1324.

Lady Audley's Secret (Braddon). M&D 181-182.

Lady Chatterley's Lover (Lawrence, D. H.). LFEng 1601-1604; RevLFEng 1974-1977, 3767.

Lady, Drop Dead (Treat). M&D 1600.

Lady Frederick (Maugham). DEng 1308-1309; RevDEng 1638.

"Lady Geraldine's Courtship" (Browning, E. B.). PEng 329; RevPEng 399.

"Lady Hsi" (Wang Wei). PFor 1685-1686.

Lady in Peril (Dent). M&D 486.

Lady in the Dark (Hart, M.). DEng 911-913; RevDEng 1134-1135.

"Lady in the Looking Glass, The" (Woolf). ShF 2456.

Lady Jane Gray. See *Tragedy of Lady Jane Gray, The.*

Lady Julie. See *Miss Julie.*

"Lady Lazarus" (Plath). PEng 2229, 3374; RevPEng 2601.

"Lady Lucifer" (O'Faoláin). ShF 2002.

"Lady Macbeth of the Mtsensk District" (Leskov). RevShF 1467; ShFSup 159.

Lady Nit-Wit, The (Vega). DFor 1936.

Lady of Dawn, The (Casona). DFor 355-357.

Lady of Lyons, The (Bulwer-Lytton). DEng 313-314; RevDEng 373-374.

Lady of Pleasure, The (Shirley). DEng 1817-1819, 2292-2293; RevDEng 2252-2254, 2811.

Lady of the Camillias, The. See *Camille.*

Lady of the Lake, The (Scott). PEng 2500, 2501-2502; RevPEng 2908, 2909.

"Lady or the Tiger?, The" (Stockton). M&D 1535-1536; RevShF 2225, 2228; ShF 588.

Lady Spider (MacDonagh). DEng 1208-1211; RevDEng 1511-1514.

Lady Susan (Austen). RevShF 121-122; ShF 897-898.

Lady Windermere's Fan (Wilde). DEng 2036, 2037; RevDEng 2535-2536.

"Lady's Dressing Room, The" (Swift). PEng 2808; RevPEng 3275.

Lady's Not for Burning, The (Fry). DEng 686-687; RevDEng 854.

Lady's Trial, The (Ford). DEng 666-669; RevDEng 811-814.

Lafcadio's Adventures (Gide). LFFor 644-645, 2139.

Laforgue, Jules. PFor 819-828, 1879.

Lagar (Mistral). PFor 1040, 1043-1044.

Lagerkvist, Pär. DFor 1146-1159, 2477-2478; **LFFor 966-977,** 2350-2351; PFor 2177-2178.

Lagerlöf, Selma. LFFor 978-990, 2344; PFor 1371.

"Lagoon, The" (Conrad). RevShF 608.

"Lágrimas que vierte un alma arrepentida" (Calderón). PFor 249.

"Lai de plaisance, Le." *See* "Lay on Pleasure, The."

"Laid in my quyett bedd" (Surrey). PEng 2789; RevPEng 3255.

Laine, Jarkko. PFor 2200.

"Lairds of Esquesing, The," 3939.

Lais, Le. See *Legacy, The.*

Lais (Marie de France). PFor 964-971; RevShF 1605; ShF 1886, 1887.

"Laissé-pour-compte, Le." *See* "Misfit, The."

"Lajwanti" (Anand). ShF 645.

"Lake, The" (Lamartine). PFor 832-833.

"Lake Isle of Innisfree, The" (Yeats). PEng 3190-3191; RevPEng 3715.

Lake of the Woods (Tesich). RevDEng 2376.

Lake Wobegon Days (Keillor). RevShF 1328.

Lakeboat (Mamet). RevDEng 1564.

Lakoff, Robin. RevPEng 3969.

Lalić, Ivan V. PFor 2257.

"Lamarck" (Mandelstam). PFor 940.

"Lamarck Elaborated" (Wilbur). PEng 3094-3095; RevPEng 3584-3585.

Lamartine, Alphonse de. LTh 1704; PFor 829-836, 1867-1868.

"Lamb, The" (Blake). PEng 209-210; RevPEng 254.

"Lamb, The" (Heyen). RevPEng 1505.

Lamb, Charles. LTh 1399, 1698, 1705, 1707, 1710; PEng 1630-1638; RevPEng 1894-1903.

"Lamb to the Slaughter" (Dahl). RevShF 656-657; ShF 1223-1224.

Lambro, powstańca grecki (Slowacki). PFor 1442.

Lambros (Solomòs). PFor 1456.

"Lame Shall Enter First, The" (O'Connor, Flannery). RevShF 1763.

"Lament, The" (Chekhov). ShF 1127-1128.

"Lament for Ignacio Sánchez Mejías" (García Lorca). PFor 21-22, 518-519.

Lament for the Bride (Reilly). M&D 1404.

"Lament for the Makaris" (Dunbar, W.). PEng 895-896; RevPEng 1031-1032.

"Lament on the Death of a Master of Arts" (Anand). ShF 646.

Lamentable Tragedy of Locrine, The (Stevenson?). DEng 2266; RevDEng 2785.

"Lamentación de Navidad" (Reyes). PFor 1322.

"Lamentation of Mr. Pages Wife, The" (Deloney). PEng 785-786.

"Lamentationen." *See* "Lamentations."

"Lamentations" (Heine). PFor 651.

Laments (Kochanowski). PFor 2119.

Lamia (Keats). PEng 1552-1553; RevPEng 1779-1780.

Lamiel (Stendhal). LFFor 1663-1664.

LaMoore, Louis Dearborn. *See* **L'Amour, Louis.**

L'Amour, Louis. LFEng 3197; LFSup 218-226; RevLFEng 1929-1939, 3854.

"Lamp, A" (Schorer). ShF 2200-2201.

"Lamp at Noon, The" (Ross, S.). ShF 638.

Lámpara maravillosa, La (Valle-Inclán). LFFor 1833-1834.

Lampe d'Aladin, La (Cocteau). PFor 370.

Lampedusa, Giuseppe Tomasi di. *See* **Tomasi di Lampedusa, Giuseppe.**

Lancashire Witches, and Tegue o Divelly the Irish Priest, The (Shadwell). DEng 1673-1674; RevDEng 2086-2087.

Lancelot (Chrétien de Troyes). PFor 1838; RevShF 545; ShF 444-445, 1140-1141.

Lancelot (Percy). LFEng 2096-2098; RevLFEng 2635-2637.

Lancelot (Robinson). PEng 2393; RevPEng 2784.

Lances de honor (Tamayo y Baus). DFor 1806-1807.

Land, The (Colum). DEng 388, 389; RevDEng 487, 488.

"Land of Exile" (Pavese). RevShF 1861.

Land of Spices, The (O'Brien, K.). RevLFEng 2564-2565.

"Land of the Dead, The" (Giusti). PFor 575.

"Land of Work" (Pasolini). PFor 1149-1150. See also "Gramsci's Ashes."

"Landarzt, Ein." *See* "Country Doctor, A."

Landessprache (Enzensberger). PFor 469.

"Landfall" (Wagoner). PEng 2992; RevPEng 3480.

Landfall (Wagoner). PEng 2992-2993; RevPEng 3479.

Landkjenning (Hauge). LFFor 800. See also *Cleng Peerson.*

Landnámabók. See *Book of Settlements.*

Last Good Kiss, The (Crumley). M&D 435.

Last Hero and Other Poems, The (Coxe). PEng 630-632.

"Last Husband, The" (Humphrey). RevShF 1234.

Last Husband and Other Stories, The (Humphrey). RevShF 1234-1235.

Last Judgement (Clarke). M&D 355-357.

"Last Kiss" (Fitzgerald). RevShF 864-865; ShF 1375-1376.

"Last Laugh" (Warren). PEng 3028.

Last Laugh, Mr. Moto (Marquand). M&D 1186.

"Last Leaf, The" (Henry). ShF 230.

"Last Leaf, The" (Holmes). PEng 1372; RevPEng 1561.

Last Letters of Jacopo Ortis (Foscolo). PFor 491, 493.

"Last Love" (Novalis). PFor 1097.

Last Man, The (Shelley, M.). LFEng 2390-2392; RevLFEng 3018-3020.

Last Mandarin, The (Becker). LFEng 203-204.

"Last Meeting" (Warren). RevPEng 3524.

Last Meeting of the Knights of the White Magnolia, The (Jones, P.). DEng 1010; RevDEng 1277. See also *Texas Trilogy, A.*

"Last Mohican, The" (Malamud). RevShF 1571-1572.

"last Night that She lived, The" (Dickinson). PEng 811-812; RevPEng 923-924.

Last of Chéri, The (Colette). LFFor 372; RevShF 2742.

Last of Mr. Moto, The. See *Stopover: Tokyo.*

Last of Mrs. Cheyney, The (Lonsdale). DEng 1171-1173; RevDEng 1473-1475.

Last of the Breed (L'Amour). LFSup 225; RevLFEng 1936.

Last of the Empire, The (Sembène). LFFor 2038.

"Last of the Light Brigade, The" (Kipling). PEng 1605; RevPEng 1845.

Last of the Mohicans, The (Cooper). LFEng 606, 611-613; RevLFEng 736, 741-743.

Last of the Wine, The (Renault). LFEng 2219-2220; RevLFEng 2811.

"Last Pennant Before Armageddon, The" (Kinsella). RevShF 1355.

Last Picture Show, The (McMurtry). LFEng 1752-1753; RevLFEng 2221-2222.

Last Poems (Lawrence, D. H.). PEng 1685-1686; RevPEng 1955.

"Last Ride of Wild Bill, The" (Brown). RevPEng 390.

"Last River, The" (Kinnell). PEng 1593.

Last Seen Wearing . . . (Waugh). M&D 1685.

Last September, The (Bowen). LFEng 264-265; RevLFEng 320-321.

Last Stand at Papago Wells (L'Amour). LFSup 222; RevLFEng 1932-1933.

"Last Stop" (Seferis). PFor 1417. See also *Logbooks.*

Last Temptation of Christ, The (Kazantzakis). LFFor 920-923.

Last Things (Jones, M.). RevLFEng 1818.

Last Tycoon, The (Fitzgerald). RevShF 864-865; ShF 1374, 1375, 1376.

"Last Word, The" (Hornung). M&D 908-909.

"Lastness" (Kinnell). PEng 1598-1599.

Låt människan leva. See *Let Man Live.*

La Taille, Jean de. LTh 277.

Late Bourgeois World, The (Gordimer). LFEng 1164; RevLFEng 1385-1386.

"Late Flowering Lust" (Betjeman). PEng 172; RevPEng 205.

Late George Apley, The (Marquand). LFEng 1817; RevLFEng 2302.

Late Hour, The (Strand). PEng 2772-2773.

Late Mattia Pascal, The (Pirandello). LFFor 1302-1304, 2239.

Late Mrs. Null, The (Stockton). M&D 1537.

"Lately, Alas, I Knew a Gentle Boy" (Thoreau). PEng 2902; RevPEng 3370.

Later (Creeley). PEng 688-690.

Later Life (Gurney). RevDEng 1070-1071.

"Latest Literary Controversies, The" (Dostoevski). LTh 396.

Lathen, Emma. M&D 1021-1026.

Latimer, Jonathan. M&D 1027-1032.

Latin mystique, Le (Gourmont). LTh 624.

Latsis, Mary Jane. *See* **Lathen, Emma.**

Laudi, Le (D'Annunzio). PFor 387-388.

Laudi del cielo del mare della terra e degli eroi. See *Laudi, Le.*

Laughable Loves (Kundera). LFFor 950, 951, 952; RevShF 1385-1389.

Laughing Matter, The (Saroyan). LFEng 2338-2339; RevLFEng 2953-2954.

Laughing Policeman, The (Sjöwall and Wahlöö). M&D 1498.

Laughing Stock (Linney). DSup 238.

Laughter! (Barnes). DSup 13-14; RevDEng 146-147.

"Laughter Beneath the Bridge" (Okri). RevShF 1807.

Laughter in the Dark (Nabokov). LFEng 1949-1950; RevLFEng 2462-2463.

Laundromat, The (Norman). RevDEng 1741. See also *Third and Oak.*

Laune des Verliebten, Die. See *Wayward Lover, The.*

Laura (Caspary). M&D 290-292.

"Laura" (Saki). M&D 1458; RevShF 2035; ShF 2172.

"Laura am Klavier." See "Laura at the Piano."

"Laura at the Piano" (Schiller). PFor 1407.

Laurel de Apolo (Vega). PFor 1603.

Laurels Are Poison (Mitchell). M&D 1233.

Laurence, Margaret. LFEng 1567-1577; LFSup 405; RevLFEng 1940-1950; RevShF 1406-1411; ShF 1775-1779; ShFSup 389.

Laurence Bloomfield in Ireland (Allingham). PEng 44-45; RevPEng 35-36.

Laurents, Arthur. DEng 1098-1108; RevDEng 1377-1388.

"Laus Deo" (Whittier). PEng 3087-3088; RevPEng 3576-3577.

"Laüstic" (Marie de France). RevShF 1606-1607; ShF 1888-1889.

Lautaro (Aguirre). DFor 37-38.

Lavers, Norman. ShF 2675.

Lavin, Mary. RevShF 1412-1418; ShF 522, 675, 1780-1787; ShFSup 389.

"Law" (Radnóti). PFor 1312.

Law, William. PEng 397-398.

"Law of Life" (London). RevShF 1498; ShF 1811-1812.

Lawd Today (Wright, R.). LFEng 2978-2979; RevLFEng 3683-3684.

Lawler, Ray. DEng 1109-1117, 2434-2435; RevDEng 1389-1398, 2957-2958.

"Lawley Road" (Narayan). RevShF 1718; ShFSup 228.

Lawley Road (Narayan). RevShF 1718.

Lawley Road and Other Stories (Narayan). ShFSup 227-228.

"Lawn in the Park" (Kraus). PFor 799.

Lawrence, D. H. LFEng 1578-1605, 3058-3059, 3316; LTh 865-870, 876, 1318, 1492; PEng 1677-1687; RevLFEng 1951-1980, 3766-3767; RevPEng 1947-1958; RevShF 1419-1428, 2736-2737; ShF 242-243-244, 520.

Lawrence, Frieda von Richthofen. LFEng 1581-1582; RevLFEng 1954-1955.

Lawrence, Lydia Beardsall. PEng 1678.

Lawrence L'Imposteur (Aldington). LFEng 39; RevLFEng 53.

Laws (Plato). LTh 1117-1118.

Lawson, Henry. RevShF 1429-1434; ShFSup 136-141.

Lawson, Todd S. J. ShF 2676.

Lawton Girl, The (Frederic). LFEng 1027; RevLFEng 1220.

Laxdœla Saga. Rev 2589-2590; ShF 392.

Laxness, Halldór. LFFor 991-1003, 2357, 2358.

Lay By (Hare and others). DSup 184.

Lay of Atli. ShF 431.

Lay of Hákon, The (Skáldaspillir). PFor 2154.

Lay of Igor's Host, The. LTh 748; PFor 2132-2133.

Lay of the Last Minstrel, The (Scott). PEng 2500, 2501-2502; RevPEng 2908, 2909.

Lay of the Sun, The. PFor 2155.

Lay of the White Steed. PFor 1974.

"Lay on Pleasure, The" (Chartier). PFor 347.

Layamon. PEng 1688-1694; RevPEng 1959-1966.

Laye, Camara. LFFor 2035-2036, 2041.

"Layers, The" (Kunitz). PSup 247, 249; RevPEng 1888, 1890.

"Laying" (Yosano Akiko). PFor 1718.

Layman's Faith, A. See *Religio Laici.*

Lays of Ancient Rome (Macaulay). PEng 1825-1826.

Lazaretti (Hochwälder). DFor 932.

Lazarillo de Tormes. LFEng 3101-3102; LFFor 2023-2024, 2376-2377; RevLFEng 3803-3804; ShF 145, 451-453.

Lazarre, Jane. ShF 2677.

"Lazarus" (Andreyev). ShF 375-376.

Lea (Kivi). DFor 1068-1069.

Leacock, Stephen. ShF 636-637.

"Lead, Kindly Light" (Newman). PEng 2102-2103.

"Leader of the People, The" (Steinbeck). ShF 2277-2278.

"leaf falls, a" (Cummings). PEng 3230-3231; RevPEng 796.

Leaf Storm (García Márquez). LFFor 615-616.

"Leaning Tower, The" (Porter). RevShF 1912-1913.

Lear (Bond). DEng 249-251; RevDEng 290-292.

Lear, Edward. PEng 1695-1702; RevPEng 1967-1975.

Lear, Peter. See **Lovesey, Peter.**

"Learning a Dead Language" (Merwin). PEng 1981.

"Leather Jacket, The" (Pavese). RevShF 1861.

Leatherstocking Tales (Cooper). LFEng 606; RevLFEng 736, 3748, 3749, 3849.

"Leave Me" (Otero). PFor 1113, 1115.

Leavenworth Case, The (Green). M&D 783-784.

Leaves of Grass (Whitman). LTh 1748; PEng 3073, 3074, 3386; RevPEng 3553-3562.

"Leavetaking" (Ungaretti). PFor 1566. See also *Allegria, L'*.

Leaving Home: A Collection of Lake Wobegon Stories (Keillor). RevShF 1326-1329.

"Leaving Seoul" (Lew). RevPEng 3916-3917.

"Leaving the Asylum" (Orr). PEng 2154; RevPEng 2524.

Leavis, F. R. LTh 148, 415-416, **871-877,** 1337, 1569.

Leavitt, David. RevShF **1435-1441.**

Lebediny stan. See *Demesne of the Swans, The.*

Leben der schwedischen Gräfen von G . . . See *Life of the Swedish Countess of G . . ., The.*

Leben des Galilei. See *Life of Galileo.*

Leben Gundlings Friedrich von Pruessen Lessings Schlaf Traum Schrei. See *Gundling's Life Frederick of Prussia Lessing's Sleep Dream Scream.*

Leben und Tod der heiligen Genoveva (Tieck). DFor 1833.

Lebensansichten des Kater Murrs. See *Life and Opinions of Kater Murr, The.*

Lebensbeschreibung der Ertzbetrügerin und Landstörtzerin Courasche. See *Courage.*

Lebenswelt. RevPEng 3961-3962.

Leblanc, Maurice. M&D **1033-1040.**

Lebrun, Ponce-Denis Écouchard. *See* Pindare-Lebrun.

Le Carré, John. LFEng **1609-1619;** LFSup 405; M&D **1041-1047;** RevLFEng **1981-1994,** 3774, 3789.

Leçon, La. See *Lesson, The.*

"Lector Aere Perennior" (Cunningham). PSup 75; RevPEng 804.

"Lecture on Modern Poetry, A" (Hulme). LTh 716.

Lecture on Poetry (Sassoon). PEng 2470; RevPEng 2872.

Lectures Chiefly on the Dramatic Literature of the Age of Elizabeth (Hazlitt). LTh 653.

Lectures on the English Poets (Hazlitt). LTh 798.

Lectures on the History of Literature Ancient and Modern (Schlegel, F.). LTh 1702.

"Léda a kertben." *See* "Leda in the Garden."

"Leda and the Swan" (Yeats). PEng 3191-3194, 3454-3455; RevPEng 3715-3719, 3989-3990.

"Leda in the Garden" (Ady). PFor 5.

Leda senza cigno, La (D'Annunzio). LFFor 414.

Lederköpfe, Die (Kaiser). DFor 1025.

"Ledi Makbet Mtsenskogo uezda." *See* "Lady Macbeth of the Mtsensk District."

Lee, Don L. *See* **Madhubuti, Haki R.**

Lee, Howard. *See* **Goulart, Ron.**

Lee, Li-Young. RevPEng 3914.

Lee, Manfred Bennington. *See* **Queen, Ellery.**

Lee, Maria Berl. ShF 2678.

Lee, Nathaniel. DEng **1118-1123;** RevDEng **1399-1405.**

Leech, Clifford. PEng 1904.

Le Fanu, Joseph Sheridan. LFEng **1620-1628;** M&D **1048-1052;** RevLFEng **1995-2004,** 3859; RevShF **1442-1449;** ShF 734, 1689, **1795-1802.**

Left Bank and Other Stories, The (Rhys). RevShF 1999-2000; ShFSup 259.

Left Hand of Darkness, The (Le Guin). LFEng 1634-1636, 3212; RevLFEng 2010-2011.

"Lefty" (Leskov). RevShF 1468; ShFSup 160.

Legacy, The (Villon). PFor 1656-1657, 1659.

"Legacy, The" (Woolf). ShF 2457-2458.

"Legal System, The" (Hogan). RevPEng 1542.

Légataire universel, Le. See *Universal Legatee, The.*

Legend Days (Highwater). RevLFEng 1625.

Legend of Good Women, The (Chaucer). PEng 482-483; RevPEng 578-579; RevShF 485; ShF 1105.

Legend of St. Catherine, The. PFor 1796.

"Legend of St. Julian, Hospitaler, The" (Flaubert). LFEng 3265, 3266-3267; RevShF 873-874, 2715-2716; ShF 1381.

"Legend of Sleepy Hollow, The" (Irving, W.). RevLFEng 3800; RevShF 1248-1249; ShF 1666.

"Legend of the Big Hat" (Asturias). RevShF 96-99; ShF 884-887.

Legend of the Centuries, The (Hugo). PFor 736-737.

Legend of the Miraculous Stag. PFor 1974.

"Legend of the Origin of the Book Tao-Tê-Ching on Lao-tsû's Road into Exile" (Brecht). PFor 225.

"Legend of Tularecito, The" (Steinbeck). RevShF 2208.

Legenda o svaté Kateřině. See *Legend of St. Catherine, The.*

"Legende de Saint-Julien l'Hospitalier, La." *See* "Legend of St. Julian, Hospitaler, The."

Légende des siècles, La. See *Legend of the Centuries, The.*

"Legende von der Entstehung des Buches Taoteking." *See* "Legend of the Origin of the Book Tao-Tê-Ching on Lao-tsû's Road into Exile."

"Legends" (Adams). RevShF 8.

Legends of Guatemala (Asturias). LFFor 84; ShF 883-884; RevShF 95.

Legends of the Fall (Harrison). RevLFEng 1541-1542.

Léger, Alexis Saint-Léger. *See* **Perse, St.-John.**

Leggett, John. ShF 2679.

Legião Estrangeira, A. See *Foreign Legion, The.*

Légitime Défense (Breton). LTh 214.

"Legs, The" (Graves). PEng 1130-1131; RevPEng 1287.

Legs (Kennedy). LFSup 195-197; RevLFEng 1852-1854. See also *Albany Cycle, The.*

Le Guin, Ursula K. LFEng 1629-1637; LFSup 405; **RevLFEng 2005-2015,** 3870. **RevShF 1450-1455;** ShF 552-553; **ShFSup 142-147.**

Lehmann, Rosamond. LFSup 227-234; **RevLFEng 2016-2024.**

Lehmann, Wilhelm. PFor 1931.

Lehre der Sainte-Victoire, Die. See *Lesson of Mont-Sainte-Victoire, The.*

Lehtonen, Joel. LFFor 2356.

Leiber, Fritz, Jr. ShF 2680.

Leibniz, Gottfried Wilhelm. LFFor 2153, 2154; LTh 78.

Leibowitz, Judith. LFEng 3251-3252.

Leiden des jungen Werthers, Die. See *Sorrows of Young Werther, The.*

Leila (Donleavy). RevLFEng 950.

Leila (Fogazzaro). LFFor 2235.

"Leilige Cäcilie: Oder, Die Gewalt der Musik, Die." *See* "St. Cecilia: Or, The Power of Music."

Leino, Eino. PFor 2173.

Lei-yü. See *Thunderstom.*

Lélia (Sand). LFFor 1492-1494.

Lem, Stanisław. LFFor 1004-1015; **RevShF 1456-1463; ShFSup 148-155.**

Lemaître, Frédéric. DFor 2343.

"Lemmings, The" (Slavitt). RevPEng 3049.

"Lemon Trees, The" (Montale). PFor 1049. See also *Bones of the Cuttlefish.*

Lena (Ariosto). DFor 108-109.

Lenau, Nikolaus. PFor 1920.

"Lend Lease" (Shalamov), 2095; ShFSup 290.

Lengua poética de Góngora, La (Alonso). LTh 26.

"Leningrad" (Mandelstam). PFor 940.

Lenngren, Anna Maria. PFor 2162.

Lentricchia, Frank. LTh 506.

Lenz, Jakob Michael Reinhold. DFor 1160-1169.

Leo Armenius (Gryphius). DFor 836.

León, Luis de. PFor 837-844.

"Leonainie" (Riley). PEng 2375; RevPEng 2765.

Leonard, Elmore. M&D 1053-1057; RevLFEng 2025-2031.

Leonard, Hugh. DEng 2449; **DSup 226-234; RevDEng 1406-1415,** 2974.

Leonard, Lionel Frederick. *See* **Lonsdale, Frederick.**

Léonard, Nicolas-Germain. PFor 1863.

"Leonard and Susan" (Coleridge, H.). PEng 526.

Leonardo's Last Supper (Barnes). DSup 12; RevDEng 145.

Leonce and Lena (Büchner). DFor 273-274.

Leoni (Ruskin). ShF 2166-2167.

Leonidas of Tarentum. PFor 845-851.

Léonie est en avance (Feydeau). DFor 606-607.

Leonor de Guzman (Boker). DEng 224-225; RevDEng 265-266.

Leonov, Leonid Maksimovich. M&D 1058-1064.

Leopard, The (Tomasi di Lampedusa). LFFor 1730-1731, 1732-1737.

"Leopardi" (Strand). PEng 2773.

Leopardi, Giacomo. LTh 367, 1019, 1702, 1704, 1706, 1710; **PFor 852-865.**

Leopold, Karl Gustaf af. PFor 2162.

"Lepanto" (Chesterton). PEng 494.

Leper of Saint Giles, The (Peters, Ellis). M&D 1323.

Le Queux, William. M&D 1065-1070.

Lermontov, Mikhail. DFor 1170-1180; LFEng 3142-3144; **LFFor 1016-1024,** 2313-2314; LTh 119; **PFor 866-876,** 2139-2140.

Lerner, Alan Jay, and Frederick Loewe. RevDEng 3001.

Leroux, Gaston. M&D 1071-1077.

"Leroy" (Baraka). PEng 86; RevPEng 97-98.

Les. See *Forest, The.*

Les Blancs. See *Blancs, Les.*

Lesage, Alain-René. DFor 1181-1192, 2338; LFEng 3103; **LFFor 1025-1036,** 2029-2030, 2305; RevLFEng 3805.

"Lesbia" (Congreve). PEng 555; RevPEng 647.

Lescarbot, Marc. RevDEng 2960.

Leskov, Nikolai. LFFor 2319; LTh 1356; **RevShF 1464-1471; ShFSup 156-163.**

Leslie, Frank. ShF 588-589.

Leśmian, Bolesław. PFor 2128.

Less Than Angels (Pym). LFEng 2180-2181; RevLFEng 2756.

Lessico famigliare. See *Family Sayings.*

Lessing, Doris. LFEng 1638-1650, 3131; LFSup 405; **RevLFEng 2032-2042,** 3774, 3775, 3833; **RevShF 1472-1478; ShF 1803-1808.**

Lessing, Gotthold Ephraim. DEng 2184-2185, 2343; **DFor 1193-1211,** 2363-2364; LFFor 2154; LTh 70, 175, 287, 370, 437, 663,

"Letters to the Princess" (Senghor). PFor 1426-1427. See also *Hosties noires*.

Letters to Yesenin (Harrison, J.). PEng 1231-1233; RevPEng 1412-1414.

Letting Go (Roth). LFEng 2301-2302; RevLFEng 2898-2899.

"Lettre du voyant." *See* "Seer Letter."

"Lettre d'un fou." *See* "Letter from a Madman."

Lettre morte. See *Dead Letter.*

Lettres à l'Amazone. See *Letters to the Amazon.*

Lettres de mon moulin. See *Letters from My Mill.*

Lettres persanes, Les. See *Persian Letters.*

Lettres portugaises. See *Portugese Letters.*

Letty Fox (Stead). LFEng 2492-2493; RevLFEng 3119, 3122.

"Letzte Liebe." *See* "Last Love."

Letzten Tage der Menschheit, Die. See *Last Days of Mankind, The.*

Leucippe and Cleitophon (Achilles Tatius). LFFor 2004-2005.

Leute von Seldwyla, Die. See *People of Seldwyla, The.*

"Levél Várady Antalhoz." *See* "Letter to Antal Várady."

Levelek Irisz koszorújából (Babits). PFor 119-120.

Levertov, Denise. PEng 1703-1711; PSup 407; **RevPEng 1976-1987.**

Levi, Carlo. LFFor 2247.

Levi, Primo. LFSup 235-240.

Levia gravia (Carducci). PFor 270.

Léviathan. See *Dark Journey, The.*

Leviathan (Hauge). LFFor 803-804.

Leviathan (Hobbes). ShF 505.

Levin, Meyer. ShF 2682.

Levin, Samuel. RevPEng 3987-3988; PEng 3452-3453.

Levine (Hanley). LFEng 1250-1251; RevLFEng 1478.

Levine, David M. ShF 2683.

Levine, Philip. PEng 1712-1718; PSup 407; **RevPEng 1988-1996.**

Lévi-Strauss, Claude. LTh 269, 503, 749, 845, **885-892,** 1280, 1761-1762, 1826.

Levnet og meninger (Ewald). LFFor 2335.

"Levsha." *See* "Lefty."

Levstik, Fran. PFor 2268.

Levy, Newman A. RevDEng 733-735.

Lew, Walter, 3916-3917.

Lewees, John. *See* **Stockton, Frank R.**

Lewes, George Henry. LFEng 872; RevLFEng 1034-1035.

Lewis, Clayton W. ShF 2685.

Lewis, C. S. LFEng 1651-1660; LTh 95-96, 893-898; PEng 164; RevLFEng 2043-2054, 3860; RevPEng 3800.

Lewis, Janet. PSup 252-257; RevPEng 1997-2002; ShF 2687.

Lewis, Mary. *See* **Brand, Christianna.**

Lewis, Matthew Gregory. DEng 1124-1140; LFEng 1661-1667, 3122-3123; RevDEng 1416-1432; RevLFEng 2055-2063, 3783, 3824-3825.

Lewis, Sinclair. LFEng 1668-1681, 3053-3054; 2064-2078, 3761-3762.

Lewis, Wyndham. LFEng 1682-1690; RevLFEng 2079-2087, 3860; **RevShF 1479-1488.**

Lexiphanes (Lucian). LTh 1644.

"Leyenda del sombrerón." *See* "Legend of the Big Hat."

Leyendas de Guatemala. See *Legends of Guatemala.*

L'Hermite, François. *See* **Tristan L'Hermite.**

Li Chih. LTh 1779.

Li Ch'ing-chao. PFor 877-884, 1789.

Li K'ai-hsiang. DFor 2323.

Li Mêng-yang. LTh 1777.

Li Po. PFor 885-893, 1540, 1542, 1785-1786.

Li Shang-yin. PFor 1787.

Li Ssu. PFor 1782.

Li Tung-yang. LTh 1777.

Liaisons dangereuses, Les. See *Dangerous Liaisons.*

Liang Ch'ên-yü. DFor 2323.

Liao-chai chih-i. See *Strange Stories from a Chinese Studio.*

"Liar!" (Asimov). RevShF 86-87; ShF 877.

"Liar, The" (Wolff). RevShF 2507.

Liars, The (Jones, H. A.). DEng 1005; RevDEng 1271.

Libation Bearers (Aeschylus). DFor 2101. See also *Oresteia.*

Libedinsky, Yuri. LFFor 2325.

Liber XXIV philosophorum. LTh 21.

Liberal Imagination, The (Trilling). LTh 1453-1454.

"Liberation, The" (Stafford). RevShF 2180; ShF 2262.

Liberties, The (Howe). PSup 195-196; RevPEng 1630-1632.

Libertine, The (Shadwell). DEng 1672; RevDEng 2085.

"Liberty" (O'Faoláin). ShF 2002.

"Liberty and Peace" (Wheatley). PEng 3056; RevPEng 3543.

"Live" (Sexton). PEng 2525; RevPEng 2935.
Live and Remember (Rasputin). RevShF 1995.
"Live Bait" (Tuohy). RevShF 2314-2315; ShF 2348-2349.
Live Bait and Other Stories (Tuohy). RevShF 2314-2315; ShF 2348.
"Live Life Deeply" (West). RevShF 2451; ShFSup 364-365.
Live Like Pigs (Arden). DEng 45; RevDEng 58-59.
Live or Die (Sexton). PEng 2524; RevPEng 2934.
"Lives" (Booth). PEng 247.
"Lives" (Rukeyser). PSup 331; RevPEng 2832.
Lives of St. Edmund and St. Fremund, The (Lydgate). PEng 1808-1809.
Lives of the Artists (Vasari). ShF 681.
Lives of the English Poets (Johnson). LTh 1259.
Lives of the Poets, The (Johnson, S.). PEng 3473-3475; RevPEng 1720, 4016-4018.
Lives of X (Ciardi). PEng 504; RevPEng 593.
"Living Alone" (Levertov). PEng 1709.
Living and the Dead, The (Boileau and Narcejac). M&D 158-159.
Living and the Dead, The (White, P.). LFEng 2864-2866; RevLFEng 3547.
Living End, The (Elkin). LFEng 892-893.
Living Flame of Love (John of the Cross). PFor 763, 766-767.
"Living Glass" (McPherson). PEng 1884.
"Living on the Box" (Gilliatt). RevShF 993.
"Living Relic, A" (Turgenev). RevShF 2320; ShF 2356-2357.
Living Room, The (Greene, G.). DEng 828-829; RevDEng 1022-1023.
Living Shadow, The (Gibson). M&D 720-721.
Living Temple, The (Fish). LTh 490.
"Living Temple, The" (Holmes). PEng 1375-1376; RevPEng 1564-1565.
Living, The Dying, and the Dead, The (Gilman). RevLFEng 3855.
Living Together (Ayckbourn). DEng 64-65; RevDEng 80-81. See also *Norman Conquests, The.*
Livings, Henry. DEng 1151-1157; RevDEng 1451-1459.
Livius Andronicus. DFor 2138; PFor 2088-2089.
"Livre de Créatures, Le" (Philippe de Thaon). PEng 3489.
Livre des masques, Le. See *Book of Masks, The.*
"Livre des quarte dames, Le." *See* "Book of Four Ladies, The."
"Livre est sur la table, Le" (Ashbery). RevPEng 56-60.

Livsslaven. See *One of Life's Slaves.*
"Livvie" (Welty). RevShF 2434-2435.
Livy. PFor 2098.
Liza. See *House of Gentlefolk, A.*
Liza of Lambeth (Maugham). LFEng 1845; RevLFEng 2333.
Lizard in the Cup, The (Dickinson). M&D 512-513.
Lizardi, José Joaquín Fernández de. LFFor 2281.
Lizárraga, Andrés. DFor 2444.
Lizzie Borden (Lowndes). M&D 1101.
Llama de amor viva. See *Living Flame of Love.*
Llanto por Ignacio Sánchez Mejías. See *Lament for Ignacio Sánchez Mejías.*
Llosa, Mario Vargas. *See* **Vargas Llosa, Mario.**
Lloyd Webber, Andrew. DEng 2477; RevDEng 3004-3005.
Llull, Ramon. PFor 1769-1771.
"L. N. Tolstoy's *Childhood* and *Boyhood* and *Military Tales*" (Chernyshevsky). LTh 289.
Lo Kuan-chung. LFFor 2081-2082, 2090, 2092-2094; ShF 135.
Lo que puede un empleo (Martínez de la Rosa). DFor 1272.
"Loaf of Bread, The" (Ponge). PFor 1264-1265.
"Lobsters" (Nemerov). PEng 2080-2081.
Local Measures (Miles). PSup 277; RevPEng 2317.
Locandiera, La. See *Mistress of the Inn, The.*
Locataire, Le. See Lodger, The.
Lock of Berenice (Callimachus). PFor 253.
Locke, John. LTh 238, 1700.
Locked House, A (Snodgrass). RevPEng 3094.
Locke-Elliott, Sumner. DEng 2434; RevDEng 2957.
"Locket, The" (Pardo Bazán). RevShF 1844; ShF 2050.
Locklin, Gerald. ShF 2689.
Lockridge, Richard, and **Frances Lockridge.** M&D 1086-1092.
Lockwood Concern, The (O'Hara). LFEng 2052-2054; RevLFEng 2587-2589.
Locrine (Swinburne). DEng 1899; RevDEng 2341.
Locura de amor, La (Tamayo y Baus). DFor 1809.
"Locus" (Hayden). PEng 1252; RevPEng 1436.
Locusts Have No King, The (Powell, D.). RevLFEng 2686-2687.
Lodge, David. RevLFEng 2088-2095.
Lodge, Thomas. DEng 1158-1164, 2271; LTh 609, 613, 1186; PEng 1729-1736; RevDEng 1460-1466, 2790; RevPEng 2013-2021; ShF 491, 495.

Long Way to Shiloh, A. See *Menorah Men, The.*
Longest Journey, The (Forster). LFEng 997-999;
  RevLFEng 1187-1189.
Longfellow, Henry Wadsworth. LTh 525, 1744;
  PEng **1744-1754,** 3343, 3344; **RevPEng**
  2029-2040, 3862.
Longing of a Blessed Heart (Breton, N.). PEng
  281; RevPEng 345.
Longinus. LTh **904-910,** 1143, 1531, 1596,
  1598, 1642; RevPEng 4009-4010.
Longstreet, Augustus Baldwin. RevShF
  1501-1506, 2659-2661; ShF 164, **1814-1819.**
Longus. LFFor 2008-2009, 2017.
Lönnrot, Elias. DFor 1060-1061; LFFor 2342.
Lonsdale, Frederick. DEng **1165-1177;**
  RevDEng 1467-1479.
"Look, The" (Teasdale). PEng 2857; RevPEng
  3330.
Look at Me (Brookner). LFSup 65-66; RevLFEng
  401-402.
Look Back in Anger (Osborne). DEng 1430-1431,
  2385-2386; RevDEng 1809-1811, 2903-2904.
Look Homeward, Angel (Wolfe). LFEng 2930,
  2931, 2932-2934, 3162; RevLFEng 3631,
  3632-3634.
Look, Stranger, On This Island Now (Gonzalez).
  LFEng 1139-1140; RevLFEng 1359-1360.
Look! We Have Come Through! (Lawrence, D.
  H.). PEng 1680, 1683; RevPEng 1953.
Looking Backward: 2000-1887 (Bellamy).
  RevLFEng 3866.
"Looking for Mr. Green" (Bellow). RevShF
  203-204; ShF 949-950.
"Looking for Work" (Carver). RevPEng 537.
"Looking Glass" (Gunn). RevPEng 1330.
Looking Glass for London and England, A (Lodge
  and Greene, R.). DEng 842, 843, 1162-1163;
  RevDEng 1037-1039, 1464.
Looking Glass War, The (le Carré). LFEng
  1614-1615; RevLFEng 1988-1989.
Lookout Cartridge (McElroy). LFSup 285-287;
  RevLFEng 2184-2186.
Loom, The (Kelly). PSup 221; RevPEng 1800.
Loon Lake (Doctorow). LFEng 778-779;
  RevLFEng 938.
"Loon's Cry, The" (Nemerov). PEng 2083-2084.
"Loot" (Kipling). PEng 1606; RevPEng 1846.
Loot (Orton). DEng 1422-1424; RevDEng
  1800-1802.
*Loot of Cities, Being the Adventures of a
  Millionaire in Search of Joy, The* (Bennett).
  M&D 108.
López Albújar, Enrique. ShF 702, 705.
López de Ayala, Pero. PFor 2213.

López de Ayala y Herrera, Adelardo. DFor
  2499-2500.
Lorca, Federico García. See **García Lorca,**
  Federico.
Lord, Albert B. PFor 1752-1754.
Lord Dragonfly (Heyen). RevPEng 1507.
Lord Hay's Masque (Campion). PEng 426-427;
  RevPEng 494-495.
"Lord, I've seen too much" (Shapiro). PEng
  2542; RevPEng 2954.
Lord Jim (Conrad). LFEng 585, 593-597, 1762;
  RevLFEng 714, 722-726.
Lord Malquist and Mr. Moon (Stoppard). DEng
  1866-1867.
Lord Mayor of Death, The (Babson). M&D 49.
Lord of the Flies (Golding). LFEng 1129,
  1130-1131; RevLFEng 1350-1351, 3768.
Lord of the Isles, The (Scott). PEng 2502;
  RevPEng 2909, 2910.
Lord of the Rings, The (Tolkien). LFEng
  2644-2646; RevLFEng 3299-3300, 3862.
Lord Weary's Castle (Lowell, R.). PEng
  1787-1789; RevPEng 2081.
Lorde, Audrey. RevPEng 2041-2047.
Lord's Masque, The (Campion). PEng 427;
  RevPEng 495.
Lorenc, Kito. PFor 1818, 1823-1824.
Lorenzaccio (Musset). DFor 1406-1408.
Lorenzaccio (Vigny). DFor 2344.
Lorris, Guillaume de. See **Guillaume de Lorris.**
"Lorry Driver, The" (Moravia). RevShF 1672;
  ShFSup 197.
"Lorsque l'enfant paraît." See "Infantile
  Influence."
Los de abajo. See *Underdogs, The.*
Los que se van (Aguilera Malta). LFSup 9.
Losing Battles (Welty). LFEng 2826-2827;
  RevLFEng 3497-3498.
"Loss of Paradise, The" (Illyés). PFor 744-745.
"Loss of Sammy Crockett, The" (Morrison).
  M&D 1244.
"Losses" (Jarrell). PEng 1480-1481; RevPEng
  1692-1693.
Lost and Found Stories of Morley Callaghan, The
  (Callaghan). RevShF 389; ShFSup 73.
"Lost Battle, The" (Mansfield). RevShF 1598.
"Lost Bodies" (Wright, C.). RevPEng 3662-3663.
"Lost Children, The" (Jarrell). PEng 1484;
  RevPEng 1696-1697.
"Lost Cottage, The" (Leavitt). RevShF 1439.
Lost Domain, The. See *Wanderer, The.*
Lost Empires (Priestley). LFEng 2144-2145;
  RevLFEng 2716-2717.

"Lost Hearts" (James, M. R.). RevShF
1270-1271; ShF 1689-1691.
Lost Honor of Katharina Blum, The (Döll). LFFor
188.
"Lost in the Funhouse" (Barth). RevShF 155-157;
ShF 928, 930-931.
Lost in the Funhouse (Barth). RevShF 153-158,
2751; ShF 928.
Lost Lady, A (Cather). LFEng 480-481;
RevLFEng 590, 593-594.
Lost Letter, The (Caragiale). DFor 348-350, 2298.
"Lost Luggage" (Adams). RevShF 8; ShFSup 2.
Lost Ones, The (Beckett). LFEng 213-214; LFFor
129-130; RevLFEng 262-263.
"Lost Phoebe, The" (Dreiser). RevShF 778; ShF
1310-1311.
"Lost Pilot, The" (Tate, J.). RevPEng 3305.
Lost Pilot, The (Tate, J.). PEng 2835-2836;
RevPEng 3304-3307.
"Lost Princess, The" (Nahman). RevShF
1709-1710; ShF 1942-1943.
Lost Profile (Sagan). LFFor 1476.
"Lost Sanjak" (Saki). M&D 1457.
"Lost Self" (Benn). PFor 173-174.
"Lost Souls" (Wright, C.). RevPEng 3663.
Lost Steps, The (Carpentier). LFFor 284-286.
"Lost Titian, The" (Rossetti, C.). PEng 2416;
RevPEng 2809.
Lost World, The (Doyle). LFEng 810-811;
RevLFEng 974-975, 3861.
"Lost World, The" (Jarrell). PEng 1484-1485;
RevPEng 1697.
Lost World, The (Jarrell). PEng 1484; RevPEng
1696-1697.
Lotman, Yuri. LTh 440, 745, **911-917.**
Lo-t'o Hsiang-tzu. See *Rickshaw Boy.*
"Lotos-Eaters, The" (Tennyson). PEng
2862-2863; RevPEng 3336-3337.
"Lottery, The" (Edgeworth). RevShF 800-801;
ShF 1327.
Lottery, The (Fielding). DEng 604; RevDEng 747.
"Lottery, The" (Jackson). RevShF 1255-1256;
ShF 795-796, 1672-1674.
Lotus (Breytenbach). PSup 56.
"Lotus, The" (Rhys). RevShF 2000; ShFSup 260.
"Lough Derg Pilgrim, The" (Carleton). RevShF
419; ShF 1060.
"Lough Neagh Sequence, A" (Heaney). PEng
1269.
"Louie, El" (Montoya). RevPEng 3923.
Louis Lambert (Balzac). LFFor 96-97.
"Louis Lebeau's Conversion" (Howells). PEng
1421.

"Louisa, Please" (Jackson). RevShF 1253; ShF
1670.
"Louise" (Smith, S.). RevPEng 3079.
Loupeznik. See *Robber, The.*
Loutherbourg, Philip James de. DEng 2227,
2325; RevDEng 2747, 2844. Louÿs, Pierre.
PFor 1573.
"Love" (Colette). RevShF 580.
"Love" (III) (Herbert). PEng 1304; RevPEng
1483.
"Love" (Lispector). RevShF 1491; ShFSup 166.
"Love" (Zoshchenko). RevShF 2560; ShFSup
381.
Love Affair, A (Buzzati). LFFor 227-228.
Love Always (Beattie). RevLFEng 252.
Love Among the Cannibals (Morris). LFEng
1912; RevLFEng 2420.
"Love and Death" (Leopardi). PFor 863. See also
Canti.
Love and Death in the American Novel (Fiedler).
LTh 486.
Love and Freindship (Austen). RevShF 120-121;
ShF 897.
Love and Friendship (Lurie). LFSup 250-253;
RevLFEng 2127-2130.
"Love and Grief" (Dunbar, P.). PSup 111-112;
RevPEng 1013-1014.
Love and Its Derangements (Oates). PEng 2118;
RevPEng 2464-2465.
Love and Like (Gold). ShF 1501-1502.
"Love and Money" (Dugan). RevPEng 1009.
Love and Napalm (Ballard). ShF 914-915.
Love and Work (Price). LFEng 2132-2134;
RevLFEng 2702.
"Love Asleep" (Guillén). PFor 626.
Love, Death, and the Changing of the Seasons
(Hacker). RevPEng 1365-1366.
"Love Decoy, The" (Perelman). RevShF 1870;
ShF 2083.
Love Eaters, The (Settle). LFSup 344-345;
RevLFEng 3004, 3005-3006.
Love Feast. See *Book of Bebb, The.*
"Love for Four Voices, A" (Hecht). RevPEng
1463.
Love for Love (Congreve). DEng 406-408;
RevDEng 505-507.
Love for Lydia (Bates). LFEng 183-184;
RevLFEng 244-245.
"Love. Friendship." (Oates). RevShF 1742.
Love Has No Alibi (Cohen). M&D 367.
Love in a Dry Season (Foote). LFEng 975-977;
RevLFEng 1158-1160.

Love in a Small Town (Wang Anyi). RevShF
2398.

Love in a Tub. See *Comical Revenge, The.*

Love in a Wood (Wycherley). DEng 2106-2107;
RevDEng 2625-2626.

"Love in fantastic triumph sate" (Behn). PEng
128; RevPEng 149, 151.

Love in Several Masques (Fielding). DEng 602;
RevDEng 745.

Love in the Ruins (Percy). LFEng 2095-2096;
RevLFEng 2634-2635.

Love Is a Dog from Hell (Bukowski). PEng
362-363; RevPEng 435-436.

"Love Is a Piece of Paper Torn to Bits"
(Bukowski). RevPEng 431; PEng 358.

Love Is Enough (Morris). PEng 2058-2059;
RevPEng 2389-2390.

Love Letter from an Impossible Land (Meredith).
RevPEng 2267-2268.

"Love Lies Sleeping" (Bishop). PEng 185;
RevPEng 228.

"Love Match, A" (Warner). RevShF 2404-2405;
ShFSup 354-355.

Love Medicine (Erdrich). RevLFEng 1066-1068.

"Love Must Not Be Forgotten" (Zhang Jie).
RevShF 2542-2543.

Love Nest, The (Sherwood). DEng 1801;
RevDEng 2235.

"Love-o'-Women" (Kipling). RevShF 1362.

"Love of Death, A" (Pinsky). PEng 2215-2218.

Love of Fame, the Universal Passion (Young).
LTh 1597.

Love of the Nightingale, The (Wertenbaker).
RevDEng 2498

Love of the Three Oranges, The (Gozzi). DFor
794-795.

Love on a Barren Mountain (Wang Anyi).
RevShF 2397-2398.

Love Poems (Sexton). PEng 2525; RevPEng 2935.

"Love Song: I and Thou" (Dugan). PEng
883-884; RevPEng 1007-1008.

"Love Song for the Future" (Miller). RevPEng
2332.

"Love Song of J. Alfred Prufrock, The" (Eliot).
PEng 942-943; RevPEng 1071-1072.

"Love Sonnet" (Updike). PSup 382-383;
RevPEng 3426-3427.

Love Space Demands, The (Shange). RevDEng
2144.

Love Suicide at Schofield Barracks, The (Linney).
DSup 238; RevDEng 1448.

Love Suicides at Amijima, The (Chikamatsu).
DFor 398-399.

Love Suicides at Sonezaki, The (Chikamatsu).
DFor 397-398, 2426.

"Love that doth raine and live within my thought"
(Surrey). PEng 2786-2787; RevPEng
3252-3253.

Love You (Randall, D.). PEng 2317; RevPEng
2707.

Lovecraft, H. P. RevShF 1507-1514; ShF
744-746, 1820-1828.

Loved and the Lost, The (Callaghan). LFEng 432,
435-437; RevLFEng 543, 546-548.

Loved One, The (Waugh). LFEng 2799-2800;
RevLFEng 3466-3467.

Lovejoy, Arthur O. LTh 1538.

Lovelace, Earl. LFEng 1700-1704; RevLFEng
2106-2111.

Lovelace, Richard. PEng 1755-1762; RevPEng
2048-2055.

Loveliest Afternoon of the Year (Guare).
RevDEng 1055-1056.

"Lover's Anger, A" (Prior). PEng 2289.

Lovers Are Never Losers (Giono). LFFor 654-655.

Lover's Melancholy, The (Ford). DEng 653-655;
RevDEng 798-800.

"Lovers of Their Time" (Trevor). RevShF
2307-2308; ShFSup 322-323.

"Lovers Relentlessly" (Kunitz). PSup 243;
RevPEng 1884.

Lover's Revolt, A (De Forest). LFEng 701;
RevLFEng 835.

Lover's Whim, The. See *Wayward Lover, The.*

"Love's Consolation" (Dixon). PEng 817-818.

"Love's Humility" (Dunbar, P.). PSup 112;
RevPEng 1014.

Love's Labour's Lost (Shakespeare). DEng
1705-1706, 2276; RevDEng 2119-2120,
2794-2795.

Love's Last Shift (Cibber). DEng 365-366, 2310;
RevDEng 443-444, 2829.

"Loves Me, Loves Me Not" (Tolstaya). RevShF
2292.

Love's Metamorphosis (Lyly). DEng 1186-1188;
RevDEng 1488-1490.

"Loves Offence" (Suckling). PEng 2781;
RevPEng 3246.

Love's Old Sweet Song (Saroyan). DEng 1657;
RevDEng 2067.

Love's Pilgrimage (Sinclair, U.). LFEng 2423;
RevLFEng 3053.

Love's Questing (Romains). LFFor 1441. See also
Body's Rapture, The.

Love's Sacrifice (Ford). DEng 658-661;
RevDEng 803-806.

Love's Victory (Moreto y Cabaña). DFor 1370-1371.

Lovesey, Peter. M&D 1093-1098.

Lovesick (Stern). RevPEng 3198.

Loving (Green). LFEng 1209-1211; RevLFEng 1434-1436.

Loving a Woman in Two Worlds (Bly). RevPEng 274.

Loving Hands at Home (Johnson, D.). RevLFEng 1771-1773.

Lovo o polku Igoreve, S. See *Lay of Igor's Host, The.*

"Low Barometer" (Bridges). PEng 286-287; RevPEng 351-352.

"Low Down" (Brown). RevPEng 390.

"Low Lands" (Davie). PSup 87; RevPEng 852.

"Low-lands" (Pynchon). RevShF 1971; ShF 2143-2144.

Löwe Leopold, Der (Kunze). PFor 801.

Lowell, Amy. PEng 1763-1772; RevPEng 2056-2066.

Lowell, James Russell. LTh 525; PEng 1773-1782; RevPEng 2067-2076.

Lowell, Robert. DEng 2408; LFEng 1255-1256; PEng 1783-1800; RevDEng 2929; RevLFEng 1491; RevPEng 2077-2095, 3886-3891.

Löwensköldska ringen. See *Ring of the Löwenskölds, The.*

Lower Depths, The (Gorky). DFor 783-784.

"Lowest Room, The" (Rossetti, C.). PEng 2420; RevPEng 2813.

"Lowlands of Holland, The" (Hill). RevPEng 1521.

Lowndes, Marie Belloc. M&D 1099-1105.

Lowry, Malcolm. LFEng 1705-1718; RevLFEng 2112-2125; ShF 639.

Lowry, Margerie Bonner. LFEng 1708; RevLFEng 2115.

Loyal Subject, The (Fletcher). DEng 637; RevDEng 782.

Loyalties (Galsworthy). DEng 715-716; RevDEng 892-893.

"Loyalty Up and Loyalty Down" (Auchincloss). RevShF 113.

Lu Ann Hampton Laverty Oberlander (Jones, P.). DEng 1010; RevDEng 1277. See also *Texas Trilogy, A.*

"Lu chaih." *See* "Deer Park."

Lu Chi. LTh 901, 918-923, 1774; PFor 1784.

Lu Hsün. LFFor 2106-2107; **RevShF 1515-1526; ShFSup 170-184.**

Lu Yu. PFor 1789-1790.

Lubbock, Percy. LTh 924-928.

Lucan. PFor 894-901, 2104-2105.

Luces de bohemia. See *Bohemian Lights.*

Lucian. LTh 929-933, 1643-1644.

Lucić, Hanibal. PFor 2260.

Lucidor, Lasse. PFor 2158.

Lucien Leuwen (Stendhal). LFFor 1657-1660.

Lucienne's Story (Romains). LFFor 1441. See also *Body's Rapture, The.*

Lucilius. LTh 697.

Lucius Annaeus Florus. *See* Florus.

Lucius Apuleius. *See* Apuleius.

Luck of Ginger Coffey, The (Moore, B.). LFEng 1888-1889; RevLFEng 2394-2395.

"Luck of Roaring Camp, The" (Harte). ShF 222-223, 587.

"Lucky Draw, The" (Zoshchenko). RevShF 2557; ShFSup 378.

Lucky Jim (Amis, K.). LFEng 63-65; PEng 3377; RevLFEng 89-91, 3775, 3808.

"Lucky Life" (Stern). PSup 371-372; RevPEng 3191-3192.

Lucky Life (Stern). PSup 370; RevPEng 3190-3192.

Lucky Poet (MacDiarmid). RevPEng 2125.

Lucky Sam McCarver (Howard, S.). DEng 976-977; RevDEng 1214-1215.

Lucrèce (Ponsard). DFor 1489, 1492.

Lucretia Borgia (Hugo). DFor 969-970.

"Lucretia Burns" (Garland). RevShF 967-968; ShF 1467-1468.

Lucretius. PFor 902-908, 2094-2095.

Lucretius Carus, Titus. *See* **Lucretius.**

Lucy Church Amiably (Stein). LFEng 2515; RevLFEng 3147.

Lucy Gayheart (Cather). LFEng 479; RevLFEng 592.

"Lucy in Her Pink Jacket" (Coppard). RevShF 629; ShF 1200.

Ludlum, Robert. M&D 1106-1111.

Ludus Coventriae. See *N-town Cycle.*

Ludvígsbakke. See *Ida Brandt.*

Ludwig, Jack. ShF 640.

Ludwig, Otto. DFor 1212-1217, 2374.

Lugar sin límites, El. See *Hell Has No Limits.*

Lugné-Poë, François. DFor 2349.

"Lui?" *See* "He?"

Luis de León. *See* **León, Luis de.**

"Luischen." *See* "Little Lizzy."

Lukáč, Emil Boleslav. PFor 1811.

Lukács, Georg. 2670-2671; LFEng 3158, 3160, 3234; LTh 416, 664, 759, **934-940,** 1814.

"Luke Havergal" (Robinson, E. A.). PEng 3518-3529; RevPEng 4035-4046.

"Lullaby" (Auden). PEng 76; RevPEng 86.

"Lullaby" (Sexton). PEng 2521; RevPEng 2931.

"Lullaby" (Silko). RevShF 2107-2108; ShFSup 296-298.

"Lullaby of Cape Cod" (Brodsky). PFor 241, 242.

Lully, Jean-Baptiste. LTh 839.

"Luna." *See* "Moon."

Luna de miel, luna de hiel. See *Honeymoon, Bittermoon.*

Luna e i falò, La. See *Moon and the Bonfires, The.*

Lunacharsky, Anatoly. LTh 122, **941-950,** 1125.

"Lunching at the Ritzmore" (Himes). RevShF 1201-1202.

Lundbye, Vagn. LFFor 2367-2368.

Lundis (Sainte-Beuve). LTh 1259, 1263.

Lundkvist, Artur. PFor 2179.

Lung ch'êng lu (Liu Tsung-yüan). ShFSup 246.

Lun-wên. See *Art of Letters, The.*

"Lupa, La." *See* "She-Wolf, The."

Lupa, La. See *She-Wolf, The.*

Lupercal (Hughes, T.). RevPEng 1648-1649.

"Lupercalia" (Hughes, T.). RevPEng 1650.

Luria, Isaac. ShF 420-421.

Lurie, Alison. LFSup 249-257; **RevLFEng 2126-2134.**

Lusiad, The (Fanshawe). RevPEng 1134.

Lusíadas, Os. See *Lusiads, The* (Camões).

Lusiads, The (Camões). PFor 262-265.

Lusiads, The (Fanshawe). PEng 1002-1003.

Lustig comedia vid nampn Tisbe, En (Asteropherus). DFor 2465.

Lute, The (Kao Ming). DFor 1038-1039, 1042-1049, 2319.

Luther (Osborne). DEng 1432-1433; RevDEng 1812-1813.

Luther, Martin. PFor 1905-1907.

Lutherbibel (Luther). PFor 1906-1907.

Luv (Schisgal). DEng 1662-1663; RevDEng 2074-2076.

Luz de domingo. See *Sunday Sunlight.*

Luzán y Claramunt, Ignacio de. LTh **951-955,** 1692; PFor 2220-2221.

Luzi, Mario. PFor 2045.

Lvov, Pavel. LFFor 2306.

Lycée (La Harpe). LTh 863.

"Lycidas" (Milton). PEng 2007-2008; RevPEng 2340-2341.

Lycophron of Chalcis. DFor 2120, 2134.

Lycus, the Centaur (Hood). PEng 1384-1385; RevPEng 1582-1583.

"Lydford Journey" (Browne). PEng 322.

Lydgate, John. PEng **1801-1813,** 3270-3271; RevDEng 2775; **RevPEng 2096-2108,** 3789-3790.

Lydie Breeze (Guare). DEng 863; RevDEng 1061-1062.

Lying Days, The (Gordimer). LFEng 1159-1161; RevLFEng 1381-1382.

"Lying in a Hammock at William Duffy's Farm in Pine Island, Minnesota" (Wright, James). PEng 3158; RevPEng 3670.

Lying Low (Johnson, D.). RevLFEng 1774-1775.

Lying Three (McInerny). M&D 1162, 1164.

Lykke-Per (Pontoppidan). LFFor 2339-2340.

Lyly, John. DEng **1178-1188,** 2269-2270; LFEng 3014; PEng **1814-1821; RevDEng 1480-1491,** 2788-2789; RevLFEng 3722; **RevShF 1527-1532;** ShF 491, 492, **1829-1833.**

Lymington, John. *See* **Chance, John Newton.**

Lynch, B. Suárez. *See* **Borges, Jorge Luis.**

Lynchers, The (Wideman). LFSup 382-383; RevLFEng 3564-3565.

"Lynching, The" (McKay). PEng 1846; RevPEng 2145.

"Lynching of Jube Benson, The" (Dunbar). ShF 576-577.

Lynds, Dennis. *See* **Collins, Michael.**Lyons, Grant. ShF 2693.

"Lyogkoe dukhanie." *See* "Light Breathing."

Lyre of Orpheus, The (Davies). RevLFEng 802-803.

"Lyric Poetry and Experiment" (Bely). LTh 127.

"Lyric Short Story, The" (Baldeshwiler). ShF 70.

Lyrical Ballads (Wordsworth and Coleridge, S. T.). LTh 1578-1579, 1581-1582, 1708; PEng 3125-3128, 3342, 3475-3477; RevPEng 3634-3637, 3860, 4018-4019; RevShF 2675; ShF 179-180.

Lyrical Poems (Dixon). PEng 819.

Lyrics and Rhythms, The (Carducci). PFor 272.

Lyrics of Love and Laughter (Dunbar, P.). PSup 112; RevPEng 1014.

Lyrics of Lowly Life (Dunbar, P.). PSup 113-114; RevPEng 1015-1017.

Lyrics of the Hearthside (Dunbar, P.). PSup 111-112; RevPEng 1013-1014.

Lys rouge, Le. See *Red Lily, The.*

Lysistrata (Aristophanes). DFor 2128.

Lytle, Andrew Nelson. ShF 2694.

Lytton, David. RevDEng 2943.

Lyubimov. See *Makepeace Experiment, The.*

"Lyubka the Cossack" (Babel). RevShF 127; ShF 900.

Lyutenant Shmidt. See *Lieutenant Schmidt.*

M

M. Butterfly (Hwang). RevDEng 1229-1230.
"M. Pigeonneau" (France). RevShF 901-902; ShF 1404.
"M. Seguin's Goat" (Daudet). RevShF 673-674; ShF 1239.
"M., Singing" (Bogan). PEng 235; RevPEng 282.
Ma Chih-yüan. DFor 2315.
"Ma Rainey" (Brown). PEng 3402-3403; RevPEng 3910-3911.
Ma Rainey's Black Bottom (Wilson, A.). RevDEng 2601.
"Maaruf the Cobbler." ShF 411.
Mabel (Creeley). RevPEng 780.
Mabou Mines. *See* Akalaitis, JoAnne.
Maça no Escuro, A. See Apple in the Dark, The.
McAfee, Thomas. ShF 2695.
McAlmon, Robert. ShF 252-253.
MacAndrew, Elizabeth. ShF 724.
Macaulay, Rose. LFSup 258-264; RevLFEng 2135-2141.
Macaulay, Thomas Babington. LFFor 2214; LTh 1730; PEng 1822-1829.
McBain, Ed. M&D 1112-1117; RevLFEng 3847.
Macbeth (Shakespeare). DEng 1720-1721, 2281, 2282-2283; PEng 1946; RevDEng 2134-2135, 2801-2802.
MacBeth, George. PEng 1830-1837; PSup 407; RevPEng 2109-2117.
McCarthy, Cormac. LFSup 265-270. RevLFEng 2142-2148.
McCarthy, Mary. LFEng 1719-1726; RevLFEng 2149-2157; RevShF 1533-1538; ShF 1834-1839; ShFSup 389.
McCartney, Dorothy. ShF 2696.
McCauley, Carole Spearin. ShF 2697.
McClure, James. M&D 1118-1123.
McClure's. ShF 589.
McCluskey, John A., Jr. ShF 2698.
McConkey, James. ShF 2699.
McCord, Howard. ShF 2700.
McCue, Lillian de la Torre Bueno. *See* De la Torre, Lillian.
McCullers, Carson. DEng 1190-1200; LFEng 1727-1737; RevDEng 1492-1503; RevLFEng 2158-2169, 3877; RevShF 1539-1547; ShF 550, 1840-1848.
MacDiarmid, Hugh. PSup 258-268; RevPEng 2118-2128.

MacDonagh, Donagh. DEng 1201-1212; RevDEng 1504-1515.
Mcdonald, Gregory. M&D 1124-1129.
MacDonald, John D. M&D 1130-1134.
Macdonald, John Ross. *See* Macdonald, Ross.
Macdonald, Ross. LFSup 271-280; M&D 1135-1140; RevLFEng 2170-2179; ShF 763-764.
McDonald, Walter. ShF 2701.
McElroy, Colleen J. ShF 2702.
McElroy, Joseph. LFSup 281-289; RevLFEng 2180-2189.
"McEwen of the Shining Slave Makers" (Dreiser). RevShF 775; ShF 1308.
Mac Flecknoe (Dryden). PEng 874-875; RevPEng 991-992.
McGerr, Patricia. M&D 1141-1147.
McGinley, Patrick. M&D 1148-1153; RevLFEng 2190-2196.
McGivern, William P. M&D 1154-1159.
McGrath, John. RevDEng 1516-1523.
McGuane, Thomas. LFSup 290-297; RevLFEng 2197-2206; RevPEng 2129-2136.
Mácha, Karel Hynek. PFor 1800.
Machado, Antonio. PFor 909-916, 2227.
Machado, Eduardo. RevDEng 1524-1533.
Machado, Manuel. PFor 910, 913.
Machado de Assis, Joaquim Maria. LFFor 1037-1048, 2285; RevShF 1548-1553; ShF 1849-1853.
Machar, Josef Svatopluk. PFor 1803.
Macherey, Pierre. LTh 416, 1767.
Machiavelli, Niccolò. DFor 1218-1226, 2396-2397; LTh 366-367, 1459, 1463.
"Machine Stops, The" (Forster). RevShF 886; ShF 1388.
Machine-wreckers, The (Toller). DFor 1860-1861.
Machineries of Joy, The (Bradbury). RevShF 306-307.
"Machtmythus" (Holz). PFor 693.
Machwe, Prabhakar. LFFor 2225.
McInerny, Ralph. M&D 1160-1166.
MacInnes, Helen. M&D 1167-1171.
"McKabe" (Gallico). ShF 1442-1443.
McKay, Claude. PEng 1838-1846; RevPEng 2137-2146, 3908; ShF 578.
MacKay, John Henry. LFFor 2181.
McKeon, Richard. LTh 1817.

Mackerel Plaza, The (De Vries). LFEng 738-739; RevLFEng 886-887.

Mackey, Ernan. *See* **McInerny, Ralph.**

Mackey, Mary. ShF 2703.

Mackintosh, Elizabeth. *See* **Tey, Josephine.**

Macklin, Charles. DEng 2523-2524.

MacLean, Alistair. M&D 1172-1176.

MacLeish, Archibald. DEng 1213-1225; PEng 1847-1860; RevDEng 1534-1547, 3026-3027; RevPEng 2147-2161.

MacLennan, Hugh. LFEng 1738-1748; RevLFEng 2207-2218.

MacLeod, Charlotte. M&D 1177-1183.

McLuhan, Marshall. LTh 956-962, 1079.

McMahon, Pat. *See* **Hoch, Edward D.**

McMillan, Florri. ShF 2704.

McMurtry, Larry. LFEng 1749-1757; LFSup 405; RevLFEng 2219-2229.

McNally, Terrence. DEng 1226-1233; DSup 407; RevDEng 1548-1558.

McNamara, Eugene. ShF 2705.

MacNeice, Louis. PEng 1861-1877; RevDEng 3033; RevPEng 2162-2179.

McNeile, Herman Cyril. *See* **Sapper.**

McPherson, James. RevPEng 3848.

McPherson, James Alan. RevShF 1554-1559; ShF 1854-1858.

McPherson, Sandra. PEng 1878-1885; PSup 407; RevPEng 2180-2189.

Macquarie (Buzo). DEng 321-322; RevDEng 381-382.

Macready, William Charles. DEng 2357, 2525.

Macrobius. LTh 963-968, 1646-1647; PFor 2109.

Macropulos Secret, The (Čapek). DFor 340.

Macskajáték. See *Catsplay.*

Mactacio Abel. See *Killing of Abel, The.*

McTeague (Norris). LFEng 2002-2004; RevLFEng 2527-2529.

Mad Hercules (Seneca). DFor 1692-1693, 2148.

Mad Lover, The (Fletcher). DEng 637; RevDEng 782.

"Mad Potter, The" (Hollander). RevPEng 1555.

Madach, Imre. DFor 1227-1234, 2287.

"Madagascar" (Davenant). PEng 738-739; RevPEng 842-843.

Madagascar (Davenant). PEng 738; RevPEng 842-844.

Madame Aubray's Ideas (Dumas, *fils*). DFor 505.

Madame Bovary (Flaubert). LFEng 3162; LFFor 550-553, 2332-2333.

"Madame de la Carlière" (Diderot). RevShF 731; ShF 1279.

Madame Delphine (Cable). LFEng 417-419; RevLFEng 527-529.

Madame de Sade (Mishima). DFor 1325-1326.

Madame d'Ora (Jensen). LFFor 881-882.

Madame Gervaisais (Goncourts). LFFor 716.

"Madame Tellier's Establishment" (Maupassant). RevShF 1636-1637, 2716; ShF 1909.

"Madame Zilensky and the King of Finland" (McCullers). RevShF 1540-1541; ShF 1842.

Mädchen aus der Feenwelt, Das. See *Maid from Fairyland, The.*

Madden, David. LFEng 1758-1768; LFSup 405; RevLFEng 2230-2242; ShF 2706.

Maddux, Rachel. ShF 2708.

Madeleine (Zola). DFor 2049.

Madeleine Férat (Zola). LFFor 1989.

"Mademoiselle de Scudéry" (Hoffman). RevShF 1215.

Mademoiselle de Scudéry (Hoffmann). ShF 1647.

"Mademoiselle Panache" (Edgeworth). RevShF 799; ShF 1325.

Madheart (Baraka). DEng 100-101; RevDEng 125-126.

Madhubuti, Haki R. PEng 1886-1897; RevPEng 2190-2202.

"Madman, The" (Maupassant). M&D 1210.

Madman and the Nun, The (Witkiewicz). DFor 2011.

Madness and Civilization (Foucault). LTh 504.

Madoc (Muldoon). RevPEng 2406-2407; RevPEng 3125.

"Madonna Mia" (Swinburne). PEng 2819; RevPEng 3287.

"Madonna Mia" (Wilde). PEng 3105; RevPEng 3596.

"Madonna of the Evening Flowers" (Lowell, A.). PEng 1771; RevPEng 2064.

"Madonna of the Hills" (Allen). RevPEng 3935.

Madras House, The (Granville-Barker). DEng 800-801; RevDEng 991-992.

Madre, La. See *Mother, The.*

Madre naturaleza, La (Pardo Bazán). LFFor 1226-1227.

Madsen, Sven Åge. LFFor 2360, 2366.

"Madwoman, The" (Maupassant). RevShF 1634.

Madwoman in the Attic, The (Gilbert and Gubar). LTh 579, 1769.

Madwoman of Chaillot, The (Giraudoux). DFor 729-730.

Maecenas. PFor 1285.

Maeterlinck, Maurice. DEng 2198, 2199; **DFor 1235-1242,** 2238, 2349; RevDEng 2718-2719.

Mafia Vendetta (Sciascia). LFFor 1519-1520.

Magda (Sudermann). DFor 1766-1767.

Magda and Callas (Innaurato). RevDEng 1251-1252.

Magellanic Clouds, The (Wakoski). RevPEng 3487-3488.

Maggie (Crane, S.). LFEng 640-641, 3177-3179; RevLFEng 773-774; RevShF 645; ShF 536, 1309.

"Maggie Meriwether's Rich Experience" (Stafford). RevShF 2178-2179; ShF 2260-2261.

Maggot, A (Fowles). RevLFEng 1213-1214.

"Magic" (Porter). RevShF 1908-1909.

"Magic Barrel, The" (Malamud). RevShF 1570-1571, 2735; ShF 1862-1863.

Magic Christian, The (Southern). LFEng 2469-2470.

"Magic Curtain, The" (Kunitz). PSup 246; RevPEng 1887.

"Magic Egg, The" (Stockton). RevShF 2226-2227; ShF 2287-2289.

Magic Kingdom, The (Elkin). RevLFEng 1050.

Magic Mountain, The (Mann). LFFor 1080-1082, 2193.

"Magic of Words, The" (Bely). LTh 126-127.

Magic Realists, The (Terry). DSup 342-343; RevDEng 2368.

"Magic Striptease, The" (Garrett). RevShF 975-976; ShF 1475-1477.

Magic Striptease, The (Garrett). LFEng 1095.

Magic Toyshop, The (Carter). LFSup 72-73; RevLFEng 566-567.

Magician of Lublin, The (Singer, Isaac). LFEng 2435-2437; LFFor 1620-1622; RevLFEng 3063-3064.

Magician's Nephew, The (Lewis, C. S.). LFEng 1657; RevLFEng 2049.

"Magician's Song" (Fletcher, J.). PEng 1014.

Mágico prodigioso, El. See *Wonder-Working Magician, The.*

Magie rouge. See Red Magic.

Magister Ludi. See *Glass Bead Game, The.*

Magistrate, The (Pinero). DEng 1501-1503; RevDEng 1886-1888.

Magnetic Mountain, The (Day Lewis). PEng 759; RevPEng 877.

Magnificence (Brenton). DSup 33-34; RevDEng 320-321.

Magnificence (Skelton). DEng 2259; RevDEng 2779.

Magnus Felix Ennodius. *See* Ennodius.

Magnus Herodes. See Herod the Great.

Magpie's Shadow, The (Winters). PSup 397; RevPEng 3626.

Magus, The (Fowles). LFEng 1012-1014; RevLFEng 1203-1205.

Mahabharata. ShF 138-139, 642.

"Mahadev and Parvati" (Anand). ShF 645.

Mahapatra, Jayanta. ShF 654.

Mahfouz, Naguib. RevShF 1560-1566.

Maia (D'Annunzio). PFor 387. See also *Laudi, Le.*

Maias, The (Eça de Queiróz). LFFor 545.

Maid from Fairyland, The (Raimund). DFor 1530-1531.

Maid Marian (Peacock). LFEng 2083-2084; RevLFEng 2621-2622.

Maid of Honour, The (Massinger). DEng 1300-1302; RevDEng 1628-1630.

Maid of Orleans, The (Schiller). DFor 1660-1663.

Maid Silja, The (Sillanpää). LFFor 1579.

"Maiden in a Tower" (Stegner). RevShF 2191; ShF 2272.

"Maiden Song" (Rossetti, C.). PEng 2420; RevPEng 2813.

Maiden's Consent, The. See *When A Girl Says Yes.*

Maiden's Dream, A (Greene). PEng 1151-1152.

"Maiden's Leap" (Kiely). RevShF 1334-1335; ShF 1744-1745.

Maidens of the Rocks, The (D'Annunzio). LFFor 411-412.

Maidens' Vows (Fredro). DSup 139.

Maids, The (Genet). DFor 681-683, 2259, 2358.

Maid's Tragedy, The (Beaumont and Fletcher). DEng 632-633, 2290; PEng 1017-1018; RevDEng 777-778, 2809.

Maigret and Monsieur Charles (Simenon). M&D 1488.

Maigret and the Loner (Simenon). LFFor 1597.

Maigret and the Strangled Stripper. See *Maigret in Montmartre.*

Maigret au Picratt's. See *Maigret in Montartre.*

Maigret et M. Charles. See *Maigret and Monsieur Charles.*

Maigret in Montmartre (Simenon). M&D 1488.

Maigret Sets a Trap (Simenon). LFFor 1597-1598.

Mailer, Norman. LFEng 1770-1787, 3064-3065; LFSup 405; **RevLFEng 2243-2263,** 3773.

"Main, La." *See* "Hand, The."

Main chaude, La (Follain). PSup 126-127.

Main Currents in American Thought (Parrington). LTh 1454.

"Main-Morte" (Reverdy). PSup 324-325.

"Main Road West" (Kennedy). PEng 1573; RevPEng 1808.

"Main Street" (Hawthorne). ShF 813.

Main Street (Lewis, S.). LFEng 1672-1675; RevLFEng 2068-2071.

"Main Street Morning" (Petesch). ShF 128-129.

Main Thing, The (Evreinov). DFor 585-586.

Main-Travelled Roads (Garland). RevShF 2713; ShF 231.

Mains sales, Les. See *Dirty Hands.*

Mair, Charles. DEng 2439; RevDEng 2962.

Mairet, Jean. DFor 1243-1251.

Maison de rendez-vous, La (Robbe-Grillet). LFFor 1417-1418.

Maison de Silvie, La. See "Sylvia's Park."

"Maison fermée, La." *See* "Within the House."

"Maison Tellier, La." *See* "Madame Tellier's Establishment."

Maître Cornélius (Balzac). LFFor 98.

Maître de Santiago, Le. See *Master of Santiago, The.*

Máj. See May.

Major, Clarence. ShF 2709.

Major Barbara (Shaw). DEng 1736-1739; RevDEng 2157-2160.

Majuma (Gryphius). DFor 839.

"Makar Chudra" (Gorky). RevShF 1047.

Makassar Reef (Buzo). DEng 322-323; RevDEng 382-383.

Make Light of It (Williams, W. C.). ShF 2442.

Make My Bed Soon (Webb). M&D 1693.

Makepeace Experiment, The (Sinyavsky). LFFor 1632-1635.

"Maker of Coffins, The" (Bates). RevShF 176; ShFSup 32.

Makers and Finders (Brooks, V.). LTh 224, 228, 316.

Making Do (Goodman). LFEng 1153-1155; RevLFEng 1374-1376.

Making Good Again (Davidson). M&D 458-459.

Making of a Saint, The (Maugham). LFEng 1845-1846; RevLFEng 2333-2334.

Making of Americans, The (Stein). LFEng 2509-2510, 2513-2515; RevLFEng 3141-3142.

"Making of Ashenden, The" (Elkin). LFEng 890-891.

Making of the Representative for Planet 8, The (Lessing). RevLFEng 2039.

"Making-up" (Boland). PSup 40; RevPEng 295.

Makioka Sisters, The (Tanizaki). LFFor 1713-1714.

Makkabäer, Die (Ludwig). DFor 1215-1216.

Maksimović, Desanka. PFor 2256.

Mal court, Le (Audiberti). DFor 2359.

Mal vu mal dit. See *Ill Seen Ill Said.*

Mała apokalipsa. See *Minor Apocalypse, A.*

Mala hora, La. See *In Evil Hour.*

Malamud, Bernard. LFEng 1788-1800, 3067; LFSup 405; **RevLFEng 2264-2277,** 3775-3776; **RevShF 1567-1576,** 2734-2735, 2757; ShF 549, **1859-1864;** ShFSup 389.

Malasangre, La (Gambaro). DSup 150-151.

Malatesta (Montherlant). DFor 1353.

Mālavikāgnimitra (Kālidāsa). DFor 1031-1033.

Malavoglia, I. See *House by the Medlar Tree, The.*

Malcolm (Purdy). LFEng 2170-2171; RevLFEng 2744-2745.

Malcontent, The (Marston). DEng 1269-1270, 2291; RevDEng 1594-1595, 2810.

Malcontents, The (Snow). LFEng 2463-2464; RevLFEng 3089-3090.

Malediction, The (Giono). LFFor 657.

"Malediction, The" (Williams, T.). RevShF 2479-2480; ShF 2434.

Malefactors, The (Gordon). LFEng 1180; RevLFEng 1402.

Maleficio de la mariposa, El. See *Butterfly's Evil Spell, The.*

Malek-Adhél (Saavedra). DFor 1615.

Malentendu, Le. See *Misunderstanding, The.*

Malgonkar, Manohar. LFFor 2223; ShF 650.

Malgudi Days (Narayan). RevShF 1717; ShFSup 226.

Malherbe, François de. LTh 838, 969-974; PFor 917-923, 1855.

Malice Aforethought (Berkeley). M&D 121.

Malign Fiesta. See *Human Age, The.*

Malik Udib, al-. See *King Oedipus.*

Malina (Beck), Judith. DEng 2481, 2482.

Malinovski, Ivan. PFor 2196-2197.

"Mall: A History, The" (Wetherell). RevShF 2760-2761.

Mallarmé, Stéphane. DEng 2198, 2199; LTh 213, 551, 555, 571-572, 623, **975-980,** 1489-1491; **PFor 924-931,** 1878; RevDEng 2718-2719.

"Mallarmé et l'idée de décadence" (Gourmont). LTh 623.

Mallea, Eduardo. LFFor 1049-1058.

Malleson, Lucy Beatrice. See **Gilbert, Anthony.**

Mallowan, Agatha Christie. See **Christie, Agatha.**

Malone, Michael Patrick. ShF 2710.

Malone, Ruth. *See* **Rice, Craig.**

Malone Dies (Beckett). LFEng 211-212; LFFor 128; RevLFEng 260-261.

Malone meurt. See *Malone Dies.*

Malory, Sir Thomas. LFEng 1801-1810; RevLFEng 2278-2287; RevShF 1577-1581; ShF 447, **1865-1869.**

Malouf, David. RevLFEng 2288-2295.

Malparte, Curzio. LFFor 2243.

Malquerida, La. See *Passion Flower, The.*

Malraux, André. LFFor 1059-1069, 2143.

Maltese Falcon, The (Hammett). LFEng 1237-1239, 3189; M&D 827; RevLFEng 1465-1466, 3846.

Maltz, Albert. ShF 268, 1870-1874; ShFSup 389.

Malvaloca (Álvarez Quinteros). DFor 56-57.

Malzberg, Barry. ShF 781.

Mama Day (Naylor). RevLFEng 2492-2493.

"Mama's Old Stucco House" (Williams, T.). RevShF 2482; ShF 2438.

"Mamay" (Zamyatin). RevShF 2536-2537; ShFSup 372.

Mamba's Daughters (Heyward and Heyward). DEng 938; RevDEng 1171.

"mame" (Cummings). PEng 706; RevPEng 797.

Mamet, David. DEng 1234-1245, 2413; DSup 407-408; RevDEng 1559-1570, 2934-2935.

"Man Alone" (Bogan). PEng 234; RevPEng 281.

Man and Boy (Morris). LFEng 1909-1910; RevLFEng 2417-2418.

Man and His Picture, A (Sudermann). DFor 1763-1765.

Man and Superman (Shaw). DEng 1733-1736, 2382; RevDEng 2154-2157, 2900.

"Man and Two Women, A" (Lessing, D.). RevShF 1476-1477; ShF 1807-1808.

Man and Wife (Collins, Wilkie). LFEng 557-558; RevLFEng 684-685.

"Man and Wife" (Purdy). ShF 2137-2138.

"Man by the Name of Ziegler, A" (Hesse). RevShF 1184-1185; ShF 1635-1636.

"Man Child, The" (Baldwin, James). RevShF 134-135; ShF 906-907.

Man-Fate (Everson). PEng 992; RevPEng 1123.

Man for All Seasons, A (Bolt). DEng 234-236; RevDEng 275-277, 3033-3034.

"Man Friday" (Hope). PSup 191; RevPEng 1596.

"Man from Mars, The" (Atwood). RevShF 102-103; ShFSup 14-15.

Man from the Norlands, The (Buchan). M&D 226.

Man from the North, A (Bennett). LFEng 241; RevLFEng 295.

"Man from the South" (Dahl). RevShF 658-659; ShF 1225-1227.

"Man from the Top of the Mind, The" (Wagoner). PEng 2988; RevPEng 3476.

Man Full of Nothing, A (Nestroy). DFor 1424-1426.

Man fun Notseres, Der. See *Nazarene, The.*

"Man I Parted from, Below, The" (Miyazawa). PSup 286.

"Man in Inhumanity" (Ady). PFor 7.

Man in the Black Coat Turns, The (Bly). PEng 226-227; RevPEng 273-274.

"Man in the Brooks Brothers Shirt, The" (McCarthy). RevShF 1535-1536; ShF 1836-1837.

"Man in the Dead Machine, The" (Hall). PEng 1202.

Man in the Divided Sea, A (Merton). PEng 1974-1975; RevPEng 2292-2293.

Man in the High Castle, The (Dick). LFSup 95-96; RevLFEng 895-896.

"Man in the Mirror, The" (Strand). RevPEng 3233.

"Man in the Room, The" (Balmer and MacHarg). ShF 753.

"Man Is Born, A" (Gorky). RevShF 1047-1048.

"Man-Moth, The" (Bishop). PEng 184; RevPEng 227.

"Man of Adamant, The" (Hawthorne). ShF 477.

Man of Character, A (Henshaw). DEng 928-929; RevDEng 1161-1162.

Man of Forty Crowns, The (Voltaire). LFFor 1902-1903.

Man of Mode, The (Etherege). DEng 572-578; RevDEng 713-719.

Man of Property, The (Galsworthy). LFEng 1062-1064; RevLFEng 1261-1263.

Man of the Forty Faces, The (Hanshew). M&D 838.

Man of the Moment (Ayckbourn). RevDEng 82-83.

Man of the People, A (Achebe). LFEng 6, 11-13; RevLFEng 6, 12-14.

"Man on a Road" (Maltz). ShF 1873.

"Man on the Wharf, The" (Booth). RevPEng 303.

Man Outside, The (Borcherdt). DFor 2380.

"man saw a ball of gold in the sky, A" (Crane, S.). PEng 664; RevPEng 760.

"Man That Corrupted Hadleyburg, The" (Twain). RevShF 2329; ShF 2363-2364.

"Man Who Became a Woman, The" (Anderson). LFEng 3288-3290; ShF 873; RevShF 73.

Man Who Came to Dinner, The (Kaufman and Hart, M.). DEng 909-910; RevDEng 1132-1133.

"Man Who Did Not Smile, The" (Kawabata). RevShF 1320.

Man Who Died, The (Lawrence). RevShF 1427.

Man Who Gave Up His Name, The (Harrison). RevLFEng 1540-1541; RevShF 1124-1125.

Man Who Had All the Luck, The (Miller). DEng 1338; RevDEng 1676-1677.

"Man Who Had No Idea, The" (Disch). RevShF 747; ShF 1290.

Man Who Had Three Arms, The (Albee). RevDEng 32.

Man Who Invented Sin and Other Stories, The (O'Faolain). RevShF 1786; ShF 1997.

Man Who Killed the Deer, The (Waters). LFEng 2785-2787; RevLFEng 3451-3453.

Man Who Laughs, The (Hugo). LFFor 855-856.

Man Who Lived His Life Over, The (Lagerkvist). DFor 1154-1155.

"Man Who Lived Underground, The" (Wright). RevShF 2520-2522; ShF 579, 2465-2467.

"Man Who Lost the Sea, The" (Sturgeon). RevShF 2241; ShF 2301.

Man Who Loved Children, The (Stead). LFEng 2490-2492; RevLFEng 3120-3122.

"Man Who Loved His Kind, The" (Woolf). RevShF 2515-2516.

Man Who Loved His Wife, The (Caspary). M&D 290-292.

Man Who Shook Hands, The (Wakoski). RevPEng 3491.

"Man Who Was Almos' a Man, The" (Wright). ShF 580.

Man Who Was There, The (Morris). LFEng 1908-1909; RevLFEng 2416-2417.

Man Who Was Thursday, The (Chesterton). RevShF 530.

"Man Who Would Be King, The" (Kipling). RevShF 2724-2725; ShF 112, 518, 1749-1751.

Man with Bags (Ionesco). DFor 1103-1104.

Man with the Blue Guitar, The (Stevens). PEng 3391.

Man with the Golden Arm, The (Algren). LFSup 26-28; RevLFEng 76-80.

Man with the Golden Arm, The (Kirkland). DEng 1053; RevDEng 1330.

Man with the Luggage, The. See *Man with Bags.*

"Man Without a Country, The" (Hale, E.). RevShF 2702; ShF 209.

Man Without a Soul, The (Lagerkvist). DFor 1155-1156.

"Man Without a Temperament, The" (Mansfield). RevShF 1599-1600; ShF 114.

Man Without Qualities, The (Musil). LFFor 1186-1191, 2194.

Manassas (Sinclair, U.). LFEng 2420; RevLFEng 3050.

Manciata di more, Una. See *Handful of Blackberries, A.*

Mandarin, The (Eça de Queiróz). LFFor 544-545.

Mandarins, The (de Beauvoir). LFFor 117-119.

Mandate, The (Erdman). DFor 2460.

Mandel, Oscar. ShF 2711.

Mandell, Marvin. ShF 2712.

Mandelstam, Osip. PFor 932-942, 2147-2148.

Mandingo (Kirkland). DEng 1053; RevDEng 1330.

Mandragola, La. See *Mandrake, The.*

Mandrake, The (Machiavelli). DFor 1222-1224, 2396-2397.

Man'en gan'nen no futtoboru. See *Silent Cry, The.*

"Manet" (Snodgrass). PEng 2662-2663; RevPEng 3091-3092.

Manette Salomon (Goncourts). LFFor 715-716.

Manfred (Byron). DEng 328; RevDEng 388.

Manfred, Frederick. ShF 2713.

Mangan Inheritance, The (Moore, B.). LFEng 1892-1893; RevLFEng 2398-2399.

Manganilla de Melilla, La (Ruiz de Alarcón). DFor 1606.

Manger, Itzik. PFor 943-953.

"Mangler, The" (King). RevShF 1348; ShFSup 123.

Manhattan Transfer (Dos Passos). LFEng 793-794; RevLFEng 957-958.

"Manhole 69" (Ballard). RevShF 142.

Manifest Detection of Dice-Play, A (Walker). ShF 453.

"Manifeste technique de la littérature futuriste." *See* "Technical Manifesto of Futurist Literature."

Manifesto of Surrealism (Breton). LTh 213-214.

Manivelle. See *Old Tune, The.*

Mann, Abel. *See* **Creasey, John.**

Mann, Heinrich. LFFor 2185-2186.

Mann, Thomas. LFEng 3333-3334; LFFor 195, **1070-1085,** 2186, 2193; LTh 937-938, **981-990,** 1316; **RevShF 1582-1593,** 2739-2740; ShF 713, **1875-1879.**

"Mann mit den Messern, Der." *See* "Men with the Knives, The."

Mann ohne Eigenschaften, Der. See *Man Without Qualities, The.*

Mannen utan själ. See *Man Without a Soul, The.*

Manner, Eeva-Liisa. PFor 2190-2191.

Manninen, Otto. PFor 2174.

Mano (Dixon). PEng 816-817.

Manon Lescaut (Prévost). LFFor 1311, 1314-1316, 2119.

Manrique, Gómez. DFor 1252-1256, 2171, 2483.

Man's Blessing, A (Sciascia). LFFor 1520-1521.

Man's Fate (Malraux). LFFor 1065-1067.

Man's Hope (Malraux). LFFor 1067-1068.

"Marie" (Woiwode). RevShF 2495.

Marie and Bruce (Shawn). DSup 336; RevDEng 2169.

Marie de France. PFor 962-971; RevShF 1604-1610, 2579, 2614-2615; ShF 380, 444-445, 1886-1892.

Marie Grubbe (Jacobsen). LFFor 2338.

Marilyn (Mailer). LFEng 1785; RevLFEng 2258.

Marina, Jeanne. ShF 2714.

"Marin-an" (Snyder). PEng 2673.

Marinetti, Filippo Tommaso. LTh 991-998; PFor 2037-2038.

Marino, Giambattista. PFor 972-977, 2017.

Marino Faliero, Doge of Venice (Byron). DEng 328-329, 339-340; RevDEng 388-389, 399-400.

Mario and the Magician (Mann). RevShF 1588, 1591, 2740; ShF 1878.

Marion de Lorme (Hugo). DFor 968.

"Marionette Theater, The." *See* "About the Marionette Theater."

Mariquita y Antonio (Valera). LFFor 1818-1819.

Maritain, Jacques. LTh 154, 301, 999-1002.

Marius the Epicurean (Pater). LFEng 2068-2075; RevLFEng 2605-2612.

Marivaux. DEng 2332; DFor 1257-1268, 2339-2340; LFFor 1095-1107, 2030-2031, 2119; RevDEng 2852.

Marivaux, Pierre Carlet de Chamblain de. See **Marivaux.**

"Marjorie Daw" (Aldrich). RevShF 2704-2705; ShF 212.

Marjorie Morningstar (Wouk). LFEng 2967-2969; RevLFEng 3669-3671.

"Mark of Apelles, The" (Pasternak). RevShF 1853; ShF 2059.

"Mark of Vishnu, The" (Singh). ShF 650.

"Mark on the Wall, The" (Woolf). RevShF 2513; ShF 2455-2456.

Markandaya, Kamala. LFFor 2222.

"Marked with D" (Harrison, T.). PSup 171; RevPEng 1425.

Markens grøde. See *Growth of the Soil.*

"Market at Turk" (Gunn). PEng 1172.

Markets of Paris, The. See *Savage Paris.*

Markham, Marion M. ShF 2715.

"Markheim" (Stevenson, R. L.). RevShF 2220-2222; ShF 2283-2285.

Marksizm i filisofiya yazyka. See *Marxism and the Philosophy of Language.*

Markurells of Wadköping (Bergman). DFor 191-192.

Marler, Robert. RevShF 2700.

Marlowe, Christopher. DEng 1246-1264, 2272-2273; PEng 1898-1907; RevDEng 1571-1589, 2791-2792; RevPEng 2203-2211; ShF 1893-1898.

Marlowe, Stephen. *See* **Queen, Ellery.**

"Marmalade Bird, The" (Sansom). RevShF 2054.

Marmion (Scott). PEng 2501-2502; RevPEng 2908, 2910.

Marnie (Graham). M&D 776-777.

Maro, Publius Vergilius. *See* **Vergil.**

Marot, Clément. PFor 1848, 1850.

Marowitz, Charles. DEng 2489; RevDEng 3017-3018.

Marquand, John P. LFEng 1811-1821; M&D 1184-1188. RevLFEng 2296-2307.

Marqués, René. DFor 2446.

Marquina, Eduardo. DFor 2503.

Marquis of Keith, The (Wedekind). DFor 1979-1980.

Marquise of O . . ., The (Kleist). RevShF 1372; ShF 1757, 1760.

"Marriage" (Berry). PEng 151.

"Marriage" (Corso). PEng 577; RevPEng 672.

Marriage, The (Gombrowicz). DFor 771-773.

Marriage à la Mode (Dryden). DEng 517-519; RevDEng 639-641.

"Marriage à la Mode" (Mansfield). RevShF 1599.

"Marriage Bond, The" (Zoshchenko). RevShF 2557; ShFSup 378.

"Marriage Ghazal" (Harrison, J.). PEng 1234; RevPEng 1415.

Marriage of Bette and Boo (Durang). DEng 104; RevDEng 673.

Marriage of Figaro, The (Beaumarchais). DFor 150-153, 2340.

Marriage of Heaven and Hell, The (Blake). PEng 211-213; RevPEng 255-257.

"Marriage of Helen and Menelaos, The" (Landor). PEng 1644; RevPEng 1909.

Marriage of Mr. Mississippi, The (Dürrenmatt). DFor 519-521.

Marriage Play (Albee). RevDEng 32.

"Marriage Portion, A" (Foote). LFEng 978-979; RevLFEng 1161.

Marriages Between Zones Three, Four, and Five (Lessing). LFEng 1648-1650; RevLFEng 2038.

Marric, J. J. *See* **Creasey, John.**

Marrow of Tradition, The (Chesnutt). LFEng 520-521; RevLFEng 636-637.

Marry Me (Updike). RevLFEng 3356.

Marrying of Anne Leete, The (Granville-Barker). DEng 798-799; RevDEng 989-990.

Mars (Zorn). LFFor 2209.

Marsden, James. *See* **Creasey, John.**
Marsh, Ngaio. M&D 1189-1194.
Marsh Hay (Denison). DEng 502-504, 2439; RevDEng 623-625, 2962.
Marshall, Paule. RevShF 1611-1616.
Marshall, Raymond. *See* **Chase, James Hadley.**
"Marshes of Glynn, The" (Lanier). PEng 1664-1666; RevPEng 1931-1933.
"Marsina stretta, La." *See* "Tight Frock Coat, The."
Marson, Una. RevDEng 2977.
Marsten, Richard. *See* **McBain, Ed.**
Marston, John. DEng 1265-1274, 2290-2291; **RevDEng 1590-1600,** 2809-2810.
Marta la piadosa (Tirso). DFor 1846.
"Marta Riquelme" (Hudson). LFEng 1383; RevLFEng 1659.
Martens, Adémar-Adolphe-Louis, *See* **Ghelderode, Michel de.**
Martereau (Sarraute). LFFor 1502-1503.
"Martha Blake" (Clarke). PSup 70; RevPEng 610.
"Martha's Lady" (Jewett). RevShF 1279-1280; ShF 1696.
Marthe (Huysmans). LFFor 861.
Martial. PFor 2104.
Martian Chronicles, The (Bradbury). RevLFEng 358-359; RevShF 303-304.
Martian Sends a Postcard Home, A (Raine). RevPEng 3901.
Martian Time-Slip (Dick). LFSup 96; RevLFEng 896.
"Martian Way, The" (Asimov). RevShF 88; ShF 879-880.
Martianus Capella. *See* Capella, Martianus.
Martin, Peter. *See* **Melville, James.**
Martin, Richard. *See* **Creasey, John.**
Martin, Stella. *See* **Heyer, Georgette.**
Martin Chuzzlewit (Dickens, C.). LFEng 749-751; RevLFEng 907-909.
Martin du Gard, Roger. LFFor 1108-1119.
Martin Eden (London). LFEng 1696-1697; RevLFEng 2101-2102; ShF 589-590.
Martin Faber (Simms). LFEng 2414; RevLFEng 3044.
Martin Salander (Keller). LFFor 934-935.
"Martin the Fisherman" (Knowles). RevShF 1381-1382; ShF 1769.
Martínez, Enrique González. *See* **González Martínez, Enrique.**
Martínez de la Rosa, Francisco. DFor 1269-1277, 2498.
Martínez Sierra, Gregorio, and María Martínez Sierra. DFor 1278-1288, 2503.

Martinsen, Martin. *See* **Follett, Ken.**
Martinson, Harry. PFor 2179-2180; **PSup 269-274.**
Mártir del Sacramento, San Hermenegildo, El (Cruz). DFor 444-445.
Marty (Chayefsky). DEng 2508.
Martyn, Edward. DEng 1275-1282; RevDEng 1601-1609.
"Martyr, A" (Rossetti, C.). PEng 2420; RevPEng 2813.
Martyrdom of Peter Ohey, The (Mrożek). DFor 1380-1381.
"Martyr's Corner, The" (Narayan). RevShF 1718; ShFSup 228.
Martz, Louis L. PEng 1904.
Marulić, Marko. PFor 2259.
Marvell, Andrew. PEng 1908-1918; RevPEng 2212-2223.
Marvellous Shoemaker's Wife, The. See Shoemaker's Prodigious Wife, The.
"Marvels Beyond Thule, The" (Antonius Diogenes). LFFor 2000, 2014.
Marx, Karl. LTh 936, 1295, 1712, 1718, 1721.
Marxism and African Literature (Ngugi). LTh 1065.
Marxism and Form (Jameson). LTh 760, 762.
Marxism and Literary Criticism (Eagleton). LTh 415.
Marxism and Literature (Williams). LTh 1542.
Marxism and the Philosophy of Language (Bakhtin). LTh 88.
Mary (Nabokov). LFEng 1949; RevLFEng 2462.
Mary Barton (Gaskell). LFEng 1099, 1103; RevLFEng 1302, 1306.
Mary Lavelle (O'Brien, K.). RevLFEng 2563-2564.
Mary O'Grady (Lavin). RevShF 1416; ShF 1780, 1785.
"Mary Postgate" (Kipling). RevShF 1366-1367.
Mary Stuart (Słowacki). DFor 1712-1714.
Marylebone Miser, The (Phillpotts). M&D 1327.
"Mary's Song" (Plath). PEng 2225-2226; RevPEng 2597-2598.
"Marzo 1821" (Manzoni). PFor 960.
"Masa." *See* "Mass."
Masamune Hakuchō. LTh 1003-1008.
Masaoka Shiki. PFor 2075.
Maschera e il volto, La. See Mask and the Face, The.
Maschinenstürmer, Die. See Machine-wreckers, The.
Masculine Dead, The (Everson). PEng 987-988; RevPEng 1118-1119.

Masefield, John. DEng 1283-1291; PEng 1919-1926; RevDEng 1610-1619; RevPEng 2224-2232.

Mashen'ka. See Mary.

Masir Sursar. See Fate of a Cockroach.

Mask and the Face, The (Chiarelli). DFor 387-390.

Mask for Dimitrios, A. See Coffin for Dimitrios, A.

Mask for Janus, A (Merwin). RevPEng 2299.

Mask of Apollo, The (Renault). LFEng 2221-2222; RevLFEng 2812-2813.

Masked Gods (Waters). LFEng 2781; RevLFEng 3447.

"Masked Woman's Song" (Bogan). PEng 234; RevPEng 281.

Maskerad. See Masquerade, The.

Masks of Drought, The (Everson). PEng 992-993; RevPEng 1123-1125.

Masnavi-ye Ma'navi (Rumi). PSup 338-340.

Mason, A. E. W. M&D 1195-1199.

Mason, Bobbie Ann. RevShF 1617-1622, 2756.

Mason, Tally. *See Derleth, August.*

"Masque of Blackness, The" (Nims). PEng 2109, 2110-2112; RevPEng 2456-2458.

"Masque of the Red Death, The" (Poe). RevShF 2687, 2688; ShF 193, 194, 474, 723-724, 792.

Masque Presented at Ludlow Castle, A. See Comus.

Masquerade, The (Clark-Bekederemo). DSup 55-56; RevDEng 452-453.

Masqueraders, The (Jones, H. A.). DEng 1004; RevDEng 1270.

"Mass" (Vallejo). PFor 1594.

"Mass for the Day of St. Thomas Didymus" (Levertov). PEng 1710.

"Massachusetts to Virginia" (Whittier). PEng 3087; RevPEng 3576.

Massacre at Paris, The (Marlowe). DEng 1256-1257; RevDEng 1581-1582.

Masse-Mensch. See Masses and Man.

Masse und Macht. See Crowds and Power.

Masses and Man (Toller). DFor 1858-1860.

Massinger, Philip. DEng 1292-1302, 2291-2292; LTh 450; RevDEng 1620-1631, 2810-2811.

"Mastectomy" (Boland). PSup 38-39; RevPEng 294.

"Master and Man" (Tolstoy). RevShF 2286-2287.

Master and Man (Tolstoy). LFEng 3268-3270.

Master and Margarita, The (Bulgakov). LFFor 208-209, 2327.

Master Builder, The (Ibsen). DFor 986-987.

"Master Glass" (Cervantes). LFEng 3231.

"MASTER HAROLD . . . and the boys" (Fugard). DEng 695, 704-705; RevDEng 863, 873-874.

"Master Misery" (Capote). RevShF 407-408; ShF 1054-1056.

Master of Ballantrae, The (Stevenson, R. L.). LFEng 2550-2551; RevLFEng 3194-3195.

Master of Hestviken, The (Undset). LFFor 1804-1805, 2352.

"Master of Prayers, The" (Nahman). RevShF 1711; ShF 1943-1944.

Master of Santiago, The (Montherlant). DFor 1353-1354.

"Master Richard" (Wain). RevShF 2373; ShF 2400-2401.

Masterpiece Theatre. RevDEng 3044.

Masters, The (Snow). LFEng 2462-2463; RevLFEng 3088-3089.

Masters, Edgar Lee. PEng 1927-1935; RevPEng 2233-2241.

Mastro-don Gesualdo (Verga). LFFor 1864-1865.

Mastronardi, Lucio. LFFor 2256.

Masuji, Ibuse. LFFor 2278.

Mat. See Mother, The.

Matchmaker, The (Nestroy). DFor 1424.

Matchmaker, The (Wilder). DEng 2051-2052; RevDEng 2550-2551.

"Mateo Falcone" (Mérimée). LFFor 1144; RevShF 1656-1657, 2667; ShF 171, 1922.

Materials, The (Oppen). PEng 2139; RevPEng 2508.

Maternus, Curiatius. DFor 2150.

Matevski, Mateja. PFor 2273.

Mathematical Principles of Natural Philosophy, The (Newton). PEng 3494.

Mather, Cotton. LTh 1741.

Mather, Richard. LTh 1740.

Mathnavī of Jalālu'ddīn Rūmī, The. See Masnavi-ye Ma'navi.

Matić, Dušan. PFor 2256.

Matilda Hunter Murder, The (Keeler). M&D 957.

Matilde (Niccolini). DFor 1431.

"Matisse" (Snodgrass). PEng 2662; RevPEng 3091.

Matka. See Mother, The.

"Matlock Bath" (Betjeman). PEng 171; RevPEng 204.

Matlock Paper, The (Ludlum). M&D 1108.

Matoš, Antun Gustav. PFor 2264.

Matrosen von Cattaro, Die. See Sailors of Cattaro, The.

"Matryona's House" (Solzhenitsyn). RevShF 2162; ShF 2249-2250.

Matsukaze. See Wind in the Pines, The.

Matsunaga Teitoku. PFor 2068-2069.
Matsuo Bashō. LTh 1790-1791; **PFor 978-985,** 2070-2071.
"Matter of Chance, A" (Nabokov). RevShF 1702-1703; ShFSup 219.
Matthews, Brander. RevShF 2677, 2714; ShF 181-182, 585-586, 588, 811, 812.
Matthews, Jack. ShF 2716.
Matthews, William. PEng **1936-1941;** PSup 407; **RevPEng 2242-2248.**
Matthiessen, F. O. LTh **1009-1014.**
Matthiessen, Peter. LFEng **1822-1833; RevLFEng 2308-2320.**
Maturin, Charles Robert. LFEng **1834-1842,** 3123, 3140-3141; **RevLFEng 2321-2330,** 3825.
Mątwa. See *Cuttlefish, The.*
"Maud" (Auchincloss). RevShF 112-113.
"Maudlin" (Plath). PEng 2227; RevPEng 2599.
Maugham, W. Somerset. DEng **1303-1313;** LFEng **1843-1852;** M&D **1200-1206; RevDEng 1632-1643; RevLFEng 2331-2340; RevShF 1623-1630;** ShF 244, 521-522, 527, 786-787, **1899-1906.**
Maupassant, Guy de. M&D **1207-1212; RevShF 1631-1639;** ShF 459-460, **1907-1912.**
Mauprat (Sand). LFFor 1494-1495.
Maurer, Georg. PFor 1817, 1821-1822.
Mauriac, François. LFFor **1120-1132,** 2142; LTh 1273.
Maurice (Forster). LFEng 1003-1004; RevLFEng 1193-1194.
Mauser (Müller). DSup 260.
Mausoleum (Enzensberger). PFor 469-470.
Mauthner, Fritz. LFFor 2189.
"Mauvais sang." *See* "Bad Blood."
Mavor, Osborne Henry. *See* **Bridie, James.**
Max (Grass). DSup 159.
"Maximin" (George). PFor 550.
Maximus Poems (Olson). PEng 3366, 3367; PSup 310-311; RevPEng 2502-2503, 3884, 3885.
Maxwell, Mary Elizabeth Braddon. *See* **Braddon, M. E.**
Maxwell, William. RevLFEng **2341-2347.**
May (Mácha). PFor 1800.
May, Karl. LFFor 2185.
May Day (Chapman). DEng 356; RevDEng 417.
"May Day Ode" (Thackeray). PEng 2875.
"May Day Sermon" (Dickey, J.). PEng 799; RevPEng 908-910.
"May Evening" (Eberhart). PEng 933.
"May Night: Or, The Drowned Maiden, A" (Gogol). RevShF 1016-1017.

"May Night" (Musset). PFor 1065-1066.
"May-Pole of Merrymount, The" (Hawthorne). RevShF 1147-1148.
"May Queen" (Robison). RevShF 2012-2013.
Mayakovsky, Vladimir. DFor **1289-1299;** LTh 947; **PFor 986-994,** 2148-2149.
"Maybe Alone on My Bike" (Stafford). RevPEng 3173.
"Mayday on Holderness" (Hughes, T.). RevPEng 1649.
Mayden's Dream, A (Greene). RevPEng 1309-1310.
Mayflower, The (Blasco Ibáñez). LFFor 169-171.
Mayhall, Jane. ShF 2717.
Mayne, Ethel Colburn. ShF 517.
Mayor of Casterbridge, The (Hardy). LFEng 1270-1271, 3050; RevLFEng 1506-1507, 3758.
Mayor of Zalamea, The (Calderón). DFor 306-307.
"Mayskaya Noch: Ili, utoplennitsa." *See* "May Night: Or, The Drowned Maiden, A."
Mąż i żona. See Husband and Wife.
"Maze" (Eberhart). PEng 928-929.
Mazeppa (Słowacki). DFor 1717-1719.
Mažuranić, Ivan. PFor 2262.
Mazzini, Giuseppe. LTh **1015-1021,** 1398.
"Me and Miss Mandible" (Barthelme). RevShF 162-163; ShFSup 24-25.
"Me and My Baby View the Eclipse" (Smith). RevShF 2157.
"Me and the Girls" (Coward). ShF 1208.
"Meadow Turned Green, The" (Novalis). PFor 1100.
Mean Rufus Throw Down (Smith, D.). PEng 2644; RevPEng 3066.
Measure for Measure (Shakespeare). DEng 1710, 2280-2281; RevDEng 2124, 2799-2800; ShF 2210.
"Meat" (Simic). PEng 2592.
"Mechón blanco, El." *See* "White Lock of Hair, The."
Meckel, Christoph. LFFor **2201; RevShF 1640-1646;** ShFSup **185-191.**
Męczeństwo Piotra Oheya. See *Martyrdom of Peter Ohey, The.*
Medea (Euripides). DFor 574-575, 2111-2112.
Medea (Grillparzer). DFor 825. See also *Golden Fleece, The.*
Medea (Seneca). DFor 1689-1690, 2148-2149.
Medici, Lorenzo de'. PFor 2010-2011.
"Medicine" (Lu Hsün). RevShF 1521; ShFSup 176-177.

Memnon: Or Human Wisdom (Voltaire). RevShF 2359-2360; ShFSup 330.
"Mémoire" (Reverdy). PSup 323-324.
Mémoires de Vidocq, chef de la police de Sûreté jusqu'en 1827. See *Memoirs of Vidocq, Principal Agent of the French Police Until 1827.*
Mémoires d'Hadrien. See *Memoirs of Hadrian.*
Mémoires d'outre-tombe. See *Memoirs* (Chateaubriand).
Mémoires d'un honnête homme. See *Memoirs of a Man of Honor.*
Mémoires et avantures d'un homme de qualité. See *Memoirs of a Man of Quality.*
Memoirs (Chateaubriand). LFFor 334-335.
Memoirs and Adventures of a Man of Quality, The. See *Memoirs of a Man of Quality.*
Memoirs Found in a Bathtub (Lem). LFFor 1011.
Memoirs in Oxford (Prince). PSup 317; RevPEng 2665.
Memoirs of a Man of Honor (Prévost). LFFor 1316-1318.
Memoirs of a Man of Quality (Prévost). LFFor 1310-1311, 1312-1314.
Memoirs of a Midget (de la Mare). LFEng 709, 710-711; RevLFEng 844, 845-846.
Memoirs of a Space Traveler (Lem). RevShF 1459-1460; ShFSup 152.
Memoirs of a Survivor, The (Lessing). LFEng 1640-1641; RevLFEng 2037-2038.
Memoirs of Hadrian (Yourcenar). LFFor 1965-1970.
Memoirs of Leonora Christina (Leonora Christina). LFFor 2334.
Memoirs of Vidocq, Principal Agent of the French Police Until 1827 (Vidocq). M&D 1651-1652.
Memorandum, The (Havel). DFor 879-880.
Memorandum on My Martinique. See *Return to My Native Land.*
Memorial de Ayres. See *Counselor Ayres' Memorial.*
Memórias póstumas de Braz Cubas. See *Posthumous Memoirs of Brás Cubas, The.*
"Memories" (Leopardi). PFor 861. See also *Canti.*
"Memories of an Auctioneer" (Auchincloss). RevShF 115.
"Memories of the Space Age" (Ballard). RevShF 143.
"Memories Sent to an Old Friend" (Akutagawa). RevShF 37; ShFSup 11.
"Memory Clearing House, The" (Zangwill). M&D 1733.

Memory of Two Mondays, A (Miller). DEng 1343; RevDEng 1681-1682.
"Memphis Blues" (Brown). RevPEng 391-392.
Me-mushiri ko-uchi (Ōe). LFFor 1196.
Men and Brethren (Cozzens). LFEng 633-634; RevLFEng 766-767.
"Men Are a Mockery of Angels" (Hill). RevPEng 1521-1522.
Men at Arms (Waugh). LFEng 2801; RevLFEng 3468-3469.
Men in Her Death, The (Morice). M&D 1238.
Men in White (Kingsley). DEng 1039-1040; RevDEng 1315-1316.
Men livet lever. See *Road Leads On, The.*
"Men Loved Wholly Beyond Wisdom" (Bogan). PEng 233; RevPEng 280.
"Men of Careful Turns" (Brooks). RevPEng 381.
Men of Good Will (Romains). LFFor 1441-1444.
Men of Maize (Asturias). LFFor 84-85.
Men on Bataan (Hersey). LFEng 1352; RevLFEng 1610.
"Men with the Knives, The" (Böll). RevShF 239.
"Menace, The" (Gunn). RevPEng 1335.
"Menace from Earth, The" (Heinlein). RevShF 1156; ShF 1618-1619.
Menachem-Mendl letters (Aleichem). RevShF 49.
Menaechmi. See *Twin Menaechmi, The.*
Menander. DEng 2144; **DFor 1300-1308,** 2131-2133; RevDEng 2664.
Menaphon (Greene, R.). PEng 1149; RevPEng 1307; RevShF 1078-1079; ShF 1551-1552.
Menashe, Samuel. RevPEng **2259-2265.**
Menčetić, Šiško. PFor 2260.
Mencius. LTh 1467.
Mencken, H. L. LTh 71-72.
Mendiant de Jerusalem, Le. See *Beggar in Jerusalem, A.*
"Mending Wall" (Frost). PEng 1047; RevPEng 1179.
Mendoza, Fray Iñigo de. DFor 2171.
Ménechmes, Les (Regnard). DFor 1543-1544.
Menéndez y Pelayo, Marcelino. LTh **1022-1026.**
Mêng fêng chi (Wang). DFor 2324.
Menneskene og maktene. See *Floodtide of Fate.*
"Menons Klagen um Diotima." *See* "Menon's Laments for Diotima."
"Menon's Laments for Diotima" (Hölderlin). PFor 687.
Menorah Men, The (Davidson). M&D 456-457.
Mensagem (Pessoa). PFor 1206-1207.
Menschen und Leidenschaften (Lermontov). DFor 1177-1178.

Menschliches, Allzumenschliches. See *Human, All Too Human.*

"Menses" (Boland). PSup 39; RevPEng 294-295.

"Menses" (Millay). PEng 2002-2003; RevPEng 2326-2327.

Mensonge romantique et vérité romanesque. See *Deceit, Desire, and the Novel.*

"Men's Room in the College Chapel, The" (Snodgrass). PEng 2661; RevPEng 3090.

Men's Wives (Thackeray). RevShF 2261-2262; ShF 2316-2317.

Mentoria (Rowson). LFEng 2317-2318; RevLFEng 2912-2913.

"Mentors" (Brooks, G.). PEng 3397; RevPEng 3905.

"Menu/1965, The" (Brautigan). RevShF 318; ShFSup 57-59.

Mercadé, Eustache. DFor 2166.

Mercer, David. DEng 2506.

Merchant, The (Wesker). RevDEng 2510.

"Merchant and the Jinni, The." ShF 410.

"Merchant of New Desires, The" (Elkin). RevShF 812; ShF 1340.

Merchant of Venice, The (Shakespeare). DEng 1706-1707, 2278; RevDEng 2120-2121, 2797; ShF 2210.

"Merchant's Tale, The" (Chaucer). PEng 487; RevPEng 583; RevShF 494-495; ShF 1113, 1115.

Mercian Hymns (Hill, G.). PEng 1346-1347, 1357, 3369; RevPEng 1524-1525, 3887.

Mercier, Louis-Sébastien. DEng 2182-2183; **DFor 1309-1318**, 2342; RevDEng 2702-2703.

Mercier and Camier (Beckett). LFEng 210-211; LFFor 126-127; RevLFEng 259-260.

Mercière assassinée, La (Hébert). LFFor 806.

"Mère Sauvage, La" (Maupassant). ShF 114.

Meredith, Anne. See **Gilbert, Anthony.**

Meredith, George. LFEng 1863-1872, 3079; **RevLFEng 2359-2369**, 3788.

Meredith, William. PEng 1952-1957; RevPEng **2266-2276.**

Merely Murder. See *Death in the Stocks.*

Meres, Francis. LTh 1184.

Merezhkovsky, Dmitry. LFFor 1133-1141, 2319.

Meri, Veijo. LFFor 2368.

Meridian (Walker). LFEng 2749-2750, 2753-2754; RevLFEng 3407, 3410-3412.

"Meriggiare pallido e assorto." See "Wall, The."

Mérimée, Prosper. LFFor 1142-1153, 2128; LTh 1395; **RevShF 1655-1659**, 2667; ShF 459, **1920-1924.**

Merle (Marshall). RevShF 1615.

Merlin (Dorst). DSup 96.

"Merlin" (Emerson). PEng 956; RevPEng 1086.

Mermaids on the Golf Course and Other Stories (Highsmith). RevShF 1195-1196.

Merope (D'Annunzio). PFor 388. See also *Laudi, Le.*

Mérope (Voltaire). DFor 1969.

Meropius Pontius Paulinus. See Paulinus of Nola.

Merril, Judith. ShF 780.

Merrill, James. PEng **1958-1969;** PSup 407; **RevPEng 2277-2287.**

Merritt, Abraham. RevLFEng 3861.

Merry Death, A (Evreinov). DFor 583-584.

Merry-Go-Round, The (Becque). DFor 171.

"Merry-Go-Round, The" (Zoshchenko). RevShF 2559; ShFSup 381.

Merry-Go-Round of Love, The (Pirandello). LFFor 1301-1302.

"Merry-Go-Round with White Swan" (Seifert). PSup 355.

Merry Pranksters, The. LFEng 1527, 1528-1529.

Merry Wives of Windsor, The (Shakespeare). DEng 1709, 2279; RevDEng 2123, 2798.

Merton, Thomas. PEng **1970-1978; RevPEng 2288-2296.**

Merton of the Movies (Kaufman and Connelly). DEng 418-419; RevDEng 518-519.

Mertz, Barbara. See **Peters, Elizabeth.**

Merveilleux Nuages, Les. See *Wonderful Clouds, The.*

Merwin, W. S. PEng **1979-1983;** PSup 407; **RevPEng 2297-2305.**

"Mes bouquins refermés sur le nom de Paphos." See "My Old Books Closed at the Name of Paphos."

Meshchane. See *Smug Citizen.*

"Message All Blackpeople Can Dig (& a few negroes too), A" (Madhubuti). PEng 1895; RevPEng 2199.

Message from Hong Kong (Eberhart). M&D 565.

"Message from the Pig-Man, The" (Wain). RevShF 2373-2374; ShF 2401.

Messe là-bas, La (Claudel). PFor 363.

Messenger, The (Kinsella). PSup 237; RevPEng 1839.

Messenius, Johannes. DFor 2465.

Messiah (Vidal). RevLFEng 3373.

Messiya. See *Akhnaton, King of Egypt.*

Mestiere di vivere, Il. See *This Business of Living.*

"Mestrović and the Trees" (Blackburn). PEng 196; RevPEng 240.

Mesyats v derevne. See *Month in the Country, A.*

Milton, John. LTh 92, 174-176, 239-240, 449, 1349; **PEng 2004-2015,** 3315, 3493; RevPEng 2337-2349.

Milton, John R. ShF 2727.

Milton's God (Empson). LTh 464.

Milton's Prosody (Bridges). PEng 289-290; RevPEng 354-355.

Milutinovič Sarajlija, Sima. PFor 2253-2254.

Mimesis (Auerbach). LTh 56-60, 712, 1394.

Mimic Men, The (Naipaul). LFEng 1961; RevLFEng 2471.

Mimologiques (Genette). LTh 563.

"Mimosa, Le." *See* "Mimosa, The."

"Mimosa, The" (Ponge). PFor 1263.

"Mimsy Were the Borogoves" (Kuttner). ShF 565.

Min son på galejan (Wallenberg). LFFor 2335.

"Min taht ila Fawq" (Mahfouz). RevShF 1565.

Mind Breaths (Ginsberg). PEng 1095; RevPEng 1233.

"Mind, Intractable Thing, The" (Moore). PEng 2048; RevPEng 2378.

"Mind Is an Enchanting Thing, The" (Moore). PEng 2046; RevPEng 2376.

Mind of My Mind (Butler, O.). RevLFEng 496.

Mind of the Maker, The (Sayers). LFEng 2357-2358; RevLFEng 2973-2974.

"Mind-Reader, The" (Wilbur). PEng 3098, 3099; RevPEng 3589.

Mind to Murder, A (James). M&D 933-934.

Mine Boy (Abrahams). LFFor 2049.

"Mine own John Poyntz" (Wyatt). PEng 3178; RevPEng 3702.

"Minek nevezzelek?" *See* "What Shall I Name You?"

Miner, Valerie. ShF 2728.

"Minerva Writes Poems" (Cisneros). RevShF 558-559.

"Mines of Falun, The" (Hoffman). RevShF 1215; ShF 1647.

Ming Huang. DFor 2305.

"Mingo: A Sketch of Life in Middle Georgia" (Harris, J.). RevShF 1118; ShF 1589.

"Minister's Black Veil, The" (Hawthorne). RevShF 1146-1147, 2684; ShF 189-190.

Minister's Wooing, The (Stowe). LFEng 2561-2563; RevLFEng 3213-3214.

Minkin, Stephen. ShF 2729.

Minna von Barnhelm (Lessing). DFor 1203-1205.

"Minneapolis Poem, The" (Wright, James). PEng 3166-3168; RevPEng 3678-3680.

Minnesota Strip (Collins, M.). M&D 382, 384.

Minor, The (Fonvizin). DFor 635-638, 2452.

Minor Apocalypse, A (Konwicki). LFFor 947, 948-949.

Minor Poets of the Caroline Period (Saintsbury). LTh 1268.

Minot, Stephen. ShF 2730.

Minstrelsy of the Scottish Border (Scott). PEng 2500; RevPEng 2908.

"Mint Quality, The" (Blackburn). PEng 200; RevPEng 244.

Minturno, Antonio. DEng 2156; **LTh 1038-1041,** 1669.

Minuta (Reyes). PFor 1322.

Miošić, Andrija Kačić. PFor 2261.

Mir zur Feier (Rilke). PFor 1328.

Mira de Amescua, Antonio. DFor 2493.

Mirabell (Merrill). RevPEng 2282-2283.

"Miracle" (Carver). RevPEng 537.

Miracle de la rose. See *Miracle of the Rose.*

Miracle de Théophile, Le (Rutebeuf). DFor 2164.

Miracle of the Rose (Genet). LFFor 629-631.

Miracle Worker, The (Gibson). DEng 752-754; RevDEng 932-934.

Miracolo d'Amore (Clarke, M.). RevDEng 475-477.

Mirikitani, Janice. RevPEng 3914-3915.

Mirour de l'Omme (Gower). PEng 1114, 1115, 1116-1118; RevPEng 1264-1266.

Mirra. See *Murrha.*

Mirror: Or, Book of Women (Roig). PFor 1772.

Mirror and the Lamp, The (Abrams). LTh 2-3, 850, 1370.

Mirror for Magistrates, A (Baldwin, W., comp.). PEng 2437-2439, 3294-3295.

Misal kneza Novaka. PFor 2259.

Misanthrope, The (Molière). DFor 1339; LTh 1687.

"Misanthrope, The" (Moravia). RevShF 1673; ShFSup 198.

"Misanthropos" (Gunn). RevPEng 1334.

"Misantropo, Il." *See* "Misanthrope, The."

"Miscarriage" (Olds). RevPEng 2492.

Miscellaneous Observations on the Tragedy of Macbeth (Johnson). LTh 775.

Miscellaneous Pieces in Prose (Aiken and Barbauld). ShF 470.

"Miscellanies" (Cowley, A.). PEng 592-593; RevPEng 698.

Mischief (Armstrong). M&D 38.

Mischief of Being Clever, The (Griboyedov). DFor 812-816.

Misérables, Les (Hugo). LFFor 854; RevDEng 3027.

Misericordia. See *Compassion.*

"Miserie" (Herbert). PEng 1303; RevPEng 1482.

"Misery" (Chekhov). RevShF 2719-2720.

Misery (King). RevLFEng 1893-1894.

"Misfit, The" (Colette). RevShF 581.

"Misfits, The" (Miller). ShF 1925, 1926-1927.

Misfortune of Being Clever, The. See *Mischief of Being Clever, The.*

Misfortunes of Arthur, The (Hughes). DEng 2265; RevDEng 2784.

Misfortunes of Elphin, The (Peacock). LFEng 2083, 2084; RevLFEng 2622.

"Misgivings" (Melville). PEng 1945-1948; RevPEng 2252-2255.

Mishima, Yukio. DFor 1319-1327, 2434; LFFor 1154-1160, 2275, 2278; RevShF 1660-1666, 2746-2747; ShF 1931-1939.

"Misoginia" (Pavese). ShF 2065-2066.

"Miss August" (Hale, N.). RevShF 1097; ShF 1570.

"Miss Brill" (Mansfield). RevShF 1598.

Miss Brown of X.Y.O. (Oppenheim). M&D 1274.

Miss Cayley's Adventures (Allen). M&D 18.

"Miss Coynte of Greene" (Williams, T.). RevShF 2482; ShF 2437-2438.

"Miss Cudahy of Stowe's Landing" (Elliott). RevShF 821-822; ShF 1349-1350.

"Miss Dulane and My Lord" (Collins, Wilkie). LFEng 561; RevLFEng 688.

Miss Firecracker Contest, The (Henley). DSup 196; RevDEng 1154.

"Miss Holland" (Lavin). RevShF 1413-1414; ShF 1782.

Miss Julie (Strindberg). DFor 1750-1752, 2475.

Miss Kilmansegg and Her Precious Leg (Hood). PEng 1386-1387; RevPEng 1584-1585.

"Miss Leonora When Last Seen" (Taylor). RevShF 2254-2255; ShF 2309.

Miss Lonelyhearts (West, N.). LFEng 2842, 2843-2844; RevLFEng 3515-3516.

Miss Mabel (Sherriff). DEng 1791; RevDEng 2225.

"Miss Marple Tells a Story" (Christie). ShF 1145-1146.

Miss Peabody's Inheritance (Jolley). LFSup 180; RevLFEng 1793.

"Miss Pinkerton's Apocalypse" (Spark). ShF 2254-2255.

Miss Pym Disposes (Tey). M&D 1582.

Miss Ravenel's Conversion from Secession to Loyalty (De Forest). LFEng 702-703; RevLFEng 834-835.

"Miss Ruth Algrave" (Lispector). RevShF 1493; ShFSup 168.

Miss Sara Sampson (Lessing). DFor 1201-1202.

"Miss Shum's Husband" (Thackeray). RevShF 2259; ShF 2313-2314.

Miss Silver Comes to Stay (Wentworth). M&D 1697-1698.

"Miss Tempy's Watchers" (Jewett). RevShF 1276; ShF 228.

Miss Universal Happiness (Foreman). DSup 122-123; RevDEng 823-824.

Missing Brontë, The. See *Case of the Missing Brontë, The.*

"Missing Dates" (Empson). PEng 968, 972; RevPEng 1102.

"Missing Person, The" (Wolff). RevShF 2507.

Mission Accomplished (Beti). LFFor 2036-2037.

Mission terminée. See *Mission Accomplished.*

"Mission Tire Factory, 1969" (Soto). RevPEng 3114.

Mission to Kala. See *Mission Accomplished.*

Missolonghi Manuscript, The (Prokosch). LFEng 2167; RevLFEng 2741.

Mist (Unamuno). LFFor 1791-1792.

Mistaken Clinic, The (Lucian). LTh 931.

Mr. Adam (Kirkland). DEng 1052-1053; RevDEng 1329-1330.

"Mr. and Mrs. Discobbolos" (Lear). PEng 1701; RevPEng 1973.

Mr. Beluncle (Pritchett). LFEng 2156-2160; RevLFEng 2728-2732.

"Mr. Bennett and Mrs. Brown" (Woolf). LTh 1574.

"Mr. Big" (Allen). RevShF 57.

Mr. Blettsworthy on Rampole (Wells). RevLFEng 3484-3485.

"Mr. -bov and the Question of Art" (Dostoevski). LTh 395.

Mr. Bridge (Connell). LFEng 579-580; RevLFEng 708-709.

Mr. Britling Sees It Through (Wells). LFEng 2813-2814; RevLFEng 3484.

Mr. Buckstone's Ascent of Mount Parnassus (Planché). DEng 1528-1529; RevDEng 1916-1917.

Mr. Bullivant and His Lambs. See *Manservant and Maidservant.*

Mr. Frivolous (Shawn). DSup 336; RevDEng 2169. See also *Three Short Plays.*

Mr. Gallion's School (Stuart). LFEng 2577; RevLFEng 3229.

"Mr. Gilfil's Love Story" (Eliot, G.). RevShF 806-807; ShF 1334.

Mister Johnson (Cary). LFEng 456-457; RevLFEng 574, 576-577.

Mr. Leonida and the Reactionaries (Caragiale). DFor 348, 2298.

Modern Ladies of Guanabacoa, The (Machado). RevDEng 1526-1527.

"Modern Landscape" (Gressmann). PFor 1822.

Modern Lover, A (Moore, G.). LFEng 1899; RevLFEng 2406.

Modern Painters (Ruskin). LTh 1247; ShF 714.

Modern Poetry and the Tradition (Brooks, C.). LTh 220-221.

"Modern Theatre" (Lagerkvist). LFFor 968, 969-970.

"Moderne Landschaft." *See* "Modern Landscape."

"Modes of Pleasure" (Gunn). PEng 1171, 1174.

Modest Art, The (Beachcroft). ShF 70-71.

Modification, La. See *Change of Heart, A.*

"Modulations" (Wright, Jay). RevPEng 3689.

Moetsukita chizu. See *Ruined Map, The.*

Mogens (Jacobsen). LFFor 2338.

"Moglie con le ali, La." *See* "Count's Wife, The."

"Moglie di Gogol, La." *See* "Gogol's Wife."

"Mohincan, The" (Nin). ShF 1949-1950.

Mohn und Gedächtnis (Celan). PFor 311-312.

Mohocks, The (Gay). DEng 731; RevDEng 910.

"Moi pervyi gus'" *See* "My First Goose."

Moi universitety. See *My Universities.*

Moira (Green). LFFor 748-749.

"Moïse" (Vigny). PFor 1639-1640.

"Mojave" (Capote). LFEng 449-450; RevLFEng 561.

Mojigata, La (Moratín). DFor 1363.

"Mold of Yancy, The" (Dick). RevShF 717.

"Mole, The" (Kawabata). RevShF 1320.

Molière. DEng 2174, 2296; **DFor 1328-1340,** 2226-2227; LTh 838, 1196; RevDEng 2694-2695, 2815.

Molina, Tirso de. *See* **Tirso de Molina.**

Molinaro, Ursule. ShF 2731.

Moll Flanders (Defoe). LFEng 691, 693-694, 3020-3021, 3104; RevLFEng 824, 826-827, 3728-3729, 3731-3732, 3806.

Møller, Poul Martin. LTh 1723.

Mollie Bailey's Traveling Family Circus (Terry). DSup 345; RevDEng 2370.

Molloy (Beckett). LFEng 211; LFFor 127-128; RevLFEng 260.

"Molly's Dog" (Adams). RevShF 10; ShFSup 4.

Mölna-elegi, En. See *Molna Elegy, A.*

Molna Elegy, A (Ekelöf). PFor 451-452.

Molnár, Ferenc. DFor 1341-1349.

Molodoi Tolstoi. See *Young Tolstoi, The.*

Molodost' (Khodasevich). PSup 225.

"Moly" (Gunn). PEng 1176; RevPEng 1334.

"Moly" (Gunn). PEng 1169-1170, 1171, 1175-1177; RevPEng 1334.

Momaday, N. Scott. PEng 2016-2022; **RevPEng 2350-2357,** 3929, 3934.

Moment in Eternity, A (MacDiarmid). PSup 260; RevPEng 2120.

"Moment of Eternity, A" (Bhattacharya). ShF 651-652.

"Moments of Being" (Woolf). ShF 2456.

"Mōmoku monogatari." *See* "Blind Man's Tale, A."

Momos de doña Isabel para su hermano don Alfonso (Manrique). DFor 1255.

"Mon rêve familier." *See* "My Familiar Dream."

"Mon Roi." *See* "My King."

Monahan, John. See **Burnett, W. R.**

Monday After the Miracle (Gibson). DEng 754; RevDEng 934-935.

"Monday, Monday" (Blackburn). PEng 200; RevPEng 244.

Monday Night (Boyle, K.). LFEng 278; RevLFEng 343.

"Monday or Tuesday" (Woolf). RevShF 2513.

Monday Tales (Daudet). RevShF 673-674; ShF 1241.

Monde comme il va, Le. See *Babouc.*

"Mondnacht." *See* "Moonlit Night."

"Monet's 'Waterlilies'" (Hayden). PEng 1249; RevPEng 1433.

Money (Amis, M.). RevLFEng 104.

Money (Bulwer-Lytton). DEng 315-316, 2366; RevDEng 375-376.

Money Changers, The (Sinclair, U.). LFEng 2422-2423; RevLFEng 3052-3053.

Money for Maria (Rasputin). RevShF 1994.

Money Order, The (Sembène). LFFor 1542, 1543.

Monk, The (Lewis, M.). LFEng 1661-1667, 2156-2160, 3126-3127; RevLFEng 2057-2061, 3824, 3828-3829; ShF 730-731.

Monk, Elizabeth Graham. ShF 2732.

Monkey. See *Journey to the West, The.*

"Monkey, The" (Dinesen). RevShF 736-737.

"Monkey, The" (King). RevShF 1347-1348.

Monkey King, The (Mo). RevLFEng 3793

"Monkey's Paw, The" (Jacobs). M&D 930.

Monkey's Raincoat (Matsuo Bashō). PFor 983.

Monkey's Wrench, The (Levi). LFSup 236-237.

Monk's-Hood (Peters, Ellis). M&D 1322.

Monkshood's Farewell (Clarke, M.). RevDEng 472-473.

Monody, Written at Matlock (Bowles). PEng 254-255; RevPEng 315-316.

"Monody Written Near Stratford Upon Avon" (Warton). PEng 3038.

"Monologue of Isabel Watching It Rain in Macondo" (García Márquez). RevShF 951.

Monroe, Harriet. PEng 2023-2030.

Monsieur (Durrell). LFEng 847, 3069.

Monsieur Beaucaire (Lonsdale). DEng 1169; RevDEng 1471-1472.

Monsieur d'Olive (Chapman). DEng 356, 357; RevDEng 417, 418.

Monsieur Lecoq (Gaboriau). M&D 684.

"Monsieur Maurice" (Colette). RevShF 581.

Monsieur Ouine. See Open Mind, The.

"Monster, The" (Crane, S.). ShF 1221.

"Monster, The" (Gunn). PEng 1174.

Monster and Other Stories, The (Crane). LFEng 645-646; RevLFEng 778-779.

"Monster Dance" (Slavitt). RevPEng 3054.

Monstre Gai. See Human Age, The.

Mont Blanc (Shelley). PEng 2552-2554; RevPEng 2965-2967.

"Mont des Oliviers, Le" (Vigny). PFor 1640-1641.

Montague, John. PEng 2031-2039; PSup 408; RevPEng 2358-2369.

Montaigne, Michel Eyquem de. LTh 1042-1048.

Montale, Eugenio. PFor 1046-1053, 2040-2042, 2048-2049.

"Montana Pastoral" (Cunningham). PSup 78; RevPEng 807.

"Monte Sant' Angelo" (Miller). ShF 1928-1929.

Montesquieu, Charles de. LFEng 3110-3112; PFor 1858; RevLFEng 3811.

Montgomery, Marion. ShF 2733.

Montgomery, Max. *See* **Davenport, Guy.**

Montgomery, Robert Bruce. *See* **Crispin, Edmund.**

Month in the Country, A (Turgenev). DFor 1906-1908.

Month of Sundays, A (Updike). LFEng 2687, 2691; RevLFEng 3358.

Montherlant, Henry de. DFor 1350-1357, 2352-2353.

Monti, Vincenzo. DFor 2407; PFor 2024-2025.

Montiano y Luyando, Agustin. LTh 1692.

Montoya, José, 3923.

Montreal Smoked Meat. See Cinq and *Like Death Warmed Over.*

"Monument, The" (Bishop). PEng 186-187; RevPEng 229-230.

"Monument" (Brodsky). PFor 239.

Moodie, Susanna. ShF 635.

"Moon" (Unamuno). PFor 1558.

Moon and Sixpence, The (Maugham). LFEng 1847-1848, 1850; RevLFEng 2335-2336.

Moon and the Bonfires, The (Pavese). LFFor 2250; ShF 2066.

"Moon-Bone Song, The" (Murray). PSup 290; RevPEng 2411.

"Moon Came Out, The" (Tolstaya). RevShF 2294-2295.

"Moon Lake" (Welty). RevShF 2436-2437.

"Moon on the Water, The" (Kawabata). RevShF 1320-1321.

"Moongate" (Everson). PEng 993; RevPEng 1124-1125.

Moonlight, The (Cary). LFEng 458; RevLFEng 578.

"Moonlight" (Verlaine). PFor 1627, 1630.

Moonlight Sonata, The (Rítsos). PFor 1350, 1970.

"Moonlit Night" (Eichendorff). PFor 441.

"Moonlit Night" (Tu Fu). PFor 1541, 1543.

"Moonshine War, The" (Stuart). RevShF 2234; ShF 2295.

Moonstone, The (Collins, W.). LFEng 560-561, 3186; M&D 389-390; RevLFEng 687-688, 3843.

Moorcock, Michael. ShF 780.

Moore, Brian. LFEng 1883-1894; LFSup 405; RevLFEng 2389-2401.

Moore, G. E. LTh 497, 1574.

Moore, George. LFEng 1895-1903, 3082; LTh 1089, 1735; RevLFEng 2402-2411; RevShF 2726; ShF 655, 656, 659-661.

Moore, Marianne. PEng 2040-2049; RevPEng 2370-2380.

Moore, Raylyn. ShF 2734.

Moortown (Hughes, T.). RevPEng 1654-1655.

Moose, Ruth. ShF 2735.

"Morada del cielo." *See* "Dwelling Place in Heaven."

Moral Tales (Edgeworth). ShF 1323-1324, 1330.

Moral Tales for Young People (Edgeworth). RevShF 798-799.

Moralitas. RevShF 2580.

Morall Fables of Esope (Henryson). RevShF 2580; ShF 143, 381.

Morall Philosophie of Doni, The. See Pañcatantra.

Moran of the Lady Letty (Norris). LFEng 2004-2005; RevLFEng 2527, 2529-2530.

Morante, Elsa. LFFor 2255.

Moratín, Leandro Fernández de. DFor 1358-1366, 2497; LTh 1692.

Moravagine (Cendrars). LFFor 320-321.

Mountain Giants, The (Pirandello). LFFor 1298.
Mountain King and Misanthrope (Raimund). DFor 1531-1532.
Mountain Meadow (Buchan). M&D 228. See also *Sick Heart River.*
"Mountain Tavern, The" (O'Flaherty). RevShF 1796; ShF 2011.
"Mountain Whippoorwill, The" (Benét). PEng 14; RevPEng 173.
Mountains and Rivers without End (Snyder). RevPEng 3106-3107.
"Mountains of Guatemala, The" (Connell). RevShF 602; ShF 1181.
Mountolive. See *Alexandria Quartet, The.*
Mourners Below (Purdy). LFEng 2176; RevLFEng 2750.
Mourning Bride, The (Congreve). DEng 408-409; RevDEng 507-508.
"Mourning Muse of Alexis, Lamenting the Death of Queen Mary, The" (Congreve). PEng 557; RevPEng 649.
"Mourning Pablo Neruda" (Bly). PEng 226-227; RevPEng 273-274.
"Mouth of Brass" (Humphrey). RevShF 1235-1236.
Mouthful of Birds, A (Churchill). RevDEng 435, 436-437.
Move, The (Betsuyaku). DFor 2435.
"Movie" (Nims). PEng 2110; RevPEng 2456.
Movie at the End of the World, The (McGrath). RevPEng 2131-2135.
"Movie-Going" (Hollander). RevPEng 1547.
Movie Star Has to Star in Black and White, A (Kennedy). DSup 215-216; RevDEng 1307-1308.
Moviegoer, The (Percy). LFEng 2091-2094; RevLFEng 2631-2633.
"Moving Again" (Matthews). PEng 1938; RevPEng 2244-2245.
"Moving Away" (Soto). RevPEng 3113-3114, 3924.
Moving On (McMurtry). LFEng 1753-1755; RevLFEng 2222-2223.
"Moving through the silent crowd" (Spender). PEng 2697, 2700; RevPEng 3141, 3144.
"Mower, The" (Bates). RevShF 174; ShFSup 30.
"Mower, The" (Larkin). RevPEng 1944-1945.
Moyes, Patricia. M&D 1252-1257.
Mozart and Salieri (Pushkin). DFor 1498-1499. See also *Little Tragedies.*
Mphahlele, Ezekiel. LTh 1054-1059.
Mrcchakatika. See *Little Clay Cart, The.*
Mrożek, Sławomir. DFor 1373-1385.

"Ms. Found in a Bottle" (Poe). ShF 2107.
"Mtsyri." *See* "Novice, The."
Much Ado About Nothing (Shakespeare). DEng 1707, 2278; RevDEng 2121, 2797.
"Much Madness is divinest Sense" (Dickinson). PEng 810; RevPEng 922.
"Mud Turtle, The" (Nemerov). PEng 2081.
Mudrooroo Narogin. RevPEng 3944.
"Muerte constante más allá del amor." *See* "Death Constant Beyond Love."
Muerte de Artemio Cruz, La. See *Death of Artemio Cruz, The.*
Muerte del cisne, La (González Martínez). PFor 612.
Muerte en el barrio (Sastre). DSup 324-325.
"Muerte y la brújula, La." *See* "Death and the Compass."
Muerte y la niña, La (Onetti). LFFor 1213-1214.
"Mugging" (Ginsberg). PEng 1095.
Muhammad (Hakim). DSup 174.
Mujer, dos hombres, y un balazo, Una. See *Woman, Two Men, and a Gunshot, A.*
Mujō to iū koto (Kobayashi). LTh 820-821.
Mukarovsky, Jan. LTh 1476, 1822.
Mukherjee, Bharati. RevShF 1685-1691.
Mukherjee, Bhudeva Chandra. LFFor 2216.
Mulata (Asturias). LFFor 85-86.
Mulata de tal. See *Mulata.*
Mulcaster, Richard. LTh 1662.
Muldoon, Paul. RevPEng 2401-2408, 3902.
Mules (Muldoon). RevPEng 2404.
Mules and Men (Hurston). LFEng 1392; RevLFEng 1668; ShF 577.
Mulford, Clarence Edward. LFEng 3195; RevLFEng 3852.
Mu-lien pien-wên. LFFor 2088.
Müller, Heiner. DFor 849-850; **DSup 255-263.**
Müllner, Adolf. M&D 1258-1263.
Mumbo Jumbo (Reed). LFSup 338-339; RevLFEng 2800, 2802-2803.
Mummer's Wife, A (Moore, G.). LFEng 1899; RevLFEng 2406.
Mumming at Bishopswood (Lydgate). PEng 1801; RevPEng 2096.
Mumming at Hertford (Lydgate). DEng 2255; RevDEng 2775.
"Mummy's Foot, The" (Gautier). RevShF 2691; ShF 197.
"Mumu" (Turgenev). RevShF 2322.
Mundo es ancho y ajeno. See *Broad and Alien Is the World.*
"Municipal Report, A" (Henry). ShF 1630.
Munk, Kaj. DFor 1386-1394, 2479-2480.

Muñoz Seca, Pedro. DFor 2503.

Munro, Alice. RevShF 1692-1698; ShF 640-641, 2738; ShFSup 208-214.

Munro, Hector Hugh. *See* **Saki.**

Mur, Le. See Wall, The.

Murasaki Shikibu. LFFor 1174-1183; LTh 1049, 1051, 1786-1787.

Murder à la Mode (Moyes). M&D 1254.

Murder All Over. See Up Jumped the Devil.

Murder at the Savoy (Sjöwall and Wahlöö). M&D 1498.

Murder by Proxy (Carmichael). M&D 263.

Murder Games. See Chelsea Murders, The.

Murder in Hospital (Bell). M&D 104.

Murder in Mimicry (Morice). M&D 1237.

Murder in the Cathedral (Eliot). DEng 548-550; RevDEng 689-691.

"Murder Lock'd In" (de la Torre). M&D 481.

Murder, Murder, Little Star (Babson). M&D 49.

Murder of My Aunt, The (Hull). M&D 918-919.

Murder of Quality, A (le Carré). LFEng 1612; RevLFEng 1986.

Murder of Roger Ackroyd, The (Christie). LFEng 539-540, 3187-3188; RevLFEng 656-657, 3844.

Murder of the Ninth Baronet (Fletcher). M&D 623.

Murder on a Mystery Tour (Babson). M&D 50-51.

Murder on the Blackboard (Palmer). M&D 1288-1289.

Murder Post-Dated (Morice). M&D 1238-1239.

"Murderer, The" (Ignatow). PEng 1470; RevPEng 1682.

Murders in Praed Street, The (Rhode). M&D 1414.

"Murders in the Rue Morgue, The" (Poe). M&D 1334-1335; RevLFEng 3842; ShF 532, 749-750.

Murdoch, Iris. LFEng 1925-1944; LFSup 405; RevLFEng 2436-2457.

Murfree, Mary Noailles. ShF 226-227.

"Murke's Collected Silences" (Böll). RevShF 238; ShF 975-976.

Murmuring Judges (Hare). RevDEng 1115.

Murphy (Beckett). LFEng 209; LFFor 125; RevLFEng 258.

Murphy, Michael. ShF 2739.

Murray, Les A. PSup 288-293; RevPEng 2409-2416.

Murrha (Alfieri). DFor 46.

Murthy, U. R. Anantha. LFFor 2226.

Murtoleide, La (Marino). PFor 975.

Murugan the Tiller (Venkataramani). ShF 643.

Muschg, Adolf. LFFor 2210.

"Muse as Medusa, The" (Sarton). PEng 2462; RevPEng 2866-2867.

"Muse of Water, A" (Kizer). PEng 1621.

"Muse qui est la grâce, La." *See* "Muse Who Is Grace, The."

"Muse Who Is Grace, The" (Claudel). PFor 361. See also *Five Great Odes.*

"Musée Imaginaire" (Montague). RevPEng 2360.

"Muses, The" (Claudel). PFor 360-361. See also *Five Great Odes.*

Muses Are Heard, The (Capote). LFEng 444; RevLFEng 556.

Muses' Elizium, The (Drayton). PEng 855-856; RevPEng 970-971.

Muses of One Mind (Trimpi). LTh 801.

Museum (Dove). RevPEng 957-958.

Museum (Howe). RevDEng 1220-1221.

Music, The (Duras). DFor 511.

"Music" (Gilchrist). RevShF 987-988.

"Music" (Thoreau). PEng 2901; RevPEng 3369.

"Music Master, The" (Allingham). PEng 44; RevPEng 35.

"Music on the Muscatatuck" (West). RevShF 2449; ShFSup 362-363.

"Music School, The" (Updike). RevShF 2754; ShF 798-799, 2374-2375.

"Musician" (Bogan). PEng 237; RevPEng 284.

Musil, Robert. LFFor 1184-1191, 2188, 2194.

"Musk-ox, The" (Leskov). RevShF 1466; ShFSup 158.

Musophilus (Daniel). PEng 729; RevPEng 827, 832-833.

Musset, Alfred de. DFor 1395-1409; LFFor 1489; LTh 1709; PFor 1063-1068, 1869-1870.

Mustapää, P. PFor 2182-2183.

Mustapha (Greville). PEng 1157; RevPEng 1316.

"Muta, La." *See* "Mute, The."

"Mutabilitie Cantos" (Spenser). PEng 2717; RevPEng 3161.

"Mute, The" (Landolfi). RevShF 1397.

"Mute Companions, The" (Narayan). RevShF 1717; ShFSup 226-227.

Mutmassungen über Jakob. See Speculations About Jacob.

Mutter Courage und ihre Kinder. See Mother Courage and Her Children.

Mutwa, Credo V. RevDEng 2942.

Muzeeka (Guare). DEng 862; RevDEng 1056, 1057.

My. See We.

My Ántonia (Cather). LFEng 476-477, 479-480; RevLFEng 589-590, 592-593; RevShF 454; ShF 1569.

"My Belongings" (Endō). RevShF 834-835.

My Bones Being Wiser (Miller). RevPEng 2332-2333.

"My Brother Went to College" (Yerby). ShF 2479-2480.

"My Brother's Hand" (Zoshchenko). RevShF 2560; ShFSup 382.

"My Brunette" (Poliziano). PFor 1255.

My Childhood (Gorky). LFFor 727.

My Children! My Africa! (Fugard). RevDEng 876.

My Client Curley (Corwin and Lucille Fletcher). RevDEng 3030-3031.

My Cousin Rachel (du Maurier). M&D 554.

"My Credo: Verbal Analysis" (Empson). LTh 462.

"My Death" (Strand). PEng 2770; RevPEng 3235.

My Dinner with André (Shawn and Gregory). DSup 337; RevDEng 2170.

"My Expensive Leg" (Böll). RevShF 239.

My Fair Lady (Lerner and Loewe). DEng 2475; RevDEng 3001.

"My Familiar Dream" (Verlaine). PFor 1628.

"My Father Is an Educated Man" (Stuart). RevShF 2235; ShF 2296.

"my father moved through dooms of love" (Cummings). PEng 707-708; RevPEng 798, 799.

"My Father Sits in the Dark" (Weidman). RevShF 2418; ShF 2410.

"My Father's Breasts" (Olds). RevPEng 2492.

"My Father's Garden" (Wagoner). PEng 2992; RevPEng 3480.

"My Father's Ghost" (Wagoner). PEng 2992; RevPEng 3480.

"My Favorite Murder" (Bierce). ShF 740.

"My First Acquaintance with Poets" (Hazlitt). LTh 652.

"My First Cousin" (Dovlatov). RevShF 759-760.

"My First Day as a Painter" (Harrison, J.). PEng 1235; RevPEng 1416.

"My First Goose" (Babel). RevShF 129, 2744-2745.

"My First Tooth" (Shalamov). RevShF 2097; ShFSup 292.

My Friend Hitler (Mishima). DFor 1325-1327.

"My Great-Grandfather's Slaves" (Berry). PEng 150.

My Head! My Head! (Graves, R.). LFEng 1194; RevLFEng 1418.

My Heart and My Flesh (Roberts). LFEng 2282; RevLFEng 2877.

My Heart's in the Highlands (Saroyan). DEng 1655-1656; RevDEng 2065-2066.

"My Heat" (O'Hara). PEng 2125-2126; RevPEng 2476-2478.

"My King" (Michaux). PFor 1000-1001.

"My Kinsman, Major Molineux" (Hawthorne). RevShF 1145-1146, 2657, 2684-2685; ShF 160, 190.

"My Lady Asks Me" (Cavalcanti). PFor 306.

My Lady Clara. See *Dreams.*

"My Last Duchess" (Browning, R.). PEng 339; RevPEng 410.

"My Life" (Strand). PEng 2770.

My Life as a Man (Roth). LFEng 2306-2307; RevLFEng 2900.

"My Life by Somebody Else" (Strand). PEng 2770.

My Life in the Bush of Ghosts (Tutuola). LFFor 1787-1788.

"My Little Utopia" (Simic). PEng 2596.

"My lute awake" (Wyatt). PEng 3177-3178; RevPEng 3701-3702.

"My Marriage to Vengeance" (Leavitt). RevShF 1438.

"My Mother" (Kincaid). RevShF 1342-1343.

"My mother's maids, when they did sew and spin" (Wyatt). PEng 3178-3179; RevPEng 3702-3703.

My Name Is Aram (Saroyan). LFEng 2335-2336; RevLFEng 2946, 2951; RevShF 2060-2061; ShF 2190.

My Name Is Asher Lev (Potok). LFSup 316-317; RevLFEng 2662-2663.

My Next Bride (Boyle, K.). LFEng 276; RevLFEng 341.

"My Oedipus Complex" (O'Connor, Frank). RevShF 1771; ShF 672, 1992-1993.

"My Old Books Closed at the Name of Paphos" (Mallarmé). PFor 927-928.

"My Older Brothers" (Dazai). RevShF 692; ShFSup 93-94.

"My Own Heart Let Me Have More Pity On" (Hopkins). PEng 1402; RevPEng 1611.

My Own Murderer (Hull). M&D 919.

"My Poetry" (Dučić). PFor 432.

"My Religion" (Unamuno). PFor 1556-1557.

"My Sad Captains" (Gunn). PEng 1170, 1175; RevPEng 1332.

My Sad Captains and Other Poems (Gunn). PEng 1169, 1170, 1171; RevPEng 1331-1332.

My Secret History (Theroux). RevLFEng 3287.

My Sister, Life (Pasternak). PFor 1157-1159.

My Sister's Hand in Mine (Bowles, J.). RevShF 273.

"My Sisters, O My Sisters" (Sarton). PEng 2458-2459; RevPEng 2862-2863.

"My Songs" (Petőfi). PFor 1223.

My Soul in China (Kavan). RevShF 1315.

"my sweet old etcetera" (Cummings). PEng 709; RevPEng 800.

My Uncle Dudley (Morris). LFEng 1908; RevLFEng 2416.

My Uncle Silas (Bates). RevShF 174-175; ShF 270-271; ShFSup 31.

My Universities (Gorky). LFFor 727-728.

My Voice Because of You (Salinas). PFor 1387-1388.

My Wife and I (Stowe). LFEng 2564; RevLFEng 3216.

"My Wife and My Sword" (Petőfi). PFor 1226.

"Mycerinus" (Arnold). PEng 50; RevPEng 49.

Myers, George, Jr. ShF 2740.

Myles, Simon. *See* **Follett, Ken.**

"Myopia: A Night" (Lowell, R.). PEng 1792; RevPEng 2086.

Myortvye dushi. See Dead Souls.

Myra Breckenridge (Vidal). RevLFEng 3376-3377.

Myrdal, Jan. LFFor 2362.

Myricae (Pascoli). PFor 1141.

Myrrour for Magistrates, A (Baldwin, W., comp.). RevPEng 3813-3814.

"Myrtho" (Nerval). PFor 1087.

"Myself" (Creeley). PEng 690.

Mysli vrasplokh. See Unguarded Thoughts.

Mystère d'Adam. See Jeu d'Adam, Le.

Mystère de la chambre jaune, Le. See Mystery of the Yellow Room, The.

Mystère de la charité de Jeanne d'Arc, Le. See Mystery of the Charity of Joan of Arc, The.

Mystère de la parole. See Mystery of the Word.

Mystère de la passion, Le (Greban). DFor 2166.

Mystère des saints innocents, Le. See Mystery of the Holy Innocents, The.

Mystères de Paris, Les. See Mysteries of Paris, The.

Mysterier. See Mysteries.

Mysteries (Hamsun). LFFor 2346.

Mysteries of Paris, The (Sue). M&D 1554-1557.

Mysteries of Udolpho, The (Radcliffe). LFEng 2201-2202, 3125-3126; M&D 1392-1393; RevLFEng 2780-2781, 3783, 3824, 3827-3828.

Mysteries of Winterthurn (Oates). RevLFEng 2538-2539.

Mysterious Affair at Styles, The (Christie). LFEng 536-537, 538-539; M&D 348-349; RevLFEng 655, 656.

Mysterious Island, The (Verne). LFFor 1874.

Mysterious Mr. Quin, The (Christie). RevShF 551-552.

Mysterium (Hauge). LFFor 800-802.

Mystery. RevDEng 3044.

Mystery and Manners (O'Connor, Flannery). LFEng 2040; RevLFEng 2574.

Mystery-bouffe (Mayakovsky). DFor 1294-1295; PFor 986, 990.

Mystery of Edwin Drood, The (Dickens). M&D 504-506.

Mystery of High Eldersham, The. See Secret of High Eldersham, The.

"Mystery of Marie Roget, The" (Poe). M&D 1335-133; RevLFEng 3842; ShF 532, 750.

"Mystery of the Blue Jar, The" (Christie). RevShF 550-551.

Mystery of the Cape Cod Players, The (Taylor). M&D 1568.

Mystery of the Charity of Charles Péguy, The (Hill). RevPEng 1527-1528.

Mystery of the Charity of Joan of Arc, The (Péguy). PFor 1180-1181.

"Mystery of the Five Hundred Diamonds, The" (Barr). M&D 92.

Mystery of the Holy Innocents, The (Péguy). PFor 1181-1182.

Mystery of the Word (Hébert). LFFor 806, 809, 815.

Mystery of the Yellow Room, The (Leroux). M&D 1074-1075.

Mystery on Southampton Water (Crofts). M&D 422.

Mystic Masseur, The (Naipaul). LFEng 1959; RevLFEng 2472.

"Myth, Fiction, and Displacement" (Frye). ShF 77.

Myth, Literature, and the African World (Soyinka). LTh 1370.

Myth of Sisyphus, The (Camus). LFFor 251.

"Myth on Mediterranean Beach: Aphrodite as Logos" (Warren). PEng 3024.

Mythistorema (Seferis). PFor 1416, 1962.

Mythologia. See Mythologies, The (Fulgentius).

Mythologies (Barthes). LTh 105.

Mythologies, The (Fulgentius). LTh 514, 518-519.

Mythologiques (Lévi-Strauss). LTh 888.

Mythomystes (Reynolds). LTh 1675.

Myths and Texts (Snyder). PEng 2671-2672; RevPEng 3105.

N

N or M? The New Mystery (Christie). LFEng 541; RevLFEng 658.

"n(o)w/the" (Cummings). PEng 705; RevPEng 796.

N-town Cycle. DEng 2248, 2250-2251; RevDEng 2768, 2770-2771.

"N'a catedral." *See* "In the Cathedral."

Na dne. See *Lower Depths, The.*

Na Drini ćuprija. See *Bridge on the Drina, The.*

"Na kraiu sveta." *See* "At the Edge of the World."

"Na noite terrível." *See* "In the Terror of the Night."

Na pełnym mrozu. See *Out at Sea.*

Na vsyakogo mudretsa dovolno prostoty. See *Scoundrel, The.*

Nabokov, Vladimir. LFEng 1945-1954; LFFor 2328-2329; RevLFEng 2458-2468; RevShF 1699-1707, 2745; ShFSup 215-223.

Nabucco (Niccolini). DFor 1431.

"Nach der Lese." *See* "After the Harvest."

Nachdenken über Christa T. See *Quest for Christa T., The.*

Nachsommer, Der (Stifter). LFFor 1672-1673.

Nacht von Lissabon, Die. See *Night in Lisbon, The.*

Nachtgesänge (Hölderlin). PFor 685-686.

Nada como el piso 16. See *Nothing Like the Sixteenth Floor.*

Nada que ver (Gambaro). DSup 148-149.

"Nadgrobnoe slovo." *See* "Epitaph, An."

Nadja (Breton). LTh 214.

Nadobnisie i koczkodany. See *Dainty Shapes and Hairy Apes.*

Naevius, Gnaeus. DFor 1410-1414, 2139; PFor 2089.

Nagarajan, K. ShF 644.

Naharro, Bartolomé de Torres. *See* **Torres Naharro, Bartolomé de.**

Nahman of Bratslav, Rabbi. RevShF 1708-1714; ShF 1940-1946.

Nahr al-junun. See *River of Madness, The.*

Naidu, Sarojini. PFor 1997-1998; RevPEng 3945.

"Nail, The" (Alarcón). RevShF 40-41; ShF 844-845.

Naipaul, V. S. LFEng 1955-1964; RevLFEng 2469-2479.

Naissance de la clinique. See *Birth of the Clinic, The.*

Naissance de l'Odyssée (Giono). LFFor 654.

Nakanune. See *On the Eve.*

Naked and the Dead, The (Mailer). LFEng 1773-1776, 3064-3065; RevLFEng 2246-2250, 3773.

"Naked and the Nude, The" (Graves). PEng 1128; RevPEng 1285.

Naked King, The (Shvarts). DFor 1698-1700.

Naked Lunch, The (Burroughs). LFEng 384, 387-389; RevLFEng 486, 487.

Naked to the Grave (Carmichael). M&D 264.

Naked Year, The (Pilnyak). LFFor 2323.

Namatianus, Claudius. PFor 2109.

Name of the Rose, The (Eco). M&D 569-572.

Names, The (DeLillo). LFSup 88-89; RevLFEng 866-867.

Names, The (Momaday). PEng 2019; RevPEng 2353-2354.

"Names" (Walcott). PEng 3005.

Names and Faces of Heroes, The (Price). RevShF 1923-1924; ShF 2122-2123, 2126.

Names of Christ, The (León). PFor 841.

"Names of Horses" (Hall). RevPEng 1375.

"Nametracks" (Brathwaite). PEng 272-273; RevPEng 334.

"Naming of Parts" (Reed, H.). PEng 2334, 2338; RevPEng 2725.

Nana (Zola). LFFor 1992-1994. See also *Rougon-Macquart, Les.*

Nan-hsi. DFor 1039, 1042-1043, 1046, 2306, 2308, 2321-2322.

Nanshokuōkagami (Saikaku). RevShF 2030; ShFSup 270.

Nansō Santomi hakkenden (Bakin). LFFor 2270-2273, 2275.

Napasta (Caragiale). DFor 350.

Napis (Herbert). PFor 657, 659.

Napoleon (Grabbe). DFor 805-806.

Napoléon Bonaparte (Dumas, *père*). DFor 487-488.

"Napoleonic Ode, The" (Manzoni). PFor 960-961.

Napoli milionaria! (De Filippo). DFor 469.

Narayan, R. K. LFEng 1965-1972; LFFor 2220-2222; LFSup 405-406; **RevLFEng 2480-2488; RevShF 1715-1720;** ShF 646-647; **ShFSup 224-230.**

Narcejac, Thomas, and **Pierre Boileau. M&D 155-160.**

"Night in the Royal Ontario Museum, A"
(Atwood). PEng 65-66; RevPEng 72.
Night Light (Justice). PEng 1530, 1531; RevPEng
1755-1756.
Night Lodging, A. See *Lower Depths, The.*
Night Mirror, The (Hollander). RevPEng 1549.
'night Mother (Norman). DSup 291-292;
RevDEng 1741-1743.
Night Music (Odets). DEng 1402; RevDEng 1778.
Night Must Fall (Williams, E.). DEng 2061-2063;
RevDEng 2561-2563.
"Night Notes" (Booth). RevPEng 305.
Night Notes (Booth). PEng 243-244.
Night of Snow (Bracco). DFor 226-227.
"Night of the Curlews" (García Márquez). ShF
1454.
Night of the Iguana, The (Williams, T.). DEng
2080-2083; RevDEng 2581-2584; RevShF
2479; ShF 2434-2435.
"Night of the Iguana, The" (Williams, T.).
RevShF 2479, 2480.
Night of the Poor (Prokosch). LFEng 2167;
RevLFEng 2740.
Night of the Twelfth, The (Gilbert, M.). M&D 735.
Night of Wenceslas, The (Davidson). M&D 456.
Night on Bald Mountain (White). DSup 395;
RevDEng 2515.
"Night Owls" (Leskov). RevShF 1469; ShFSup
161.
"Night Ride" (Tomlinson). RevPEng 3380.
Night Rider (Warren). LFEng 2773-2775;
RevLFEng 3439-3440.
"Night Scene Before Combat" (Dugan). RevPEng
1009-1010.
"Night-Sea Journey" (Barth). RevShF 155; ShF
929-930.
"Night Song of a Nomadic Shepherd in Asia"
(Leopardi). PFor 862. See also *Canti.*
"Night Taxi" (Gunn). RevPEng 1336.
"Night Thoughts" (Coulette). RevPEng 691.
Night Thoughts (Young, E.). PEng 3325-3326,
3327; RevPEng 3846.
"Night Thoughts over a Sick Child" (Levine).
PEng 1714; RevPEng 1990.
Night-World (Bloch). M&D 147.
"Nightfall" (Asimov). RevShF 87-88; ShF
878-879.
"Nightingale, The" (Andersen). RevShF 65-66;
ShF 864-865.
Nightmare Abbey (Peacock). LFEng 2082-2083;
RevLFEng 2620-2621.
Nightmare Begins Responsibility (Harper). PSup
164; RevPEng 1403-1404.

"Nightmare by Day" (Untermeyer). PEng 2950;
RevPEng 3418.
Nights and Days (Merrill). RevPEng 2279.
Nights at the Circus (Carter). LFSup 75;
RevLFEng 569-570.
"Night's for Cryin', The" (Himes). ShF 1641.
Nightspawn (Banville). LFSup 44-45; RevLFEng
201-202.
"Nightwalker" (Kinsella). PSup 232-235;
RevPEng 1834-1835, 1836-1837.
Nightwatchmen (Hannah). RevLFEng 1483-1484.
Nightwing (Smith). M&D 1503-1506.
Nihon shoki. See *Chronicles of Japan.*
Niihara, Ryūnosuke. *See* **Akutagawa,
Ryūnosuke.**
"Nikal Seyn" (Coxe). PEng 631-632.
"Nikki-Rosa" (Giovanni). PEng 3400; RevPEng
3908.
"Nile, The" (Hunt). PEng 1464; RevPEng 1675.
Nile, Dorothea. *See* **Avallone, Michael.**
Nils Holgerssons underbara resa genom Sveriga.
See *Further Adventures of Nils, The* and
Wonderful Adventures of Nils, The.
Nimphidia (Drayton). RevPEng 970.
Nims, John Frederick. PEng 2107-2115;
RevPEng 2453-2461.
Nin, Anaïs. LFEng 1986-1997; RevLFEng 2381,
**2510-2522; RevShF 1721-1726; ShF
1947-1952.**
Nine Coaches Waiting (Stewart). M&D
1528-1529.
Nine Days to Mukalla (Prokosch). LFEng 2165;
RevLFEng 2738-2739.
"Nine Monsters, The" (Vallejo). PFor 1592. See
also *Human Poems.*
Nine Stories (Salinger). ShF 290-291, 2176.
Nine Tailors, The (Sayers). LFEng 2359-2361,
3187; M&D 1476; RevLFEng 2975-2977,
3844.
Nineteen, The (Fadeyev). LFFor 2324.
Nineteen Eighty-Four (Orwell). LFEng
2061-2063, 3211; RevLFEng 2597-2599.
1968 (Coulette). RevPEng 689-690.
1919 (Dos Passos). LFEng 796-797; RevLFEng
960-961.
1913 (Sternheim). DFor 1738-1739.
1939 (Boyle, K.) RevLFEng 344; LFEng 279.
"Nineteen Fifty-five" (Walker). RevShF
2382-2383; ShFSup 340.
"95 Theses 95" (Keillor). RevShF 1326-1327.
"99.6" (West). RevShF 2448-2449; ShFSup
361-362.
"90 North" (Jarrell). PEng 1480; RevPEng 1692.

Nonsequences/Selfpoems (Middleton, C.). PEng 1986-1988; RevPEng 2308-2310.

"Noon Wine" (Porter). RevShF 1910.

Noon Wine (Porter). LFEng 2105-2106, 3307-3308; RevLFEng 2653-2654, 3876-3877.

Noonday Demons (Barnes). DSup 12; RevDEng 145.

Noone, Edwina. *See* **Avallone, Michael.**

Nordenflycht, Hedvig Charlotta. PFor 2160.

"Nordsee, Die." *See* "North Sea, The."

Norén, Lars. LFFor 2362; PFor 2194.

"Norfolk sprang thee" (Surrey). PEng 2788-2789; RevPEng 3254-3255.

Norinaga, Motoori. *See* **Motoori Norinaga.**

Norm and Ahmed (Buzo). DEng 320-321; RevDEng 380-381.

Norman, Marsha. DEng 2411; **DSup 288-293; RevDEng 1738-1745,** 2932.

Norman Conquests, The (Ayckbourn). DEng 62, 66; RevDEng 80-81.

Normance. See Féerie pour une autre fois.

Norne-Gæst (Jensen). LFFor 883. See also *Long Journey, The.*

Norris, Frank. LFEng 1998-2006; RevLFEng 2523-2532, 3797; **RevShF 1727-1733;** ShF 234-235, 536-537, **1953-1960.**

North (Heaney). PEng 1264, 1266, 1271-1272, 3369-3370; RevPEng 1447-1448, 3887-3888.

"North, The" (Zamyatin). RevShF 2535-2536; ShFSup 370-371.

North, Anthony. *See* Koontz, Dean R.

North, Howard. *See* **Trevor, Elleston.**

"North American Sequence" (Roethke). PEng 2409; RevPEng 2802.

"North American Time" (Rich). RevPEng 2759.

North and South (Gaskell). LFEng 1100-1101, 1102, 1104-1105, 3165; RevLFEng 1303-1304, 1305, 1307-1308.

"North Central" (Niedecker). PSup 296-297; RevPEng 2445-2446.

"North Light" (Helprin). RevShF 1164-1165.

North of Grand Central (Marquand). LFEng 1818; RevLFEng 2303.

"North Sea, The" (Heine). PFor 649.

North Ship, The (Larkin). PEng 1671; RevPEng 1939.

Northanger Abbey (Austen). LFEng 124-125; RevLFEng 166-167.

"Northern Hoard, A" (Heaney). PEng 1270.

Northern Lass, The (Brome). DEng 285-286; RevDEng 341-342.

Northern Passion. DEng 2247; RevDEng 2767.

"Northhanger Ridge" (Wright, C.). RevPEng 3658.

"Northumberland Bagpipe, The" (D'Urfey). PEng 912.

Norton, Charles Eliot. ShF 587.

Norton, Thomas, and **Thomas Sackville. DEng 1370-1381; RevDEng 1746-1757.**

Norwid, Cyprian Kamil. PFor 2126.

Nosce Teipsum (Davies). PEng 747, 749-750; RevPEng 864, 866-867.

"Nose, The" (Akutagawa). RevShF 35; ShFSup 9.

"Nose, The" (Gogol). RevShF 1019-1020; ShF 715-716, 1496, 1497-1499.

"Nostalgia" (Mukherjee). RevShF 1687.

"Nostalgia" (Viereck). RevPEng 3460.

"Nostalgic and Narrative" (Sissman). PEng 2618; RevPEng 3022.

Nostradamus Traitor, The (Gardner, J.). M&D 697.

Nostri atenti, I. See *Our Ancestors.*

"Not-Being" (Oates). RevPEng 2467.

Not By Bed Alone (Feydeau). DFor 604-606.

Not Honour More (Cary). LFEng 461, 462, RevLFEng 581, 582.

"Not palaces, an era's crown" (Spender). PEng 2697; RevPEng 3141.

Not the Murderer (Werfel). LFFor 1909-1910.

Not to Disturb (Spark). LFEng 2477; RevLFEng 3106.

"Not to Tell Lies" (Booth). RevPEng 305-306.

"Not Waving but Drowning" (Smith, S.). RevPEng 3082-3083.

"Not Writing My Name" (Harrison, J.). PEng 1234-1235; RevPEng 1416.

Notable Discovery of Coosenage, A (Greene, R.). RevShF 1079; ShF 1552.

"Note on Local Flora" (Empson). PEng 970-971; RevPEng 1100.

"Note on the Mystic Writing Pad" (Freud). LTh 359.

Notebook (Lowell, R.). PEng 1795-1796; RevPEng 2090.

Notebook 1967-68 (Lowell, R.). PEng 1795-1796; RevPEng 2088-2090.

Notebooks 1960-1977 (Fugard). DEng 692, 699; RevDEng 861, 868.

"Notes for an Elegy" (Meredith). PEng 1955; RevPEng 2268.

"Notes from a Lady at a Dinner Party" (Malamud). RevShF 1574-1575.

Notes from the Castle (Moss). PEng 2066-2067; RevPEng 2398-2399.

"Notes from the Delivery Room" (Pastan). PEng 2176.

Notes from the Land of the Dead and Other Poems (Kinsella). PSup 235; RevPEng 1837.

Notes from the Underground (Dostoevski). LFEng 3147-3148, 3286-3288; LFFor 508-509; LTh 288, 396; RevShF 2697-2698, 2718; ShF 204-205, 1292-1294.

"Notes from Various Pasts" (Atwood). PEng 65.

"Notes on 'Camp'" (Sontag). LTh 1364.

"Notes on Scottish Song" (Burns). PEng 373; RevPEng 447.

"Notes on the American Short Story Today" (Kostelanetz). ShF 81.

"Notes prises pour un oiseau." *See* "Notes Taken for a Bird."

"Notes Taken for a Bird" (Ponge). PFor 1265.

"Notes Toward Lessons to Be Learned at Thirty" (Oppenheimer). PEng 2145; RevPEng 2515.

"Nothin' to Say" (Riley). PEng 2379; RevPEng 2769.

Nothing (Green). LFEng 1211-1212; RevLFEng 1436-1437.

"Nothing" (Södergran). PSup 365-366.

"Nothing Is Really Hard But to Be Real" (Ciardi). PEng 504; RevPEng 593.

Nothing Like the Sixteenth Floor (Vilalta). DSup 377.

Nothing Like the Sun (Burgess). LFEng 368-369; RevLFEng 467.

Noticen des Feuerwerkers Christopher Magalan, Die (Meckel). RevShF 1643-1644; ShFSup 189.

"Notre Dame" (Mandelstam). PFor 937. See also *Stone.*

"Notre Dame de Chartres" (Meredith). PEng 1955-1956; RevPEng 2270.

Notre-Dame de Paris. See *Hunchback of Notre Dame, The.*

Notre-Dame des Fleurs. See *Our Lady of the Flowers.*

Notte di neve. See *Night of Snow.*

Nourritures terrestres, Les. See *Fruits of the Earth.*

Nouveau Discours du récit (Genette). LTh 563.

Nouveaux Essais de critique et d'histoire (Taine). LTh 1391, 1419-1420.

Nouvelle critique ou nouvelle imposture? See *New Criticism or New Fraud?*

Nouvelle Héloïse, La. See *New Héloïse, The.*

Nouvelles méditations poétiques (Lamartine). PFor 833.

Nov. See *Virgin Soil.*

Nova (Delany). LFEng 718; RevLFEng 854.

Nova Express (Burroughs). LFEng 387-388, 390; RevLFEng 486-487.

Novalis. LFFor 2165, 2166; LTh 437-438, 1697, 1701-1702, 1706, 1709; **PFor 1090-1101,** 1916-1917.

"Novel and the Story—The Long and Short of It, The" (Gold, Herbert). ShF 77.

Novel of Master F. J., The (Gascoigne). RevShF 2626; ShF 489, 490.

Novelas Ejemplares. See *Exemplary Novels, The.*

Novelle (Goethe). LFEng 3239-3242; RevShF 1010; ShFSup 101-102.

Novelle napoletane. See *Neapolitan Short Stores.*

Novellino. ShF 677-678, 680.

Novels and Novelists (Mansfield). ShF 815.

"November" (Pastan). PEng 2173.

"November Cotton Flower" (Toomer). RevShF 2298; ShF 2340-2341.

November 1918 (Döblin). LFFor 478-479.

November Twenty-six, Nineteen Sixty-three (Berry). RevPEng 179.

"Novice, The" (Lermontov). PFor 869, 870.

"Novice, A" (Rossetti, C.). PEng 2420; RevPEng 2813.

Novikov, Nikolay. LTh 1694.

Novius. DFor 2136.

"Novotny's Pain" (Roth). RevShF 2021-2022; ShF 2161-2162.

Novum Organum (Bacon). LTh 76-77.

"Now and Then" (Baraka). ShF 924.

"Now, Dear Me!" (de la Mare). PEng 776.

"Now, Dear Me" (de la Mare). RevPEng 896.

"Now in These Days" (Everson). PEng 988; RevPEng 1119.

Now That April's Here and Other Stories (Callaghan). RevShF 386-388; ShFSup 70-71.

"Now the Sky" (Van Doren). PEng 2958; RevPEng 3436.

Nowhere but Light (Belitt). RevPEng 157-158.

Nowhere City, The (Lurie). LFSup 252-253; RevLFEng 2129-2130.

Noyes, Stanley. ShF 2749.

"NRACP, The" (Elliott). RevShF 818-819; ShF 1345-1347.

Nü Chuang Yüan (Hsü). DFor 2323-2324.

"Nube que trae un viento, La." *See* "Cloud That Bears Wind, The."

Nubes, Las (Cernuda). PFor 321-323.

"Nude" (Guillén). PFor 626.

9, El. See *Number 9.*

"+9 de febrero de 1913" (Reyes). PFor 1320.

"Nueve monstruos, Los." *See* "Nine Monsters, The."

O

O Babylon! (Walcott, D. A.). DEng 2002-2003; RevDEng 2472.

"O Basne i basniakh Krylova" (Zhukovsky). LTh 1612-1613.

O Beulah Land (Settle). LFSup 345-346; RevLFEng 3006-3007. *See also* Beulah Quintet, The.

"O Cheese" (Hall). PEng 1206.

"O Corpo" (Lispector). RevShF 1493.

"O Daedalus, Fly Away Home" (Hayden). PEng 1248; RevPEng 1432.

"O. Genri i teoriia novelly." *See* "O. Henry and the Theory of the Short Story."

"O happy dames, that may embrace" (Surrey). PEng 2788; RevPEng 3254.

"O. Henry and the Theory of the Short Story" (Eikhenbaum). LTh 443; ShF 75.

"O literaturnoy evolyutsii." *See* "On Literary Evolution."

O locura o santidad. See *Folly or Saintliness.*

O noapte furtunoasa. See Stormy Night, A.

Ô Pays, mon beau peuple! (Sembène). LFFor 1538-1540, 2045-2046.

O Pioneers! (Cather). LFEng 478; ShF 1569; RevLFEng 591.

"O poete i sovremennom ego znachenii" (Zhukovsky). LTh 1614.

"O pokolenii, rastrativshem svoikh poetov." See "On a Generation That Squandered Its Poets."

"O repertuare dramatischeskikh teatov i merakh po ego ulucheniiu." *See* "On the Repertoire of the Dramatic Theaters and Measures for Its Improvement."

"O satire i satirakh Kantemira" (Zhukovsky). LTh 1613.

O scrisoare pierduta. See *Lost Letter, The.*

"O Shekspire i o drame." *See* "Shakespeare and the Drama."

"O Sol, di cui questo bel sol è raggio" (Bembo). PFor 167.

"O stepeni uchastiia narodnosti v razvitii russkoi literatury" (Dobrolyubov). LTh 388.

"O Vanke Kaine, slavnom vore i moshennike kratkaya povest." LFFor 2306.

"O Yes" (Olsen). RevShF 1814; ShF 2022.

"O Youth and Beauty" (Cheever). RevShF 502-503.

"O zhurnalnoy kritike." *See* "On Journal Criticism."

O-Zone (Theroux). RevLFEng 3287.

"Oaks, The" (Castro). PFor 280. See also *Beside the River Sar.*

Ōan shinshiki. See *Renga shinshiki.*

"O-A-O-A" (Sachs). PFor 1375-1376.

Oasis, The (McCarthy, M.). LFEng 1721-1722; RevLFEng 2152.

Oates, Joyce Carol. LFEng 2007-2016; LFSup 406; PEng 2116-2121; PSup 408; RevLFEng 2533-2541; RevPEng 2462-2472; RevShF 1734-1743, 2753, 2754-2755; ShF 552, 1961-1968; ShFSup 389.

Oath, The (Wiesel). LFFor 1927-1928.

Obaka san. See *Wonderful Fool.*

Obermann (Senancour). LFFor 2123-2124.

Oberon (Weber). DEng 2460; RevDEng 2984.

"Obit" (Lowell, R.). PEng 1796; RevPEng 2090.

"Object of Virtue" (Hale, N.). RevShF 1097; ShF 1570.

"Objects and Apparitions" (Paz). PEng 184.

"Oblako, ozero, bashnya." *See* "Cloud, Castle, Lake."

Oblako v shtanakh. See *Cloud in Pants, A.*

Oblivion Ha-Ha, The (Tate, J.). PEng 2836; RevPEng 3307-3308.

Oblomov (Goncharov). LFFor 705-707, 2315-2316; LTh 389.

"Oblong Box, The" (Poe). M&D 1333-1334.

"Oblong Room, The" (Hoch). RevShF 1209.

Oboler, Arch. RevDEng 3030-3031.

Obra gruesa (Parra). PFor 1134.

Obrestad, Tor. LFFor 2363-2364; PFor 2195.

O'Brien, Edna. LFEng 2017-2023; RevLFEng 2542-2550; RevShF 1744-1750; ShF 1969-1976; ShFSup 390.

O'Brien, Edward J., 2643-2644, 2676; ShF 561.

O'Brien, Fitz-James. RevShF 1751-1755; ShF 1977-1981.

O'Brien, Flann. LFEng 2024-2032; ShF 666; RevLFEng 2551-2559.

O'Brien, Kate. RevLFEng 2560-2566.

O'Brien, Tim. RevShF 2760.

Obryv. See *Precipice, The.*

Obscene Bird of Night, The (Donoso). LFFor 498-500.

Obsceno pájaro de la noche, El. See *Obscene Bird of Night, The.*

"Observance" (Berry). PEng 149.

"Of the lady who can sleep when she pleases" (Waller). PEng 3013-3014; RevPEng 3510-3511.

"Of the last verses in the book" (Waller). PEng 3017; RevPEng 3514.

"Of the Monastic Life" (Rilke). PFor 1330. See also *Book of Hours, The.*

"Of the Muse" (Sarton). PEng 2464; RevPEng 2868.

Of the Progress of the Soule (Donne). PEng 834, 835; RevPEng 940.

Of Thee I Sing (Kaufman and Ryskind). DEng 1032-1034; RevDEng 1300-1302.

Of Time and the River (Wolfe). LFEng 2934-2936; RevLFEng 3630-3631, 3634-3636.

Of Women and Their Elegance (Mailer). LFEng 1785; RevLFEng 2258.

O'Faolain, Seán. RevShF 1783-1790, 2673; ShF 177, 253, 666, 669-670, 671-672, 673-674, 1996-2004; ShFSup 390.

"Off the Trail" (Snyder). RevPEng 3110.

Offending the Audience (Handke). DFor 858-859.

"Offering for Mr. Bluehart, An" (Wright, James). PEng 3160-3161; RevPEng 3672-3673.

"Offerings" (Mason). RevShF 1619-1620.

"Office Romances" (Trevor). RevShF 2307; ShFSup 322.

Officers and Gentlemen (Waugh). LFEng 2801-2802; RevLFEng 3469.

Oficio de tinieblas, 5 (Cela). LFFor 299-300.

O'Flaherty, Liam. RevShF 1791-1798; ShF 253, 669-671, 2005-2012; ShFSup 390.

"Often I Am Permitted to Return to a Meadow" (Duncan). PEng 902; RevPEng 1039.

Ogier, François. LTh 310.

Ogiwara Seisensui. PFor 2076.

Ognall, Leopold Horace. *See* Carmichael, Harry.

"Ogni bol'shogo goroda." *See* "Big-City Lights."

Ogniem i mieczem. See *With Fire and Sword.*

"Ogon', ty slyshish'." *See* "Fire Is Dying Down, The."

Ogre, The (Tournier). LFFor 1743-1745.

Oh Dad, Poor Dad, Mamma's Hung You in the Closet and I'm Feelin' So Sad (Kopit). DEng 1070-1071; RevDEng 1349-1350.

"Oh, I could laugh to hear the midnight wind" (Lamb). PEng 1634; RevPEng 1898.

"Oh Thy Bright Eyes Must Answer Now" (Brontë). PEng 297-298; RevPEng 363-364.

"Oh, Welcome May" (Poliziano). PFor 1254-1255.

"Oh! were my Love" (Allingham). PEng 41-42; RevPEng 32.

Oh What a Paradise It Seems (Cheever). LFEng 502; RevLFEng 625-626.

"Oh, Whistle, and I'll Come to You, My Lad" (James, M. R.). RevShF 1271-1272; ShF 1691-1693.

O'Hara, Frank. PEng 191-192, 2122-2129; RevPEng 2473-2481.

O'Hara, John. LFEng 2041-2054; RevLFEng 2576-2590; RevShF 1799-1805; ShF 267, 546-547, 2013-2019.

Ohio State Murders, The (Kennedy). RevDEng 1309.

Ohmann, Richard. RevPEng 3987; PEng 3452.

Ohrfeige und Sonstiges, Eine. See *Slap in the Face et cetera, A.*

Oidipous epi Kolōnōi. See *Oedipus at Colonus.*

Oidipous Tyrannos. See *Oedipus Tyrannus.*

"Oil of Dog" (Bierce). M&D 127-128.

"Oiseau blanc, L'." *See* "White Bird, The."

Oiseaux. See *Birds.*

"Oiseaux sont en neige" (Cocteau). PFor 371. See also *Vocabulaire.*

Ojciec zadżumionych. See *Father of the Plague-Stricken, The.*

Ojos de los enterrados, Los. See *Eyes of the Interred, The.*

Okhlopkov, Nikolai. DEng 2238-2239.

Okigbo, Christopher, 3947.

Oklahoma! (Rodgers and Hammerstein). DEng 1591, 1595, 2471; RevDEng 1995, 1999, 2997.

Økland, Einar. LFFor 2364; PFor 2195.

Okno bez krat (Slonimski). PFor 1434.

Okri, Ben. RevShF 1806-1811.

Oktave (Pavlović). PFor 1165.

Oku no hosomichi. See *Narrow Road to the Deep North, The.*

Ōkuma Kotomichi. PFor 2073.

Okura, Yamanoe no. *See* Yamanoe no Okura.

Ōkura Toraaki. LTh 1789.

Okuretekita seinen (Ōe). LFFor 1195-1197.

Olav Audunssøn. See *Master of Hestviken, The.*

"Old Address, The" (Kavan). RevShF 1314.

Old and New Poems (Hall). RevPEng 1377.

Old and the Young, The (Pirandello). LFFor 1302.

"Old Apple Tree, The" (Dunbar, P.). PSup 117-118; RevPEng 1019-1020.

"Old Apple Trees" (Snodgrass). RevPEng 3094.

Old Bachelor, The (Congreve). DEng 402-404; RevDEng 501-503.

Old Cap. Collier Library. ShF 759.

Old Creole Days (Cable). ShF 225, 534, 616.

Old Devils, The (Amis, K.). RevLFEng 90, 95-98.

"Old Doc Rivers" (Williams, W. C.). RevShF 2487; ShF 2442-2443.

Old English Apollonius of Tyre, The. LFFor 2014-2015.

Old English Peep Show, The (Dickinson). M&D 511.

"Old Familiar Faces, The" (Lamb). PEng 1635; RevPEng 1899.

"Old Fashioned Cincinnati Blues, The" (Young). PEng 3215; RevPEng 3739.

"Old Fools, The" (Larkin). PEng 1675; RevPEng 1943.

Old Fortunatus (Dekker). PEng 767-768; RevPEng 886-887.

"Old Friends" (Endō). RevShF 838.

"Old Gods, The" (Kizer). RevPEng 1855.

"Old Gypsy, The" (Vörösmarty). PFor 1669.

"Old Halvorson Place, The" (Woiwode). RevShF 2495.

Old Heads and Young Hearts (Boucicault). DEng 268; RevDEng 311.

Old House in the Country, The (Reese). PEng 2346; RevPEng 2733.

"Old Ironsides" (Holmes). PEng 1371-1372; RevPEng 1560-1561.

"Old King, The" (de la Mare). PEng 775-776; RevPEng 895.

Old Man (Gorky). DFor 785.

"Old Man and Jim, The" (Riley). PEng 2379-2380; RevPEng 2769-2770.

Old Man and the Sea, The (Hemingway). LFEng 1339, 1347-1348, 3061-3062, 3272-3274; RevLFEng 1605-1607, 3769-3770, 3875.

Old Man Dies, The (Simenon). LFFor 1600.

Old Man Rubbing His Eyes (Bly). PEng 225.

Old Man Savarin and Other Stories. ShF 636.

"Old Man's Journey" (MacLeish). PEng 1859; RevPEng 2159.

"Old Manuscript, An" (Kafka). ShF 1732.

"Old Master, The" (O'Faolain). RevShF 1784-1785.

Old Men at the Zoo, The (Wilson, Angus). LFEng 2903-2904; RevLFEng 3593-3594.

"Old Morality, The" (Fuentes). RevShF 927.

"Old Mortality" (Porter). RevShF 1909-1910, 2732.

Old Mortality (Porter). LFEng 2104-2105; RevLFEng 2652-2653; ShF 13.

Old Mortality (Scott). LFEng 2371-2373; RevLFEng 2989-2991.

"Old Neighborhood, The" (Dreiser). RevShF 777-778; ShF 1309-1310.

"Old Night and Sleep" (Dubie). PSup 107; RevPEng 1003.

Old Ones, The (Wesker). DEng 2018-2019; RevDEng 2508-2509.

"Old Order, The" (Porter). RevShF 1911.

Old Saint Paul's (Ainsworth). LFEng 31-32; RevLFEng 45-46.

"Old Swimmin'-Hole, The" (Riley). PEng 2381-2382; RevPEng 2771-2772.

"Old Town" (Saba). PSup 347.

"Old Trip by Dream Train, The" (Galvin). PEng 1057; RevPEng 1190.

Old Tune, The (Pinget). DSup 305.

"Old Vicarage, Grantchester, The" (Brooke). PEng 304-305; RevPEng 370-371.

Old Wives' Tale, The (Bennett). LFEng 242-244; RevLFEng 296-297.

Old Wives' Tale, The (Peele). DEng 1492-1494; RevDEng 1876-1878.

Old Woman, The (Godwin). LFSup 137-138.

"Old Woman, The" (O'Flaherty). ShF 2009.

Old Woman Broods, The (Różewicz). DFor 1585-1586.

"Old Woman Izergil" (Gorky). RevShF 1047.

Oldest Living Graduate, The (Jones, P.). DEng 1010-1011; RevDEng 1277-1278. See also *Texas Trilogy, A.*

Oldest Olafs saga helga. See *St. Olaf's Saga.*

Oldham, John. PEng 2130-2135; RevPEng 2482-2488.

Olds, Sharon. RevPEng 2489-2494.

Oldtown Folks (Stowe). LFEng 2563-2564; RevLFEng 3215-3216.

Ole Bienkopp (Strittmatter). LFFor 2203.

Oleanna (Mamet). RevDEng 1567-1568.

Olesha, Yury. LFFor 2322-2323.

"Olga Poems" (Levertov). PEng 1706-1708, 1709, 1710; RevPEng 1983-1984.

Olimpia. See *Olympia.*

Olimpia, L' (Della Porta). DFor 477.

Olimpiade, L'. See *Olympiad, The.*

Olinger Stories (Updike). ShF 2367-2368.

Oliver Twist (Dickens, C.). LFEng 3077; RevLFEng 3786.

Olives, The. See *Deleitoso, El.*

Olney Hymns (Cowper). PEng 610; RevPEng 719.

Olor Iscanus (Vaughan). PEng 2971-2972; RevPEng 3450-3451.

Olsen, Tillie. RevShF 1812-1817; ShF 2020-2024.

Olson, Charles. LTh 1072-1078, 1160; PEng 60, 3378; PSup 303-312. RevPEng 2495-2504, 3884-3885, 3896.

Olson, Elder. LTh 1755, 1817.

Olson, Toby. ShF 2750.

"On the Morning of Christ's Nativity" (Milton). PEng 2006-2007; RevPEng 2339-2340.

On the Motion and Immobility of Douve (Bonnefoy). PSup 44-45.

"On the Move" (Gunn). PEng 1171-1172, 1176; RevPEng 1331.

On the Nature of Things. See De rerum natura.

On the Origin of Species (Darwin). PEng 3348.

On the Principles of Human Action (Hazlitt). LTh 798.

"On the Puppet Theatre" (Kleist). LFEng 3247-3248.

"On the Receipt of My Mother's Picture Out of Norfolk" (Cowper). PEng 613-615; RevPEng 720-721.

"On the Repertoire of the Dramatic Theaters and Measures for Its Improvement" (Zhdanov). LTh 1603.

On the Road (Kerouac). LFEng 1520-1522, 1524; RevLFEng 1865-1867, 3808.

"On the Road to San Romano" (Breton). PFor 234.

"On the Short Story" (Canby). ShF 72-73.

On the Sublime (Longinus). LTh 904-909, 1596, 1642, 1679-1680; PEng 3466-3467; RevPEng 4009-4010.

On the Sublime (Schiller). LTh 1298-1299.

"On the Supernatural in Poetry" (Radcliffe). ShF 472.

"On the Teaching of Modern Literature" (Trilling). LTh 1455.

"On the Tram" (Kafka). ShF 1734.

On the Twofold Abundance of Words and Things. See De Duplici Copia Verborum ac Rerum.

"On the Universality and Other Attributes of the God of Nature" (Freneau). PEng 1036-1037; RevPEng 1167-1169.

"On the Violence of Self-Death" (Oates). RevPEng 2468.

"On the Walpole Road" (Freeman). ShF 370-371.

"On this auspicious, memorable morn" (Byrom). PEng 395-396.

"On Trains" (McPherson). ShF 582-583.

"On Wit and Humour" (Hazlitt). LTh 653.

On World Government (Dante). PFor 390.

On Your Toes (Rodgers and Hart, L.). DEng 903-904; RevDEng 1126-1127.

Once and Future King, The (White, T.). RevLFEng 3862

Once in a Lifetime (Kaufman and Hart, M.). DEng 908-909; RevDEng 1131-1132.

"Once Only" (Seifert). PSup 354.

"Once-Over, The" (Blackburn). PEng 199; RevPEng 243.

Once Removed (Machado). RevDEng 1531.

Oncle Charles s'est enfermé (Simenon). LFFor 1598-1599.

Onde estivertes de noite (Lispector). RevShF 1492-1493; ShFSup 168.

"Ondes." See "Waves."

"Ondine" (Barnard). PSup 28-29; RevPEng 111-112.

"1(a" (Cummings). PEng 705; RevPEng 796.

"One Against Thebes" (Gordon). RevShF 1041-1042; ShF 1521-1522.

"One Arm" (Kawabata). RevShF 1321-1322.

"One Arm" (Williams, T.). RevShF 2483-2484; ShF 2438-2439.

"One Autumn Night" (Gorky). RevShF 1048.

"One Bone to Another" (Popa). PFor 1270.

One Day, The (Hall). RevPEng 1376.

One Day in the Life of Ivan Denisovich (Solzhenitsyn). LFFor 1636-1637, 1642-1643, 2327-2328.

"One Evening at Home" (Petőfi). PFor 1218.

One Flew over the Cuckoo's Nest (Kesey). LFEng 1526, 1532 1534; RevLFEng 1877-1879, 3808.

One Foot in the Grave (Dickinson). M&D 513.

One for My Dame (Webb). M&D 1692-1693.

"One for the Road" (King). RevShF 1347.

"One Holy Night" (Cisneros). RevShF 559-560.

158-Pound Marriage, The (Irving, J.). LFEng 1420-1421; RevLFEng 1697-1698.

150,000,000 (Mayakovsky). PFor 989-990.

One Hundred More Poems from the Japanese (Rexroth, trans.). PFor 1716.

One Hundred Years of Solitude (García Márquez). LFFor 617-619.

"One-Legged Man, The" (Sassoon). PEng 2472; RevPEng 2878.

One Lonely Night (Spillane). M&D 1511.

One Million Dead (Gironella). LFFor 663-665.

£1,000,000 Bank Note, The (Twain). RevShF 2328-2329; ShF 2363.

One, None and a Hundred-Thousand (Pirandello). LFFor 1305-1306.

One O'Clock! (Lewis). DEng 1137-1139; RevDEng 1429-1431.

One of Life's Slaves (Lie). LFFor 2341.

One of Our Girls (Howard, B.). DEng 971; RevDEng 1208.

One of Ours (Cather). LFEng 480; RevLFEng 590, 593.

"One of These Days" (Garcia Márquez). ShF 702-704.

One Sentence on Tyranny (Illyés). PFor 742, 744.

"Orchards, The" (Thomas). RevShF 2269; ShF 2324.

Orchestra (Davies). PEng 747, 750-753, 754, 3290; RevPEng 864, 865, 867-870.

Orczy, Baroness. M&D 1279-1285; ShF 752-753.

Ordeal of Richard Feverel, The (Meredith). LFEng 1865-1867; RevLFEng 2361-2363.

"Ordeal of the Bier" (Arany). PFor 82.

Order, The (Hochwälder). DFor 931-932.

"Order of Insects" (Gass). RevShF 980; ShF 1480.

Orderly Life, An (Yglesias). LFEng 2997-2999; RevLFEng 3703-3705.

Ordet. See *Word, The.*

"Ordinance of Wine" (Neruda). PFor 1076. See also *Residence on Earth.*

Ordinary Life, An (Čapek). LFFor 278.

Ordinary Love (Smiley). RevShF 2148-2149.

Ördög, Az. See *Devil, The.*

Oreach Nata Lalun. See *Guest for the Night, A.*

"Oread" (H. D.). PEng 1257-1261, 1262; RevPEng 1350-1356.

Oregon Message, An (Stafford). RevPEng 3172-3173.

Oresteia (Aeschylus). DFor 20-21, 2101, 2103.

Orestes (Euripides). DFor 2117.

Orestēs (Rítsos). PFor 1970.

Orfalea, Greg. ShF 2752.

Orfeo (Poliziano). DFor 2394; PFor 1249, 1251-1252, 2011.

"Orgy: An Idyll, The" (de la Mare). RevShF 698; ShF 1252.

Oriani, Alfredo. LFFor 2238.

Oricellari, Orti. LTh 1459.

Orientales, Les (Hugo). PFor 733.

Origen. LTh 1644.

"Origin of Sadness, The" (Morris). RevShF 1681-1682; ShFSup 206.

Origin of the Brunists, The (Coover). LFEng 620-621; RevLFEng 751-752.

"Origin of the Praise of God, The" (Bly). RevPEng 272-273.

Original Child Bomb (Merton). PEng 1976; RevPEng 2294.

"Origins" (Walcott). RevPEng 3497.

"Orion" (Rich). RevPEng 2755.

Orison (Arrabal). DFor 2261.

Örkény, István. DSup 294-301.

Orlandino (Edgeworth). ShF 1329.

Orlando furioso (Ariosto). LTh 131, 366, 584, 1662; PFor 97-100, 2012-2014; ShF 138.

Orlando Furioso (Greene, R.). DEng 839-840; RevDEng 1034-1035.

Orlando innamorato (Boiardo). PFor 97-98, 2012-2013.

Orléans, Charles d'. *See* **Charles d'Orléans.**

Orley Farm (Trollope). LFEng 2654-2656; RevLFEng 3310-3312.

Orlock, Carol. ShF 2753.

"Orlov Married Couple" (Gorky). RevShF 1048.

Ormond (Edgeworth, M.). LFEng 867-868; RevLFEng 1023-1024, 1028-1029.

Ornithes. See *Birds, The.*

Ørnsbro, Jess. PFor 2196.

Oroonoko (Behn). DEng 168-170; LFEng 222, 301; RevDEng 204, 206; RevLFEng 270, 272, 3727; ShF 502.

Oroonoko (Southerne). DEng 2451; RevDEng 2976.

Orphan, The (Otway). DEng 1440-1441, 1449-1450; RevDEng 1820-1821, 1829-1830.

Orphan, The (Rabe). DEng 1549-1550; RevDEng 1941-1942.

Orphan Island (Macaulay). LFSup 261; RevLFEng 2138.

"Orpheus" (Snodgrass). PEng 2659; RevPEng 3088.

Orr, Gregory. PEng 2148-2155; PSup 408; RevPEng 2518-2525.

Orrego Luco, Luis. LFFor 2286-2287.

Orrie's Story (Berger). RevLFEng 315.

Országh-Hviezdoslav, Pavol. DFor 2285.

Ortadirek. See *Wind from the Plain, The.*

Ortega y Gasset, José. LFEng 3224-3225; LTh 194.

Orthodoxy (Chesterton). PEng 496.

Ortiz, Simon, 3935.

Orton, Joe. DEng 1418-1427; RevDEng 1796-1806.

O'Ruddy, The (Crane and Barr). LFEng 646; RevLFEng 779.

Örvar-Odds saga. LFFor 2333.

Orwell, George. LFEng 2055-2064; PEng 1699-1700; RevLFEng 2591-2601, 3798.

Orzeszkowa, Eliza. LFFor 2063.

Osanai Kaoru. DFor 2432-2433.

Osborn, Carolyn. ShF 2754.

Osborne, John. DEng 1428-1437, 2385-2386; RevDEng 1807-1817, 2903-2904.

"Oskar" (Walser, R.). RevShF 2390; ShFSup 347.

Osman (Gundulić). PFor 2260-2261.

Osman (Tristan). DFor 1893-1895.

Ossi di seppia. See *Bones of the Cuttlefish.*

Ossian. LTh 669-671.

Ossian tales (Macpherson). PEng 3329.

"Ostanovka v pustyne." *See* "Halt in the Wilderness, A."

Osterman Weekend, The (Ludlum). M&D 1107.

Östersjöar. See *Baltics.*

Ostrekoff Jewels, The (Oppenheim). M&D 1275.

"Ostrov Borngolm." *See* "Song of Bornholm, The."

Ostrovityane. See *Islanders, The.*

Ostrovsky, Alexander. DFor 1443-1452, 2454.

Osudy dobrého vojáka Švejka ve světove války. See *Good Soldier Schweik, The.*

O. T. (Andersen). LFFor 2336.

Otero, Blas de. PFor 1109-1118.

Otfrid von Weissenburg. PFor 1897.

Othello (Shakespeare). DEng 1717-1719, 2281, 2282; RevDEng 2131-2133, 2801.

Other, The (Unamuno y Jugo). DFor 1914-1915.

Other Inquisitions (Borges). LTh 192.

Other Karen, The (Johnston). M&D 940.

"Other Kingdom" (Forster). RevShF 887-888; ShF 1388-1389, 1390-1391.

Other Men's Daughters (Stern). LFSup 364-365; RevLFEng 3167-3168.

"Other Paris, The" (Gallant). RevShF 939-940; ShF 1438-1439.

Other Paris, The (Gallant). LFEng 1052-1053; RevLFEng 1250-1251.

Other People (Amis, M.). RevLFEng 103-104.

Other Side of the River, The (Wright, C.). RevPEng 3662-3663.

Other Times (Lawler). DEng 1117; RevDEng 1397. See also *Doll Trilogy, The.*

"Other Two, The" (Wharton). ShF 707.

"Other Voices, The" (Hogan). RevPEng 1543.

Other Voices, Other Rooms (Capote). LFEng 444, 445-446, 447-448; RevLFEng 556, 557-558.

"Other Way, The" (Grau). RevShF 1058; ShF 1531.

"Other World, The" (Zhang Jie). RevShF 2544-2545.

Other Worlds (Cyrano). LFFor 396-403.

Otherwise Engaged (Gray). DEng 809-811; RevDEng 1002-1004.

Ōtomo no Tabito. PFor 2057.

Ōtomo no Yakamochi. PFor 2057-2058.

Otoño del patriarca, El. See *Autumn of the Patriarch, The.*

Otras inquisiciones. See *Other Inquisitions.*

Otro, El. See *Other, The.*

Ottar Trallings leftnads-målning (Cederborgh). LFFor 2335.

"Ottawa Valley, The" (Munro). RevShF 1695; ShFSup 211-212.

"Otto and the Magi" (Connell). RevShF 602-603; ShF 1181.

8 anime in una bomba (Marinetti). LTh 223, 859, 996.

Ottsy i deti. See *Fathers and Sons.*

Otuel. RevShF 2616; ShF 445.

Otway, Thomas. DEng 1438-1452. RevDEng 1818-1833.

Otzhitoye vremya. See *Case, The.*

Our Ancestors (Calvino). LFFor 237, 238.

Our Betters (Maugham). DEng 1309-1310; RevDEng 1638-1639.

"Our Bog Is Dood" (Smith, S.). RevPEng 3080.

Our Country's Good (Wertenbaker). RevDEng 2499-2500.

"Our Cousin, Mr. Poe" (Tate). LTh 1428.

"Our English Syllabus" (Lewis). LTh 896.

Our Father's Failing (Horovitz). DEng 962; RevDEng 1197-1198.

Our Flowers & Nice Bones (Middleton, C.). PEng 1988-1989; RevPEng 2310-2311.

Our Gang (Roth). LFEng 2304; RevLFEng 2900.

Our Husband Has Gone Mad Again (Rotimi). DEng 1624-1625, 1629; RevDEng 2031, 2035.

Our Lady of the Flowers (Genet). LFFor 628-629.

Our Late Night (Shawn). DSup 335; RevDEng 2168.

Our Mrs. McChesney (Ferber and Hobart). DEng 586, 589; RevDEng 729, 732.

Our Mutual Friend (Dickens, C.). LFEng 754-755; RevLFEng 912-913.

"Our Story Begins" (Wolff). RevShF 2507.

Our Time Is Gone. See Fury Chronicle, The.

Our Town (Wilder). DEng 2046-2049; RevDEng 2546-2548.

Ours: A Russian Family Album (Dovlatov). RevShF 757-758, 760.

Ours (Robertson). DEng 1608-1609; RevDEng 2012-2013.

"Ourselves or Nothing, 1159.

Oursler, Fulton. *See* **Abbot, Anthony.**

Ousmane Sembène. *See* **Sembène, Ousmane.**

Out at Sea (Mrożek). DFor 1381.

Out of Africa (Dinesen). ShF 1281.

Out of His Head (Aldrich). M&D 12; ShF 750-751.

"Out of Lycophron" (Sedley). PEng 2507; RevPEng 2916.

"Out-of-the-Body Travel" (Plumly). PEng 2237.

Out-of-the-Body Travel (Plumly). PEng 2237-2238; RevPEng 2605-2606, 2609.

"Out of the Cradle Endlessly Rocking" (Whitman). PEng 3071; RevPEng 3558.

Out of the Shelter (Lodge). RevLFEng 2091.
Out of the Silent Planet (Lewis, C. S.). LFEng 1654-1655, RevLFEng 2046.
Outcast, The (Pirandello). LFFor 1301.
"Outcasts of Poker Flat, The" (Harte). RevShF 1131-1134; ShF 587, 594-595, 1594-1597.
Outcry, The (James, H.). DEng 995; RevDEng 1260-1262.
Outer Dark (McCarthy, C.). LFSup 267-268; RevLFEng 2145.
"Outlaw, The" (Heaney). PEng 1269.
Outlyer and Ghazals (Harrison, J.). PEng 1229-1231; RevPEng 1410-1412.
"Outpost of Progress, An" (Conrad). RevShF 608.
"Outside" (Lorde). RevPEng 2044.
"Outsider, The" (Lovecraft). RevShF 1508-1509; ShF 1822.
Outsider, The (Sabato). LFFor 1464-1465.
Outsider, The (Wright, R.). LFEng 2981-2983; RevLFEng 3686-3688.
Outsider in Amsterdam (van de Wetering). M&D 1629-1631.
Ou-yang Hsiu. PFor 1788.
"Oval Portrait, The" (Poe). ShF 474.
"Ove romita e stanca si sedea" (Bembo). PFor 167-168.
Over ævne, annet stykke. See Beyond Our Power.
Over ævne, første stykke. See Pastor Sang.
"Over Colorado" (Walcott). PEng 3005.
"Over Sir John's Hill" (Thomas, D.). PEng 2886-2887; RevPEng 3353-3355.
"Over the Carnage Rose Prophetic a Voice" (Whitman). PEng 3072; RevPEng 3559.
"Over the Rivers That Flow" (Camões). PFor 262.
"Over 2000 Illustrations and a Complete Concordance" (Bishop). PEng 185-186; RevPEng 228.
"Overcoat, The" (Gogol). RevShF 1019, 2666, 2682.
Overcoat, The (Gogol). LFEng 3267, 3276-3278; ShF 120, 187-188.
"Overcoat II, The" (Boyle, T.). RevShF 294-295.
Overholser, Stephen D. LFEng 3198; RevLFEng 3855.
Overkomplet, En (Drachmann). LFFor 2339.
Overlaid (Davies). DEng 468; RevDEng 578.

Øverland, Arnulf. PFor 2183.
Overland Monthly. ShF 587.
Overskou, Thomas. DFor 2469.
Overstreet, Bonaro. RevShF 2715.
Overture to Death (Marsh). M&D 1192.
Ovid. LTh 1654; **PFor 1119-1128,** 1282, 1283, 2097; **RevShF 1818-1827,** 2567; **ShF 2025-2034.**
"Ovid in the Third Reich" (Hill). RevPEng 1523.
Ovid's Banquet of Sence (Chapman). PEng 458-460; RevPEng 553-554.
Ovonramwen Nogbaisi (Rotimi). DEng 1625, 1626-1627; RevDEng 2032-2033.
"Ovtsebyk." *See* "Musk-ox, The."
Owen, Philip. *See* **Pentecost, Hugh.**
Owen, Wilfred. PEng 2156-2163; RevPEng 2526-2533.
Owens, Rochelle. DEng 1453-1462; RevDEng 1834-1844.
Owl Answers, The (Kennedy). DSup 214-215; RevDEng 1306-1307.
"Owl King, The" (Dickey, J.). PEng 796.
Ox-Bow Incident, The (Clark). LFEng 545-546, 548-550; RevLFEng 662, 663, 666-667; ShF 607.
"Ox Cart, The" (Petőfi). PFor 1221.
"Oxenhope" (Warner). RevShF 2407; ShFSup 357-358.
Oxford Blood (Fraser). M&D 658.
Oxherding Tale (Johnson, C.). RevLFEng 1765-1766.
"Oxychloride X" (Oboler). RevDEng 3031.
Oxyrhynchus (MacLennan). LFEng 1741; RevLFEng 2210.
Oyono-Mbia. DFor 2268, 2270-2271.
"Oyster, The" (Ponge). PFor 1263, 1264.
Ozaki, Hōsai. PFor 2076.
Ozhog. See Burn, The.
Ozick, Cynthia. RevShF 1828-1834, 2757; **ShF 2035-2039;** ShFSup 390.
Ozidi (Clark-Bekederemo). DSup 57-58; RevDEng 454-456.
Ozu Norinaga. *See* **Motoori Norinaga.**
"Ozymandias" (Shelley). PEng 1608; RevPEng 1848.

P

P., W. S. *See* **Henry, O.**
Pa Chin. LFFor 2107.
Pabellón de reposo. See *Rest Home.*
Pachmuss, Temira. LFEng 3297-3298.
Packer, Nancy Huddleston. ShF 2755.
Pact with Satan, A (Holton). M&D 902.
Pacuvius, Marcus. DFor 2146.
Padmasambhava. PFor 2242.
Padrona, La (Betti). DFor 207-208.
"Paean to Place" (Niedecker). PSup 299-300;
　RevPEng 2446-2447, 2448-2449.
"Paese infido" (Calvino). ShF 1044.
Paesi tuoi. See *Harvesters, The.*
Pagan Place, A (O'Brien, E.). LFEng 2021;
　RevLFEng 2546.
"Pagan Rabbi, The" (Ozick). RevShF 1829-1831.
Pagan Salute (Radnóti). PFor 1312.
Page, Thomas Nelson. ShF 616.
"Page d'écriture" (Prévert). PFor 1278.
Pagenstreiche (Kotzebue). DFor 1087-1088.
"Pages from Cold Point" (Bowles, P.). RevShF
　278.
Paige, Richard. See **Koontz, Dean R.**
Pai-mao mü. See *White-Haired Girl, The.*
"Pain, Le." See "Loaf of Bread, The."
"Pain for a Daughter" (Sexton). PEng 2524-2525;
　RevPEng 2934-2935.
"Painful Case, A" (Joyce). RevShF 1295, 1297;
　ShF 1722.
Painted Bird, The (Kosinski). LFEng 1559-1561;
　RevLFEng 1921-1923.
Painted Face, The (Stubbs). M&D 1549-1551.
Painted Lady, The (Sagan). LFFor 1478.
"Painted Skin, The" (P'u Sung-ling). RevShF
　1948-1950; ShFSup 246-248.
"Painter Dreaming in the Scholar's House, The"
　(Nemerov). PEng 2088.
Painter of His Dishonor, The (Calderón). DFor
　308-309.
Painter of Signs, The (Narayan). LFEng 1971;
　RevLFEng 2486.
Painting Churches (Howe). RevDEng 1221-1222.
"Painture" (Lovelace). PEng 1761; RevPEng
　2054.
Pair of Drawers, A. See *Bloomers, The.*
"Pair So Unequal" (Salinas). PFor 1388-1389.
　See also *Sea of San Juan, The.*

Paixão Segundo G. H., A (Lispector). LFSup 244.
"Pajamas" (Olds). RevPEng 2492.
"Pájaro, El." *See* "Bird, The."
Pal Joey (Rodgers and Hart, L.). DEng 904;
　RevDEng 1127.
"Palace, The" (Bates). RevShF 174; ShF 270;
　ShFSup 31.
Palace of Eternal Youth, The (Hung). DFor 2326.
Palace of Pleasure, The (Painter). ShF 147, 487.
"Palace of Sleep, The" (Kavan). RevShF 1313.
"Palace of the Moorish Kings, The" (Connell).
　RevShF 600.
Palace of the Peacock (Harris, W.). LFSup
　144-147; RevLFEng 1526-1529. See also
　Guiana Quartet, The.
Palacký, František. PFor 1799-1800.
"Palais de Justice" (Helprin). RevShF 1165;
　ShFSup 119.
"Palamon and Ersyte." *See* "Knight's Tale, The."
Palazzeschi, Aldo. LFFor 2240-2241.
Pale Fire (Nabokov). LFEng 1953; RevLFEng
　2466.
"Pale Horse, Pale Rider" (Porter). RevShF 1911.
Pale Horse, Pale Rider (Porter). LFEng
　2106-2107; RevLFEng 2654-2655.
"Pale Pink Roast, The" (Paley). RevShF 1837;
　ShF 2042.
Pale View of Hills, A (Ishiguro). RevLFEng
　1707-1708, 3793.
**Paley, Grace. RevShF 1835-1839, 2751; ShF
　551, 2040-2044;** ShFSup 390.
Palimpsestes (Genette). LTh 563.
Palm, Göran. PFor 2192.
Palm-Wine Drinkard, The (Tutuola). LFFor
　1785-1787.
Palmàs, Kostìs. PFor 1952-1954.
"Palmatoria de cobre, La." *See* "Copper Ferule,
　The."
Palmer, Leslie John. *See* **Beeding, Francis.**
Palmer, Stuart. M&D 1286-1292.
Palombe (Camus, J. P.). ShF 498.
Palomino (Jolley). LFSup 178-179; RevLFEng
　1791-1792.
Pálsson, Sigurthur. PFor 2200-2201.
Paludan, Jacob. LFFor 2354.
Paludan-Müller, Frederik. PFor 2166-2167.
Pamela (Richardson, S.). LFEng 2246,
　2248-2250, 3013, 3072-3073, 3112-3114;

RevLFEng 2839-2840, 3721, 3732, 3781-3782, 3814, 3816. See also *Shamela.*
"*Pamiętnik.*" *See* "Monument."
Pamiętnik znaleziony w wannie. See *Memoirs Found in a Bathtub.*
Pan (Hamsun). LFFor 771-773, 2346
"Pan and Pitys" (Landor). PEng 1644; RevPEng 1909.
Pan Cogito (Herbert). PFor 657, 659.
Pan Geldhab (Fredro). DSup 137-138.
Pan Jowialski (Fredro). DFor 2277; DSup 140.
Pan Ku. LTh 1773-1774.
Pan Michael (Sienkiewicz). LFFor 1565, 1573, 1574-1575.
Pan Tadeusz (Mickiewicz). PFor 1017, 1022-1024, 2125.
Pan Wołodyjowski. See *Pan Michael.*
Panama (McGuane). LFSup 293-294; RevLFEng 2200.
Pañcatantra. LFFor 2214.
"Pandora" (Nerval). RevShF 2691-2692; ShF 197-198.
Pandora's Box (Wedekind). DFor 1976-1978.
Pandosto, the Triumph of Time (Greene). ShF 492-493.
Panduro, Leif. LFFor 2365.
Pane e vino. See *Bread and Wine.*
"Panegyrick to my Lord Protector, A" (Waller). PEng 3016; RevPEng 3513.
P'ang-huang. See *Wandering.*
"Pangolin, The" (Moore). PEng 2045; RevPEng 2375.
Panic (MacLeish). DEng 1218; RevDEng 1539.
Pannonius, Janus. PFor 1975.
Panova, Vera. LFFor 2326, 2327.
Pansies (Lawrence, D. H.). PEng 1681, 1684-1685; RevPEng 1954-1955.
Pantagleize (Ghelderode). DFor 695-697.
Pantagruel. See *Gargantua and Pantagruel.*
Panteleón y las visitadoras. See *Captain Pantoja and the Special Service.*
"Panthea" (Wilde). PEng 3106; RevPEng 3597.
Panthée (Tristan). DFor 1891-1892.
"Panther, The" (Rilke). PFor 1331. See also *New Poems.*
Panther and the Lash, The (Hughes, L.). PEng 1435; RevPEng 1643.
Pantomime (Walcott, D. A.). DEng 2004; RevDEng 2472-2473.
Panzini, Romagnol Alfredo. LFFor 2240.
Paolo Paoli (Adamov). DFor 18-19, 2258, 2358.
Papa Hamlet (Holz). LTh 692.

"Papa Love Baby" (Smith, S.). RevPEng 3077-3078.
Papa verde, El. See *Green Pope, The.*
Papaleo, Joseph. ShF 2756.
Papeleros, Los (Aguirre). DFor 34-35.
Papeles del infierno, Los (Buenaventura). DFor 2445.
Paper Men, The (Golding). RevLFEng 1357.
"Paper Pills" (Anderson). RevShF 72; ShF 872.
"Paper Route, The" (Galvin). PEng 1055; RevPEng 1189.
Paphnutius (Hroswitha). DFor 2153-2154.
"Papillon, Le." *See* "Butterfly, The."
Papin perhe (Canth). DFor 327-328.
Papin rouva (Aho). LFFor 2342-2343.
Papin tytär (Aho). LFFor 2342.
Papini, Giovanni. PFor 2045.
Pâques à New York, Les (Cendrars). LFFor 317.
Para esta noche (Onetti). LFFor 1211.
Para una tumba sin nombre (Onetti). LFFor 1213.
Parable and Paradox (Politzer). RevShF 1304.
"Parable of the Stairs" (Illyés). PFor 745.
Parables (Fletcher, J. G.). PEng 1027.
Parábola del náufrago. See *Hedge, The.*
Parade's End (Ford, F.). LFEng 988-989; RevLFEng 1171-1172.
Paradísarheimt. See *Paradise Reclaimed.*
Paradise (Barthelme). RevLFEng 236.
Paradise (Dante). PFor 411-416. See also *Divine Comedy, The.*
"Paradise" (O'Brien, Edna). ShF 1970-1973.
Paradise and Other Stories (Moravia). RevShF 1673-1674; ShFSup 198.
Paradise Lost (Milton). LTh 239-240; PEng 2008-2012, 3492-3493; RevPEng 2341-2345; ShF 135, 471.
Paradise Lost (Odets). DEng 1399-1400; RevDEng 1775-1776.
"Paradise Lounge, The" (Trevor). RevShF 2309; ShFSup 325-326.
Paradise Poems (Stern). PSup 376; RevPEng 3196-3198.
Paradise Reclaimed (Laxness). LFFor 997-998.
"Paradise Re-entered" (Lawrence, D. H.). PEng 1683; RevPEng 1953.
Paradise Regained (Milton). PEng 2012-2013; RevPEng 2345-2346.
Paradisi, Agostini. LTh 1691.
Paradiso, Il. See *Paradise and Other Stories.*
"Paradox" (Warren). RevPEng 3524.
Paradox, King (Baroja). LFFor 109.
"Paradox Lost" (Brown). ShF 564.
Paradox of Acting, The (Diderot). LTh 374.

Paterson (Williams, W. C.). PEng 3113-3119, 3366-3367, 3392; RevPEng 3612-3618, 3884-3885.

Path, The (Delibes). LFFor 449-450.

Path to the Nest of Spiders, The (Calvino). LFFor 234-236, 2251.

Patience (Gilbert and Sullivan). DEng 764-765; RevDEng 945-946.

Patience (Pearl-Poet). PEng 2197, 2200-2202, 3254; RevPEng 2568, 2571-2573; ShF 2068, 2069-2070.

"Patience, Hard Thing" (Hopkins). PEng 1402; RevPEng 1611.

"Patience of Job in Detroit, The" (Berrigan). ShF 372-373.

Patmore, Coventry. PEng 2184-2195; RevPEng 2555-2566.

"Patmos" (Hölderlin). PFor 688.

Patraput (Tagore). PFor 1484-1485.

Patrasket (Bergman). DFor 190-191.

"Patriarch, The" (Colette). ShF 1165-1166.

"Patricia, Edith and Arnold" (Thomas). RevShF 2267-2268; ShF 2322.

Patrick, John. DEng 1463-1471; RevDEng 1845-1853.

Patrick, Q. *See* **Quentin, Patrick.**

Patrick, Robert. DEng 1472-1480; RevDEng 1854-1863.

Patrick Pearse Motel, The (Leonard). DSup 229-230; RevDEng 1410-1411.

Patrie (Sardou). DFor 1634-1637.

Patriot, The (Connell). LFEng 577-578; RevLFEng 706-707.

"Patriotic Debate, The" (Chartier). PFor 347-348.

Patriotic Gore (Wilson). LTh 1549.

"Patriotism" (Mishima). RevShF 1664, 2746-2747; ShF 1937-1938.

Patriots, The (Kingsley). DEng 1042; RevDEng 1318.

"Patrol, The" (Lem). RevShF 1460-1416; ShFSup 153.

Patron Happiness (McPherson). RevPEng 2187.

Pattee, Frederick Lewis. RevShF 2653, 2669, 2676-2679, 2702.

"Pattern, The" (Creeley). RevPEng 779.

"Pattern of Perfection, The" (Hale, N.). RevShF 1098; ShF 1571.

Pattern of Perfection, The (Hale, N.). RevShF 1098; ShF 1570-1571.

Patternmaster (Butler, O.). RevLFEng 496.

Patterns of Childhood (Wolf). LFFor 1933.

Pattes de mouche, Les. See Scrap of Paper, A.

Paul, Jean. See **Jean Paul.**

Paul Among the Jews (Werfel). DFor 1999.

Paul and Mary. See Paul and Virginia.

Paul and Virginia (Saint-Pierre). LFFor 2121.

Paul Campenhaye, Specialist in Criminology (Fletcher). M&D 622.

Paul Lange and Tora Parsberg (Bjørnson). DFor 219-220.

Paul Schippel Esq. (Sternheim). DFor 1742-1743.

Paulding, James Kirke. LTh 1743.

Paulinus of Nola. PFor 2109-2110.

"Paul's Case" (Cather). RevShF 452-453, 2714; ShF 252, 800-801, 1077-1078.

Paulus unter den Juden. See Paul Among the Jews.

"Paura alla Scala." *See* "Scala Scare, The."

Pause Under the Sky (Beck). ShF 935.

Pauvre Christ de Bomba, Le. See Poor Christ of Bomba, The.

Pavese, Cesare. LFFor 1240-1250, 2249; PFor 2048, 2049; RevShF 1859-1865; ShF 2064 2067.

Pavić, Milorad. PFor 2257-2258.

Pavičić, Ante Tresić. PFor 2264.

Pavlović, Miodrag. PFor 1163-1168, 2257; PSup 408.

"Pavlovic Variations" (Middleton, C.). PEng 1988-1989; RevPEng 2310-2311.

Pavlovski, Radovan. PFor 2273.

Pavlovsky, Eduardo. DFor 2445.

Pavšič, Vladimir. *See* Bor, Matej.

Pawnbroker, The (Wallant). LFEng 2762-2763; RevLFEng 3420-3421.

"Pawnbroker's Wife, The" (Spark). RevShF 2167.

Payack, Paul J. J. ShF 2758.

Payment Deferred (Forester). M&D 641-643.

Payne, John Howard. DEng 1481-1487, 2397; RevDEng 1864-1871, 2918.

"Payoff" (Queen). RevShF 1981.

"Paysages tristes." *See* "Sad Landscapes."

Paysan parvenu, Le. See Fortunate Peasant, The.

"Paysans, Les." *See* "Peasants, The."

Paz, Octavio. PFor 1169-1175, 2228; PSup 408.

Pazos de Ulloa, Los. See Son of the Bondwoman, The.

p'Bitek, Okot. RevPEng 3947, 3947-3948.

Pea, Enrico. LFFor 2240.

Peabody, Richard Myers, Jr. ShF 2759.

Peace (Aristophanes). DFor 2126.

"Peace" (Brooke). PEng 306; RevPEng 372.

"Peace" (Rítsos). PFor 1350.

Peace After War (Gironella). LFFor 665.

"Peace and Plenty" (Kennedy). PEng 1573; RevPEng 1808.

Persian Eclogues (Collins). PEng 550; RevPEng 642.

Persian Letters (Montesquieu). LFEng 3110-3112; LFFor 2118; RevLFEng 3811, 3812-3814.

Persian Nights (Johnson, D.). RevLFEng 1775-1776.

Persians, The (Aeschylus). DFor 24-26, 2090, 2099-2100.

Persidskie motivi (Esenin). PFor 480.

"Persistent Mystery of the Modern Short Story." ShF 87.

Persius. PFor 1198-1203, 2104.

Personae (Pound). PEng 2267-2268; RevPEng 2642.

"Personal Ad" (Ginsberg). RevPEng 1234.

"Personal Episode, A" (Zoshchenko). RevShF 2556-2557; ShFSup 378.

Personal Heresy, The (Lewis). LTh 896.

Personal Matter, A (Ōe). LFFor 1197, 1198.

Persons, Truman Streckfus. *See* Capote, Truman.

Persuasion (Austen). LFEng 125-127; RevLFEng 167-168.

Perto de coraçao selvagem (Lispector). LFSup 242-243.

"Perusing yesternight, with idle eyes" (Nashe). PEng 2071-2072; RevPEng 2420.

"Pervaia liubov." *See* "First Love" (Babel).

"Pervaya lyubov." *See* "First Love" (Turgenev).

"Perviy zub." *See* "My First Tooth."

Perzival (Chrétien de Troyes). ShF 1141.

Peščanik (Kiš). LFSup 214-215.

Pesetsky, Bette. ShF 2762.

"Peshchera." *See* "Cave, The."

Peshkov, Aleksey Maksimovich. *See* **Gorky, Maxim.**

"Pesn' torzhestvuiushchei liubvi." *See* "Song of Triumphant Love, The."

"Pesnia o Burevestnike." *See* "Song of the Stormy Petrel, The."

"Pesnia o sokole." *See* "Song of the Falcon, The."

Pessoa, Fernando. PFor 1204-1211.

Peste, La. See *Plague, The.*

"Pet Deer, The" (Tate, J.). RevPEng 3307-3308.

Pet Sematary (King). LFSup 208-210; RevLFEng 1890-1892.

Petals of Blood (Ngugi wa Thiong'o). LFEng 1983-1984; RevLFEng 2506-2508.

"Peter Grimes" (Crabbe). PEng 642-643; RevPEng 736-737.

Peter Pan (Barrie). DEng 123-125; RevDEng 158-160.

Peter Pencilcase's Son. *See* **Twain, Mark.**

"Peter Rabbit" (McPherson). RevPEng 2184.

Peter Whiffle (Van Vechten). LFEng 2707, 2708-2709; RevLFEng 3363-3365.

"Peters" (Tolstaya). RevShF 2293.

Peters, Bill. *See* **McGivern, William P.**

Peters, Elizabeth. M&D 1311-1317.

Peters, Ellis. M&D 1318-1324.

Peters, Lawrence. *See* **Davies, L. P.**

Peters, Lenrie. LFFor 2048-2049.

Peters, S. H. *See* **Henry, O.**

Peter's Pence (Cleary). M&D 362.

Petersburg (Bely). LFFor 2320.

Petersen, Kaj Harald Leininger. *See* **Munk, Kaj.**

Petersen, Nis. LFFor 2355; PFor 2185.

Peterson, Mary. ShF 2763.

Petit Chose, Le. See *Little Weakling, The.*

Petit Prince, Le. See *Little Prince, The.*

Petit Testament, Le. See *Legacy, The.*

Petite Palace of Pettie His Pleasure, A (Pettie). ShF 488.

"Petite Ville en Siberie." *See* "Little Town in Siberia."

"Petition" (Coulette). RevPEng 692.

Petits poèmes en prose. See *Paris Spleen.*

Petőfi, Sándor. PFor 77, 1212-1229, 1981-1983.

Petrarca, Francesco. *See* **Petrarch.**

Petrarch. LTh 133-135, 169-171, 1091-1096, 1658-1660; PFor 1230-1239, 2007-2009, 2114-2115.

Petri, Olaus. DFor 2465.

Petrified Forest, The (Sherwood). DEng 1805-1806, 2403; RevDEng 2239-2240, 2924.

Petronius. LFFor 2009-2010, 2011; LTh 1143; RevShF 1878-1884; ShF 2091-2097.

Petroski, Catherine. ShF 2764.

Petrov, Evgeni. LFFor 2325.

Petty Bourgeois, The. See *Smug Citizen.*

Petursson, Hannes. PFor 2192.

"Pevtsky." See "Singers, The."

Peyton Place. RevDEng 3041.

Pfarrer von Kirchfeld, Der (Anzengruber). DFor 88-89.

Pfeil, Fred. ShF 2765.

Pfisters Mühle (Raabe). LFFor 2175.

Phaedra (Racine). DFor 1519-1521.

Phaedra (Seneca). DFor 1690-1691.

Phaedra (Unamuno y Jugo). DFor 1911-1912.

Phaedrus. PFor 2105; RevShF 2578-2579; ShF 379-380.

Phaedrus (Plato). LTh 1114-1116, 1118, 1634-1635; PFor 1747, 1748.

Phalereus, Demetrius. ShF 379.

"Phantasie an Laura." *See* "Fantasy, to Laura."
Phantasterne (Schack). LFFor 2337.
Phantasus (Holz). PFor 690-696.
Phantom Lady, The (Calderón). DFor 301-302.
Phantom Lady (Woolrich). M&D 1727.
"Phantom of the Movie Palace, The" (Coover). RevShF 620.
"Phantom 'Rickshaw, The" (Kipling). RevShF 1362; ShF 1751.
"Phares, Les." *See* "Beacons."
Pharisienne, La. See *Woman of the Pharisees, A.*
Pharsalia (Lucan). PFor 894, 896-901.
Pharsamond (Marivaux). LFFor 1099-1100.
Pheander the Mayden Knight (Roberts, H.). ShF 495-496.
"Pheasants" (Woiwode). RevShF 2494-2495.
Phèdre. See *Phaedra.*
"Phelim O'Toole's Courtship" (Carleton). RevShF 419-420.
Phelps, Samuel. DEng 2357.
"Phenomenology of Reading" (Poulet). LTh 1149-1150.
Phenomenology of Spirit, The (Hegel). LTh 656, 658.
Pherecrates. DFor 2122.
"Phihellene" (Cavafy). PFor 298.
Philadelphia Comedy, The. See *City Looking Glass, The.*
Philadelphia, Here I Come! (Friel). DEng 674; RevDEng 840-841.
Philadelphia Story, The (Barry). DEng 135; RevDEng 171.
Philaster (Beaumont and Fletcher). DEng 631-632, 2290; RevDEng 776-777, 2809.
Philby, Kim. LFEng 1217; RevLFEng 1443.
Philemon. DFor 2133-2134.
Philip. See *Phillip II.*
Philip Sparrow (Skelton). PEng 2637.
Philipe, Gérard. DFor 2354.
Philips, Judson. *See* **Pentecost, Hugh.**
Philistines, The. See *Smug Citizen.*
Philistion of Nicaea. DFor 2135.
"Phillida and Coridon" (Breton, N.). PEng 278-279; RevPEng 341, 342-343.
Phillip II (Alfieri). DFor 47, 2406.
Phillips, Jayne Anne. RevShF 1885-1888.
Phillips, Louis. ShF 2766.
Phillips, Robert. ShF 2767.
Phillips, Thomas. *See* **Davies, L. P.**
Phillis (Lodge). PEng 1733; RevPEng 2017.
"Phillis: Or, The Progress of Love" (Swift). PEng 2808; RevPEng 3275.

Phillpotts, Eden. M&D 1325-1330.
Philoctetes (Müller). DSup 259-260.
Philoctetes (Sophocles). DFor 2108-2109.
Philoktet. See *Philoctetes.*
Philoktētēs (Rítsos). PFor 1351, 1970.
Philosophe sans le savior, Le (Sedaine). DFor 2342.
"Philosopher, The" (Anderson). RevShF 70-71; ShF 870-871.
"Philosopher, The" (Brontë, E.). PEng 297; RevPEng 363.
"Philosopher, The" (Graves). PEng 1129; RevPEng 1286.
Philosopher's Stone, The (Lagerkvist). DFor 1156-1157, 2478.
Philosophes classiques du XIXe siècle en France, Les (Taine). LTh 1419-1421.
Philosophes français du XIXe siècle, Les. See *Philosophes classiques du XIXe siècle en France, Les.*
Philosophiae Naturalis Principia Mathematica. See *Mathematical Principles of Natural Philosophy, The.*
Philosophic Words (Wimsatt). LTh 1556.
Philosophical Enquiry into the Origin of Our Ideas of the Sublime and Beautiful, A (Burke, E.). LTh 238, 1218, 1601, 1700; ShF 470.
"Philosophy of Composition" (Poe). LTh 1135-1136; PEng 2248; RevPEng 2621; RevShF 439.
Philosophy of the Short Story, The (Matthews). ShF 82.
Philotas (Lessing). DFor 1202-1203.
"Phineas" (Knowles). RevShF 1380-1381; ShF 1767-1769.
Phlyakes. DFor 2137.
"Phoebe's Garden." See *Quality Street.*
Phoenician Women, The (Euripides). DFor 2116-2117.
Phoenician Women, The (Seneca). DFor 2148.
Phoenissae (Phrynichus). DFor 2090.
"Phoenix, The" (Colette). RevShF 581.
Phoenix and the Tortoise, The (Rexroth). PEng 2353; RevPEng 2740.
"Phoenix and the Turtle, The" (Shakespeare). PEng 2529.
Phoenix and the Turtle, The (Shakespeare). RevPEng 2940.
Phoenix Nest, The (Breton, N.). PEng 278; RevPEng 342.
Phormio (Terence). DFor 1827, 2143.
"Photo Album, The" (Dovlatov). RevShF 762.

"Pillow of Stone" (Grau). RevShF 1058; ShF
1531.
Pilnyak, Boris. LFFor 2323-2324.
"Pilot from the Carrier, A" (Jarrell). PEng 1481;
RevPEng 1693.
Pilote de guerre. See *Flight to Arras.*
"Pilot's Story, The" (Howells). PEng 1421.
Pinakes (Callimachus). LTh 1637; PFor 253.
Pincher Martin (Golding). LFEng 1129-1130,
1133; RevLFEng 1352-1353.
Pincherle, Alberto. See **Moravia, Alberto.**
Pinchi-Ran'na chōsho (Ōe). LFFor 1202-1203.
Pindar. PFor 1240-1247, 1945-1946.
Pindare-Lebrun. PFor 1862.
"Pindarique Odes" (Cowley, A.). PEng 593-594;
RevPEng 699.
**Pinero, Arthur Wing. DEng 1496-1509;
RevDEng 1881-1895.**
Ping Pong (Adamov). DFor 17-18, 2257-2258.
**Pinget, Robert. DSup 302-308; LFFor
1286-1294.**
P'ing-hsi opera. DFor 2334.
Pinocchio. See *Adventures of Pinocchio, The.*
Pinsky, Robert. PEng 2210-2219; PSup 408;
RevPEng 2581-2591.
Pint of Murder, A (MacLeod). M&D 1182.
**Pinter, Harold. DEng 1510-1520, 2387-2388;
DSup 408; RevDEng 1896-1908, 2905-2906,
3033.**
Pintor de su deshonra, El. See *Painter of His
Dishonor, The.*
Pioneers, The (Cooper). LFEng 607-611;
RevLFEng 737-741.
Pioniere in Ingolstadt (Fleisser). DFor 608,
620-621.
P'i-p'a chi. See *Lute, The.*
Pippa Passes (Browning). DEng 294-295;
RevDEng 351-352.
Pir vo vryemya chumy. See *Feast in Time of the
Plague, The.*
Piraksa (Hakim). DSup 175-176.
**Pirandello, Luigi. DFor 384, 386, 465-466,
1464-1472, 2412-2413; LFFor 1295-1307,
2239; LTh 144, 148, 1097-1103; RevShF
1889-1895; ShF 688-689, 2098-2102.**
Pirates of Penzance, The (Gilbert and Sullivan).
DEng 763-764; RevDEng 944-945.
Pisan Cantos, The (Pound). PEng 2273-2274;
RevPEng 2647-2649.
Pisarev, Dmitri. LTh 1104-1110.
Piscator, Erwin. DEng 2239.
Pisemsky, Aleksei. DFor 2454; LFFor 2318.
Pisma bez adresa. See *Unaddressed Letters.*

"Pisma iz vtorogo i tretego putishestivij po
Europe" (Fonvizin). LFFor 2308.
Pisma russkogo puteshestvennika. See *Letters of
a Russian Traveler.*
"Pis'mo." *See* "Letter, A."
Pisti a vérzivatarban (Örkény). DSup 299.
Pit, The (Norris). LFEng 2005-2006; RevLFEng
2527, 2530-2531.
"Pit and the Pendulum, The" (Poe). RevShF
2659, 2687-2688; ShF 193-194, 2107.
"Pit Strike" (Sillitoe). RevShF 2116-2117; ShF
2227, 2230.
"Pitch Pines" (Galvin). PEng 1054-1055;
RevPEng 1187-1188.
"Pitcher, The" (Ponge). PFor 1265.
Pitoëff, Georges. DFor 2351.
"Pity" (Ungaretti). PFor 1568-1569. See also
Sentimento del tempo.
"Pity. We Were Such a Good Invention, A"
(Amichai). PSup 7.
Più forte, Il. See *Stronger, The.*
**Pixérécourt, Guilbert de. DEng 2187; DFor
1473-1480, 2343; RevDEng 2707, 2869.**
Pizarro (Sheridan). DEng 1781; RevDEng 2214.
"Pkhentz" (Sinyavsky). RevShF 2141.
"Place, The" (Eberhart). PEng 932.
"Place for No Story, The" (Jeffers). PEng
1494-1495; RevPEng 1707-1709.
Place I've Never Been, A (Leavitt). RevShF
1437-1438.
Place of Dead Roads, The (Burroughs).
RevLFEng 490.
"Place of Pain in the Universe, The" (Hecht).
PEng 1281.
Place on the Magdalena Flats, A (Jones, P.).
DEng 1011-1012; RevDEng 1278-1279.
"Place That Is Feared I Inhabit, The" (Forché).
RevPEng 1157-1158.
Place to Come To, A (Warren). LFEng 2778;
RevLFEng 3443.
Place with the Pigs, A (Fugard). RevDEng 876.
Placeres prohibidos, Los (Cernuda). PFor
320-321.
Plague, The (Camus). LFFor 259-262.
Plague Column, The (Seifert). PSup 357.
Plagued by the Nightingale (Boyle, K.). LFEng
275; RevLFEng 340.
Plaidoyer d'un fou, Le. See *Confessions of a
Fool, The.*
Plain-Chant (Cocteau). PFor 372.
Plain-Dealer, The (Wycherley). DEng
2111-2113; RevDEng 2630-2632.

"Plain Language from Truthful James" (Harte). PEng 1239, 1242-1243.

Plain Murder (Torcotor). MſtD 643

"Plain Pleasures" (Bowles, J.). RevShF 272.

Plain Song (Harrison, J.). PEng 1226-1228, 1229; RevPEng 1407-1409.

Plains Song, for Female Voices (Morris). LFEng 1911, 1912-1913; RevLFEng 2419, 2420-2421.

"Plaint of the Poet in an Ignorant Age" (Kizer). PEng 1617.

"Plainview: 1" (Momaday). PEng 2019, 2020; RevPEng 2354.

"Plainview: 2" (Momaday). PEng 2019, 2020; RevPEng 2354.

"Plainview: 3" (Momaday). PEng 2019, 2020; RevPEng 2354.

"Plainview: 4" (Momaday). PEng 2019, 2020; RevPEng 2354.

Plaisir du texte, Le. See *Pleasure of the Text, The.*

Plan d'un divertissement. See *Est-il bon? Est-il méchant?*

Planché, James Robinson. DEng **1521-1530,** 2194, 2355-2356, 2361; RevDEng **1909-1919,** 2714, 2873-2874, 2879.

Planchon, Roger. DFor 2354.

"Planctus, The" (Hope). PSup 190; RevPEng 1595.

Planetarium, The (Sarraute). LFFor 1503-1505.

"Plant, The" (McPherson). RevPEng 2181-2182.

Plante, David. LFSup **306-312;** RevLFEng **2642-2648.**

"Planting Crocus" (Slavitt). RevPEng 3049-3050.

Plath, Sylvia. PEng **2220-2231,** 3374; PSup 408-409; RevPEng **2592-2603,** 3892.

Plato. DEng 2139, 2142-2143; LFEng 1941-1942, 2217-2219; LTh 21, 529, 532, 958, 965, 1039, 1043, **1111-1119,** 1320, 1347, 1404-1405, 1634-1636, 1702; PFor 1747-1748; RevDEng 2659, 2661; RevLFEng 2452-2453, 2808-2810; RevPEng 4005-4006.

"plato told" (Cummings). PEng 709; RevPEng 800.

Platonov, Andrey. LFFor 2323, 2327.

Plautus. DEng 2146-2147, 2263; **DFor 1481-1487,** 2141-2142, 2158; LTh 1666; RevDEng 2666-2667, 2782.

Plave legende (Dučić). PFor 432.

Play (Beckett). RevDEng 189.

Play and Place of Criticism, The (Krieger). LTh 827.

Play It As It Lays (Didion). LFEng 761-763; RevLFEng 927-928.

Play of Love, The (Heywood, J.). DEng 943-944; RevDEng 1176-1177.

Play of the Sibyl Cassandra, The (Vicente). DFor 1956-1957.

Play of the Weather, The (Heywood, J.). DEng 944, 2256; RevDEng 1177, 2776.

Play the Piano Drunk Like a Percussion Instrument Until the Fingers Bleed a Bit (Bukowski). PEng 363-364; RevPEng 436-437.

"Playback" (Beattie). RevShF 183; ShFSup 40-41.

Playbill (Rattigan). DEng 1561; RevDEng 1953.

Playboy of the Western World, The (Synge). DEng 1907-1910; RevDEng 2350-2353.

Playe of the Foure P.P., The. See *Four P.P, The.*

Player Piano (Vonnegut). LFEng 2724-2725; RevLFEng 3380-3381.

Players and the Game, The (Symons). M&D 1564.

Playes Confuted in Fiue Actions (Gosson). LTh 613.

"Playhouse Called Remarkable, The" (Spark). RevShF 2167; ShF 2253-2254.

Playhouse 90. RevDEng 3037.

Playhouse to Be Lett, The (Davenant). DEng 459-461; RevDEng 568-570.

"Playroom" (Barnard). PSup 24; RevPEng 107.

Plays of Clara Gazul, The (Mérimée). LFFor 1146.

Play's the Thing, The (Molnár). DFor 1346-1347.

Playwright as Thinker, The (Bentley). LTh 147-149.

Plaza Suite (Simon). RevDEng 2265.

"Plea, A" (Dunbar, P.). PSup 112-113; RevPEng 1014-1015.

"Plea of the Midsummer Fairies, The" (Hood). PEng 1384; RevPEng 1582.

Plea of the Midsummer Fairies, The (Hood). PEng 1384, 1385; RevPEng 1582-1583.

Pleasant Historie of Lazarillo de Tormes, The. See *Lazarillo de Tormes.*

Pleasant Memoirs of the Marquis de Bradomín, The (Valle-Inclán). LFFor 1834-1835, 1836-1837.

"Please Don't Talk About Me When I'm Gone" (Algren). RevShF 53; ShF 857.

Pleasure-Dome (Madden). LFEng 1766-1767; RevLFEng 2238-2239.

"Pleasure of Her Company, The" (Smiley). RevShF 2146.

Pleasure of the Text, The (Barthes). LTh 107.

"Pleasure Pier" (Pinsky). RevPEng 2586.

"Pleasures" (Levertov). PEng 1706.

"Pleasures of Melancholy, The" (Warton). PEng 3035-3037.

"Pleasures of Peace, The" (Koch). PEng 1626-1627; RevPEng 1865-1866.

"Poem for My Twenty-ninth Birthday" (Ciardi). PEng 502; RevPEng 591.
"Poem for the Governments, A" (Williams, C. K.). PSup 389; RevPEng 3604.
Poem in Progress (Logan). PEng 1741-1743; RevPEng 2025-2027.
"Poem (Lana Turner has collapsed!)" (O'Hara). PEng 2128-2129; RevPEng 2479-2480.
"Poem of Pure Imagination, A" (Warren). LTh 1525.
"Poem of Summer's End" (Merrill). PEng 1962-1963.
Poem of the Cid. PFor 2205-2206.
"Poem on St. James' Park as lately improved by His Majesty, A" (Waller). PEng 3016-3017; RevPEng 3513-3514.
"POEM, OR BEAUTY HURTS MR. VINAL" (Cummings). PEng 709; RevPEng 800.
"Poem Some People Will Have to Understand, A" (Baraka). PEng 88; RevPEng 99.
"Poem to a Woman" (Dučić). PFor 430-431.
"Poem to Shout in the Ruins" (Aragon). PFor 69-70.
"Poem with One Fact" (Hall). PEng 1204; RevPEng 1373.
Poem Without a Hero, The (Akhmatova). PFor 14-15.
"Poem written by Sir Henry Wotton, in his youth, A" (Wotton). PEng 3143-3144.
Poema bez geroa. See *Poem Without a Hero, The.*
Poema de Chile (Mistral). PFor 1044.
Poema de Fernán González. PFor 2209-2210.
"Poema de un día." *See* "Poem for a Day."
Poema paradisiaco (D'Annunzio). PFor 386.
Poemas (Drummond de Andrade). PSup 101.
Poemas humanos. See *Human Poems.*
Poemas y antipoemas. See *Poems and Antipoems.*
"Poemat dla doroslych." *See* "Poem for Adults."
"Poème à crier dans les ruines." *See* "Poem to Shout in the Ruins."
Poème pulvérisé, Le (Char). PFor 335.
Poèmes saturniens (Verlaine). PFor 1627.
Poemetti (Pascoli). PFor 1142.
Poems (Beaumont). PEng 95-96.
Poems (Burns). PEng 380-381; RevPEng 450-455.
Poems (Cowley, A.). PEng 591, 592-593; RevPEng 697.
Poems (Drummond of Hawthornden). PEng 864-866; RevPEng 980-982.
Poems (Ignatow). PEng 1470; RevPEng 1682-1683.
Poems (Tuckerman). PEng 2938; RevPEng 3405-3406.

Poems (Vaughan). PEng 2971; RevPEng 3450.
Poems (Warton). PEng 3037-3038.
Poems (Wilde). PEng 3104-3105; RevPEng 3594, 3595-3598.
Poems and Antipoems (Parra). PFor 1130, 1133.
Poems and Ballads (Swinburne). PEng 2818-2819; RevPEng 3286-3287.
Poems and Ballads: Second Series (Swinburne). PEng 2820-2822; RevPEng 3288-3290.
Poems and Fancies (Newcastle). PEng 2091-2092, 2093; RevPEng 2435-2438.
"Poems and Romances of Alfred de Vigny" (Mill). LTh 1029.
Poems Before Congress (Browning, E. B.). PEng 326; RevPEng 396.
Poems by Doveglion (Villa). PEng 2979; PFor 1647; RevPEng 3466.
Poems from Centre City (Kinsella). RevPEng 1839-1840.
Poems in Persons (Holland). LTh 685-686.
Poems in Prose (Wilde). PEng 3108; RevPEng 3599-3600.
Poems in Slang (Villon). PFor 1659-1660.
Poems 1934-1969 (Ignatow). PEng 1470; RevPEng 1682.
"Poems of Death" (Dučić). PFor 431.
Poems of Doctor Zhivago, The (Pasternak). PFor 1161-1162.
Poems of Felicity (Traherne). PEng 2927-2928.
"Poems of Our Climate" (Stevens). PEng 2745-2746; RevPEng 3206-3207.
"Poems of the Times" (Heine). PFor 650.
Poems of the War (Boker). DEng 219; RevDEng 260.
Poems Old and New, 1918-1978 (Lewis). PSup 254; RevPEng 1999.
Poems on Several Occasions (Cotton). PEng 586-587; RevPEng 683-684.
Poems on Several Occasions (Miles). PSup 277; RevPEng 2317.
"Poems to God" (Dučić). PFor 431.
Poems, with "The Muses Lookingglasse" and "Amyntas" (Randolph). PEng 2320.
Poems Written Before Jumping out of an 8 Story Window (Bukowski). PEng 360; RevPEng 433.
Poemut o czasie zastyglym (Miłosz). PFor 1032.
"Poesía." *See* "Poetry."
Poesía de San Juan de la Cruz (desde esta ladera), La (Alonso). LTh 27.
Poesía española (Alonso). LTh 25-26.
Poesia in forma di rosa (Pasolini). PFor 1150-1151.
Poesie a Casarsa (Pasolini). PFor 1148.

Prinz Zerbino (Tieck). DFor 1839-1840.

Prior, Matthew. PEng 2287-2292; RevPEng 2668-2673.

"Prioress's Tale, The" (Chaucer). RevShF 492; ShF 1112.

"Prism and Lens" (Hacker). PEng 1191-1192.

Prison-House of Language, The (Jameson). LTh 758; ShF 80.

"Prisoner, The" (Brontë, E.). PEng 229; RevPEng 365.

Prisoner of Grace (Cary). LFEng 461; RevLFEng 581.

Prisoner of the Caucasus, The (Pushkin). LTh 1178.

Prisonnière, La. See *Captive, The.*

Prisons (Settle). LFSup 347; RevLFEng 3008. See also Beulah Quintet, The.

Pritam, Amrita. LFFor 2226.

Pritchett, V. S. LFEng 2148-2160; LFSup 406; ShF 271-272, 524, 526-527, 2128-2133; ShFSup 390; RevLFEng 2720-2733; RevShF 1929-1939.

"Private Lies" (Mason). RevShF 1621-1622.

Private Lives (Coward). DEng 430; RevDEng 530.

Private Memoirs and Confessions of a Justified Sinner, The (Hogg). LFEng 3146-3147; RevLFEng 3858.

Private Papers of Henry Ryecroft, The (Gissing). LFEng 1115; RevLFEng 1325.

Private View (Havel). DFor 881.

Privates on Parade (Nichols). DSup 282-283; RevDEng 1731-1732.

Prize, Matthew. See **Hoch, Edward D.**

Prličev, Grigor. PFor 2272.

Pro eto. See *About That.*

"Pro Femina" (Kizer). PEng 1614-1617; RevPEng 1856-1858.

Pro Patria (Sender). LFFor 1549-1550.

"Problem, The" (Emerson). PEng 957; RevPEng 1087.

"Problem of Cell Thirteen, The" (Futrelle). M&D 676.

"Problem of the General Store, The" (Hoch). RevShF 1208-1209.

"Problem of the Text in Linguistics, Philology, and Other Human Sciences, The" (Bakhtin). LTh 87.

Problem of Verse Language, The (Tynyanov). LTh 1477-1479.

Problema stikhotvornogo iazyka. See *Problem of Verse Language, The.*

"Problema teksta v lingvistike, filologii, i drugikh gumanitarnykh naukakh." *See* "Problem of the Text in Linguistics, Philology, and Other Human Sciences, The."

Probleme der Lyrik (Benn). PFor 176.

Problème du style, Le (Gourmont). LTh 624.

"Problems in the Study of Literature and Language" (Jakobson). LTh 747.

Problems of Dostoevsky's Poetics (Bakhtin). LTh 84-86.

"Problemy izucheniya literatury i yazykha." *See* "Problems in the Study of Literature and Language."

Problemy poetiki Dostoevskogo. See *Problems of Dostoevsky's Poetics.*

"Probuzhdenie." *See* "Awakening, The" (Babel).

Procedures for Underground (Atwood). RevPEng 74-75.

Proceed, Sergeant Lamb (Graves, R.). LFEng 1196.

Procession, The (Gibran). PEng 1083-1084; PFor 566-567; RevPEng 1219-1220.

Procession (Sircar). DFor 2391.

Processus Noe Cum Filiis. See *Noah.*

"Proclamation and Petit Four" (Ponge). PFor 1265.

"Procura de uma dignidade, A" (Lispector). RevShF 1492-1493; ShFSup 168.

"Procurator de Judée, Le." *See* "Procurator of Judea, The."

"Procurator of Judea, The" (France). RevShF 900-901; ShF 1404-1405.

"Prodigal Son, The." ShF 363-364.

"Prodigal Son, The" (Bly). RevPEng 273.

"Prodigal Son, The" (Różewicz). PFor 1364-1366.

"Prodiges de la liberté, Les" (Prévert). PFor 1279.

"Prodigiosa tarde de Baltazar, La." *See* "Baltazar's Marvellous Afternoon."

"Prodigioso miligramo, El." *See* "Prodigious Milligram, The."

"Prodigious Milligram, The" (Arreola). RevShF 79-80.

"Prodotti, I." *See* "Products."

"Products" (Moravia). RevShF 1673; ShFSup 198-199.

"Proem" (Miyazawa). PSup 284.

Profane Hymns and Other Poems (Darío). PFor 423.

Profesores, Los (Parra). PFor 1134.

Professor, The (Brontë, C.). LFEng 300-301; RevLFEng 384-385.

"Professor" (Hughes). RevShF 1227-1228; ShF 1658-1659.

"Punishment" (Heaney). RevPEng 1448.

Punishment Without Revenge. See Justice Without Revenge.

Pupil of Nature, The. See Ingenuous.

"Pupils of the Eyes That Talked, The" (P'u Sung-ling). RevShF 1946-1947; ShFSup 244-245.

Puppet Play of Don Cristóbal, The. See In the Frame of Don Cristóbal.

Purcell, Henry. RevDEng 2981.

"Purchase's Living Wonders" (Bates). RevShF 174; ShF 270; ShFSup 31.

Purdy, James. LFEng 2169-2177; LFSup 406; RevLFEng 2743-2752; RevShF 1953-1960; ShF 2134-2140.

"Pure and Impure Poetry" (Warren). LTh 1524; PEng 3430, 3432-3433; RevPEng 3974, 3976-3977.

Pure and the Impure, The (Colette). LFFor 369.

"Pure Diamond Man, The" (Laurence). ShF 1778-1779.

Purgatory (Dante). PFor 405-411. See also *Divine Comedy, The.*

Purgatory (Yeats). DEng 2120-2121; RevDEng 2640-2641.

Purgatory of St. Patrick, The (Marie de France). ShF 1891.

Purity. See Cleanness.

"Purloined Letter, The" (Poe). M&D 1336; RevLFEng 3842; RevShF 1901-1902; ShF 750, 2108.

"Purple Dress, The" (Henry). RevShF 1179; ShF 1630.

Purple Dust (O'Casey). DEng 1390; RevDEng 1766.

"Purple Jar, The" (Edgeworth). RevShF 797; ShF 1322.

Purple Land, The (Hudson). LFEng 1382-1384; RevLFEng 1658-1660.

Purposes of Love. See Promise of Love.

Purse of Coppers, A (O'Faolain). RevShF 1784-1785; ShF 1997.

"Purse Seine, The" (Blackburn). PEng 198; RevPEng 242.

"Pursuit, A" (Atwood). PEng 66.

Pursuit of Happiness. RevDEng 3030.

Pushkin, Alexander. DFor 1494-1502, 2453; LFFor 1359-1372, 2309, 2311, 2312; LTh 119, 287, 388, 398-399, 747-748, 946, 1108, 1176-1183; PFor 873, 1292-1302, 2136-2138; RevShF 1961-1968, 2665; ShF 169-170; ShFSup 250-257.

Puss-in-Boots (Tieck). DFor 1833-1836.

Putem zerna (Khodasevich). PSup 226-227.

Puteshestvie iz Peterburga v Moskvu. See Journey from St. Petersburg to Moscow, A.

Putnam's Monthly. ShF 588.

"Putois" (France). RevShF 902; ShF 1406.

Puttenham, George. LTh 1184-1187.

"Putting Granny Out to Die" (Dazai). RevShF 692-693; ShFSup 94.

"Puzyry zemli" (Blok). PFor 199. See also *Nechayannaya radost.*

Puzzle for Fools, A (Quentin). M&D 1386.

Puzzle for Players (Quentin). M&D 1386-1387.

Puzzle of the Briar Pipe, The. See Puzzle of the Red Stallion, The.

Puzzle of the Red Stallion, The (Palmer). M&D 1288-1289.

"Pylons" (Spender). PEng 2701-2702; RevPEng 3145.

Pym, Barbara. LFEng 2178-2185; LFSup 406; RevLFEng 2753-2762.

Pynchon, Thomas. LFEng 2186-2194; RevLFEng 2763-2773, 3777; RevShF 1969-1975; ShF 2141-2147; ShFSup 390.

Pyramid, The (Golding). LFEng 1135-1136; RevLFEng 1354-1355.

"Pyramus and Thisbe" (Cowley, A.). PEng 591; RevPEng 696.

Pythagorean Silence (Howe). PSup 196-197; RevPEng 1632-1633.

Pythian Ode 8 (Pindar). PFor 1246-1247.

Pythian Ode 10 (Pindar). PFor 1245.

Q

Qashtamar (Mahfouz). RevShF 1564.

Q.E.D. See *Things as They Are.*

Quaderni di Serafino Gubbio, operatore, I. See *Shoot! The Notebooks of Serafino Gubbio, Cinematograph Operator.*

"Quail for Mr. Forester" (Humphrey). RevShF 1235.

"Quaker Graveyard in Nantucket, The" (Lowell, R.). PEng 1787-1788; RevPEng 2081-2082.

"Qualcosa era successo." *See* "Catastrophe."

Quality of Mercy, A (West, P.). LFSup 370; RevLFEng 3521-3522.

"Quality of Sprawl, The" (Murray). PSup 292; RevPEng 2413.

Quality Street (Barrie). DEng 119-121; RevDEng 154-156.

Quand le navire . . . See *Love's Questing.*

"Quand vous serez bien vieille." *See* "When You Are Old."

"Quangle Wangle's Hat, The" (Lear). PEng 1701-1702; RevPEng 1973.

Quare Fellow, The (Behan). DEng 164-165; RevDEng 199-200.

Quarles, Francis. PEng 2293-2300; RevPEng 2674-2681.

Quarry, The (Dürrenmatt). M&D 559.

Quartet (Rhys). LFEng 2228; RevLFEng 2819.

Quartet in Autumn (Pym). LFEng 2182, 2184-2185; RevLFEng 2757, 2759-2760.

Quartier Nègre (Simenon). LFFor 1599.

"Quartz Pebble, The" (Popa). PFor 1269-1270. See also *Bark.*

Quasimodo, Salvatore. PFor 1303-1309, 2032, 2043-2044, 2046, 2049.

"14 juillet, Le." *See* "July 14."

Quatre-vingt-treize. See *Ninety-three.*

"Que bien sé yo la fonte." *See* "Although by Night."

"¿Que lle digo?" *See* "What Should I Tell Her?"

Que ma joie demeure. See *Joy of Man's Desiring.*

Que trata de España (Otero). PFor 1116-1117.

Que van quedando en el camino, Los (Aguirre). DFor 35-37.

Queen, Ellery. M&D 1375-1383; RevLFEng 3845; **RevShF 1976-1983;** ShF 526, 763. *See also* **Hoch, Edward D.**

Queen After Death (Montherlant). DFor 1352-1353.

Queen Is Dead, The. See *Queen on Tour, The.*

Queen Mary (Tennyson). DEng 1915-1917; RevDEng 2358-2360.

Queen of Spades, The (Pushkin). RevShF 1966-1967, 2665; ShF 170; ShFSup 255-256.

Queen on Tour, The (Abell). DFor 6.

Queene of Navarres Tales, The. See *Heptameron, The.*

Queen's Comedy, The (Bridie). DEng 278; RevDEng 333.

Queen's Husband, The (Sherwood). DEng 1801-1802; RevDEng 2235-2236.

"Queer Client" (Dickens). RevShF 721-722.

Quem quaeritis. DEng 2150, 2244-2245; DFor 2155-2156.

Queneau, Raymond. LFSup 322-332; LTh 269, 1234; PFor 1890.

Quentin, Patrick. M&D 1384-1388.

Quer pasticciaccio brutto de via Merulana. See *That Awful Mess on Via Merulana.*

Querelle of Brest (Genet). LFFor 631-633.

Qu'est-ce que la littérature? See *What Is Literature?*

Quest for Christa T., The (Wolf). LFFor 1935-1938.

Quest for Karla, The. See *Tinker, Tailor, Soldier, Spy, Honourable Schoolboy, The,* and *Smiley's People.*

Quest of the Absolute, The (Balzac). LFFor 92, 93.

Quest of the Gole, The (Hollander). PEng 1364.

"Quest of the Holy Grail, The" (Malory). RevShF 1579.

"Question of the Existence of Waring Stohl, The" (Auchincloss). RevShF 116.

Question of Upbringing, A (Powell, A.). LFEng 2117-2118; RevLFEng 2676-2677.

"Question Poem, The" (Booth). RevPEng 304.

Question Time (Davies). DEng 467-468, 471-472; RevDEng 578, 580-582.

Questions de critique (Brunetière). LTh 235.

Questions of Travel (Bishop). PEng 187; RevPEng 228, 230.

"Quia Multum Amavit" (Swinburne). PEng 2820; RevPEng 3288.

Quiet American, The (Greene, G.). LFEng 1221; RevLFEng 1447.

Quiet as a Nun (Fraser). M&D 657-658.

"Quiet Work" (Arnold). PEng 53; RevPEng 52.

R

Raabe, Wilhelm. LFFor **1373-1386,** 2174-2176.
"Rabbi" (Babel). RevShF 130.
Rabbi of Lud, The (Elkin). RevLFEng 1050.
Rabbit at Rest (Updike). RevLFEng 3354-3355.
Rabbit Is Rich (Updike). LFEng 2698-2699;
RevLFEng 3354.
Rabbit Race, The (Walser, M.). DSup 385-386.
Rabbit Redux (Updike). LFEng 2695-2698;
RevLFEng 3353-3354.
Rabbit, Run (Updike). LFEng 2689, 2692-2695;
RevLFEng 3352-3353, 3806, 3808.
Rabe, David. DEng **1545-1554,** 2413; DSup 408;
RevDEng **1936-1946,** 2933.
Rabelais, François. LFFor **1387-1394,** 2022,
2111-2112.
Rabelais and His World (Bakhtin). LTh 85.
Rabinowitz, Solomon. *See* Aleichem, Sholom.
Racconto d'autunno (Landolfi). RevShF 1394;
ShFSup 129.
Race Rock (Matthiessen). LFEng 1823-1824,
1826; RevLFEng 2309-2310, 2312.
"Race," Writing, and Difference (Gates). LTh
550.
"Racer's Widow, The" (Glück). PSup 135;
RevPEng 1245, 1246.
Rachel Papers, The (Amis, M.). RevLFEng 102.
Rachlin, Nahid. ShF 2774.
Racin, Kosta. PFor 2272.
Racine, Jean. DEng 2173; DFor **1510-1522;**
LTh 669, 708-709, 837, 839-840, 880,
1195-1201, 1306, 1393, 1419; RevDEng
2692-2693.
Racine, Louis. PFor 1861.
Racine and Shakespeare (Hugo). LTh 709.
Racine and Shakespeare (Stendhal). LTh
1393-1395, 1696.
Racing Demon (Hare). RevDEng 1115.
"Radagon in Dianem" (Greene). PEng
1149-1150; RevPEng 1307-1308.
Radcliffe, Ann. LFEng **2195-2204,** 3122, 3126;
M&D **1389-1394;** RevLFEng **2774-2784,**
3783, 3824; ShF 472, 730.
Radetzky March, The (Roth). LFFor 1452-1453.
RADI OS I-IV (Johnson, R.). PSup 214; RevPEng
1716.
Radiance of the King, The (Laye). LFFor
2035-2036.
Radiation (McPherson). RevPEng 2184-2185.

Radičević, Branko. PFor 2253-2254.
Radishchev, Aleksandr. LFFor 2308.
Raditzer (Matthiessen). LFEng 1824-1825, 1826;
RevLFEng 2310-2311. 2312.
Radnóti, Miklós. PFor **1310-1316,** 1986-1987.
Radović, Burislav. PFor 2258.
Radunitsa (Esenin). PFor 478.
"Radwechsel, Der." *See* "Changing the Wheel."
"Rady." *See* "Counsels."
"Rafaelova 'Madonna'" (Zhukovsky). LTh 1613.
Raffel, Burton. ShF 2775.
Raffles, the Amateur Cracksman. See *Amateur
Cracksman, The.*
Raft (Clark-Bekederemo). DSup 56-57; RevDEng
453-454.
Raft of the Medusa, The (Kaiser). DFor
1025-1026.
Ragged Dick (Alger). RevLFEng 3795.
"Raggedy Man, The" (Riley). PEng 2380-2381;
RevPEng 2770-2771.
"Ragman's Daughter, The" (Sillitoe). ShF 2227.
Ragtime (Doctorow). LFEng 770, 777-778;
RevLFEng 937-938.
"Ragtime" (Nin). RevShF 1723-1724; ShF
1950-1951.
Rai Sanyō. PFor 2073.
Raičković, Stevan. PFor 2258.
Railroad (McPherson and Williams, M.). ShF
1855.
Raimann, Jakob. *See* Raimund, Ferdinand.
Raimund, Ferdinand. DFor 1523-1534, 2372.
"Rain" (Booth). PEng 246-247.
"Rain, The" (Creeley). PEng 679-680.
"Rain" (Maugham). RevShF 1627-1628; ShF
1903-1904.
"Rain" (Ponge). PFor 1263-1264.
"Rain Down Home" (Foote). LFEng 978;
RevLFEng 1161.
Rain from Heaven (Behrman). DEng 186, 187;
RevDEng 223, 224.
Rain in the Trees, The (Merwin). RevPEng 2302.
"Rain on the Cumberlands" (Still). PEng 2764;
RevPEng 3227.
Rainbow, The (Lawrence, D. H.). LFEng
1589-1591; RevLFEng 1962-1964, 3767.
"Rainbow" (Plumly). PEng 2238; RevPEng 2610.
Raine, Craig. RevPEng 3901.
"Rainy Moon, The" (Colette). ShF 1166-1167.

"Rainy Mountain Cemetery" (Momaday). PEng 2021; RevPEng 2355.

"Raise High the Roof Beam, Carpenters" (Salinger). RevShF 2042.

Raisin in the Sun, A (Hansberry). DEng 877, 878-880; RevDEng 1086, 1087-1089.

"Raison d'Être of Criticism in the Arts, The" (Forster). LTh 498.

Raj Duszny (Biernat of Lublin). PFor 2119.

Raj Mohan's Wife (Chatterjee). LFFor 2216; ShF 642.

Rājā. See *King of the Dark Chamber, The.*

Rake's Progress, The (Auden and Kallman). DEng 56-57; RevDEng 70-71.

Rakić, Milan. PFor 2255.

Rakosi, Carl. RevPEng 2682-2689.

Rakovy korpus. See *Cancer Ward.*

Raktakarabi. See *Red Oleanders.*

Raleigh, Sir Walter. LFEng 1094-1095; **PEng 2301-2309; RevPEng 2690-2699.**

Ralph Roister Doister (Udall). DEng 1960-1963; RevDEng 2418-2422.

"Ram in the Thicket, The" (Morris). RevShF 1678-1679; ShFSup 202-203.

Ramayana. ShF 137, 642.

"Ramble in St. James's Park, A" (Rochester). PEng 2400-2401; James's Park, A" (Rochester). RevPEng 2792-2793.

Rambler, The (Johnson, S.). LTh 771, 773-774, 777, 1685; RevShF 1284-1285, 2642-2643; ShF 1707, 1708-1709.

Rame, Franca. DSup 108-109.

Rameau's Nephew (Diderot). LFFor 464-465, 2120.

Ramos, José Antonio. DFor 2442.

Ramsay, Allan. PEng 3334.

Ramus, Petrus. LTh 1081.

Ranch, Hieronymus Justesen. DFor 2464.

Randall, Dudley. PEng 2310-2318; PSup 409; **RevPEng 2700-2709.**

Randisi, Robert J. *See* **Carter, Nick.**

Randolph, Georgiana Ann. *See* **Rice, Craig.**

Randolph, Thomas. PEng 2319-2323.

Ranger, Ken. *See* **Creasey, John.**

Ransom (Cleary). M&D 363.

Ransom, John Crowe. LTh 158, 1011, 1148, **1202-1207,** 1424-1425, 1522, 1554, 1753, 1818; **PEng 2324-2333; RevPEng 2710-2720,** 3976.

"Ransom of Red Chief, The" (Henry). RevShF 1181; ShF 1632.

Rao, Raja. LFEng 2205-2215; LFFor 2220; **RevLFEng 2785-2796;** ShF 648.

"Rape" (Rich). ShF 124.

Rape of Lucrece, The (Shakespeare). PEng 2529; RevPEng 2940; ShF 2210.

Rape of the Bucket, The (Tassoni). PFor 2018.

Rape of the Lock, The (Pope). PEng 2255-2257, 3324; RevPEng 2629-2631.

Rape upon Rape (Fielding). DEng 603; RevDEng 746.

"Rapids, The" (Barnard). PSup 26; RevPEng 109.

Rapin, René. LTh 277.

Raport z obleżonego miasta (Herbert). PFor 659-660.

"Rappaccini's Daughter" (Hawthorne). RevShF 1149-1150, 2685-2686; ShF 191, 369-370, 475, 801, 1612.

"Rapsodhia skeseon" (Pentzíkis). PFor 1189. See also *Ikones.*

"Rapture" (Purdy). RevShF 1958.

"Rapture, to Laura" (Schiller). PFor 1406-1407.

"Rapunzel" (Grimm). RevShF 1086-1087; ShF 1558-1559.

"Rapunzel" (Morris). PEng 2054, RevPEng 2385.

Raquel encadenada (Unamuno y Jugo). DFor 1913-1914.

Rasa, Risto. PFor 2200.

"Rashiroshi." *See* "Retreating Figures."

"Rashōmon" (Akutagawa). RevShF 35; ShFSup 9.

Rask, Rasmus. PFor 1732.

Raspberry Picker, The (Hochwälder). DFor 931-932.

Rasputin, Valentin. RevShF 1992-1997.

Rasselas, Prince of Abyssinia (Johnson, S.) LFEng 1468-1473; RevLFEng 1783-1787; RevPEng 1719; RevShF 1285-1288.

"Rasskas o tom, kak zhena ne razreshila muzhu umeret." *See* "Hen-Pecked."

"Rasskaz o samom glavnom." *See* "Story About the Most Important Thing, A."

Rastell, John. DEng 2258-2259; RevDEng 2778-2779.

Rat Man of Paris (West, P.). LFSup 376-377; RevLFEng 3527-3528.

Ratablillo de don Cristóbal, El. See *In the Frame of Don Cristóbal.*

Ratner's Star (DeLillo). LFSup 87-88; RevLFEng 865-866.

Rats (Horovitz). DEng 961-962; RevDEng 1197.

"Rats in the Walls, The" (Lovecraft). ShF 735.

Rat's Mass, A (Kennedy). DSup 215; RevDEng 1307.

Rattigan, Terence. DEng 1555-1565; **RevDEng 1947-1958.**

Rattray, Simon. *See* **Trevor, Elleston.**

Räuber, Die. See *Robbers, The.*

"Rautavaara's Case" (Dick). RevShF 715-716.

Ravagers, The (Hamilton). M&D 819-820.

"Ravages of Spring, The" (Gardner). RevShF 958-959.

Ravenna (Wilde). PEng 3103-3104; RevPEng 3594-3595.

"Ravens, the Sexton, and the Earthworm, The" (Gay). PEng 1076-1077; RevPEng 1211-1212.

"Raven's Wing" (Oates). RevShF 1741.

Ravenswood (McNally). See *Bad Habits.*

Ravishing of Lol Stein, The (Duras). LFFor 534, 537-538.

Ravisht Soule, and the Blessed Weeper, The (Breton, N.). PEng 280-281; RevPEng 344-345.

Raw Flesh (Popa). PFor 1272.

Raw Youth, A (Dostoevski). LFFor 514-515.

Ray (Hannah). RevLFEng 1484-1485.

Ray, David. ShF 2776.

Ray, Raja Rammohan. LFFor 2214.

Raymond, Marcel. LTh 1151, 1808.

Raymond, René Brabazon. *See* **Chase, James Hadley.**

Rayner, Olive Pratt. *See* **Allen, Grant.**

Rayons et les ombres, Les (Hugo). PFor 734.

Rayuela. See *Hopscotch.*

"Razglednicas" (Radnóti). PFor 1316.

Razgovor na bolshoy doroge. See *Conversation on the Highway, A.*

Razgovor ugodni naroda slovinskoga (Miošić). PFor 2261.

Razgrom. See *Nineteen, The.*

Razón de amor (Salinas). PFor 1387.

"Razor, The" (Nabokov). RevShF 1701-1702; ShFSup 218.

Razor's Edge, The (Maugham). LFEng 1849-1850; RevLFEng 2337-2338.

"Razrushenie estetiki" (Pisarev). LTh 1107.

Razvan si Vidra (Hasdeu). DFor 2297.

Re cervo, Il. See *King Stag, The.*

Re Torrismondo, Il (Tasso). DFor 1819-1821.

"Re Travicello, Il." See "King Travicello."

"Reach, The" (King). ShFSup 125.

"Reaching In" (Booth). RevPEng 307.

"Reaching Out with the Hands of the Sun" (Wakoski). RevPEng 3487.

Read, Sir Herbert. LTh 1208-1213.

Reade, Hamish, *See* **Gray, Simon.**

"Reader, The" (Lewis). PSup 255; RevPEng 2000.

"Reading" (Slavitt). RevPEng 3054.

Reading and Feelings (Bleich). LTh 1764.

"Reading and Writing of Short Stories, The" (Welty). ShF 93, 815-816.

"Reading Nijinsky's Diary" (Young). PEng 3213-3214; RevPEng 3737-3738.

Reading the Spirit (Eberhart). PEng 928.

"Readville Stars, The" (Hale, N.). RevShF 1098; ShF 1570.

Real Life of Sebastian Knight, The (Nabokov). LFEng 1951; RevLFEng 2464.

Real People (Lurie). LFSup 251, 253; RevLFEng 2128, 2130.

"Real Thing, The" (James, H.). RevShF 1262, 2712; ShF 1680-1682.

Real Thing, The (Stoppard). DEng 1877-1879; RevDEng 2317-2318.

Realidad (Pérez Galdós). DFor 2501.

Realism in Our Time (Lukács). LTh 938.

"Realists, The" (Pisarev). LTh 1107-1108.

"Realisty." *See* "Realists, The."

Realities of Fiction, The (Hale, N.). RevShF 1100-1101; ShF 1573.

Reality and the Poet in Spanish Poetry (Salinas). PFor 1383, 1389-1390.

"Reality (dreamed), A" (Ekelöf). PFor 450-451.

"Reality in America" (Trilling). LTh 1454.

Realms of Gold, The (Drabble). LFEng 823-825; RevLFEng 988-990.

"Realpolitik and the Death of Galba" (Slavitt). RevPEng 3049.

Reaney, James. DEng 1566-1578; RevDEng 1959-1972.

"Rear Window." *See* "It Had to Be Murder."

Reardon Poems, The (Blackburn). PEng 200-201; RevPEng 244-245.

"Reasonable Use of the Unreasonable, A" (O'Connor, Flannery). RevShF 1759.

Reasons for Moving (Strand). PEng 2769; RevPEng 3233-3234.

Reasons of State (Carpentier). LFFor 286-287.

"Reassurances and Revisions" (Biermann). PFor 190.

Rebecca (du Maurier). M&D 553-554.

Rebel Angels, The (Davies). LFEng 671; RevLFEng 798-799, 801-802.

Rebels, The (Ngugi). DSup 269-270; RevDEng 1718.

Rèbora, Clemente. PFor 2045.

Recapitulation (Stegner). LFEng 2502-2503; RevLFEng 3133-3134.

"Recapture of the Storyable, The" (Munson). ShF 84.

Recensenten og dyret (Heiberg, J.). DFor 902-903.

"Research on the Technique of the Novel" (Butor). LTh 251.

"Resemblance Between a Violin Case and a Coffin, The" (Williams, T.). RevShF 2480-2481; ShF 2435-2436.

Residence on Earth (Neruda). PFor 1075-1076, 1077.

Residencia en la tierra. See *Residence on Earth.*

"Residential Streets" (Hall). PEng 1199-1200.

"Residents and Transients" (Mason). RevShF 1620.

"Resignation" (Schiller). PFor 1407-1408.

"Resigning from a Job in the Defense Industry" (McPherson). RevPEng 2183.

Resistance to Theory, The (de Man). LTh 351.

Resisting Reader, The (Fetterley). RevPEng 3970.

"Resolution and Independence" (Wordsworth). ShF 180.

Résponce aux injures et calomnies de je ne sçay quels predicans et ministres de Genève (Ronsard). PFor 1359.

"Response to a Request" (Walser, R.). RevShF 2390; ShFSup 348.

"Rest" (Newman). PEng 2104.

Rest Home (Cela). LFFor 292.

Rest in Pieces (McInerny). M&D 1162.

Restif de la Bretonne, Nicholas. LFFor 2121.

Restless Serpents (Zamora). RevPEng 3925.

Restlessness of Shanti Andia, The (Baroja). LFFor 110.

Resurrection, The (Gardner, J.). LFEng 1071-1072; RevLFEng 1271-1272.

Resurrection (Tolstoy). LFFor 1722.

Resurrection of the Word (Shklovsky). LTh 1341.

Resurreicão (Machado de Assis). LFFor 1042.

"Resuscitation of a Vampire, The" (Rymer). ShF 732.

"Reszket a bokor, mert." *See* "Bush Trembles, Because, The."

Retablo de las maravillas, El. See *Wonder Show, The.*

Retenue d'amours (Charles d'Orléans). PFor 340.

"Retornos de Chopin a través de unas manos ya idas." *See* "Returns: Chopin by Way of Hands Now Gone."

Retornos de lo vivo lejano (Alberti). PFor 22-23.

"Retornos del amor en una noche de verano." *See* "Returns: A Summer Night's Love."

Retour imprévu, Le. See *Unexpected Return, The.*

Retreat, The (Appelfeld). LFSup 39.

"Retreating Figures" (Endō). RevShF 835-836.

Retrieval System, The (Kumin). RevPEng 1874-1876.

"Return, The" (Berry). PEng 151.

Return, The (de la Mare). LFEng 709-710; RevLFEng 844-845.

"Return" (Sikelianos). PFor 1957-1958.

"Return, The" (Warren). RevPEng 3520.

Return from the Stars (Lem). LFFor 1010-1011.

"Return of a Private, The" (Garland). RevShF 969; ShF 1469-1470.

Return of A. J. Raffles, The (Greene, G.). DEng 833; *J. Raffles, The* (Greene, G.). RevDEng 1027.

Return of Ansel Gibbs, The (Buechner). LFEng 351-352; RevLFEng 447-448.

"Return of Aphrodite, The" (Sarton). PEng 2461; RevPEng 2865.

"Return of Iphigenia, The" (Rítsos). PFor 1970.

Return of Moriarty, The (Gardner, J.). M&D 696.

Return of Peter Grimm, The (Belasco). DEng 196-197; RevDEng 234-235.

"Return of the Goddess" (Graves). PEng 1132; RevPEng 1289.

Return of the King, The. See *Lord of the Rings, The.*

Return of the Native, The (Hardy). LFEng 1268-1270; RevLFEng 1504-1506.

Return of the Sphinx (MacLennan). LFEng 1746-1747; RevLFEng 2215-2216.

"Return to Hinton" (Tomlinson). PEng 2909; RevPEng 3377.

Return to My Native Land (Césaire). PFor 327-328, 329.

Return to Región. See *Volverás a Región.*

"Return Trips" (Adams). RevShF 9.

Returning to Earth (Harrison, J.). PEng 1233-1234; RevPEng 1414-1415.

"Returns: A Summer Night's Love" (Alberti). PFor 23.

"Returns: Chopin by Way of Hands Now Gone" (Alberti). PFor 23.

Reuben (Wideman). RevLFEng 3567.

Reuben, Reuben (De Vries). LFEng 740; RevLFEng 888-889.

"Reuben, Reuben" (Harper). PSup 162; RevPEng 1402.

"Reunion" (Goethe). PFor 588. See also *West-Eastern Divan.*

Reunion (Mamet). RevDEng 1568.

Reunion in Vienna (Sherwood). DEng 1803-1804; RevDEng 2237-2238.

Reuter, Christian. LFFor 2152.

Revard, Carter, 3936.

"Revelation" (O'Connor, Flannery). RevShF 1763.

"Revelation and Evolution" (Gullason). ShF 78.
"Revelation in the Short Story" (Sullivan, W.). ShF 91.
Revenge (Fredro). DFor 2277.
Revenge (Harrison). RevLFEng 1539-1540; RevShF 1123-1124.
"Revenge, The" (Pardo Bazán). RevShF 1843-1844; ShF 2049-2050.
Revenge for Love, The (Lewis, W.). LFEng 1687; RevLFEng 2084.
Revenge of Bussy d'Ambois, The (Chapman). DEng 359-360, 2288; RevDEng 420-421, 2807.
"Revenge of Hannah Kemhuff, The" (Walker). RevShF 2380; ShFSup 337-338.
Revenge of the Lawn (Brautigan). RevShF 315-316; ShFSup 55.
Revengers' Comedies, The (Ayckbourn). RevDEng 77.
Revenger's Tragedy, The (Tourneur). DEng 1934-1941, 2292; RevDEng 2393-2400, 2811.
Reverdy, Pierre. PFor 1888-1889; PSup 319-327.
"Reverend Father Gaucher's Elixir, The" (Daudet). RevShF 674; ShF 1239-1240.
"Reversion to Type, A" (Norris). RevShF 1730; ShF 1957.
Reviczky, Gyula. PFor 1983.
"Review, The" (Rakosi). RevPEng 2688.
"Review of *Twice-Told Tales*" (Poe). RevShF 2678; ShF 87-88.
Revizor. See *Inspector General, The.*
Revolt of Islam, The (Shelley). LTh 1334, 1336.
"Revolt of 'Mother,'" (Freeman, M.). RevShF 911-912; ShF 1417-1418.
Revolt of the Angels, The (France). LFFor 579.
Revolt of the Fishermen, The (Seghers). LFFor 1526-1527.
Révolte des anges, La. See *Revolt of the Angels, The.*
Revolution der Lyrik (Holz). LTh 693.
"Revolution in the Revolution in the Revolution" (Snyder). PEng 2674.
"Revolutions, Les" (Lamartine). PFor 834-835. See also *Harmonies poetiques et religieuses.*
"Revolver, The" (Pardo Bazán). RevShF 1844; ShF 2050-2051.
Rexroth, Kenneth. PEng 2348-2355; RevPEng 2735-2742.
Reyes, Alfonso. PFor 1317-1323.
Reymont, Władysław. LFFor 1404-1411, 2063.
Reynolds, Henry. LTh 1675.
Reynolds, Sir Joshua. LTh 91, 1214-1220.

Reznikoff, Charles. PEng 2356-2362; RevPEng 2743-2750.
"R. F. at Bread Loaf His Hand Against a Tree" (Swenson). PEng 2798; RevPEng 3264.
Rhesis. RevDEng 2653-2654.
Rhesus (Euripides?). DFor 2130-2131.
"'Rhetoric' and Poetic Drama" (Eliot). LTh 448.
Rhetoric of Fiction, The (Booth). LTh 184-186, 560; ShF 299.
"Rhetoric of Hitler's 'Battle,' The" (Burke, K.). LTh 246.
Rhetoric of Irony, A (Booth). LTh 186.
Rhetoric of Religion, The (Burke, K.). LTh 247.
Rhetoric, Romance, and Technology (Ong). LTh 1082.
Rhetorica ad Herrenium (Cicero). LTh 1653.
Rhinoceros (Ionesco). DFor 1001-1002, 2253-2255, 2357.
Rhinthon of Tarentum. DFor 2137.
Rhodanes et Simonis. See *Babyloniaca.*
Rhode, John. M&D 1412-1419.
Rhodes, Eugene Manlove. ShF 603, 604-605.
Rhodius, Apollonius. *See* **Apollonius Rhodius.**
"Rhodora, The" (Emerson). PEng 959; RevPEng 1089.
R'Hoone, Lord. *See* **Balzac, Honoré de.**
"Rhotruda" (Tuckerman). PEng 2939; RevPEng 3406.
"Rhyme" (Bogan). PEng 235; RevPEng 282.
Rhymes, The (Bécquer). PFor 154, 155-158.
Rhymes (Petrarch). See *Canzoniere.*
Rhymes of a Red Cross Man (Service). PEng 2514; RevPEng 2923.
Rhys, Jean. LFEng 2226-2233; RevLFEng 2817-2824; RevShF 1998-2003; ShF 244-245, 2779; ShFSup 258-263.
Riba, Carles. PFor 1774-1775.
Ribman, Ronald. DSup 309-316; RevDEng 1973-1981.
Ricahembra, La (Tamayo y Baus). DFor 1805-1806.
Rice, Craig. M&D 1420-1426.
Rice, Elmer. DEng 1579-1588. RevDEng 1982-1992.
Riceyman Steps (Bennett). LFEng 246.
Riceyman Steps (Bennett). RevLFEng 300.
"Rich" (Gilchrist). RevShF 986.
Rich, Adrienne. PEng 2363-2371; PSup 409; RevPEng 2751-2761, 3970.
Rich and Famous (Guare). RevDEng 1060.
"Rich Boy, The" (Fitzgerald). RevShF 862; ShF 1372.
"Rich Brother, The" (Wolff). RevShF 2509.

"Rinconete and Cortadillo" (Cervantes). RevShF 464-465; ShF 1090-1092.

Rinehart, Mary Roberts. M&D 1427-1433.

Ring and the Book, The (Browning, R.). PEng 344-346; RevPEng 415-417.

Ring of the Löwenskölds, The (Lagerlöf). LFFor 985-986, 2344.

"Ringing the Bells" (Sexton). PEng 2521; RevPEng 2931.

Ringwood, Gwen Pharis. DEng 2440-2441; RevDEng 2963-2964.

Rintala, Paavo. LFFor 2369.

Río, un amor, Un (Cernuda). PFor 320-321.

Riotous Assembly (Sharpe). RevLFEng 3847-3848.

"Rip Van Winkle" (Irving, W.). RevLFEng 3800; RevShF 1247-1248, 2653-2655; ShF 157-159, 1664-1665.

Riprap (Snyder). RevPEng 3103-3104.

Rise of Silas Lapham, The (Howells). LFEng 1375-1376, 3049, 3086; RevLFEng 1651-1652, 3757, 3795.

"Rise of the Short Story, The" (Harte). ShF 79.

Rishel, Mary Ann. ShF 2780.

Rising and Falling (Matthews). RevPEng 2244-2245.

"Risurrezione, La" (Manzoni). PFor 958-959. See also *Sacred Hymns, The.*

"Rite, The" (Randall, D.). PEng 2316-2317; RevPEng 2706-2707.

"Rites and Ceremonies" (Hecht). RevPEng 1456-1458.

Rites of Passage (Brathwaite). PEng 268; PFor 212.

Rites of Passage (Golding). LFEng 1136; RevLFEng 1356.

"Rites of Passage" (Gunn). PEng 1176.

Rítsos, Yánnis. PFor 1344-1352, 1967-1970.

Ritt über den Bodensee, Der. See *Ride Across Lake Constance, The.*

"Ritter Gluck" (Hoffman). RevShF 1214; ShF 1646.

"Ritual I" (Blackburn). PEng 196-197; RevPEng 240-241.

"Ritual IV" (Blackburn). PEng 197; RevPEng 241.

Ritz, The (McNally). DEng 1232-1233; RevDEng 1553-1554.

Rival Queens, The (Lee). DEng 1119-1121; RevDEng 1400-1402.

Rivals, The (Sheridan). DEng 1774-1776; RevDEng 2207-2209.

Rivas, Duke of. See **Saavedra, Ángel de.**

Riven Doggeries (Tate, J.). PEng 2839-2840; RevPEng 3310-3311.

"River," *See* "Arethusa, The First Morning."

"River, The" (Patmore). PEng 2189; RevPEng 2560.

River Between, The (Ngugi wa Thiong'o). LFEng 1978-1980; LFFor 2041, 2044; RevLFEng 2498, 2501-2504.

"River by Our Village, The" (Tu Fu). PFor 1543.

River of Heaven, The (Hongo). RevPEng 1573-1574.

River of Madness, The (Hakim). DSup 175.

"Riverman, The" (Bishop). PEng 186; RevPEng 229.

"Rivers, The" (Ungaretti). PFor 1566. See also *Allegria, L'.*

Rivers and Forests, The (Duras). DFor 511.

"Rivers and Mountains" (Ashbery). RevPEng 59.

Rivière, Jacques. LFFor 24, 25, 26.

Road, The (Martinson). LFFor 2351.

Road, The (Soyinka). DEng 1851-1854; RevDEng 2291-2293.

Road Block (Waugh). M&D 1685-1686.

"Road from Colonus, The" (Forster). RevShF 888; ShF 1391.

Road Leads On, The (Hamsun). LFFor 768.

Road to Mecca, The (Fugard). DEng 705-707; RevDEng 875-876.

Road to Rome, The (Sherwood). DEng 1799-1801; RevDEng 2233-2235.

"Road to Shu Is Hard, The" (Li Po). PFor 891-892.

Road to the City, The (Ginzburg). LFSup 129.

Roads of Destiny (Henry). RevShF 1180; ShF 1631.

Roads to Freedom (Sartre). LFFor 1514-1517.

"Roan Stallion" (Jeffers). PEng 1492; RevPEng 1705.

Roaring Girl, The (Middleton and Dekker). DEng 1327-1329; RevDEng 1664-1666.

Rob Roy (Scott). LFEng 2373-2377; RevLFEng 2991-2995.

"Roba, La." *See* "Property."

Robbe-Grillet, Alain. LFFor 1412-1422, 2146-2147; LFSup 406; LTh 251, 1233-1238; M&D 1434-1441; ShF 2153-2157.

Robber, The (Čapek). DFor 336-337.

Robber Bridegroom, The (Welty). LFEng 2822-2823; RevLFEng 3493-3494; ShF 481.

Robbers, The (Schiller). DFor 1657, 2367-2368.

Robe rouge, La. See *Red Robe, The.*

Robert Browning (Chesterton). ShF 714.

"Robert Kennedy Saved from Drowning" (Barthelme). RevShF 165; ShF 99-100; ShFSup 25.

Roberts, Charles G. D. ShF 636.

Roberts, Elizabeth Madox. LFEng 2274-2283; RevLFEng 2869-2879.

Roberts, James Hall. M&D 1442-1447.

Roberts, Lawrence. See **Fish, Robert L.**

Robertson, Mary Elsie. ShF 2781.

Robertson, Thomas William. DEng 1599-1611, 2364-2365; DFor 2237; **RevDEng 2003-2016,** 2882-2883.

Robeson, Kenneth. See **Dent, Lester, and Goulart, Ron.**

Robin, Ralph. ShF 2782.

"Robin Redbreast" (Kunitz). PSup 245-246; RevPEng 1886-1887.

Robinson, Edwin Arlington. PEng 2384-2394, 3388; **RevPEng 2775-2786.**

Robinson, Lennox. DEng 1612-1621; RevDEng 2017-2027.

Robinson, Leonard Wallace. ShF 2784.

Robinson, Nugent. ShF 589.

Robinson Crusoe (Defoe). LFEng 688-690, 3019-3020; RevLFEng 821-824, 3727-3728, 3733.

Robinson Crusoë (Pixérécourt). DFor 1479-1480.

Robison, Mary. RevShF 2010-2017.

"Robles, Los." See "Oaks, The."

Robles, Alfred, 3917-3918.

Robortello, Francesco. LTh 310, 1664.

"Robot" (Davenport). RevShF 681.

Robson, Deborah. ShF 2785.

Rocannon's World (Le Guin). LFEng 1632-1633; RevLFEng 2008-2009.

Rocher, Jean-Antoine. PFor 1862.

Rochester, John Wilmot, Earl of. PEng 2395-2404; RevPEng 2787-2797.

Rock Garden, The (Shepard). RevDEng 2193.

"Rock-of-the-Mas" (Corkery). ShF 667, 668.

"Rock Springs" (Ford). RevShF 880-881.

Rock Wagram (Saroyan). LFEng 2337-2338; RevLFEng 2952-2953.

Rocket to the Moon (Odets). DEng 1401-1402; RevDEng 1777-1778.

Rocket to the Morgue (Boucher). M&D 171.

"Rocking-Horse Winner, The" (Lawrence, D. H.). ShF 115, 481, 520, 786, 1792-1793.

"Rockpile, The" (Baldwin). ShF 581.

"Rocks, The" (Creeley). PEng 682.

Röda rummet. See *Red Room, The.*

Roderick Random (Smollett). LFEng 2447-2448, 3104; RevLFEng 3072-3073, 3735, 3782, 3806.

Roderick, the Last of the Goths (Southey). PEng 2682-2683; RevPEng 3125-3126.

"Rodez" (Davie). PSup 87; RevPEng 852.

Rodgers, Richard, and Oscar Hammerstein II. RevDEng 1995, 1999, 2997.

Rodgers, Richard, and **Lorenz Hart. DEng 896,** 898-899, 900, 901; RevDEng 1119, 1121-1127.

Rodríguez Álvarez, Alejandro. See **Casona, Alejandro.**

Roethke, Theodore. PEng 2405-2415; RevPEng 2798-2808.

"Roger Malvin's Burial" (Hawthorne). RevShF 1145; ShF 114.

Rogers, Samuel Shepard. See **Shepard, Sam.**

Roger's Version (Updike). RevLFEng 3358.

Rogue Cop (McGivern). M&D 1156.

"Rogul'ka." See "Buoy, The."

Rohmer, Sax. M&D 1448-1453.

Rohrberger, Mary. RevShF 2678.

Roi des aulnes, Le. See *Ogre, The.*

Roi sans divertissement, Un (Giono). LFFor 657.

Roi se meurt, Le. See *Exit the King.*

Rojas, Fernando de. DFor 2483; RevDEng 2681.

Rojas Zorrilla, Francisco de. DFor 2495.

Roksolanki (Zimorowic). PFor 2121.

Roland, Alan, PEng 3425; RevPEng 3960.

Roland, Betty. RevDEng 2956.

Roland and Vernagu. RevShF 2616.

Roland Barthes by Roland Barthes (Barthes). LTh 104.

Role of the Reader, The (Eco). LTh 425.

Rolland, Romain. LFFor 1423-1432, 2141-2142.

Rolls, Anthony. See **Vulliamy, C. E.**

"Romagna, The" (Pascoli). PFor 1141.

Romains, Jules. DFor 1547-1556, 2350-2351; LFFor 1433-1445.

Roman bourgeois. See *City Romance.*

Roman comique, Le. See *Comical Romance, The.*

Roman de Brut (Wace). ShF 441.

Roman de la Rose, Le. See *Romance of the Rose, The.*

Roman de Renart. PFor 1840.

Roman Elegies (Goethe). PFor 584, 586-587, 1913.

Roman expérimental, Le. See *Experimental Novel, The.*

"Roman Fever" (Wharton). ShF 539.

Roman Forgeries (Traherne). PEng 2924; RevPEng 3397.

"Rosa" (Barnes). RevDEng 147.
"Rosa" (Ozick). RevShF 1831-1833.
Rosa, João Guimarães. *See* **Guimarães Rosa, João.**
"Rosa Alchemica" (Yeats). RevShF 2528.
Rosa do povo, A (Drummond de Andrade). PSup 99-100.
Rosalynde (Lodge). ShF 492.
"Rosalynds Madrigal" (Lodge). PEng 1732; RevPEng 2016.
Rosamond (Addison). DEng 4-6; RevDEng 4-6.
"Rosanna" (Edgeworth). RevShF 802; ShF 1326-1327.
"Rosas amo dos jardins do Adónis, As." *See* "Roses of the Gardens of Adonis, The."
"Rose, The" (Creeley). PEng 680.
"Rose, The" (Fanshawe). PEng 999-1000; RevPEng 1131-1132.
Rose (Lee). RevPEng 3914.
Rose, Wendy, 3936.
Rose Bernd (Hauptmann). DFor 873-874.
Rose caduche (Verga). DFor 1943-1944.
"Rose for Ecclesiastes, A" (Zelazny). ShF 371.
"Rose for Emily, A" (Faulkner). M&D 586-587; RevShF 849-852, 2731; ShF 112, 1360-1363.
Rose Garden, The (Sa'di of Sheraz). PFor 1377, 1381-1382; RevShF 2568.
Rose of Dutcher's Coolly (Garland). LFEng 1087; RevLFEng 1290.
Rose of Solitude, The (Everson). PEng 991-992; RevPEng 1122-1123.
Rose of Tibet, The (Davidson). M&D 457.
"Rosebush on the Hillside" (Petőfi). PFor 1225.
"Roselily" (Walker). RevShF 2379-2380; ShFSup 336-337.
"Rosemary" (Moore). PEng 2047; RevPEng 2377.
Rosen by Any Other Name, A (Horovitz). RevDEng 1199.
Rosencrantz and Guildenstern Are Dead (Stoppard). DEng 1872-1873; RevDEng 2311-2312.
Rosenfeld, Rita L. ShF 2787.
Rosengarten, Theodore. ShF 627.
Rosenstock, Sami. *See* **Tzara, Tristan.**
Rosenthal, Carole. ShF 2788.
"Roses and Revolution" (Randall, D.). PEng 2315-2316; RevPEng 2705-2706.
"Roses of the Gardens of Adonis, The" (Pessoa). PFor 1209-1210.
Roshwald, Mordecai. ShF 2789.
"Rosina Alcona to Julius Branzaida." *See* "Remembrance."
Rosmersholm (Ibsen). DFor 983-985.

Ross (Rattigan). DEng 1562-1563; RevDEng 1955.
Ross, Bernard L. *See* **Follett, Ken.**
Ross, Sinclair. LFEng 2284-2297; RevLFEng 2880-2894; ShF 638.
Rossetti, Christina. PEng 2416-2423; RevPEng 2806-2816, 3867.
Rossetti, Dante Gabriel. LTh 1398, 1734, 1822; PEng 2424-2434; RevPEng 2817-2828, 3867.
Rossia i intelligentsia (Blok). PFor 196.
"Rosso Malpelo" (Verga). RevShF 2347; ShF 2381.
Rostand, Edmond. DFor 1557-1567, 2350.
Rosten, Norman. ShF 2790.
"Rot, The" (Lewis). RevShF 1484.
"Rot" (Williams, J.). RevShF 2475.
Roth, Joseph. LFFor 1446-1453, 2191.
Roth, Philip. LFEng 2298-2310, 3324-3325; LFSup 406; RevLFEng 2895-2905, 3877; RevShF 2018-2023; ShF 2158-2162.
"Rothschild's Fiddle" (Chekhov). RevShF 516.
Rotimi, Ola. DEng 1622-1630; RevDEng 2028-2037.
Rotrou, Jean de. DFor 1568-1577.
Rotting Hill (Lewis). RevShF 1483, 1484-1486.
Rouge et le noir, Le. See *Red and the Black, The.*
Rough Field, The (Montague). PEng 2037-2038; RevPEng 2363-2364.
"Rough Justice" (Nebel). M&D 1266.
Rougon-Macquart, Les (Zola). LFFor 1988, 1989-1995.
Round and Round the Garden (Ayckbourn). DEng 65-66; RevDEng 80-81. See also *Norman Conquests, The.*
"Round Dozen, The" (Maugham). ShF 1904.
Rounding the Horn (Slavitt). RevPEng 3052.
Rousseau, Jean-Baptiste. PFor 1859-1860.
Rousseau, Jean-Jacques. LFEng 3114-3115; LFFor 1454-1460, 2120-2121; LTh 1239-1244, 1381, 1393-1394, 1696, 1709; RevLFEng 3737, 3816-3817; RevShF 2645-2646.
Rousset, Jean. LFEng 3118; LTh 1151.
Route antique des hommes pervers, La. See *Job, the Victim of His People.*
Route des Flandres, La. See *Flanders Road, The.*
"Route of Evanescence, A" (Dickinson). PEng 806; RevPEng 918.
Roux, Paul. *See* Roux, Saint-Pol.
Roux, Saint-Pol. PFor 1880.
Rover, The (Behn). DEng 176-177; RevDEng 212-213.
Rovetta, Gerolamo. DFor 2409-2410.

Russell, William. ShF 751.

Russet Mantle (Riggs). DEng 1595-1596; RevDEng 1999-2000.

Russia House, The (le Carré). RevLFEng 1993.

"Russian at the Rendez-vous, The" (Chernyshevsky). LTh 289.

Russian Life in the Interior. See *Sportsman's Sketches, A.*

"Russkii chelovek na rendez-vous." *See* "Russian at the Rendez-vous, The."

Russo, Albert. ShF 2792.

Russo, Fernando. PFor 2035.

Rusteghi, I. See *Boors, The.*

"Rustic Chivalry" (Verga). DFor 1944-1945, 2411; RevShF 2346-2347; ShF 2479-2380.

Rusticus (Poliziano). PFor 1256. See also *Sylvae.*

Rutebeuf. DFor 2164.

Ruth. ShF 352-356.

Ruth (Gaskell). LFEng 1098, 1103-1104; RevLFEng 1301, 1306-1307.

"Ruth's Blues" (Harper). PSup 162-163; RevPEng 1402-1403.

Ruy Blas (Hugo). DFor 968-969.

Ryan, Tim. *See* **Dent, Lester.**

Rydberg, Viktor. LFFor 2337-2338; PFor 2167.

Ryder, Jonathan. *See* **Ludlum, Robert.**

Ryga, George. DEng 1639-1648; RevDEng 2047-2057.

Rymer, Thomas. LTh 1250-1255, 1688.

Ryskind, Morrie. RevDEng 1300-1302.

Rytsar nashego vremeni (Karamzin). LFFor 2307.

Ryum, Ulla. LFFor 2366.

S

S. (Updike). RevLFEng 3358-3359.
"S ANGEL" (Chabon). RevShF 468-469.
"S veselym rzhaniem pasutsia tabuny." See "Happily Neighing, the Herds Graze."
S/Z (Barthes). LTh 106, 1765.
Saar, Ferdinand von. LFFor 2187.
Saarikoski, Pentti. PFor 2198-2199.
Saavedra, Ángel de. DFor 1612-1619, 2498.
Saavedra, Miguel de Cervantes. See **Cervantes, Miguel de.**
Saba, Umberto. PFor 2042-2043; PSup 342-349.
Sabato, Ernesto. LFFor 1461-1469, 2295-2296.
"Sabato del villaggio, Il." See "Saturday Evening in the Village."
"Sabbatha and Solitude" (Williams, T.). RevShF 2481; ShF 2437.
Sabbaths (Berry). RevPEng 185.
"Sacajawea's Gold" (Hoch). RevShF 1208.
Sachs, Hans. DFor 1620-1627, 2178-2179.
Sachs, Leonie. See **Sachs, Nelly.**
Sachs, Nelly. PFor 1370-1376.
Sackett's Land (L'Amour). LFSup 223; RevLFEng 1934.
Sackful of News, The. ShF 497.
Sackler, Howard. DEng 1649-1653; RevDEng 2058-2063.
Sackville, Thomas. PEng 2435-2443; RevPEng 2838-2846.
Sackville, Thomas, and **Thomas Norton.** DEng 1370-1381; **RevDEng 1746-1757.**
Sacred Hymns, The (Manzoni). PFor 958-960.
"Sacred Mound, The" (Foote). LFEng 979; RevLFEng 1162.
"Sacrifice, The" (Herbert). PEng 1302; RevPEng 1481.
"Sad Fate of Mr. Fox, The" (Harris, J.). RevShF 1117; ShF 1588.
"Sad Hour of Your Peace, The" (Young). PEng 3215-3216; RevPEng 3740.
"Sad Landscapes" (Verlaine). PFor 1628.
Sad Shepherd, The (Jonson). DEng 2286; RevDEng 2805.
Saddest Summer of Samuel S., The (Donleavy). LFEng 785; RevLFEng 948.
Sade, Marquis de. LFFor 2122.
Sa'di. PFor 1377-1382.
Sadler, Mark. See **Collins, Michael.**

"Sadness and Happiness" (Pinsky). PEng 2214-2215; RevPEng 2584-2585.
Sadness and Happiness (Pinsky). PEng 2212-2214; RevPEng 2583-2588.
Sado kōshaku fujin. See *Madame de Sade.*
Šafárik, Pavol Jozef. PFor 1799, 1808.
"Safe" (Johnson, J.). ShF 1702-1703, 1705.
"Safe Place, The" (Morris). RevShF 1679-1680; ShFSup 203-204.
"Safety" (Brooke). PEng 306; RevPEng 372.
Safety Net, The (Böll). LFFor 188.
Saga of Gisli, The. LFFor 2332; RevShF 2590; ShF 393.
Saga of the Volsungs, The. See *Volsunga Saga.*
Sagan (Bergman). DFor 188.
Sagan, Françoise. LFFor 1470-1479.
Sagan om Fatumeh (Ekelöf). PFor 453.
"Sage in the Sierra, The" (Van Doren). PEng 2957-2958; RevPEng 3435.
Sagesse (Verlaine). PFor 1628, 1631-1632.
"Saget mir ieman, waz ist Minne?" See "What Is Loving?"
Saggio metafisico sopra l'entusiasmo nelle belle arti (Paradisi). LTh 1691.
Sahgal, Nayantara. LFFor 2223.
Said, Edward. LTh 506.
"Said King Pompey" (Sitwell). PEng 2629; RevPEng 3033.
Saikaku, Ihara. PFor 2070; RevShF 2024-2032; ShFSup 264-272.
Saikaku okimiyage (Saikaku), RevShF 2030-2031; ShFSup 271.
Saikaku skokoku-banashi (Saikaku). RevShF 2029; ShFSup 270.
Saiko, Georg. LFFor 2206.
"Sail, The" (Lermontov). PFor 871.
"Sailing to Byzantium" (Yeats). PEng 3362; RevPEng 3727-3729.
"Sailor, The" (Wescott). RevShF 2442.
"Sailor-Boy's Tale, The" (Dinesen). RevShF 739-740, 2740-2741.
"Sailor off the Bremen" (Shaw). RevShF 2100-2101; ShF 2222-2223.
Sailors of Cattaro, The (Wolf). DFor 2020-2021.
Sailors Song (Hanley). LFEng 1250; RevLFEng 1478.
"St. Agnes' Eve" (Fearing). RevPEng 1139.

"Saint Augustine's Pigeon" (Connell). RevShF 602; ShF 1181.

"St. Cecilia: Or, The Power of Music" (Kleist). RevShF 1374-1375; ShF 1762.

"St. Columba and the River" (Dreiser). RevShF 778; ShF 1311.

St. Edmund and Fremund (Lydgate). RevPEng 2104.

St. Elsewhere. RevDEng 3042.

"St. Emmanuel the Good, Martyr" (Unamuno). LFEng 3303-3304.

Saint Erkenwald (Pearl-Poet). PEng 2196; RevPEng 2567.

Saint Genet: Actor and Martyr (Sartre). DFor 2259; Lth 1274.

St. Helena (Sherriff). DEng 1790-1791; RevDEng 2224-2225.

Saint Jack (Theroux). LFEng 2630, 2631-2632; RevLFEng 3284-3285.

Saint Joan (Shaw). DEng 1739-1742; RevDEng 2160-2163, 2900.

"St. John" (Dixon). PEng 817.

St. John on Patmos (Dixon). PEng 819.

"Saint Judas" (Wright, James). PEng 3163-3164; RevPEng 3675-3676.

Saint Judas (Wright, James). RevPEng 3671-3676.

Saint Maker, The (Holton). M&D 901.

Saint Manuel Bueno, Martyr (Unamuno). LFFor 1793-1796.

St. Mawr (Lawrence). RevShF 1426.

St. Olaf's Saga (Sturluson, Snorri). RevShF 2586; ShF 388.

St. Patrick's Day (Sheridan). DEng 1781-1782; RevDEng 2214-2215.

"St. Paul" (Dixon). PEng 817.

"Saint Paul" (Smith). RevShF 2156.

Saint Paul of Lavanthal. DFor 2178.

St. Peter's Complaint (Southwell). PEng 2689-2690, 3293; RevPEng 3132-3133, 3812.

"Saint Scholastica" (Castro). PFor 281. See also *Beside the River Sar.*

St. Urbain's Horseman (Richler). LFEng 2259-2260; RevLFEng 2849, 2851-2852.

Saint-Aubin, Horace de. *See* **Balzac, Honoré.**

Sainte Carmen of the Main (Tremblay). DSup 352-353.

"Sainte Lucie" (Walcott). PEng 3005.

"Sainte Mary Magdalen or The Weeper" (Crashaw). PEng 670-672; RevPEng 767-769.

Sainte-Beuve, Charles-Augustin. LTh 111, 555, 753, 1087, 1173, 1180, **1256-1263,** 1418, 1421.

Saint-Exupéry, Antoine de. LFFor 1480-1486, 2143.

Saint-Lambert, Jean François, Marquis de. PFor 1861.

"Saints" (Everson). PEng 990; RevPEng 1122.

Saints and Sinners (Jones, H. A.). DEng 1002-1003; RevDEng 1268-1269.

Saint's Day (Whiting). DEng 2025-2027; RevDEng 2524-2526.

"Saint's Encouragement, The" (Fanshawe). PEng 998-999; RevPEng 1130-1131.

Saintsbury, George. LFEng 1802; **LTh 1264-1269,** 1735; RevLFEng 2279.

Saint-Sorlin, Jean Desmarets de. LTh 1683.

"Sa'iq al-qitar" (Mahfouz). RevShF 1562-1563.

Saison au Congo, Une. See *Season in the Congo, A.*

Saison en enfer, Une. See *Season in Hell, A.*

Saito Mokichi. PFor 2075.

Saki. M&D 1454-1459; RevShF 2033-2037; ShF 516, **2170-2174.**

Śakuntalā (Kālidāsa). DFor 1032-1036, 2387-2388.

Salaam, Huey Newton, Salaam (Bullins). RevDEng 366.

Salah al-mala 'ikah. See *Angels' Prayer.*

Salama, Hannu. LFFor 2369.

"Salami" (Levine). PEng 1716; RevPEng 1992.

Salammbô (Flaubert). LFFor 553-554.

'Salem's Lot (King). LFSup 205-206; M&D 989; RevLFEng 1887-1888.

Salernitano, Massuccio. ShF 680.

Salinas, Pedro. PFor 1383-1390, 2212-2213.

Salinas, Raul. RevPEng 3923.

Salinger, J. D. LFEng 2321-2329; RevLFEng 2929-2938, 3808; **RevShF 2038-2047;** ShF 551, **2175-2181.**

Sallust. PFor 2094.

Sally (Fuller). RevDEng 883.

"Sally Go Round the Moon" (Bates). RevShF 174; ShFSup 30.

Salmacis and Hermaphroditus (Beaumont). PEng 94-95, 97.

Salmagundi (Irving). RevShF 1246; ShF 1663.

Salomé (Wilde). DEng 2034-2036; RevDEng 2533-2535.

"Salon of 1846" (Baudelaire). LTh 1697.

Salt (Soto). RevPEng 3925.

Salt Garden, The (Nemerov). PEng 2078-2079; RevPEng 2428-2429.

Salt Is Leaving (Priestley). M&D 1358-1359.

"Salt Water" (Pinsky). RevPEng 2586.

Salter, James. RevLFEng 2939-2944.

Santob. *See* Sem Tob.

"Santorini" (Merrill). RevPEng 2285.

Santos, Bienvenido N. ShF 2793.

"Sapeur, Le" (Follain). PSup 130-131.

Sapho and Phao (Lyly). DEng 1182; PEng 1819; RevDEng 1484.

Sapientia (Hroswitha). DFor 2153.

Sapper. M&D 1467-1471.

Sappho. PFor 1391-1400, 1759-1761.

Sappho (Daudet). LFFor 424-426.

"Sappho's Last Song" (Leopardi). PFor 860. See also *Canti*.

Sara. ShF 2794.

Sara Videbeck (Almqvist). LFFor 2337.

Sarah (Sackler). DEng 1651; RevDEng 2060.

Sardanapalus (Byron). DEng 329, 340-341; RevDEng 390-391, 400-401.

Sardou, Victorien. DFor 1628-1637, 2346.

Sarmiento, Domingo Faustino. LFFor 2282, 2290, 2294.

Saroyan, William. DEng 1654-1659; LFEng 2330-2342; RevDEng 2064-2071; RevLFEng 2945-2957; RevShF 2057-2062; ShF 264-265, 547, 2187-2192.

Sarraute, Nathalie. LFFor 1500-1508, 2143, 2146.

Sarton, May. LFEng 2343-2352; LFSup 406; PEng 2454-2465; PSup 409; RevLFEng 2958-2968; RevPEng 2858-2871.

Sartor Resartus (Carlyle). LTh 1248.

Sartre, Jean-Paul. DFor 72, 1638-1652, 2356; LFFor 1123-1124, **1509-1517,** 2143; LTh 104, 808, **1270-1276,** 1806; RevShF **2063-2071,** 2742-2743; ShF **2193-2196.**

"Sarugashima." *See* "Island of Monkeys, The."

Sarumino. See *Monkey's Raincoat.*

"Saruzuka." *See* "Mound of the Monkey's Grave, The."

Sarvig, Ole. LFFor 2364-2365; PFor 2188-2189.

Sasame-yuki. See *Makioka Sisters, The.*

Sa-skya Pandita. PFor 2247.

Sassoon, Siegfried. PEng 2466-2475; RevPEng 2872-2881.

Sastre, Alfonso. DFor 2507; DSup 317-325.

"Sat." *See* "Clock, The."

Satan in Goray (Singer, Isaac). LFEng 2433-2434; LFFor 1619-1620; RevLFEng 3060-3061.

Satan in Search of a Wife (Lamb). PEng 1637-1638; RevPEng 1901-1902.

Satan Says (Olds). RevPEng 2490-2491.

Satanic Verses, The (Rushdie). RevLFEng 2919, 2925-2927, 3777, 3793.

Sathianandan, Kamala. ShF 642.

Satin Slipper, The (Claudel). DFor 410-411, **2352.**

Satir (Reljković). PFor 2261.

"Satire Against Mankind, A" (Rochester). PEng 2402-2403; RevPEng 2794.

Satires (Ariosto). PFor 97.

Satires, The (Boileau). LTh 1687.

Satires (Horace). LTh 695-698; PFor 714-715; RevShF 2578.

Satires (Juvenal). ShF 1724-1728.

Satires (Persius). PFor 1198-1203, 2261.

Satires of Circumstance (Hardy). PEng 1221; RevPEng 1394.

Satires upon the Jesuits (Oldham). PEng 2132-2133.

"Satiric Short Story, The" (Fitzgerald, G.). ShF 76.

Satiromastix (Dekker). DEng 2288; RevDEng 2807.

Satokagura. DFor 2417.

Satura. PFor 2085.

Satura (Montale). PFor 1052.

Saturae. RevDEng 2665.

"Saturday Afternoon" (Caldwell). RevShF 370; ShF 1030.

"Saturday Evening in the Village" (Leopardi). PFor 859, 861-862. See also *Canti*.

Saturday Evening Post. ShF 589, 778.

Saturday Night and Sunday Morning (Sillitoe). LFEng 2398-2399, 2400-2401; RevLFEng 3029.

Saturn over the Water (Priestley). M&D 1356-1357.

Saturnalia, The (Macrobius). LTh 963-964, 966, 1646-1647; PFor 2109.

Satyricon, The (Petronius). LFEng 3219; LFFor 2009-2010, 2011-2012; RevShF 1878-1883, 2571; ShF 2091-2092, 2095, 2096.

Satyrs upon the Jesuits (Oldham). RevPEng 2484-2485.

Sauce for the Goose (De Vries). RevLFEng 889.

Saul (Alfieri). DFor 47, 2406.

Saul (Heavysege). DEng 2438; RevDEng 2961.

Saul, George Brandon. ShF 2795.

Saunders, Hilary Aidan St. George. *See* **Beeding, Francis.**

Sauser, Frédéric Louis. *See* **Cendrars, Blaise.**

Sauspiel, Das (Walser, M.). DSup 388-389.

Saussure, Ferdinand de. LTh 105, 422, 549, 559, 828, 849, 912-913, 1229, 1277-1281, 1480, 1627, 1761-1762, 1813, 1827, 1829; PFor 1736; RevPEng 3996-3997.

Savage Mind, The (Lévi-Strauss). LTh 887.

Savage Paris (Zola). LFFor 1989-1990. See also *Rougon-Macquart, Les.*

Savage Streets (McGivern). M&D 1157.

"Savages" (O'Brien, E.). RevShF 1748.

Save Every Lamb (Stuart). RevShF 2235; ShF 2296.

Saved (Bond). DEng 245-247; RevDEng 286-288.

Saving the Appearances (Barfield). LTh 98.

Saving the Queen (Buckley). M&D 234.

Saving the Text (Hartman) 645.

Savings (Hogan). RevPEng 1542.

Saviors of God, The (Kazantzakis). LFFor 918; PFor 786-787, 789-790.

Savon, Le. See *Soap.*

"'Savonarola' Brown" (Beerbohm). RevShF 198-199; ShF 943, 944-945.

"Savoy" (O'Hara). PEng 2127; RevPEng 2478.

Savva (Andreyev). DFor 62-63.

Sawbones Memorial (Ross). LFEng 2295-2297; RevLFEng 2885, 2891-2893.

Saxe-Meiningen, George II, Duke of. DEng 2232.

Saxo Grammaticus. LFFor 2333.

Saxon, Alex. *See* **Pronzini, Bill.**

Saxon, John. *See* **Harvester, Simon.**

"Say Could That Lad Be I" (Lavin). RevShF 1415-1416; ShF 1784.

Say Pardon (Ignatow). PEng 1471-1472; RevPEng 1683-1685.

Sayers, Dorothy L. LFEng 2353-2363; M&D **1472-1481;** RevLFEng 2969-2981, 3844; ShF 758.

Sayings of the High One, The. PFor 2153.

"Scala Scare, The" (Buzzati). RevShF 351; ShFSup 62-63.

Scaliger, Julius Caesar. DEng 2156; LTh 780, **1282-1287,** 1347, 1664.

"Scandal in Bohemia, A" (Doyle). RevShF 767; ShF 1300.

"Scandalous Woman, A" (O'Brien, E.). RevShF 1746-1747.

Scannabue, Aristarco. LTh 92.

Scapegoat, The (Girard). LTh 592.

Scapegoat, The (Settle). LFSup 348-349; RevLFEng 3009-3010. *See also* Beulah Quintet.

Scarcity of Love, A (Kavan). LFEng 1511; RevLFEng 1836.

"Scariboo" (Morgenstern). PFor 1057. See also *Gallows Songs, The.*

Scarlatti Inheritance, The (Ludlum). M&D 1107.

Scarlet Letter, The (Hawthorne). LFEng 1320-1322, 3129; RevLFEng 1575-1577, 3831.

Scarron, Paul. LFFor 2028.

Scars on the Soul (Sagan). LFFor 1476-1477.

Scattered Returns (Sissman). PEng 2616-2618; RevPEng 3020-3022.

"Scene at Rome" (Hallam). PEng 1211; RevPEng 1383.

Scenes from American Life (Gurney). DSup 165-166; RevDEng 1067-1068.

Scenes of Childhood (Warner). RevShF 2407-2408; ShFSup 358.

Schade, Jens August. PFor 2184-2185.

Schaffner, Jakob. LFFor 2208.

Schäffrey von der Nimphen Hercinie, Der (Opitz). LFFor 2151.

Schakels. See *Links.*

"Schalken the Painter" (Le Fanu). RevShF 1443-1445; ShF 1796-1798.

Schaubühne als eine moralische Anstalt betrachtet, Die. See *Theater as a Moral Institution, The.*

Schechner, Richard. DEng 2484.

Schelling, Friedrich Wilhelm Joseph von. LFFor 2164; LTh 117, 599, **1288-1294,** 1302, 1358, 1360, 1696, 1702.

Schernberg, Dietrich. DFor 2169-2170.

Schiller, Friedrich. DEng 2185-2186; DFor 734, **1653-1664,** 2367-2368; LFFor 2160-2161; LTh 118, 437, 531, 596, 599, 663, 670, 790, 985-986, **1295-1300,** 1302, 1305-1306; PFor 682, **1401-1411,** 1914; RevDEng 2705-2706.

Schimmelreiter, Der. See *Rider on the White Horse, The.*

Schindler's Ark. See *Schindler's List.*

Schindler's List (Keneally). LFSup 185; RevLFEng 1841.

Schionatulander and Sigune (Wolfram von Eschenbach). PFor 1700-1701.

Schisgal, Murray. DEng **1660-1665;** DSup 408; RevDEng **2072-2078.**

Schlacht bei Lobositz, Die (Hacks). DFor 852.

Schlaf, Johannes. LTh 1719-1720.

Schlafwandler, Die. See *Sleepwalkers, The.*

"Schlechte Zeit für Lyrik." *See* "Bad Time for Poetry."

Schlegel, August Wilhelm. DFor 2369; LTh 599, 642, 663, 710, **1301-1307,** 1309, 1360-1361, 1392, 1405, 1697, 1699.

Schlegel, Friedrich. LFEng 3141, 3232-3233; LFFor 2166; LTh 433, 437, 599, **1308-1313,** 1360-1361, 1696-1697, 1699, 1702, 1704, 1708, 1710.

Schleiermacher, Friedrich. LFFor 2164; LTh 377-378, 529-530, 1359, 1702, 1809.

"Schloimele" (Singer). RevShF 2134.

Schloss, Das. See *Castle, The.*

Seasons, The (Thomson). PEng 3326; RevPEng 2845.

Season's Difference, The (Buechner). LFEng 348, 350, 351; RevLFEng 444, 447.

Season's Greetings (Ayckbourn). RevDEng 81-82.

"Seasons of the Soul" (Tate, A.). PEng 2829-2831; RevPEng 3298-3300.

Sebastopol (Tolstoy). RevShF 2282-2283.

Secchia rapita, La. See *Rape of the Bucket, The.*

"Sechzigjährige dankt, Der" (Zweig). PFor 1726-1727.

"2nd Air Force" (Jarrell). PEng 1480; RevPEng 1692.

Second *Aliya.* LFFor 20.

Second Birth, The (Pasternak). ShF 2062.

Second Coming, The (Percy). LFEng 2098-2099; RevLFEng 2637-2638.

"Second Coming, The" (Yeats). PEng 3194-3199; RevPEng 3719-3723.

"Second Conversations with Ogotemmêl" (Wright, Jay). RevPEng 3687.

"Second Didactic Poem" (Levertov). RevPEng 1985.

"Second Eclogue" (Garcilaso). PFor 524-525.

"Second Eclogue" (Radnóti). PFor 1313-1314.

"Second Eye of the World, The" (Wright, Jay). RevPEng 3689.

Second Flowering, A (Cowley). LTh 316, 319.

Second Man, The (Behrman). DEng 185, 186; RevDEng 222, 223.

Second Man and Other Poems, The (Coxe). PEng 627-628.

Second Manifesto of Surrealism (Breton). LTh 214.

Second Mrs. Tanqueray, The (Pinero). DEng 1507-1509; RevDEng 1892-1894.

Second Round, The (Peters). LFFor 2048-2049.

Second Sex, The (Beauvoir). PEng 1615.

Second Shepherds' Play, The (Wakefield Master). DEng 1993-1994; RevDEng 2462, 2463.

"Second Song" (Bogan). PEng 235; RevPEng 282.

Second Sophistic. LFFor 2003, 2004.

"Second Variety" (Dick). RevShF 717-718.

Secondary Heaven (Popa). PFor 1270, 1272-1273.

Secondat, Charles-Louis de. *See* Montesquieu.

Secret Adversary, The (Christie). LFEng 540-541; RevLFEng 657-658.

Secret Agent, The (Conrad). RevLFEng 3789.

"Secret Garden, The" (Chesterton). RevShF 532.

"Secret Integration, The" (Pynchon). RevShF 1973-1974; ShF 2146-2147.

Secret Journey, The. See *Fury Chronicle, The.*

Secret Ladder, The (Harris, W.). LFSup 146-148; RevLFEng 1530. See also *Guiana Quartet, The.*

Secret Life, The (Granville-Barker). DEng 801-802; RevDEng 992-993.

"Secret Life of Walter Mitty, The" (Thurber). RevShF 2274; ShF 2328.

Secret Masters, The. See *Great Wash, The.*

"Secret of Father Brown, The" (Chesterton). RevShF 530.

Secret of Heaven, The (Lagerkvist). DFor 1153-1154.

Secret of High Eldersham, The (Rhode). M&D 1416.

Secret of Luca, The (Silone). LFFor 1589-1590.

"Secret of the Short Story, The" (O'Faoláin). ShF 85.

Secret Rendezvous (Abe). LFFor 8.

"Secret Room, The" (Robbe-Grillet). ShF 2156-2157.

Secret Rose, The (Yeats). RevShF 2527; ShF 657.

Secret Service (Gillette). DEng 2398-2399; RevDEng 2919-2920.

"Secret Sharer, The" (Conrad). LFEng 3295-3296; RevShF 612-613, 2725; ShF 477-478, 795, 1186-1188.

Secret Sharer, The (Conrad). RevLFEng 3876.

Secret Vengeance for Secret Insult (Calderón). DFor 305-306.

"Secret Woman, The" (Colette). ShF 707-708.

Secrets (Besier). DEng 200-201; RevDEng 239-240.

Secrets (Hale, N.). RevShF 1099-1100; ShF 1571-1572.

Secrets and Surprises (Beattie). RevShF 180-181; ShFSup 38.

Secuestro del general, El. See *Babelandia.*

Secular Masque, The (Dryden). PEng 872; RevPEng 989.

Secular Scripture, The (Frye). LTh 508, 512.

Secunda Pastorum. See *Second Shepherds' Play, The.*

Sedaine. DFor 2342.

Sédécie. See *Juives, Les.*

Sedley, Sir Charles. PEng 2504-2511; RevPEng 2913-2920.

Seduction by Light (Young). RevLFEng 3717-3719.

Seduction of the Minotaur (Nin). LFEng 1966; RevLFEng 2516, 2519-2520.

Sedulius. PFor 2113-2114.

"See the Moon" (Barthelme). ShFSup 23.

Seeberg, Peter. LFFor 2365.

Send No More Roses. See *Siege of the Villa Lipp, The.*
Sender, Ramón José. LFFor 1546-1554.
Senderos ocultos, Los (González Martínez). PFor 611-612.
Seneca. DEng 2146, 2263; **DFor 1685-1694,** 2148-2149; LTh 1045; PFor 2103-2104; RevDEng 2666, 2782.
"Senex" (Betjeman). PEng 172; RevPEng 205.
Senghor, Léopold. LTh 1055-1057; **PFor 1419-1429.**
Senilità. See *As a Man Grows Older.*
"Senility" (Lavin). RevShF 1416; ShF 1785.
"Senility of the Short Story, The" (Cory). ShF 74.
Senlin (Aiken). PEng 24; RevPEng 25.
Sennik współczesny. See *Dreambook for Our Time, A.*
Šenoa, August. LFFor 2076; PFor 2263.
"Señor muy viego con unas alas enormes, Un." *See* "Very Old Man with Enormous Wings."
Señor Presidente, El. See *Mr. President.*
Sense and Sensibility (Austen). LFEng 118-119; RevLFEng 160-161.
Sense in Sex and Other Stories (Ayyar). ShF 643.
Sense of an Ending, The (Kermode). LTh 810.
"Sense of Humour" (Pritchett). RevShF 1932-1933; ShF 2131-2132.
Sense of Movement, The (Gunn). PEng 1169, 1170, 1171-1173.
"Sense simbolisme." *See* "Without Symbolism."
Sensenheimer Lieder (Goethe). PFor 1913.
Sensible Wege (Kunze). PFor 806-807.
Sent for You Yesterday (Wideman). LFSup 384-385. See also *Homewood Trilogy, The.*
Sent på jorden (Ekelöf). PFor 448.
Sentence, The. See *Judgment, The.*
"Sentence" (Barthelme). RevShF 167-168.
Sentences (Nemerov). RevPEng 2431.
"Sententious" (Shalamov). RevShF 2095-2096; ShFSup 291.
"Sententious Man, The" (Roethke). PEng 2412; RevPEng 2805.
"Sententsiya." *See* "Sententious."
Sentiero dei nidi di ragno, Il. See *Path to the Nest of Spiders, The.*
"Sentimental Colloquium" (Verlaine). PFor 1630.
"Sentimental Education" (Brodkey). RevShF 331-332.
Sentimental Education, A (Flaubert). LFFor 554-555.
Sentimental Journey, A (Sterne). LFEng 2534, 2540-2542; RevLFEng 3178, 3182-3185.
"Sentimental Walk" (Verlaine). PFor 1628-1629.

Sentimento del tempo (Ungaretti). PFor 1567-1569.
Sentimento do mundo (Drummond de Andrade). PSup 99-100.
Sentiments de l'Académie française sur "Le Cid," Les (Chapelain). LTh 309-310.
"Sentinel, The" (Clarke, A.). RevShF 571-572; ShF 1158-1159.
"Separating" (Updike). RevShF 2339.
Separations (Hacker). RevPEng 1361-1362.
"Sephestia's Song to Her Child" (Greene). PEng 1149; RevPEng 1307.
"September" (Coleridge, H.). PEng 530.
September September (Foote). LFEng 979-980; RevLFEng 1162-1163.
"Sequence for Francis Parkman, A" (Davie). PSup 87; RevPEng 852.
"Sequence on the Virgin Mary and Christ, The" (Southwell). PEng 2688-2689; RevPEng 3131.
"Sequence, Sometimes Metaphysical" (Roethke). PEng 2413; RevPEng 2806-2807.
Séquestrés d'Altona, Les. See *Condemned of Altona, The.*
"Ser Cepparello" (Boccaccio). RevShF 232; ShFSup 48.
"Sera del dì di festa, La." *See* "Sunday Evening."
Serafimovich, Aleksandr. LFFor 2324.
Serao, Matilde. LFFor 2234.
"Seraph and the Poet, The" (Browning, E. B.). PEng 332-333; RevPEng 402-403.
"Seraph and the Zambezi, The" (Spark). RevShF 2166-2167.
Seraph on the Suwanee (Hurston). LFEng 1393; RevLFEng 1669.
"¿Serás, amor?" *See* "Will You Be, Love?"
Serena Blandish (Behrman). DEng 185; RevDEng 222.
"Serenade" (Sitwell). PEng 2626; RevPEng 3030.
Serenade to the Big Bird (Stiles). ShF 274.
Sergeant Lamb of the Ninth. See *Sergeant Lamb's America.*
Sergeant Lamb's America (Graves, R.). LFEng 1196; RevLFEng 1420.
Serious Money (Churchill). RevDEng 436.
Serjeant Musgrave's Dance (Arden). DEng 46-47; RevDEng 59-61.
Serling, Rod. RevDEng 3037.
Serlio, Sebastiano. DEng 2216.
Serment de Kolvillàg, Le. See *Oath, The.*
"Sermon Fourteen" (Taylor). PEng 2847-2849; RevPEng 3320-3322.
"Sermon in a Churchyard" (Macaulay). PEng 1825.

"Sermon on the Warpland" (Brooks, G.). PEng 315; RevPEng 381-382.

Sermoni (Manzoni). PFor 957.

Sermons and Soda Water (O'Hara). LFEng 2051-2052; RevLFEng 2586-2587.

Serpent and the Rope, The (Rao). LFEng 2210-2212; RevLFEng 2790-2792; ShF 648.

"Serpent Knowledge" (Pinsky). PEng 2218-2219.

Serpent of Division, The (Lydgate). PEng 1801; RevPEng 2096.

Serpent's Egg, A (Ribman). DSup 316.

Serpiente de oro, La. See *Golden Serpent, The.*

Service, Robert W. PEng 2512-2518; RevPEng 2921-2928.

Servius. LTh 1650.

"Ses purs ongles très haut dédiant leur onyx." *See* "Her Pure Fingernails on High Offering Their Onyx."

Sestra moia zhizn. See *My Sister, Life.*

Set This House on Fire (Styron). LFEng 2592, 2594-2595, 2598-2599; RevLFEng 3244, 3250-3251.

Seth's Brother's Wife (Frederic). LFEng 1028-1029; RevLFEng 1221-1222.

Sette giornate del mondo creato, Le (Tasso). PFor 1497-1498.

"Sette messaggeri, I." *See* "Seven Messengers."

Settembrini, Luigi. LTh 365.

Setting Free the Bears (Irving, J.). LFEng 1415-1416, 1417-1418; RevLFEng 1694-1696.

Setting in the American Short Story of Local Color (Rhode). ShF 88.

Setting Sun, The (Dazai). LFFor 431-433.

"Setting Suns" (Verlaine). PFor 1628.

Setting the World on Fire (Wilson, Angus). LFEng 2905-2906; RevLFEng 3596.

Settle, Mary Lee. LFSup 342-350; RevLFEng 3003-3012.

Settled out of Court. See *Body in the Silo, The.*

"Settlers, The" (Atwood). RevPEng 72.

Settlers of the Marsh (Grove). LFEng 1225-1227; RevLFEng 1452-1454.

Seugamme (Gryphius). DFor 835.

Seuils (Genette). LTh 563.

"Seurat's Sunday Afternoon Along the Seine" (Schwartz). PEng 2493-2494; RevPEng 2900-2901.

Seven Against Reeves (Aldington). LFEng 45; RevLFEng 59.

Seven Against Thebes (Aeschylus). DFor 2100.

Seven Brothers (Kivi). LFFor 2342.

Seven Conundrums, The (Oppenheim). M&D 1275.

Seven Deadly Sisters, The (McGerr). M&D 1144-1145.

"Seven Destinations of Mayerling" (Cassity). PSup 61; RevPEng 543.

"Seven Floors" (Buzzati). RevShF 351; ShFSup 62.

Seven Gothic Tales (Dinesen). RevShF 736-741; ShF 1281.

Seven Hills Away (Gonzalez). LFEng 1139; RevLFEng 1359.

Seven Lamps of Architecture, The (Ruskin). LTh 1248.

Seven Men (Beerbohm). RevShF 197-199; ShF 943.

"Seven Messengers" (Buzzati). RevShF 350-351; ShFSup 61-62.

Seven Rivers West (Hoagland). LFSup 155-156; RevLFEng 1632-1633.

Seven Serpents and Seven Moons (Aguilera Malta). LFSup 12-13; LFFor 2295.

"7:VII" (Snyder). PEng 2673.

"Seven Sides and Seven Syllables" (Kizer). RevPEng 1858.

Seven Sisters, The (Prokosch). LFEng 2165-2166; RevLFEng 2739.

"Seven Songs for an Old Voice" (Wagoner). PEng 2990; RevPEng 3478.

Seven Suspects (Innes). M&D 923-924.

Seven Types of Ambiguity (Empson). LTh 461-463, 465.

Seven Who Fled, The (Prokosch). LFEng 2164-2165; RevLFEng 2737-2738.

"7 Years from Somewhere" (Levine). PEng 1717; RevPEng 1993.

"17-18 April, 1961" (Oppenheimer). PEng 2144-2145; RevPEng 2514-2515.

"XVII Machines" (Heyen). PEng 1326.

Seventh Cross, The (Seghers). LFFor 1527-1528.

"Seventh House" (Narayan). RevShF 1718-1719; ShFSup 228.

Seventh Ring, The (George). PFor 549-550.

Seventh Sinner, The (Peters, Elizabeth). M&D 1313.

"Sever." *See* "North, The."

Several Perceptions (Carter). LFSup 73-74; RevLFEng 567-568.

"Several Voices out of a Cloud" (Bogan). PEng 234; RevPEng 281.

Sewamono. DFor 2427-2428, 2430.

Sexton, Anne. PEng 2519-2526; RevPEng 2929-2937.

Sexual Perversity in Chicago (Mamet). DEng 1237-1240; RevDEng 1564.

Sexual Politics (Millett). LTh 1768.

Shackles (Césaire). PFor 328-330.
"Shades of Spring, The" (Lawrence). RevShF 1422.
Shadow, The. RevDEng 3031-3032.
"Shadow, The" (Andersen). RevShF 63-65; ShF 862-863.
Shadow, The (Shvarts). DFor 1698-1699.
Shadow Before, The (Davies). M&D 462-463.
Shadow Behind the Curtain (Johnston). M&D 941.
"Shadow Figure, The" (Endō). RevShF 837.
Shadow Flies, The (Macaulay). LFSup 262; RevLFEng 2139.
"Shadow in the Rose Garden, The" (Lawrence). RevShF 1421-1422.
Shadow Knows, The (Johnson, D.). RevLFEng 1773-1774.
Shadow-Line, The (Conrad). LFEng 3313-3315.
Shadow of a Gunman, The (O'Casey). DEng 1386, 1388-1389; RevDEng 1762, 1764-1765.
"Shadow of Cain, The" (Sitwell). PEng 2630-2631; RevPEng 3034-3035.
Shadow of Night, The (Chapman). PEng 457-458; RevPEng 552-553.
Shadow of the Glen, The. See *In the Shadow of the Glen*.
"Shadow of the Goat, The" (Carr). RevShF 430.
Shadow of the Mountain (Wilkinson). LFEng 2893-2894.
Shadow Show (Flower). M&D 632-633.
Shadows (Gardner). RevLFEng 1282-1283.
Shadows from the Past (Neely). M&D 1271.
Shadows on the Rock (Cather). LFEng 482-483; RevLFEng 595-596.
Shadwell, Thomas. DEng 1666-1675, 2297-2298; **RevDEng 2079-2089,** 2816-2817.
Shaffer, Anthony. DEng 1676, 1677; RevDEng 2090, 2091.
Shaffer, Peter. DEng **1676-1688,** 2389; **RevDEng 2090-2102,** 2907.
Shaft, The (Tomlinson). RevPEng 3381.
Shaftesbury, Earl of.
Shaftesbury, Third Earl of (Anthony Ashley Cooper). LTh 240, **1319-1324,** 1531; PEng 3325; RevPEng 3844.
"Shag" (Booth). PEng 245-247; RevPEng 305.
Shah, Indries. RevShF 2672; ShF 177.
Shahnamah (Firdusi). PSup 119-123.
Shakespeare, William. DEng **1689-1724,** 2165-2166, 2273-2285; DFor 2228; LTh 90, 301-302, 305, 448, 450, 597, 636, 641-642, 669, 709-710, 774-776, 783, 826, 862, 880, 883, 1144-1145, 1181, 1204, 1253, 1304-1305,

1393, 1398, 1517, 1671-1673, 1688, 1698; **PEng 2527-2537,** 3319-3320; **RevDEng 2103-2138,** 2686, 2792-2803; **RevPEng 2938-2949;** ShF 146-150, **2209-2220.**
Shakespeare and Society (Eagleton). LTh 415.
"Shakespeare and the Drama" (Tolstoy). LTh 1445.
"Shakespeare and the Stoicism of Seneca" (Eliot). LTh 450.
"Shakespeare at Sonnets" (Ransom). LTh 1204.
Shakespeare's Game (Gibson). DEng 748; RevDEng 928.
Shakespeare's Sisters (Gilbert and Gubar). LTh 580.
Shalako (L'Amour). RevLFEng 3854.
Shalamov, Varlam. RevShF 2092-2098; ShF 2806; **ShFSup 287-293.**
Shame (Rushdie). RevLFEng 2919, 2922-2925, 3793.
Shamela (Fielding, H.). LFEng 943, 945-947; RevLFEng 1124, 1126-1128.
Shams al-Nahar. See *Princess Sunshine*.
"Shancoduff" (Kavanagh). PEng 1538-1539; RevPEng 1764-1765.
Shange, Ntozake. DSup 326-331; **RevDEng 2139-2145.**
Shannon, Dell. See **Linington, Elizabeth.**
Shape of a Stain, The. See *Don't Monkey with Murder*.
"Shape of Light, A" (Goyen). RevShF 1053-1055; ShF 1527-1528.
Shapes of Sleep, The (Priestley). M&D 1357-1358.
Shapiro, Karl. PEng 2538-2543; PSup 409; **RevPEng 2950-2956.**
Shard, Jerome. See **Halliday, Brett.**
"Shark, The" (Pratt). PEng 2283; RevPEng 2656.
"Shark's Parlor, The" (Dickey, J.). PEng 797-798.
Sharp, Luke. See **Barr, Robert.**
Sharpe, Tom. RevLFEng 3847.
Shattered (Koontz). M&D 1007.
"Shattered Like a Glass Goblin" (Ellison). RevShF 826.
Shaughraun, The (Boucicault). DEng 269-270; RevDEng 312-313.
Shaw, Felicity. See **Morice, Anne.**
Shaw, George Bernard. DEng 1725-1742, 2192, 2369, 2380-2382; LTh 146-147, **1325-1331,** 1739; **RevDEng 2146-2164,** 2712, 2887, 2898-2900.
Shaw, Irwin. RevShF 2099-2104; ShF 267-268, 548, **2221-2225; ShFSup 390.**
"Shawl, The" (Ozick). RevShF 1831.

"Shiloh, a Requiem" (Melville). PEng 1948-1949; RevPEng 2255-2256.

Shimamura Hōgetsu. DFor 2432.

Shining, The (King). LFSup 206; M&D 987-988; RevLFEng 1888.

Shinjū ten no Amijima. See *Love Suicides at Amijima, The.*

Shintaishisho. PFor 2074.

Shiosai. See *Sound of Waves, The.*

"Ship, The" (Booth). PEng 245.

Ship, The (Ervine). DEng 561, 562, 563; RevDEng 702, 703, 704.

"Ship Island" (Spencer). RevShF 2174.

"Ship of Death, The" (Lawrence, D. H.). PEng 1686; RevPEng 1956.

Ship of Fools (Brant). ShF 141.

Ship of Fools (Porter). LFEng 2101-2102, 2107-2109; RevLFEng 2655-2657.

Ship of Heaven, The (Vicente). DFor 1958.

Ship of the Righteous, The (Evreinov). DFor 586.

Ships and Other Figures (Meredith). RevPEng 2268-2269.

Shipyard, The (Onetti). LFFor 1212-1213.

"Shirei Ziyyon." See "Ode to Zion."

Shires, The (Davie). PSup 89; RevPEng 854.

Shirley (Brontë, C.). LFEng 302-303; RevLFEng 386-387.

Shirley, James. DEng 1810-1823, 2292-2293; **RevDEng 2245-2258,** 2811-2812.

"Shisei." See "Tattooer, The."

"Shita de wakareta sakki no hito." See "Man I Parted from, Below, The."

Shklovsky, Viktor. LFEng 3226; LFFor 2322; LTh 913-914, 975, **1339-1344,** 1505, 1758, 1803, 1822.

Shock of Recognition, The (Anderson, R.). DEng 39; RevDEng 51. See also *You Know I Can't Hear You When the Water's Running.*

Shock to the System, A (Brett). M&D 207-208.

Shockley, Ann Allen. ShF 2814.

Shoemakers, The (Witkiewicz). DFor 2011, 2279.

Shoemaker's Holiday, The (Dekker). DEng 485-488; PEng 768-770; RevDEng 597-600; RevPEng 887-889.

Shoemaker's Prodigious Wife, The (García Lorca). DFor 658-660.

Shōfū. PFor 980.

Sholokhov, Mikhail. LFFor **1555-1562,** 2324-2325.

Shoot! The Notebooks of Serafino Gubbio, Cinematograph Operator (Pirandello). LFFor 1304-1305.

"Shooting-match, The" (Longstreet). RevShF 1504-1505; ShF 1818.

"Shooting Party, The" (Woolf). ShF 2456.

"Shooting Whales" (Strand). PEng 2773; RevPEng 3236.

"Shootout at Gentry's Junction" (Coover). RevShF 619-620.

"Shoreline" (Barnard). PSup 25; RevPEng 108.

Short, Luke. LFEng 3196-3197; RevLFEng 3853-3854.

"Short Essay on Critics, A" (Fuller). LTh 523.

"Short Friday" (Singer). ShF 422.

"Short Happy Life of Francis Macomber, The" (Hemingway). RevShF 1173-1176; ShF 1626-1627.

Short Letter, Long Farewell (Handke). LFFor 785-787.

"Short Song of Congratulation, A" (Johnson, S.). PEng 1506; RevPEng 1727.

Short View of Tragedy, A (Rymer). LTh 1254, 1688.

Shōsetsu shinzui (Tsubouchi). LTh 1005, 1793.

Shosha (Singer, Isaac). LFEng 2439-2441; LFFor 1625-1627; RevLFEng 3065.

"Shot, The" (Pushkin). RevShF 1962-1964; ShFSup 252-253.

Shoten an Goray. See *Satan in Goray.*

"Shoveling Out" (Galvin). PEng 1056; RevPEng 1189.

Show Boat (Kern and Hammerstein). DEng 2469-2470; RevDEng 2995-2996.

"Show me, dear Christ" (Donne). PEng 836; RevPEng 942.

Showalter, Elaine. LTh 1769, 1807.

"Shower of Gold, A" (Barthelme). RevShF 163; ShFSup 24.

"Shower of Gold" (Welty). ShF 2418-2419.

Shōyō, Tsubouchi. See Tsubouchi Shōyō.

Shrapnel Academy, The (Weldon). RevLFEng 3476-3477.

Shred of Evidence, A (Sherriff). DEng 1793; RevDEng 2225.

Shrewsbury Fragments. DEng 2246; RevDEng 2766.

Shrimp and the Anemone, The (Hartley). LFEng 1299; RevLFEng 1553.

"Shrine, The" (H. D.). PEng 1259; RevPEng 1352.

"Shrine Whose Shape I Am, The" (Menashe). RevPEng 2261-2262.

Shroud for a Nightingale (James, P.). LFSup 165-166; M&D 935; RevLFEng 1732-1733.

"Shrubs Burnt Away" (Hall). RevPEng 1375.

Shui-hu chuan. See *Water Margin.*

"Some General Instructions" (Koch). PEng 1628; RevPEng 1867.

"Some Grist for Mervyn's Mill" (Richler). RevShF 2007-2008; ShF 2151-2152.

"Some Like Them Cold" (Lardner). RevShF 1403-1404; ShF 1773.

"Some Notes for an Autobiographical Lecture" (Trilling). LTh 1456.

"Some Notes on Recent American Fiction" (Bellow). ShF 949, 951.

"Some of Us Had Been Threatening Our Friend Colby" (Barthelme). ShF 725.

"Some Parishioners" (Moore). ShF 660.

Some Prefer Nettles (Tanizaki). LFFor 1713; RevShF 2246-2247; ShFSup 315-316.

"Some Recent Fiction" (Young). PEng 3217; RevPEng 3741.

Some Versions of Pastoral (Empson). LTh 461, 463.

Someday, Maybe (Stafford). RevPEng 3171-3172.

Somers, Paul. *See* **Garve, Andrew.**

Somerset Masque, The (Campion). PEng 427; RevPEng 492, 495.

Something About a Soldier (Harris, M.). LFEng 1278, 1282-1284; RevLFEng 1519-1521.

"Something Else" (Zhang Jie). RevShF 2545-2546.

Something Happened (Heller). LFEng 1334-1335; RevLFEng 1591-1592.

Something I'll Tell You Tuesday (Guare). RevDEng 1055.

"Something Out There" (Gordimer). RevShF 1034-1035, 1036; ShFSup 109-111.

Something Short and Sweet (Bates). RevShF 174; ShFSup 31.

"Something Terrible, Something Lovely" (Sansom). RevShF 2051.

Something Terrible, Something Lovely (Sansom). RevShF 2051-2052; ShF 275.

"Something That Happened" (Phillips). RevShF 1887-1888.

"Something There" (Beckett). PEng 106; PFor 149; RevPEng 124.

Something to Be Desired (McGuane). LFSup 295-297; RevLFEng 2202-2204.

Something Wicked This Way Comes (Bradbury). RevLFEng 361.

Sometimes a Great Notion (Kesey). LFEng 1534-1536; RevLFEng 1879-1881.

Sommergeschichten (Storm). ShF 463.

"Somnambule Ballad" (García Lorca). PFor 517.

"Somo zenjitsu." *See* "Day Before, The."

Son Avenger, The (Undset). LFFor 1805. See also *Master of Hestviken, The.*

"Son du cor, Le." *See* "Sounding of the Hunting Horn, The."

Son Excellence Eugène Rougon. See *His Excellency.*

Son of Don Juan, The (Echegaray). DFor 532-533.

Son of Learning, The (Clarke, A.). DEng 375-376; RevDEng 463-464.

Son of Perdition, The (Cozzens). LFEng 631; RevLFEng 764.

Son of the Bondwoman, The (Pardo Bazán). LFFor 1221-1226.

Son of the Soil, A. *See* **Fletcher, J. S.**

"Son smeshnago cheloveha." *See* "Dream of a Ridiculous Man, The."

Sonata de otoño. See *Autumn Sonata.*

Sonata tou selēnophōtos, Ē. See *Moonlight Sonata, The.*

Sonatas. See *Pleasant Memoirs of the Marquis de Bradomín, The.*

"Sonatina in Green" (Justice). PEng 1533; RevPEng 1758.

Sondheim, Stephen. DEng 2477-2478; RevDEng 3003-3005.

Sondhi, Kuldip. RevDEng 2940-2941.

"Soñé con un verso . . ." (González Martínez). PFor 611.

"Sonet." *See* "Sonnet."

Sonetni venec (Prešeren). PFor 2268.

Sonetos espirituales (Jiménez). PFor 752.

Sonette an Orpheus, Die. See *Sonnets to Orpheus.*

"Sonetti" (Foscolo). PFor 493-494.

Sonety krymskie. See *Sonnets from the Crimea.*

Sonezaki shinjū. See *Love Suicides at Sonezaki, The.*

"Song" (Congreve). PEng 554-555; RevPEng 646-647.

"Song" (Creeley). PEng 682.

"Song: when Phillis watched her harmless sheep" (Etherege). PEng 976; RevPEng 1107.

Song (Harper). PSup 163; RevPEng 1403.

"Song: Adieu, farewell earths blisse" (Nashe). PEng 2073-2074; RevPEng 2422, 2423.

"Song: Autumn Hath all the Summer's Fruitfull Treasure" (Nashe). PEng 2073; RevPEng 2422.

"Song: Fayre Summer droops" (Nashe). PEng 2073; RevPEng 2422.

"Song" (Radnóti). PFor 1314.

"Song: My dear Mistress has a heart, A" (Rochester). PEng 2399-2400; RevPEng 2791-2792.

"Song" (Schuyler). PEng 2480; RevPEng 2886.

"Song: Not *Celia*, that I juster am" (Sedley). PEng 2509; RevPEng 2918.

"Song: *Phillis* is my only Joy" (Sedley). PEng 2508; RevPEng 2917.

"Song: *Phillis*, let's shun the common Fate" (Sedley). PEng 2508; RevPEng 2917.

Song, Cathy. RevPEng 3917.

Song and Idea (Eberhart). PEng 930.

"Song Coming Toward Us" (Forché). RevPEng 1157.

"Song for a Slight Voice" (Bogan). PEng 235; RevPEng 282.

"Song for Billie" (Hughes, L.). PEng 3402; RevPEng 3910.

"Song for My Comrades" (Biermann). PFor 191.

"Song for St. Cecilia's Day, A" (Dryden). PEng 878; RevPEng 995.

"Song in Dialogue, For Two Women" (Congreve). PEng 555; RevPEng 647.

"song in praise of a Ladie, A" (Heywood, J.). PEng 1335; RevPEng 1516.

"Song Now" (Stafford). RevPEng 3172.

Song of a Goat (Clark-Bekederemo). DEng 2422; DSup 53-54; RevDEng 451-452, 2944.

"Song of a Man Who Has Come Through" (Lawrence, D. H.). PEng 1683; RevPEng 1953.

"Song of Autumn" (Verlaine). PFor 1629.

Song of Bernadette, The (Werfel). LFFor 1912.

"Song of Bornholm, The" (Karamzin). LFFor 2307.

Song of Death, The (Hakim). DSup 177.

"Song of Grendel, The" (Gardner). ShF 1459-1460.

Song of Hiawatha, The (Longfellow). PEng 1752; RevPEng 2037.

Song of Hildebrand, The. See *Hildebrandslied*.

Song of Los, The (Blake). PEng 215-216; RevPEng 259.

"Song of Love" (Carducci). PFor 271.

"Song of Myself" (Whitman). PEng 3066-3068, 3386; RevPEng 3553-3555.

"Song of Queene Isabel, A" (Deloney). PEng 787.

Song of Roland, The. LFFor 2110; PFor 1747, 1766-1767, 1830, 1831; RevShF 2616; ShF 134, 135.

Song of Solomon. ShF 348-349.

Song of Solomon (Morrison). LFEng 1919-1922; RevLFEng 2427-2431.

"Song of the Bell, The" (Schiller). PFor 1402, 1410.

"Song of the Borderguard, The" (Duncan). PEng 901; RevPEng 1038.

"Song of the Chattahoochee" (Lanier). PEng 1662-1663; RevPEng 1929-1930.

"Song of the Falcon, The" (Gorky). RevShF 1046-1047.

"Song of the Fort Donald Railroad Gang" (Brecht). PFor 222-223.

"Song of the Horseman, The" (García Lorca). PFor 516.

Song of the Lark, The (Cather). LFEng 478-479; RevLFEng 591-592.

"Song of the Shirt, The" (Hood). PEng 1388; RevPEng 1586.

"Song of the Son" (Toomer). PEng 2917; RevPEng 3389.

"Song of the Stormy Petrel, The" (Gorky). RevShF 1048.

Song of the World, The (Giono). LFFor 655-656.

"Song of Triumphant Love, The" (Turgenev). RevShF 2323-2324.

Song 6 (Sidney, R.). PEng 2585-2586; RevPEng 2993-2994.

Song to David, A (Smart). RevPEng 3058-3061.

"Song, To my inconstant Mistress" (Carew). PEng 433-434; RevPEng 501-502

"Song Turning Back into Itself, The" (Young). RevPEng 3739.

Song Turning Back into Itself, The (Young). PEng 3215; RevPEng 3739.

"Song Which the Old Man Heard in His Dreams, The" (Castro). PFor 280. See also *Beside the River Sar*.

"Songbook of Sebastian Arrurruz, The" (Hill). RevPEng 1523-1524.

Songe de Vaux, Le (La Fontaine). PFor 812, 813, 814-815.

Songe en complainte (Charles d'Orléans). PFor 341-343.

Songes and Sonettes. See *Tottel's Miscellany*.

"Songs" (p'Bitek). RevPEng 3947-3948.

Songs and Lyrics from the Plays (MacDonald, H., ed.). PEng 96-97.

Songs Before Sunrise (Swinburne). PEng 2819-2820; RevPEng 3287-3288.

"Song's Eternity" (Clare). PEng 512; RevPEng 602.

"Songs for Signare" (Senghor). PFor 1427-1428. See also *Nocturnes*.

Songs of Dream and Death, The (George). LTh 575.

Songs of Experience (Blake). PEng 207, 208-209; RevPEng 252-255, 3849.

Songs of Innocence (Blake). PEng 207, 208-209; RevPEng 252-255.

"Songs of Reba Love Jackson, The" (Wideman). RevShF 2464.

"Songs of Sorrow" (Awoonor). PFor 112-113.

Spitteler, Carl. LFFor 2186-2187.

Spivak, Gayatri Chakravorty. PEng 3969; RevPEng 3969.

Spleen de Paris, Le. See *Paris Spleen.*

Splendid Lives (Gilliatt). RevShF 994-995.

Splendid Mummer (Elder). RevDEng 677.

Spoil of Office, A (Garland). LFEng 1085-1086; RevLFEng 1288-1289.

Spoiled (Gray). DEng 807; RevDEng 999.

Spoilers, The (Bagley). M&D 54.

Spoils, The (Bunting). PEng 371; RevPEng 445.

Spöksonaten. See *Ghost Sonata, The.*

"Spondi's Two Pages" (Arany). PFor 80.

Sponge Room, The (Hall and Waterhouse). DEng 872, 873; RevDEng 1080, 1081.

Spook Sonata, The. See *Ghost Sonata, The.*

"Spool, The" (Belitt). RevPEng 157.

Spoon River Anthology (Masters). PEng 1929-1932; RevPEng 2235-2238; ShF 869.

"Spooniad, The" (Masters). PEng 1932; RevPEng 2238.

Spór o Istnienie świata (Ingarden). LTh 726.

Sporedno nebo. See *Secondary Heaven.*

Sport of Nature, A (Gordimer). RevLFEng 1392-1393.

Sporting Club, The (McGuane). LFSup 291-292; RevLFEng 2198-2199.

Sportsman's Sketches, A (Turgenev). LFFor 2316; RevShF 2319-2321, 2694-2697; ShF 206.

Sportswriter, The (Ford, R.). RevLFEng 1178-1179.

Sposi promessi, Gli. See *Betrothed, The.*

"Spouse Night" (Leavitt). RevShF 1439-1440.

"Sprache." *See* "Language."

"Sprache als Hort der Freiheit, Die" (Böll). ShF 972.

Sprachgitter. See *Speech-Grille.*

Sprat, Thomas. PEng 3496.

Spreading the News (Gregory). DEng 852, 853; RevDEng 1048, 1049.

"Spring, The" (Barnard). PSup 27; RevPEng 110.

"Spring" (Hopkins). PEng 1400; RevPEng 1609.

Spring and Asura (Miyazawa). PSup 283-284.

"Spring in Fialta" (Nabokov). RevShF 1705; ShFSup 221-222.

Spring of the Thief (Logan). PEng 1741; RevPEng 2025.

"Spring on Troublesome Creek" (Still). PEng 2764; RevPEng 3227.

Spring Snow (Mishima). LFFor 1159.

"Spring Sowing" (O'Flaherty). ShF 2009.

Springer, Mary Doyle. LFEng 3253-3254.

Springer, Norman. RevShF 2701.

Springhouse, The (Dubie). PSup 106-107; RevPEng 1002-1003.

"Springing of the Blade, The" (Everson). PEng 989-990; RevPEng 1121.

Spring's Awakening (Wedekind). DFor 1975-1976.

"Spunk" (Hurston). RevShF 1242.

Sputniki. See *Train, The.*

Spy in the House of Love, A (Nin). LFEng 1995; RevLFEng 2516, 2519.

Spy in the Vodka. See *Cold War Swap, The.*

Spy Who Came in from the Cold, The (le Carré). LFEng 1612-1614; RevLFEng 1986-1988.

"Spy Who Came Out of the Night, The" (Hoch). RevShF 1207.

"Spy Who Came to the End of the Road, The" (Hoch). RevShF 1207.

Square, The (Duras). DFor 510.

Square in the Eye (Gelber). DEng 743-744; RevDEng 923-924.

Square One (Tesich). RevDEng 2379.

Square Root of Wonderful, The (McCullers). DEng 1198-1200; RevDEng 1500-1502.

"Squares" (Hollander). PEng 1364.

"Squire's Daughter, The" (Pushkin). RevShF 1965-1966; ShFSup 255.

"Sredni Vashtar" (Saki). M&D 1455; RevShF 2035-2036; ShF 2173.

S.S. San Pedro (Cozzens). LFEng 631-632; RevLFEng 764-765.

Sšu-k'ung T'u. LTh 1776.

Stab in the Dark, A (Block). M&D 151-152.

Stadler, Ernst. PFor 1928-1929.

Staël, Madame de. LFFor 2124; LTh 863, 1243, 1302, 1306, **1378-1384,** 1392, 1696, 1699, 1704, 1706; PFor 1864-1865.

Staff, Leopold. PFor 2128.

Stafford, Jean. RevShF 2177-2182; ShF 2259-2263.

Stafford, William. PEng 2719-2723; PSup 410; RevPEng 3163-3175.

Stage Door (Kaufman and Ferber). DEng 593-594; RevDEng 736-737.

Stage for Poetry, A (Bottomley). DEng 255-256; RevDEng 297-298.

Stagge, Jonathan. *See* **Quentin, Patrick.**

Stagnelius, Erik Johan. LFFor 2335; PFor 2165.

Stained Glass (Buckley). M&D 234-235.

Stallerhof. See *Farmyard.*

Stallings, Laurence. RevDEng 38, 2921.

"Stalnaia cikada." *See* "Steel Cicada, The."

Stalnaya ptitsa. See *Steel Bird, The.*

Stampa, Gaspara. PFor 1459-1465.

Stones of Venice, The (Ruskin). LTh 1248-1249.

"Stony Limits" (MacDiarmid). PSup 263-264; RevPEng 2124.

Stony Limits and Other Poems (MacDiarmid). PSup 263-264; RevPEng 2123-2125.

Stop It, Whoever You Are (Livings). DEng 1155; RevDEng 1455.

Stopfkuchen. See *Tubby Schaumann.*

Stopover: Tokyo (Marquand). M&D 1187.

Stoppard, Tom. DEng 1866-1879, 2204, 2389; DSup 408; **RevDEng 2308-2320,** 2724, 2907.

"Stopping a Kaleidoscope" (Eberhart). PEng 934.

"Stopping by Woods on a Snowy Evening" (Frost). PEng 3388; RevPEng 1178.

Stops of Various Quills (Howells). PEng 1424-1425.

Storey, David. DEng 1880-1891; RevDEng 2321-2333.

Storia della letteratura. See *History of Italian Literature.*

Storia di una capinera (Verga). LFFor 1860.

"Storie of Wyllyam Canygne, The" (Chatterton). PEng 470, 473; RevPEng 566-567, 569.

"Stories" (Heine). PFor 651.

"Stories" (Jarrell). ShF 80.

Stories and Texts for Nothing (Beckett). ShF 939.

Stories from Indian Christian Life (Sathianandan). ShF 642.

Stories of Liam O'Flaherty, The (O'Flaherty). ShF 2006.

Stories of Red Hanrahan (Yeats). RevShF 2527; ShF 657, 2472.

Stories of Three Burglars, The (Stockton). M&D 1536-1537.

"Storm, The" (Chopin). RevShF 540; ShF 1135.

Storm, The (Drinkwater). DEng 509; RevDEng 630.

Storm, The (Ostrovsky). DFor 1450-1451, 2454.

Storm, Elliott. *See* **Halliday, Brett.**

Storm, Theodor. LFFor 1675-1684, 2172-2173; PFor 1921, 1922.

Storm and Echo (Prokosch). LFEng 2167; RevLFEng 2740.

Storm and Other Poems, The (Montale). PFor 1051-1052.

Storm in Shanghai. See *Man's Fate.*

Storm over Chandigarh (Sahgal). LFFor 2223.

Stormy Night, A (Caragiale). DFor 346-347, 2298.

"Story, The" (Pasternak). RevShF 1855-1856; ShF 2061-2062.

"Story About the Most Important Thing, A" (Zamyatin). RevShF 2537; ShFSup 372.

Story and Discourse (Chatman). ShF 120-121.

"Story by Maupassant, A" (O'Connor, Frank). RevShF 1771-1772.

Story of a Bad Boy, The (Aldrich). LFEng 51-53; RevLFEng 66-68.

"Story of a Contraoctave, The" (Pasternak). RevShF 1853; ShF 2059.

Story of a Novel, The (Wolfe). LFEng 2932; RevLFEng 3634.

"Story of a Panic" (Forster). RevShF 886, 887.

"Story of an Hour, The" (Chopin). RevShF 537; ShF 707, 1133.

Story of Belphagor the Arch Demon, The (Machiavelli). ShF 1681.

Story of Burnt Njal, The. RevShF 2591.

Story of Gísli the Outlaw, The. See *Gísli saga.*

Story of Gösta Berling, The. See *Gösta Berling's Saga.*

Story of Him, The (Vilalta). DSup 377-378.

"Story of Justin Martyr, The" (Trench). PEng 2943.

Story of Marie Powell, Wife to Mr. Milton, The (Graves, R.). LFEng 1197-1198; RevLFEng 1421-1422.

"Story of Maupassant, A" (O'Connor, Frank). ShF 1993.

"Story of My Dovecote, The" (Babel). RevShF 126.

"Story of Our Lives, The" (Strand). PEng 2771; RevPEng 3235-3236.

Story of Our Lives, The (Strand). PEng 2771-2772; RevPEng 3235-3236.

"Story of Phoebus and Daphne, applied, The" (Waller). PEng 3014, 3015; RevPEng 3511-3512.

"Story of Richard Maxfield, The" (Wakoski). RevPEng 3490.

Story of Rimini, The (Hunt). PEng 1463-1464; RevPEng 1674-1675.

"Story of Serapion, The" (Hoffman). RevShF 1214; ShF 1646.

Story of Sigurd the Volsung and the Fall of the Nibelungs, The (Morris). PEng 2060; RevPEng 2390-2391.

"Story of Stories, A" (Dreiser). RevShF 776; ShF 1308.

Story of the Stone, The. See *Dream of the Red Chamber.*

Story of Thebes, The (Lydgate). PEng 1804; RevPEng 2099.

Story Teller's Story, A (Anderson, S.). ShF 815.

"Story Without an End, The" (Bates). RevShF 174; ShFSup 30.

"Storyteller, The" (Benjamin). ShF 71.

Strife (Galsworthy). DEng 714-715; RevDEng 891-892.
Strike Out Where Not Applicable (Freeling). M&D 663.
Strike the Father Dead (Wain). LFEng 2738, 2740-2741; RevLFEng 3395, 3397-3398.
Strindberg, August. DEng 2196; **DFor 1745-1756,** 2239, 2475-2476; **LFFor 1685-1696,** 2340; LTh 1724; RevDEng 2715-2716.
"String, The" (Dickey, J.). PEng 795.
String Game, The (Owens). DEng 1457-1458; RevDEng 1457-1458.
"String Quartet, The" (Woolf). ShF 2455.
Striptease (Mrożek). DFor 1381-1382.
Stritar, Josip. PFor 2268.
Strittmatter, Erwin. LFFor 2203.
Strittmatter, Eva. PFor 1817, 1824.
Strong Are Lonely, The (Hochwälder). DFor 928-929.
"Strong Men" (Brown). RevPEng 389.
Strong Wind (Asturias). LFFor 87.
Strongbox, The (Sternheim). DFor 1740-1742.
Stronger, The (Giacosa). DFor 708-710.
Stronger Climate, A (Jhabvala). ShF 650-651.
Stronghold (Ellin). M&D 576.
Strophe. See *Turning Point.*
"Strophi." *See* "Turn."
"Struck by a Boomerang" (Stockton). M&D 1535.
"Structural Analysis in Linguistics and in Anthropology" (Lévi-Strauss). LTh 888.
Structural Anthropology (Lévi-Strauss). LTh 1762.
"Structural Study of Myth, The" (Lévi-Strauss). LTh 888.
"Structuralism and Literary Criticism" (Genette). LTh 559.
Structure of Complex Words, The (Empson). LTh 463-465.
"Structure of Rime, The" (Duncan). PEng 903; RevPEng 1040.
Structure of Scientific Revolutions, The (Kuhn). LTh 765.
"Structure, Sign and Play in the Discourse of the Human Sciences" (Derrida). LTh 354, 1765.
Strudlhofstiege, Die (Doderer). LFFor 484.
Struna swiatla (Herbert). PFor 657.
Stseny iz rytsarskikh vryemen (Pushkin). DFor 1501.
Stuart, Ian. See **MacLean, Alistair.**
Stuart, Jesse. LFEng 2567-2578; LFSup 407; **RevLFEng 3219-3230; RevShF 2230-2236;** ShF 262, **2291-2296;** ShFSup 390.

Stuart, Sidney. See **Avallone, Michael.**
Stub, Ambrosius. PFor 2160.
"Stub-Book, The" (Alarcón). RevShF 43; ShF 847.
Stub sećanja (Pavlović). PFor 1165.
Stubbs, Jean. M&D 1548-1552.
Studenbuch, Das. See *Book of Hours, The.*
Studenti, I. See *Pretenders, The.*
Studia z estetyki. See *Selected Papers in Aesthetics.*
Studies in Classic American Literature (Lawrence, D H.). LTh 867-868; ShF 814.
Studies in the History of the Renaissance (Pater). LTh 1734.
"Studies in the Literature of Sherlock Holmes" (Knox). M&D 998.
Studies in the Narrative Technique of the First-Person Novel (Romberg). ShF 120.
Studio One. RevDEng 3037-3038.
Studium przedmiotu (Herbert). PFor 657, 659.
Studs Lonigan: A Trilogy (Farrell, James). LFEng 909-910; RevLFEng 1076-1077, 3770.
Study in Scarlet, A (Doyle). LFEng 810; RevLFEng 974, 3843.
"Study of Poetry, The" (Arnold). LTh 48; PEng 3482, 3483-3484; RevPEng 4025-4027.
Study of Prose Fiction, A (Perry). ShF 182.
Study of Thomas Hardy (Lawrence). LTh 867.
Stuff of Sleep and Dreams (Edel). LTh 428-429.
"Stumble Between Two Stars" (Vallejo). PFor 1593. See also *Human Poems.*
Stundeslose, Den. See *Fussy Man, The.*
Stupid Lady, The. See *Lady Nit-Wit, The.*
Štúr, Ludovít. PFor 1808-1809.
Sturgeon, Theodore. LFEng 2579-2588; LFSup 407; **RevLFEng 3231-3240; RevShF 2237-2243;** ShF **2297-2303;** ShFSup 390. *See also* **Queen, Ellery.**
Sturhahn, Lawrence. ShF 2845.
Sturlunga saga (Narfason). LFFor 2332.
Sturluson, Snorri. RevShF 2584, 2587; ShF 389-390.
Sturm, M. *See* **Millar, Margaret.**
"Stuttgart Trilogy" (Raabe). LFFor 1380-1381.
"Style" (Durrell). PEng 918-919; RevPEng 1048.
"Style" (Moore). PEng 2047; RevPEng 2377.
Styles of Radical Will (Sontag). LTh 1365.
Styron, William. LFEng 2589-2603, 3154-3155; **RevLFEng 3241-3256,** 3839-3840.
Su Pao-pi. DFor 2304.
"Su persona." *See* "Her Person."
Su T'ung-p'o. PFor 1788-1789.
Su único hijo. See *His Only Son.*

MAGILL INDEX TO CRITICAL SURVEYS

Subhasitaratnanidhi (Sa-skya Pandita). PFor 2247.
Subida del Monte Carmelo, La. See *Ascent of Mount Carmel, The.*
Subject Was Roses, The (Gilroy). DEng 776-779; RevDEng 958-961.
Subjective Criticism (Bleich). LTh 688, 1764.
Sublette, Walter. ShF 2846.
"Sublimating" (Updike). RevShF 2338.
"Sublime Adventure, The" (Guillén). PFor 627. See also *Homenaje.*
Substance of Fire, The (Baitz). RevDEng 88-90.
Subterraneans, The (Kerouac). LFEng 1522-1523, 1524; RevLFEng 1867-1868.
"Suburban Mad Song" (Corso). PEng 578; RevPEng 673.
Success (Amis, M.). RevLFEng 103.
"Success" (Empson). PEng 972; RevPEng 1102.
Succession, The (Garrett). RevLFEng 1297.
"Such hap as I am happed in" (Wyatt). PEng 3177; RevPEng 3701.
Such Is My Beloved (Callaghan). LFEng 432-435; RevLFEng 542, 544-545.
Suchbild (Meckel). RevShF 1644; ShFSup 190.
Suckling, Sir John. PEng 2775-2783; RevPEng 3240-3249.
Suckow, Ruth. RevShF 2673; ShF 177, 541-542.
Sud idyot. See *Trial Begins, The.*
Sudermann, Hermann. DFor 1757-1770; LTh 1722.
Sudraka. DFor 2386-2387.
Suds in Your Eye (Kirkland). DEng 1052; RevDEng 1329.
Sue, Eugène. M&D 1553-1559.
Suekichi, Aono. LTh 1006.
"Suelo." See "Soil."
Sueño de la razón, El. See *Sleep of Reason, The.*
Suetonius. LTh 964.
"Suffolk" (Davie). PSup 89; RevPEng 854.
Suffrage of Elvira, The (Naipaul). LFEng 1959; RevLFEng 2473.
"Sugawn Chair, The" (O'Faolain). RevShF 1786-1787.
Sugimori Nobumori. See **Chikamatsu Monzaemon.**
Suhrawardy, Shahid. PFor 2001.
Sui principi di belle lettere (Parini). LTh 1691.
"Suicide Eaters, The" (Smith, D.). PEng 2644; RevPEng 3066.
"Suicides" (Pavese). RevShF 1862.
Suicide's Wife, The (Madden). LFEng 1761-1762, 1766; RevLFEng 2233-2234, 2238.
"Suicidi." See "Suicides."

"Suicidio al parco" (Buzzati). RevShF 352-353; ShFSup 64.
"Suigetsu." See "Moon on the Water, The."
Suitable Match, A (Fontane). LFFor 561-562, 2177.
Suits for the Dead (Slavitt). RevPEng 3048.
Sukenick, Ronald. ShF 817.
Sukhovo-Kobylin, Alexander. DFor 1771-1778.
Sula (Morrison). LFEng 1917-1918; RevLFEng 2426-2427.
Sulayman al-hakim. See *Wisdom of Solomon, The.*
Sulkin, Sidney. ShF 2847.
Sullen Lovers, The (Shadwell). DEng 1669-1670, 2297-2298; RevDEng 2082-2083.
Sullivan, Sir Arthur. See **Gilbert, W, S.**
"Sullivan's Trousers" (O'Faoláin). ShF 2001.
Sult. See *Hunger.*
Sultan, Stanley. ShF 2848.
Sultan al-ha'ir, al-. See *Sultan's Dilemma, The.*
Sultaness, The. See *Bajazet.*
Sultan's Dilemma, The (Hakim). DSup 175.
Sumarokov, Aleksandr Petrovich. DFor 1779-1788, 2451; LTh 1693.
"Sumerki svobody." See "Twilight of Freedom, The."
Summer (Wharton, Edith). LFEng 2855-2856; RevLFEng 3537-3538.
Summer Anniversaries, The (Justice). PEng 1529; RevPEng 1754-1755.
Summer Before the Dark, The (Lessing). RevLFEng 2037.
Summer Bird-Cage, A (Drabble). LFEng 817; RevLFEng 982.
"Summer Cannibals" (Ballard). ShF 915.
Summer Celestial (Plumly). RevPEng 2610.
Summer Evening (Shawn). DSup 335-336; RevDEng 2168-2169. See also *Three Short Plays.*
Summer Folk (Gorky). DFor 784-785.
"Summer Gone, A" (Moss). PEng 2065, 2066; RevPEng 2397-2398.
"Summer Home" (Heaney). PEng 1270-1271.
Summer Knowledge (Schwartz). PEng 2492-2493; RevPEng 2899-2900.
"Summer My Grandmother Was Supposed to Die, The" (Richler). RevShF 2005-2007; ShF 2149-2151.
"Summer Night" (Bowen). RevShF 262-263; ShF 984-985.
Summer 1914. See *World of the Thibaults, The.*
"Summer of the Beautiful White Horse, The" (Saroyan). RevShF 2060; ShF 2190.

320

Summer of the Seventeenth Doll, The (Lawler). DEng 1109, 1110-1115, 2434-2435; RevDEng 1389, 1390-1395, 1396, 2957-2958. See also *Doll Trilogy, The.*

"Summer People, The" (Merrill). PEng 1906-1961.

"Summer Pilgrim, A" (Tuohy). RevShF 2314; ShF 2348.

Summer's Last Will and Testament (Nashe). DEng 1364-1369; PEng 2073; RevDEng 1705-1710; RevPEng 2422-2423.

"'Summertime and the Living . . .'" (Hayden). PEng 1253; RevPEng 1437.

Summing Up, The (Maugham). DEng 1308; RevDEng 1637.

"Summing Up, A" (Woolf). RevShF 2516.

Summoned by Bells (Betjeman). PEng 169; RevPEng 204.

Summoning of Stones, A (Hecht). PEng 1275; RevPEng 1454-1456.

"Summons, The" (Vörösmarty). PFor 1668.

Sump'n Like Wings (Riggs). DEng 1594; RevDEng 1998.

"Sun" (Moore). PEng 2047-2048; RevPEng 2377-2378.

Sun Also Rises, The (Hemingway). LFEng 1338, 1340-1343; RevLFEng 1598-1601, 3769.

Sun Chemist, The (Davidson). M&D 457.

Sun, He Dies, The (Highwater). LFEng 1364-1366; RevLFEng 1622-1624.

Sun Rock Man (Corman). PEng 569-570; RevPEng 663-664.

Suna no onna. See *Woman in the Dunes, The.*

"Sunčane pesme" (Dučić). PFor 429-430.

Sunday (Simenon). LFFor 1600.

"Sunday" (Tzara). PFor 1549.

"Sunday Afternoon Hanging" (Stuart). RevShF 2233-2234; ShF 2294-2295.

"Sunday Evening" (Leopardi). PFor 858-859. See also *Canti.*

"Sunday Morning" (Stevens). PEng 2747-2748; RevPEng 3208-3209.

Sunday of Life, The (Queneau). LFSup 329-330.

"Sunday Painter, The" (Cassill). RevShF 447; ShF 1070, 1072.

Sunday Sunlight (Pérez de Ayala). LFFor 1258.

Sundial, The (Jackson). LFEng 1428-1430.

Sundman, Per Olaf. LFFor 2360-2361.

Sundog (Harrison). RevLFEng 1544.

"Sunflower Kid, The" (Gill). ShF 1487.

"Sunflower Sutra" (Ginsberg). PEng 1092.

"Sunlight" (Gunn). PEng 1176-1177.

"Sunlight and Shadow" (Pirandello). RevShF 1891-1892.

Sunlight Dialogues, The (Gardner, J.). LFEng 1074-1076; RevLFEng 1274-1276.

Sun's Darling, The (Ford and Dekker). DEng 652-653; RevDEng 797-798.

"Super Flumina Babylonis" (Swinburne). PEng 2820; RevPEng 3288.

"Supermarket in California, A" (Ginsberg). PEng 1092; RevPEng 1229.

Superstition (Barker). DEng 105, 112-113; RevDEng 131, 138-139.

Supervielle, Jules. PFor 1888.

"Supper, The" (Borowski). RevShF 258.

Supplement to Bougainville's Voyage (Diderot). RevShF 731-732; ShF 1279.

Suppliants, The (Aeschylus). DFor 2090, 2100-2101.

Suppliants, The (Euripides). DFor 2114.

Supposes (Gascoigne). DEng 726, 2257, 2264; RevDEng 904-905, 2777, 2783.

"Supposition with Qualification" (Booth). RevPEng 303.

"Supremacy of the Hunza, The" (Greenberg). RevShF 1063-1065; ShF 1536-1538.

"Suprugi Orlovy." *See* "Orlov Married Couple."

"Sur" (Le Guin). RevShF 1454.

"Sur la Route de San Romano." *See* "On the Road to San Romano."

Sur le Fil (Arrabal). DFor 129-130.

Sur Racine. See *On Racine.*

"Sur une morte." *See* "On a Dead Woman."

Suréna (Corneille). DFor 436.

Surface of the Earth, The (Price). LFEng 2134-2135; RevLFEng 2704-2707.

Surfacing (Atwood). LFEng 96-98; RevLFEng 135-136.

Surgeon of His Honor, The (Calderón). DFor 302-303.

"Surprises" (Kumin). RevPEng 1877.

Surrey, Henry Howard, Earl of. PEng 2784-2792; RevPEng 3250-3258.

Surviving and Other Essays (Bettleheim). ShF 290.

Survivor (Butler, O.). RevLFEng 495-496.

"Survivor in Salvador, A" (Tuohy). RevShF 2313; ShF 2347.

Survivors of the Chancellor (Verne). LFFor 1874-1875.

"Susanna at the Beach" (Gold). ShF 1503.

Suspense. RevDEng 3032-3033.

"Sussex" (Davie). PSup 90; RevPEng 855.

Sutras (Pānini). PFor 1731.

T

T Zero (Calvino). LFFor 244-245.

Ta'am li-kull fam, al-. See *Food for the Millions*.

"Tabacaria." *See* "Tobacco-Shop."

Tabermann, Tommy. PFor 2199-2200.

Tabito, Ōtomo no. *See* Ōtomo no Tabito.

Table for Critics, A (Lowell, J. R.). PEng 1779-1780.

Table Manners (Ayckbourn). DEng 63-64; RevDEng 80-81. See also *Norman Conquests, The*.

"Table of Balin, The" (Malory). ShF 1866-1867.

"Tables of the Law, The" (Yeats). RevShF 2528; ShF 2473.

Tabte land, Det (Jensen). LFFor 882. See also *Long Journey, The*.

Tacey Cromwell (Richter). LFEng 2268-2270; RevLFEng 2862-2864.

Tacitus, Cornelius. LTh 1193.

Tade kuu mushi. See *Some Prefer Nettles*.

"Tag, Der." *See* "Day, The."

"Tag der Gesichter, Der" (Bernhard). PFor 181. See also *Auf der Erde und in der Hölle*.

"Tagebuchblatt 1980." *See* "Diary Page 1980."

Tagger, Theodor. *See* **Bruckner, Ferdinand.**

Tagore, Rabindranath. DFor 1789-1799; LFFor 2215; PFor 1477-1485, 1998-1999.

"Tahta al-mizalla." *See* "Beneath the Shelter."

"Taibele and Her Demon" (Singer). RevShF 2131-2132.

Tai-ching T'ang shin-hua (Wang Shih-chen). LTh 1780.

Taine, Hippolyte-Adolphe. LTh 231, 235, 260, 753, 1122-1123, 1258, 1391, **1416-1423.**

Takamura Kōtarō. PFor 2077.

Takarai Kikaku. PFor 2071.

Take a Girl Like You (Amis, K.). LFEng 63-64, 65-67; RevLFEng 89, 91-92, 97-98.

"Take It and Like It" (Nebel). M&D 1266.

Takemoto Gidayū. DFor 2426.

"Taken" (Kohu). RevPEng 3943.

"Taking a Poem to Pieces" (Sinclair, J.). PEng 3455.

"Taking Care" (Williams, J.). RevShF 2473.

Taking Care (Williams, J.). RevShF 2473-2474.

"Taking Notice" (Hacker). PEng 1192-1193.

Taking Notice (Hacker). RevPEng 1362-1363.

Taking of Miss Janie, The (Bullins). DEng 306-307; RevDEng 364-365.

Taking Steps (Ayckbourn). RevDEng 81.

Taking the Side of Things (Ponge). PFor 1260, 1261.

"Taking the Wen Away" (Dazai). RevShF 694; ShFSup 95.

Takitarō, Shimamura. See **Hōgetsu, Shimamura.**

Taková láska (Kohout). DSup 221-222.

Tala (Mistral). PFor 1040, 1042-1043.

Talanta, La (Aretino). DFor 99-100.

"Talbot Road" (Gunn). RevPEng 1336.

Tale for Midnight, A (Prokosch). LFEng 2167; RevLFEng 2740.

Tale of a Tub, A (Swift). LFEng 2606-2608; LTh 1690.; RevLFEng 3259-3261.

"Tale of Balin, The" (Malory). RevShF 1578-1579.

Tale of Gamelyn, The. PEng 3251.

Tale of Genji, The (Murasaki). LFFor 1174-1175, 1177-1182, 2259, 2260-2265, 2275; LTh 1049, 1051, 1786-1787; RevShF 2575.

Tale of Hemetes the Hermit, The (Gascoigne). LTh 542.

"Tale of King Arthur, The" (Malory). RevShF 1578; ShF 1866.

Tale of Mystery, The (Pixérécourt). DFor 1477-1478.

Tale of Orpheus (Henryson). PEng 1288, 1291-1292; RevPEng 1468-1469.

Tale of Sunlight, The (Soto). RevPEng 3114.

Tale of the Heike, The. See *Heike monogatari*.

"Tale of the Hunchback, The." ShF 412-413.

"Tale of the Ragged Mountains, A" (Poe). ShF 2107.

"Tale of the Seven Beggars, The" (Nahman). RevShF 1711-1713; ShF 1944-1946.

"Tale of the Squint-eyed Left-handed Gunsmith from Tula and the Steel Flea, The." *See* "Lefty."

Tale of Two Cities, A (Dickens, C.). LFEng 3153; RevDEng 3030; RevLFEng 3838.

Talented Mr. Ripley, The (Highsmith). M&D 869.

Tales (Baraka). ShF 923.

Tales and Short Stories in Verse (La Fontaine). PFor 815-816.

"Tales from a Family Album" (Justice). PEng 1530; RevPEng 1755.

Tales from the Calendar (Brecht). RevShF 322-325; ShF 1006.

"Telling Stories" (Moffett). ShF 83.

Tem, Steve Rasnic. ShF 2854.

Tembladera (Ramos). DFor 2442.

"Temnoe tsarstvo." *See* "Kingdom of Darkness, The."

Témoins, Les. See *Witnesses, The.*

Tempest, The (Césaire). DSup 43.

Tempest, The (Shakespeare). DEng 1712-1713, 2284; PEng 1946, 1949-1950; RevDEng 2126-2127, 2803; ShF 149, 2218-2219.

Tempête, d'après "La Tempête" de Shakespeare, Une. See *Tempest, The.*

Temple, The (Herbert). PEng 1296-1297, 1299-1300, 1302, 1303-1304; RevPEng 1475-1483.

Temple, Mary (Minny). LFEng 1438; RevLFEng 1717.

Temple, Sir William. LTh 1689-1690.

Temple Beau, The (Fielding). DEng 602; RevDEng 745.

Temple of the Golden Pavilion, The (Mishima). LFFor 1157-1158.

Temporary Kings (Powell, A.). LFEng 2121; RevLFEng 2677, 2680-2681.

Temps retrouvé, Le. See *Time Regained.*

Temps sauvage, Le (Hébert). LFFor 806.

Temptation of Eileen Hughes, The (Moore, B.). LFEng 1893; RevLFEng 2399.

Temptation of Saint Anthony, The (Flaubert). LFFor 555-556.

"Temptation of St. Ivo, The" (Gardner). RevShF 959.

Tempter, The (Jones, H. A.). DEng 1004; RevDEng 1270.

Ten. See *Shadow, The.*

Ten Little Indians (Christie). RevLFEng 3845.

Ten North Frederick (O'Hara). LFEng 2048-2051; RevLFEng 2583-2586.

"Tenant, The" (Mukherjee). RevShF 1689.

"Tenants" (Sinyavsky). RevShF 2139-2140.

Tenants of Moonbloom, The (Wallant). LFEng 2764-2765; RevLFEng 3422-3423.

Tender Buttons (Stein). PEng 2738; RevPEng 3183-3184; RevShF 2199-2200; ShFSup 305-307.

Tender Hands (Hakim). DSup 176.

Tender Husband, The (Steele). DEng 1860-1862; RevDEng 2301-2303.

Tender Is the Night (Fitzgerald, F. S.). LFEng 964-966; RevLFEng 1146-1148; RevShF 862-863; ShF 1373.

Tender Only to One (Smith, S.). RevPEng 3082.

"Tender Shoot, The" (Colette). RevShF 580.

"Tendril in the Mesh" (Everson). PEng 992; RevPEng 1123.

Tenebrae (Hill, G.). PEng 1353-1354; RevPEng 1526.

Ténébreuse Affaire, Une. See *Historical Mystery, An.*

Tenement of Clay (West, P.). LFSup 370-372; RevLFEng 3522-3523.

Tennessee (Linney). DSup 238. See also *Laughing Stock.*

"Tennessee's Partner" (Harte). RevShF 2702-2704; ShF 210-211.

Tennis Handsome, The (Hannah). RevLFEng 1485-1486.

Tennyson, Alfred, Lord. DEng 1912-1921; PEng 1207-1208, 1209, **2859-2870,** 3345-3346, 3497; **RevDEng 2355-2364; RevPEng 3333-3345,** 3863-3864.

Tenor, The (Wedekind). DFor 1978-1979.

"Tension in Poetry" (Tate). LTh 1427.

Tentativa del hombre infinito (Neruda). PFor 1073-1075.

"Tenth Clew, The" (Hammett). M&D 826.

Tents of Wickedness, The (De Vries). LFEng 739; RevLFEng 887.

"Tenzone" (Ciardi). PEng 504; RevPEng 593.

"Teoría prosaica" (Reyes). PFor 1321.

"Teoriia 'formalnogo metoda.'" *See* "Theory of the 'Formal Method,' The."

Teppich des Lebens und die Lieder von Traum und Tod, mit einem Vorspiel, Der. See *Tapestry of Life, The.*

Terence. DEng 2147-2148, 2263; DFor 1823-1829, 2142-2144, 2153; RevDEng 2667-2668, 2782.

Teresa (Unamuno). PFor 1555.

Teresa and Other Stories (O'Faoláin). ShF 1997.

"Terminal Beach, The" (Ballard). RevShF 144; ShF 914.

Ternura (Mistral). PFor 1043.

"Terra dei morti, La." *See* "Land of the Dead, The."

"Terra d'esilio." *See* "Land of Exile."

Terra nostra (Fuentes). LFFor 594-595.

Terra promessa, La (Ungaretti). PFor 1570-1571.

"Terrapin, The" (Highsmith). RevShF 1191.

Terras do sem fim. See *Violent Land, The.*

Terre des hommes. See *Wind, Sand and Stars.*

Terrible Twos, The (Reed). LFSup 340; RevLFEng 2804.

Territorial Rights (Spark). LFEng 2476; RevLFEng 3105.

"Territory" (Leavitt). RevShF 1438.

"Terror" (Tanizaki). RevShF 2245-2246; ShFSup 315.

Terror and Decorum (Viereck). RevPEng 3458-3459.

Terror Tales. ShF 741.

Terry, Megan. DEng 2486-2487; **DSup 340-346; RevDEng 2365-2373,** 3010, 3014-3015.

Terternikov, Fyodor. *See* Sologub, Fyodor.

Tertz, Abram. *See* **Sinyavsky, Andrei.**

"Terzinen." *See* "Stanzas in Terza Rima."

Tesich, Steve. RevDEng 2374-2380.

Tess of the D'Urbervilles (Hardy). LFEng 1271-1274; RevLFEng 1507-1510, 3758.

"Test, The" (Lem). RevShF 1460, 1461; ShFSup 153.

Testament (Jean de Meung). PFor 614.

Testament (Lydgate). PEng 1805; RevPEng 2100.

Testament, The (Wiesel). LFFor 1928-1929.

Testament d'un poète juif assassine. See *Testament, The.*

Testament of Beauty, The (Bridges). PEng 288-289; RevPEng 353-354.

Testament of Cresseid (Henryson). PEng 1287, 1288, 1290-1291, 3278-3279; RevPEng 1468-1469, 3797-3798.

Testarium. See *Prophets, The.*

Testi, Fulvio. PFor 2018.

Testimony (Reznikoff). PEng 2361-2362; RevPEng 2748-2749.

Testing Tree, The (Kunitz). PSup 244-245, 247; RevPEng 1885-1888.

Testor, A. See *Guardsman, The.*

Testori, Giovanni. LFFor 2256.

Tête d'Or (Claudel). DFor 404-405.

"Tetemre hívas." *See* "Ordeal of the Bier."

Tetmajer, Kazimierz Przerwa. PFor 2127.

Tetradio gymnasmaton. See *Book of Exercises.*

Teufels General, Des. See *Devil's General, The.*

Teutonic Knights, The. See *Knights of the Cross, The.*

Tevye stories (Aleichem). RevShF 47-48.

Texas (Michener). LFSup 304-305; RevLFEng 2376-2377.

Texas Trilogy, A (Jones, P.). DEng 1009-1010, 1011; RevDEng 1276-1278.

Texasville (McMurtry). RevLFEng 2222.

Tey, Josephine. M&D 1579-1583.

Thackeray, William Makepeace. LFEng 2613-2627, 3078; **PEng 2871-2877; RevLFEng 3266-3280,** 3787; **RevShF 2257-2263; ShF 2312-2318.**

Thaïs (France). LFFor 575-576; RevShF 900; ShF 1404.

Thalaba the Destroyer (Southey). PEng 2681-2682; RevPEng 3124-3125.

"Thalia" (Aldrich). PEng 33.

Thalia Rediviva (Vaughan). PEng 2974-2975; RevPEng 3453-3454.

"Thanatopsis" (Bryant). PEng 350-352; RevPEng 422-424.

Thanatos Syndrome, The (Percy). RevLFEng 2638-2640.

"Thank-You Letter, A" (Swenson). RevPEng 3265.

"Thank-You Ma'am" (Hughes). RevShF 1227; ShF 1658.

"Thanksgiving" (Glück). PSup 134; RevPEng 1245.

"Thanksgiving, The" (Herbert). PEng 1303; RevPEng 1482.

"Thar's More in the Man Than Thar Is in the Land" (Lanier). PEng 1660-1661; RevPEng 1927-1928.

That Awful Mess on Via Merulana (Gadda). LFFor 608-610.

"That Evening Sun" (Faulkner). RevShF 2731; ShF 623.

That Hideous Strength (Lewis, C. S.). LFEng 1655-1656; RevLFEng 2047-2048.

"That in Aleppo Once . . ." (Nabakov). ShF 114.

That Lady (O'Brien, K.). RevLFEng 2565.

"That Nature Is a Heraclitean Fire and of the Comfort of the Resurrection" (Hopkins). PEng 1402-1403; RevPEng 1611-1612.

"That Silent Evening" (Kinnell). RevPEng 1829-1830.

"That Straightlaced Christian Thing Between Her Legs" (Simic). PEng 2592-2593.

That Summer—That Fall (Gilroy). DEng 779-781; RevDEng 961-963.

"That the pear delights me" (Hoffman). PEng 1358; RevPEng 1533.

That Voice (Pinget). LFFor 1292.

"Thatcher" (Heaney). RevPEng 1442-1443.

"Theater" (Toomer). RevShF 2300; ShF 2342.

Theater and Its Double, The (Artaud). DFor 2256.

Theater as a Moral Institution, The (Schiller). LTh 1296.

Théâtre de Clara Gazul, Le. See *Plays of Clara Gazul, The.*

Théâtre de Neptune dans la Nouvelle France, Le. See *Theatre of Neptune, The.*

Théâtre et son double, Le. See *Theater and Its Double, The.*

Theatre of Gods Judgements, The (Beard, Thomas). RevShF 2634-2635; ShF 499.

Theatre of Neptune, The (Lescarbot). DEng 2437; RevDEng 2960.

Theatre of the Absurd, The (Esslin). DFor 2255-2256.

Theatre of the Soul, The (Evreinov). DFor 584-585.

Thebaid. See *Thebais.*

Thebais (Statius). PFor 1471-1475; ShF 150.

Theban Mysteries, The (Cross). M&D 428.

Theft, A (Bellow). RevLFEng 287.

"Theft" (Porter). RevShF 1909.

"Theft of the General's Trash, The" (Hoch). RevShF 1209.

Their Eyes Were Watching God (Hurston). LFEng 1393, 1395-1397; RevLFEng 1669, 1671-1673.

"Them" (Galvin). PEng 1055; RevPEng 1189.

Them (Oates). LFEng 2012-2013.

"Thematics" (Tomashevsky). ShF 92-93.

Then Came Violence (Ball). M&D 70.

"Then the Ermine" (Moore). PEng 2047; RevPEng 2377.

Theocritus. PFor 1503-1510.

Theognidea (Theognis). PFor 1511-1515.

Theognis. PFor 1511-1516, 1761-1762.

Theogony (Hesiod). PFor 662, 663, 664-666, 1757-1758.

Theōn dialogoi. See *Dialogues of the Gods.*

Theophilus. DFor 2169.

Theophilus North (Wilder). LFEng 2887-2888; RevLFEng 3577-3578.

Theophrastus. LTh 384; ShF 155.

Théorie des Romans, Die. See *Theory of the Novel, The.*

Theory and Practice of Rivers, The (Harrison, J.). RevPEng 1417-1418.

Theory of Criticism (Krieger). LTh 828.

Theory of Flight (Rukeyser). PSup 330; RevPEng 2831.

Theory of Literature (Wellek and Warren, A.). LTh 1426, 1535-1536, 1758; RevShF 2669-2670.

"Theory of the 'Formal Method,' The" (Eikhenbaum). LTh 443.

Theory of the Novel, The (Lukács). LTh 936; ShF 174-175.

"There Are Chaste Charms" (Mandelstam). PFor 937. See also *Stone.*

"There Is No End" (Kavan). RevShF 1313.

There Is No Natural Religion (Blake). LTh 1700.

There Shall Be No Night (Sherwood). DEng 1808-1809; RevDEng 2242.

"There Was a Jesus" (Ady). PFor 7.

"There was One I met upon the road" (Crane, S.). PEng 662; RevPEng 758.

Thérèse (Mauriac). LFFor 1127-1129.

Thérèse Desqueyroux. See *Thérèse.*

Thérèse Raquin (Zola). DFor 2050; LFFor 1989.

Theriault, Yves. ShF 639-640.

Theroux, Paul. LFEng 2628-2634; LFSup 407; RevLFEng 3281-3289.

These Are the Ravens (Everson). PEng 985-986; RevPEng 1116.

"These Are Things I Tell To No One" (Kinnell). RevPEng 1828.

"These Images Remain" (Sarton). PEng 2461; RevPEng 2865.

"These Trees Stand . . ." (Snodgrass). PEng 2659; RevPEng 3088.

These Twain (Bennett). LFEng 245-246; RevLFEng 299-300.

Thésée. See *Theseus.*

Theseus (Gide). LFFor 639, 649.

Thesmophoriazusae (Aristophanes). DFor 2127.

"They" (Kipling). RevShF 1366; ShF 1749, 1751-1753.

"They" (Sassoon). PEng 2472; RevPEng 2878.

"They are all gone into the world of light" (Vaughan). PEng 3314-3315; RevPEng 3833-3834.

They Are Dying Out (Handke). DFor 863.

They Came Like Swallows (Maxwell). RevLFEng 2343-2344.

"They Clapped" (Giovanni). PEng 1102; RevPEng 1241.

"They Feed, They Lion" (Levine). PEng 1716; RevPEng 1992.

"They flee from me, that sometime did me seek" (Wyatt). PEng 3175-3176; RevPEng 3699-3700.

They Found Him Dead (Heyer). M&D 862-863.

They Hanged My Saintly Billy (Graves, R.). LFEng 1195-1196; RevLFEng 1419-1420.

They Knew What They Wanted (Howard, S.). DEng 975-976; RevDEng 1213-1214.

"They Say That Plants Do Not Speak" (Castro). PFor 280. See also *Beside the River Sar.*

They Sleep Without Dreaming (Gilliatt). RevShF 995-996.

They Were Defeated. See *Shadow Flies, The.*

They Wouldn't Be Chessmen (Mason). M&D 1198.

Thibaudet, Albert. LTh 1421.

Thibault, Jacques-Anatole-François. *See* **France, Anatole.**

Tierra de nadie (Onetti). LFFor 1210-1211.

Tiersten, Irene. ShF 2857.

Tiet etäisyyksiin (Haavikko). PSup 142-143.

Tieta, the Goat Girl (Amado). LFFor 1260-1261.

"Tiger, The" (Blake). PEng 209-211; RevPEng 254-255.

Tiger, The (Schisgal). DEng 1663-1664; RevDEng 2076.

Tiger and the Horse, The (Bolt). DEng 231-234; RevDEng 273-275.

Tiger at the Gates (Giraudoux). DFor 727-729.

"Tiger of Chao-ch'êng, The" (P'u Sung-ling). RevShF 1945-1946; ShFSup 243-244.

Tigers Are Better-Looking (Rhys). RevShF 2000-2001; ShFSup 260.

"Tiger's Claw, The" (Narayan). RevShF 1718; ShFSup 227.

"Tight Frock Coat, The" (Pirandello). ShF 2101.

Tightrope Walker, The (Gilman). M&D 748.

Tijdkrans (Gezelle). PFor 558-559, 560.

Tikhii Don. See *Silent Don, The.*

Tikkanen, Henrik. LFFor 2370.

Tikkanen, Märta. LFFor 2370; PFor 2200.

Tilim Yid, Der. See *Salvation.*

"Till September Petronella" (Rhys). RevShF 2000-2001; ShFSup 260-261.

Till We Have Faces (Lewis, C. S.). LFEng 1658-1660; RevLFEng 2050-2051.

Tillray, Les. *See* **Gardner, Erle Stanley.**

Tilton, Alice. *See* **Taylor, Phoebe Atwood.**

Timber (Jonson). LTh 1676; RevPEng 1734-1735.

"Time" (Bates). RevShF 174; ShFSup 30.

Time and a Place, A (Humphrey). RevShF 1235-1236.

Time and Free Will (Bergson). LTh 154.

"Time and Music" (Lewis). PSup 256; RevPEng 2001.

Time and Narrative (Ricœur). LTh 1763.

Time and the Conways (Priestley). DEng 1538-1540; RevDEng 1927-1929.

Time and the White Tigress (Barnard). PSup 30-31; RevPEng 113-114.

Time and Time Again (Ayckbourn). RevDEng 79-80.

"Time Considered as a Helix of Semiprecious Stones" (Delany). RevShF 704.

"Time in Santa Fe" (Adams). RevShF 9; ShFSup 3.

Time Machine, The (Wells). LFEng 3208; RevLFEng 3481-3482, 3867.

Time Must Have a Stop (Huxley). LFEng 1408; RevLFEng 1684.

Time of Hope (Snow). LFEng 2461-2462; RevLFEng 3087-3088.

Time of Indifference, The (Moravia). LFFor 1167-1168.

"Time of Learning, A" (West). RevShF 2450; ShFSup 363-364.

Time of Man, The (Roberts). LFEng 2281-2282; RevLFEng 2876-2877.

Time of Predators, A (Gores). M&D 759.

Time of the Cuckoo, The (Laurents). DEng 1102-1104; RevDEng 1382-1383.

Time of the Hero, The (Vargas Llosa). LFFor 1847-1848.

Time of Your Life, The (Saroyan). DEng 1656-1657; RevDEng 2066-2067.

Time Out of Joint (Dick). LFSup 95; RevLFEng 895.

"Time Poems" (George). PFor 549-550.

Time Regained (Proust). LFFor 1342-1345. See also *Remembrance of Things Past.*

"Time the Tiger" (Lewis). RevShF 1484-1485.

Time Traveller, The (Oates). RevPEng 2469-2470.

Time Will Darken It, 2344-2345.

Time's Laughingstock and Other Verses (Hardy). PEng 1220; RevPEng 1393.

Time's Power (Rich). RevPEng 2760.

"Time's Song" (Praed). PEng 2279.

Timoleon (Alfieri). DFor 45.

"Timon" (Rochester). PEng 2401-2402; RevPEng 2793-2794.

Timon of Athens (Shakespeare). DEng 1717, 2283-2284; RevDEng 2131, 2802-2803.

Timotijević, Božidar. PFor 2258.

Timour the Tartar (Lewis). DEng 1131, 1136-1137; RevDEng 1423, 1428-1429.

Tin Can Tree, The (Tyler). LFEng 2676-2677; RevLFEng 3334-3335.

Tin Drum, The (Grass). LFFor 734-736.

"Tinder" (Heaney). PEng 1270.

Tine (Bang). LFFor 2339.

Ting I. DFor 2333.

Tinieblas en las cumbres (Pérez de Ayala). LFFor 1255-1256.

Tinka (Braun). DSup 23-24.

Tinker, Chauncey Brewster. LTh 1011.

Tinker, Tailor, Soldier, Spy (le Carré). LFEng 1615-1616; M&D 1043-1045; RevLFEng 1989-1990.

Tinódi, Sebestyén. PFor 1975-1976.

"Tintagel" (Reed, H.). PEng 2338; RevPEng 2725.

Tiny Alice (Albee). DEng 17-19; RevDEng 26-28.

"Tip on a Dead Jockey" (Shaw). RevShF 2101; ShF 2223-2224.

"Tipo medio." *See* "Middling Type, A."

Tiptree, James, Jr. ShF 781-782.

"Tirade for a Minic Muse" (Boland). PSup 36-37; RevPEng 291-292.

"Tirade for the Lyric Muse" (Boland). RevPEng 297.

Tirando Banderas. See *Tyrant, The.*

"Tire Hangs in the Woods, The" (Smith, D.). PEng 2647-2648; RevPEng 3069-3070.

Tirso de Molina. DFor 1842-1849, 2492-2493.

"'Tis not your saying that you love" (Behn). PEng 128; RevPEng 151.

'Tis Pity She's a Whore (Ford). DEng 661-664, 2289-2290; RevDEng 806-809, 2808.

"Tischrede des Dichters." *See* "Poet's Table Speech, The."

Titan (Jean Paul). LFFor 874-875.

Titanic, The (Pratt). PEng 2284; RevPEng 2657.

Títeres de Cachiporra, Los. See *Tragicomedy of Don Cristóbal and Doña Rosita, The.*

Titurel. See *Schionatulander and Sigune.*

Titus and Berenice (Otway). DEng 1445; RevDEng 1825.

Titus Andronicus (Shakespeare). DEng 1714, 2275; RevDEng 2128, 2794.

Titus Calpurnius Siculus. *See* Calpurnius Siculus.

Titus Livius. *See* Livy.

Titus Lucretius Carus. *See* **Lucretius.**

"Tiva's Tapestry" (Hogan). RevPEng 1541-1542.

"Tlactocatzine, del Jardín de Flandes." *See* "Flemish Garden, A."

"Tlön, Uqbar, Orbis Tertius" (Borges). RevShF 2748; ShF 979-980.

"To a Bramble in Winter" (Dixon). PEng 819.

"To a Child of Quality of Five Years Old" (Prior). PEng 2289; RevPEng 2670.

"To a Child Trapped in a Barber Shop" (Levine). PEng 1715; RevPEng 1991.

"To a Deaf and Dumb Little Girl" (Coleridge, H.). PEng 527.

"To a Defeated Savior" (Wright, James). PEng 3160; RevPEng 3672.

"To a Face in a Crowd" (Warren). RevPEng 3519-3520.

"To a Falling Leaf" (Novalis). PFor 1094, 1095.

"To a Lady, Asking Him How Long He Would Love Her" (Etherege). PEng 977; RevPEng 1108.

"To a Lady Singing" (Trench). PEng 2935.

"To a Man on His Horse" (Prince). PSup 315; RevPEng 2663.

"To a Poet" (Annensky). PFor 43-44.

"To a Poor Old Woman" (Williams, W. C.). PEng 3113; RevPEng 3612.

"To a Town Poet" (Reese). PEng 2342; RevPEng 2729.

"To a Very Young Lady" (Etherege). PEng 978; RevPEng 1109.

"To a Waterfowl" (Hall). PEng 1204; RevPEng 1373.

To All Appearances (Miles). PSup 278; RevPEng 2318.

"To Althea, from prison" (Lovelace). PEng 1759; RevPEng 2052.

"To Amaranta Whom He Fell in Love with at a Play-House" (Sedley). PEng 2508-2509; RevPEng 2917-2918.

"To an Artist, To Take Heart" (Bogan). PEng 236; RevPEng 283.

"To an Officer in the Army" (Byrom). PEng 394-395.

"To an Old Lady" (Empson). PEng 969; RevPEng 1099.

"To Angelo Mai" (Leopardi). PFor 859. **See also** *Canti.*

"To Any Reader" (Stevenson). PEng 2755-2756; RevPEng 3217-3218.

To Asmara (Keneally). RevLFEng 1847-1848.

"To Autumn" (Keats). PEng 1555-1556; RevPEng 1782-1783.

To Be a Pilgrim (Cary). LFEng 458, 459-460; RevLFEng 578, 579-580.

To Be, or Not to Be? (Andersen). LFFor 2336.

To Bedlam and Part Way Back (Sexton). PEng 2521; RevPEng 2931-2933.

"To Begin" (Strand). PEng 2771.

"To Blossoms" (Herrick). RevPEng 1496.

"To Build a Fire" (London). RevShF 1497-1498; ShF 95-97, 788, 1810-1811.

"To Carry the Child" (Smith, S.). RevPEng 3080-3081.

"To Christ Crucified" (León). PFor 841-842.

"To Christ Our Lord" (Kinnell). RevPEng 1827-1828.

To Circumjack Cencrastus (MacDiarmid). PSup 263; RevPEng 2123.

"To Cloris: *Cloris:* I justly am betray'd" (Sedley). PEng 2510; RevPEng 2919.

"To Crickley" (Gurney). PEng 1184; RevPEng 1345.

"To Da-duk, In Memoriam" (Marshall). ShF 582.

"To Die in Bilbao" (Otero). PFor 1117.

"To Dives" (Belloc). PEng 138-139; RevPEng 167-168.

"To Do: A Book of Alphabets and Birthdays" (Stein). RevShF 2202.

"Tombeaux" (Cocteau). PFor 371. See also *Vocabulaire.*

Tomlinson, Charles. PEng 2905-2911; PSup 410; **RevPEng 3374-3383.**

Tomodachi. See *Friends.*

"Tomorrow—Fairly Cloudy" (Perelman). RevShF 1868-1869; ShF 2081-2082.

"Tomorrow Morning" (Cowley, M.). PEng 606; RevPEng 712.

"Tomorrow-Tamer, The" (Laurence). RevShF 1408; ShF 1776-1778.

"Tomorrow's Song" (Snyder). PEng 2675.

"Tone in the Short Story" (Howe). ShF 79.

"Tonging at St. James Harbor" (Heyen). PEng 1323.

"Tonight at Seven-Thirty" (Auden). PEng 78; RevPEng 89.

Tonio Kröger (Mann). LFFor 1079, 2186; RevShF 1585-1586, 1590-1591; ShF 1876-1877.

Tono-Bungay (Wells). LFEng 2810-2811; RevLFEng 3483.

Tonson, Jacob. *See* **Bennett, Arnold.**

"Tontine Curse, The" (de la Torre). M&D 479-480.

"Tony's Story" (Silko). ShF 570-571.

"Too Late to Marry, Too Soon to Die" (Gill). ShF 1487.

Too Many Husbands. See *Home and Beauty.*

Toomer, Jean. PEng 2912-2920; RevDEng 2948; **RevPEng 3384-3393; RevShF 2297-2303; ShF** 251-252, 554-555, **2339-2344.**

"Tooth, The" (Jackson). ShF 1670.

Tooth of Crime, The (Shepard). DEng 1761; RevDEng 2196.

Top Girls (Churchill). RevDEng 435.

Topelius, Zacharias. LFFor 2342.

"Topoghrafia" (Pentzíkis). PFor 1189.

Topology of a Phantom City (Robbe-Grillet). LFFor 1419-1421.

Tor-ha-pela'ot. See *Age of Wonders, The.*

Tor und der Tod, Der. See *Death and the Fool.*

"Torch Song" (Cheever). RevShF 2734.

Torelli, Achille. DFor 2409.

Tornimparte, Alessandra. *See* **Ginzburg, Natalia.**

Törnrosens bok (Almqvist). LFFor 2337.

"Török Bálint" (Arany). PFor 80.

Torquato Tasso (Goethe). DFor 740-741, 2366.

Torquemada cycle (Pérez Galdós). LFFor 2387.

"Torrent, The" (Hébert). LFFor 811.

Torres Naharro, Bartolomé de. DEng 2162; **DFor 1866-1876,** 2484-2485; **RevDEng 2682.**

Torrie, Malcolm. *See* **Mitchell, Gladys.**

Torse 3 (Middleton, C.). PEng 1987; RevPEng 2309.

Tortilla Flat (Kirkland). DEng 1051; RevDEng 1328.

Tory Lover, The (Jewett). LFEng 1461-1463; RevLFEng 1748-1750.

Tosa Diary (Tsurayuki). LTh 1470.

Tosa Nikki. See *Tosa Diary.*

"Toska." *See* "Depression."

Tot, kto poluchayet poshchechiny. See *He Who Gets Slapped.*

"Total Stranger" (Cozzens). RevShF 639-640; ShF 1211-1212.

Tóték. See *Tóts, The.*

Toten bleiben jung, Die. See *Dead Stay Young, The.*

Tóth, Árpád. PFor 1985.

Tóts, The (Örkény). DSup 299.

Tottel's Miscellany (Surrey). PEng 3286-3288; RevPEng 3250, 3805-3806.

Totten, Caroline B. ShF 2859.

Tou Ô yüan. See *Injustice Done to Tou Ngo, The.*

Touch (Gunn). PEng 1169-1171; RevPEng 1333.

Touch Not the Cat (Stewart). M&D 1531.

"Touch of Nutmeg Makes It, The" (Collier). RevShF 592.

Touch of Silk, The (Roland). DEng 2433; RevDEng 2956.

Tough Guys Don't Dance (Mailer). RevLFEng 2261-2262.

Touissant l'Ouverture (James, C. L. R.). DEng 2452; RevDEng 2977.

"Toupee Artist, The" (Leskov). RevShF 1469; ShFSup 161.

Tour de Force (Brand). M&D 195.

Tour de Nesle, La (Dumas, *père*). DFor 489-490.

Tour du monde en quatre-vingts jours, Le. See *Around the World in Eighty Days.*

Tour du Pin, Patrice de la. PFor 1890.

"Tournament, The" (Chatterton). PEng 471; RevPEng 567.

Tournament (Foote). LFEng 973-974; RevLFEng 1156-1157.

Tourneur, Cyril. DEng 1933-1944, 2292; LTh 450; **RevDEng 2392-2403,** 2811.

Tournier, Michel. LFFor 1738-1748; LFSup 407.

Tous contre tous (Adamov). DFor 16-17.

Tous les hommes sont mortels. See *All Men Are Mortal.*

"Tout le long du jour" (Senghor). PFor 1424. See also *Chants d'ombre.*

"Toute l'âme résumée. . . ." *See* "All the Soul Indrawn. . . ."

"Towards an Open Universe" (Duncan). PEng 905; RevPEng 1041.

Towards the Last Spike (Pratt). PEng 2286; RevPEng 2659.

Tower, The (Hofmannsthal). DFor 941-942.

Tower of Babel, The. See Auto-da-Fé.

Tower of London, The (Ainsworth). LFEng 30-31; RevLFEng 44-45.

Towers of Trebizond, The (Macaulay). LFSup 263; RevLFEng 2140.

Towiański, Andrzej. PFor 1446.

Town, The (Richter). LFEng 2271-2272; RevLFEng 2865-2866.

Town and the City, The (Kerouac). LFEng 1518-1520; RevLFEng 1863-1865.

Town Beyond the Wall, The (Wiesel). LFFor 1922-1924.

Town Fop, The (Behn). DEng 176; RevDEng 212.

"Town of Hill, The" (Hall). PEng 1205; RevPEng 1373.

Town of Hill, The (Hall). PEng 1197-1198, 1204-1205; RevPEng 1373-1374.

Towneley Cycle. RevDEng 2458-2459, 2769-2770.

Toxophilus (Ascham). LTh 1662.

Toynbee Convector, The (Bradbury). RevLFEng 362.

"Toys" (Dazai). RevShF 692; ShFSup 93.

Tozzi, Federico. LFFor 2241.

Trabajos de Urbano y Simona, Los. See Honeymoon, Bittermoon.

"Traceleen at Dawn" (Gilchrist). RevShF 988.

Trachinai. See Women of Trachis, The.

"Track" (Eberhart). PEng 933.

Track of the Cat, The (Clark). LFEng 545-546, 550-552; RevLFEng 663, 667-669.

Tracks (Erdrich). RevLFEng 1070-1071.

"Tractable Man, A" (Michaux). PFor 1000.

"Trade, The" (Snyder). PEng 2674.

"Tradition and the Individual Talent" (Eliot). LTh 446, 448, 451, 1012, 1261, 1556; PEng 3486-3487; RevPEng 4029-4030.

Tragaluz, El (Buero Vallejo). DFor 279-281.

Tragédie du Roi Christophe, La. See Tragedy of King Christophe, The.

Tragedie of Gorboduc, The (Sackville). RevPEng 2838.

Tragedies of the Last Age, The (Rymer). LTh 1254.

Tragedy at Law (Hare). M&D 843.

Tragedy of Alzira, The. See Alzire.

"Tragedy of Being a Character, The" (Pirandello). ShF 2100.

Tragedy of Doctor Faustus, The (Marlowe). ShF 1895.

Tragedy of Faust, The. See Faust.

Tragedy of Ferrex and Porrex, The. Se Gorboduc.

Tragedy of Jane Shore, The (Rowe). DEng 1636-1637; RevDEng 2043-2044.

Tragedy of King Christophe, The (Césaire). DSup 42.

Tragedy of Lady Jane Gray, The (Rowe). DEng 1637; RevDEng 2044.

Tragedy of Love, The (Heiberg, G.). DFor 895-896.

Tragedy of Man, The (Madách). DFor 1230-1234, 2287.

Tragedy of Nan, The (Masefield). DEng 1288-1289; RevDEng 1615-1616.

Tragedy of Philotas, The (Daniel). PEng 722.

Tragedy of Pompey the Great, The (Masefield). DEng 1289; RevDEng 1616.

Tragedy of Pudd'nhead Wilson, The (Twain). LFEng 2669; M&D 1613-1614; RevLFEng 3326.

"Tragedy of the Leaves, The" (Bukowski). PEng 358; RevPEng 431.

Tragedy of Tragedies, The (Fielding). DEng 606-607; RevDEng 749-750.

Tragedy of Zara, The. See Zaïre.

Tragic Vision, The (Krieger). LTh 826.

Tragicomedia de Calixto y Melibea. See Celestina, La.

Tragicomédia de dom Duardos (Vicente). DFor 1959.

Tragicomedy of Don Cristóbal and Donã Rosita, The (García Lorca). DFor 658.

"Tragio conmigo un cuidado" (Cruz). PFor 380-381.

Tragoudi tēs adelphēs mou, To (Rítsos). PFor 1348.

Traherne, Thomas. PEng 2921-2930; RevPEng 3394-3403.

Traherne's Poems of Felicity (Traherne). RevPEng 3400-3402.

Traición de Rita Hayworth, La. See Betrayed by Rita Hayworth.

Traidor, inconfeso y mártir (Zorrilla y Moral). DFor 2065-2066.

Trail of Ashes, A (Babson). M&D 51.

Train, The (Panova). LFFor 2326.

"Train Whistled, The" (Pirandello). ShF 2100.

"Traitor, The" (Maugham). M&D 1203.

Trakl, Georg. PFor 1517-1525, 1928.

Trip to Niagara, A (Dunlap). DEng 531; RevDEng 654.

Trip to Scarborough, A (Sheridan). DEng 1782; RevDEng 2215.

Triple Echo, The (Bates). LFEng 185; RevLFEng 246.

Triple Thinkers, The (Wilson). PEng 3407.

Triptych (Frisch). DFor 2380-2381.

"Triptych" (Reed, H.). PEng 2338-2339; RevPEng 2725.

Triptych (Simon). LFFor 1611-1613.

Trissino, Giangiorgio. DFor 1877-1885, 2395; LTh 585-586, 1458-1464.

Tristan (Mann). LFFor 1079-1080, 2186; ShF 1876.

Tristan L'Hermite. DFor 1886-1896.

"Tristesse" (Lamartine). PFor 833-834. *See also* "Lake, The."

"Tristesse d'Olympio" (Hugo). PFor 734. See also *Rayons et ombres, Les.*

Tristi amori. See *Unhappy Love.*

"Tristia" (Mandelstam). PFor 938.

Tristia (Mandelstam). PFor 937-938, 941.

Tristram Shandy (Sterne). LFEng 2529-2530, 2532, 2534-2540, 3073; RevLFEng 3179-3182, 3733, 3782.

Triton (Delany). LFEng 722-723; RevLFEng 855, 857-859.

Triumph of Achilles, The (Glück). PSup 137-138; RevPEng 1248-1249.

Triumph of Death, The (D'Annunzio). LFFor 411.

"Triumph of Summer" (George). PFor 548.

"Triumph of the Whale, The" (Lamb). PEng 1636; RevPEng 1900.

"Triumph of Time, The" (Swinburne). PEng 2818; RevPEng 3286.

Triumphs (Petrarch). LTh 1658; PFor 1230-1231, 1236-1237.

Triumphs of Eugène Valmont, The (Barr). M&D 90-91.

Triumphs of God's Revenge, Against Murther, The (Reynolds). ShF 499.

Triunfo del amor, El (Encina). DFor 541-542, 2179.

Trivadi, V. D. DFor 2391.

Trivia (Gay). PEng 1077; RevPEng 1212.

Trōades. See *Trojan Women, The.*

Trœtte mænd (Garborg). LFFor 2341.

Troia Britannica (Heywood, T.). PEng 1338-1341.

Troilus and Cressida (Shakespeare). DEng 1716-1717, 2281; RevDEng 2130-2131, 2800.

Troilus and Criseyde (Chaucer). LTh 281, 283; PEng 476, 480, 483-485, 486, 1290, 3490;

RevPEng 579-582; RevShF 485-488, 2617; ShF 1105-1108.

Trois Filles de M. Dupont, Les. See *Three Daughters of M. Dupont, The.*

"Trois Messes basses, La." *See* "Three Low Masses, The."

Trois Mousquetaires, Les. See *Three Musketeers, The.*

Trois Prétendants . . . un mari. See *Three Suitors One Husband Until Further Notice.*

Trojan Horse, The (MacLeish). DEng 1219-1220; RevDEng 1540-1541.

"Trojan Horse" (Queen). ShF 763.

Trojan Women, The (Euripides). DFor 2115.

Trojan Women, The (Seneca). DFor 2148.

Trollope, Anthony. LFEng 2648-2659, 3034, 3078-3079; RevLFEng 3304-3316, 3742-3743, 3787, 3788.

"Tropic Death" (Walrond). ShF 578.

Tropic Moon (Simenon). LFFor 1599.

Tropic of Cancer (Miller). LFEng 1873-1874, 1878-1879; RevLFEng 2383-2385.

Tropic of Capricorn (Miller). LFEng 1879-1881; RevLFEng 2380.

"Tropics in New York, The" (McKay). PEng 1843-1844; RevPEng 2142-2143.

Tropisms (Sarraute). LFFor 2143.

Troteras y danzaderas (Pérez de Ayala). LFFor 1257.

Trotsky, Leon. LTh 1058.

Trotsky in Exile (Weiss). DFor 1990.

"Trouble, The" (Powers). RevShF 1919; ShF 2120.

Trouble at Turkey Hill, The (Knight). M&D 991-992.

"Trouble Man, The" (Rhodes). ShF 603-604.

Trouble on Triton. See *Triton.*

"Trouble with Bubbles, The" (Dick). RevShF 716.

Troubled Sleep (Sartre). LFFor 1515-1516. See also *Roads to Freedom.*

Troubles (Farrell, J. G.). LFSup 110; RevLFEng 1084-1085.

Troublesome Raigne of John King of England, The. DEng 2265-2266, 2276; RevDEng 2785, 2795.

Trout Fishing in America (Brautigan). LFEng 294; RevLFEng 377; RevShF 311, 313-315; ShFSup 53-54.

"Trout Fishing on the Bevel" (Brautigan). RevShF 314-315; ShFSup 54.

"Trout Stream, The" (Welch). RevShF 2426.

Troy Book (Lydgate). PEng 1804; RevPEng 2099.

Troy Romances (Dictys). LFFor 2014.

"Tune: Song of Picking Mulberry" (Li Ch'ing-chao). PFor 882.

"Tune: Spring at Wu-ling" (Li Ch'ing-chao). PFor 881-882.

"Tune: Tipsy in the Flowers' Shade" (Li Ch'ing-chao). PFor 880-881.

"Tuned In Late One Night" (Stafford). RevPEng 3172.

Túnel, El. See *Outsider, The.*

Tung-hai Huang-kung. DFor 2302-2303.

"T'ung-hên yü." *See* "Pupils of the Eyes That Talked, The."

"Tunnel, The" (Strand). RevPEng 3232.

Tunnel of Love, The (De Vries). LFEng 737-738; RevLFEng 885-886.

Tuohy, Frank. RevShF 2311-2316; **ShF 2345-2349;** ShFSup 391.

Tupac Amaru (Dragún). DFor 2444.

"Tupeinyi khudozhnik." *See* "Toupee Artist, The."

Turandot (Gozzi). DFor 796-797.

Turberville, George. PEng 3289.

"Turbine, The" (Monroe). PEng 2028.

Turcaret (Lesage). DFor 1187-1189.

Turco, Lewis. ShF 2861.

Turgenev, Ivan. DFor 1897-1908; LFEng 3172; LFFor 504, 702-703, **1769-1780,** 2316; LTh 120, 290, 387, 947, 1106; **RevShF 2317-2325; ShF** 201, 203, 460, 533, **2350-2359.**

Turista, La (Shepard). RevDEng 2194-2195.

"Turkey, The" (O'Connor, Flannery). RevShF 1759.

"Turkey-Cock" (Lawrence, D. H.). PEng 1683; RevPEng 1953.

Turm, Der. See *Tower, The.*

"Turn" (Pentzíkis). PFor 1190.

Turn of the Screw, The (James, H.). LFEng 3262-3265; RevLFEng 3874-3875; ShF 109, 478, 479, 480.

"Turn with the Sun, A" (Knowles). RevShF 1378-1380; ShF 1765-1767, 1769.

Turnbull, Dora Amy Elles Dillon. *See* **Wentworth, Patricia.**

"Turning Point." *See* "Turn."

Turning Point (Seferis). PFor 1415-1416, 1961.

Turning Wind, A (Rukeyser). PSup 331; RevPEng 2832.

Turno, Il. See *Merry-Go-Round of Love, The.*

Turoldo, David Maria. PFor 2046-2047.

"Turtle, The" (Kees). PEng 1565-1566; RevPEng 1793-1794.

"Turtle" (Lowell, R.). PEng 1799-1800; RevPEng 2093-2094.

Turtle Island (Snyder). PEng 2674-2675; RevPEng 3108.

Tutilo. DEng 2244; DFor 2155.

Tutor, The (Lenz). DFor 1163-1166.

"Tutti-Frutti" (Sansom). RevShF 2052.

Tutti i nostri ieri. See *Dead Yesterdays.*

Tutuola, Amos. LFFor **1781-1788.**

Tvorchestvo Fransua Rable i narodnaya kul'tura srednevekov'ya i Renessansa. See *Rabelais and His World.*

Twain, Mark. LFEng 52, **2660-2670,** 3041, 3042, 3043; LTh 1749; **M&D 1609-1615; RevLFEng 3317-3328,** 3745, 3750, 3751, 3795, 3807, 3860; **RevShF 2326-2331,** 2660-2661; **ShF** 614-615, **2360-2365.**

'Twas All for the Best (Bird). DEng 213-214; RevDEng 253-254.

"'Twas like a Maelstrom, with a notch" (Dickinson). PEng 810; RevPEng 922.

Twelfth Juror, The (Gill). M&D 742.

Twelfth Night (Shakespeare). DEng 1708-1709, 2279; RevDEng 2122-2123, 2798.

Twelve, The (Blok). PFor 200.

Twelve Deaths of Christmas, The (Babson). M&D 49-50.

$1200 a Year (Ferber and Levy). DEng 590-592; RevDEng 733-735.

"12 O'Clock News" (Bishop). PEng 188; RevPEng 231.

"Twelve Seasons, The" (Hall). RevPEng 1375.

12:30 from Croydon, The (Crofts) M&D 49-50.

Twelve Words of the Gypsy, The (Palamàs). PFor 1953-1954.

Twentieth-Century Cycle (Bullins). DEng 307; RevDEng 365-366, 2950.

Twenty Love Poems and a Song of Despair (Neruda). PFor 1073.

"Twenty Rules for Writing Detective Stories" (Van Dine). M&D 1635-1636.

Twenty Thousand Leagues Under the Sea (Verne). LFFor 1872-1874.

Twenty Years After (Dumas, *père*). LFFor 525-526.

"Twenty-eight and Twenty-nine" (Praed). PEng 2278.

"25th Anniversary" (Pastan). PEng 2175-2176.

Twenty-fifth Hour, The (Kelly). M&D 962.

"21st Anniversary" (Pastan). PEng 2175.

Twenty-fourth of February, The (Werner). DFor 2370.

"Twenty-nine Sonnets of Étienne de La Boétie" (Montaigne). LTh 1044.

"Twenty-One Love Poems" (Rich). RevPEng 2757-2758.

Tyler, Royall. DEng 1945-1954; RevDEng 2404-2413.

Tylney Hall (Hood). PEng 1377; RevPEng 1575.

Tynyanov, Yury. LTh 1476-1482.

Työmiehen vaimo (Canth). DFor 325.

"Tyomnye allei." *See* "Dark Paths."

Typee (Melville). LFEng 1856; RevLFEng 2351.

Types of Shape (Hollander). RevPEng 1549.

"Typhoon" (Conrad). RevShF 610-611; ShF 1186.

"Typical Optical" (Updike). PSup 381; RevPEng 3425.

Tyrant, The (Valle-Inclán). LFFor 1837-1840.

Tyutchev, Fyodor. PFor 2141-2142.

Tzara, Tristan. DEng 2203; DFor 2238; LTh 214; PFor 1545-1553, 1885.

Tzili (Appelfeld). LFSup 38-39.

Tzu yeh. See *Midnight.*

345

U

"U nas, w Auschwitzu." *See* "Auschwitz, Our Home."

"Ubasute." *See* "Putting Granny Out to Die."

Über Anmut und Würde. See *On Grace and Dignity.*

Über das Erhabene. See *On the Sublime* (Schiller).

"Über das Marionetten theater." *See* "Marionette Theater, The."

"Über das Studium der griechischen Poesie" (Schlegel, F.). LTh 1697.

"Über das Wesen des Dramas" (Grillparzer). LTh 636.

"Über den gegenwärtigen Zustand der dramatischen Kunst in Deutschland" (Grillparzer). LTh 635.

"Über Dichtung." *See* "On Poetry."

Über die neuere deutsche Literatur (Herder). LTh 670-671.

Über die Religion. See *On Religion.*

Über naïve und sentimentalische Dichtung. See *On Naïve and Sentimental Poetry.*

"Über Shakespeare" (Herder). LTh 669.

"Über Vergänglichkeit" (Hofmannsthal). PFor 674-675.

Überlebensgross Herr Kott (Walser, M.). DSup 386.

Ubik (Dick). LFSup 97; RevLFEng 897.

Ubohý vrah. See *Poor Murderer.*

Ubu Cuckolded (Jarry). DFor 1013-1014.

Ubu roi (Jarry). DEng 2203; DFor 1010-1013; RevDEng 2723.

Udall, Nicholas. DEng 1955-1964; RevDEng 2414-2423.

Uden fædreland, De. See *Denied a Country.*

"Uder." *See* "Blow, The."

Ughniyah al-mawt. See *Song of Death, The.*

"Ugly Little Boy, The" (Asimov). RevShF 85; ShF 876.

Uhland, Ludwig. LTh 438.

Új versek. See *New Verses.*

Ujević, Tin. PFor 2265.

"Ulalume" (Poe). PEng 2244-2246; RevPEng 2617-2619.

"Ultima calaverada, La." *See* "Last Escapade, The."

"Ultima giornata, L." *See* "Last Day, The."

"Última ilusión de Don Juan, La." *See* "Don Juan's Last Illusion."

"Ultima Ratio Regum" (Spender). PEng 2698; RevPEng 3142.

Ultima Thule (Longfellow). PEng 1751; RevPEng 2036.

Ultimate Good Luck, The (Ford, R.). RevLFEng 1177-1178.

Ultime lettere di Jacopo Ortis, Le. See *Last Letters of Jacopo Ortis.*

"Ultimo canto di Saffo." *See* "Sappho's Last Song."

"Ultimo viene il corvo." *See* "Crow Comes Last, The."

Ultramarine (Carver). RevPEng 535-537.

Ulysses (Joyce). LFEng 1502-1505, 3057, 3105-3106; LTh 1574; RevLFEng 1826-1829, 3765, 3807; RevPEng 3878; ShF 11, 14.

"Ulysses" (Saba). PSup 346, 348.

"Ulysses" (Tennyson). PEng 2863-2867; RevPEng 3337-3341.

"Ulysses and Circe" (Lowell, R.). PEng 1799; RevPEng 2093.

Ulysses in Traction (Innaurato). DSup 203; RevDEng 1248-1249.

"Umanitari." *See* "Humanitarians, The."

Umarła Klasa. See *Dead Class, The.*

Umbstaetter, Herman Daniel. ShF 589.

Umi to dokuyaku. See *Sea and the Poison, The.*

Umorismo, L'. See *Humor.*

Un de Baumugnes. See *Lovers Are Never Losers.*

Un di Velt hot geshvign. See *Night.*

Un millón de muertos. See *One Million Dead.*

Una, nessuno e centomila. See *One, None and a Hundred-Thousand.*

Una cosa è una cosa. See *Command and I Will Obey You.*

"Una-ha vez tiven un cravo." *See* "I Used to Have a Nail."

Unaddressed Letters (Plekhanov). LTh 1123-1124.

Unamuno y Jugo, Miguel de. DFor 1909-1916, 2503; LFEng 3303-3305; **LFFor 1789-1797,** 2390-2391; **LTh 1483-1488;** PFor 911, **1554-1560.**

Unbearable Lightness of Being, The (Kundera). LFFor 956-957.

Unclassed, The (Gissing). LFEng 1112-1113; RevLFEng 1322-1323.

"Uncle" (Narayan). RevShF 1718; ShFSup 228.

Uncle Abner, Master of Mysteries (Post). M&D 1345.

"Uncle Ben's Choice" (Achebe). RevShF 3-4; ShF 821-822.

"Uncle Ernest" (Sillitoe). RevShF 2114; ShF 2227-2228.

"Uncle Grant" (Price). ShF 2123-2124.

"Uncle Leopold" (Dovlatov). RevShF 760.

Uncle Silas (Le Fanu). LFEng 1626-1627; M&D 1050-1051; RevLFEng 2001-2002; RevShF 1443; ShF 1796.

Uncle Tom's Cabin (Stowe). LFEng 2558-2559; RevLFEng 3209-3211, 3750; ShF 530.

Uncle Tom's Children (Wright). ShF 579.

"Uncle Valentine" (Cather). RevShF 453; ShF 1078-1079.

Uncle Vanya (Chekhov). DFor 376-378.

"Uncle Wellington's Wives" (Chesnutt). RevShF 525-526; ShFSup 89.

"Uncle Wiggily in Connecticut" (Salinger). RevShF 2041; ShF 291, 2177.

Uncommon Women and Others (Wasserstein). RevDEng 2478-2480.

Unconditional Surrender. See End of the Battle, The.

"Under a Glass Bell" (Nin). RevShF 1723; ShF 1949.

Under a Glass Bell and Other Stories (Nin). RevShF 1722-1725; ShF 1949, 1951-1952.

"Under Ben Bulben" (Yeats). PEng 3206-3207; RevPEng 3730-3731.

"Under Libra: Weights and Measures" (Merrill). PEng 1963-1964.

Under Milk Wood (Thomas). DEng 1924-1931; RevDEng 2383-2389, 3033.

"Under Mount Sion" (Ady). PFor 6.

"Under the Banyan Tree" (Narayan). RevShF 1719; ShFSup 228-229.

Under the Banyan Tree and Other Stories (Narayan). RevShF 1719; ShFSup 228.

"Under the Lion's Paw" (Garland). RevShF 967; ShF 1467.

"Under the Moon's Reign" (Tomlinson). RevPEng 3380.

Under the Net (Murdoch). LFEng 1931-1933; RevLFEng 2441-2444.

"Under the Oaks" (Arany). PFor 83.

"Under the Rose" (Pynchon). RevShF 1973; ShF 2145.

Under the Shadow of Etna (Verga). LTh 1496-1497; ShF 2379.

Under the Sun of Satan. See Star of Satan, The.

Under the Volcano (Lowry, Malcolm). LFEng 1705-1706, 1709-1718; RevLFEng 2116-2125.

Under the Willows and Other Poems (Lowell, J. R.). PEng 1780; RevPEng 2074.

Underdogs, The (Azuela). LFFor 2288-2289.

Underground Man, The (Macdonald, R.). M&D 1138-1139; LFSup 277-278; RevLFEng 2176-2177.

Underground Woman, The (Boyle, K.). LFEng 280-281; RevLFEng 345-346.

Underhill, Charles. *See* **Hill, Reginald.**

Underpants, The. See Bloomers, The.

"Understanding But Not Forgetting" (Madhubuti). PEng 1892; RevPEng 2196.

Understanding Fiction (Warren). LTh 1522.

Understanding Poetry (Warren). LTh 1522.

"Undertaker, The" (Pushkin). RevShF 1964; ShFSup 253-254.

"Undertaking, The" (Glück). PSup 136; RevPEng 1247.

"Underwear" (Ferlinghetti). PEng 1007; RevPEng 1149.

Underwoods (Stevenson). PEng 2756; RevPEng 3218.

Undesignated (Sondhi). DEng 2418; RevDEng 2940.

Undetective, The (Graeme). M&D 771.

"Undine" (Heaney). PEng 1269.

Undivine Comedy, The (Krasinski). DFor 1095, 1099-1103, 2276.

Undset, Sigrid. LFFor 1798-1806, 2351-2352.

"Unearthing Suite" (Atwood). RevShF 106-107; ShFSup 18.

Unexpected Return, The (Regnard). DFor 1542.

Unfair Exchange (Babson). M&D 49.

Unfinished Clue, The (Heyer). M&D 860-861.

"Unfinished Ode to Mud" (Ponge). PFor 1263.

Unfinished Portrait (Christie). LFEng 535; RevLFEng 652.

"Unfinished Story, An" (Henry). RevShF 1180; ShF 1631-1632.

Unfortunate Traveller, The (Nash, Thomas). LFEng 3016-3017; PEng 2068-2069; RevLFEng 3725, 3806; RevPEng 2421; RevShF 2630; ShF 146, 453, 455, 494.

Ungaretti, Giuseppe. PFor 1561-1570, 2039-2040, 2046.

"Unge Mand med Nelliken, Den." *See* "Young Man with the Carnation, The."

"Ungrateful Garden, The" (Kizer). RevPEng 1855.

Unguarded Thoughts (Sinyavsky). LTh 1355.

"Unhappy Lot of Mr. Knott, The" (Lowell, J. R.). PEng 1778; RevPEng 2072.

Unhappy Love (Giacosa). DFor 704-705

Unholy Loves (Oates). LFEng 2014-2015.

"Unidentified Flying Object" (Hayden). PEng 1253; RevPEng 1437.

"Uninvited, The" (Abse). PEng 4; RevPEng 4.

"Union Buries Its Dead, The" (Lawson). RevShF 1431-1432; ShFSup 138-139.

Union libre, L'. See *Free Union.*

"Unique Effect of the Short Story, The" (May). ShF 83.

Unique Hamlet, The (Starrett). M&D 1517.

Universal Baseball Association, The (Coover). LFEng 621-624; RevLFEng 752-754.

Universal English Shorthand, The (Byrom). PEng 391.

"Universal Fears, The" (Hawkes). ShF 1600-1603.

Universal Gallant, The (Fielding). DEng 603-604; RevDEng 746-747.

Universal Legatee, The (Regnard). DFor 1544-1545.

Unknown Eros and Other Odes, The (Patmore). PEng 2193-2194; RevPEng 2564-2565.

"Unknown Girl in the Maternity Ward" (Sexton). PEng 2522-2523; RevPEng 2932-2933.

"Unknown Knyght, The." *See* "Tournament, The."

Unknown Man No. 89 (Leonard). M&D 1055.

Unknown Masterpiece, The (Balzac). RevShF 148-149.

Unknown Masterpiece, The (Balzac). LFFor 97; ShF 919-920.

Unlimited Dream Company, The (Ballard). LFEng 152; RevLFEng 196.

"Unlucky for Pringle" (Lewis). RevShF 1484.

Unmade Bed, The (Sagan). LFFor 1477.

"Unmailed, Unwritten Letters" (Oates). ShF 1964-1965.

Unmasked Ball, The (Evreinov). DFor 586-587.

Unnamable, The (Beckett). LFEng 212-213; LFor 128-129; RevLFEng 261.

Unnatural Combat, The (Massinger). DEng 1296-1297; RevDEng 1624-1625.

Uno von Trasenberg (Cederborgh). LFFor 2335.

uNosilimela (Mutwa). DEng 2420; RevDEng 2942.

"Unparalleled Adventure of One Hans Pfaall, The" (Poe). ShF 770.

"Unresolved" (Levertov). PEng 1710.

"Unrest-Cure, The" (Saki). M&D 1457-1458.

Unrest-Field (Popa). PFor 1270.

"Uns et les autres, Les" (Follain). PSup 131.

Unschuldige, Der (Hochwälder). DFor 930-931.

Unseen Hand, The (Shepard). RevDEng 2195.

"Unsettled Motorcyclist's Vision of His Death, The" (Gunn). PEng 1172.

Unsichtbare Loge, Die. See *Invisible Lodge, The.*

"Unspoiled Monsters" (Capote). LFEng 450; RevLFEng 561.

Unsuitable Attachment, An (Pym). LFEng 2178-2179; RevLFEng 2753-2754.

Unsuitable Job for a Woman, An (James, P.). LFSup 166; RevLFEng 1733.

Unsuspected, The (Armstrong). M&D 38.

Untamed, The (Faust). RevLFEng 3851.

Unter dem Eisen des Mondes (Bernhard). PFor 183.

"Unter Zeiten." *See* "Among Tenses."

Untergang der Titanic, Der. See *Sinking of the Titanic, The.*

Unterhaltungen deutscher Ausgewanderten. See *Conversations of German Emigrés.*

Untermeyer, Louis. PEng 2942-2953; RevPEng 3410-3422.

"Unterschiede." *See* "Differences."

Untilled Field, The (Moore). ShF 659-661.

Unto This Last (Ruskin). LTh 1248.

Untouchable (Anand). LFFor 2218-2219.

Untouchables, The. RevDEng 3040.

Untriangulated Stars (Robinson). PEng 2384-2385; RevPEng 2775-2776.

Unüberwindlichen, Die (Kraus). DFor 1116; PFor 794, 798.

Unvanquished, The (Fast). RevLFEng 3838

Unvernünftigen sterben aus, Die. See *They Are Dying Out.*

"Unwanted" (Lowell, R.). PEng 1800; RevPEng 2094.

"Unwritten Story, The" (Schorer). ShF 2201.

"Unzen" (Endō). RevShF 835.

Uomini e no (Vittorini). LFFor 2244-2245, 2251.

Uomo e galantuomo (De Filippo). DFor 468.

Up Above the World (Bowles). LFSup 57-58; RevLFEng 331-332.

Up Country (Kumin). RevPEng 1873-1874.

"Up in the Gallery" (Kafka). ShF 1734.

Up Jumped the Devil (Adams). M&D 8-9.

Up the Rhine (Hood). PEng 1377-1378; RevPEng 1575-1576.

Upanishads. PFor 1481.

Updike, John. LFEng 2686-2704; LFSup 408; PSup 379-386; RevLFEng 3347-3360, 3808; RevPEng 3423-3431; RevShF 2332-2343, 2754; ShF 559-560, **2366-2376;** ShFSup 391.

Updyke, James. *See* **Burnett, W. R.**

Uper Thoulēn apista, Ta. *See* "Marvels Beyond Thule, The."

Upfield, Arthur W. M&D 1616-1621.

"Upon Appleton House" (Marvell). RevPEng 2219-2222.

Upon Appleton House (Marvell). PEng 1915-1918.

"Upon Apthorp House" (Hollander). RevPEng 1548.

"Upon Christmas Eve" (Suckling). PEng 2778; RevPEng 3243.

"Upon Meeting Don L. Lee, in a Dream" (Dove). RevPEng 956-957.

"Upon my Lady Carliles walking in Hampton-Court garden" (Suckling). PEng 2779-2780; RevPEng 3244-3245.

"Upon some Alterations in my Mistress, after my Departure into France" (Carew). PEng 432-433; RevPEng 500-501.

"Upon T. C. having the P." (Suckling). PEng 2779; RevPEng 3244.

"Upon the death of Sir Albert Morton's *Wife"* (Wotton). PEng 3142.

"Upon the Image of Death" (Southwell). PEng 2688; RevPEng 3131.

"Upon the losse of his Little Finger" (Randolph). PEng 2321-2322.

"Upon the sudden Restraint of the Earle of Somerset, *then falling from favor"* (Wotton). PEng 3142-3143.

Uppdal, Kristofer. LFFor 2351.

"Upper Meadows, The" (Winters). PSup 397; RevPEng 3626.

Upstairs, Downstairs. RevDEng 3044.

"Upstairs in a Wineshop" (Lu Hsün). RevShF 1523-1524; ShFSup 179-180.

Uptight. See *Max.*

"Upturned Face, The" (Crane, S.). ShF 789-790.

Ur-Hamlet. DEng 1096, 2270.

"Urania" (Manzoni). PFor 957.

Urban, Milo. LFFor 2069.

"Urban Ode" (McPherson). PEng 1884-1885; RevPEng 2187.

Urfaust. See *Faust.*

Urfé, Honoré d'. LFFor 1807-1812, 2026.

Urick, Kevin. ShF 2862.

"Uriel" (Emerson). PEng 958; RevPEng 1088.

Urista, Alberto. *See* Alurista.

Urlicht (Innaurato). DSup 201; RevDEng 1246.

"Uroki francuzskogo." *See* "French Lessons."

"Urteil, Das." *See* "Judgment, The."

Urteil, Das. See *Judgment, The.*

"Urworte, Orphisch." *See* "Primeval Words, Orphic."

"U.S. Detective, A." *See* **Hanshew, Thomas W.**

U.S. 1 (Rukeyser). PSup 331; RevPEng 2832.

U.S.A. trilogy (Dos Passos). LFEng 794-798; RevLFEng 958-962, 3766.

"Uscita di sicurezza." *See* "Emergency Exit."

Use of Poetry and the Use of Criticism, The (Eliot). PEng 3485; LTh 795; RevPEng 4028.

Uses of Literature, The (Calvino). LTh 269.

"Uses of the Erotic, The" (Lorde). RevPEng 2045.

"Ushanan-Jampi" (López Albújar). ShF 694, 699-702.

Usigli, Rodolfo. DFor 2442-2443; DSup 358-365.

Using Biography (Empson). LTh 464.

"Ustcp." *See* "Digression."

Utage no ato. See *After the Banquet.*

"Utensil, The" (Ponge). PFor 1265.

"Úti levelek Kerényi Frigyeshez." *See* "Travel to Frigyes Kerenyi."

Utopia (More). LFFor 2022.

"Utro." *See* "Morning."

Utstein Monastery Cycle. LFFor 799, 802.

"Utyos." *See* "Cliff, The."

Uyezdnoye. See *Provincial Tale, A.*

V

V. (Pynchon). LFEng 2188-2190; RevLFEng 2766-2768.

V As in Victim (Treat). M&D 1598-1599.

V lyudyakh. See *In the World.*

"V Peterburge my soidemsia snova." *See* "In Petersburg We Shall Meet Again."

"V podvale." *See* "In the Basement."

"V stepi." *See* "In the Steppe."

Vade-mecum (Norwid). PFor 2126.

Vadim (Lermontov). LFFor 1020, 2313.

Vagabonds (Hamsun). LFFor 775-776.

Vägen till Klockrike. See *Road, The.*

Vägvisare till underjorden. See *Guide to the Underworld.*

Vajanský, Svetozár Hurban. LFFor 2068; PFor 1809.

Vajda, János. PFor 1983.

"Valaida" (Wideman). RevShF 2465.

Valaská škola (Gavlovič). PFor 1807.

Valčik no roz oučenou. See *Farewell Party, The.*

Valdez, Luis Miguel. DSup 366-372; RevDEng 2424-2432.

"Vale of teares, A" (Southwell). PEng 2689; RevPEng 3132.

"Vale of Tears" (Leskov). RevShF 1469; ShFSup 161.

"Valediction: Forbidding Mourning, A" (Donne). PEng 831-832; RevPEng 937-938.

Valentine (Sand). LFFor 1490-1491.

Valentine, Jo. *See* **Armstrong, Charlotte.**

"Valentines to the Wide World" (Van Duyn). PEng 2962; RevPEng 3441.

Valentinian (Fletcher). DEng 635; RevDEng 780.

Valera, Juan. LFFor 1813-1829, 2384.

"Valeria" (Monroe). PEng 2027.

Valeria and Other Poems (Monroe). PEng 2027.

Valerius Catullus, Gaius. *See* **Catullus.**

Valéry, Paul. LTh 213, 555-556, 858, 979, **1489-1494; PFor 1572-1583,** 1881, 1883.

"Valiant Woman, The" (Powers). RevShF 1918-1919; ShF 2119-2120.

Validity in Interpretation (Hirsch). LTh 809.

Valin, Jonathan. M&D 1622-1627.

Valis (Dick). RevLFEng 898-899.

Valle-Inclán, Ramón María del; DFor 1917-1927, 2503-2504; **LFFor 1830-1843,** 2389.

Vallejo, César. PFor 1584-1595, 2228.

Valle Peña, Ramón José Simón. *See* **Valle-Inclán, Ramón María del.**

"Valley, The" (Lamartine). PFor 833. See also *Poetical Meditations, The.*

"Valley Between, The" (Marshall). RevShF 1614.

Valley of Bones, The (Powell, A.). LFEng 2120; RevLFEng 2679.

Valley of the Many-colored Grasses (Johnson, R.). PSup 211; RevPEng 1713-1714.

Valley of the Moon, The (London). LFEng 1698; RevLFEng 2103.

Vallfart och vandringsår (Heidenstam). LFFor 817, 820.

"Vallon, Le." *See* "Valley, The."

Valperga (Shelley, M.). LFEng 2389-2390; RevLFEng 3017-3018.

Valse aux adieux, La. See *Farewell Party, The.*

Valse des toréadors, La. See *Waltz of the Toreadors.*

"Value is an Activity" (Empson). PEng 969; RevPEng 1099.

Vampire, The (Planché). DEng 1524-1525; RevDEng 1912-1913.

"Vampyre, The" (Polidori). ShF 476.

Vanbrugh, Sir John. DEng 1965-1977. RevDEng 2433-2445.

Vance, Arthur. ShF 589.

Vance, John Holbrook. *See* **Queen, Ellery.**

Vance, Ronald. ShF 2863.

Vančura, Vladislav. LFFor 2066.

Vandaleur's Folly (Arden and D'Arcy). DEng 48; RevDEng 61-62.

Van de Wetering, Janwillem. M&D 1628-1633.

Van Dine, S. S. M&D 1634-1640; RevLFEng 3845; ShF 756. *See also* Wright, Willard Huntington.

Van Doren, Mark. PEng 2954-2959; RevPEng 3432-3438.

Vandover and the Brute (Norris). LFEng 2002, 2004; RevLFEng 2527.

Van Druten, John. RevDEng 45.

Van Duyn, Mona. PEng 2960-2967; RevPEng 3439-3446.

Van Dyke, Henry. ShF 2864.

"Van Gogh" (Snodgrass). PEng 2663; RevPEng 3092.

Van Gulik, Robert H. M&D 1641-1647.

"Vanishing Point" (Pastan). PEng 2172.

Verbrecher, Die. See *Criminals, The.*

Verdacht, Der. See Quarry, The.

Verdud suspechosa, La. See *Truth Suspected, The.*

Verdaguer, Jacint. PFor 1773.

Verdun. See *Battle, The.*

Verfolgung und Ermordung Jean-Paul Marats, dargestellt durch die Schauspielgruppe des Hospizes zu Charenton unter Ankitung des Herrn de Sade, Der. See *Marat/Sade.*

Verga, Giovanni. DFor 1940-1949, 2411; LFFor 1855-1865, 2232-2233; LTh 1495-1500; RevShF 2344-2349; ShF 685, 686-687, 2377-2383.

Verge, The (Glaspell). RevDEng 970.

Vergil. LFFor 2021; LTh 64, 411-412, 515, 517, 965-966, 1043, 1143-1144, 1650, 1654; PEng 2790; PFor 399, **1606-1618,** 2097, 2098-2099; **RevShF 2350-2355,** 2570, 2572.ShF 135, **2384-2390.**

Vergini della rocce, Le. See *Maidens of the Rocks, The.*

"Verglia funebre, La." *See* "Funeral Wake, The."

Vergne, Marie-Madeleine Pioche de la. *See* **La Fayette, Madame de.**

Vergonzoso en palacio, El (Tirso). DFor 1845.

Verhaeren, Émile. PFor 1619-1624, 1879.

Véritable Saint-Genest, La (Rotrou). DFor 1575-1576.

Verkehrte Welt, Die (Tieck). DFor 1836-1839.

"Verklighet *(drömd),* En." *See* "Reality *(dreamed),* A."

Verlaine, Paul. PFor 1625-1633, 1876, 1877.

Verliebtes Gespente und die gelible Dornrose. See *Beloved Hedgerose, The.*

Verlorene Ehre der Katharina Blum, Die. See Lost Honor of Katharina Blum, The.

"Verlorenes Ich." *See* "Lost Self."

"Vermont: Indian Summer" (Booth). PEng 242.

"Vermont Tale, A" (Helprin). RevShF 1164; ShFSup 118-119.

Vernacular Republic, The (Murray). RevPEng 2412.

Verne, Jules. LFFor 1866-1878; RevLFEng 3866, 3867.

Vernisáž. See *Private View.*

Verre d'eau, La. See *Glass of Water, The.*

Vérrokonok. See *Blood Relations.*

"Vers dorés." *See* "Golden Verses."

Verschwender, Der. See *Spendthrift, The.*

Verschwörung des Fiesko zu Genua, Die. See *Fiesco.*

Verschwundene Mond, Der (Hochwälder). DFor 933.

Verses (Rossetti, C.). PEng 2417; RevPEng 2810.

Verses About the Beautiful Lady. See *Stikhi o prekrasnoy dame.*

"Verses on Sir Joshua Reynold's Painted Window" (Warton). PEng 3039.

Verses on the Death of Dr. Swift (Swift). LFEng 2606; PEng 2809; RevPEng 3276; RevLFEng 3759.

"Verses to the Memory of Garrick" (Sheridan). PEng 2565.

"Verses wrote in a Lady's Ivory Table-Book" (Swift). PEng 2804-2805; RevPEng 3271-3272.

Versi et regole della nuova poesia toscana (Tolomei). LTh 1663.

Versi sciolti (Paradisi). LTh 1691.

Versos de salón (Parra). PFor 1133.

Versos del capitán, Los. See *Captain's Verses, The.*

Versprechen, Das. See *Pledge, The.*

Verstörung. See *Gargoyles.*

Versty I (Tsvetayeva) PFor 1534, 1536.

Versuch einer kritischen Dichtkunst vor die Deutschen (Gottsched). LTh 617.

Versuch über Schiller (Mann). LTh 986.

"Versuch über uns." *See* "Attempt About Us."

Verte y no verte. See *To See You and Not to See You.*

Verteidigung der Wölfe (Enzensberger). PFor 469.

"Vertical Ladder, The" (Sansom). RevShF 2051-2052; ShF 2184.

Vertical Man (Kinsella). PSup 236; RevPEng 1838.

Veruntreute Himmel, Der. See *Embezzled Heaven.*

"Verwandlung, Die." *See* "Metamorphosis, The."

Verwirrungen des Zöglings Törless, Die. See *Young Törless.*

Very Heaven (Aldington). LFEng 44-45; RevLFEng 58-59.

"Very Old Man with Enormous Wings, A" (García Márquez). RevShF 953; ShF 1456-1457.

Very Rich Hours of Count von Stauffenberg, The (West, P.). LFSup 375-376; RevLFEng 3526-3527.

Vesaas, Tarjei. LFFor 2352-2353; PFor 2189-2190.

Veselovsky, Alexander. LTh 1341, 1501-1506.

"Vesna v Fialte." *See* "Spring in Fialta."

Vestris, Madame. DEng 2357.

Vesyolaya Smert. See *Merry Death, A.*

Vetere, Richard. ShF 2865.

Vetezović, Pavao Ritter. PFor 2261.

"VI Dirge" (Rakosi). RevPEng 2688.

Via crucis do corpo, A (Lispector). RevShF 1493; ShFSup 168.

Via del male, La (Deledda). LFFor 439.

Viaduct Murder, The (Knox). M&D 999-1000.

Viaducts of Seine-et-Oise, The (Duras). DFor 511.

"Viagem a Petrópolis." *See* "Journey to Petrópolis."

"Viaggio, La." *See* "Adrianna Takes a Trip."

"Viaggio di nozze." *See* "Wedding Trip."

Viaje de invierno, Un (Benet). LFFor 140-142.

Vialis, Gaston. *See* **Simenon, Georges.**

Viallis, Gaston. *See* **Simenon, Georges.**

Vic Makropulos. See *Macropulos Secret, The.*

"Vicar, The" (Praed). PEng 2278-2279.

Vicar of Tours, The (Balzac). LFFor 95-96.

Vicar of Wakefield, The (Goldsmith). RevLFEng 3736.

Vicente, Gil. DFor **1950-1960,** 2172-2173, 2484.

Viceré, I. See *Viceroys, The.*

Viceroys, The (De Roberto). LFFor 2223.

Vico, Giambattista. LTh 31, 329, **1507-1512.**

Vicomte de Bragelonne, The (Dumas, *père*). LFFor 526.

Victim, The (Bellow). LFEng 226-227; RevLFEng 277-278.

"Victim No. 5" (Keeler). M&D 955.

Victim of the Aurora, A (Keneally). LFSup 188-189; RevLFEng 1844-1845.

"Victor and Vanquished" (Longfellow). RevPEng 2036.

"Victor Hugo romancier" (Butor). LTh 253.

Victorian Village, A (Reese). PEng 2342; RevPEng 2727.

Victories of Love, The (Patmore). PEng 2192; RevPEng 2563.

Victory (Conrad). LFEng 597-600; RevLFEng 726.

Victory Over Japan (Gilchrist). RevShF 987-988.

Vida breve, La. See *Brief Life, A.*

Vida de Don Quixote y Sancho. See *Life of Don Quixote and Sancho, The.*

Vida de Lazarillo de Tormes y de sus fortunas y adversidades, La. See *Lazarillo de Tormes.*

Vida de Santa Maria Egipciaca. PFor 2207.

Vida es sueño, La. See *Life Is a Dream.*

Vida y dulzura (Martínez Sierras). DFor 1283-1284.

Vida y obra de Medrano (Alonso). LTh 27.

Vidaković, Milovan. LFFor 2075.

Vidal, Gore. LFEng 2712-2721, 3154; LFSup 408; **RevLFEng 3369-3378,** 3839. *See also* **Box, Edgar.**

Vidocq, François-Eugène. M&D 1648-1653; ShF 749.

Vidrić, Vladimir. PFor 2264.

Vie de Marianne, La. See *Life of Marianne, The.*

Vie de Rancé (Chateaubriand). LFFor 2124.

Vie de Shakespeare (Guizot). DEng 2188; RevDEng 2708.

Vie est ailleurs, La. See *Life Is Elsewhere.*

Vie Passionée of Rodney Buckthorne, La (Cassill). LFEng 468.

Viebig, Clara. LFFor 2183.

"Vieja moralidad." *See* "Old Morality, The."

Viejo celoso, El. See *Jealous Old Husband, The.*

Viejo y la niña, El (Moratín). DFor 1361-1362.

"Vielleicht" (Gomringer). PFor 594-595.

Vienna: Lusthaus (Clarke, M.). DSup 65-66; RevDEng 473-474.

Vienna (Spender). PEng 2697-2698; RevPEng 3141.

Viento fuerte. See *Strong Wind.*

Viereck, Peter. RevPEng 3456-3462.

Vierte Gebot, Das. See *Fourth Commandment, The.*

Vierundzwanzigste Februar, Der. See *Twenty-fourth of February, The.*

Vierzig Tage des Musa Dagh, Die. See *Forty Days of Musa Dagh, The.*

Viet Rock (Terry). DSup 343; RevDEng 2368-2369.

Vietnam Discourse (Weiss). DFor 1989-1990.

Vietnam Project, The. See *Dusklands.*

"Vietnam War, The" (Bly). RevPEng 269.

Vietnamization of New Jersey, The (Durang). DSup 102.

"View, A" (Van Duyn). PEng 2965-2966; RevPEng 3444-3445.

"View from an Attic Window, The" (Nemerov). PEng 2081-2082.

View from the Bridge, A (Miller). DEng 1343-1345; RevDEng 1682-1684.

"View of Birds" (George). PFor 547-548. See also *Algabal.*

"Views of My Father Weeping" (Barthelme). RevShF 166.

"Vigil Strange I Kept on the Field One Night" (Whitman). PEng 3072; RevPEng 3559.

Vigny, Alfred de. DFor 2344; LTh 1029-1030, 1702; **PFor 1634-1643,** 1868-1869.

Vikrama and Urvaśī (Kālidāsa). DFor 1031-1033.

Vikramorvaśiya. See *Vikrama and Urvakt.*

Vilalta, Maruxa. DSup 373-379.

Vilar, Jean. DFor 2354.

Vilhjálmsson, Thor. LFFor 2371.

Villa, Die (Dorst). DSup 96.

Villa, José Garcia. PEng 2976-2984; PFor 1644-1652; PSup 410, RevPEng 3163-3172, 3917.

Village, The (Crabbe). PEng 634, 637-640; RevPEng 731, 732-734.

Village: A Party, The (Fuller). RevDEng 880.

"Village of the Dead" (Hoch). RevShF 1206-1207.

Village Romeo and Juliet, A (Keller). LFFor 930-931. See also *People of Seldwyla, The.*

"Villager, The" (Jackson). RevShF 1252; ShF 1669-1670.

Villages illusoires, Les (Verhaeren). PFor 1623.

Villano en su rincón, El. See *King and the Farmer, The.*

Ville, La. See *City, The.*

Ville de la chance, La. See *Town Beyond the Wall, The.*

Villette (Brontë, C.). LFEng 303-304; RevLFEng 387-388.

Villette, Reverend John. ShF 748.

Villiers, George. DEng 1978-1985; RevDEng 2446-2453.

"Villon" (Bunting). PEng 370; RevPEng 444.

Villon, François. PFor 1653-1661, 1845-1846.

"Villon's Epitaph" (Villon). PFor 1660.

Vinaver, Stanislav. PFor 2256.

Vine, Barbara. *See* **Rendell, Ruth.**

Vinegar Tom (Churchill). RevDEng 435.

Vineland (Pynchon). RevLFEng 2771-2772, 3771, 3777.

Vingt Ans après. See *Twenty Years After.*

Vingt Mille Lieues sous les mers. See *Twenty Thousand Leagues Under the Sea.*

Vino e pane. See *Bread and Wine.*

Vintage Murder (Marsh). M&D 1193.

"Vintage Thunderbird, A" (Beattie). RevShF 180-181; ShFSup 38.

Violence and the Sacred (Girard). LTh 591.

Violence et le Sacré, La. See *Violence and the Sacred.*

Violent Bear It Away, The (O'Connor, Flannery). LFEng 2038-2039; RevLFEng 2569, 2572-2573.

Violent Land, The (Amado). LFFor 52-53.

"Violet." *See* "Epilogue II."

Violet Clay (Godwin). LFSup 138-139; RevLFEng 1342-1343.

Violio, G. *See* **Simenon, Georges.**

"Viotti Stradivarius, The" (de la Torre). M&D 480-481.

Viper Jazz (Tate, J.). PEng 2839; RevPEng 3310.

Vipers' Tangle (Mauriac). LFFor 1124, 1129-1131.

Virgiliana continentia. See *Content of Virgil.*

Virgin Martyr, The (Massinger and Dekker). DEng 1295-1296; RevDEng 1623-1624.

Virgin Soil (Turgenev). LFFor 1778-1779.

Virgin Soil Upturned (Sholokhov). LFFor 1556, 1559, 1561-1562.

"Virgin Violeta" (Porter). RevShF 1908.

Virginia (Alfieri). DFor 44-45.

Virginia (Glasgow). LFEng 1121-1122; RevLFEng 1331-1332.

"Virginia" (Macaulay). PEng 1827.

Virginia (Montiano y Luyando). LTh 1692.

Virginia (Tamayo y Baus). DFor 1807-1808.

"Virginia Britannia" (Moore). PEng 2045; RevPEng 2375.

Virginian, The (Wister). LFEng 3192-3193; RevLFEng 3849; ShF 593-594.

Virginians, The (Thackeray). LFEng 2624-2626; RevLFEng 3271, 3277-3279.

Virginius (Knowles). DEng 1056-1057, 1061; RevDEng 1334-1335, 1339.

"Virility" (Dzick). ShF 2038-2039.

"Virtue" (Maugham). RevShF 1628; ShF 1904.

Virtuous Orphan, The. See *Life of Marianne, The.*

Visconte dimezzato, Il. See *Cloven Viscount, The.*

Viscount of Blarney, The (Clarke, A.). DEng 377-378; RevDEng 465-466.

Vises sten, De. See *Philosopher's Stone, The.*

Vishnyovy sad. See *Cherry Orchard, The.*

"Vision and Form" (Harris, W.). ShF 78-79.

"Vision Between Waking and Sleeping in the Mountains" (Wright, James). PEng 3158-3159; RevPEng 3670-3671.

"Vision of a Garden, A" (Merrill). RevPEng 2279.

Vision of Delight, The (Jonson). LTh 1677.

Vision of Judgment, The (Byron). LTh 258.

"Vision of Mizrah, The" (Addison). RevShF 16; ShF 826-827.

"Vision of Repentance, A" (Lamb). PEng 1635; RevPEng 1899.

"Vision of Spring in Winter, A" (Swinburne). PEng 2821; RevPEng 3289.

Vision of the Last Judgment, A (Blake). LTh 1700.

Vision of William, Concerning Piers the Plowman, The (Langland). PEng 1646-1655, 3256-3257; RevPEng 1914-1920, 3775-3776.

Visionary, The (Lie). LFFor 2341.

Visions from the Ramble (Hollander). RevPEng 1548.

Visions of the Daughters of Albion (Blake). PEng 216-217; RevPEng 260-261.

Völuspá: The Song of the Sybil. PFor 2153.

Volverás a Región (Benet). LFFor 135-138.

"Vom armen B.B." *See* "Of Poor B.B."

Von Dalin, Olaf. LFFor 2334.

Von dem Einfluss und Gebrauche der Einbildungs-Krafft (Bodmer). LTh 176.

Von deutscher Art und Kunst (Herder). LTh 669.

Von Linné, Carl. *See* Linnaeus.

Von morgens bis mitternachts. See *From Morn to Midnight.*

Von Schwelle zu Schwelle (Celan). PFor 312-313.

Vonnegut, Kurt, Jr. LFEng 2722-2732; LFSup 408; **RevLFEng 3379-3389**, 3870, 3878; **RevShF 2364-2371; ShF 2391-2398.**

"Voprosy izucheniya literatury yazyka" (Tynyanov and Jakobson). LTh 1477.

Voprosy literatury i estetiki. See *Dialogic Imagination, The.*

Vor. See *Thief, The.*

"Vor dem Gesetz." *See* "Before the Law."

Vor dem Sturm (Fontane). LFFor 566-567.

Vor Sonnenaufgang. See *Before Dawn.*

Vorlesungen über Ästhetik (Solger). LTh 1360, 1362.

Vorlesungen über dramatische Kunst und Literatur. See *Course of Lectures on Dramatic Art and Literature, A.*

Vörösmarty, Mihály. DFor 2286-2287; **PFor 1662-1670,** 1980.

"Vorrede aus dem Jahre 1881" (Storm). LFFor 1679.

Vortex, The (Coward). DEng 426-427; RevDEng 526-527.

Voskreseniye. See *Resurrection.*

Voskreshenie slova. See *Resurrection of the Word.*

Voskresshiye bogi. See *Romance of Leonardo da Vinci, The.*

Voss (White, P.). LFEng 2869-2870; RevLFEng 3550-3551.

Voss, Arthur. RevShF 2669.

Voss, Johann Heinrich. LTh 663.

"Vowels" (Rimbaud). PFor 1338.

Vox Clamantis (Gower). PEng 1113, 1114, 1115, 1118-1120; RevPEng 1266-1268.

"Voyage, Le." *See* "Trip, The."

Voyage au bout de la nuit. See *Journey to the End of the Night.*

Voyage de M. Perrichon, Le. See *Journey of Mr. Perrichon, The.*

Voyage en Orient. See *Journey to the Orient.*

Voyage of St. Brendan. RevShF 2603; ShF 432-433.

Voyage of the Dawn Treader, The (Lewis, C. S.). LFEng 1658; RevLFEng 2050.

Voyage Out, The (Woolf). LFEng 2945-2946; RevLFEng 3646-3647.

Voyage Round My Father, A (Mortimer). DEng 1356-1358; RevDEng 1696-1697.

Voyage to Arcturus, A (Lindsay). RevLFEng 3860.

Voyage to Tomorrow (Hakim). DSup 177-178.

"Voyages" (Levine). RevPEng 1994.

Voyageur sans bagage, Le. See *Traveller Without Luggage.*

"Voyelles." *See* "Vowels."

Voyeur, Le. See *Voyeur, The.*

Voyeur, The (Robbe-Grillet). LFFor 1414-1415; M&D 1438-1439.

Voyna i mir. See *War and Peace.*

Voysey Inheritance, The (Granville Barker). DEng 799-800; RevDEng 990-991.

Voz a tí debida, La. See *My Voice Because of You.*

"Vozmezdie" (Blok). PFor 197.

Voznesensky, Andrei. PFor 2150.

Vraz, Stanko. PFor 2262.

Vrchlický, Jaroslav. DFor 2282; PFor 1802-1803.

Vreme smrti (Ćosić). LFFor 389-391.

Vsyakaya vsyachina. LTh 1694.

Vučić, Ivan Bunić. PFor 2261.

Vučja so. See *Wolf Salt.*

"Vuillard" (Snodgrass). PEng 2662; RevPEng 3091.

Vujić, Joakim. DFor 2291.

Vulliamy, C. E. M&D 1659-1664.

Vultures, The (Becque). DFor 171-172, 2347.

Vybor guvernera. See *Choice of a Tutor, The.*

"Vying" (Davie). PSup 86; RevPEng 851.

"Vykhozhu odin ya na dorogu. . . ." *See* "I Walk Out Alone onto the Road. . . ."

Vyrozumění. See *Memorandum, The.*

Vysokaya bolezn. See *High Malady.*

"Vystrel." *See* "Shot, The."

W

W Szwajcarii. See *In Switzerland.*

"Waage der Baleks, Die." *See* "Balek Scales, The."

Wackenroder, Wilhelm Heinrich. LTh 437, 1699, 1706.

Waclaw (Słowacki). PFor 1443.

Wade, Henry. M&D 1665-1670.

"Wading at Wellfleet" (Bishop). PEng 188; RevPEng 231.

Wagatomo Hittora. See *My Friend Hitler.*

Wage War on Silence (Miller). RevPEng 2331-2332.

Wager, The (Giacosa). DFor 702-704.

Wager, The (Medoff). DSup 242-243; RevDEng 1646-1647, 1648.

Wages of Zen, The (Melville, J.). M&D 1214.

Wagner, Richard. DEng 2197; DFor 2374-2375; LTh 987, 1068-1069, 1328-1329; RevDEng 2717.

Wagner the Were-Wolf (Reynolds). ShF 732.

Wagon (Ważyk). PFor 1695.

Wagoner, David. PEng 2985-2993; PSup 410; RevPEng 3473-3481.

Wahlöö, Per, and Maj Sjöwall. M&D 1495-1501.

Wahlöö, Peter. *See* **Wahlöö, Per.**

Wahlverwandtschaften, Die. See *Elective Affinities.*

Wahre Muftoni, Der (Meckel). RevShF 1645; ShFSup 190.

Wahrheit und Methode. See *Truth and Method.*

Wain, John. RevLFEng 3390-3403, 3808; LFEng 2733-2745; LFSup 408; RevShF 2372-2376; ShF 2399-2402.

"Wait by the Door Awhile, Death, There Are Others" (Dorn). PEng 842; RevPEng 948.

"Wait for Me" (Tate, J.). RevPEng 3309-3310.

"Wait Not Till Slaves Pronounce the Word" (Thoreau). PEng 2901; RevPEng 3369.

"Waiting" (Pinsky). RevPEng 2584.

Waiting for Dolphins (McGrath). RevDEng 1521.

Waiting for Godot (Beckett). DEng 150-152, 2384; DFor 158-160, 2245-2246, 2359; LFFor 122; RevDEng 186-187, 2902.

Waiting for Lefty (Odets). DEng 1397-1398; RevDEng 1773-1774.

"Waiting for My Life" (Pastan). RevPEng 2545.

Waiting for My Life (Pastan). PEng 2173-2174; RevPEng 2541, 2544.

Waiting for Sheila (Braine). LFEng 284, 287, 288; RevLFEng 371.

"Waiting for the Barbarians" (Cavafy). PFor 297-298.

Waiting for the Barbarians (Coetzee). LFSup 80-81; RevLFEng 675-676.

Waiting for the End (Fiedler). LTh 487.

Waiting for the King of Spain (Wakoski). RevPEng 3490.

Waiting Room, The (Harris, W.). LFSup 148-149; RevLFEng 1530-1531.

Wake in Ybor City, A (Yglesias). LFEng 2995-2997; RevLFEng 3701-3703.

Wake of Jimmy Foster, The (Henley). DSup 196-197; RevDEng 1154-1155.

Wake Up, Stupid (Harris, M.). LFEng 1284-1285; RevLFEng 1521-1522.

"Wakefield" (Hawthorne). RevShF 1146; ShF 112.

Wakefield Cycle. RevDEng 2768, 2769-2770.

Wakefield Master. DEng 1986-1996, 2250; RevDEng 2455-2465, 2770.

"Waking, The" (Roethke). RevPEng 2804-2805.

Waking, The (Roethke). PEng 2411-2412.

"Waking Early Sunday Morning" (Lowell, R.). PEng 1794; RevPEng 2088.

Wakoski, Diane. PEng 2994-3000; PSup 410; RevPEng 3482-3493.

Walahfrid Strabo. PFor 2113.

Walcott, Derek, A. DEng 1997-2005, 2453-2454; PEng 3001-3007; PSup 411; RevDEng 2466-2475, 2978-2979; RevPEng 3494-3504, 3944-3945.

Walcott, Roderick. DEng 2453; RevDEng 2978.

"Walcourt" (Verlaine). PFor 1631.

"Wald, Der" (Walser, R.). RevShF 2389, 2391; ShFSup 347.

Walden (Thoreau). PEng 2897; RevPEng 3365.

Waldo, Edward Hamilton. *See* **Sturgeon, Theodore.**

"Walesi bardok, A." *See* "Welsh Bards, The."

Walk and Other Stories, The (Walser, R.). RevShF 2391; ShFSup 348-349.

Walk in the Night, A (La Guma). LFFor 2050.

Walk on the Wild Side, A (Algren). LFSup 28-29; RevLFEng 80-81.

357

Wang Yu-ch'eng. *See* Wang Wei.

"Want Bone, The" (Pinsky). RevPEng 2590-2591.

"Wanting to Die" (Sexton). PEng 2524; RevPEng 2934.

"Wants" (Paley). RevShF 1838; ShF 2043.

Wapshot Chronicle, The (Cheever). LFEng 504-506, 507; RevLFEng 617-619.

Wapshot Scandal, The (Cheever). LFEng 506-508; RevLFEng 619-621.

War and Peace (Tolstoy). LFFor 1722-1725, 2317.

War and Remembrance (Wouk). LFEng 2971-2972; RevLFEng 3673-3674, 3837.

"War Baby, The" (Lewis). RevShF 1485-1486.

War Between the Tates, The (Lurie). LFSup 251; RevLFEng 2128, 2129.

"War Diary" (Radnóti). PFor 1313.

"War Generation, The" (Endō). RevShF 838.

"War God, The" (Spender). PEng 2698; RevPEng 3142.

War of Dreams, The. See Infernal Desire Machines of Doctor Hoffman, The.

War of the End of the World, The (Vargas Llosa). LFFor 1851-1853.

War of the Mice and the Crabs, The (Leopardi). PFor 856-857.

"War of the Secret Agents, The" (Coulette). RevPEng 688-689.

War of the Worlds, The (Wells, H, G.). RevDEng 3028; RevLFEng 3482.

"War of Vaslav Nijinsky, The" (Bidart). RevPEng 212-213.

War on Tatem, The (Medoff). DSup 241-243.

"War Requiem, A" (Sissman). PEng 2616-2617; RevPEng 3020-3021.

War Stories (Nemerov). RevPEng 2432.

"Warawanu Otoko." *See* "Man Who Did Not Smile, The."

Warborough, Martin Leach. *See* **Allen, Grant.**

Ward, Alfred C. RevShF 2676-2677.

Ward, Arthur Henry Sarsfield. *See* **Rohmer, Sax.**

"Ward No. 6" (Chekhov). LFEng 3301-3302.

"Warden, The" (Gardner). RevShF 959.

Ware the Hawk (Skelton). PEng 2637; RevPEng 3042.

Warera no jidai (Ōe). LFFor 1196.

Wariat i zakonnica. See Madman and the Nun, The.

Warlock (Harrison). LFEng 1291-1294; RevLFEng 1542-1544.

Warner, Sylvia Townsend. RevShF 2401-2409; ShF 273, 522; **ShFSup 351-359.**

"Warning, The" (Creeley). RevPEng 777-778.

Warren, Austin. LTh 1426, 1535, 1755.

Warren, Robert Penn. LFEng 2767-2780; LTh 158, 1148, 1424-1425, **1521-1527,** 1554, 1753, 1818; **PEng 3019-3029;** PSup 411; **RevLFEng 3432-3446,** 3772; **RevPEng 3516-3526,** 3974, 3976-3977; **RevShF 2410-2416;** ShF 546, **2403-2408.**

Wars of Caesar and Pompey, The (Chapman). DEng 359; RevDEng 420.

Wartah, al-. See Incrimination.

Warton, Joseph, and **Thomas Warton.** LTh **1528-1533.**

Warton, Thomas. PEng 3030-3040.

"Warum gabst du uns die tiefen Blicke?" *See* "Why Did You Give Us the Deep Glances?"

"Was I never yet of your love grieved" (Wyatt). PEng 3174; RevPEng 3698.

"Was it some sweet device of Faery" (Lamb). PEng 1634; RevPEng 1898.

"Washing My Face" (Orr). PEng 2150; RevPEng 2520.

Washington, D.C. (Vidal). RevLFEng 3376.

Washington Square (James, H.). LFEng 1441; RevLFEng 1720.

Wasps, The (Aristophanes). DFor 2125-2126.

Wasserstein, Wendy. RevDEng 2476-2483.

Wästberg, Per. LFFor 2360.

Waste (Granville-Barker). DEng 800; RevDEng 991.

Waste Land, The (Eliot). PEng 943-946, 3356, 3363, 3364, 3389; RevPEng 1072-1076, 3874, 3881.

Waste of Timelessness and Other Early Stories (Nin). RevShF 1722; ShF 1949.

"Wasted Evening, A" (Musset). PFor 1066-1067.

"Watakushi." *See* "Thief, The."

"Watashi no mono." *See* "My Belongings."

Watch on the Rhine (Hellman). DEng 923-924; RevDEng 1147-1148.

Watch That Ends the Night, The (MacLennan). LFEng 1746; RevLFEng 2215.

Watch the North Wind Rise (Graves, R.). LFEng 1202; RevLFEng 1426.

Watchboy, What of the Night? (Cassity). PSup 62; RevPEng 544-545.

"Watcher by the Dead, A" (Bierce). M&D 126.

Watchers (Koontz). M&D 1007.

"Water" (Creeley). PEng 682.

"Water Ballet, A" (Zoshchenko). RevShF 2560.

"Water Carrier, The" (Montague). RevPEng 2360-2361.

"Water Hen, The" (O'Flaherty). ShF 2006-2007.

We Walk the Way of the New World (Madhubuti). PEng 1892; RevPEng 2199-2200.

"We Wear the Mask" (Dunbar, P. L.). PEng 1844, 3400.

Wealth (Jones, H. A.). DEng 1003; RevDEng 1269.

"Wealthy Lady" (Oates). RevPEng 2466-2467.

Weapons of Happiness (Brenton). DSup 34; RevDEng 321-322.

"Weary Blues, The" (Hughes, L.). PEng 1433; RevPEng 1641.

Weary Blues, The (Hughes, L.). PEng 1432-1433; RevPEng 1640-1642.

Weather Breeder, The (Denison). DEng 501-502; RevDEng 622-623.

Weathers, Winston. ShF 2872.

Weaver, Gordon. ShF 2873.

"Weaver Bird, The" (Awoonor). PFor 113.

Weavers, The (Hauptmann). DFor 871-873, 2375-2376; LTh 1721-1722.

"Weaver's Grave, The" (O'Kelly). ShF 667-668.

Web and the Rock, The (Wolfe). LFEng 2936-2937; RevLFEng 3636-3637.

Webb, Bernice Larson. ShF 2875.

Webb, Christopher. *See* **Holton, Leonard.**

Webb, Frances. ShF 2876.

Webb, Jack. M&D 1689-1693.

Webb, Richard. *See* **Quentin, Patrick.**

Webber, Andrew Lloyd. *See* Lloyd Webber, Andrew.

Weber, Die. See *Weavers, The.*

Weber, Carl Maria von. RevDEng 2984.

Webster, John. DEng 2006-2011, 2289; **RevDEng 2484-2494,** 2808.

"Wedding, The" (O'Flaherty). ShF 2009-2010.

Wedding, The (Shirley). DEng 1813-1815; RevDEng 2248-2250.

Wedding, The (Wyspiański). DFor 2031-2034.

"Wedding Day" (Boyle, K.). RevShF 283-286; ShF 996-998.

"Wedding Dress, A" (Callaghan). RevShF 385; ShFSup 69.

Wedding Feast, The (Wesker). RevDEng 2509.

Wedding Guest, The. See *Italian Straw Hat, The.*

"Wedding Trip" (Pavese). RevShF 1861-1862.

Wedekind, Frank. DFor 1972-1983, 2376; LFFor 2185.

"Weed, The" (Bishop). PEng 184; RevPEng 227.

Week on the Concord and Merrimack Rivers, A (Thoreau). PEng 2896-2897; RevPEng 3370.

Weekend for Murder. See *Murder on a Mystery Tour.*

Weep Not, Child (Ngugi wa Thiong'o). LFEng 1976-1978; RevLFEng 2498, 2500-2501.

Weg der Verheissung, Der. See *Eternal Road, The.*

Wegner, Robert. ShF 2877.

Weh' dem, der lügt. See *Thou Shalt Not Lie!*

Wei, Wang. See **Wang Wei.**

Wei dem Herrn Mockingpott das Leiden ausgetrieben wird. See *How Mr. Mockingpott Was Cured of His Suffering.*

Wei Hung. LTh 1773, 1785.

Weib im Brunnen, Das (Sachs). DFor 1626.

Weidman, Jerome. RevShF 2417-2421; ShF 2409-2412.

Weight of the World, The (Handke). LFFor 789.

Weil, Simone. LFEng 1936; RevLFEng 2447.

Weill, Kurt. DEng 2472-2473; RevDEng 2998-2999.

Weinheber, Josef. PFor 1932.

Weinstein, Nathan. *See* **West, Nathanael.**

Weird Tales. ShF 741-742, 773.

Weisengrund, Theodor. *See* **Adorno, Theodor.**

Weiss, Peter. DFor 1984-1991, 2382.

Weite Land, Das. See *Vast Land, The.*

Welburn, Ron. ShF 2878.

Welch, Denton. RevShF 2422-2429.

Welch, Rowland. *See* **Davies, L. P.**

"Welcome and Farewell" (Goethe). PFor 585.

Welcome to Hard Times (Doctorow). LFEng 770-773; RevLFEng 935.

"Welcome to the Monkey House" (Vonnegut). RevShF 2366-2367; ShF 2392.

Welcome to the Monkey House (Vonnegut). RevShF 2365; ShF 2392.

"Welcoming Party, A" (Montague). RevPEng 2361.

Weldon, Fay. RevLFEng 3473-3479, 3871.

Welhaven, Henrik. PFor 2168.

Well, The (Jolley). LFSup 181-182; RevLFEng 1794-1795.

Well, The (Ross). LFEng 2288-2289, 2291-2293; RevLFEng 2884, 2887-2889.

"Well, I have lost you" (Millay). PEng 2001-2002; RevPEng 2325-2326.

"Well of Lycopolis, The" (Bunting). PEng 370-371; RevPEng 445.

Well Wrought Urn, The (Brooks, C.). LTh 220-221, 1555; PEng 3433-3434, 3435-3436; RevPEng 3977-3978, 3979-3980.

Wellek, René. LTh 726-729, 1256, 1426, **1534-1539,** 1554, 1755, 1758, 1822.

Welles, Orson. RevDEng 3026-3030, 3032, 3034.

"Wellfleet Whale, The" (Kunitz). PSup 250-251; RevPEng 1891-1892.

Wells, H. G. LFEng 1132, 2805-2816, 3082, 3207-3208; RevLFEng 3480-3487, 3791, 3866, 3867, 3869; ShF 771-772, 777.

"Welsh Bards, The" (Arany). PFor 80-81.

Welt als Wille und Vorstellung, Die. See *World as Will and Idea, The.*

Welt von Gestern, Die. See *World of Yesterday, The.*

Welty, Eudora. LFEng 2817-2829; ShF 262-263, 547-548, 815-816, 2413-2420; RevLFEng 3488-3500; RevShF 2430-2439; ShFSup 391.

Wên fu. See *Essay on Literature.*

Wên I-to. LTh 1782; PFor 1794.

Wên-hsin tiao-lung. See *Literary Mind and the Carving of Dragons, The.*

"Wenn nicht dein Brunnen, Melusine." *See* "Melusine, If Your Well Had Not."

Wentworth, Patricia. M&D 1694-1699.

Weöres, Sándor. PFor 1986.

We're Friends Again (O'Hara). LFEng 2052; RevLFEng 2587.

"Were there no warres" (Nashe). RevPEng 2421.

"Werewolf, The" (Housman). LFEng 3204.

"Werewolf Raspberries" (Brautigan). RevShF 317; ShFSup 57.

Werewolf Trace, The (Gardner, J.). M&D 696-697.

Werfel, Franz. DFor 1992-2001; **LFFor** 1905-1914, 2196; PFor 1929.

Wergeland, Henrik. DFor 2470; LFFor 2338; PFor 2168.

Werner (Byron). DEng 330, 337-339; RevDEng 390, 397-399.

Werner, Zacharias. DFor 2370.

Wertenbaker, Timberlake. RevDEng 2495-2501.

Werther, der Jude (Jacobowsky). LFFor 2182.

"Werwolf, Der." *See* "Banshee, The."

Wescott, Glenway. LFEng 2830-2839; RevLFEng 3501-3511; RevShF 2440-2446; ShF 2421-2425.

Wesele. See *Wedding, The.*

Wesker, Arnold. DEng 2012-2019, 2387; RevDEng 2502-2511, 2905.

Wessel, Johan Herman. DFor 2467.

Wessex Poems (Hardy). PEng 1218-1219; RevPEng 1391-1392.

West, Edward. *See* **Household, Geoffrey.**

West, Jessamyn. RevShF 2447-2453; ShFSup 360-365.

West, Martin. *See* **Christie, Agatha.**

West, Nathanael. LFEng 2840-2847; RevLFEng 3512-3519.

West, Owen. *See* **Koontz, Dean R.**

West, Paul. LFSup 369-377; RevLFEng 3520-3529; ShF 2879.

West-Eastern Divan (Goethe). PFor 584, 588.

West Indian, The (Cumberland). DEng 447-448, 2330; RevDEng 555-556, 2849.

West of Suez (Osborne). DEng 1435-1436; RevDEng 1814-1815.

West of Your City (Stafford). RevPEng 3167.

West-östlicher Divan. See *West-Eastern Divan.*

"West-Running Brook" (Frost). PEng 1047; RevPEng 1179.

West Side Story (Laurents and Bernstein). DEng 2474; RevDEng 3000.

"Westering" (Heaney). PEng 1271.

Western Lands, The (Burroughs). RevLFEng 490.

Westlake, Donald E. M&D 1700-1706.

Westmacott, Mary. *See* **Christie, Agatha.**

Wetherell, W. D. RevShF 2760.

"W. H. Auden and Mantan Moreland" (Young). PEng 3218; RevPEng 3742.

"Whale's Tale, The" (Berrigan). ShF 374-375.

"Wharf Rats" (Walrond). ShF 578.

Wharton, Edith. LFEng 2848-2858, 3054; RevLFEng 3530-3542, 3762; RevShF 2454-2460; ShF 539, 707, 2426-2432.

Wharton, Edward (Teddy) Robbins. LFEng 2851; RevLFEng 3533.

"What Are Years?" (Moore). PEng 2045-2046; RevPEng 2375-2376.

What Did I Do Tomorrow? (Davies). M&D 462.

"What Do the Trees Say?" (Heyen). PEng 1327-1328.

What Do You Want, Peire Vidal? (Owens). DEng 1460; RevDEng 1460.

What D'ye Call It, The (Gay). DEng 731-732; RevDEng 910-911.

"What Happened to the Short Story?" (Brickell). ShF 72.

"What Have I Been Doing Lately" (Kincaid). RevShF 1342.

"What I Believe" (Forster). LTh 500.

"What I Found in the Sea" (Stockton). M&D 1536.

What If You Died Tomorrow (Williamson). DEng 2092; RevDEng 2594.

What I'm Going to Do, I Think (Woiwode). LFSup 394-395; RevLFEng 3621-3622.

"What Is a Classic?" (Eliot). LTh 449.

"What Is a Story?" (Saroyan). ShF 88.

"What Is an Initiation Story?" (Marcus). ShF 81.
What Is Art? (Tolstoy). LTh 790, 1445.
What Is Literature? (Sartre). LTh 104, 1272; PSup 52.
"What Is Loving?" (Walther). PFor 1675.
"What Is Oblomovism?" (Dobrolyubov). LTh 390.
What Is Pure French? (Gourmont). LTh 624.
"What Is the Connection Between Men and Women" (Oates). ShF 1963.
What Is the Short Story? (Current-Garcia and Patrick, eds.). ShF 74.
What Is to Be Done? (Chernyshevsky). LTh 285-286, 396.
"What Jorkens Has to Put Up With" (Dunsany). RevShF 791; ShF 1317-1318.
"What Kind of Day Did You Have?" (Bellow). RevShF 206.
"What Makes a Short Story Short?" (Friedman, N.). ShF 76.
"What Metre Is" (MacBeth). PEng 1834; RevPEng 2113.
"What of the Night?" (Kunitz). PSup 248; RevPEng 1889.
What Price Glory? (Anderson, M., and Stallings). DEng 27, 2400; RevDEng 38, 2921.
"What Shall I Name You?" (Petőfi). PFor 1225.
What Shall We Tell Caroline? (Mortimer). DEng 1355; RevDEng 1694-1695.
"What Should I Tell Her?" (Castro). PFor 279. See also *Follas novas.*
"What the Bones Know" (Kizer). RevPEng 1859.
What the Butler Saw (Orton). DEng 1425-1427; RevDEng 1803-1805.
"What the Chimney Sang" (Harte). PEng 1244.
"What the Doctor Said" (Carver). RevPEng 539.
"What the Mouth of the Shadow Says" (Hugo). PFor 736. See also *Contemplations, Les.*
"What the Tapster Saw" (Okri). RevShF 1810-1811.
"What the White Had to Say" (Simic). PEng 2593-2594.
"What Was It?" (O'Brien, F.). RevShF 1754, 2699-2700; ShF 206-207, 1980.
What Was Literature? (Fiedler). LTh 487-488.
"What We Don't Know Hurts Us" (Schorer). ShF 2199-2200.
"What We Talk About When We Talk About Love" (Carver). ShFSup 78-80.
What We Talk About When We Talk About Love (Carver). RevShF 437-439.
"What Would You Do If You Lost It?" (Ginsberg). PEng 1095.

"What You Hear from 'Em?" (Taylor). RevShF 2254; ShF 2309.
"Whatever Happened to Corporal Cuckoo?" (Kersh). M&D 982.
What's Become of Waring (Powell, A.). LFEng 2117; RevLFEng 2676.
What's Bred in the Bone (Davies). RevLFEng 801, 802.
"What's It Like Out?" (Gilliatt). RevShF 993.
"What's Wrong with Him?" (Zhang Jie). RevShF 2543-2544.
Wheat That Springeth Green (Powers). RevLFEng 2695-2697.
Wheatcroft, John. ShF 2881.
Wheatley, Dennis. M&D 1707-1712.
Wheatley, Phillis. PEng 1031, **3050-3061,** 3395-3396; **RevPEng 3537-3548,** 3903-3904.
Wheel, The (Berry). RevPEng 184.
Wheel of Fortune, The (Cumberland). DEng 450-451; RevDEng 558-559.
"Wheelbarrow, The" (Pirandello). ShF 2100-2101.
Wheeler, Hugh. *See* **Quentin, Patrick.**
Wheelwright, Philip. LTh 1756.
When a Girl Says Yes (Moratín). DFor 1363-1365, 2497.
"When a Man's Far Away from His Country" (Amichai). PSup 5.
"When Boyhood Dreams Come True" (Farrell). RevShF 842; ShF 1353.
"When first Amintas charmed my heart" (Etherege). PEng 976; RevPEng 1107.
When Five Years Pass (García Lorca). DFor 660-662.
"When Flowers Spring Out of the Grass" (Walther). PFor 1676-1677.
"When he was at sea" (Waller). PEng 3015; RevPEng 3512.
When I Grow Rich (Fleming, J.). M&D 619.
"When I Was Thirteen" (Welch). RevShF 2424-2425.
"When I Was Young, the Whole Country Was Young" (Amichai). PSup 3.
When I Whistle (Endō). LFSup 105-106.
"When Jemmy first began to love" (Behn). PEng 128; RevPEng 149.
"When Lilacs Last in the Dooryard Bloom'd" (Whitman). PEng 3073; RevPEng 3560.
"When My Girl Comes Home" (Pritchett). RevShF 1933-1934.
When No Man Pursueth (Lowndes). M&D 1100-1101.
"When Psyche-Life Descends to the Shades" (Mandelstam). PFor 938, 939. See also *Tristia.*

Wilder, Thornton. DEng 2042-2055; LFEng 2880-2888; RevDEng 2541-2555; RevLFEng 3570-3579.

"Wilderness, The" (Coxe). PEng 628-629.

Wilderness (Warren). LFEng 2778; RevLFEng 3443.

Wilderness and Other Poems, The (Coxe). PEng 628-629.

Wilderness of Mirrors, A (Frisch). LFFor 587-589.

Wilderness Road (Green). DEng 821-822; RevDEng 1014-1015.

Wilderness Tips (Atwood). RevShF 107-108.

"Wilding, The" (Booth). RevPEng 302.

Wildlife (Ford, R.). RevLFEng 1179-1180; RevShF 881-882.

Wilhelm Meister's Apprenticeship (Goethe). LFFor 673-676.

Wilhelm Meisters Lehrjahre. See Wilhelm Meister's Apprenticeship.

Wilhelm Meister's Theatrical Mission (Goethe). LFFor 673-64.

Wilhelm Meister's Travels (Goethe). LFFor 678-681.

Wilkes, John. PEng 3333.

Wilkinson, Sylvia. LFEng 2889-2896; ShF 2884.

Will to Power, The (Nietzsche). LTh 1070.

"Will You Be, Love?" (Salinas). PFor 1388.

Will You Please Be Quiet, Please? (Carver). RevShF 436-437; ShFSup 76-77.

Wille, zur Macht, Der. See Will to Power, The.

Willehalm (Wolfram von Eschenbach). PFor 1700, 1701-1703.

Willey, Mary Louise. ShF 2885.

William Blake: A Critical Essay (Swinburne). PEng 2813; RevPEng 3281.

William Faulkner: First Encounters (Brooks, C.). LTh 221.

William Faulkner: The Yoknapatawpha Country (Brooks, C.). LTh 221.

William Shakespeare (Hugo). LTh 709, 712, 1706.

William Tell (Knowles). DEng 1061-1062; RevDEng 1339-1340.

William Tell (Schiller). DFor 2368-2369.

"William Wilson" (Poe). ShF 477, 478, 739.

Williams, Charles. RevLFEng 3860.

Williams, C. K. PSup 387-392; RevPEng 3602-3608.

Williams, Ella Gwendolen Rees. *See* **Rhys, Jean.**

Williams, Emlyn. DEng 2056-2065; RevDEng 2556-2566.

Williams, Heathcote. RevDEng 3022-3023.

Williams, John Alfred. ShF 2886.

Williams, Joy. RevShF 2472-2477.

Williams, Paulette. *See* **Shange, Ntozake.**

Williams, Raymond. LTh 414, 416, 418, 1540-1545.

Williams, Tennessee. DEng 2066-2084, 2405; RevDEng 2567-2586, 2926; RevShF 2478-2485; ShF 2433-2440; ShFSup 391.

Williams, Thomas. ShF 2888.

Williams, William Carlos. PEng 3110-3121, 3392; RevPEng 3609-3621; RevShF 2486-2491; ShF 266, 694, 2441-2446.

Williamson, David. DEng 2085-2094; RevDEng 2587-2598.

Willie Master's Lonesome Wife (Gass). LFEng 3329-3330; LFSup 124-126; RevLFEng 1315-1316, 3878.

Willing to Die (Le Fanu). LFEng 1627-1628; RevLFEng 2002-2003.

Williwaw (Vidal). LFEng 2716-2717.

"Willkommen und Abschied." *See* "Welcome and Farewell."

Willoughby, Lee Davis. *See* **Avallone, Michael,** and **DeAndrea, William L.**

"Willowwood" (Rossetti, D. G.). PEng 2433; RevPEng 2826.

Wilmot, John. *See* **Rochester, John Wilmot, Earl of.**

Wilson, A. N. LFSup 386-391; RevLFEng 3580-3586.

Wilson, Angus. LFEng 2897-2906; RevLFEng 3587-3597; ShF 276, 523-524.

Wilson, August. RevDEng 2599-2605, 2951-2952.

Wilson, Barbara. ShF 2889.

Wilson, Edmund. LTh 315-316, 319, 865, 1546-1552.

Wilson, Ethel. LFEng 2907-2916; RevLFEng 3598-3607; ShF 638.

Wilson, J. Arbuthnot. *See* **Allen, Grant.**

Wilson, Lanford. DEng 2095-2103, 2412; RevDEng 2606-2615, 2933-2934.

Wilson, Robert. DEng 2488; DSup 398-403; RevDEng 2616-2622, 3015-3016.

Wilson, Robley, Jr. ShF 2890.

Wilson, Snoo. DEng 2493-2494; RevDEng 3022.

Wilson, Thomas. LTh 1666.

Wimsatt, William K., Jr. LTh 1553-1559, 1753-1754, 1812.

"Winchester Wedding, The" (D'Urfey). PEng 912.

Winckelmann, Johann Joachim. DFor 2366; LTh 669-670, 1560-1564, 1691.

Wind (Simon). LFFor 1605-1607.

"Wind and the Snow of Winter, The" (Clark). ShF 607-609.

"Wind and Tree" (Muldoon). RevPEng 2404.

367

"Wind Blows, The" (Mansfield). ShF 1881-1883.
Wind Blows Death, The. See *When the Wind Blows.*
Wind from Nowhere, The (Ballard). LFEng 148; RevLFEng 192.
Wind from the Plain, The (Kemal). LFFor 941-942.
Wind in the Pines, The (Zeami). DFor 2039-2040.
Wind, Sand and Stars (Saint-Exupéry). LFFor 1483, 1484-1485.
Windham, Donald. ShF 2891.
"Windharp" (Montague). RevPEng 2364.
"Windhover, The" (Hopkins). PEng 1397-1399; RevPEng 1606-1608.
"Winding River, The" (Tu Fu). PFor 1543.
"Window Poems" (Berry). PEng 151; RevPEng 182.
Window to Criticism, A (Krieger). LTh 826.
Winds of April, The (Gonzalez). LFEng 1142; RevLFEng 1362.
Winds of Morning (Davis). LFEng 678-679; RevLFEng 810-811;
Winds of War, The (Wouk). LFEng 2971-2972; RevLFEng 3673-3674, 3837.
Windsor Forest (Pope). PEng 2255; RevPEng 2629.
Windsor Magazine, The. ShF 771.
Windy McPherson's Son (Anderson). LFEng 73, 75; RevLFEng 110, 112.
"Wine" (Gay). PEng 1071-1072; RevPEng 1209.
Wine of Astonishment, The (Lovelace). LFEng 1703-1704; RevLFEng 2109-2110.
Wine of the Puritans, The (Brooks, V.). LTh 226.
"Wine Song" (Petőfi). PFor 1228.
Winesburg, Ohio (Anderson). LFEng 76-78, 79; RevLFEng 113-115, 116; RevShF 69-72; ShF 247-248, 723, 869-870, 871, 872.
Wings (Kopit). DEng 1073-1075; RevDEng 1352-1353.
Winners, The (Cortázar). LFFor 377-379.
"Winter: 1978" (Beattie). RevShF 182-183; ShFSup 39-40.
"Winter" (Cotton). PEng 586; RevPEng 683.
"Winter Chemistry" (Williams, J.). RevShF 2473-2474.
"Winter Come, A" (Moss). PEng 2065-2066; RevPEng 2397-2398.
"Winter Diary, A" (Van Doren). PEng 2957; RevPEng 3434-3435.
"Winter Dreams" (Fitzgerald). RevShF 861-862; ShF 1371-1372.
"Winter Evening" (Barnard). PSup 26-27; RevPEng 109-110.

"Winter in the Air" (Warner). RevShF 2403-2404; ShFSup 353-354.
Winter in the Hills, A (Wain). LFEng 2738, 2741-2742; RevLFEng 3395, 3398-3399.
"Winter Insomnia" (Carver). RevPEng 533.
"Winter Landscapes" (Davie). PSup 87; RevPEng 852.
"Winter Night" (Boyle, K.). RevShF 288-289; ShF 1001-1002.
"Winter Noon" (Saba). PSup 347.
Winter of Artifice (Nin). LFEng 1992; RevLFEng 2515-2516.
"Winter on the River" (Meredith). RevPEng 2273-2274.
"Winter Orchard, The" (Johnson, J.). ShF 1701-1702.
Winter Palace, The (Haavikko). PSup 144.
"Winter Runner, The" (Galvin). PEng 1054; RevPEng 1187.
"Winter Sleepers" (Atwood). PEng 65.
Winter Song. See Fury Chronicle, The.
"Winter Song" (Kizer). RevPEng 1859-1860.
"Winter Verse for His Sister" (Meredith). RevPEng 2272.
"Wintergreen Ridge" (Niedecker). RevPEng 2446, 2450.
Wintering Out (Heaney). PEng 1264, 1266, 1269-1271; RevPEng 1445.
Winters, Yvor. LTh 158, 1206, **1565-1570;** **PSup 253, 255-256, 393-400; RevPEng 3622-3630;** RevShF 2686.
"Winter's Day, A" (Leskov). RevShF 1469; ShFSup 161.
Winter's Tale. (Helprin). RevShF 1160.
Winter's Tale, The (Shakespeare). DEng 1712; RevDEng 2126; ShF 2217-2218.
Winter's Tales (Dinesen). ShF 1281.
Winterset (Anderson, M.). DEng 2403; RevDEng 2924.
Winterton, Paul. *See* **Garve, Andrew.**
Winther, Christian. PFor 2166.
"Wiper, The" (MacNeice). PEng 1875-1876; RevPEng 2176-2177.
Wir werden schon noch handeln (Walser, M.). DSup 388.
Wire Harp, The (Biermann). PFor 190.
"Wireless." *See* "Where There's a Will."
"Wireless" (Kipling). ShF 1751.
Wisdom Amok (Innaurato). DSup 201; RevDEng 1246.
Wisdom of Solomon, The (Hakim). DSup 175.
Wisdom of Solomon, Paraphrased, The (Middleton, T.). PEng 1994-1995.

Wisdom of the Sands, The (Saint-Exupéry). LFFor 1485.

Wise Blood (O'Connor, Flannery). LFEng 2036-2038; RevLFEng 2569, 2570-2572, 3874, 3875.

Wise Child (Gray). DEng 806; RevDEng 998-999.

Wise Virgin (Wilson, A. N.). LFSup 389-390; RevLFEng 3583.

Wise Woman of Hogsdon, The (Heywood, T.). DEng 953-955; RevDEng 1187-1189.

"Wiser Than a God" (Chopin). RevShF 537; ShF 1132.

"Wish House, The" (Kipling). RevShF 1366.

"Wissler Remembers" (Stern). RevShF 2214.

Wister, Owen. LFEng 3192-3193; RevLFEng 3849; ShF 595, 596, 597, 609.

Wit and Mirth (D'Urfey). PEng 910.

Wit and Science (Redford). DEng 2259; RevDEng 2779.

Wit at Several Weapons (Fletcher). DEng 634; RevDEng 779-780.

Wit Works Woe. See Mischief of Being Clever, The.

Witch of Edmonton, The (Ford, Dekker, and Rowley). DEng 651-652; RevDEng 796-797.

"Witch Trial at Mount Holly, A" (Franklin). ShF 1412-1413.

Witch Wood (Buchan). LFEng 330; RevLFEng 425.

Witches' Brew, The (Pratt). PEng 2285-2286; RevPEng 2658.

Witches of Eastwick, The (Updike). RevLFEng 3356-3357.

"Witching" (Boland). PSup 39-40; RevPEng 295.

Witching Times (De Forest). LFEng 699-700, 702; RevLFEng 833-834, 836.

Witch's House, The (Armstrong). M&D 37-38.

With Eyes at the Back of Our Heads (Levertov). PEng 1706.

With Fire and Sword (Sienkiewicz). LFFor 1565, 1572-1574.

"With Garments Flowing" (Clare). PEng 512-513; RevPEng 602-603.

With Ignorance (Williams, C. K.). PSup 390; RevPEng 3605.

"With rue my heart is laden" (Housman). PEng 1412; RevPEng 1622.

With Shuddering Fall (Oates). LFEng 2010-2011; RevLFEng 2534-2535.

With Strings (Sondhi). DEng 2418; RevDEng 2940.

"Withered Arm, The" (Hardy). RevShF 1109-1110; ShF 1580-1581.

Within a Budding Grove (Proust). LFFor 1327-1330. See also *Remembrance of Things Past.*

"Within the House" (Claudel). PFor 358, 361-362. See also *Five Great Odes.*

"Without Ceremony" (Miller). RevPEng 2331-2332.

Without Feathers (Allen). RevShF 56.

"Without Love" (Pasternak). RevShF 1854; ShF 2059.

Without My Cloak (O'Brien, K.). RevLFEng 2562-2563.

"Without Symbolism" (Foix). PFor 487-488.

"Without that one clear aim, the path of flight" (Spender). PEng 2702; RevPEng 3146.

Witiko (Stifter). LFFor 1673-1674.

Witkacy. *See* **Witkiewicz, Stanisław Ignacy.**

Witkiewicz, Stanisław Ignacy. DFor 2002-2012, 2279; LFFor 2064.

"Witness" (Heyen). PEng 1323-1324.

Witness (McNally). RevDEng 1552.

"Witness, The" (Sansom). RevShF 2051.

"Witness for the Prosecution" (Christie). ShF 1147-1148.

Witnesses, The (Różewicz). DFor 1583-1584.

Witnesses, The (Simenon). LFFor 1599.

"Wits, The" (Suckling). PEng 2775-2776, 2782; RevPEng 3247.

Wittgenstein, Ludwig. DEng 1868-1869, 1870, 1871; DFor 194, 860-862; LFFor 155, 782-783; LTh 958; PFor 178.

Witts, The (Davenant). DEng 455-456; RevDEng 564-565.

Witty and Witless (Heywood, J.). DEng 943; RevDEng 1176.

Wivallius, Lars. PFor 2158.

Wives and Daughters (Gaskell). LFEng 1105-1106; RevLFEng 1308-1309.

Wniebowstąpienie (Konwicki). LFFor 947.

Wo es war, soll ich werden (Davenport). RevShF 687-688.

"Wo ich nahe, wo ich lande. . . ." *See* "Where I Near and Where I Land. . . ."

Wo warst du, Adam? See Adam, Where Art Thou?

Wobble to Death (Lovesey). M&D 1094.

Wodehouse, P. G. LFEng 2917-2926; RevLFEng 3608-3618; ShF 541.

Wodwo (Hughes, T.). RevPEng 1650-1651.

Woiwode, Larry. LFSup 392-397; RevLFEng 3619-3626; RevShF 2492-2498.

Wolf (Harrison). LFEng 1288-1289; RevLFEng 1536-1537.

Wolf, Christa. LFFor 1930-1940, 2203.

Women of Trachis, The (Sophocles). DFor 2105.
Women on the Porch, The (Gordon). LFEng 1178-1179; RevLFEng 1400-1401.
"Women Whose Lives Are Food, Men Whose Lives Are Money" (Oates). RevPEng 2466.
Women Whose Lives Are Food, Men Whose Lives Are Money (Oates). PEng 2119-2120; RevPEng 2466-2468.
Women's Town, The (Álvarez Quinteros). DFor 55-56.
Wonder of Women, The. See *Sophonisba.*
Wonder Show, The (Cervantes). DFor 366-367.
Wonder Stories. ShF 774.
Wonder-Working Magician, The (Calderón). DFor 307.
Wonderful Adventures of Nils, The (Lagerlöf). LFFor 978, 2344.
Wonderful Clouds, The (Sagan). LFFor 1475.
Wonderful Fool (Endō). LFSup 103-104.
"Wonderful Glass, The" (Grimm). RevShF 1086; ShF 1558.
"Wonderful Tar-Baby Story, The" (Harris, J.). RevShF 1117; ShF 1588.
Wonderful Year, The (Dekker). PEng 770; RevPEng 889.
Wonderland (Oates). LFEng 2013-2014; RevLFEng 2536-2537.
Wonders of the Peake, The (Cotton). PEng 585-586; RevPEng 682-683.
"Wondersmith, The" (O'Brien, F.). RevShF 1752-1753; ShF 1978, 1979.
Wood Daemon, The. See *One O'Clock!*
Woodcraft (Simms). LFEng 2411-2412; RevLFEng 3041-3042.
Woodford, Bruce P. ShF 2893.
Woodlanders, The (Hardy). LFEng 1266-1267; RevLFEng 1502-1503.
"Woodnotes" (Emerson). PEng 960; RevPEng 1090.
"Woodrow Wilson's Necktie" (Highsmith). RevShF 1194.
Woods, The (Mamet). DEng 1243.
Woods, The (Plante). LFSup 308-309; RevLFEng 2644-2645. See also *Francoeur Novels, The.*
Wooing of Etain. RevShF 2606; ShF 435.
Woolf, Virginia. LFEng 2940-2960, 3055-3056; LTh 580, **1571-1577; RevLFEng 3641-3662,** 3763-3764; RevPEng 3966, 3967; **RevShF 2511-2517; ShF 2454-2461.**
Woolrich, Cornell. M&D 1723-1729.
Woolson, Constance Fenimore. ShF 535-536.
Word, The (Munk). DFor 1390-1391, 2479-2480.

"Word Poem (Perhaps Worth Considering)" (Giovanni). PEng 1100; RevPEng 1239.
Words (Creeley). PEng 681; RevPEng 779.
"Words" (Plath). PEng 2229-2230; RevPEng 2601-2602.
"Words" (Simpson). RevPEng 3013.
Words About Words About Words (Krieger). LTh 829.
Words for the Wind (Roethke). PEng 2412; RevPEng 2805-2806.
Words upon the Window-pane, The (Yeats). DEng 2120; RevDEng 2640.
Words Without Music. RevDEng 3030.
Wordsworth (Read). LTh 1212.
Wordsworth, William. LTh 3-5, 43, 258-259, 299, 904, 1247, 1291, 1334-1335, **1578-1584,** 1696, 1705, 1708-1709; PEng 168, 526-527, 2408, 2744, 2745, **3122-3138,** 3342; **RevPEng 3631-3648,** 3860, 3991, 4018-4020.
"Wordsworth at Glenarbach: An Apisode" (Hallam). PEng 1211; RevPEng 1383.
"Work" (Miyazawa). PSup 285.
"Work of Art in the Age of Mechanical Reproduction, The" (Benjamin). LTh 139, 1366.
"Workday" (Hogan). RevPEng 1543.
"Worker in Mirror, at His Bench" (Kinsella). PSup 232; RevPEng 1834.
Workers in the Dawn (Gissing). LFEng 1112; RevLFEng 1322.
Workhouse Ward, The (Gregory). DEng 853; RevDEng 1049.
"Working Late" (Simpson). RevPEng 3011-3012.
Works and Days (Hesiod). PFor 662, 663, 666-669, 1758; RevShF 2567, 2577; ShF 135, 378.
Works of Love, The (Morris). LFEng 1910; RevLFEng 2418.
"World, The" (Creeley). PEng 684.
World According to Garp, The (Irving, J.). LFEng 1416, 1417, 1421-1423; RevLFEng 1698-1700.
"World According to Hsu, The" (Mukherjee). RevShF 1686.
World as It Is, The. See *Babouc.*
World as Will and Idea, The (Schopenhauer). LTh 1067.
"World Box-Score Cup" (Dorn). PEng 843; RevPEng 949.
World Doesn't End, The (Simic). RevPEng 3002.
World Enough and Time (Warren). LFEng 2776-2778; RevLFEng 3441-3443.
"World in an Eare-Ring, A" (Newcastle). PEng 2093-2094; RevPEng 2437.

X

X. *See* **Simenon, Georges.**

$X = O$ (Drinkwater). DEng 509-510; RevDEng 630-631.

X, Mr. *See* **Hoch, Edward D.**

Xala (Sembène). LFFor 1542, 1543-1544.

Xenophanes of Colophon. LTh 1634.

Xenophon of Athens. LFFor 2000.

Xenophon of Ephesus. LFFor 2003-2004.

"Xionia" (Wright, C.). RevPEng 3664-3665.

Y

Y nos dijeron que éramos inmortales (Dragún). DFor 2443-2444.

Ya tali' al-shajarah. See *Tree Climber, The.*

"Yabu no naka." *See* "In a Grove."

Yakamochi, Ōtomo no. *See* Ōtomo no Yakamochi.

Yama no oto. See *Sound of the Mountain, The.*

Yamanoe no Okura. PFor 2057.

Yang Shên. DFor 2324.

Yang Wan-li. LTh 1776-1777.

Yankee Ranger. See *Tory Lover, The.*

"Yao." *See* "Medicine."

Yard of Sun, A (Fry). DEng 688-689; RevDEng 856.

Yasunari Kawabata. *See* **Kawabata, Yasunari.**

"Yawahada no." *See* "You Have Yet to Touch."

Yayá Garcia. See *Iaia Garcia.*

Ye Bare and Ye Cubb. See *Bare and Ye Cubb, Ye.*

Year Before Last (Boyle, K.). LFEng 275-276; RevLFEng 340-341.

Year 1905, The (Pasternak). PFor 1159-1160.

Year of the Dragon, The (Chin). DSup 48-51; RevDEng 428-430.

Year of the Soul, The (George). LTh 575; PFor 548-549.

Years, The (Woolf). LFEng 2955-2957; RevLFEng 3656-3658.

"Years Behind, The" (Awoonor). PFor 114.

"Years Go By, The" (Niedecker). PSup 296, 299; RevPEng 2445, 2448.

Yeats, William Butler. DEng **2115-2122,** 2199, 2375, 2376, 2379, 2445, 2446; LTh 979, 1412-1413, **1585-1590,** 1737; PEng **3181-3209,** 3349, 3361-3362; PSup 411; RevDEng **2635-2642,** 2719, 2893-2894, 2897, 2969-2970; RevPEng **3705-3733,** 3879-3880, 3989-3990; RevShF **2524-2530;** ShF 292, **2468-2474.**

Yegor Bulychov and Others (Gorky). DFor 786.

Yellen, Samuel. ShF 2895.

Yellow Back Radio Broke-Down (Reed). LFSup 338; RevLFEng 2802.

"Yellow Dog, The" (Guest). PEng 1165; RevPEng 1325.

Yellow House on the Corner, The (Dove). RevPEng 956-957.

"Yellow Light" (Hongo). RevPEng 1570-1571.

Yellow Light (Hongo). RevPEng 1570-1573.

Yellow Room, The (Hall). PEng 1202-1204; RevPEng 1373.

Yemassee, The (Simms). LFEng 2413; RevLFEng 3043.

Yen Hsieh. LTh 1778.

Yen Yü. LTh 1777.

"Yentl the Yeshiva Boy" (Singer). ShF 2243-2244.

Yeomen of the Guard, The (Gilbert and Sullivan). DEng 766-767; RevDEng 947-948.

Yerby, Frank. LFEng **2985-2992;** LFSup 408; RevLFEng **3691-3698;** ShF **2475-2480.**

Yerkes, C. T. LFEng 835; RevLFEng 1001.

Yerma (García Lorca). DFor 663-664, 2505.

"Yes" (Harvey). ShF 129.

"Yes, Too Much of Everything" (Salinas). PFor 1387-1388.

Yesenin, Sergei. *See* Esenin, Sergei.

"Yesterday and To-morrow" (Dunbar, P.). PSup 115; RevPEng 1017.

"Yet Do I Marvel" (Cullen). PEng 694-696; RevPEng 785-787.

"Yeux d'Elsa, Les." *See* "Elsa's Eyes."

Yevtushenko, Yevgeny. PFor **1704-1712,** 2150.

"Yew-Trees" (Wordsworth). PEng 3458-3459; RevPEng 3993-3994.

Yglesias, José. LFEng **2993-3003;** RevLFEng **3699-3709.**

Yin, Leslie Charles Bowyer. *See* **Charteris, Leslie.**

"Yin and Yang" (Rexroth). PEng 2351; RevPEng 2738.

"Ynn Auntient Dayes" (Chatterton). PEng 471; RevPEng 567.

Yö ja päivä (Kivi). DFor 1068-1069.

Yogi and the Commissar and Other Essays, The (Koestler). LFEng 1549; RevLFEng 1910.

Yogi of Cockroach Court, The (Waters). LFEng 2787-2788; RevLFEng 3453-3454.

York, Jeremy. *See* **Creasey, John.**

York Cycle. RevDEng 2768, 2769.

Yorke, Henry Vincent. *See* **Green, Henry.**

Yosano Akiko. PFor **1713-1719,** 2075.

Yoshimoto, Nijō. LTh **1591-1595,** 1787-1788.

Yoshioka Minoru. PFor 2078.

Yosimochi, Ki no. LTh 1785.

You and I (Monroe). PEng 2028.

"You and I" (Sinyavsky). RevShF 2140.

Yüan-ch'ü hsüan wai-pien (Sui). DFor 2318.
"Yü-fu." *See* "Fisherman."
Yukiguni. See *Snow Country.*
"Yūkoku." *See* "Patriotism."

"Yume no ukihashi." *See* "Bridge of Dreams, The."
Yvain (Chrétien de Troyes). RevShF 543-544; ShF 1139-1140.

Z

"Zaabalawi" (Mahfouz). RevShF 1563.
"Zabavnoe prikliuchenie." *See* "Amusing Adventure, An."
Zabawa. See *Party, The.*
"Zabitye liudi" (Dobrolyubov). LTh 389.
Zacharias, Lee. ShF 2896.
Zadig (Voltaire). LFFor 1895-1898; M&D 1655-1657; RevShF 2358-2359.
Zagoskin, Mikhail. LFFor 2310-2311.
"Zähle die Mandeln." *See* "Count the Almonds."
Zahradní salvnost. See *Garden Party, The.*
"Zaiachii remiz." See "March Hare, The."
Zaïde. See Zayde.
Zaïre (Voltaire). DFor 1967-1968.
Zakani, 'Ubaid, 2567-2568.
Zalacaín el aventurero (Baroja). LFFor 109-110.
Zalán futása (Vörösmarty). PFor 1665-1666.
Zami (Lorde). RevPEng 2044.
Zamora, Bernice. RevPEng 3925-3926; *Restless Serpents.* RevPEng 3925.
Zamyatin, Yevgeny. LFFor 1973-1981, 2323; RevShF 2531-2539.
Zangirimono. DFor 2432.
Zangwill, Israel. M&D 1730-1734; ShF 516.
Zanzotto, Andrea. PFor 2050.
Zapatera prodigiosa, La. See *Shoemaker's Prodigious Wife, The.*
Zapatero y el rey, El (Zorrilla y Moral). DFor 2062-2063.
"Zapechatlennyi angel." See "Sealed Angel, The."
Zapiski iz myortvogo doma. See *House of the Dead, The.*
Zapiski iz podpolya. See *Notes from the Underground.*
Zauberberg, Der. See *Magic Mountain, The.*
"Zauberin im Walde, Die." *See* "Sorceress in the Forest, The."
Zavist. See *Envy.*
Zavrian, Suzanne Ostro. ShF 2897.
Zayde (La Fayette). LFFor 959-961.
Zazie in the Metro (Queneau). LFSup 330-332.
Zdarzenia (Ważyk). PFor 1695.
Ze wspomnień Ijona Tichego: Kongres futurologiczny. See *Futurological Congress, The.*
"Ze wspomnień Ijona Tichyo." *See* "Further Reminiscences of Ijon Tichy."

Ze zivota hrnyzu. See *Insect Play, The.*
Zeami Motokiyo. DFor 2036-2043, 2422-2423; LTh 1788-1789.
Zebra-Striped Hearse, The (Macdonald). LFSup 275; RevLFEng 2174.
Žebrácká opera (Havel). DFor 881.
Zee & Co. (O'Brien, E.). LFEng 2021-2022; RevLFEng 2547.
"Zeitgedichte" (George). *See* "Time Poems."
"Zeitgedichte" (Heine). *See* "Poems of the Times."
"Zeitl and Rickel" (Singer). RevShF 2133.
Zeko (Andrić). LFFor 67-69.
Zelazny, Roger. ShF 2898.
Zelman, Anita. ShF 2899.
Zement. See *Cement.*
Zemganno Brothers, The (Goncourt, E.). LFFor 717.
Zemsta. See *Revenge* and *Vengeance, The.*
Zeno, Apostolo. DFor 2402.
Zensur, Die (Wedekind). DFor 1981-1982.
"Zero" (Salinas). PFor 1389.
Zeromski, Stefan. LFFor 2063.
Zerrissene, Der. See *Man Full of Nothing, A.*
Žert. See *Joke, The.*
Zesen, Philipp von. LFFor 2151.
Zhang Jie. RevShF 2540-2547.
Zhdanov, Andrey. LTh 1125, 1505, 1603-1608.
"Zheleznaia volia." *See* "Iron Will."
Zhelezny potok. See *Iron Flood, The.*
Zhirmunsky, V. M. LTh 1504.
"Zhitie inzhenera Kipreeva." *See* "Life of Engineer Kipreev, The."
Zhizn cheloveko. See *Life of Man, The.*
Zhizn Matveya Kozhemyakina. See *Life of Matvei Kozhemyakin, The.*
Zhukovsky, Vasily. LTh 118-119, 1609-1614; PFor 2135-2136.
Ziemia obiecana. See *Promised Land, The.*
Zig-Zag Walk, The (Logan). PEng 1741; RevPEng 2025.
"Zima Junction" (Yevtushenko). PFor 1708-1709.
Zimmerschlacht, Die (Walser, M.). DSup 387-388.
Zimpel, Lloyd. ShF 2900.
Zinberg, Leonard S. *See* **Lacy, Ed.**
Zindel, Paul. DEng 2123-2131; RevDEng 2643-2652.

Zinnes, Harriet. ShF 2901.
"Zio acquatico, Lo." *See* "Aquatic Uncle, The."
"Zip!" (Davie). PSup 85; RevPEng 850-851.
Živo meso. See Raw Flesh.
Život a dílo skladatele Foltýna. See Cheat, The.
Zivot de jinde. See *Life Is Elsewhere.*
Zmaj, Jovan Jovanović. PFor 2254.
Żmija (Słowacki). PFor 1441.
Zola, Émile. DEng 2195; DFor 2044-2057; LFEng 3170, 3174-3175; LFFor 1982-1995, 2134; LTh 233, 690, 1420, 1497, 1615-1621, 1710-1719, 1750, 1794, 1816-1817; RevDEng 2715; RevShF 2548-2553; ShF 234, 2481-2486.
Zona sagrada. See *Holy Place.*
"Zone" (Apollinaire). PFor 48, 54.
Zone, The (Dovlatov). RevShF 761.
Zone Journals (Wright, C.). RevPEng 3663.
"Zoo, The" (Smith, S.). RevPEng 3076.
Zoo Story, The (Albee). DEng 2408-2409; RevDEng 2929-2930.
"Zooey" (Salinger). RevShF 2043-2045.
Zooman and the Sign (Fuller). RevDEng 881-882.
Zoot Suit (Valdez). DSup 371; RevDEng 2430.
Zorba the Greek (Kazantzakis). LFFor 919-920.
Zorn, Fritz. LFFor 2209.
Zorrilla y Moral, José. DFor 2058-2067, 2498.
Zoshchenko, Mikhail. LTh 1607; RevShF 2554-2562.

Zrínyi, Miklós. PFor 1976.
Ztížená možnost soustředění. See *Increased Difficulty of Concentration, The.*
Zuckerman Unbound (Roth). LFEng 2309-2310, 3325-3326; RevLFEng 2902-2903.
Zuckmayer, Carl. DFor 2068-2077, 2380.
Zukofsky, Louis. PEng 3220-3226; RevPEng 3744-3751.
"Zum Gedächtnis des Schauspielers Mitterwurzer" (Hofmannsthal). PFor 676-677.
Župančič, Oton. PFor 2269.
Zur Geschichte der neuenen romantischen Poesie in Deutschland (Eichendorff). LTh 435.
Zur Geschichte der Religion und Philosophie in Deutschland. See *On the History of Religion and Philosophy in Germany.*
Zur Geschichte des Dramas (Eichendorff). LTh 437.
Zvezdnyi bilet. See *Ticket to the Stars, A.*
"Zvonok." *See* "Doorbell, The."
Zwei Ansichten. See *Two Views.*
"Zwei Gesellen, Die." *See* "Two Companions, The."
"Zwei Läufer." *See* "Two Runners."
Zweig, Stefan. LFFor 2191; PFor 1720-1727.
"Zwielicht." *See* "Twilight."
Żywot Ezopa Fryga (Biernat of Lublin). PFor 2119.

DATE DUE	